THE ROUTLEDGE COMPANION
TO THE TUDOR AGE

This new *Companion* is an invaluable guide to one of the most colourful periods in history. Covering everything from the Reformation, controversies over the succession and the prayer book to literature, the family and education, this highly accessible reference tool contains commentary on the key events in the reigns of the five Tudor monarchs from Henry VII to Elizabeth I.

Opening with a general introduction, it includes a wealth of chronologies, biographies, statistics and maps, as well as a glossary and a guide to the key works in the field. Topics covered include:

- the establishment of the Tudor dynasty; monarchs and their consorts; rebellions against the Tudors
- the legal system – central and ecclesiastical courts
- government – central and local; the monarchy and parliament
- the Church – structure and changes throughout this tumultuous period
- Ireland – timeline of key events
- Population – numbers and distribution
- the World of Learning – education; literature; religion
- the key debates in the field – from religion, the economy and foreign policy to education and gender.

This indispensible resource offers thorough coverage of ecclesiastical, cultural and educational issues, as well as diplomatic, administrative and military affairs, and will be essential reading for all those with an interest in the Tudor Age.

Rosemary O'Day is Professor of History at the Open University.

ROUTLEDGE COMPANIONS TO HISTORY
Series Advisors: Chris Cook and John Stevenson

Routledge Companions to History offer perfect reference guides to key historical events and eras, providing everything that the student or general reader needs to know. These comprehensive guides include essential apparatus for navigating through specific topics in a clear and straightforward manner – including introductory articles, biographies and chronologies – to provide accessible and indispensable surveys crammed with vital information valuable for beginner and expert alike.

THE ROUTLEDGE COMPANION
TO THE TUDOR AGE

Rosemary O'Day

LONDON AND NEW YORK

First published 2010
by Routledge
2 Park Square, Milton Park, Abingdon, Oxon OX14 4RN

Simultaneously published in the USA and Canada
by Routledge
270 Madison Ave, New York, NY 10016

Previously published in 1995 by Pearson Education Limited

Routledge is an imprint of the Taylor & Francis Group, an informa business

© 2010 Rosemary O'Day

Typeset in Times New Roman by
Book Now Ltd, London
Printed and bound in Great Britain by
TJ International Ltd, Padstow, Cornwall

British Library Cataloguing in Publication Data
A catalogue record for this book is available from the British Library

Library of Congress Cataloging in Publication Data
The Routledge companion to the Tudor age/Rosemary O'Day.
p. cm.—(Routledge companions to history)
Based on the author's earlier work The Longman companion to the Tudor age,
published in 1995.
Includes bibliographical references and index.
1. Great Britain—History—Tudors, 1485–1603—Handbooks, manuals, etc.
2. Great Britain—History—Tudors, 1485–1603—Chronology.
3. Tudor, House of—Handbooks, manuals, etc.
4. England—Civilization—16th century—Handbooks, manuals, etc. I. O'Day, Rosemary. Longman
companion to the Tudor age. II. Title. III. Title: Companion to the Tudor age.
DA315.O33 2010
942.05—dc22   2009049713

ISBN10: 0–415–44564–7 (hbk)
ISBN10: 0–415–44565–5 (pbk)
ISBN10: 0–203–85046–7 (ebk)

ISBN13: 978–0–415–44564–1 (hbk)
ISBN13: 978–0–415–44565–8 (pbk)
ISBN13: 978–0–203–85046–6 (ebk)

I dedicate this book to Barbara Lewis of Gnosall, Staffordshire, with thanks for her excellent teaching and support through the years.

CONTENTS

INTRODUCTION

This volume is based on my earlier *Companion to the Tudor Age* (1995). While it retains many of the features of that work, this is a new book. The changed form of the book owes much to the changing emphases within the discipline of history since 1995. Interdisciplinarity is now fashionable and, whereas in 1995 I had to justify the inclusion of literary and artistic figures (for example, in the biographical index), there has been no such necessity in 2009 to explain the need to cover those who made a cultural contribution. Some of the best historical work now emanates from scholars working on historical themes in the disciplines of literature, art history and music. Historians now seek to compare developments in England with those in Scotland, Ireland and Wales. Benchmarking across the sector has meant that post-graduates and undergraduates alike are expected to embark on original archival research: it has, therefore, seemed appropriate to cater for their special needs throughout the book.

The present work, while retaining many of the features of its predecessor, includes a considerably improved general chronology (which has been expanded to cover religious developments, Irish and Welsh affairs and, to the extent that space permits, events in Scotland and western Europe); an enlarged biographical section (which has been checked against the new *Oxford Dictionary of National Biography* and other authorities); new sections on the structure of the Church in England, and the ecclesiastical courts; an enhanced glossary, a new bibliography section and an updated debates section.

Details and dates

A conscientious attempt has been made to ensure accuracy in respect of details and dates. Standard texts, such as the new *Oxford Dictionary of National Biography* and the Royal Historical Society's *Handbook of British Chronology* and other handlists, as well as authoritative monographs and editions, have been used to establish and check details and dates throughout. A caveat should be issued in this regard, however, because such sources are frequently in conflict and the student will, from time to time, find discrepancies. While such conflict is one of the frustrations of historical research, one of its joys lies in the attempt to resolve such problems.

The *Companion* does not pretend to contain every fact that a student and scholar will need for their work nor to provide uniform coverage of all areas. Indeed, the book intentionally provides more detailed treatment of ecclesiastical, cultural and educational affairs than of diplomatic, administrative or military history. This decision was taken in the light of the current interest in Tudor history on the part of literary, cultural, religious and educational scholars as well as history scholars. Nevertheless, the *Companion* provides a wealth of information in an easily accessible format, suitable for students studying general history of the period.

Bibliographies

The book contains highly selective bibliographies. The aim has been to provide pointers to a large number of subjects within Tudor history and, where possible, to include the best recent authorities. Categorisation has been difficult because so many books and articles cover several different subjects – for instance, some books and articles in the politics and central administration area might fit equally well into the finance or the law sections and a biography of a bishop, for example, obviously contains material relevant to religion and ecclesiastical affairs. Books published before 1950 are generally useful mainly from a historiographical point of view. Many books and articles published between 1950 and 2000 remain the standard authorities on particular subjects. Others remain useful for establishing facts, chronology and interpretative positions, even when superseded by more recent interpretations. The place of publication for all entries is London, unless otherwise stated. Places of publication have not been traced for books published prior to 1951. Dates are given for main editions but not for reprints.

Biographies

This chapter includes a large number of short biographies of prominent men and women of the period but it is, necessarily, not exhaustive. I have given special prominence to women because they have been largely neglected in most standard works of reference and yet are increasingly important in modern historical and cultural studies. Equally, I have included references to contemporary authors, dramatists, poets, musicians, artists, educationalists, scientists and professionals often overlooked in history reference books. The length of a biography does *not* equate to the importance of the subject. Indeed, some of the longer biographies relate to less well-known individuals (because their identity and importance are often less well explained, especially in general and political histories, than that of great men such as Thomas Cromwell, Thomas More and William Cecil, around whom the narrative and debates often revolve). Space in other biographies is used to explain complicated relationships and circumstances (for example, the relationships between the de la Poles and the Yorkist kings) or to correct common misconceptions and myths (for instance, surrounding the paternity of Mary Boleyn's children, Katherine and Henry Carey). The chronology of the activities of lesser players often requires more explication than that of kings, queens and statesmen (amply covered in the chronologies). Biographies of monarchs and their spouses have been treated separately for convenience and listed under their first names. There are a few exceptions (e.g. Earl of Bothwell and Lord Guildford Dudley appear in Section 12.2: Biographical index). The biographies of monarchs are not comprehensive – the reader should consult the general chronology for details of their reigns. There are cross-references to individuals treated separately in other sections of the book. Individuals are listed under the name that will be most familiar (e.g. Mary Boleyn not Mary Carey). Some spellings have been regularised (e.g. Katherine not Catherine or Katharine of Aragon, Howard, Parr, Willoughby, Carey, Grey but Catherine de Medici and Catherine (Co(o)ke) Killigrew).

Use of the biographical section

The biographies provide a first port of call, especially useful when immediate identification is required or when pertinent examples are sought. The new *Oxford Dictionary of National Biography* will provide more detailed narrative and interpretative biographies of most of these individuals. Where there is doubt about dates or details, I have, in general, relied upon those given in the new *Oxford Dictionary of National Biography* biographies, although these sometimes conflict with one another between different biographies. Where modern book-length or book-chapter biographies are available, I have cited them. With few exceptions, articles from learned journals are not cited in the biographies; for these, the reader should consult the select bibliography. Where there is especial controversy concerning an individual, I have tried to cite books representing alternative interpretations. As in the Bibliographies, the place of publication is London, unless otherwise stated.

The biographies may also be used as the basis for elementary exercises in prosopographical analysis; for example, how many individuals were married more than once, how many attended one of the universities and/or the Inns of Court, how many prominent Protestant reformers had an early career in the monastic orders, what kind of literature did women write or translate? Where such details are not given, they are not available.

General chronology

This chronology is designed to provide a year by year, month-by-month chronicle of major events in England and Wales. Occasionally it has been impossible to date an event precisely. In such cases, the event has either been placed in approximate sequence or at the end of the year concerned. Coverage of Scottish, Irish and European events has been provided where relevant to England and Wales and when space permitted.

Glossary

Words set in bold in the text of the General Chronology and elsewhere signal entries in the Glossary. This section also contains explanations of many other unfamiliar or difficult to understand terms.

Abbreviations

In general, the meaning of abbreviations should be evident from the context. A full list is printed separately for reference in case of doubt.

Acknowledgements

I have taken great pains with this *Companion*, in the hope and expectation that it will prove just that for generations of students and teachers. As a result, however, I have doubtless tried the patience of the publisher and my editor by taking far too long to hand over the book. I thank them for their long-suffering generosity and understanding. I mention Emily Kindleysides in particular in this context. I am especially grateful to the general editor of the series, Dr John Stevenson, whose suggestion it was that I produce this *Companion*. My debts to the countless historians who have researched and written about the topics covered in this work are too numerous to mention but are nonetheless immense.

I also extend thanks to my family, friends and colleagues who have supported me during this work. I mention especially, in this context, Andrew O'Day, Dan and Matthew Englander, Janet Dawson, Sheila Taylor, Yvonne Alton, Sian Lewis and Meg Kesten. Finally, I thank Barbara Lewis and Jean Forrester, who first introduced me to the joys of scholarship and the historical importance of the Tudor period when I attended the Orme Girls' School, Newcastle-under-Lyme, and Professors Claire Cross and Patrick Collinson, who consolidated their work in that respect when I moved on to the universities of York and London.

Rosemary O'Day
The Open University, Milton Keynes, September 2009

ABBREVIATIONS

(In general, the meaning of abbreviations should be evident from the context. Here is a full list for reference in case of doubt.)

Archbp = archbishop
archd. = archdeacon
app'd = appointed
arr'd = arrived
b. = born
BA = Bachelor of Arts
betw. = between
BofCP = Book of Common Prayer
bp = bishop
bpric = bishopric
c. = circa (about)
Cambr. = Cambridge
consecr. = consecrated
cr. = created
d. = died or death
dau. = daughter
decl. = declared
dep. = deputy
depr. = deprived
dioc. = diocese
eccles. = ecclesiastical or ecclesiastic
ed'n = edition
Eng. = Eng/land/ish
est'd = established
excl. = exclud/e/ed/ing
exec. = executed
fl. = *floruit* [flourishing]
Fr.= France or French
FS = Free School
GS = Grammar School
h. = heir

h.w. = his wife
HofC = House of Commons
HofL = House of Lords
illegit. = illegitimate
impr. = imprison/ed/ment
incl. = includ/e/ed/ing
incr. = increas/e/ed/ing
infl. = influenc/e/ed/ing
JP = Justice of the Peace
KB = Knight of the Bath
KG = Knight of the Garter
lieut. = lieutenant
m. = marr/iage/ied/y
MA = Master of Arts
matric. = matriculated
MP = member of Parliament
nego. = negotiated, negotiations
oppo.= oppo/sed/sition
ord. = ordained
Oxf. = Oxford
parl. = parliament/ary
PC = Privy Council[lor]
poss. = possibl/e/y
pr. = priest
Presbyt. = presbyterian
proclam. = proclamation
pub'd = published
pub'n = publication
QC = Queen's Counsel
q.v. = to be found in these biographies
R = Rector/y
RC = Roman Catholic/s
re = with reference to
res. = resigned
rest. = restor/ation/ed
s. = son
s. & h. = son and heir
SJ = Society of Jesus/Jesuit
Sp. = Spain or Spanish
subdeac. = subdeacon
suppr. = suppress/ed/ion
Tower = Tower of London
Tr. = treaty
tr. = treason

transl. = translat/e/ed/or/ion
V = Vicar/age
v. = against
w. = with or wife
wid. = widow/er/ed
wound. = wounded

1

GENERAL CHRONOLOGY

1483   9 Apr.: Edward IV d.; protectorate of Richard of Gloucester; s. of Edward IV decl. illegit.; 26 June: Richard accepted Crown by proclam.; 6 July: Richard III crowned; Edward V & Richard Duke of York impr. in Tower; Queen Elizabeth Woodville in **sanctuary** w. daus in Westminster Abbey; Hastings exec.; Margaret Beaufort nego. w. Richard III & proposed m. betw. Princess Elizabeth & Henry Tudor; failed attempt to reinstate Edward V; princes never seen again in public; autumn plot by Woodvilles & Margaret Beaufort to place Henry Tudor & Elizabeth of York on throne; Thomas Grey, Marquis of Dorset joined Henry in exile after failed plot.

1484   Feb.: betrothal of Katherine, illegit. dau. of Richard III to William Herbert, Earl of Huntingdon; Apr.: Richard's s. Edward d.; Margaret Beaufort spared **attainder** because of her husb's loyalty to Richard III; Thomas Stanley app'd Steward of Household & Constable of England; Henry VI's body moved to Windsor.

Henry VII

1485   Mar.: John of Pontefract, Richard III's illegit. s. app'd Captain of **Calais**; 22 Aug.: **Battle of Bosworth**; Henry VII proclaimed King by Sir William Stanley, brother-in-law of Margaret Beaufort; 7 Sept.: Henry VII entered London; Margaret Beaufort granted Coldharbour House; Elizabeth of York, Edward Stafford, child duke of Buckingham, & Edward Plantagenet, s. of Clarence, Ralph, s. of Earl of Westmorland, & Cecily of York placed in Margaret's charge; Margaret nego. m. betw. Thomas Grey, s. of Marquis of Dorset) & Eleanor St John (one of her kin); 30 Oct.: coronation of Henry VII by Cardinal Archbp Bourchier; 7 Nov.–10 Dec.: parl.: attainder of Richard's closest followers; petitioned Henry to m. Elizabeth of York; re-enacted 1397 **statute** decl. the Beauforts legit. & omitted 1407 clause barring them from succession; Thomas Grey rest. as Marquis of Dorset & John de Vere as Earl of Oxford; John Alcock, Bp of Worcester, made Archbp of York; Dr Richard Fox app'd Secretary of State; John Welles, half-brother of Queen Mother, rest. to barony of Welles; John Morton cr. Archbp of Canterbury & chancellor, John, Lord Dynham app'd treasurer of the exchequer; Thomas Stanley cr. Earl of Derby & Sir William Stanley app'd chamberlain of household; Margaret Beaufort decl. *femme sole.*

1486 18 Jan.: Henry VII m. Elizabeth of York; Mar.: King's **progress** to north & west, both as a public relations exercise & to quash potential rebellion; 27 Mar.: **Pope** issued **bull** excomm. anyone who challenged validity of Henry VII's m. (they both descended from John of Gaunt); Apr. risings at Middleham (led by Francis Lord Lovell) & West Midlands (led by Stafford brothers); 20 Apr.: Henry VII's triumphant entry to York; May: Staffords dragged from sanctuary at Culham; during the trial of Humphrey Stafford the King attacked privilege of sanctuary, declaring that only King could grant sanctuary for **treason**. Later Pope Innocent VIII issues bull withdrawing right of sanctuary for second offenders. July: exec. of Humphrey Stafford; 20 Sept.: b. of Prince Arthur, Duke of Cornwall, at Winchester; m. of Cecily of York & Ralph Scrope dissolved. Sweating sickness grips the kingdom.

1487 Passage of Star Chamber Act, vesting PC w. considerable power to act v. sedition and corruption; those charged w. high tr. were denied right of sanctuary; Feb.: Lambert Simnel in Ireland, supported by John de la Pole, Earl of Lincoln; Henry parades Edward Earl of Warwick before Londoners; 24 May: ten-yr-old Simnel crowned Edward VI in Dublin; 2,000 German troops arrive in Ireland to assist Simnel in invasion of Eng., headed by John de la Pole, Earl of Lincoln; 4 June: Simnel landed in Cumbria; 16 June: Henry VII routed Simnel at **Battle of Stoke**, nr Newark; Henry was so relieved that he sent the royal standard to Walsingham (centre of pilgrimage); Earl of Lincoln exec.; 25 Nov.: coronation of Queen Elizabeth; Margaret Beaufort's half-brother, John Viscount Welles m. Cecily of York.

1488 11 June: James III of Scotland d. at Sauchieburn; Dec.: ceremonial re-burial of Edmund Beaufort, last Duke of Somerset (d.1471) & his brother John at Tewksbury Abbey marks culmination of rehabilitation of Henry VII's maternal family; Margaret Beaufort begins rebuilding of Corfe Castle, Beaufort family residence; Queen Mother & Queen, wearing identical gowns, adm. to Order of Garter.

1489 14 Feb.: Britanny & Eng. sign defensive Tr. of Redon v. Fr.; Apr.: Yorkshire rising, led by Sir John Egremont, v. 4th Earl of Northumberland; 4th Earl assassinated; rising quashed by Earl of Surrey; 28 Nov.: b. of Princess Margaret; 17 Mar.: Eng. & Spanish Tr. of Medina Del Campo agrees m. betw. Arthur & Katherine of Aragon; 30 Nov.: Arthur cr. Prince of Wales & Earl of Chester; further restrictions on benefit of clergy.

1490 11 Aug.: Firth of Forth sea battle betw. Scots & Eng.; one of several incidents despite official truce since 1486.

1491 Jan.: Sir Robert Chamberlain's plot uncovered; Mar.: Queen's uncle, Richard Earl Rivers d.; 4 July: b. of Prince Henry; 1 Sept.: Prince Henry baptised; Dec.: Perkin Warbeck in Cork; impersonated Richard of York, 2nd s. of Edward IV & had the support of Margaret of Burgundy, Edward IV's sister.

1492   Mar.: Warbeck brought to Fr. court; June: Kildare removed as Dep. of
        Ireland; 2 July: Princess Elizabeth b. (d. in infancy); Prince Arthur sets
        up household in Ludlow; d. of Dowager Queen Elizabeth (Woodville),
        Edward IV's widow & mother-in-law of Henry VII; Edmunde de la Pole
        became King's Ward; 3 Nov.: Tr. of Etaples betw. Charles VIII of France
        and Henry VII compensated Eng. for Fr. involvement in campaign and
        ensured that Fr. would not support Warbeck or other pretenders to the
        English throne.

1493   26 Feb.: Edmund de la Pole accepted title of Earl of Suffolk; John
        Radcliffe, Lord Fitzwalter & Sir William Stanley plot in Warbeck's
        favour; May: commissioners app'd to investigate treasons; diplomatic
        attempts to stop Margaret of Burgundy supporting Warbeck fail; ban on
        trade with Netherlands; 15 Oct.: riots v. the Steelyard, home of Hanseatic
        merchants; Nov.: Henry & Kildare in discussions & Kildare pardoned.

1494   Warbeck, pretending to be Richard Duke of York, won support from
        Emp. Maximilian at Vienna; Aug.: Warbeck at Emp. Maximilian's court
        in Low Countries; Sept.: Sir Edward Poynings app'd Dep. of Ireland; 31
        Oct.: Prince Henry cr. Duke of York; declaration via this ceremony that
        Richard, Duke of York was dead and Perkin Warbeck was an impostor;
        attainder of Kildare for tr.

1495   Feb.: Kildare arrested; (?1495) Lord Gerald Fitzgerald (1487–1534),
        Kildare's heir, came to Eng. as hostage; Jan.: exec. of plotters; 16 Feb.:
        Sir William Stanley exec.; 31 May: Cecily, grandmother of Queen
        Elizabeth d.; Queen Elizabeth arranged m. of sisters Anne of York (to the
        heir of earl of Surrey) & Katherine (to William Courtenay, heir of Earl
        of Devon); 20 Nov.: James IV welcomed Warbeck as Richard IV at
        Stirling; Dec.: Poynings recalled; Princess Elizabeth d.

1496   13 Jan.: m. of Warbeck & Lady Katherine Gordon, distant relative of
        James of Scotland; Feb.: *Magnum Intercursus*, Anglo-Burgundian trade
        treaty, denied Warbeck sanctuary; 18 Mar.: b. of Princess Mary; June:
        Scots Parl. orders s. of nobility to attend GS; July: joined Holy League
        but did not commit to war v. Fr.; 3 July: Warbeck's invasion failed at
        Deal, Kent; Aug.: Kildare swore to uphold Poynings Law, to surrender
        traitors & rebels to Crown & to cease quarrels w. Butlers; 17 Sept.:
        Kildare returned to Ireland as Dep.; 21 Sept.: James IV & Warbeck
        invaded Eng.; 26 Sept.: James IV withdrew; Henry VII began tomb at
        Windsor for himself & Henry VI. John Colet, humanist scholar, lectured
        at Oxford on Paul's Epistle to the Romans.

1497   Syphilis reaches Scotland via Warbeck's Neapolitan **mercenaries**, gar-
        risoned at Aberdeen. Jan.: Jesus College, Cambr. founded; May: **Cornish
        rebellion**; risings in Somerset; 20 May: John Cabot set out on voyage of
        exploration to the Americas, partly funded by King; 17 June: Henry
        victorious over rebels at Blackheath; 6 Aug.: Cabot returned to Bristol
        following discovery of Nova Scotia; Aug.: proxy betrothal of Prince
        Henry & Katherine of Aragon at Woodstock; 7 Sept.: rebels welcomed
        Warbeck at Whitesand Bay; 17 Sept.: siege of Exeter by rebels; defeated

by Earl of Devon; 21 Sept.: Warbeck escaped; 30 Sept.: Anglo-Scottish truce; 5 Oct.: Warbeck brought before King, confessed he was not Richard, Duke of York & was accepted at court; 13 Dec.: Cabot granted pension of £20 p.a. by crown; Dec.: royal palace at Sheen destroyed by fire. Those charged w. petty treason were denied right of sanctuary.

1498 9 June: Warbeck escaped; 18 June: Warbeck impr. in Tower; July: Henry VI's body to be removed to Westminster Abbey (never happened); King, Queen & Queen Mother visited Cambr.; Henry VII founded Franciscan Observant Houses.

1499 The Eng. Province of the Observants was established and new convents were opened at Newcastle upon Tyne and Canterbury; 21/ 22 Feb.: b. of Prince Edmund; Mar.: 1st Irish Parl. under **Poynings Law** opened; May: confirmation of *Magnum Intercursus* of 1486; 1 July: Suffolk fled to St Omer, Picardy, to beg assistance of his aunt, Margaret of York, dowager duchess of Burgundy; July: Anglo-Scottish peace treaty; Margaret Beaufort took vow of chastity despite m. to Thomas Stanley; her council at Collyweston, nr Stamford, functions as unofficial council of the midlands; 3 Aug.: plot to free Warbeck & Earl of Warwick uncovered; Sept.: Suffolk's return by Philip the Fair secured after threat of trade embargo; 16 Nov.: Warbeck tried; 23 Nov.: Warbeck hanged at Tyburn; 28 Nov. (in some accounts the 24th): Edward Earl of Warwick beheaded for treason.

1500 Archbp John Morton d.; 19 Feb.: Flemish engineer, Matthew Hake, contracted by Crown to build dam and sluice on river Witham at Boston to stop serious fen flooding, which was adversely affecting the properties of Queen Mother, Margaret Beaufort, in the area; 1 Oct.: John Alcock, Bp of Ely d.; 2nd proxy m. betw. Arthur & Katherine of Aragon; Prince Edmund d.; House of Observants founded at Richmond.

1501 Henry VII made Baynard's Castle his principal residence; Richmond Palace completed; 26 May: Henry Deane transl. Archbp of Canterbury; Aug.: Suffolk again fled kingdom without royal licence, going w. his brother Richard de la Pole to **the court** of Emp. Maximilian; 2 Oct.: Katherine of Aragon arrived in Eng; 14 Nov.: Prince Arthur & Katherine of Aragon m. at Old St Paul's; a month of pageants and celebrations.

1502 24 Jan.: Tr. of Perpetual Peace betw. Scotland and Eng., m. betw. James IV of Scotland and Princess Margaret Tudor agreed; 2 Apr.: Prince Arthur d.; Lord Gerald Fitzgerald has prominent part in Arthur's funeral; 6 May: Sir James Tyrell, Commander of Guines near Calais, exec. for plotting v. King w. other Yorkist sympathisers, incl. Edmund & William de la Pole, s. of one of Edward IV's sisters; Margaret Beaufort's ambitious building programme at Collyweston for royal visit of Princess Margaret; Oct.: Prince Henry cr. Duke of Cornwall; 26 Dec.: exiled Edmund de la Pole, Earl of Suffolk outlawed; wid. Cecily of York banished from court for m. a mere esquire without royal permission; foundation of Lady Margaret Lectureships in theology at Oxf. & Cambr.

1503 Edinburgh High School founded; 2 Feb.: premature b. of Princess Katherine (d. shortly afterwards); 11 Feb.: Queen Elizabeth d.; 15 Feb.:

Henry Deane, Archbp of Canterbury d.; 23 Feb.: Queen Elizabeth bur.; June: Anglo-Spanish treaty specified m. betw. Prince Henry & Katherine of Aragon after papal dispensation, payment of **dowry** & Henry being 15; 23 June: Tr. of **marriage** specifying m. *per verba de praesenti*; 25 June: Prince Henry betrothed to Katherine; July: progress of Princess Margaret to Collyweston; 16 July: Elizabeth Zouche (a Beaufort) & Lord Gerald Fitzgerald (1487–1534), hostage heir to Kildare (& later 9th Earl), m.; Aug.: Kildare, Fitzgerald & h.w. returned to Ireland; 8 Aug.: Princess Margaret m. James IV of Scotland; 8 Nov.: Sir Thomas Lovell elected Speaker of HofC; 29 Nov.: Papal transl. of William Warham from London to Canterbury; Thomas Marowe discussed whether *feme sole* could be appointed a justice by royal **commission**; Margaret Beaufort at Collyweston successfully arbitrated dispute betw. Town & Gown at Cambr.; Dec.: Sir John Hussey app'd Master of Court of Wards & Liveries.

1504 21 Jan.: Warham app'd Lord Chancellor; Jan.: parl. attainder of Edmund and Richard de la Pole & others; Feb.: Fitzgerald app'd Treasurer of Ireland; 23 Feb.: Prince Henry cr. Prince of Wales; Mar.: Warham enthroned Archbp; Mar.: papal dispensation for Prince Henry's m. received; 3 Mar.: Henry VII signed m. treaty made the previous year; Apr.: Sir Thomas More led parl. to reduce parl. grant by two-thirds; Henry VII cr. post of royal printer & app'd William Faques; 30 Oct.: founding of Lady Margaret preacher at Cambr.; 26 Nov.: Queen Isabella of Castile d.; Kildare defeated Ó Briain & Clanricarde in pitched battle at **Knockdoe**; Kildare cr. **Knight of the Garter**.

1505 Feb.: Prince Henry formally repudiated betrothal to Katherine of Aragon, alleging no consent on his part, in diplo. attempt to keep m. options open; John Fisher elected President of Queens' College, Cambr. at Margaret Beaufort's behest; re-foundation of God's House as Christ's College, Cambr. by Margaret Beaufort.

1506 6 Jan.: Richard Pynson app'd King's printer; 17 Jan.: Philip and Joanna, king & queen of Castile, landed in Dorset, due to storm; escorted to King Henry VII's court; 24 Apr.: Edmund de la Pole impr. in Tower; Henry VII made loan to Philip of the Low Countries to invade Spain.

1507 Royal printing press est'd in Edinburgh; winter: Henry VII seriously ill; June: Prince Henry displayed prowess at tournament; 24 Dec.: George Neville, Lord Bergavenny, heavily fined for raising a large private army and instigating a riot in Kent in 1503.

1508 Feb.: Spanish ambass. brought dowry; Henry angling for m. of Princess Mary w. future Charles V; Mar.: Henry VII so seriously ill that his mother, with her **servants**, moved into Richmond to watch over him; late in the year: plans made for Katherine's return to Spain.

Henry VIII

1509 Mar.: Margaret Beaufort travels betw. Coldharbour and Richmond to attend Henry VII in last illness; 21 Apr.: Henry VII d.; on deathbed

Henry made Margaret chief executrix of will; kept secret until 23 Apr. John, Edmund & Richard de la Pole excepted from general pardon; 24 Apr.: impr. of Edmund Dudley & Sir Richard Empson, two of Henry VII's most unpopular ministers, for plotting v. Henry VIII's accession; 11 May: Lady Margaret Beaufort accorded precedence over all other royal women at funeral; 11 June: Henry VIII m. Katherine at Greenwich; 24 June: coronation of Henry VIII & Katherine by Warham; 29 June: d. of Margaret Beaufort, Countess of Richmond & Derby, Henry VIII's paternal grandmother; Nov.: Henry VIII promotes Thomas Wolsey, Dean of Lincoln, to position of Almoner; Erasmus arr. in Eng. for extended visit.

1510   31 Jan.: Queen miscarried dau.; Pynson prints statutes; 8 Nov.: Kildare confirmed as Dep. of Ireland.

1511   1 Jan.: Henry, Prince of Wales, b.; 12–13 Feb.: allegorical Tournament of Westminster to celebrate birth; 22 Feb.: Prince Henry d.; (by) June: Wolsey joined PC; Aug.: Erasmus made 1st professor of Greek & Divinity at Cambr.; Nov.: Eng. joined Holy League w. Pope Julius II, Venetian Republic & Ferdinand of Aragon v. Louis XII of France; Henry founds Royal Armoury at Greenwich; Erasmus working on his Latin transl. of New Testament.

1512   Completion of chapel of Henry VII at **Westminster**; Pietro Torrigiano continued to work on tomb of Henry VII & Elizabeth; Richard Pynson secured exclusive right to print statutes & proclamations; James IV of Scotland renewed alliance w. Fr. & refused to join Holy League; 4 Feb.: 2nd parl. of reign opened; Act of Parl. consolidated Henry VII's legislative attacks on benefit of clergy in case of serious crimes; Mar.: Pope granted Henry title of Most Christian King; 10 Apr.: b. of Prince James of Scotland; Henry VIII decl. war v. Fr.; May: troops sent to Basque country; May: foundation of St Leonard's College, St Andrews; June: Louis XII supporter of Richard de la Pole's claim to Eng. throne; 15 June: Mercers' Company to run St Paul's School; Oct.: Eng. troops return home after mutiny in Spain; Dec.: Richard de la Pole fights w. Louis XII v. Eng. in Navarre.

1513   Mar.: invaded Fr.; 5 Apr.: **Emperor** joined Holy League; 4 May: Edmund de la Pole, 8th Earl of Suffolk, exec. without trial; Richard de la Pole decl. himself duke of Suffolk & claimed Eng. throne; 30 June to 21 Oct.: Queen regent during Henry's absence on campaign in Fr.; 16 Aug.: Battle of Spurs at Therouanne when Richard de la Pole fought Eng.; 22 Aug.: Scots invaded Eng.; 22 Aug.: Therouanne surrendered to Henry; Henry took Tournai in person; 3 Sept.: Kildare d.; Sept.: 8th Earl of Kildare d.; Henry confirmed app't of Gerald, 9th Earl of Kildare (his boyhood friend) as Lord Dep. of Ireland; 9 Sept.: Thomas Howard, Earl of Surrey, defeated Scots at **Flodden** Field; James IV d. in the battle; ? infant b. to Queen Katherine; 21 Sept.: infant James V crowned & 24-yr-old Queen Margaret (sister of Henry VIII) made Queen Regent; 23 Sept.: Tournai surrendered to Holy League; 25 Sept. Henry rode triumphant into Tournai.

1514 1 Feb.: Thomas Howard cr. Duke of Norfolk & s. Thomas cr. Earl of Surrey; 1 Feb.: Charles Brandon cr. 1st Duke of Suffolk; June: Louis XII & Richard de la Pole planned invasion of Eng.; 7 Aug.: Anglo-French peace treaty; provided for m. of Princess Mary to Louis XII; 2 Sept.: Richard de la Pole under protection of Duke of Lorraine; Sept.: Wolsey, previously Bp of Lincoln, made Archbp of York; 6 Nov.: Mary entered Paris as Queen of France; Nov. or Dec.: prince stillborn; Richard Hunne sued in London Consistory Court for refusal to pay **mortuary** fine; Hunne lost case & impr. but retaliated by suing the priest under the statutes of *praemunire*; Dec.: Richard Hunne d. in gaol; rumours of murder; rumours that King has mistress; Wolsey acquired Hampton Court; Erasmus left Eng. for good.

1515 1 Jan.: François I succeeded cousin Louis as King of France; mid-Feb: Princess Mary secretly m. Charles Brandon in Paris; parl. debates bills to abolish mortuary fees and to limit **benefit of clergy**. In connection with Hunne's case, Dr Richard Kidderminster, Abbot of Winchcombe, and Dr Henry Standish, the Crown's appointee, debated the right of secular courts to try clergy and, therefore, independence of the church and its servants from state jurisdiction. **Convocation** summoned Standish to answer for his criticisms of the church but the King secured his release and later rewarded him with dioc. of St Asaph. A compromise, which included the suppression of all **anti-clerical** bills and the exaction of fines from guilty parties in the Hunne case, was worked out. Apr.: Eng. soldiers at Tournai threatened to defect to Richard de la Pole, who was supported by François; 13 May: public m. of Brandon & Princess Mary at Greenwich; Anglo-Spanish alliance; 10 Sept.: Pope made Wolsey Cardinal; 15 Nov.: Wolsey received Cardinal's hat; 24 Dec.: Wolsey replaced Warham as Lord Chancellor.

1516 Jan.: Ferdinand d.; succeeded by Charles V; 18 Feb.: Princess Mary b.; Henry VIII impr. 5th Earl of Northumberland in Fleet.

1517 Kildare invaded Tyrone in support of O'Neill; Kildare visited Court; 1 May: Norfolk suppr. **'Evil May day'** riots in London; Queen pleaded for pardon for rioters; June: Wolsey seriously ill; summer: Richard de la Pole visited Milan & Venice.

1518 Jan.: Wolsey attempted to enforce quarantine as remedy for plague; Aug.: Wolsey & Campeggio cr. papal **legates** for period; 2 Oct.: Tr. of Universal Peace (aka Tr. of London); returned Tournai to Fr.; 5 Oct.: proxy betrothal of Dauphin François to Princess Mary; 9/10 Nov.: princess stillborn (Queen's last delivery).

1519 12 Jan.: Emp. Maximilian d.; succeeded by grands. Charles V; King acknowl. b. of illegit. s. Henry Fitzroy; Sept.: Kildare visited Court & detained; 28 Oct.: **Star Chamber** punished Sir William Bulmer for wearing Duke of Buckingham's **livery**; Pope extended Wolsey's Legatine powers for three years; Wolsey undertook visitation of Westminster Abbey.

1520 Hugh Latimer, Thomas Cranmer, Miles Coverdale, Robert Barnes, John Frith & others met regularly at White Horse tavern, Cambr. This discussion group was characterised by a broadly sympathetic attitude to church reform; publ'n of Luther's *On the Babylonish Captivity of the Church*; May: Kildare forbidden to leave London area; Chas V met w. King in London; 7–24 June: Wolsey, Charles Brandon & Kildare (among others) accompanied King at **Field of Cloth of Gold**; late summer: Kildare impr.; Nov.: Kildare released.

1521   Jan.: Pope Leo X **excommunicating** Martin Luther; spring: Kildare again impr.; Wolsey acted v. importation of Lutheran books; 12 May: Bp Fisher preached at burning of Lutheran books in St Paul's Churchyard; 17 May: Edward Stafford, 3rd Duke of Buckingham exec. for tr.; heretics in London **diocese** persecuted; many heretics burnt; May: Henry VIII pub'd rebuttal of Luther in *Assertio septem sacramentorum*; 2 Oct.: presented *Assertio* to Leo X; rewarded w. title *Fidei Defensor* (Defender of the Faith).

1522   26 May: Chas V came to Eng.; 16 June: Anglo-Imperial Tr. v. Fr.; 19 June: secret treaty confirmed betrothal of Chas V to Mary; Fr. invaded; Wolsey instituted permanent Legatine court w. John Allen as chancellor; 'general proscription' or survey to measure military preparedness, & used to assess & raise a non-parl. forced loan; Kildare m. Lady Elizabeth Grey, King's cousin; Martin Luther publ'd his German translation of the New Testament, which was based on Erasmus's text.

1523   Queen brought Juan Luis Vives to Eng.; Queen commissioned Vives to write *De institutione foeminae Christianae*; Kildare & h.w. went to Ireland; Aug.: Suffolk led invasion of Fr.; Oct.: Brandon's Fr. campaign began w. early successes & fall of Paris expected; autumn: early promise of Fr. campaign petered out; Nov.: conflict betw. Ormond & Kildare culminated in murder of sheriff of Dublin; mid-Dec.: Eng. troops retreated to Calais; 28-year-old scholar, William Tyndale, sought but did not receive support from Bp Tunstall of London for English transl. of **Bible**.

1524   Jan.: Pope cr. Wolsey Legate for life; pub'n of Vives' *De institutione foeminae Christianae*; 21 May: 2nd Duke of Norfolk d.; summer: commissioners composed Geraldine-Butler feud; Kildare app'd Dep.; Tyndale visited Hamburg, Wittenberg and Cologne. He based his Eng. translation of the New Testament on Erasmus & Luther.

1525   Robert Barnes, a friar in the Austen House at Cambridge, attacked relig. Ceremonies; Wolsey suppressed 29 religious houses & transferred their financial resources to Cardinal College, Oxford; Jan.: Wolsey began building of Cardinal College, Oxford & gave Hampton Court Palace to King; Princess Mary's household est'd at Ludlow & her council of Wales & Welsh Marches; Richard Featherstone app'd Latin tutor to Princess Mary; 23/24 Feb: Charles V at Pavia impr. François I of France; Richard de la Pole d. at battle of Pavia; Apr.: Henry asked parl. for 'Amicable Grant' to finance war; 11 May: East Anglian rebellion crushed; 18 June: Henry Fitzroy cr. Duke of Richmond; June: Charles V refused to m. Princess Mary; Aug.: Richmond app'd Warden of Northern

Marches & Lieut.-Gen. of North; 30 Aug.: Anglo-French treaty of The More; joined papal Holy League of Cognac; Tyndale's English Bible being printed in Cologne but, because of intervention by Church authorities, had to be transferred to & completed at Worms.

1526 Erasmus dedicated *Christiani matrimonii institutio* to Queen; Wolsey intro'd Eltham Ordinances for royal household; reorganised Council of Wales; 26 Jan.: 3 Hanse merchants arrested for smuggling heretical books into Eng.; Margaret of Scotland bigamously m. Henry Stewart, treasurer & Lord Chancellor of Scotland; Shrove Tuesday: King smitten by Anne Boleyn; Apr.: copies of Tyndale's New Testament on sale in Eng. Bp of London forbade its dissemination or possession in his diocese, 6,000 copies of Tyndale's Eng. Bible seized in London & a copy burnt at Paul's Cross. New ed'n printed by Christopher Endhoven at Antwerp.; Aug.: King publicly favoured Anne Boleyn; Hans Holbein the younger welcomed to court; Aug.: Kildare & Ormond summoned to court; recoinage.

1527 Thomas Bilney impr. in Tower for **heresy**; 30 Apr.: Anglo-French Tr. of Westminster; May: Wolsey demanded that Henry secretly answer charge that he was living in sin w. his bro. Arthur's wid.; June: sack of Rome by Emp. Chas V; 22 June: King informed Katherine of Aragon of **divorce** plans; July: Katherine informed Pope & Emperor that her m. w. Arthur was never consummated & therefore void; July: Edward Seymour accompanied Wolsey on embassy to Fr.; Aug.: King sought papal dispensation to m. Anne; Aug.: Anglo-French Peace of Amiens finalised; Dec.: King requested papal legatine commission of Wolsey & Campeggio to try matter of divorce.

1528 Jan.: war decl. v. Charles V;.23 Feb.: Piers Butler cr. Earl of Ossory & his former title, Earl of Ormonde, conferred upon Thomas Boleyn; Cardinal Wolsey prosecuted some, incl. Thomas Garrett of Oxford, for distributing Tyndale's New Testament; 6 July: 16-year-old James V entered Edinburgh to assert right to rule; Kildare impr.; 4 Aug.: Piers Butler, Earl of Ossory cr. Dep. of Ireland; 20,000 Irish supporters of Kildare emigrated to Pembrokeshire.

1529 22 June: Duke of Richmond app'd Lieut. of Ireland; 31 May: Legatine Court formally opened at Blackfriars to hear divorce case; 18 June to 31 July: King's divorce proceedings at Blackfriars; 1 July: King registered 'scruple of conscience' by several bps regarding validity of his m.; 31 July: case deferred to Oct.; 4 Aug.: Dublin Council dismissed Ossory; Oct.: Wolsey charged w. *Praemunire*; 18 Oct.: Wolsey surrendered Great Seal; 25 Oct.: More app'd Lord Chancellor; Thomas Cranmer app'd royal chaplain; Stephen Gardiner app'd principal **secretary**; 3 Nov.–17 Dec.: 1st session of Reformation Parl. which opened w. renewed calls for **ecclesiastical** reform. Acts passed to regulate burial & **probate** fees; to remove **Benefit of Clergy** from those charged with murder or robbery; to limit **pluralism**; to limit clerical involvement in trade & commerce; to remove possibility of papal dispensations. HofC drew up a Supplication directed v. the bps.

1530   12 Feb. Wolsey pardoned by King (after Cromwell's intercession); 14 Feb.: Wolsey rest. to Archbpric of York; Hoochstraten of Antwerp pub'd Tyndale's Eng. version of Pentateuch (first five books of the Old Testament). Endhoven pub'd a new ed'n of Tyndale's New Testament. Henry VIII set up **commission** of inquiry into need for Eng. Bible, which reported back favourably. George Joye pub'd *Psalms* in Eng. Pope was petitioned by 22 abbots to approve divorce betw. Henry VIII & Katherine of Aragon. Henry VIII's agents toured the major European universities soliciting academic support for divorce. *Praemunire* charges brought v. leading churchmen who had had financial dealings w. Wolsey. 8 Apr.: univs of Oxf. & Cambr. decl. in favour of royal divorce; 22 June: Sir William Skeffington app'd Dep. of Ireland; summer: presentation to King of 'Collectanea Satis Copiosa' (the sufficiently full collections) regarding papal jurisdiction; Aug.: Kildare given general pardon & returned to Ireland; 4 Nov.: Wolsey arrested for tr.; 29 Nov.: Wolsey d. at Leicester; King took possession of Hampton Court (given to him by Wolsey in 1525); Thomas Cromwell joined King's Council.

1531   Jan. to Mar.: 2nd Session of Reformation Parl.; late Jan.: King charged clergy w. *praemunire* & demanded £100,000 from **convocation** of Canterbury for pardon; church agreed to pay; King's further demands incl. recognition of him as 'the only protector and supreme head of the English church and clergy', King gave general pardon when clergy agreed 'as far as the law of Christ allows'; parl. confirmed this as Act for the Pardon of the Clergy; Mar.: Bilney exec. at Norwich; 11 July: last audience of Katherine of Aragon w. Henry VIII; 14 July: King moved into Woodstock Palace w. Anne Boleyn; Nov.: Stephen Gardiner cr. Bp of Winchester; King asked southern Convocation to recognise him as 'Supreme Head of the Church of England'; Nov.: pub'n of *Determinations of the . . . Universities.*

1532   15 Jan.: 3rd session of Reformation Parl. assembled; Reginald Pole retired to Italy; Gardiner in convocation led oppo. to supremacy; . 25 Jan.: Pope threatened Henry VIII w. excomm.; Mar.: Archbp Warham excomm. Hugh Latimer; Mar.: Act for the Conditional Restraint of Annates; 18 Mar.: Commons' Supplication v. the ordinaries handed to King; Stephen Gardiner penned 'Answer of the Ordinaries'; Thomas More led oppos'n to this; spring: Kildare & Ossory recalled to Eng.; 14 Apr.: Cromwell app'd Master of the Jewels; 14 May: parl. **prorogued**; May: King suspended legis. business in Convocation and ordered inquiry into canon law; 15 May: Warham & seven bps signed 'Submission of the Ordinaries'; 16 May: More resigned Chancellorship; 5 July: 9th Earl of Kildare app'd Dep. of Ireland; 22 Aug.: Warham d.;1 Sept.: Anne Boleyn cr. Marchioness (Marquis) of Pembroke in her own right; Sept.: pub'n of *A Glasse of the Truthe*; Oct: Henry & Anne Boleyn met Francis I at Calais.

1533   25 Jan.: Cranmer secretly m. King & Anne Boleyn at **Whitehall**; 26 Jan.: Sir Thomas Audley app'd Lord Chancellor; 4 Feb.: parl. recalled to legitimise m.; Apr.: Act in Restraint of Appeals to Rome; 30 Mar.:

Cranmer consecr. Archbp of Canterbury (w. papal bull); 9 Apr.: Katherine of Aragon informed she is no longer Queen; 12 Apr.: Cromwell app'd Chancellor of Exchequer; Pope excomm. Henry VIII; 10 May: King's m. to Katherine of Aragon tried *in absentia* at Dunstable; 23 May: Cranmer annulled m. to Katherine of Aragon; 28 May: decl. m. to Anne valid; 1 June: Anne Boleyn crowned; Sept.: Pope excomm. Henry VIII; Sept.: Kildare recalled to London to answer charges of maladministration; 7 Sept.: Princess Elizabeth b. at Greenwich; 23 Nov.: Elizabeth Barton impr. for tr.; 3 Dec.: Cranmer enthroned at Canterbury.

1534 German Bible pub'd at Wittenberg. New ed'n of Tyndale's New Testament pub'd at Antwerp. Miles Coverdale started work on English Bible at Antwerp; creation of Canterbury Mint; Jan. to Mar.: session of parl. intro. imp. legisl'n; Act of Dispensations; new Act in Restraint of Annates; Act for Submission of the Clergy; 23 Mar.: Pope decl. m. w. Katherine valid; 26 Mar.: Act of Succession; 30 Mar.: Act forbidding flocks of more than 2,000 sheep; 30 Mar.: Audley gave royal assent to all this legisl'n; MPs swore oath accepting Act of Succession before parl. prorogued; 13 Apr.: oath to succession admin. to London clergy; 17 Apr.: Thomas More impr. in Tower; 18 Apr.: Citizens of London to swear to succession; 20 Apr.: London guildsmen swore oath to succession; Elizabeth Barton 'Holy Maid of Kent', Dr Edward Bocking & two others hanged at Tyburn; Apr.: Cromwell app'd Principal Secretary & Chief Minister; Act of Treasons; 19 Apr.: Rowland Lee consecr. Bp of Coventry & Lichfield & Thomas Goodrich consecr. Bp of Ely & made to swear to both supremacy & succession; May: Katherine of Aragon under house arrest in Cambridgeshire; Rowland Lee, Bp of Coventry & Lichfield, app'd President of Council of Marches & Wales; May: Cranmer's metropolitical visitation began; 1 May: new Dublin parl. assembled; 11 May: Anglo-Scots peace treaty; 11 June: Kildare's s., Lord Offaly 'Silken Thomas' rebelled; 29 June: Kildare impr. in Tower; 27/28 July: Lord Offaly's supporters murdered John Alen, Archbp of Dublin; 30 July: Sir William Skeffington replaced Kildare as Lord Dep.; 2 Sept.: Kildare d. & was replaced by h.s. Lord Offaly; Offaly besieged Dublin; 24 Oct.: Skeffington arrived to quash rebellion; 11 Nov.: Cranmer replaced Legatine powers w. Metropolitical authority; Nov.: parl. reconvened: Nov.–Dec.: important legisl'n – 17 Nov.: Act of Supremacy; followed by Treason Act; Acts concerning **First Fruits and Tenths**. The Oath of Supremacy was administered to all religious houses. The Observant Houses were closed. All houses of friars visited. Dec.: **Convocation** petitioned King for Eng. Bible. Cranmer organised modification of Tyndale's New Testament but project was unsuccessful. In this year Cromwell and others discuss financial nationalisation of English Church, but discarded the plan; 19 Dec.: truce betw. Eng. & Kildare.

1535 21 Jan.: Cromwell made **vicegerent** or vicar-general; compilation of *Valor ecclesiasticus* (King's Book of the values of church property); visitation of the monasteries; Feb.: Margaret Chanseler alleged to have called Anne Boleyn 'a goggyll eyed hoore' & brought before JPs; Apr.:

Cromwell ordered impr. of clergy preaching papal supremacy; 23 Mar.: defeat of Kildare at Maynooth Castle; 4 May: three priors of Carthusians hanged at Tyburn; 20 May: John Fisher cr. Cardinal; 3 June: Vicegerent Cromwell ordered bps & prs to preach in support of supremacy; 19 June: three more Carthusians exec.; 22 June: John Fisher exec.; June–Sept.: King & Queen on progress to west country; 6 July: More exec.; Aug.: Kildare surrendered; 31 Dec.: Skeffington d.

1536   **Privy Council** replaced King's Council; 7 Jan.: Katherine of Aragon d. at Kimbolton, Hunts; 29 Jan.: Anne Boleyn miscarried boy for second time; 4 Feb.: last session of Reformation parl. began; 6 Feb.: Cranmer preached v. Pope as Anti-Christ; Mar.: Anne oppo. Cromwell's secularisation policy; Mar.–Apr.: Anne quarrelled w. Cromwell; Mar.: book of complaints v. the monasteries (*Compendium compertorum*) brought before parl.; 3 Mar.: Edward Seymour app'd Gent. of Privy Chamber; Edward Seymour, h.w. & his sister Jane installed in apartment in Greenwich Palace; 18 Mar.: Act of Suppr. of religious houses worth less than £200 p.a.; **Court of Augmentations** set up to carry out suppr. & administer former monastic lands; suppr. of 243 of the 419 smaller monasteries began; Statute of **Uses**; 14 Apr.: Act of Union betw. Eng. & Wales 'act for laws and justice to be ministered in Wales in like forms as it is in this realm'; 18 Apr.: King tried to persuade Emp. to recognise Anne as queen; 30 Apr.: arrest of Mark Smeaton; 2 May: Anne Boleyn impr. in Tower; 15 May: Anne stood trial w. Rochford; 17 May: Cranmer decl. m. null & void; 19 May: Anne exec.; 19 May: Cranmer signed dispensation for King to m. Jane Seymour within degrees of **affinity**; 30 May: King m. Jane Seymour privately; May: Irish parl. posthumously attainted 9th Earl of Kildare; 8 June: new parl. assembled; 9 June: Convocation assembled; June: Act of Exchange; 18 June: Thomas Boleyn resigned Privy Seal; 2 July: Cromwell app'd Lord Privy Seal; 7 July: Edward Seymour app'd governor & captain of Jersey; 11 July: **Ten Articles**; Cromwell issues the first Royal **Injunctions**, by which the clergy are ordered to preach quarterly sermons, to provide religious instruction in English for the young, to sustain the poor and to discourage what was seen as the superstitious devotion to **shrines** and images; 15 June: Princess Mary swore oath of supremacy; 22 July: Richmond d.; June: Princess Mary acknowl. royal supremacy & her own illegitimacy; July: 2nd Act of Succession illegitimated Mary & Elizabeth & vested succession in Henry & Jane's children; Aug.: Tyndale condemned for obstinate heresy; 6 Oct.: Tyndale exec. in Low Countries; 2–12 Oct.: Lincolnshire rising: 2 Oct.: start of **Pilgrimage of Grace** at Louth, Lincs; 9 Oct.: outbreak of revolt in Yorkshire, Lancashire & the north, known as the Pilgrimage of Grace; 16 Oct.: rebels occupied York; 20 Oct.: rebels took Pontefract & were joined by Lord Darcy; 8 Dec.: leaders of Pilgrimage offered pardon by Duke of Norfolk; poor law enacted.

1537   1 Jan.: James V of Scotland m. Princess Madeleine of France; Jan.: riots in north; Jan.: second Yorkshire rising under Sir Francis Bigod; 3 Feb.:

'Silken Thomas' 10th Earl of Kildare & his five uncles exec. for tr. at Tyburn; Mar.–Apr.: Pilgrimage rebels incl. Robert Aske arrested; Apr.: Furness Abbey, Cumbria, one of the greater monasteries, was first to 'voluntarily surrender' to King; 22 May: Edward Seymour PC; June: London Charterhouse (Carthusian) surrendered to King & more Carthusian monks exec.; 30 June: Henry Percy, Earl of Northumberland d.; July: exec. of Robert Aske at York; 7 July: Madeleine of Scotland d.; Aug.: Thomas Mathew (alias John Rogers, a friend of Tyndale) pub'd the 'Mathew Bible', based on Tyndale and more Protestant than Coverdale's translation, with King's permission. Sept.: reorganisation of Council of North; King criticised Hugh Latimer's paper condemning doctrine of **purgatory**; Sept.: pub'n of The *Institution of a Christian Man* (aka '**Bishops' Book**'); King criticised its contents; 12 Oct.: Prince Edward b. at Hampton Court; 15 Oct.: Prince Edward baptised; 18 Oct.: Edward Seymour cr. Earl of Hertford; 24 Oct.: Queen Jane d.; 13 Nov.: Queen Jane bur. at Windsor; court in mourning until 2 Feb 1538; Dec.: Henry VIII amended so-called Bishops' Book in unpredicted fashion. He excluded astrology from list of prohibitions & altered wording of 1st Commandment to read that Christians must pray only to Christ, not God the Father; 3 Dec.: Abbot of Rievaulx, North Yorkshire, signed deed of surrender; during this year many **religious** voluntarily withdrew from their orders, some taking pension, others not.

1538 Hans Holbein toured European courts making portraits of suitable brides for Henry VIII; Jan.: King attempted revision of Bishops' Book; May: King seriously ill; 4 May: James V of Scotland m. Mary of Guise by proxy; 10 June: Mary of Guise arrived in Scotland; 18 June: Fr. & the **Empire** signed Tr. of Nice; June: Plot to crown Gerald Fitzgerald, heir to Kildare, King of Ireland; Aug.: impr. of Geoffrey de la Pole & others; Sept.: Royal injunctions ordered cessation of superstitious worship & rituals; destruction of shrines; 8 Sept.: destruction of shrine of St Thomas Becket at Canterbury; John Bale's play v. Becket performed at court; 16 Nov.: cult of Thomas Becket outlawed; 16 Nov.: King presided over trial of John Lambert; 12 Nov.: Countess of Salisbury interrogated for high tr.; 22 Nov.: building of renaissance Nonsuch Palace, Surrey began; 17 Dec.: Pope Paul III reissued bull excomm. Henry VIII; 19 Dec.: Henry exchanged church lands w. Charles Brandon & placed him in East Anglia to keep the peace; Cranmer worked on revised, vernacular Breviary, that replaced eight church services w. two (morning & evening prayer); royal injunctions instructed all Eng. parishes to supply vernacular Bible; Bp Edmund Bonner (under Cromwell's instruction) supervised project to print in Fr. a Bible transl. overseen by Miles Coverdale.

1539 Eng. put on alert v. possible invasion by Franco-Imperial alliance; Calais fortifications strengthened; Feb.: new castles for defence ordered in Kent (Deal, Sandown & Walmer); 28 Apr.: parl. assembled; Act for the Dissolution of the Greater Monasteries (31 Henry VIII, cap. 13) led to closure of those still extant; Apr.: 1st ed'n of Great Bible available in

Eng.; Apr.: Proclamation on Uniformity in Religion was cautious on popular Bible reading & made it private; Cranmer abandoned 1st version of Eng. liturgy; spring: evangelicals arrested in Calais; May: Margaret Pole, Countess of Salisbury attainted; June: bps debated Act of 6 Articles & demoted auricular confession to something merely 'expedient'; 16 June: conservative Act of 6 Articles passed; 1 July: Bps of Worcester & Salisbury res.; July: Cranmer sent wife to Germany; Miles Coverdale left Eng.; Act of Proclamations; Holbein painted daus of Duke of Cleves; Kildare faction defeated at Bellahoe by Deputy, Lord Leonard Grey; 27 Oct.: Hugh Cook, Abbot of Benedictine monastery of Reading condemned to d. for treason; by Nov.: Countess of Salisbury impr. in Tower; mid-Nov.: Calais evangelicals released; 15 Nov.: Richard Whiting, Abbot of Benedictine monastery of Glastonbury, hanged for tr.; 27 Dec.: Anne of Cleves arrived.

1540 5 Jan.: King tried to stop Cleves m.; 6 Jan.: King m. Anne of Cleves; Jan.–May 1540: Henry unable to consummate the m.; 16 Feb.: Cluniac Priory of Thetford surrendered; 21 Mar.: Gerald Fitzgerald escaped to St Malo; Mar.: Robert Barnes, Wm Jerome & Thomas Garrett impr. in Tower; Apr./May: 2nd ed'n of Great Bible, w. preface by Cranmer (hence 'Cranmer's Bible'), pub'd. Berthelet pub'd cheap ed'n. A young London layman, John Porter, was arrested by Bp of London for reading aloud and commenting upon the Bible in St Paul's; Apr.: Cromwell cr. Earl of Essex & Lord Great Chamberlain; Waltham Abbey was last of the greater monasteries to surrender 'voluntarily' to the crown; summer: committee set up to revise Bishops' Book of 1537; King supported evangelical anti-clerical position on many points; 10 June: Cromwell impr. at PC meeting; 19 June: HofL accused Cromwell of tr.; June: King took Katherine Howard as mistress; Lord Leonard Grey, Dep. of Ireland, impr.; **Statute of Wills**; 9 July: both Convocations annulled m. to Anne; 29 June: parl. passed Act of Attainder v. Cromwell; 12 July: m. to Anne of Cleves annulled by parl.; 28 July: Cromwell exec.; 28 July: King m. Katherine Howard at Oatlands; **Court of Wards** & Court of First Fruits and Tenths estab'd; 8 Aug.: Katherine proclaimed Queen; burning of Protestant Robert Barnes, William Jerome & Thomas Garrett at Smithfield balanced by execs of three Catholics for tr.; Eng. Bible ordered in every church; 12 Aug.: Sir Anthony St Leger app'd Dep. of Ireland.

1541 Jan.: Sir Ralph Sadler & Thomas Wyatt impr.; twin sons of James V & Mary of Guise d.; 9 Jan.: Edward Seymour KG; 27 May: Countess of Salisbury exec.; June–Sept.: Henry & Katherine's progress to York accompanied by John Leland, antiquary; Henry VIII snubbed by James V's failure to meet him at York; 18 June: Henry decl'd King of Ireland by Dublin parl. thus transforming Ireland from lordship into kingdom; 28 June: Lord Leonard Grey exec. for tr.; July: ceremonies such as app't of boy bps on St Nicholas' Day were abolished by royal proclam.; 6 Aug.: Tyrconnell submitted to St Leger; Great Bible went into 5th ed'n;

sees of Chester, Gloucester, Peterborough created; July: many ancient customs connected with **Holy Days** abolished; Oct.: abolition of all **shrines** ordered. Catholic plot discovered in Yorkshire. Order reinforces instruction that Great Bible must be set up in all parish churches; 18 Oct.: Margaret (Tudor) of Scotland d.; 14 Nov.: Katherine Howard under house arrest at Syon House; 22 Nov.: Katherine deposed; 10 Dec.: Francis Dereham & Thomas Culpepper exec.; 28 Dec.: Conn O'Neill submitted to St Leger.

1542   Creation of sees of Oxford & Bristol. Conservatives in **Convocation** secure agreement that Great Bible will be revised in a more conservative fashion in the light of the Vulgate transl. Cranmer initiates this but the project is transferred by Henry to the universities and it never bears fruit. The Great Bible is still available. 21 Jan.: attainder of Katherine Howard & Lady Rochford by HofL; 10 Feb.: Katherine Howard moved to Tower; 11 Feb.: King gave assent to Bill of Attainder; 13 Feb.: Katherine Howard & Lady Rochford exec.; Apr.: Cranmer accused of heresy but cleared; 1 Oct.: Conn O'Neill cr. Earl of Tyrone; 24 Nov.: Eng. defeat Scots at battle of Solway Moss; 8 Dec.: Mary of Guise gave b. to Princess Mary; 14 Dec. James V of Scotland d.; 28 Sept.: Edward Seymour app'd Lord High Admiral; 29 Dec.: Henry VIII released Scots nobles captured at Solway Moss in exchange for their support of m. betw. Prince Edward & infant Mary Queen of Scotland; beginnings of debasement of **coinage** to raise money.

1543   Philip II (aged 16) became nominal ruler of Spain & m. Maria of Portugal; pub'n of *The Necessary Doctrine & Erudition for any Christian Man* (**King's Book**), rejected **justification by faith** but was critical of masses for the dead; Act for the Advancement of True Religion authorised King's Book as official doctrine; 3 Jan. (& 12 Mar. in parl.); 2nd Act of Union betw. Eng. & Wales; Act extended all Eng. law to Wales; Jan.: James Hamilton, Earl of Arran, app'd Regent of Scotland & tutor to Queen Mary; 27 Jan.: Arran dismissed Cardinal Beaton from Scots chancellorship; Arran announced conversion to Protestantism; 11 Feb.: Anglo-Imperial alliance v. Fr.; 16 Feb.: Edward Seymour app'd Lord Great Chamberlain; 13 Mar.: Ralph Sadler ambass. in Edinburgh; 12–17 Mar.: Scots Parl. allowed reading of vernacular Bible; 24 Mar.: charges laid v. Cranmer; July: Bp Gardiner exec. Protestants; 1 July: Anglo-Scots treaty of Greenwich provided for m. betw. Edward & Mary of Scotland in 1552; 12 July: Henry m. Katherine Parr – Prince Edward, Princesses Mary & Elizabeth attended; Sept.: King presented Cranmer w. allegations that he was 'the gretest heretique in Kent' & charged Cranmer to investigate the Canterbury Prebendaries plot; Act of Advancement of True Religion forbids the lower sort and all women below the rank of gentlewoman from reading the Scriptures. Conservative Bps Salcot, Heath and Thirlby, are ordered by the King to revise the Bishops' Book of 1537. They produce *The Necessary Doctrine and Erudition of a Christian Man*, which defends the doctrines of **transubstantiation** and salvation by works; 9 Sept.: Mary crowned Queen of Scotland; Nov.: King protected Cranmer from attacks in PC; 11 Dec.: Scots Parl. (infl. by Beaton) rejected Treaty of Greenwich.

1544   Mar.: Edward Seymour app'd Lieut.-gen. in north; 3 May: Hertford burnt Edinburgh & surrounds & sacked Holyrood; 10 June–July: Mary of Guise attempted coup; June: Eng. invaded Fr.; 11 June: King ordered use of Eng. liturgy; July: Protestant humanist scholar, Sir John Cheke, appointed tutor to Prince Edward (aged 6); 14 July: King joined troops at Calais; Katherine Parr app'd Regent & brought Elizabeth out of exile from Ashridge; Act of Succession rest. Mary & Elizabeth to places in succession but did not legitimise them; Edward Seymour app'd lieut of the kingdom under Queen Katherine's regency; Elizabeth reinstated at Court; 14–18 Sept.: King & Brandon besieged & took Boulogne; Edward Seymour joined King; Treaty of Crepy betw. Fr. & Emp.; 7 Nov.: battle of Lothian betw. Eng. & troops of Mary of Guise & Earl of Arran; Cranmer pub'd Eng. Litany; debasement of Eng. coinage.

1545   Jan.: Earl of Arran admitted Mary of Guise to Council; Edward Seymour in command at Boulogne & fought off the Fr.; 27 Feb.: Scots defeat Eng. at battle of Ancrum Moor; 2 May: Hertford again app'd Lieut.-gen. of north; May: Cranmer, etc. pub'd official vernacular *King's Primer* – substituted scriptural readings for traditional piety; 29 May: Katherine Parr pub'd *Prayers or Meditations*; 20 July: *Mary Rose* sank in Solent; 22 Aug.: Charles Brandon d.; 9 Sept.: Earl of Hertford launched counteroffensive on Scottish borders; Sept.: John Dudley, Lord Admiral, raided Fr. coast; Surrey cr. lieut-gen. of Eng's continental possessions; 24 Dec.: King in speech marking end of parl. session called for religious unity.

1546   7 Jan.: Henry Howard, Earl of Surrey & Governor of Boulogne, routed by Fr. army at St Etienne; c. 19 Feb.: Surrey replaced by Earl of Hertford as lieut.-gen.; Feb. to July: Stephen Gardiner & others plotted v. Katherine Parr; 21 Mar.: Surrey ordered home; Mar.: Hertford defended Boulogne; 29 May: Cardinal Beaton murdered; 6/7 June: Anglo-French Tr. of Camp or Ardres (incl. Scotland as Fr. ally) gave Eng. control of Boulogne till 1554; 16 July: Anne Askew burnt at Smithfield for heresy; Sept.: Henry VIII ill; Oct.: Sir Anthony Denny, Hertford's ally, app'd Chief Gentleman of King's Privy Chamber; 28 Oct.: d. of James Butler, Earl of Ormond & Ossory; 2 Dec.: Stephen Gardiner refused to exchange church lands w. Crown; 12 Dec.: Surrey sentenced to d. for treason; 26 Dec.: Hertford (Seymour), Lisle (Dudley), Paget & Denny witnessed changes to Henry VIII's will; Stephen Gardiner excl. from **executors**; regency by PC; place of Mary & Elizabeth in succession recognised but they were not legitimised; will signed by **stamp**.

Edward VI

1547   Jan.: Henry VIII seriously ill; 13 Jan.: Surrey tried; 16 Jan.: Henry VIII received ambassadors for last time; 19 Jan.: Surrey beheaded; 28 Jan.: Henry VIII d.; body embalmed & displayed at Whitehall Palace until 14

Feb.; 30 Jan.: Edward informed of H's d. at Enfield; 31 Jan. or 1 Feb.: Hertford app'd Lord Protector & governor of the king's person by executors; **iconoclasm** in London; arrival of Peter Martyr & Martin Bucer; 16 Feb.: Henry VIII bur. at Windsor; 17 Feb.: Hertford cr. Duke of Somerset; Somerset began building **Somerset House**; Elizabeth joined Katherine Parr's household; Feb.: large amount of monastic plate from Christ Church priory melted down for coining; 6 Mar.: Thomas Wriothesley depr. of lord chanc.; 12 Mar.: Patent gives Somerset authority w/out reference to regency council; c. June: Katherine Parr m. Thomas Seymour; summer: PC suspended powers of bps & sent commissioners throughout the dioceses; clergy ordered to use Nicholas Udall's transl. of Erasmus's *Paraphrases*; scandalous rumours circulate regarding Thomas Seymour & Elizabeth; 31 July: vernacular Book of Homilies pub'd & Cranmer reissued 1538 Injunctions; 22 Sept.: City of London orders survey of churches to curtail wanton destruction of church statues & stained glass; 25 Sept.: Bp Gardiner impr. in Fleet for opposing *Book of Homilies*; late Aug.: royal visitation of kingdom began; 10 Sept.: Arran routed at Battle of Pinkie by Somerset; Oct.–Dec: parl. passed radical legisl'n incl. Act dissolving the **chantries** & Act v. revilers & receiving in both kinds & repealed **Act of Six Articles**; parl. passed harsh act v. vagabonds; 25 Nov.: Ridley consecr. Bp of Rochester; Nov.: Katherine Parr pub'd *The Lamentation of a Sinner*; Dec.: Peter Martyr & Bernardino Ochino welcomed by Cranmer.

1548   Jan.–Mar.: Council ordered abol'n of many ceremonies & encouraged destruction of images & stone altars; Jan.: Cranmer issued Eng. *Order of the communion*; Jan.: Roger Ascham assumed control of Elizabeth's education; 20 Feb.: Gardiner freed after pledging obedience; 22 Feb.: orders from PC for destruction of all religious images & statues & abolition of various ceremonies, including use of holy water; 7 Mar.: Hugh Latimer preaches before Edward VI; 1 Apr.: this version of the part of the mass in which the laity took **communion** was made compulsory; Apr.: rising in Cornwall v. the Prayer Book and **enclosures**; May: Elizabeth joined household of Sir Anthony Denny; June: Cranmer issued openly Lutheran official **catechism**; **Convocation** debates Cranmer's English **Prayer Book**. Several bps, including Bonner of London and Tunstall of Durham, oppose it; 1 June: Royal proclamation to restrict enclosures; 6 July: m. betw. Mary of Scotland & Dauphin of France (later Francis II); 29 June: Gardiner imprisoned in Tower after preaching before Edward VI and making clear his implacable opposition to protestantising policies; 29 July: Mary travelled to Fr. court; 5 Sept.: Katherine Parr d. in childbirth; Dec.: foreign Protestants granted permission to establish congregation in London. 14 Dec.: Cranmer decl. belief in spiritual presence in the **Eucharist**; 17 Dec.: House of Lords begins debate on the new English Prayer Book.

1549   Jan.: parl. passed Act of Uniformity; 17 Jan.: arrest of Thomas Seymour; Feb.: clerical marriage sanctioned by parl.; Mar.: 1st Prayer Book pub'd;

9 June: use of 1st Prayer Book made compulsory; tax imposed on sheep & woollen cloth; priests allowed to m.; general unrest incl. rebellion in Devon & Cornwall in favour of old religion; 20 Mar.: Thomas Seymour exec.; July: rebels formed camps in East Anglia, led by **Robert Kett**; 8 July: Somerset set up enclosure commission; 21 July: Cranmer preached v. rebels at Paul's Cross; 22 July: Kett's men occupied Norwich; trial of Bp Edmund Bonner of London; 18 Aug.: John, Lord Russell routed the rebels at Sampford Courtenay, near Okehampton; return of John Hooper from exile; he became Somerset's Chaplain; 27 Aug.: John Dudley, Earl of Warwick defeated Kett's men at Dussindale; 1 Oct.: Bp Edmund Bonner of London depr. of see for oppo. Prayer Book; 6 Oct.: Somerset moved King to Windsor; 11 Oct.: John Dudley, Earl of Warwick led privy council *coup d'état* v. Protector Somerset; 13 Oct.: Somerset's protectorship revoked; Somerset impr. in Tower; Dec.: Wriothesley & others plotted further coup.

1550 John Hooper a prominent preacher at **court**. Emperor Chas V decided that h.s. Philip wd inherit Spain & Netherlands while Chas's brother Ferdinand wd inherit the imperial title & Ger. & Austrian Hapsburg lands; 14 Jan.: parl. confirmed Somerset's deposition; 6 Feb.: Somerset released; 8 Feb.: Somerset pardoned; Feb.: Ridley transl. Bp of London; Mar.: Cranmer pub'd ordinal; 24 Mar.: Anglo-French treaty of Boulogne (incl. Scots); Mar.: intro. of Eng. **Ordinal** & abolition of **Minor Orders**; 1 Apr.: Nicholas Ridley made Bp of London (incorporating Henrician See of Westminster); 10 Apr.: Somerset re-adm. to PC; Act for the Abolition of Divers Books and Images ordered destruction of all statues and images, incl. rood screens; gov't tried to put brake on radical Protestantism; May: **anabaptist** Joan Bocher burnt at stake; 14 May: Somerset re-app'd Gent. of **King's Chamber**; 3 June: Anne Seymour m. John Dudley, Viscount Lisle; Somerset est'd Flemish cloth manu. at Glastonbury; June: Bp Nicholas Heath impr.; 29 June: John Ponet consecrated Bp of Rochester in Ridley's place; July: Hooper nominated Bp of Gloucester; refused to wear vestments for consecration (*see* **Vestiarian Controversy**); bps (including Ridley and Hooper) issued Visitation **Injunctions** ordering removal of altars & screens from parish churches; Sept.: William Cecil joined PC & became 3rd Sec. of State; Nov.: Council ordered removal of altars & replacement by tables; 25 Dec.: Edward rebuked Princess Mary for Catholicism; 15 Dec.: trial of Bp Stephen Gardiner of Winchester; Gardiner impr. in Tower.

1551 Cranmer & Gardiner debated the Eucharist in print; Jan.: Hooper impr. in Fleet; Feb.: Bp Gardiner of Winchester depr. & replaced by John Ponet, radical Protestant; 3 Mar.: PC orders removal of plate from parish churches; 8 Mar.: Hooper consecr. Bp of Gloucester in vestments; 18 Mar.: Princess Mary rejected BofCP & **Mass** continued to be said in her Essex home; 10 June: Anglo-Scottish treaty of Norham; Eng. withdrew troops from Scotland; Unitarian, George van Parris, burnt at stake; 11 Oct.:

John Dudley cr. Duke of Northumberland & Henry Grey cr. Earl of Suffolk; 16 Oct.: Somerset impr.; work on 2nd BofCP began; Hooper a vigorous bishop; 16 Oct.: Somerset sent to Tower on charges of high treason; Oct.: Nicholas Heath deprived of See of Worcester; Mary of Guise visited Eng.; Dec.: Edward ordered sister Mary to renounce her Catholicism; she remained defiant; 1 Dec.: Somerset tried & found guilty of felony.

1552 22 Jan.: Somerset exec.; King's guard & trained bands kept peace; William Cecil, Somerset's secretary, now joined Northumberland's service; Apr.: Act of Uniformity ordered use of radical 2nd BofCP (which abol'd mass, prayers for dead & confession, etc.) as from Nov.; King ill; 26 Apr.: Hooper resigned See of Gloucs to King; 20 May: Hooper named as Bp of both Gloucester & Worcester dioceses including Gloucester archdeac. Sept.: Ridley & Edmund Grindal paid visit to Princess Mary but were rebuffed; Knox objected to kneeling, etc. in Prayer Book; printing halted; Oct./Nov: 2nd BofCP pub'd after insertion of **Black rubric** to placate radicals; henceforth, the **Mass** is totally abolished; prayers for the dead and private confession followed suit; gov't planned to issue a set of articles and held talks with divines, incl. John Knox; Cranmer in Kent investigating anabaptism; Dec: Hooper consecr. Bp of Gloucs & Worcs.

Mary I

1553 Jan.: commission of Sir Richard Cotton to seize **church plate** & vestments; Edward VI ill w. tuberculosis; Mar.: Northumberland stopped Cranmer's reform of canon law in its passage through HofL; May: pub'n of catechism, primer; May/June: **fourty-two articles** issued v. anabaptism; defined Eucharist in Zwinglian terms; asserted justification by faith & denied purgatory; 21 June: Princesses Mary & Elizabeth decl. illegit.; 6 July: Edward d.; July: Jane Grey proclaimed Queen; 19 July: Mary proclaimed Queen; July: Ridley impr. in Tower w. Cranmer, Latimer & John Bradford; release of Bps Bonner & Gardiner; 5 Sept.: Cranmer appeared before royal commissioners to answer questions about Lady Jane Grey coup & ordered to appear in Star Chamber on 14 Sept; 1 Oct.: Mary I crowned; autumn: parl. reassembled & passed 1st Act of Repeal, which undid Edwardian reformation by revoking legisl'n such as Act of Uniformity (1552) & Act for m. of priests (1550) but kept Act of Supremacy & work of reformation parl.;13 Nov.: Archbp Cranmer depr. & stood trial for tr. alongside Lady Jane Grey & the Dudley brothers; St Leger re-app'd Lord Dep. of Ireland; Dec.: Elizabeth left court & set up house at Ashridge.

1554 Jan.: mass exodus of Protestants to Germany and Switzerland, predating official persecution of m. clergy; Jan.: Thomas Wyatt led Kentish rising v. Mary's m. to Philip of Spain; 12 Feb.: Lady Jane Grey (Dudley) & Guildford Dudley exec.; 23 Feb.: Henry Grey exec.; Elizabeth returned to Whitehall; 18 Mar.: Elizabeth impr. in Tower; Mar.: Cranmer, Latimer & Ridley moved to impr. in Bocardo, Oxford; Mar.: Mary issues Royal

Injunctions ordering bps to suppress heresy, remove m. clergy, divorce **ex-religious**, re-ordain clergy who had been ordained under English **Ordinal** & restore **Holy Days**, processions & ceremonies; Bp Gardiner began depr. of m. pr.; eventually betw. 10 & 25 per cent of **parish** clergy depr. for m.; some reinstated when they conformed; 11 Apr.: Sir Thomas Wyatt exec.; 14–20 Apr.: Cranmer, Latimer & Ridley debated Eucharist; parl. eventually agreed to reintro. of heresy laws in exchange for assurance that former monastic lands will not be returned to relig. houses; 13 May: Gerald Fitzgerald rest. Earl of Kildare (this had lapsed w. exec. of his father in 1537); h.w. Mabel favoured at court; 19 May: Elizabeth under house arrest at Woodstock; 21 May: Elizabeth met Mary; 25 July: Mary m. Philip of Spain; Aug.: ceremonial entry of Philip of Spain into London; Nov.: Cardinal Pole arrived in Eng.; 2nd Act of Repeal (revoking work of Henry VIII's reformation parl.) passed & Eng. rest'd to Catholic communion; 28 Nov.: thanksgiving service at St Paul's for pregnancy of Queen; plot v. Philip; Dec.: Philip II tried to org. m. of Elizabeth to Count Emmanuel of Savoy.

1555 Richard Chancellor's Muscovy company obtained Eng. & Russian charters to trade betw. the two countries; 4 Feb.: John Rogers (biblical translator & 1st Prot. martyr of reign) is burnt under rest. heresy laws; late Apr.: false rumour that Queen had given birth (she was not pregnant); 7 June: Pope invested Philip & Mary as king & queen of Ireland; Sept.: John Knox returned to Scotland from exile; 12 Sept.: Cranmer, Latimer & Ridley tried; Sept.: Philip left Eng.; Oct.: Elizabeth returned to Hatfield; 15 Oct.: Ridley depr. of bpric; 16 Oct.: Latimer & Ridley burnt at stake in Oxford; 25 Oct.: Philip became ruler of Netherlands; 12 Nov.: Bp Gardiner of Winchester d.; Archbp Nicholas Heath of York repl. Gardiner as Chancellor; 13 Nov.: Cranmer depr. of Archbp Canterbury; 3 Dec.: Reginald Pole named Archbp of Canterbury; 11 Dec.: Cranmer moved to house arrest at Christ Church, Oxford; refoundation of Benedictine House at Westminster under Abbot John Feckenham.

1556 16 Jan.: Chas V abdicated; Philip made King of Spain & Netherlands; Ferdinand made Emperor; 24 Feb.: writ for Cranmer's exec. issued; 26 Feb.: Cranmer recanted; 18 Mar.: Sir Henry Dudley arrested for plot to place Elizabeth on throne; Philip II intervened to halt investigation; 18 Mar.: Cranmer withdrew recantation in writing; 20 Mar.: Cranmer publicly withdrew recantation; 21 Mar.: Cranmer burnt at stake in Oxford; 22 Mar.: Reginald Pole consecr. Archbp of Canterbury; 28 Apr.: plantation of Co. Laois & Offaly; 26 May: Thomas Radcliffe, Lord Fitzwalter replaced St Leger (recalled on charges of embezzlement) as Dep. of Ireland; July: Fitzwalter campaigned v. Scots in Ulster; Sept.: Philip's war v. Papacy jeopardises Eng.'s rel'ns w. papacy; worst harvest of century & dearth of corn; Eng. printing **monopoly** granted to Stationers' Company; Benedictine Westminster Abbey refounded.

1557 Forfeited Irish lands in Laois & Offaly used to form King's & Queen's Counties; Feb.: Fitzwalter inherited Earldom of Sussex; 18 Mar.: return of Philip II to beg for financial assistance; 25 Apr.: performance before Mary & Philip at Whitehall of 'Great Mask of Almains, pilgrims, & Irishmen'; late Apr.: Fr. attacked Scarborough; 7 June: Queen decl. war on Fr.; June: Pole recalled to Rome to answer charges of heresy; Mary I refused to allow him to go and rejected Friar William Peto the papal app. as Pole's replacement as Legate; 6 July: Philip II left for Fr.; 16 July: Anne of Cleves d.; Dec.: Queen announced pregnancy to Philip II.

1558   7 Jan.: Calais surr. to Fr.; Feb.: Count of Feria arrived to congratulate Queen on pregnancy & muster support for Philip II's Fr. war; 9 Mar.: Sussex cr. Lord Dep. of Ireland; 30 Mar.: Mary I excl. Elizabeth from succession; 24 Apr.: Mary of Scotland m. Fr. dauphin, Francis; 1 Sept. Prot. riots in Edinburgh; pub'n of Knox's *First Blast of the Trumpet*; 10 Nov.: 5 Protestants burnt at stake at Canterbury; **17 Nov.: d. of Mary I & accession of Elizabeth**; William Cecil made secretary of state; c.18 Nov.: Archbp Pole d.; c.18 Nov.: 1st informal meeting of PC, w. William Cecil as secretary; 23 Nov.: Elizabeth entered London; 12 Dec.: Henry Sidney app'd Lord Justice of Ireland; 25 Dec.: Elizabeth commanded Bp Oglethorpe to omit **elevation of the host** from the **Mass** in royal chapel; she left chapel when he refused.

Elizabeth I

1559   c. 10 Jan.: Philip II proposed m. to Elizabeth; 13 Jan.: Edward Seymour eldest s. of Protector was rest. to blood & cr. Earl of Hertford; 15 Jan.: coronation of Elizabeth; Elizabeth again displayed displeasure at **elevation of the host**; 25 Jan.: 1st parl. of reign assembled; Feb.: Elizabeth initiated currency reform; 2 Feb.: Select Committee of HofC petitioned Queen to m.; 10 Feb.: Elizabeth announced to parl. she had no m. plans; 3 Apr.: Peace of **Cateau-Cambrésis** w. Fr.; 29 Apr.: Act of Supremacy passed (oath of supremacy administered to clergy, royal officials, etc.); Act of Uniformity (imposing Prayer Book) passed; thus there was a new religious settlement, which declared that Elizabeth was Supreme Governor of the Church of England w. power of visitation, by reviving all the legislation which Mary's parliaments had repealed, by revoking the heresy acts & the Papal supremacy & by enforcing conformity to Prayer Book **liturgy**. **Prayer Book** provided 'a remarkable latitude of Eucharistic belief', omitted the **Black rubric** of 1552 & amended **Ornaments rubric** of 1552; issue of Royal **Injunctions**, which reinforced the new settlement; 11 May: John Knox preached inflammatory sermon at Perth; May: 1st parl. closed; May–June: Protestant riots in Perth v. Mary of Guise; 5 June: Queen rejected m. proposal from Archduke Charles of Austria; Erik XIV of Sweden a persistent suitor; 13 June: Injunctions drawn up for visitation of realm; 3 July–30 Aug.: Sussex Lord Dep. of Ireland; 7 July: Scots Protestants occupied Edinburgh; 10 July: Henri II of France d. & succeeded by Francis & Mary of Scots; c. 16 July: Conn O'Neill d. & succession by grandson.

Brien as Earl of Tyrone; Shane O'Neill (Conn's s. & h.) – excl. by patent from succession in 1542 – asserted right to earldom; 24 July: Mary of Guise signed truce w. Scots Protestant Lords of the Congregation; 21 Oct.: Mary of Guise depr. of regency; Queen ordered rest. of crucifix to Chapel Royal; 17 Dec.: Matthew Parker consecr. Archbp of Canterbury; depr. of Marian bps & small number of 'papist' clergy.

1560 Sir Henry Sidney app'd President of Council of Marches in Wales; Jan.–Feb.: Dublin parl. passed Act of Uniformity; 21 Jan.: John Jewel consecr. Bp of Salisbury; 27 Feb.: Eng/Scots Tr. of Berwick; 24 Mar.: Thomas Bentham consecr. Bp of Coventry and Lichfield; Mar./Apr.: Bps at Lambeth Synod produced 'Interpretations'; Apr.: Eng. entered Scotland; 6 May to 25 June: Sussex re-app'd Lord Lieut. of Ireland; subjugation of Shane O'Neill ordered; Gerald fitz James Fitzgerald, 14th Earl of Desmond opens renewed rivalry w. Butler, Earl of Ormond; Ormond & Desmond summoned before Elizabeth; Ormond appeared but Desmond did not; June: Cecil personally nego. w. Scots & Fr.; 11 June: Mary of Guise d.; 6 July: Anglo-Fr. Treaty of Edinburgh under which Fr. were expelled from Scotland & a Protestant regency was est'd; Scots parl. abolished papal jurisdiction; summer: ten-week royal progress; Aug.: Scots adopted **Calvinism**; 1 Sept.: John Parkhurst consecr. Bp of Norwich; pub'n of William Whittingham's Eng. transl. of the *Geneva Bible*, w. strongly Calvinist notes; this, w. its oddly-worded transl. of Genesis III, v. 7 as 'They sewed fig-leaves together and made themselves breeches', has led to it being nicknamed 'The Breeches Bible'; it was the most popular Elizabethan text of the Bible; 8 Sept.: Amy Robsart, w. of Leicester, d.; Nov.: Archbp Parker instigated survey of clergy in southern province; 5 Dec.: Francis II of France d.; Sir Thomas Smith's 'Dialogue on the queen's marriage', advocating m. w. Dudley, circulated in ms.

1561 10 Jan.: Cecil cr. Master of Wards; 27 Jan.: Church of Scotland intro. *First Book of Discipline*; Mar./Apr.: 2nd Lambeth Synod, 'Resolutions and Orders'; 25 May to 5 June: Sussex Lord Lieut. of Ireland; June: Sussex decl. Tyrone a traitor; Sussex defeated in Ireland; 13 July: Elizabeth denied Mary of Scotland safe passage though Eng.; Aug.: discovery of (heir presumptive) Lady Katherine Grey's clandestine m. w. Edward Seymour; 19 Aug.: Mary of Scotland landed in Scotland; Elizabeth began to express pref. for claims of Mary to Eng. succession; Sept.: Lady Katherine Grey & Seymour impr. in Tower; Christmas: Sackville & Norton's *Gorboduc*, implicitly advocating m. of queen to Dudley, performed at **Inns of Court**; 26 Dec.: Ambrose Dudley cr. Earl of Warwick; Eng. transl. of Calvin's *Institutes* pub'd.

1562 6 Jan.: Shane O'Neill paid homage to Elizabeth in London; Aug.: recoinage rest. Eur. confidence; May: Desmond appeared before Queen but refused homage; Desmond impr.; 20 Sept: Tr. w. Fr. achieves help for Fr. Protestants in exchange for Le Havre; Oct.: Elizabeth ill w. smallpox at Hampton Court & Robert Dudley app'd Protector; 28 Oct.: Mary

Queen of Scots defeated Earl of Huntly, 'cock o' the north', at Corrichie, Aberdeenshire; Huntly d. of heart attack; 2 Nov.: exec. of Huntly's s.; Nov.: Shane O'Neill plundered Co. Fermanagh; Nov.: Duke of Norfolk cr. PC; Dec.: O'Neill campaigned to take Ulster; John Hawkins began slaving expeditions to Africa; pub'n of Jewel's *Apology*.

1563 12 Jan.: parl. assembled; attempt to debate succession stymied; Eliz. promised to m.; Jan.: Act of Parl. obliged graduates, schoolmasters and MPs to take Oath of Supremacy; Bps drew up 'Certen Articles' and 'Generall Notes' for further eccles. reformation; Jan.: 1st Canterbury Convocation assembled; Feb.: Protestant attempts in **Convocation** to introduce Book of Discipline & reform **Prayer Book** in a more radical direction are narrowly defeated; the reforms would have abolished **Holy Days**, use of the sign of the cross, compulsory wearing of **surplice**, practice of kneeling for the sacrament and also use of organs in churches; Feb.: Convocation agreed 39 Articles of Religion; mid-Feb.: Queen accepted them after modification & resubmission (see 1571); Mar.: civil war betw Fr. Protestants & Catholics; 2 Mar.: Adam Loftus consecr. Archbp of Armagh & app'd to Irish PC; Apr.: Statute of Artificers regulated wages & employ't conditions; parl. ordered Welsh transl. of Prayer Book; Desmond released but kept in Eng.; Sussex led campaign v. O'Neill in Ireland; 28 July: Warwick surrendered Le Havre to Fr., under terms of Treaty of Amboise; 11 Sept.: O'Neill subm. to Sussex, who nevertheless failed to restore order; severe plague epidemic; Oct.: Desmond attacked Ormond; Hugh Brady app'd Protestant Bp of Meath.

1564 Winter: deep freeze in Scots Highlands, following upon dearth & inflation, led to depopulation of whole valleys; 1563/4: pub'n of 2nd Book of Homilies; 25 Mar.: Queen gave approval to Book of Homilies; Mar.: Elizabeth proposed m. betw. Robert Dudley & Mary Queen of Scots; 11 Apr.: Anglo-Fr. Tr. of Troyes – Calais handed to Fr.; 25 May: recall of Sussex from Ireland; replaced by Sir Nicholas Arnold; 29 Sept.: Robert Dudley cr. Earl of Leicester; Oct.: Ct of High Commission estab'd in Ireland to enforce relig. conformity; riots in Queen's & King's Counties, Ireland; Dec.: Thomas Sampson, Dean of Christ Church, Oxf., and Laurence Humphrey, President of Magdalen College, Oxf., brought before Parker re use of vestments; pub'n of Eng. transl. of Jewel's *Apology*. 1564–65: many parish clergy deprived for refusal to wear the surplice.

1565 25 Jan.: Elizabeth required Archbp of Canterbury to act v. clerical nonconformity (2nd **Vestiarian Controversy**); 30 Jan.: Parker ordered Grindal to convey royal command to bps; 28 Feb.: deadline for diocesan certification of conformity; activities of a group of Puritan hardliners, centred on St John's College, Cambr., caused unease at **Court** & made Queen & Archbp Parker yet more determined to protect status quo; 8 Feb.: Desmond defeated by Ormond at Affane; Desmond & Ormond subm. to Queen; **Jesuits** opened school in Limerick; 22 Feb.: Archbp of Armagh impr. in Tower; 20 Mar.: Sampson, Humphrey & 18 other leading clergy petitioned the eccles. commissioners for permission to follow consciences in matter of vestments; three out of five commissioners agreed; 29 Apr.: final attempt to persuade Sampson, Humphrey, etc.; 8 May: Edward Brocklesby, **vicar** of Hemel Hempstead, depr. for refusing to wear vestments; 26 May: Sampson depr.; simultaneously persecution of Catholics at Oxf. sent William Allen into exile; May: Elizabeth indicated intention to m. Archduke Chas; 2 May: O'Neill defeated MacDonnells at Glenshesk, Co. Antrim; 29 July: Mary of Scotland & Henry Stuart, Lord Darnley, gt grandson of Henry VII, m. at Holyrood; summer: Queen visited Coventry during progress; Aug.: Lady Mary Grey impr. for clandestine m. to Thomas Keys; 6 Oct.: Mary Queen of Scots defeated James Earl of Moray & anglophiles in Borders; Moray fled to Eng.; Oct.: Sir Henry Sidney cr. Lord Dep. of Ireland; 1 Oct.: Adam Loftus heads Irish eccles. commission; Jesuit school in Limerick sacked; rift betw. Mary of Scots & Darnley because she refused him crown matrimonial; RC pamphleteers use term 'puritan' for hotter kind of Protestant; work began on the Bishops' Bible.

1566 20 Jan.: Sidney returned to Ireland as Lord Dep.; cr. Munster Presidency; joined by Christopher Goodman as his chaplain; late Jan.: Grindal assembled all London clergy to view & accept 'modified' correct clerical attire; 9 Mar.: murder of David Rizzio at Holyrood; Darnley implicated; 20 Mar.: Mary resumed control in Edinburgh; 20 Mar.: Parker summoned London clergy to Lambeth; 26 Mar.: London clergy shown correct attire & ordered to subscribe within three months: 'Volo – I will' or be depr.; Mar.: c. 37 London clergy suspended for refusing to wear vestments; by late 1566 all but 15 had subscribed; Mar.: Matthew Parker issued *Advertisements*, without royal approval, of standard of conformity; 19 June: birth of Prince James Stuart of Scotland; 29 June: Stationers' Company monopoly granted; July–Sept.: Elizabeth's progress to Stamford, Woodstock & Oxf.; Munster in disorder; Sept.: parl. assembled; Queen came close to promising to m. to prevent debate on succession; 3 Aug.: O'Neill burned Armagh Cathedral & was decl'd traitor; autumn & winter campaign by Sidney v. O'Neill; 25 Oct.: Mary of Scots seriously ill; Dec.: Alphabetical Bills on relig. issues intro'd into parl. incl., on 5 Dec., Bill 'A' on 39 Articles – all quashed by Elizabeth; 17 Dec.: RC **baptism** of Prince James; 24 Dec.: royal pardon for Rizzio's murderers; wrangles in Eng. Parl. re succession & religion; Cecil drafted parl. petition to Elizabeth to m.; continental reformers, Theodore Beza and Heinrich Bullinger (appealed to in the matter of vestments) counselled submission to the Elizabethan Settlement.

1567 Early: Sussex went to Vienna to nego m. betw. Elizabeth & Archduke Chas; 20 Jan.: Mary of Scots brought syphilitic Darnley back to Kirk o'field Edinburgh; 9–10 Feb.: Darnley murdered at Kirk o'field; 24 Apr.: James Hepburn, Earl of Bothwell, abducted & impr. Mary of Scots at Dunbar; 15 May: Mary m. Bothwell; 2 June: Shane O'Neill murdered; 15 June: Scots nobles victorious at Carberry Hill; Bothwell fled; 20 June: Mary impr.; 2 July: papacy severed links w. Mary of Scots; 24

July: Mary of Scotland abdicated in favour of infant s.; 29 July: James VI proclaimed King; 9 Aug.: Adam Loftus Archbp of Dublin; 22 Aug.: Earl of Moray cr. Regent of Scotland; Oct.: Sidney returned from Ireland; Desmond impr. in Tower; Dec.: Elizabeth ended nego. for m. w. Archduke Chas. A **separatist** congregation discovered in London. Welsh translations of the BofCP and the New Testament pub'd.

1568 ?22 Jan.: d. of Lady Katherine Grey, who under Henry VIII's will had a statutory right to the succession; Sir Henry Sidney app'd President of Council of North (while still Pres. of Wales & Lord Dep. of Ireland); 2 May: Mary Stuart escaped & joined supporters in southern Scotland;13 May: Mary defeated by Moray at Langside, nr Glasgow; 16 May: Mary Stuart fled to Eng.; Aug.: Moray appeared before commission of inquiry at York & presented Casket Letters, implicating Mary in Darnley's murder; Mary refused to renounce crown & accept asylum in Eng.; autumn: Sidney returned to Ireland; 21 Sept.–Dec: Anglo-Sp. crisis sparked when John Hawkins attacked Sp. treasure ships in Mexico; 5 Oct.: Bishops' Bible presented to Queen; William Allen founds College at Douai, Flanders, to train Eng. Catholic priests.

1569 Jan.: Mary Stuart impr. at Tutbury; proposed m. betw. Mary & Norfolk & restoration to Scotland oppo. by Cecil; Feb.: fierce plague in Edinburgh; May–June: Cecil quarrelled w. Norfolk; June: Sidney crushed rebellion in Munster & south Leinster v. Eng. rule; mid-July: Norfolk intrigue w. Leicester, etc. to m. Mary Stuart to an Eng. nobleman (Norfolk) uncovered; Sept.: Elizabeth heard of the plot; Oct.: Norfolk under house arrest; 1 Nov.: Norfolk impr. in Tower; Nov.: revolt of the Northern Earls supp'd by Sussex & the Yorks; gentry; 2nd Elizabeth Irish parl. met; quarto revised ed'n of Bishops' Bible pub'd; Thomas Cartwright app'd Lady Margaret Professor at Cambr.; Dec.: Catholic earls fled.

1570 A total of 450 participants in rebellion of the Earls exec.; 21 Jan.: Moray assassinated; pro-Marian reaction; Mary placed under house arrest w. Earl & Countess of Shrewsbury at Sheffield; Feb.: Pope Pius V issued *Regnans in Excelsis*, excommunicating Elizabeth; 20 Feb.: Dacre rising supp'd by Hunsdon; spring: Thomas Cartwright sketched out Presbyt. form of church gov't in inaugural lectures on Acts at Cambr.; early June: pub'n of Alexander Nowell's *Catechism*; 11 June: Wm Chaderton, Regius Prof., Cambr. complained about Cartwright; June: unrest of Huguenot workers in Norwich was quashed; 3 Aug.: Norfolk released from Tower but placed under house arrest; Sept.: Eliz was considering m. w. Archduke Chas; 25 Sept.: Queen assented to new Cambr. Statutes; John Felton exec. for pinning *Regnans in Excelsis* on Bp of London's door; m. betw. Elizabeth & Henry Duke of Anjou proposed; Nov.: Whitgift cr. vice-chanc. of Cambr.; 11 Dec.: Cartwright depr. of chair & banned from preaching at Cambr.; midwinter: Desmond released into house arrest in London; pub'n of *An Homelie against Disobedience and Wylfull Rebellion*.

1571 25 Feb.: Cecil cr. Baron Burghley; 27 Feb.: Sir John Perrot, President of Munster, arrived at Waterford; 25 Mar./1 Apr.: Sidney relinquished Lord Dep of Ireland; repl. by Sir William Fitzwilliam; Apr.: Queen vetoed parl. bill to incr. penalties for non-attendance at church & to enforce annual reception of sacrament by so-called 'church-papists'; 6 Apr.: Wm Strickland spoke in parl. v. dispensations & **simony**; Treasons Act, Act v. Papal Bulls & Act v. fugitives over the sea passed; parl. ratified 39 Articles of Religion; subscription required of all clergy at **ordination** and entry to benefices – consequent depr. of John Field; Convocation reformed dispensations; Henry Duke of Anjou continued suit for Elizabeth; Ridolfi plot to m. Norfolk to Elizabeth; Sept.: Archbp Parker presented Bullinger's *Bullae papisticae* to Elizabeth; 7 Sept.: Norfolk impr. in Tower; Treason Acts passed; every cathedral & church in Eng. ordered to obtain & display Foxe's *Acts & Monuments* (Book of Martyrs); Matthew Stuart, Earl of Lennox & regent of Scotland, killed by Mary Stuart's supporters; Dec.: Sir John Perrot began anglicisation programme in Munster by enforcing clothing regulation; ed'n of 2nd Book of Homilies incl. *An Homelie against Disobedience and Wylfull Rebellion* of 1570.

1572 16 Jan.: Norfolk found guilty of tr.; 21 Apr.: Anglo-Fr. **Treaty of Blois**; May: parl. assembled; 17 May: parl. bill to allow dispensations from requirement to wear vestments & observe ceremonies; late May: Queen forbade parl. to introduce relig. bills without permission of bps & so stifled parl. debate re relig. matters; pub'n of Casket Letters; 2 June: Norfolk exec.; 13 June: Poor Law passed; June: Thomas Wilcox pub'd *First Admonition to the Parliament*, asking parl. to intro. Genevan form of church gov't; Queen issued proclamation re seditious puritan pamphlet, *An Admonition to Parliament*; Wilcox & John Field impr. briefly; 27 June: Bp Cooper of Lincoln preached v. Presbyt. At Paul's Cross; m. betw. Elizabeth & François, duke of Alençon proposed; 27 June to Sept.: Perrot successfully laid siege to Castlemaine; 15 July: Burghley app'd Lord Treasurer; summer: Queen visited Warwick during progress; 24 Aug.: **St Bartholomew's Day Massacre** of Protestants in Paris; 27 Aug.: Huguenots sought refuge at Rye, Sussex; 29 Aug.: Francis Drake seized Sp. treasure in West Indies; 28 Oct.: Earl of Mar, regent of Scotland, d.; Earl of Morton cr. regent of Scotland; Cartwright pub'd *A Second Admonition to the Parliament*; Nov.: Whitgift pub'd *Answer to the Admonition*; 24 Nov.: John Knox d.; Cartwright returned to Cambr. but was depr. of fellowship by Whitgift; 2nd folio ed'n of Bishops' Bible, incl. revised New Testament; **prophesyings** instituted in east Kent w. Archbp Parker's agreement; Parker pub'd *De Antiquitate Britannicae Ecclesiae*, history of his archiepiscopal ancestors.

1573 Feb.: augmented ed'n of Whitgift's *Answer to the Admonition* pub'd; 23 Feb.: James Fitzmaurice FitzGerald, rebel leader, cousin of Desmond, submitted to Sir John Perrot in Ireland; 25 Mar.: Desmond returned to Ireland from Eng. impr.; rearrest of Desmond & impr. in Dublin Castle;

Apr.: Carwright pub'd *Replye to an Answere of Dr Whitgifte*; 28 May: fall of Edinburgh castle; Protestant regency in Scotland; 11 June: proclam. v. Presbyt. writings; July: Perrot returned to Eng. from Ireland for health reasons; 9 Aug.: Drake brought treasure to Plymouth; Oct.: Essex & Hugh O'Neill of Dungannon clashed w. Bryan O'Neill of Clandeboye; 20 Oct.: royal proclam. insisted on rigorous enforcement of Act of Uniformity; 11 Nov.: Desmond escaped; Desmond reclaimed Munster lands, etc.; Dec.: Sir Francis Walsingham app'd 2nd secretary of state; Walter Devereux, 1st Earl of Essex, began Ulster plantations under royal licence; Whitgift again Cambr. vice-chanc.; trade w. Netherlands reopened.

1574 Pub'n of Walter Travers' *Ecclesiasticae disciplinae*;Whitgift pub'd *Defense of the Aunswere to the Admonition Against the Replie of T.C.*; Thomas Cartwright at Heidelberg; 26 Mar.: Whitgift preached defence of episcopacy in New Year's sermon before Elizabeth; Archbp Parker tricked into believing in Presbyt. plot to murder Cecil; 7 May: Elizabeth renewed Tr. of Blois but lent money to Fr. Huguenots; 8 May: Bryan O'Neill submitted to Essex; summer: Queen's progress to Bristol; 2 Aug.: Desmond subm. to Fitzwilliam; 2 Sept.: Bryan O'Neill subm. to Fitzwilliam, vice-deputy; Nov.: Essex ordered exec. of Bryan O'Neill & sparked rebellion; anti-Catholic feeling diminishing & several RCs released from gaol; Catholic missionary pr. arrived from Douai & Rheims & made contact w. Eng. Catholic families.

1575 Mar.: James Fitzmaurice Fitzgerald went to Fr. to seek support; 17 May: Matthew Parker Archbp of Canterbury d.; 18 Sept.: Sir Henry Sidney cr. Lord Dep. of Ireland; 29 Dec.: Edmund Grindal Archbp of York nominated Archbp of Canterbury.

1576 HofC led by Peter Wentworth petitioned Queen re eccles. abuses; Queen referred complaints to Convocation; 8 Feb.: Parl. Committee examined Peter Wentworth for speech in which he spoke of Mary of Scotland as 'Jezebel'; 15 Feb.: Edmund Grindal Archbp of York confirmed as Archbp of Canterbury; **Convocation** passed new Canons (*see* **Canon law**) to curb abuses; Dec.: Queen ordered Grindal to suppr. **prophesyings**. Archbp Grindal wrote to Queen refusing & denied her authority in spiritual matters, 'I choose rather to offend your earthly majesty than to offend the heavenly majesty of God'; collapse of Sp. power in Netherlands; Elizabeth supported States General w. a loan.

1577 25 Feb.: Pope Gregory XIII urged Irish to support James Fitzmaurice Fitzgerald; 8 Mar.: Edwin Sandys app'd Archbp of York; 24 Mar.: John Aylmer consecr. Bp of London; 12 May: John Whitgift enthroned Bp of Worcester by proxy; Whitgift app'd Vice-President of Council of Marches of Wales; Whitgift acted v. recusants; May–July: James Fitzmaurice Fitzgerald unsuccessfully sought support in Madrid & Lisbon; autumn: Burghley supported States General v. Don Juan in Netherlands; Nov.: Cuthbert Mayne, a seminary pr., exec. at Launceston, Cornwall.

1578   Jan.: victory at Battle of Gembloux; Elizabeth contemplated employing mercenary troops v. Sp. in Netherlands; Feb.: John Nelson, seminary pr. from Douai, hanged at Tyburn; Thomas Sherwood, a Catholic layman, hanged a few days later; Archbp Edwin Sandys of York intro. Quarterly Synods in attempt to improve clerical edu. in dioc.; Mar.: Queen ordered recall of Sidney from Ireland; summer: Queen's progress into East Anglia; Thomas Churchyard's plays & masques celebrating the Queen's virginity performed before her in Norwich; 12/14 Sept.: Sidney resigned & returned from Ireland to Eng.; Sidney active at Ludlow; 21 Sept.: Leicester m. Lettice (Knollys) Devereux; François, duke of Alençon (now Anjou), in person revived suit for Elizabeth & supported by Burghley.

1579   Eng. SJ College founded at Rome; 18 July: James Fitzmaurice Fitzgerald landed in Kerry; 1 Aug.: Desmond's brothers joined 2nd Desmond rebellion; 18 Aug.: James Fitzmaurice Fitzgerald killed; proposed m. betw. Elizabeth & Alençon; 6 Oct.: Burghley gave speech opposing the Alençon m.; PC decl. oppo. to m. w. Alençon; controversial pub'n of John Stubbe's *The Discoverie of a Gaping Gulf whereinto England is Like to be Swallowed*; Nov.: trial & exec. of Stubbe; Edmund Spenser's *The Shepheardes Calender* allegorically celebrated Virgin Queen; 2 Nov.: Desmond attainted as traitor.

1580   Mar.–Apr.: seizure of Desmond's lands; 2nd Desmond rebellion spread outside Munster; 6 Apr.: Old St Paul's damaged in earthquake; June: Jesuit missionaries (Edmund Campion & Robert Parsons) arr'd at Dover & conducted mission to Catholic families; Aug.: Lord Grey of Wilton app'd Lord Dep. of Ireland; 4 Aug.: exec. of Sir James Fitzmaurice Fitzjames, Desmond's brother; 12–13 Sept.: papal troops landed at Smerwick, to support Desmond; Sept.: Drake completed circumnavig'n of globe; 7–9 Nov.: garrison surrendered to Grey & were massacred; 31 Dec.: Earl of Morton arrested in Edinburgh.

1581   Mar.: widespread rebellion in Munster; parl. prepared penal code v. RCs (bill 'to retain the Queen's majesty's subjects in their due obedience') in wake of Jesuit missionary activity; Elizabeth modified the legisl.; Queen rejected Peter Wentworth's move in parl. for **public** fast on grounds that this was infringement of royal **prerogative**; Commons petition to Crown for church reform was considered by the bps and rejected; John Field & Walter Travers app'd to London **lecture/ships**, thus raising profile of Puritans in the capital; 4 Apr.: Drake knighted on *Golden Hind*; summer: match betw. Elizabeth & Alençon finally abandoned; 2 June: Morton exec. in Edinburgh; 17 July: Edmund Campion arrested; 5 Aug.: Esme Stuart cr. Duke of Lennox; 2 Nov.: François duc d'Alençon arr'd in London to nego. m. w. Eliz.; 1 Dec.: Campion exec.; Parsons, condemned to death in absentia, fled to Fr.

1582   Presbyterian *classes* began to meet in East Anglia; Desmond rebellion; Grey began campaign of brutal repression in Ireland; starvation resulted in about 30,000 deaths in Munster; Feb.: Alençon left Eng. after failure of m. nego.; Aug.: James VI impr. at Ruthven Castle by the Protestant Earls (Gower, Mar & Angus); 31 Aug.: Lord Grey de Wilton, Lord Dep., recalled from Ireland for savagely repressive policies.

1583   6 July: Archbp Grindal d.; July: exec. of three separatists at Bury St Edmunds for vilifying Queen as 'Jezebel'; Sept.: mob destr. house of John Dee at Mortlake; 23 Sept.: John Whitgift consecr. Archbp of Canterbury; 8 Oct.: Dermot O'Hurley, RC Archbp of Cashel, presented to Irish lord justices; 23 Oct.: Whitgift enthroned Archbp of Canterbury; 11 Nov.: Desmond beheaded by Daniel O'Kelly & rewarded by crown; 17 Nov.: subscription to three articles required by all clergy; Nov.: Mary Queen of Scots implicated in Throckmorton plot, uncovered by Walsingham; Robert Parsons and other **Jesuits** deeply implicated in the Throckmorton plot; 11 Nov.: Earl of Desmond d.; end of Munster rebellion; Dec.: renewal of eccles. High Commission; betw. 300 & 400 ministers refused to subscribe to Whitgift's three articles; Philip Stubbes' controversial Puritanical denunciation of the times, *The Anatomy of Abuses*, pub'd; Alençon (Anjou) & Prince of Orange d.

1584   Jan.: Sp. Ambass. Mendoza expelled for complicity in Throckmorton plot; 17 Jan.: John Perrott app'd Lord Dep. of Ireland; John Field & eight other clergy depr. for non-subscrip. to three articles; Apr.: coup attempted to remove gov't of Earl of Arran; 2 May: Wm Ruthven, Earl of Gowrie, exec. for part in coup v. Arran; May: Whitgift issued 24 articles to be sworn under oath *ex officio mero* before ct of high commission; & secured subscription of most clergy who had refused to sign previously; May: Scots Parl. decl'd James VI 'head of the church'; June: Alençon d.; Henri of Navarre now heir to Fr. throne; 21 June: Perrot arr'd in Dublin; July: Wm of Orange assassinated; Sept.: Burghley, etc. oppo'd actions v. non-subscribing clergy; 19 Oct.: **Bond of Association** for defence of the Queen & prosecution to death of those who attempted assassination, sponsored by PC; Nov.: Perrott proposed Ulster plantation; Nov.: complaints in parl. about Whitgift's policies and petitions from Essex, Warwickshire and Lincolnshire about his curtailment of preaching under the articles; Elizabeth continues strong support for Whitgift and his policies; 1 Dec: parl. began to debate Act for Security of Queen's Royal Person; 14 Dec.: Peter Turner proposes bill to intro. Presbyt. order with Genevan **liturgy** – known as 'The Bill and Book' – but it was denied a reading; winter: RC threats of assassination v. Elizabeth; Burghley proposed enlarged Council but oppo. by Elizabeth; Archbp of Cashel tortured & exec. by martial law; Sir Walter Mildmay founded Emmanuel College, Cambr. for training of preaching ministers.

1585   Jan.: Mary Queen of Scots under close impr. by Sir Amyas Paulet at Tutbury; Whitgift campaigned to prevent Puritans being elected to parl.; 22 Feb.: Burghley reminded parl. of royal prohibition on relig. debate; Feb.: parl. banished Catholic prs & recalled Eng. from seminaries abroad; 13 Mar.: Act for Security of Queen's Royal Person passed as 27 Elizabeth I, c. 1; Bond of Association (now given legal force) proposed commission for trial of Mary Queen of Scots; in HofL Queen ordered bps to suppress the Puritans; HofC defied royal displeasure to discuss bill concerning clerical recruitment; in **Convocation**, Whitgift pursued reforms relating to edu. standards of cler. recruits & residence of **benefice** holders; parl. passed Act v. **Jesuits**, seminary prs & other suchlike disobedient persons; Apr.: 3rd Elizabeth Irish parl. met; May: Philip II ordered seizure of Eng. ships in Atlantic ports; July/Aug.: Elizabeth plotted v. Arran gov't; 10 Aug.: Tr. of Nonsuch w. Dutch; Eng. pledged assistance to Dutch army v. Sp. rule; 18 Oct.: Grenville brought news of colonisation of Roanoake, VA; 2 Nov.: Arran gov't collapsed after Eng. backed coup; Thomas Cartwright returns from exile to employment w. Earl of Leicester; winter: campaign v. bps in HofC; Dec.: Mary Queen of Scots impr. at Chartley, Staffs seat of Earl of Essex.

1586 Feb.: Leicester alienated Elizabeth by accepting Gov.-Generalship of Netherlands & refusing to resign; 2 Feb.: Whitgift joined PC; Mar.: Whitgift revoked Walter Travers' preaching licence; 5 May: d. of Sidney at Ludlow; May–July: Babington conspiracy, Mary Stuart implicated when she wrote w. suggestions to Babington on 17 July; June: Decree of Star Chamber tightened press censorship; June: Drake evacuated Eng. from Roanoake; 7 July: Anglo-Scots tr. of mutual defence; 20 Sept.: Anthony Babington & six others exec.; 11 Oct.: Mary of Scotland tried by special commission & found guilty of treason at Fotheringay Castle, Northants; 14 Oct.: Mary decl. guilty of treason; Oct.: parl. assembled & Whitgift & two others deputised for queen; twelve RC pr. & three laity exec.; Margaret Clitheroe exec. in York for giving refuge to pr.; Oct.: parliament presses for and secures heavier **recusancy** fines of £20 a month. Peter Wentworth to the forefront in unsuccessful attempt in parliament to replace BofCP with Genevan Forme of Prayer; 17 Oct.: Sir Philip Sydney killed at battle of Zutphen, Flanders v. Sp.; Hawkins brought news of Sp. **Armada**; Nov.: Leicester recalled; 4 Dec.: Royal Proclamation of guilt of Mary of Scotland.

1587 1–3 Feb.: Queen signed Mary Queen of Scots' exec. warrant, presented to her by Davison; 3 Feb.: PC signed commission for the exec.; 8 Feb.: Mary exec. at Fotheringhay; Elizabeth furious & Davison & Burghley withdrew from court; Davison found guilty before Star Chamber, impr. & fined; Feb.: Eng. surrendered to Sp. Duke of Parma; 27 Feb.: Anthony Cope re-intro'd Presbyt. 'bill & book' for relig. reform to parl.; 23 Mar.: Cope, Wentworth & others impr. in Tower; Queen vetoed parl. attempts to stop use of *ex officio mero* oath v. Puritans; 8 May: Raleigh set out to colonise America; 'singeing of King of Spain's beard' at Cadiz; 18 June: Essex app'd Master of the Horse; 7 Aug.: William Allen cr. Cardinal; Oct.: London **separatist** leaders, Henry Barrow & John Greenwood, impr.; .Nov.: Leicester again recalled from Netherlands; 4 Dec.: Lord Willoughby replaced Leicester as commander-in-chief in Netherlands; Dec.: Leicester returned home in disgrace.

1588 17 Feb.: Perrott recalled from Ireland after its pacification & replaced by Fitzwilliam; Mar.: John Field d.; 23 Apr.: Essex cr. KG; 30 May: Sp.

Armada sailed from Lisbon; June: James VI quashed Catholic rebellion at Dumfries; Eng. & Wales prepared defences v. poss. Sp. invasion; gov't determination to crush Catholicism led to exec. of 31 prs; 30 June: Sir Wm Fitzwilliam sworn in as Lord Dep. of Ireland; July: Perrot returned to Eng.; 19 July: Sp. Armada spotted off Scilly Isles; 28 July: Eng destr. much of Armada in Calais port; 29 July: battle of Gravelines; 7 Aug.: Eng. sent eight fire ships into Sp. Armada; 8 & 9 Aug.: Elizabeth inspected troops at Tilbury, attended by Essex; 4 Sept.: Leicester d.; 11 Sept.: storm destr. 25 Sp. ships off Irish coast; Oct.: pub'n of satire *The Epistle of Martin Marprelate*, from underground press of Robert Waldegrave; **Marprelate** controversy; Nov.: Willoughby triumphed at siege of Bergen; Nov.: Marprelate Press moved to Sir Richard Knightley's house at Fawsley, Northants; 4 Nov.: Fitzwilliam led campaign v. Sp. & Irish supporters; Fitzwilliam ordered exec. of 50 Sp. gents.: 24 Nov.: public thanksgiving at Old St Paul's for salvation from Armada; Dec.: Fitzwilliam returned victorious to Dublin; Christmas: rivalry betw. Raleigh & Essex almost led to duel.

1589   Marprelate Press moved to White Friars, Coventry; Perrot continued to exert infl. in Ireland, to Fitzwilliam's annoyance; 4 Feb.: parl. assembled; Sir Christopher Hatton opened parl. w. speech denouncing Catholics & Puritans; 9 Feb.: Richard Bancroft preached defence of episcopacy at Paul's Cross; Mar.: pub'n of Marprelate tract *Hay any Worke for Cooper*; 8 Apr.: Drake's expedition to place Don Antonio on Portuguese throne; 17 Apr.: James VI suppr's Catholic rebellion nr Aberdeen; July: Drake returned from disastrous voyage; 22 July: Henri III murdered; Henri of Navarre proclam'd King Henri IV by troops; Aug.: Marprelate press uncovered; arrest of Marprelate printers but John Penry escaped to Scotland; royal **proclamation** v. printers of seditious works; winter: proceedings in high commission v. clerical *classes* in midlands; Aug.: Willoughby finally resigned command in Netherlands; Sept.: Willoughby app'd general of troops in Normandy to support Henri of Navarre; Oct.: Perrot accused Fitzwilliam of bribery & corruption; Essex & Lady Rich made overtures to James VI as probable successor to Elizabeth; 23 Dec.: Fitzwilliam began campaign to rest. order in Connacht; Sir Francis Vere triumphed over Sp. in Netherlands.

1590   14 Jan.: Willoughby's troops captured Honfleur but returned home; proceedings in high commission v. clerical *classes* in midlands; nine clergy, incl. Thomas Cartwright, depr. but all refused *ex officio* oath; 20 Feb.: Warwick d.; May: Fitzwilliam suppr'd mutiny v. Sir Thomas Norris; Feb.: Fitzwilliam accused Perrot of treason; Apr.: Sir Francis Walsingham d.; May: Perrot impr. at Burghley's house on Strand; Oct.: Essex's secret m. w. Frances (Walsingham) Sidney became public.

1591   Jan.: b. of Robert Devereux (later 3rd Earl of Essex); Feb.: John Udall sentenced to d. by assize court for his *Demonstration of Discipline* but then exiled; Mar.: Perrot impr. in Tower; 11 May: trial of Cartwright transferred to Star Chamber; Royal **Proclamation** v. pr., **Jesuits** and seminaries; links Catholicism w. Sp. Threat; commissioners appointed in every county to investigate; May: Lord Howard and Grenville set off from Plymouth to seize Sp. treasure ships in Azores; July: Hacket conspiracy implicated Cartwright; Wm Hacket exec.; Robert Cecil cr. PC; Essex app'd Lieut.-Gen. of Queen's army in Normandy; 2 Aug.: Essex took 4,000 men to Fr. to assist Henri of Navarre; Essex's friendship w. Henri infuriated Elizabeth; 23 Sept.: royal progress to Earl of Hertford's home in Hampshire marks return to favour of Edward Seymour; Sept.: chastened Howard returns with fleet to Plymouth; Story of Grenville and the *Revenge* recounted; 7 Oct.: Stephen Trefulack, gentleman, indicted at Sessions in London for sorcery; 1 Nov.: capture of father Edmund Jennings, SJ by Richard Topcliffe; 3 Nov.: Brian O'Rourke exec. at Tyburn; 5 Nov.: proclamation against vagrant soldiers who were to be treated as vagabonds unless they substantiated their service claims; 20 Nov.: Sir Christopher Hatton, Lord Chancellor, d.; 21 Nov.: proclamation v. Jesuits; Raleigh pub'd *The Last Fight of the Revenge* after his cousin Grenville's d. on 2 Sept.; Nov.: Christopher Hatton d.; repl. by Sir John Puckering as chancellor & by Sir Walter Raleigh as Captain of the Guard; Raleigh & Lady Elizabeth Throckmorton secretly m.; failure of Essex's Normandy campaign; 10 Dec.: 7 RCs exec., including four Jesuits; 26 Dec.: Hugh Roe O'Donnell, s. & h. of Hugh O'Donnell, lord of Tyrconnell, escaped impr. in Dublin.

1592   14 Jan.: Essex returned to court; 7 Feb.: James Stewart, 2nd Earl of Moray murdered in Edinburgh by Catholic Earl of Huntly; Robert Parsons established further seminary in Seville, seeming to underline message of the Royal **Proclamation**; Jesuit poet Robert Southwell pub'd defence of Catholic loyalty to Queen, *An Humble Supplication to her Majestie*; 20 Feb.: Thomas Pormort, seminary pr., hanged in St Paul's churchyard; 25 Feb.: lord Mayor petitioned Archbp of Canterbury re corrupting infl. of plays on apprentices & servants; 27 Apr.: Perrot tried for treason at Westminster; 3 Mar.: charter granted Trinity College, Dublin w. Adam Loftus 1st Provost; 3 May: Hugh Roe O'Donnell cr. Lord of Tyrconnell on resign. of his father Hugh; Ditchley portrait of Elizabeth by Marcus Gheeraerts the younger, celebrated her visit to house of Sir Henry Lee, in Oxon; May: Queen placed Walter & Bess Raleigh under house arrest; 12 June: Southwark feltmakers' apprentices & servants rioted; 26 June: Perrot found guilty & condemned to d.; 28 June: Bothwell's unsuccessful attempt to capture James VI; 7 Aug.: Walter & Bess Raleigh impr'd in Tower; masterless Irishmen ordered to be deported to repopulate Ireland; Sept.: Raleigh released from Tower to recapture Sp. treasure; 17 Sept.: Thame fair postponed because of fear of plague; 28 Sept.: Elizabeth progressed to Oxf.; 21 Oct.: central courts moved to Hertford because of continuing plague; 3 Nov.: Perrot d. (poss. poisoned); Dec.: Catholic bps assembled in Convocation at Tyrconnell; 22 Dec.: Bess Raleigh released.

1593   1 Jan.: Sp. plot uncovered v. James VI; 21 Jan.: plays & games banned because of plague; 19 Feb.: parl. assembled; gov't sought to intro. severe measures v. RCs (£10 monthly fines; removal of Catholic children over the age of seven from their homes; exclusion of Catholics from office); HofC resisted & passed legisl. to identify RCs, directed v. Catholics who were demonstrably 'seditious sectaries and disloyal persons' (the Act against popish recusants and the Act to retain the Queen's subjects in obedience); Act v. Protestant Sectaries; 24 Feb.: Sir Peter Wentworth & Sir Henry Bromley petitioned Lord Keeper for HofL & HofC to join in pleading w. Queen to entail succession; Wentworth impr. & d. in gaol; 25 Feb.: Essex cr. PC; 22 Mar.: John Penry captured; 6 Apr.: separatists Henry Barrow & John Greenwood exec.; John Penry, active in Marprelate campaign, exec.; Essex cr. PC; 7 Apr.: exec. at Huntingdon of Alice & John Samuel & their daughter Agnes for bewitching to death Lady Cromwell, wife of Sir Henry, & bewitching daughters of Robert Throckmorton; 16 May: Elizabeth recalled Fitzwilliam at his request; 28 May: Stratford Bow Goose Fair forbidden, to prevent disorder; 29 May: John Penry hanged for role in Marprelate; 30 May: Christopher Marlowe stabbed to death in tavern brawl; 5 June: Londoners forbidden to enter Windsor in attempt to keep it clear of plague for Queen's visit; 29 June: city feasts curtailed because of plague; June: Anthony Bacon, on Essex's behalf, opened indirect nego. w. James VI; 1 July: London fairs abandoned because of plague; 19 July: Surrey Assizes held in a tent in St George's Field because of plague; 24 July: Bothwell stages coup and controls James VI's court at Holyrood; James spared when he agrees to withdraw witchcraft charges v. Bothwell; 12 Aug.: Fitzwilliam left Ireland; winter: Burghley rejected Francis Bacon's suit to become Attorney-General; pub'n of Richard Hooker's, *On the Laws of Ecclesiastical Polity*, which defended moderate Protestant position; Richard Bancroft attacked Presbyt. position w. his *A Surveye of the Pretended Holy Discipline* & *Dangerous Positions and Proceedings*.

1594   6 Jan.: Twelfth Night revels at Court: Earl of Essex at Queen's side; 2 Feb.: Eng. captured Enniskillen, Co. Fermanagh; 19 Feb.: Prince Henry of Scotland b. ; 26 Mar.: Queen refused to promote Francis Bacon to Solicitor-Generalship & fell out w. Essex over it; 28 Feb.: torture and arraignment of Queen's physician, Roderigo Lopez, at Essex's instigation; 3 Apr.: Bothwell failed to capture Edinburgh; 16 May: Sir William Russell appointed Lord Dep.; June: Maguire and Tyrconnell besiege Enniskillen; 3 June: Bp John Aylmer of London d.; 7 June: Lopez exec. at Tyburn; 7 June: Walter Travers app'd Provost of Trinity College, Dublin; 26 July: John Boste, SJ exec. for high tr.; 20 Aug.: discovery of Sp. assisted plot by Father Holt, Sir William Stanley & Captain Edmund Yorke to kill Queen; 30 Aug.: English led by Russell raised siege of Enniskillen; 3 Oct.: Huntly and Catholic rebels defeat King's Lieut., Earl of Argyll, at Glenlivet; 16 Oct.: Cardinal Allen d.; 24 Dec.: pamphlet, *A Conference about the next succession to the Crown of England* (dedicated to Earl of Essex, promoting claims of the Sp. Infanta & supposedly by Robert Parsons SJ) circulated in Eng. & alienated Eng. Catholics from **Jesuits**; arguments in Wisbech Castle, the official prison for Catholics, betw. SJs & other pr. underlined the breach; Essex supported claims of James VI .

1595 Hugh O'Neill, 2nd Earl of Tyrone, decl'd traitor; 6 Feb.: Raleigh set out in search of El Dorado; Essex began to build diplomatic support, incl. foreign agents; Essex remained supporter of Henri IV while Elizabeth & Burghley withdrew their support; 29 Apr.: William Barrett, fellow of Caius College, Cambr., attacked Calvinist belief in predestination & began controversy; he was forced to recant; 13–16 June: apprentices and masterless men rioted in London; 23 June: Southwark apprentices and servants involved in disorder; 29 June: unruly youths in riot on Tower Hill; 4 July: proclamation against unlawful assemblies prompted by disorders; 18 July: Provost Marshal appointed to oversee order in London; 24 July: youths involved in Tower Hill riot hanged and disembowelled on Tower Hill; July: Sp. attack on Cornwall; 7 Aug.: fear of new Sp. Armada; Essex to fore in preparations v. Sp.; 23 Aug.: Tyrconnell and Tyrone invite Archduke Albert, Governor of the Low Countries, to be King of Ireland; 28 Aug.: Drake and Hawkins sail for West Indies; 15 Sept.: great fire at Woburn, Beds, consumes much of town; 18 Oct.: Dublin gov't makes peace with Tyrone and Tyrconnell, Oct.: Sp. fleet intending to invade Ireland is lost at sea; 6 Nov.: Essex's loss of favour signalled by Queen's refusal to make Francis Bacon Solicitor General; 11/12 Nov.: Sir John Hawkins d. at Puerto Rico; 20 Nov.: nine Calvinist **Lambeth Articles** issued; Dec.: Elizabeth forbade pub'n of Whitgift's Calvinist Lambeth Articles; 14 Dec.: Henry Hastings, Earl of Huntingdon, 'the Puritan earl', Lord President of the **Council of the North**, d. at York.

1596 Jan.: Peter Baro appealed v. Lambeth Articles; 27 Jan.: Francis Drake d. at sea off Panama; 23 Feb.: Middlesex justices ordered to suppress building of 'base tenements and disorderly houses' erected in the sub-urbs of London which have attracted beggars and unemployed people and encouraged the spread of sickness, thievery and sedition; 17 Mar.: Sp. raid near Plymouth; 20–21 June: Eng. fleet destr. Sp. at Cadiz; Queen refused to allow Essex to garrison Cadiz; 5 July: Robert Cecil cr. Secretary of State; 22 July: plays forbidden in City because of plague; 16 or 19 Aug.: b. of Princess Elizabeth Stuart; 18 Aug.: touching for the **Queen's Evil**; Edmund Spenser's *A Vewe of the Present State of Ireland*; one of the worst harvests of the century; food riots in Kent; Sp. captured Calais; Essex's affair w. Elizabeth Stanley, countess of Derby.

1597 Protestant bills v. eccles. fees & subscription to the 39 Articles with-drawn because of weakness of Puritan group in parl.; **Convocation** approved 'Constitutions' to tackle eccles. abuses; 18 Mar.: Essex app'd Master of Ordinance; 10 July: abortive Essex expedition v. Sp. left Plymouth; 17 Aug.: Essex led fleet to await Sp. silver ships off the Azores but an ignominious failure; Oct.: Essex's dispersal of 2nd Sp. Armada off Cornwall; Nov.: Fr. ambass. sought Eng. agreement to nego. gen. peace w. Sp.; Walter & Bess Raleigh rest. to favour.

1598   Essex's relationship w. Elizabeth Brydges, dau. of 3rd Lord Chandos; 2 May: Fr./Sp. Tr. of Vervins, 30 June/1 July: Essex openly argued w. Elizabeth regarding appointment of new Lord Dep. for Ireland; Essex angrily withdrew from Court; Essex raised dangerous questions regarding royal authority; 4 Aug.: Burghley d.; 14 Aug.: Tyrone defeats Eng. at Yellow Ford; 25 Aug.: Essex cr. Chancellor of Oxf. University; Sept.: Essex's illness led to reconciliation; 10 Sept.: Essex returned to PC; 12 Sept.: Essex met w. Queen; 5 Nov.: Lincs., Northants., Hunts., Isle of Ely, Sussex and Surrey are devastated by floods; 9 Nov.: arraignment of Edward Squire for conspiracy to kill Queen & Essex; 5 Dec.: Queen seeks and obtains loan from City to finance army in Ireland; 30 Dec.: Essex app'd Lord Lieut. of Ireland; George Blackwell was made **Archpriest** of England by **Papacy**; **Archpriest Controversy**: **Jesuits** excl. from his jurisdiction; Eng. Catholics enraged; their attempt to petition Pope was quashed when Parsons ordered their return from Rome.

1599   Some anti-Jesuit pr. negotiate with Bp Bancroft; bps eager to exploit divisions within Catholicism; 14 Apr.: Essex arrived in Dublin; 15 Apr.: Essex cr. Lord Lieut. in Dublin; Elizabeth sent 17,000 troops to Ireland; ineffectual military progress of Essex to Leinster; 21 May: Cecil app'd Master of Wards; 14 July: witch hanged at St Edmondsbury, Suffolk; Aug.: Spanish fleet sent to invade Ireland is defeated off Brittany; Lord Howard of Effingham entrusted w. defence of realm v. Sp. Armada threat; 6–8 Sept.: Essex made truce w. Tyrone on River Lagan; Elizabeth repudiated the truce; 28 Sept.: Essex confronted Queen at Nonsuch Palace; Tyrone proclaimed independent Ireland; 1 Oct.: Essex placed under house arrest, supervised by Egerton; Essex reprimanded by special commission of PC; Nov.: Charles Blount, Lord Mountjoy, app'd Lord Dep. of Ireland; 4 Dec.: Anne Kerke hanged as witch at Tyburn; 15 Dec.: Essex seriously ill.

1600   Jan.: Tyrone invaded Munster; Queen refused Essex's **New Year gifts**; Feb.: Mountjoy left for Ireland; 11 Feb: Will Kemp, stage-clown, began 130 mile morris dance from London to Norwich; pub'n of *Kemp's Nine Daies Wonder* (1600) as publicity; 13 Feb.: projected trial of Essex before Star Chamber cancelled after he wrote submissive letter to Elizabeth; 20 Mar.: house arrest of Essex; 5 June: Essex tried at York House; 13 June: Ormond escapes; 18 June: Somerset grain riots; 21 Aug.: exec. of two seminary pr at York; July–Aug.: Chas Blount, 8th Baron Mountjoy, began suppr. of Tyrone's rebellion; Ulster stormed; Munster subdued; 26 Aug.: Essex released; Sept.: Essex out of favour; *Richard II* revived at Globe Theatre; 5 Oct.: James VI survives Gowrie Plot, Perth; Oct.: Mountjoy enters Tyrone's lands in Ulster; 30 Oct.: Essex deprived of main source of income, duties on sweet wines; 1 Dec.: Essex reported to be resentful and rebellious; 22 Dec.: Essex returned to London and kept open house at Essex House.

1601   2 Jan.: Essex House preachers opined that superior magistrates of the realm had power to restrain monarchs; 3 Feb.: Essex supporters met at

Drury House; 7 Feb.: Essex disobeyed summons to appear before the PC; 7 Feb.: *Richard II* performed at *The Globe* at request of Essex supporters; 8 Feb.: Essex staged coup by march w. 200 followers on City of London; coup failed & Whitgift's men arrested Essex; 15 Feb.: non-Londoners ordered out of the capital by royal proclam.; 19 Feb.: Essex & Southampton tried for treason; 25 Feb: Essex exec.; 27 Feb.: exec. of Father Barkworth, pr. at Tyburn, along w. a Jesuit & a lay recusant woman; 1 Mar.: Dr Barlow preached v. Essex at Paul's Cross; 5 Mar.: Essex collaborators arraigned; 13 Mar.: exec. of Merrick & Cuffe, two Essex conspirators; 15 Mar.: exec. of Sir Christopher Blount & Sir Chas Danvers, two more Essex conspirators; Apr.–June: Cecil conducts secret corresp. w. James VI; 25 May: inquiry into wealth of realm; July: Anglo-Dutch forces defended Ostend v. Sp. invasion; Sept.: 5,000 Sp. troops intervened on Tyrone's side in Ireland; 27 Oct.: parl. assembled; 20 Nov.: bill concerning abuse of monopolies intro'd; parl. oppo. to monopolies; 30 Nov.: Elizabeth granted parl. demands & delivered 'golden speech'; 19 Dec.: Queen's last speech before parl.; 24 Dec.: Mountjoy defeated Tyrone at Kinsale; 27 Dec.: Tyrone withdrew to Ulster; Tyrconnell escaped to Sp.

1602 2 Jan.: Sp. Commander submitted to Mountjoy; 22 June: proclam. sought to restrict new building in London, claiming that such building acted as magnet to poor from outside the capital; 2–3 Aug.: Queen visited Lord Keeper at Harefield; 5 Nov.: royal **proclamation** v. priests discriminated in favour of non-Jesuits; **Jesuits** to leave Eng. immediately & actively to be sought out; other pr. given until 1603 to leave but encouraged to submit & promised favourable treatment if they did; 6 Dec.: Robert Cecil entertained Queen at Strand; Dec.: Tyrone finally subm. unconditionally to Mountjoy; 27 Dec.: Queen noted to be infirm.

1603 24 Mar.: Queen d. at Richmond; Robert Cecil read out proclamation decl. James VI King; late Mar.: Tyrone submitted to Mountjoy & Eng. rule; King met Cecil at York; Cecil retained as Secretary of State; 28 Apr.: Elizabeth buried at Westminster Abbey; Apr.: Mountjoy app'd Lord Lieut. of Ireland & PC; May: King stayed at Theobalds (Cecil's home) en route to London.

2

REBELLIONS AGAINST THE TUDORS: CHRONOLOGIES

Yorkist risings against Henry VII, 1486–87 March 1486: Francis Lord Lovell attempted unsuccessfully to raise North Yorkshire v. Henry.

March 1486: Thomas and Humphrey Stafford failed to raise the West Country v. Henry. The Staffords claimed sanctuary at Culham, Oxon. but were removed. July: Humphrey Stafford executed.

16 June 1487: Lambert Simnel defeated at Battle of Stoke near Newark; supported by Earl of Lincoln. Execution of Lincoln.

The Yorkshire Rebellion, 1489 Earl of Northumberland murdered while collecting parliamentary subsidy for the war in Brittany. Rioting led by Sir John Egremont. Earl of Surrey suppressed riot.

The Cornish Rebellion, 1497 15,000 Cornish rebels marched against London to protest against taxes for a war on Scotland. The leaders were Lord Audley, Michael Joseph (a blacksmith) and Thomas Flamank (a lawyer).

16 June 1497: rebels camped on Blackheath.

17 June 1497: rebel numbers reduced by half through desertion; defeated by royal troops; leaders executed; rebels fined heavily.

Resistance to the Amicable Grant, 1525 Widespread resistance, especially in Suffolk, to Wolsey's **Amicable Grant** to finance the French war. Henry VIII heeded the mood of the people, relinquished the grant and gave up the idea of war.

The Pilgrimage of Grace, 1536 1 October: rising at Louth, Lincolnshire – it collapsed within a fortnight; Duke of Suffolk's threat of armed intervention effective. Rising spread to Yorkshire as Pilgrimage of Grace.

16 October: Robert Aske and York pilgrims occupied York. 20 Oct.: Rebels took Pontefract. Duke of Norfolk forced to parley with rebels at Doncaster in face of 30,000-strong rebel force.

4 December: Aske delivered demands to Norfolk who on 8 Dec. persuaded rebels to disperse with the promise to award royal pardons and to summon a free parliament.

January and February 1537: fresh northern risings. Henry revoked pardon. A total of 216 rebels executed. July 1537: Robert Aske hanged.

There is much debate among historians concerning the motivation for the pilgrimage and the rebels' membership. Their demands showed general hostility towards Cromwell's regime and the religious innovations in particular, but also concern about the regional economy.

The Western Rebellion, 1549   June 1549: rising in West of England against **Prayer Book** and Edward VI's religious programme in general.

6 August 1549: Lord Russell, aided by Italian mercenaries, relieved six-week siege of Exeter.

17/18 August 1549: rebellion finally crushed at Sampford Courtenay.

Kett's Rebellion, 1549   12 July 1549: Robert Kett (Norfolk tanner and landowner) and rebels encamped on Mousehold Heath, near Norwich, in protest against enclosures and exploitation. They also expressed grievances against the clergy but actually adopted the new **Prayer Book**.

27 August: rebellion crushed at Battle of Dussindale by Earl of Warwick, using foreign mercenaries.

Wyatt's Rebellion, 1554   January 1554: Sir Thomas Wyatt led 4,000 men from Kent to London. The rebels crossed the Thames at Kingston but were stopped at Ludgate, where Wyatt surrendered on 7 February. Wyatt was executed on 11 April 1554. The rebellion was part of a wider plot to depose Mary I and thus prevent her marriage to Philip II of Spain.

The Rebellion of the Northern Earls, 1569   November 1569: when the Duke of Norfolk was imprisoned in the Tower and the Earls of Northumberland and Westmorland were summoned to court to answer for their part in a conspiracy to marry Norfolk to Mary Stuart, the Earls rebelled. On 14 November the rebels entered Durham and restored Catholic worship in its cathedral. They retreated when the Earl of Sussex raised an army against them.

January 1570: a separate rebellion was staged by Leonard Dacre but he was defeated in battle between Hexham and Carlisle.

The Essex Rebellion, 1601   In late 1599, the Earl of Essex was placed under house arrest for his conduct in Ireland. He hatched a conspiracy and, on 8 February 1601, attempted to raise London in his defence. He was executed on 25 February 1601.

3

IRELAND

Chronology

Ireland had been conquered by the Normans in the twelfth century and a feudal ruling class had been imposed. The Kings of England claimed to be lords of Ireland but ruled little of it. The area which was ruled by the English – the **Pale** – was little more than a stretch of coast extending 50 miles north from Dublin. Anglo-Irish families, such as FitzGeralds (Geraldines) and Butlers, had become as Irish as the Irish themselves. Ireland in Tudor times was made up of the Pale under English rule (stretching from Dundalk to Dublin and beyond) and four provinces, each under the control of tribal chiefs. As Map 1 indicates, the extent of the Pale was increased under Mary (by the inclusion of King's County and Queen's County) and under Elizabeth (see Chapter 18: Maps). The term 'Geraldine' is applied to the followers of both Kildare and Desmond.

The reign of Henry VII

When Henry VII ascended the throne, the Irish chiefs were using the English dynastic struggle as a vehicle for their own fight for independence. Kildare and Desmond espoused the Yorkist cause while their enemies, the Butlers under the Earl of Ormond, supported the Lancastrians. Ireland was a springboard for pretenders to the English throne. Kildare gave assistance to Lambert Simnel (1487) and, despite Henry VII's subsequent forbearance, proceeded to aid Warbeck (1491). Henry finally deprived Kildare of the Deputyship and put in his own men.

1493	Henry pardons Kildare after personal submission.
1494	Sir Edward Poynings is made Deputy (the nominal governor of Ireland is Prince Henry). Poynings plans to conquer Ulster and impose English constitution. Poynings fails to take Ulster. Dec.: Irish parliament at Drogheda enacts **Poynings' Law** which destroys legislative independence of Irish parliament; attainder of Kildare – sent to Tower.
1496	Henry VII effectively gives up on problem of imposing English rule in Ireland. Recall of Poynings; Kildare made Lord Deputy.
1497	26 July: Warbeck lands at Cork.

The reign of Henry VIII

1521	Surrey recalled from Ireland. Ireland effectively ruled by Sir Piers Butler and Gerald, Earl of Kildare, in succession.
1526	Kildare imprisoned in Tower. Skeffington rules Ireland.
1529	Return of Kildare.
1532	Kildare made Lord Deputy. Disorder.
1534	Kildare dies in the Tower. His son besieges Dublin. Skeffington and Brereton lead relief of Dublin.
1536	Lord Leonard Grey replaces Skeffington as Lord Deputy.
1537	'Silken Thomas' FitzGerald, Earl of Kildare, and others executed in London. Geraldine power finally crushed.
1540	Sir Anthony St Leger made Lord Deputy.
1541	June: Henry assumes title of King of Ireland and Head of the Irish Church.
1542	First Jesuit mission to Ireland lands.

The reign of Edward VI

1548	Sir Edward Bellingham replaces St Leger.
1549	Bellingham suppresses rebellions in King's and Queen's Counties.
1550	St Leger returns as Lord Deputy.
1550	St Leger recalled for alleged Catholicism.
1552	Privy Council acquits St Leger.

The reign of Mary I

1553	St Leger again Lord Deputy.
1556	St Leger charged with embezzlement and recalled; died; Earl of Sussex is made Lord Deputy; Shane O'Neill supreme in Ireland.

The reign of Elizabeth I

1560	Elizabeth orders crushing of O'Neill.
1561	Defeat of Sussex in Ireland.
1562	Shane O'Neill submits to Queen in London.
1563	Failure of Sussex's attempts to restore order.
1564	Sussex recalled.
1566	Henry Sidney appointed Lord Deputy.
1567	Shane O'Neill dies.
1568	Devon Adventurers attempt to colonise Munster.
1569	Revolt of the Desmonds (FitzGerald) led by James FitzMaurice FitzGerald. Elizabeth's second Irish parliament meets.
1573	Desmond crushed. Plantation of Ulster attempted.
1576	Henry Sidney returns as Lord Deputy.
1579	Desmond revolt under Gerald FitzGerald, Earl of Desmond. Destruction of Munster. July: Spanish troops arrive to aid revolt.
1580	Lord Grey de Wilton made Lord Deputy.

1582	Famine in Munster.
1583	Death of Gerald FitzMaurice FitzGerald, 14th Earl of Desmond. Plantation of Munster initiated.
1584	John Perrot(t) made Lord Deputy.
1585	Apr.: Elizabeth's third parliament meets.
1588	When Perrot(t) is replaced by Fitzwilliam, Ireland is at peace.
1589	Commission set up to assess progress of plantation of Munster.
1591	Royal foundation of Trinity College, Dublin. Sir Henry Bagnal appointed Chief Commissioner for Government of Ulster.
1594	Earl of Tyrone (Hugh O'Neill) leads Ulster revolt and appeals to Spain for help.
1595	Sir John Norreys, commander of the English forces, fails to crush the Ulster revolt.
1597	Lord Burgh is made Lord Deputy but dies in Oct. 1597.
1597–	Truce.
June 1598	
1598	Aug.: at Battle of the Yellow Ford the English army under Bagnal is defeated. Hugh O'Neill supreme in Ireland.
1599	Essex made Lord Lieutenant. 15 Apr.: Essex reaches Dublin. 8 Sept.: Essex treats with Tyrone and gives him a breathing space to await Spanish assistance. English army wasting away with disease. 24 Sept.: Essex leaves Ireland. 28 Sept.: Essex in London.
1600	Jan.: Tyrone invades Munster. Mountjoy is made Lord Deputy. July–Aug.: order restored in English Pale. Sept.–Oct.: Tyrone forced to go north. Nov.: Earl of Desmond captured.
1601	Spanish occupy port of Kinsale. Mountjoy and Carew occupy Kinsale. Battle of Kinsale with Irish troops. Tyrone and Tyrconnel(l) (Hugh Roe O'Donnell) routed.
1603	Mar.: Tyrone surrenders.

Governors of Ireland

LJ = Lord Justice
KL = King's Lieutenant
LD = Lord Deputy
LL = Lord Lieutenant
D = Deputy

21 Aug. 1484   John de la Pole, Earl of Lincoln, KL.

The reign of Henry VII

11 Mar. 1486   Jasper Tudor, Duke of Bedford, KL.
24 May–Oct. 1487   Gerald, 8th Earl of Kildare, KL.
11 Sept. 1494   Prince Henry, KL (there was a series of Deputies, the most important being Sir Edward Poynings, D from Sept. 1494 to Dec. 1495).

The reign of Henry VIII

8 June 1509–d. 3 Sept. 1513   Gerald, 8th Earl of Kildare, LJ and LD.
4 Sept. 1513–26 Nov. 1515   Gerald, 9th Earl of Kildare, LJ and LD.
13 Apr. 1515   William Preston, Viscount Gormanston, LJ.
Before Sept. 1515–Sept. 1519   Gerald, 9th Earl of Kildare, LD.
After Sept. 1519–Mar. 1520   Maurice FitzGerald of Lackagh, LJ.
10 Mar. 1520–6 Mar. 1522   Thomas Howard, Earl of Surrey, LL.
6 Mar. 1522–13 May 1524   Piers Butler, pretended 8th Earl of Ormond, LD.
13 May 1524–Nov. 1526   Gerald, 9th Earl of Kildare, LD (appointment secret until
    4 Aug.).
1527–15 May 1528   Richard Nugent, Baron Devlin, LJ.
15 May 1528–4 Aug. 1528   Thomas FitzGerald, LJ.
4 Aug. 1528–22 June 1529   Piers Butler, 1st Earl of Ossory, LD.
22 June 1529–d. 22 July 1536   Henry FitzRoy, Duke of Richmond, LL (22 June
    1530–35 July 1532 William Skeffington D; 5 July 1532 to Feb. 1534
    Gerald, 9th Earl of Kildare, D; Feb.–June 1534 Thomas, Lord Offaly, D.
June–Aug. 1534   Richard Nugent, acting D.
23 July 1534–d. 31 Dec. 1535   William Skeffington, LD.
23 Feb. 1536–1 Apr. 1540   Leonard, Lord Grey, LD.
1 Apr. 1540–7 July 1540   Sir William Brereton, LJ.
7 July 1540–22 Apr. 1548   Anthony St Leger, LD (12 Oct. 1543–1 Dec. 1546
    William Brabazon LJ and D).

The reign of Edward VI

22 Apr. 1548–27 Dec. 1549   Edward Bellingham, LD.
27 Dec. 1549–2 Feb. 1550   Francis Bryan, LJ.
2 Feb.–4 Aug. 1550   William Brabazon, LJ.
4 Aug. 1550–29 Apr. 1551   Anthony St Leger, LD.
29 Apr. 1551–6 Dec. 1552   Thomas Cusack and Gerald Aylmer, LJs.

The reign of Mary I

Oct. 1553–27 Apr. 1556   Anthony St Leger, LD.
27 Apr. 1556–Dec. 1558   Thomas Radcliff, Lord Fitzwalter (1557: Earl of Sussex),
    LD (Jan.–Dec. 1558: Henry Sidney, LJ, D).

The reign of Elizabeth I

12 Dec. 1558–3 Jul. 1559   Henry Sidney, LJ.
3 July 1559–13 Oct. 1565   Thomas Radcliff, Earl of Sussex, LD and then LL (dur-
    ing this period there was a D. 18 Jan. 1560–2 May 1564: William Fitzwilliams
    was LJ and D; 2 May 1564–9 Oct. 1567: Nicholas Arnold was LJ and D).
13 Oct. 1565–1 Apr. 1571   Henry Sidney, LD (9 Oct. 1567: Robert Weston and
    William Fitzwilliams were appointed Ds when Sidney was recalled to London to
    discuss Irish programme).

1 Apr. 1571–5 Aug. 1575   William Fitzwilliams, LJ and then LD.

5 Aug. 1575–12 Sept. 1578 (resigned)   Henry Sidney, LD.

27 Apr. 1578–11 Oct. 1579   William Drury, LJ.

11 Oct. 1579–15 July 1580   William Pelham, LJ.

15 July 1580–25 Aug. 1582   Arthur, Lord Grey de Wilton, LD.

25 Aug. 1582–7 Jan. 1584   Adam Loftus, Archbishop of Dublin, and Henry Wallop, LJs.

7 Jan. 1584–17 Feb. 1588   John Perrot(t), LD.

17 Feb. 1588–16 May 1594   William Fitzwilliam(s), LD.

16 May 1594–5 Mar. 1597   William Russell, LD.

5 Mar. 1597–29 Oct. 1597   Thomas, Lord Burgh, LD (29 Oct. 1597: Thomas, 10th Earl of Ormond, appointed in charge of military affairs).

29 Oct. 1597–15 Nov. 1597   Thomas Norreys, LJ.

15 Nov. 1597–12 Mar. 1599   Adam Loftus, Archbishop of Dublin, and Richard Gardiner, LJs.

12 Mar. 1599–24 Sept. 1599   Robert Devereux, 2nd Earl of Essex, LL.

24 Sept. 1599–21 Jan. 1600   Adam Loftus, Archbishop of Dublin, and George Cary, LJs.

21 Jan. 1600–30 May 1603   Charles Blount, Lord Mountjoy, LD, LJ, LD and LL.

30 May 1603–1 Feb. 1605   Sir George Cary, LD.

4

THE WORLD OF LEARNING

Universities

In the Middle Ages the universities of Oxford and Cambridge had been small, with varying student numbers (in 1500, each admitted about 150 men) and almost exclusively concerned with the education of a pool of clergy from which would be drawn the Church's leadership and the King's chief servants. During the Tudor period the universities grew in size and altered in character. By 1600, they each admitted between 400 and 500 men per annum. The colleges developed as institutions for the tuition, residence and supervision of undergraduate students. Prior to this, most teaching was undertaken by the university and students lived in halls or town lodgings. These undergraduate students now included large numbers of well-born students who had no intention of pursuing a career in the church, as well as men from humbler backgrounds who eventually took holy orders and, much more often than not, entered the Church in humble positions. Corpus Christi College, Oxford, and Emmanuel College, Cambridge, for instance, were both established with the training of ministers uppermost in the minds of their founders. University education was not open to all: it was expensive and it was seen as appropriate only to some vocations. The universities educated distinct groups of students for different roles in society. They combined the roles of fashionable colleges for young gentlemen, who frequently completed their education at the Inns of Court in London, and secular seminaries for determined professional recruits to the church and government service. The curriculum and teaching offered was influenced by the student composition of the colleges.

Chronology

1481   Building of Duke Humfrey's Library, Oxford.
1483   John Russell, Bishop of Lincoln, made Chancellor of Oxford.
1485   Thomas Rotherham, Archbishop of York, made Chancellor of Cambridge.

1490	Thomas Cosyn made Chancellor of Cambridge.
1494	John Blythe, Bishop of Salisbury, made Chancellor of Cambridge. John Morton, Archbishop of Canterbury, made Chancellor of Oxford.
1496	John Alcock, Bishop of Ely, founded Jesus College, Cambridge.
1497	Readerships in Divinity at Oxford and Cambridge founded by Lady Margaret Beaufort, mother of Henry VII. George Fitzhugh made Chancellor of Cambridge.
1499	A humanist, John Dogget, appointed Provost of King's College, Cambridge. Thomas Rotherham made Chancellor of Cambridge.
1500	William Grocyn began to lecture on Greek at Oxford. Richard Fox, Bishop of Durham, made Chancellor of Cambridge. William Smyth, Bishop of Lincoln, made Chancellor of Oxford.
1501	John Fisher appointed Vice Chancellor of Cambridge. He was chaplain to Lady Margaret Beaufort.
1502	George Fitzhugh made Chancellor of Cambridge.
1503	Thomas Ruthall made Chancellor of Cambridge. He later became Bishop of Durham. Richard Mayew, Bishop of Hereford, made Chancellor of Oxford.
1504	John Fisher made Bishop of Rochester and Chancellor of Cambridge.
1505	John Fisher made Provost of Queens' College, Cambridge. Refoundation of God's House, Cambridge, as Christ's College; statutes stipulated college lectures.
1506	William Warham appointed Chancellor of Oxford. Erasmus visited Fisher.
1509	Foundation of Brasenose College, Oxford.
1511	Lady Margaret Beaufort founded St John's College, Cambridge and stipulated college lectures in statutes. Erasmus returned to lecture in Greek at Cambridge; appointed as Lady Margaret Professor of Divinity.
1514	Erasmus left Cambridge.
1517	Corpus Christi College, Oxford, founded by Richard Fox, Bishop of Winchester; inaugurated lectures in Greek, Latin and Divinity. Wolsey appointed several other lecturers at Oxford. A printing press was established in Oxford.
1518	Richard Croke lectured in Greek and lectureships in Logic, Philosophy and Rhetoric endowed at Cambridge by Sir Robert Reade.
1520	Beginnings of printing at Cambridge.
1524	Medical lectures established at Oxford by Thomas Linacre.
1525	Attempt to eradicate Lutheranism at Cambridge following Robert Barnes' sermon attack on Wolsey.
1526	Thomas Wolsey founded Cardinal College, Oxford.
1530	Universities debated royal divorce. Examination of dangerous books by special committees.
1532	John Longland, Bishop of Lincoln, made Chancellor of Oxford. Henry VIII refounded Cardinal College, Oxford, as King's College.

1535	Reform of the university statutes following royal visitation of the universities. Thomas Cromwell appointed Chancellor of Cambridge.
1536	End of monastic colleges.
1540	Foundation of Regius Professorships in Divinity, Law, Hebrew, Greek and Medicine. Stephen Gardiner became Chancellor of Cambridge.
1542	Thomas, Lord Audley founded Magdalene College, Cambridge.
1546	Foundation of Trinity College, Cambridge, by Henry VIII; college lectures stipulated in statutes. Refoundation of King's College, Oxford, as Christ Church.
1547	Chantry Act exempted colleges of the universities from its terms. Somerset made Chancellor of Cambridge. Richard Cox, Dean of Christ Church, made Chancellor of Oxford.
1549	Reform of university statutes following royal visitation. Destruction of images and 'popish' books. Martin Bucer and other foreign reformers arrived in England.
1551	College lectures in Logic and Sophistry at Clare College, Cambridge.
1552	John Dudley, Duke of Northumberland, made Chancellor of Cambridge. Sir John Mason made Chancellor of Oxford.
1553	Order that all members of the universities subscribe to the new articles of religion not carried out due to death of Edward VI. Marian Government ordered graduates to declare Catholic faith and deprived many college heads of their positions.
1554–55	Foundation of Trinity College, Oxford, by Sir Thomas Pope, Treasurer of Court of Augmentations. Sir Thomas White, Alderman of London, founded St John's College, Oxford.
1556–57	Reginald Pole made Chancellor of Oxford. His visitations of the university enforce Catholic worship and **creed**.
1557	John Caius refounded Gonville Hall as Gonville and Caius College, Cambridge.
1559	Henry Fitzalan, Lord Arundel, made Chancellor of Oxford. Sir John Mason made Elizabeth's first Chancellor of Oxford and William Cecil her first Chancellor of Cambridge. Royal visitations resulted in removal of Catholic heads of many colleges at Oxford. Revival of the Edwardian Statutes.
1564	Queen's visit to Cambridge. Robert Dudley, Earl of Leicester made Chancellor of Oxford.
1565	Oxford received new statutes. Oxford Arts course lasted seven years; BA after four years' study of Grammar, Rhetoric, Dialectics or Logic; MA after three years' study of Greek, Geometry, Natural, Moral and Metaphysical Philosophy. Gentlemen could graduate BA after three years, presumably because they knew sufficient Latin grammar before they started to be exempt from this part of the course. Cambridge academics protested against Matthew Parker's plans for imposing orthodoxy.
1566	Elizabeth visited Oxford.
1569	Thomas Cartwright, the new Lady Margaret Professor of Divinity at Cambridge, demanded Church reform from the pulpit.

1570	John Whitgift, Vice-Chancellor of Cambridge, deprived Thomas Cartwright of Chair. New statutes received at Cambridge. Cambridge Arts course to cover seven years; BA after four years' study of Rhetoric, Logic and Philosophy; followed by MA after further three years' study of Natural, Moral and Metaphysical Philosophy, Astronomy, Drawing and Greek.
1571	Dr Hugh Price, Chancellor of St David's Diocese, founded Jesus College, Oxford; strong and continuing Welsh links.
1574	Peter Baro, opponent of Calvinism, appointed Lady Margaret Professor of Divinity, Cambridge.
1576	Ordered that all graduands subscribe to 39 **Articles of Religion**.
1580	Ordered that all graduands take Supremacy Oath.
1581	All those at Oxford required to take oath of subscription.
1584	Sir Walter Mildmay, Chancellor of the Exchequer, founded Emmanuel College, Cambridge. Dudley Fenner published translation of Pierre de la Ramée's work, which substituted scriptural for classical examples.
1585	Cambridge University Press founded. Sir Thomas Bromley deputised for Leicester as Chancellor of Oxford.
1588	Sir Christopher Hatton appointed Chancellor of Oxford.
1589	Two fellows of Christ's College, Cambridge, imprisoned for sedition.
1591	Thomas Sackville, Lord Buckhurst made Chancellor of Oxford.
1592	Elizabeth visited Oxford.
1595	John Whitgift silenced William Barrett's attack on Calvinism at Cambridge.
1596	Peter Baro silenced and left Cambridge. Lady Frances Sidney, Dowager Countess of Sussex, founded Sidney Sussex College, Cambridge.
1598	Robert Devereux, Earl of Essex, made Chancellor of Cambridge.
1601	Robert Cecil, Earl of Salisbury, made Chancellor of Cambridge.
1602	Thomas Bodley re-established University Library with 2,000 volumes. Not a lending library and restricted to graduates.

Education

Sixteenth-century England was not a schooled society like our own and we must avoid the temptation to identify an 'educational system' as such. The upbringing of most children was still firmly rooted in the family, the Church and the workshop. For centuries, academic learning had been the preserve of the clergy and potential clergy, because only they needed advanced literacy for their work. There did, however, emerge a movement for the schooling of society. Renaissance scholars saw in education along classical lines a way to improve society: the school was thought to counteract the evil influences of family and society upon the young. Out of this belief grew the grammar schools, endowed in large numbers in our period. But the town grammar schools owed a good deal also to demand among tradesmen and craftsmen for basic vernacular literacy. It was common for the grammar schools, therefore, to combine a classical side (with a curriculum of Latin Grammar, Logic and Rhetoric) with a vernacular side (offering Writing, Arithmetic and more 'modern' subjects) and for boys within them to be thus 'streamed'. Alongside the grammar schools there existed a plethora of more ephemeral establishments, ranging from ABC or 'dame' schools, which taught little more than reading and basic numeracy, to the classical education offered by the local clergyman or freelance schoolmaster to groups of boys. Wealthier homes employed private tutors to teach their sons and daughters. Important though these developments were, we should resist the belief that the majority of children attended school.

Chronology

Single place names indicate foundation or refoundation of a school at that date.

1487	Stockport.
1490s	First editions of Erasmus' *Adagia* (Adages).
1502	Macclesfield.
1509	St Paul's School, London.
1512	Publication of Erasmus' *De Copia*. Giggleswick, Yorkshire.
1513	Nottingham.
1515	Wolverhampton, Staffordshire; Manchester.
1519	First publication of Erasmus' *Colloquies*. Pocklington, Yorkshire; King's, Bruton, Somerset.
1520	Cranbrook, Kent.
1522	King's College, Taunton, Somerset.
1524	Bolton.
1525	Sedburgh, Yorkshire.
1529	Bingley, Yorkshire.
1532	Bristol.
1536	Royal injunctions ordered clergy to teach the young in their care. Wealthier clergymen were to provide scholarships to finance able boys, either at grammar school or university.
1538	Royal injunctions ordered the provision of an English Bible in every parish church. The clergy were to expound this to their parishioners.
1539	Crypt, Gloucester; Colchester, Essex.
1540–42	Official Latin grammar issued. Known as Lily's Latin Grammar, although merely based on an earlier work by William Lily.
1541	Berkhamstead, Hertfordshire; Canterbury, Kent; Northampton; Christ's College, Brecon; King's, Worcester; King's, Chester.
1542	King's, Rochester, Kent.
1543	Devizes, Wiltshire; King's, Ely. Access to vernacular Bible denied to all but gentlemen.
1545	Newcastle.
1547	Royal injunctions restore access to vernacular Bible. Priests ordered to buy Erasmus' *Paraphrases* on the Gospels to improve their scriptural understanding. Chantry priests ordered to teach young to read and write and bring them up in good manners. Chantry Act surrenders to Crown all chantry and college endowments with the exception of those belonging to colleges of Oxford and Cambridge, Winchester and Eton.

1548	Survey of educational institutions, most of which were accorded stipend for continuance. Some schools protected by Act of Parliament.
1549	Maidstone, Kent; Wellingborough, Northants (refoundation); Ilminster (refoundation). Publication of a new royal Latin grammar.
1550	Bury St Edmund's, Suffolk; Sherborne, Dorset; Bruton; Stafford; Stourbridge, Worcestershire; Marlborough. Many of the former chantry schools receive new endowments from the Chancellor of the Court of Augmentations.
1551	High Wycombe, Bucks; King Edward's, Chelmsford, Essex; Louth; Great Yarmouth; Leeds; Spilsby; Sedburgh, Yorkshire (refoundation).
1552	Christ's Hospital, London; King Edward's, Poole; King Edward's, Birmingham; Leeds; Bedford (refounded 1566); Shrewsbury; East Retford; Macclesfield; Ludlow, Shropshire (refoundation); Bath (refoundation); Abingdon; Beverley, Yorkshire; Stratford-upon-Avon; Morpeth (refoundation); Nuneaton, Warwickshire.
1553	Tonbridge, Kent (refoundation); Stratford-on-Avon, Warwickshire (re-endowment); St Alban's; Guildford; Totnes; Tavistock; Christ's College, Giggleswick (refoundation); Bradford; Ripon. Publication of official catechism by John Ponet; Thomas Wilson, *Art of Rhetoric*.
1554	Queen Mary's, Walsall; Gresham's, Holt, Norfolk; Leominster, Herefordshire (refoundation).
1555	Derby; Boston, Lincolnshire.
1556	Oundle, Northamptonshire.
1557	Brentwood, Essex; Repton, Derbyshire. All new schoolmasters to be licensed by bishop of diocese in which they intend to work.
1559	Act provided for statutory foundation of schools left incomplete at Mary's accession. Act dissolved Marian chantry and monastic foundations but preserved educational establishments attached to them.
1561	Merchant Taylors', London.
1562	High Wycombe, Buckinghamshire (refoundation).
1563	Elizabeth College, Buxton, Derbyshire; Sir Roger Manwood's School, Sandwich, Kent.
1564	Felsted, Essex; Wyggeston, Leicestershire.
1565	Rochdale, Lancashire; Highgate, Middlesex.
1567	Blackburn, Lancashire; Rugby, Warwickshire.
1569	Publication of John Harte, *Orthography*. Dorchester, Dorset.
1570	Derby (refoundation). Publication of Roger Ascham, *The Scholemaster*; John Harte, *Method*.
1571	Andover, Hampshire; St Olave's, London; Harrow, Middlesex. All teachers ordered by Convocation to subscribe to 39 Articles of Religion and the Prayer Book. Those who refused were deprived. Catechism by Alexander Nowell prescribed for general use.
1572	Queen Elizabeth's, Barnet.
1574	Norwich.
1580	Wrexham, Wales.
1581	Publication of Richard Mulcaster, *Positions . . . The Training up of Children*.

1582	Publication of Richard Mulcaster, *The First Part of the Elementarie*.
1584	Oakham, Rutland; Uppingham, Rutland.
1585	The practice of sending Catholics abroad for their education is declared illegal and offenders are fined £100.
1588	Publication of William Kempe, *Education of Children in Learning*.
1590	Wallasey, Cheshire.
1591	Wakefield, Yorkshire.
1595	Wellingborough, Northamptonshire refoundation.
1596	Publication of Edmund Coote, *The English Schoolmaster*.
1597	Alleyn's, London; Aldenham, Hertfordshire.
1598	Aylesbury Grammar School, Buckinghamshire.
1599	Blundell's, Tiverton, Somerset.

Books of the Tudor period

Select bibliography of important contemporary works by title

This is a brief list of works often referred to by title rather than author in student texts and monographs. See Authors listing (below) for additional works of importance. Early English Books Online (popularly referred to as EEBO) provides a searchable full-text database of a very large number of published books of the period.

Acts and Monuments (*see* Book of Martyrs)
Adages (*see* Erasmus, Desiderius)
Admonition to the people of England: against Martin Marprelate, An (1589) The Bishop of Winchester's defence of the bishops and attack on the writings of Martin Marprelate.
Admonition to the Parliament, An (1572) Important Puritan manifesto. Edited by W.H. Frere and C.E. Douglas, *Puritan Manifestoes, 1954*. John Field and Thomas Wilcox. 'Polemic of the highest order, measured and serious, but with shafts of infectious satire' directed against episcopal government and arguing for full reformation. Thomas Wilcox responsible for solemn admonition proper and John Field for 'vituperative and journalistic' attack on 'popish abuses yet remaining in the English church'. Autumn 1572: authors sentenced to a year's imprisonment.
Admonition to the Parliament, A Second (1572) Sometimes attributed to Thomas Cartwright.
Anglica Historica (1485–1537) Polydore Vergil. A prime source for the events of the reign of Henry VII. Printed by Denys Hay in Camden Society, 3rd series, LXXIV, 1950.
Annales Rerum Anglicarum et Hibernicarum, Regnante Elizabetha (1615) William Camden. Fed the myth of Elizabeth as the second Deborah.
Apology of the Church of England (1562) John Jewel, Bishop of Salisbury. Written from the point of view that the monarchy was the bulwark against the threat of restored Catholicism. Believed that the Church would be protected by the Crown, which would leave it free to perform its spiritual functions without interference.

Assertio Septem Sacramentorum (1521)   Henry VIII. Important treatise. English translation printed with Latin original, by L. O'Donovan, New York, 1908.

Autobiography of an Elizabethan (manuscript in circulation)   William Weston. Superior of the Jesuit mission in England, 1584. A persecuted Catholic priest during the reign of Elizabeth. Translation by Philip Caraman, published 1955.

Autobiography of John Gerard (manuscript in circulation from early seventeenth century)   A persecuted Jesuit priest in Elizabeth I's reign. Translation 1951.

Boke named the Governour, The (1531)   Sir Thomas Elyot. Treats of the education of the aristocracy.

Book of Martyrs (*see* Dialogi Sex, Confutation)   John Foxe's seminal history of the Christian church. Latin text published in 1559. Much-revised English version published in 1563 by John Day during the succession crisis. It provided a vivid account of events leading up to Elizabeth I's accession, concentrating on the edifying lives and deaths of the martyrs of the Reformation. It also supplied a history of the Reformation within the context of providential history. There was a struggle between Christ and Antichrist and Elizabeth was a second Deborah sent to rescue the nation from Antichrist and restore the rule of Christ. The Church of England was not revolutionary and innovatory: rather, it represented a return to the primitive and pristine early Christian church. The book had a wider circulation than any other English book, apart from the Bible.

Catechism, The (reign of King Edward VI)   Thomas Becon. Important Protestant teaching from reign of Edward VI. Edited by John Ayre for The Parker Society, Cambridge, 1844.

Chronicles of England (1580)   John Stowe. Presented, in chronicle form, the legend of English as a people chosen by God for His own purposes.

Chronicles of England, Scotland and Ireland, The (1578, revised 1587)   Raphael Holinshed 1587 version, based on Stow's *Chronicles*, is useful for reign of Elizabeth up to 1586.

Collectanea Satis Copiosa (1530)   Collaborative index, sponsored by Edward Foxe and Thomas Cromwell, of over 200 citations from scripture, the early Fathers and medieval works addressing the questions of royal and ecclesiastical jurisdiction and power. The work supported the idea of a royal supremacy in spiritual matters but also propounded the view that each province of the Church had its own jurisdictional independence.

Colloquies (*see* Erasmus, Desiderius)

Confutation (1565) (*see* Book of Martyrs)   Thomas Harding. Attacked Foxe's account and conclusions in *Book of Martyrs*.

De Antiquitate Britannicae Ecclesiae (1572)   Matthew Parker, Archbishop of Canterbury. Aimed to trace the apostolic origins of the English church.

De Copia (*see* Erasmus, Desiderius)

De Vera Obedentia (1535)   Bishop Stephen Gardiner's influential work, which saw Church and **commonwealth** as a unitary body politic, comprehensive of all the people, and ruled over by a single person, head of the Church and King of the commonwealth, to whom God ordered obedience.

Dialogue between Reginald Pole and Thomas Lupset, A (1535)   Thomas Starkey. Major humanist political treatise. Presented in fashionable dialogue form a programme of reforms for the public good. Attacked growing individualism and lack of concern for commonweal.

Dialogi Sex (1566) (*see* Book of Martyrs) Nicholas Harpsfield, under the alias Alan Cope. Refutation of Foxe's *Book of Martyrs*.

Discourse of the Common Weal of this Realm of England. (c.1549, unpublished until 1581) Variously attributed to John Hales and Sir Thomas Smith. Current opinion favours Smith. Sophisticated survey of contemporary politics and economy from the perspective of one who urged action for the good of the commonweal.

Discourse on Usury (Elizabethan) Thomas Wilson. Important treatise. Edited by R.H. Tawney, New York, 1925.

Elementarie, The First Parte of the (1582) (*see* Richard Mulcaster)

First and Chiefe Grounds of Architecture, The (1563) John Shute. This is the principal Elizabethan work on architecture.

Harborowe for Faithful and True Subjectes, An (April 1559) John Aylmer, later Bishop of London. Presents Elizabeth as having been saved from martyrdom only by divine intervention (death of Mary I), so that the English nation was committed to her preservation. Conspiracies against Elizabeth were conspiracies against the true Church.

How superior powers ought to be obeyd (1558 edn) Christopher Goodman. Tract by **Marian exile** on obedience due to secular powers.

If you know not me you know nobody; or the Troubles of Queen Elizabeth (1603) Thomas Heywood. Protestant historiographical propaganda presenting Elizabeth as second Deborah.

Laws of Ecclesiastical Polity, The (1593) Richard Hooker. Portrays the monarch as guardian of the Church of England but is implicitly critical of the way in which the Queen was exercising the royal supremacy. This part, Book 8, was published posthumously in 1662.

Lily's Latin Grammar In the late 1530s, a royal commission was set up to produce a Latin grammar based on the St Paul's texts of John Colet, William Lily and Desiderius Erasmus, the multiplicity of different grammars having caused confusion. The composite version was known as Lily's Latin Grammar and was prescribed for use in grammar schools until 1604. Ten thousand copies were published annually.

Marchants Aviso, The (Elizabethan) John Browne, Bristol merchant during Elizabeth's reign. A manual for merchants and factors involved in overseas trade. Edited by Patrick McGrath, Boston, 1957.

Obedience of a Christian Man (1528) William Tyndale traced the long-drawn-out contest between clergy and the Crown, casting the English monarchs as the dupe of the Roman clergy and only potentially as saviours of the Church.

Positions . . . The Training up of Children (1581) (*see* Mulcaster, Richard)

Praise of Folly (*see* Erasmus, Desiderius)

Reformatio Legum Ecclesiasticarum (1571) Reprinted in English translation as *The Reformation of the ecclesiastical laws as attempted in the reigns of King Henry VIII, King Edward VI and Queen Elizabeth*, Oxford, 1850.

Scholemaster, The (1570) (*see* Ascham, Roger) Ascham saw this book as showing his sons Giles and Dudley 'the right way to good learning'. The first book gives the character of the ideal tutor and scholar and draws heavily on Plato; the second treats the method of instruction by double translation, using proper imitation of classical models, and draws equally heavily upon Cicero. He discussed how best to judge the aptitude of a pupil, how best to encourage a student, how best to inculcate a love of learning. This book, which popularised the educational views of Renaissance Englishmen, has made Ascham famous among educational theorists,and one of the most influential of their number. He was concerned to rear an élite, capable of assuming what he considered their proper place in serving the commonweal, and he wrote in English to guarantee as wide an audience as possible, thus opening up ideas previously hidden from those who knew no classical languages. He has been singled out for bringing to an English audience the educational ideas of Johann Sturm. *The Scholemaster* was published in 1570 by John Daye (q.v.) at the request of Ascham's widow, Margaret, went through five editions between 1570 and 1590 and has been repeatedly republished and referred to both in English and in translation.

Sermon on the Ploughers or Sermon on the Plough (1548)   Hugh Latimer. One of a series of four sermons based on Christ's Parable of the Sower. The clergy are the ploughers, who prepare the land (the people) to receive the seed (the Word of God). Much of the sermon is an attack on preachers (or 'prelates' as Latimer calls them) who are failing in their duty. A remarkable sermon, characterised by powerful use of language. Some controversy as to Latimer's approach to England's problems in the 1540s. It is now accepted that he was not a member of a 'commonwealth party' (*see* Crowley, Brinklow, Smith) and, indeed, he rarely mentions the word 'commonwealth'. But to see him, even primarily, as a socio-economic critic or as a champion of the poor is probably a mistake. He regarded the material evils of the day as the by-products of England's failure to follow God's word: in this regard the poor were as guilty as the rich.

Short Treatise of Politicke Power, A (1556)   John Ponet. Marian exile's advocacy of limited monarchy. Published in Strasbourg.

Supplication for the Beggars, A (1529)   Simon Fish described the excesses of the Roman clergy, showed them to be seditious and prescribed a political remedy to be administered by the Crown. F.J. Furnivall and J.M. Cooper (eds), Early English Text Society, extra series, XIII, 1871.

Tree of the Commonwealth, The (1509?)   (*see* **Dudley, Edmund**)

Troubles at Frankfurt, A Briefe Discourse of the Troubles at Frankfort, 1554–58   Variously attributed to William Whittingham and Thomas Wood. An account of conflicts between the Marian exiles.

Union of the Two Noble and Illustre Famelies of Lancastre and York, The (1548)   Edward Hall. Good example of native writing, which assumed that dynamic monarchs caused change.

Utopia (*see* More, Thomas)

Valor Ecclesiasticus (1535)   Enormous survey of ecclesiastical benefices commissioned by Thomas Cromwell as vicegerent.

Vitae Romanorum Pontificum (1536)   Robert Barnes demonstrated that the very decline of the Church of Rome was due, in large part, to the Papacy's usurpation of temporal powers. The King might defend the faith by banishing the clerical estate to its own sphere but it would still be the clergy who would determine the form of religion in accord with Scripture.

Wolsey, The Life and Death of (c. 1554–58) George Cavendish. Written by a servant of Wolsey. Printed version in Richard S. Sylvester, Early English Text Society, original series, vol. CCXLIII, 1959.

Authors of the Tudor period

Included here are some European authors whose work was extremely influential in Tudor England as well as many of the English authors most frequently mentioned in student texts and monographs. Excluded are collections of letters and other manuscript materials, such as diaries and autobiographies, which have since been published.

Agrippa, Henry Cornelius (1486–1535)

His important *De nobilitate et praecellentia feminei sexus* (1534) was translated into English immediately; women have been forced to give place by male tyranny not by incapacity.

The English translation was: David Clapham, *A Treatise of the Nobilitie and Excellencye of Woman Kynde* (1534, 1542).

Ascham, Roger (1515–68)

Toxophilus (1540). Treatise on archery.

The Scholemaster (1570). Subtitled 'A plain and perfect way of teaching children to understand, write and speak, the Latin tongue'. 'Teach yourself' manual.

Bale, John (1495–1563)

A Comedy Concerning Three Laws (1532, pub. 1538). First Protestant morality play in English. Attack on papacy and monasticism.

A Tragedy of John, King of England (1538). Good King is duped by Archbishop and the Papacy. Use of allegory.

Image of Both Churches (1541). Detailed scholarly paraphrase book of Revelations, casting the Pope as Antichrist.

The Acts of English Votaries (1546). Scurrilous attack on veneration of saints, via descriptions of sexual exploits of saints, forms part of the argument justifying the Henrician break with Rome.

Barnes, Robert (1495–1540)

That Men's Constitutions, which are not Grounded in Scripture, Bind not the Conscience of Man (pub. with *Supplication* in 1534). It is God who institutes political authority and men are bound to obedience by Him. Resistance is in no circumstances justifiable but there is a distinction between disobedience and resistance.

Becon, Thomas (1512–67)

Thomas Becon. Works, ed. by J. Ayre in three volumes, Parker Society, Cambridge, 1843–44. Includes influential *Catechism* and also much of socioeconomic as well as religious interest.

Bilson, Thomas (1547–1616)

The Perpetual Government of Christ's Church (1593). Defence of episcopacy.

Brinklow, Henry (d. 1546)

The Complaint of Roderick Mors (1546). Prototype of the so-called 'Commonwealth tracts' which angrily chastised the exploitative activities of nobles and landlords.

Browne, Robert (?1550–?1633)

A Treatise of Reformation without Tarrying for Anie (1582). Sets out separatist position on the Church and presents separatist attack on Puritans.

Cartwright, Thomas (1533–1603)

A reply to an answere made of M Dr Whitgifte agaynste the Admonition to Parliament (1574).
The second replie of T.C. against Master Doctor Whitgift's second answer, touching the church discipline (1575).
The rest of the second replie . . . (1577). Part of important debate concerning manner of Church government (whether by episcopacy or not) sparked off by John Field and Thomas Wilcox's *Admonition to the Parliament* (1572). The latter work is detailed under 'Books of the Tudor Period' above.

Cleaver, Robert (fl. 1590s)

Godlie Forme of Householde Government: For the Ordering of Private Families, According to the Direction of God's Word (1598). This is normally cited in its 1612 edition and attributed to John Dod and Robert Cleaver. A popular marriage conduct book designed for the middle classes. It describes 'a way of ordering the famelie aright'.

Coote, Edmund (fl. 1590s)

The English Schoolmaster (1596). The most popular manual for teaching of reading. Twenty-six editions between 1596 and 1656; still used in the eighteenth century.

Upper- and lower-case alphabets; vowels and consonants; graded syllable-based vocabularies using verses to produce mechanical accuracy but with little attention to comprehension; syllabification; rules of pronunciation; spelling contest; reading practice; rules of behaviour and number.

Cranmer, Thomas (1489–1556)

The Works of Thomas Cranmer, ed. by J.E. Cox in three volumes, Parker Society, Cambridge, 1844–46. Important for understanding religious developments in Henry VIII's and Edward VI's reigns.

Crowley, Robert (?1518–88)

The Way to Wealth (1550). Angry work of protest against those who undermine the common good by pursuing their own advancement. One of the so-called 'Commonwealth tracts'. See Brinklow, Henry, above.

The Voice of the Last Trumpet (1550). Versified critique of those merchants and others who pursue their own selfish concerns at the expense of the public good.

Dee, John (1527–1608)

Translation of Euclid's *Elements of Geometry* with important preface (1570). Preface treats diverse subjects such as music, navigation and astronomy. Defends translation of learned book for wide audience. Suggests practical applications of mathematical principles.

Dudley, Edmund (1462–1510)

The Tree of the Commonwealth (1510). Extravagant allegory of the commonwealth as a tree rooted in love of God, justice, fidelity, concord and peace. Portrays 'prince' as defender of these roots, often against clerical encroachment. Marked hostility to the clergy as an estate.

Elyot, Sir Thomas (?1490–1546)

The Boke of the Governour (1531) (also referred to as 'The Boke Called the Governor'; 'The Boke Named the Governor'). The paramount importance of education for the nobility as a preparation for public life is stressed and an ideal humanist curriculum proposed.

Latin–English Dictionary (1538). Widely used in grammar schools.

Erasmus, Desiderius (c. 1469–1536)

Adagiorum Collectanea. Adages (several editions beginning with 1490s). A collection of pithy sayings with their meanings compiled by Erasmus as a teaching aid.

Adages, according to Erasmus, have four chief uses: to sum up basic philoso-
phies; to assist persuasive argument; to be decorative; to aid understanding of
classical authors. The collection was heavily relied on by generations of English
and other European schoolboys as part of an attempt to enrich the Latin then in
use and to make the language more effective.

Ciceronianus (1527). Dialogue debating the approach of humanists to the ancient
authors. Erasmus does not favour slavish imitation of, for example, Cicero, but
rather creative use of ancient forms.

Colloquies (first edition, 1519). Dialogues designed to illustrate forms of speech and
address and to familiarise students with Latin as an everyday language. Widely used
in grammar schools and universities. Success, and historical significance, ensured
by treatment within the dialogues of issues of contemporary importance – for
example, the corruptions and abuses apparent in the Church; the relationships
between men and women, husbands and wives; the nature of true religion. See
especially: *A Pilgrimage for Religion's Sake* (1526); *The Exorcism or Apparition;
Courtship* (1523); *Marriage* (1523); *The Religious Banquet*.

Conscribendis Epistolis [*On Letter Writing*] (1522). Published as a textbook on the
fashionable art of letter writing. Immensely successful because of its widespread
use in schools and universities. Long lists of sample classical letters from Cicero,
Pliny and Horace. Erasmus turned it into a lively book by treating each class of
letters to a discrete study and by using vivid contemporary examples containing
absorbing subject matter.

De Copia [*De Duplici Verborum ac Rerum*] (1512). Standard work throughout
Europe for teaching of Latin rhetoric and composition. Went through 100 editions
during the sixteenth century alone. Contained extended vocabulary to diversify
expression.

Enchiridion Militis Christi (1503); published in English as *The Handsome Weapon
of a Christian Knight*. Here Erasmus sees the Christian life as a war in which the
chief weapons are knowledge and prayer. He pleads for the inwardness of the
spiritual life and attacks outward, ritualistic religion. He sees study of the classical world as preparing the Christian to study the Scriptures and receive the revelation of God's Word. Secular learning is therefore a means to a spiritual end.
Important work in the development of Christian **humanism**.

The Institution of Christian Marriage (1526). Significant work on Christian mar-
riage translated into English and published by Richard Tavernour, *A Ryght
Fruteful Epystle Devysed by the Most Excellent Clerke Erasmus, in Laude and
Prayse of Matrymony*, 1532.

New Testament (Greek version, Latin translation) (1516). *Paraclesis* (or introduction) seeks to open up the scriptures to everyone.

The Praise of Folly (*Moriae Encomium*) (1509). Folly defends herself and enumer-
ates her admirers, which include the lawyers, the princes and their courtiers and
the Pope and all churchmen. Their position depends upon folly: 'were wisdom to
descend on them, how it would inconvenience them!' by depriving them of
wealth and honour. The oration concludes with an attack on the corruptions and
abuses of the church and the Papacy. Completed 1510; first pub'd 1511.

Foxe, Edward (c. 1496–1538)

The True Difference Between the Regal Power and the Ecclesiastical Power (1534). Part of justification for royal divorce and supremacy.

Foxe, John (1516–87)

Actes and Monuments of these Latter and Perilous Days (1563). *See* 'Books of the Tudor Period' above.

Froissart, Sir John (?1337–?1410)

Chronicles (c. 1400). Translated into English by John Bourchier Berners (1469–1533). Provided Shakespeare with details for *Richard II*. Froissart lived in England from 1360 to 1366, partly as clerk to Queen Philippa of Hainault, wife of Edward III. He revisited England in 1395, when he met Richard II.

Gardiner, Stephen (1483–1555)

De Vera Obedientia (*The Oration of True Obedience*) (1535). Support for royal supremacy. Vindication of royal divorce. Markedly Lutheran view of temporal and spiritual authority. Princes reign by God's authority and resistance to their rule is resistance to God. There are no parallel temporal and spiritual jurisdictions. Papal and ecclesiastical power is usurped from the King. There continues to be an area of spiritual activity, but not of separate spiritual jurisdiction.

Discourse on the Coming of the English and Normans to Britain (1555). Advice book to Philip II, thinly disguised as history of early Britain. Advocates Machiavellian idea that reason of state is an acceptable defence for any ruler to employ 'unvirtuous' strategies to protect the interests of the commonwealth. First northern European humanist to provide defence of Machiavelli.

Goodman, Christopher (?1520–1603)

How Superior Powers ought to be Obeyed of their Subjects (1558). Goodman, Edwardian Lady Margaret Professor of Divinity at Cambridge, wrote this tract while pastor of English congregation at Geneva. All rulers under obligation to defend the true faith. Assigned a monarchy limited by God. Private-law doctrine used to justify forcible resistance: when 'kings and rulers are become altogether blasphemers of God, and oppressors and murderers of their subjects . . . [then] . . . ought they to be accounted no more for kings or lawful magistrates, but as private men, and to be examined, accused, condemned and punished by the law of God, whereunto they are and ought to be subject'.

Grindal, Edmund (?1519–83)

Grindal's Remains, ed. by W. Nicholson, Parker Society, Cambridge, 1843.

Hall, Edward (1498–1547)

The Union of the Two Noble and Illustre Famelies of Lancastre and York (1548). Chronicle of English history from Henry IV to Henry VIII which influenced all sixteenth-century historians, including Holinshed and Shakespeare, with its moralistic view of history.

Harte, John (d. 1574)

Orthography (1569) and *Method* (1570). Early printed manuals of instruction for teachers.

Holinshed, Raphael (?1530–?80)

History of England. History of Scotland (translation of Hector Boece). Formed part of *The Chronicles of England, Scotland and Ireland* (1577 and 1587). Second edition of 1587 was principal source for Shakespeare's later history plays and, together with Hall, for the earlier cycle from Henry VI to Richard III.

Hooker, Richard (?1554–1600)

Of the Lawes of Ecclesiasticall Politie (Books I–IV, 1594; Book V, 1597; Books VI and VII, 1644; Book VIII, 1662). Authorship of Book VI doubtful; Books VII and VIII constructed from Hooker's rough notes. Defence of Elizabethan Church against Puritan criticism. Extremely important contribution to sixteenth-century political thought.

Hooper, John (d. 1555)

Early Writings of John Hooper, ed. by S. Carr in two volumes, Parker Society, Cambridge, 1843. *Later Writings of John Hooper*, ed. by C. Nevinson in two volumes, Parker Society, Cambridge, 1852. Crucially important for primitivist Protestant thought – regarding, for example, the nature of the ministry and of worship and the question of **adiaphora** or 'things indifferent'.

Jewel, John (1522–71)

Works of John Jewel, ed. by J. Ayre in four volumes, Parker Society, Cambridge, 1840–50. *Apology* (1562) is included in Volume 3. This was the first important defence of the Elizabethan Church of England.

Joye, George (1490–1553)

The Psalms (1530) English translation of the psalms.

Kempe, William (d. 1601)

Education of Children in Learning (1588). Treatise which displays influence of Pierre de Ramée, who emphasised the utility of knowledge.

Latimer, Hugh (c. 1485–1555)

Sermons by Hugh Latimer, ed. by G.E. Corrie, Parker Society, Cambridge, 1844. *Sermons and Remains of Hugh Latimer*, ed. by G.E. Corrie, Parker Society, Cambridge, 1845. Forty-one sermons survive, most preached during the reign of Edward, either at court or on preaching tours. These were taken down verbatim by an amanuensis and not revised for publication. They are conveniently collected together in this nineteenth-century edition. Contain much valuable socio-economic comment. For *Sermon on the Ploughers* see 'Books of the Tudor Period' above.

Machiavelli, Niccolo (1469–1527)

The Prince (1532). Spirited defence of reason of state as justification for political action. Considerable historical debate as to its influence on English thought.

Marprelate, Martin

Nom de plume of author or authors of tracts against the bishops. See Job Throckmorton, John Penry, John Udall, Robert Waldegrave.

Marshal, William (fl. 1530s)

Defender of Peace (1535). Translation into English of Marsiglio of Padua's *Defensor Pacis*. Commissioned by Thomas Cromwell. Translation omitted passages on the popular origins of political authority. Preface maintained that the book proved that popes have always been usurpers of power.

More, Sir Thomas (1478–1535)

Apology (*see* St German, Christopher). Counterattack to St German's blast against the legal jurisdiction of the Church.

Dialogue concerning Heresies (1529) (*see* Tyndale, William). Accuses Tyndale of arguing in favour of rebellion. Enters into debate about access to Bible: Church must supervise translation; no indiscriminate access to Bible.

Debellacion between Salem and Bizance (1533) (*see* St German, Christopher). Rejoinder to St German's dialogue.

Utopia (1516). 'Unquestionably the greatest contribution to the political theory of the northern Renaissance, it also embodies by far the most radical critique of humanism written by a humanist . . . [It] believes that one of the most urgent tasks of social theory is to discover the root causes of injustice and poverty . . . [and believes] that these evils are mainly caused by the misuse of private property' (Skinner, *Foundations of Modern Political Thought*, Vol. I, pp. 256–62). Use of mythical state of Utopia to explore ideas. Through humanist belief that virtue constitutes the only true nobility, More attacks both hereditary **aristocracy** and the 'comfortable social philosophy' of many fellow humanists, such as Elyot. Attacks whole concept of hierarchical society. Denunciation of Italianate preoccupation with the art of war. Latin text.

Morrison, Richard (d. 1556)

Apomaxis Calumniarum (1537). Account of the schism, which includes an attack on Thomas More and John Fisher.

Lamentation (1536) and *Remedy for Sedition* (Oct. 1536) showed the consequences of sedition and rebellion in the wake of the Pilgrimage of Grace.

Invective against the Great and Detestable Vice, Treason (1539). The Northern rebellion.

An Exhortation to Stir all Englishmen in Defence of their Country (1539). Patriotic view of the reformation settlement, written against the background of reimposition of Clement VII's excommunication of Henry VIII, which released Catholic subjects from allegiance. Extremely influential. Reiterates Lutheran call to non-resistance in all circumstances. Denounces his former patron, 'pestiferous Pole', alongside Catholics in general.

Mulcaster, Richard (?1530–1611)

Positions . . . The Training up of Children (1581) and *The First Part of the Elementarie* (1582). These two books provided Mulcaster with a platform to deal with two fundamental problems facing the humanist education programme: ill-qualified and uncommitted teachers and poor method that turned pupils away from learning. He recommended a teacher-training college; physical education; the direction of the best teachers to the elementary forms; full-time commitment to teaching; a carefully planned and standardised curriculum; standard teaching methodology; fundamental spelling reform.

Perkins, William (1558–1602)

The Works of William Perkins. Extremely influential Protestant Cambridge divine during reign of Elizabeth. His works of pastoral theology particularly important. No complete modern edition of his voluminous writings exists.

Pole, Reginald (1500–58)

Apology to Charles V (1539). Includes attack on Machiavelli's ideas as destructive of the virtues.

A Defence of Ecclesiastical Unity (1536). A Latin tract defending impossibility of royal supremacy. Church is gift of God but kingship is creation of the people themselves who 'spontaneously submit' to an authority set up in their own self-interest. Weakened by vitriolic attack on King as head of church of Satan.

Includes attack on Machiavelli's ideas as destructive of the virtues. Contributed to downfall and eventual execution of his brother, Henry, Lord Montague and his mother Margaret, Countess of Salisbury.

Ponet, John (?1514–56)

Short Treatise of Politicke Power (1556). Justification of forcible resistance written during Marian exile in Frankfurt by Edwardian Bishop of Winchester.

Sadoleto, Jacopo (1477–1547)

The Right Education of Boys (1534).

Sampson, Richard (d. 1554)   (see Foxe, Edward and Gardiner, Stephen)

Oration to Teach Everyone that they must be Obedient to the Will of the King (1534).

Shakespeare, William (1564–1616)

Chronology of writing of Shakespeare's Elizabethan plays

1588–94
Titus Andronicus
Henry VI, Part I
The Comedy of Errors
The Two Gentlemen of Verona
Henry VI, Part 2
Henry VI, Part 3
King John
Love's Labour's Lost
Richard III
The Taming of the Shrew

1594–96
Romeo and Juliet
Richard II (published 1597 apart from abdication scene)
A Midsummer Night's Dream
Henry IV, Parts 1 and 2

1596–98
The Merry Wives of Windsor
The Merchant of Venice
Henry V
Much Ado About Nothing

1599–1601
As You Like It
Twelfth Night
Julius Caesar
Hamlet

1602–03
All's Well That Ends Well
Troilus and Cressida

Sidney, Sir Philip (1554–86)

Arcadia (1593). A pastoral romance. Two versions. The first, a straightforward affair, was not published until the twentieth century. A second version, incomplete but richer and more complex, was published as *Countess of Pembroke's Arcadia* in 1593.

Smith, Henry (?1550–91)

A Preparative to Marriage (1591). Contains attack on wet-nursing. Discusses relationship between husbands and wives and nature of woman.

Smith, Sir Thomas (1513–77)

De Republica Anglorum. The Maner of Government or policie of the Realme of England (1583). Otherwise known as *The Commonwealth of England*. Description of English constitution and government.
Discourse of the Common Weal (1549, unpublished until 1581). Disputed authorship. Sometimes attributed to John Hales (d. 1571) but currently most commonly attributed to Smith. Sophisticated survey of polity and economy from perspective of **commonwealthmen** of Edward's reign.

Spenser, Edmund (1552–97)

The Faery Queen (1589–96). A lengthy allegorical pastoral poem which represented a new departure in English poetry and combined epic and romance with styles derived from Chaucer. Spenser introduced a new form of stanza of nine lines (known as the Spenserian). Only six of the intended twelve books were completed. His poetry became the inspiration for many in the early Stuart period, especially Michael Drayton, and greatly influenced John Milton.

Starkey, Thomas (?1499–1538)

A Dialogue Between Reginald Pole and Thomas Lupset (1535). Major treatise of humanist political thought. A series of reform proposals for the commonwealth presented in fashionable dialogue form. The universities were designed to educate clergy, therefore there was a need for a separate academy in London for the education of the elite.

An Exhortation to the People (1535, published 1536). Defence of the Reformation settlement inspired by and perhaps revised by Thomas Cromwell. Instructed people to 'unity and obedience'. Stresses the power of statute.

St German, Christopher (c. 1460–1540)

Dialogue between a Doctor and a Student (Latin version 1523; English version 1531). Dialogue about the foundations of law and, especially, the relationship between the eternal law, the laws of nature and the law of God on the one hand and the laws of England on the other. The conclusion is that the customary laws of England are supreme. The English version included a second dialogue (published separately in 1530) which brought out the anti-clerical aspects of St German's thought on the law.

Treatise (concerning the division between the spiritual and the temporal) (1532) (*see* Thomas More, *Apology* and *Debellacion of Salem and Bizance*. Attack on clerical estate and its claim to legal jurisdiction. Opening salvo in war, in which Thomas More campaigned on the clergy's behalf with the *Apology*.

Dialogue (between Salem and Bizance) (1532). More responded to this with *Debellacion between Salem and Bizance*.

Answer to a Letter (1535). All power is secular. The common law is supreme and legislative authority is vested in the King in Parliament. The King is resuming his headship of the church, which had been delegated by his forbears to the Papacy, and this headship includes even the power to determine doctrine. This provided useful independent support for the Government's propaganda in support of the break with Rome.

Tilney, Edmund (d. 1610)

A Briefe and Pleasaunt Discourse of Duties in Marriage (1568). The author was Master of Revels in the royal household, 1579–1609.

Travers, Walter (?1548–1635)

Ecclesiasticae discipliniae et Anglicanae ecclesiae . . . explicatio (1574). English translation, *A Full and Plain Declaration of Ecclesiastical Discipline*, published in 1574, generally attributed to Thomas Cartwright. Not to be confused with Puritan *Book of Discipline* (Directory which is also often attributed to Travers).

A Directory of Church Government . . . Found in the Study of . . . Cartwright after his decease (1644). Late version of document, *Book of Discipline*, produced by Puritans in the 1580s. Sometimes attributed to Cartwright and sometimes to Travers. Modern scholarship plumps for composite authorship of a document of which Travers was draftsman.

Tyndale, William (c. 1494–1536) (see 'The Bible and Biblical Scholarship' below)

The Obedience of a Christian Man (1531). Lutheran emphasis on distinction between disobedience and resistance. Rulers must be obeyed in all things because God has so ordered it. Forcible resistance is never justifiable. The subject enjoined by the powers that be to do evil must desist but must suffer death rather than resist the civil authorities. The Church, defined as a purely spiritual body, is not exempt from this obligation. The ruler has a duty to rule the people as God wants, for they are God's people. All jurisdiction is secular and, therefore, the Pope and the Church have usurped the power of the King.
Answer to Sir Thomas More's Dialogue (1531).

Vives, Jean Luis (sometimes given as Ludovico) (1492–1540)

De Instructione Feminae Christianae (1524) translated by Richard Hyrde as *Instruction of a Christian Woman*. A manual which, while advocating a humanistic education for girls, nevertheless emphasised that a woman's domestic vocation dictated the limits of her educational needs.
De Tradendis Disciplinis (1531). Suggested value of technique of double translation (from Latin into English and back again) which was, in consequence, widely used in English grammar schools.
Latinae Linguae Exercitatio (1539). **Colloquies** particularly useful for schoolboys.
Office and Duty of a Husband (1550).

Whitgift, John (?1530–1604) (see Cartwright, Thomas; Admonition)

An Answere to a Certen Libel Entituled an Admonition to the Parliament (1572).
The Defense of the Aunswere to the Admonition, Against the Replie of T.C. (1574).

Wilson, Thomas (?1525–81)

Rule of Reason (1551). Manual for teaching of logic.
Art of Rhetoric (1553). Manual for teaching of rhetoric (i.e. oral communication).

The Bible and biblical scholarship

Chronology

1496/97   John Colet lectured at Oxford on St Paul's Epistle to the Romans. The lectures were unusual because Colet set the text in its historical context. Moreover, Colet employed St Paul's arguments to criticise the contemporary Church and to call for a return to primitive Christianity.

1499   Erasmus visited England and was received by John Colet who encouraged Erasmus's dislike of scholasticism and directed him towards scriptural study. Erasmus thought that he did not possess the technical expertise to translate the Old Testament as Colet suggested, but vowed to acquire such expertise.

1503	Erasmus published the *Enchiridion Militis Christiani* (*The Handbook of the Christian Soldier*).
1504	Erasmus wrote to Colet urging him to publish his work on St Paul and the Gospels.
1509	Erasmus returned to England.
1511–14	Erasmus working on translation of Greek New Testament while at Cambridge University.
1516	Erasmus published translated New Testament, which included *Paraclesis*, exhorting people to read the scriptures; Colet begged Erasmus to produce detailed commentaries on his scriptural translations to make entirely clear his interpretation of the 'philosophia Christi'.
1522	Publication at Wittenberg of Martin Luther's German New Testament (based on Erasmus' translation).
1523	William Tyndale unsuccessfully sought patronage of Cuthbert Tunstal, Bishop of London for translation of Bible into English. Tyndale associated with Protestants. Publication at Wittenberg of Luther's German translation of the Pentateuch (first five books of the Old Testament).
1524	Humphrey Monmouth, a London merchant, assisted Tyndale to visit Germany. Tyndale visited Cologne, Hamburg and Wittenberg.
1525	Tyndale's English New Testament, based on Luther's and Erasmus's translations, completed. Printing began at Cologne but was interrupted by the Church authorities and had to continue at Worms.
1526	April: Tyndale's New Testament on sale in England. The Bishop of London banned its sale and use in his diocese and a copy was burned at **St Paul's Cross**. Second edition printed by Christopher Endhoven of Antwerp.
1528	Cardinal Wolsey prosecuted several, including Thomas Garrett of Oxford, for circulating Tyndale's New Testament.
1530	Hoochstraten of Antwerp printed Tyndale's translation of the Pentateuch. Endhoven printed third edition of New Testament. Henry VIII set up commission of inquiry into need for English Bible and this reported in favour of an official translation. George Joye translated Psalms into English from Martin Bucer's Latin translation.
1531	George Joye published translation of Book of Isaiah.
1533	Winken de Worde publishes Tyndale's English translation of Erasmus' *Enchiridion* under title *The Manuell of the Christen Knyght*.
1534	Publication of German Bible at Wittenberg. Fourth edition of Tyndale's New Testament published at Antwerp. George Joye published Book of Jeremiah. Miles Coverdale began work on English translation of Old Testament at Antwerp. December: Canterbury Convocation petitioned King for English Bible. At Cranmer's request a group of bishops and scholars set to work to amend Tyndale's New Testament, but the project bore no fruit.

1535	Arrest and imprisonment of Tyndale at Vilvorde Castle, near Brussels. Coverdale put together Tyndale's translation of the Pentateuch and New Testament and his own translation of the rest of the Old Testament to publish complete English Bible at Cologne; Henry VIII gave the printer James Nicholson permission to print Coverdale's Bible but did not give it official approval.
1536	Execution of Anne Boleyn put an end to Cromwell's plan to make English Bible compulsory in parish churches. Tyndale executed at Vilvorde in October.
1537	Nicholson printed two revised editions of Coverdale's Bible, claiming official sanction. August: John Rogers published 'Mathew Bible', based on Tyndale's, at Antwerp with the permission of the King. It was so called because Rogers used the pseudonym Thomas Mathew.
1538	Coverdale, in Paris, worked to modify the radical Protestantism of the Mathew Bible; publication was interrupted by the French authorities but moved to London. Cromwell's injunctions ordered an English Bible to be placed in every church.
1539	Coverdale's Great Bible printed. Richard Taverner, one of Cromwell's protégés, also produced a modified Mathew Bible.
1540	Second edition of Great Bible with preface by Cranmer. Berthelet printed first cheap edition of Great Bible. Bishop of London arrested John Porter for reading English Bible aloud in St Paul's and offering commentary.
1541	Fifth edition of Great Bible. Order for English Bible to be placed in every parish church repeated.
1542	Conservative revision of Great Bible (to be based on Vulgate version) demanded. Cranmer appointed panel of 15 bishops to examine New Testament but Henry VIII handed the task to the universities. No revision was forthcoming.
1543	Act for the advancement of true religion passed. Right to read vernacular scriptures restricted.
1551	William Salesbury published Welsh translation of Epistles and Gospels.
1553–58	English Bibles destroyed.
1556	English translation of the Psalms produced at Geneva by William Whittingham and William Kethe.
1557	Whittingham translated New Testament.
1559	Royal injunctions order English Bible to be set up in every church. Elizabethan **Book of Common Prayer** (excluding **Black Rubric** of 1552).
1560	April: William Whittingham, Anthony Gilby and Richard Sampson produced 'Geneva Bible' or 'Breeches Bible'. This Bible was Calvinist, relatively cheap and more accessible to the reader; it was printed in roman type and the text was divided into chapters and verses.
1563	Commission of bishops of Bangor, St David's, St Asaph's, Llandaff and Hereford set up to translate Bible into Welsh.
1566	Edition of Great Bible. Matthew Parker directed amended translation of Bible.

1567	Bible in Welsh published. William Salesbury largely responsible.
1568	Parker's Bible (the Bishops' Bible) published.
1572	Revised version of Bishops' Bible published.
1576	Geneva Bible first published in England.
1578	Work begun on Rheims/Douay Catholic translation of the Bible into English by Gregory Martin. William Allen supervised this translation of the Vulgate.
1582	Martin New Testament published.
1588	William Morgan, Bishop of St Asaph, published first Welsh Bible.
1596	Hugh Broughton published English translation of Book of Daniel from the Hebrew.
1611	Authorised Version of Bible published.

5

CENTRAL GOVERNMENT: (1) THE MONARCHY AND THE ROYAL HOUSEHOLD

The monarchy

England was governed by a monarch. Changes to the royal style occurred during Henry VIII's reign. In 1521, Pope Leo X conferred the title of *fidei defensor* (defender of the faith) on Henry VIII. Henry was the first monarch to place a numeral after his or her name (1525). In 1541, Henry was declared King rather than Lord of Ireland by statute (33 Henry VII, c. 1). Both Henry and his son Edward maintained the style: *Dei Gratia Angliae, Franciae, et Hiberniae Rex, Fidei Defensor, et in terra Ecclesiae Anglicanae et Hibernicae supremum caput* (by the grace of God king of England, France and Ireland, Defender of the Faith, and Supreme Head of the Church of England and Ireland on earth). The Act of 1 & 2 Ph. & Mary repealed the statute of 1541 (35 Henry VIII, c. 3) by which it was declared high treason to deprive the monarch of this title and the claim to supremacy was dropped. Philip's titles were added to those of Mary. When Elizabeth succeeded she adopted the style: 'Dei Gratia Angliae, Franciae et Hiberniae regia, fidei defensor . . .'.

Monarchs

Henry VII, b. 28 January 1457, d. 21 April 1509. Ruled 1485–1509.
Henry VIII, b. 28 June 1491, d. 28 January 1547. Ruled 1509–47.
Edward VI, b. 12 October 1537, d. 6 July 1553. Ruled 1547–53.
'Queen Jane Grey', b. October 1537, d. 12 February 1554. 'Ruled' 6–14 July 1553.
Mary I, b. 18 February 1516, d. 17 November 1558. Ruled 1553–58.
Elizabeth I, b. 7 September 1533, d. 24 March 1603. Ruled 1558–1603.

The Tudor dynasty *ruled* England. It did so with the assistance of a council, occasional **Great Councils**, a parliament and a number of officers of state. The period was one of experiment. Henry VII, for example, carried on medieval experiments with chamber financial administration while, under King Henry VIII, new courts were created to deal with new sources of revenue. Under Henry VIII and his heirs, the Secretaryship of State became an increasingly important office and the Lord Chancellorship's executive role shrank in relation to his position as chief legal officer of the Crown.

Listings of office holders below are restricted to the major offices of state (Lord Chancellor, Keeper, Keeper of the Privy Seal, Secretaries of State).

The Royal Council

The monarch selected a council of advisers from among the powerful of the realm, both lay and ecclesiastical. In medieval times, the royal council was large and unwieldy, made up of bishops and magnates, who assembled to advise the King only during the legal terms because they had to attend to other business during much of the year. The monarch, of course, needed constant advice and not just while the law courts were sitting, so he habitually consulted those councillors who were always present (often members of his household) and who came to form a more influential and select Privy Council. Thomas Cromwell's reform of the council and establishment of the Privy Council in the 1530s as the supreme executive was a formalisation of an existing tendency in royal government.

Chronology

15th century	Council at its most important.
Henry VII	Large council of 40 to 50 members; some functional divisions made the council more effective by reducing its size in particular circumstances: e.g. Star Chamber; Court of Requests; small group of itinerant councillors who accompanied the king. Council managed by the Lord Chancellor, backed by the **Chancery**.
Henry VIII	Also had large council but largely relied on Wolsey for advice and action:
1526	In the Eltham Ordinances, Wolsey proposed a smaller council of about 20 members but this came to nothing when he fell from power.
Mid-1530s	Cromwell revived idea of smaller council and established a Privy Council of 19 office holders and royal servants sitting under the King's chairmanship by 1536: Thomas Cromwell, as Principal Secretary, initiated and organised the business of the Privy Council and enjoyed much executive power as a result.
1540	Cromwell fell from office and a permanent clerk to the council was appointed who kept the minutes. The administrative and judicial work of the council was thereafter kept strictly separate, although the Star Chamber and Court of Requests were staffed by Privy Council members.
Edward VI	Large and ineffective council of about 40 members, riven by faction, which worked through committees. Proposals for reform mooted but impossible to arrive at agreement.

Mary I   Council grew even larger and more unmanageable; Crown relied on a very few advisers, such as Cardinal Reginald Pole, and this had repercussions for the success of the Government.

Elizabeth I   Privy Council drawn from about 58 men and at any one time numbered about a dozen; deliberate return to small Privy Council; extremely effective in managing the Government and keeping it in touch with the rest of the nation. Used the JPs and Lords Lieutenant to implement its acts. Controlled and purged membership of local commissions of the peace (e.g. of recusants) to ensure compliance. Worked through special agencies of the regional councils (e.g. Council of the North), which received a stream of orders from the Privy Council and also sought the council's advice. Decline of the Privy Council in the later years of the century because of political factionalism.

- Thomas Cromwell reduced size and increased efficiency of the Royal Council in the 1530s, thus building on Wolsey's ideas.
- Reversion to larger and ineffective council under the middle Tudors.
- Effective partnership between Privy Council and local agencies during Elizabeth's reign.
- Decline of the Privy Council under Elizabeth as it became an arena for the manoeuvrings of Cecil, Essex, Walsingham and Leicester.

The following listings of the membership of the Privy Council may be used to illustrate its changing size and composition.

Membership of Privy Council, 1526 (Eltham Ordinances), 20 members

Thomas Wolsey, Chancellor; Duke of Norfolk, Treasurer; Cuthbert Tunstall, Bishop of London and Keeper of Privy Seal; Duke of Suffolk, Marshal of England; Marquess of Dorset; Marquess of Exeter; Earl of Shrewsbury, Steward of Household; Earl of Oxford, Lord Chamberlain; John Clerk, Bishop of Bath; John Longland, Bishop of Lincoln; Lord Sandys, Chamberlain of the Household; Sir William FitzWilliam, Treasurer of Household; Sir Henry Guilford, Comptroller; Richard Pace, Secretary; Sir Thomas More, Chancellor of Duchy of Lancaster; Richard Sampson, Dean of King's Chapel; Sir Henry Wyatt, Treasurer of King's Chamber; Sir Richard Wingfield, Vice Chamberlain; Sir William Kingston, Captain of the Guard; Doctor Wolman, Almoner.

Membership of the Privy Council, 1540, 18 members

Thomas Cranmer, Archbishop of Canterbury; Thomas, Lord Audley, Chancellor; Thomas, Duke of Norfolk, High Treasurer; Charles, Duke of Suffolk, Master of King's Household and President of the Council; William, Earl of Southampton and Lord Privy Seal; Robert, Earl of Sussex and Great Chamberlain; Edward Seymour, Earl of

Hertford; John, Lord Russell, Great Admiral; Cuthbert Tunstall, Bishop of Durham; Stephen Gardiner, Bishop of Winchester; William, Lord Sandys, King's Chamberlain; Sir Thomas Cheyney, Lord Warden of the **Cinque Ports** and Treasurer of Household; Sir Anthony Browne, Master of the King's Horse; Sir William Kingston, Comptroller of Household; Sir Anthony Wingfield, Vice Chamberlain of Household; Sir Thomas Wriothesley, Secretary; Sir Richard Rich, Chancellor of Court of Augmentations; Sir John Baker, Chancellor of Court of First Fruits and Tenths.

Membership of the Privy Council, 1553 (Edward VI), 39 members

Thomas Cranmer, Archbishop of Canterbury; Thomas Goodrich, Bishop of Ely and Lord Chancellor; The Marquess of Winchester, Lord Treasurer; The Duke of Northumberland; Lord John Russell, Lord Privy Seal; The Duke of Suffolk; The Marquess of Northampton; The Earl of Shrewsbury; The Earl of Westmorland; The Earl of Huntingdon; The Earl of Pembroke; The Viscount Hereford; Lord Clinton, Lord Admiral; Lord Darcy, Lord Chamberlain; The Lord Cobham; The Lord Rich; Sir Richard Cotton, Mr Comptroller; Sir Thomas Cheyney, Mr Treasurer; Sir John Gates, Mr Vice Chamberlain; William Petre, Secretary; William Cecil, Secretary; Sir Philip Hoby; Sir Robert Bowes; Sir John Gage; Sir John Mason; Mr Ralph Sadler; Sir John Baker; Judge Bromley; Judge Montague; Mr Wotton; Mr North; Nicholas Ridley, Bishop of London; Thomas Thirlby, Bishop of Norwich; Sir Thomas Wrothe; Sir Richard Cotton; Sir Walter Mildmay; Edward Griffyn, former solicitor; Mr Coke; Mr Lucas.

Membership of Privy Council, 1591, 10 members

John Whitgift, Archbishop of Canterbury; Sir Christopher Hatton, Lord Chancellor; Sir William Cecil, Lord Burghley, Lord High Treasurer; Charles Howard, Baron Effingham, Lord Admiral; Henry Carey, Lord Hunsdon, Lord Chamberlain; Thomas, Lord Buckhurst, Lord High Butler; Sir Francis Knollys, Treasurer of the Queen's Household; Sir Thomas Heneage, Vice Chamberlain to the Queen, Chancellor of the Duchy of Lancaster; Mr John Wolley, Esq., Secretary for the Latin Tongue and Chancellor of the Order of the Garter; Mr John Fortescue, Esq., Master of the Great Wardrobe and Under Treasurer of the Exchequer.

Membership of Privy Council, 1601, 13 members

John Whitgift, Archbishop of Canterbury; Sir Thomas Egerton, Lord Keeper; Sir Thomas Sackville, Lord Buckhurst, Lord High Treasurer; Charles, Earl of Nottingham, Lord High Admiral; Gilbert, Earl of Shrewsbury; Edward, Earl of Worcester, Master of the Horse; Sir George Carey, Lord Hunsdon, Lord Chamberlain; Sir William Knollys, Comptroller of Household; Sir John Stanhope, Vice Chamberlain and Treasurer of the Chamber; Sir Robert Cecil, Principal Secretary and Master of Court of Wards; Sir John Foretscue, Chancellor and Under-Treasurer of the Exchequer; Sir John Popham, Lord Chief Justice; Mr John Herbert, Secretary.

Henry VII also summoned five Great Councils between 1487 and 1502. These occasional assemblies of peers of the realm and councillors (and sometimes burgesses) were called to give advice and provide authority for war and taxation and should not be confused with the King's Council as described above. Rather, they demonstrate Henry VII's attempts to govern consensually and his belief that Great Councils were important to this process whereas parliament had no part in the making of policy.

Government by ministers

The seals

Traditionally, government was by the seals: the Great Seal of England (held by the Lord Chancellor), the Privy Seal and the Signet. Henry VII and Henry VIII continued this tradition. All the work of the Government was handled by the offices of the Keepers of the seals, who authorised all decisions by applying the relevant seals. It was the Lord Chancellor who managed the work of the Government. However, the Tudor period witnessed the decline of government by the seals. There was, for example, no Lord Chancellor during the periods 1558–79 and 1592–96. during these periods the seal was held by a Lord Keeper. The Lord Chancellor, when there was one, was important chiefly as a the principal legal officer of the Crown. The Keepers of the Privy Seal derived their importance, not so much from control of the seal, as from their simultaneous occupancy of the Secretaryship of State. The mid-century saw the development of government by ministers as a replacement for the medieval government by seals.

Lord Chancellors and [Lord] Keepers [of the Great Seal]

1485 Thomas Rotherham, Archbishop of York
1485–87 John Alcock, Bishop of Worcester and then Ely
1487–1500 John Morton, Archbishop of Canterbury
1500–02 Henry Deane, Archbishop of Canterbury (Keeper)
1502–04 William Warham, Bishop of London and then Archbishop of Canterbury (Keeper of the Seal until he became Chancellor in 1504)
1504–15 William Warham, Archbishop of Canterbury
1515–29 Thomas Wolsey, Cardinal Archbishop of York and Papal Legate
1529–32 Sir Thomas More
1532–33 Sir Thomas Audley (Keeper)
1533–44 Sir Thomas Audley (created first Lord Audley, 1538)
1544–47 Thomas Wriothesley, first Lord Wriothesley (created first Earl of Southampton, 1547)
1547 Paulet, first Lord St John (Keeper)
1547–51 Richard Rich, first Lord Rich
1551–52 Thomas Goodrich, Bishop of Ely (Keeper of the Seal until he became Lord Chancellor in 1552)
1552–53 Thomas Goodrich, Bishop of Ely
1553–55 Stephen Gardiner, Bishop of Winchester
1556–58 Nicholas Heath, Archbishop of York
1558–79 Sir Nicholas Bacon (Lord Keeper)
1579–87 Sir Thomas Bromley

1587–91 Sir Christopher Hatton
1592–96 Sir John Puckering (Lord Keeper)
1596–1603 Sir Thomas Egerton (Lord Keeper), created first Lord Ellesmere, 1603

- Up to and including Wolsey, the Lord Chancellor or Keeper was normally a high-ranking cleric. Mary I reverted to this policy with the appointment of Gardiner.
- Under Thomas Cromwell's Secretaryship (1533–40) the Lord Chancellor was pushed into a subsidiary role as principal legal officer of the Crown.

Keepers of the Privy Seal

1485–87 Peter Courtenay, Bishop of Exeter
1487–1516 Richard Fox
1516–23 Thomas Ruthall, Bishop of Durham
1523 Sir Henry Marny, first Lord Marny
1523–30 Cuthbert Tunstal, Bishop of London
1530–36 Thomas Boleyn, first Earl of Wiltshire and Ormonde
1536–40 Thomas Cromwell, first Lord Cromwell (created first Earl of Essex, 1540), Secretary of State
1540–42 William FitzWilliam, first Earl of Southampton
1542–55 John Russell, first Lord Russell (created first Earl of Bedford, 1550)
1555 William Paget
1559–72 William Cecil (created first Lord Burghley, 1571)
1572–73 William Howard, first Lord Howard of Effingham
1573–76 Sir Thomas Smith, Secretary of State
1576–90 Sir Francis Walsingham, Secretary of State
1590–98 Lord Burghley
1598–1603 Robert Cecil

Secretaries and Principal Secretaries of State

Until the 1530s, the Secretary of State was the King's personal secretary and keeper of the signet. He was not on a par with the great officers of state. After the fall of Cromwell in 1540, there were normally two secretaries, one of whom assisted the Principal Secretary. Throughout the century, the office was poorly defined and its relative importance within the government tended to depend on the men who held it. So, both Thomas Cromwell and William Cecil made it the principal office of government while, under Sir Thomas Smith, the office achieved little.

Function of the office

- Provided a link between Crown and council, parliament and people.
- Managed the agenda of the council.
- Represented the Crown in parliament.

- Headed the diplomatic service.
- Guarded the peace of the realm.

Secretaries of State

1485	Dr Richard Fox
1487	Dr Owen King
1500	Dr Thomas Ruthall
1516	Dr Richard Pace
1526	Dr William Knight
1528	Dr Stephen Gardiner (from 1531 Bishop of Winchester)
1533	Thomas Cromwell

Principal Secretaries

1540–44	Sir Thomas Wriothesley
1540–43	Sir Ralph Sadler
1543–48	Sir William Paget
1544–57	Sir William Petre
1548–49	Sir Thomas Smith
1549–50	Sir Nicholas Wotton
1550–53	Sir William Cecil
1553	Sir John Cheke
1553–58	Sir John Bourne
1557–58	Sir John Boxall
1558–72	Sir William Cecil
1572–76	Sir Thomas Smith
1573–90	Sir Francis Walsingham
1577–81	Thomas Wilson
1586–87	William Davison
1596–1603	Sir Robert Cecil
1600	John Herbert

The royal household

The Exchequer

(The development of the Exchequer is dealt with in further detail on pp. 96–97.) The Exchequer consisted of two sections:

- Exchequer of Receipt
    - for receipt and disbursement of revenue
    - main work carried out by the Under-Treasurer and the Chamberlains
- Upper Exchequer or Exchequer of Account
    - for audit
    - Chancellor of the Exchequer: a relatively unimportant office.

Treasurer

- Honorary position.
- Henry VIII bestowed it upon peers of the realm.
- 1572–99 William Cecil, Lord Burghley Treasurer.

- Free of embezzlement
- Most royal revenue anticipated so Exchequer dealt in tallies rather than money
- Audit was very slow
- Medieval monarchs had turned Wardrobe and Chamber into secondary financial institutions which permitted receipt and disbursement
- Henry VII sought to make Chamber centre of administration of his revenues. Treasurer of Chamber was to receive all revenues except customs, which remained with Exchequer.

The Household/the Chamber

In the fifteenth century the household officers of the Crown had enjoyed considerable influence in government. The Tudor period saw household government in decline but offices were bestowed as a mark of royal favour, or withheld as a mark of disapproval. The following were the chief offices within the household and, when a new household was set up (for example, for a young prince or princess), these offices would be duplicated in that household:

- Treasurers of the Household
- Comptrollers of the Household
- Lords Stewards of the Household
- Treasurers of the Chamber
- Keepers of the Jewel House
- Chief Butlers of England.

Royal financial administration

Chamber finance

There was one significant exception to the decline of the household, namely the development of the Chamber as a financial department.

Monarchical government was financed from a large number of sources: receipts from royal lands; customs; sale of **wardships**; subsidies granted by parliament and Convocation; **benevolences**; fines (after the break with Rome) first fruits and tenths; monastic and chantry endowments.

Court of Augmentations

- Established by statute in 1536 (27 Henry VIII c. 27) to administer the transfer of the dissolved monasteries' lands to the Crown.
- Chief officials were Chancellor and Treasurer and, after 1547, General Surveyor.
- 1547: amalgamated with Court of General Surveyors.

Court of General Surveyors of the King's Lands

- Established in 1515 by parliament (6 Henry VIII c. 24) from one parliament to the next to administer Crown lands acquired by Henry VII and Wolsey.
- Established as permanent office in 1535.
- General surveyors of the King's lands.
- 1547: amalgamated with Court of Augmentations.

Court of Wards and Liveries

- Regular Master of the Wards appointed from 1503.
- Statute of 1540 (32 Henry VIII c. 46) made court responsible for feudal revenues.
- Chief officers are: Master of King's or Queen's Wards; Surveyor of Liveries; Receiver-General; Attorney.
- Under Elizabeth, used as powerful instrument for control of aristocracy and for raising revenue.

Court of First Fruits and Tenths

- Established in 1540 (32 Henry VIII, c. 45).
- Officers are: Chancellor; Attorney; Treasurer; Auditor.

Court of Duchy of Lancaster

- Ancient court administering lands of the duchy.

The Chamber: chronology

Under Henry VII all revenues (except customs, which continued to go to the Exchequer) were diverted to the Chamber. Disbursement by word of mouth or signet warrant. King audited accounts. Rapid audit.

1491	Henry VII levied benevolence.
1500	Regular committee collected fines on penal statutes.
1503	Appointment of Master of Wards, with bureaucracy, to secure revenues from feudal wardships owned by the Crown.
1504 and 1508	Temporary commissions of inquiry search for prerogative rights, etc.

1508	Office of Surveyor of King's Prerogative established to replace temporary commissions. Very short-lived.
1512	Experiments with graduated poll tax.
1514	Wolsey's first **subsidy**.
1515	Appointment of two General Surveyors of Crown lands who audited not only the Chamber accounts but also those of other revenue-collecting courts. Given temporary statutory authority (6 Henry VIII c. 24).
1523	Wolsey offered anticipation discounts to those who paid their subsidy early.
1528	Sir Brian Tuke appointed Treasurer of the Chamber and reorganised the office.
1531	Praemunire fine on clergy raised £118,000.

Cromwell's financial administration reforms

1535	Powers of King's General Surveyors made permanent.
1536	Statute created Court of Augmentations (27 Henry VIII, c. 27).
1540	Statute made First Fruits and Tenths office a court (32 Henry VIII, v. 45). Statute made Court of Wards and Liveries responsible for feudal revenues (32 Henry VIII, c. 46).
1545	Henry VIII levied benevolence.
1547	Augmentations and General Surveyors merged into second Court of Augmentations.
1536–40	Crown seized monastic endowments. Administered by Court of Augmentations.
1554	New courts absorbed into Exchequer as specialised sub-departments. Court of Wards and Duchy of Lancaster remain independent of Exchequer.
Later sixteenth century	Lord Treasurer becomes Minister of Finance. Chancellor of Exchequer became officer of importance as did the Auditor of the Receipt.

- Henry VII made Chamber centre of revenue administration but did so on informal basis, supervised carefully by himself.
- Under Henry VIII, Wolsey (and, at first, Cromwell) continued this policy of Chamber administration but they institutionalised it.
- New revenue from monastic lands, etc. made Cromwell think that more fundamental reforms were required. He broke the links between the Chamber and the Household and created new departments (known as courts) for specific sections of the revenue: Augmentations, First Fruits and Tenths; Exchequer; Duchy of Lancaster; Wards and Liveries; General Surveyors.
- Too diverse; too many officials. Eventual amalgamation of courts into a reformed Exchequer.

6

CENTRAL GOVERNMENT: (2) PARLIAMENT

Parliament was an established part of the King's government but it was an intermittent part, called for special purposes, usually the granting of money. Originally it had been the King's most important court but, by the sixteenth century, the function of settling legal problems had devolved to the **conciliar** courts (see Chapter 7: Central courts) and Parliament was not used for trials. The Reformation Parliament of 1529–36 signalled enormous changes in the nature and function of Parliament, both because the monarch chose to implement a revolution through it and also because the legislation it produced incorporated Parliament fully into the system of government of Church and state.

Parliamentary officers

The Speaker of the House of Commons
Clerk of the Parliaments
Gentleman Usher of the Black Rod
Clerk of the Crown in Chancery

The Speaker

Sir Thomas Lovell, MP for Northamptonshire (d. 1524), elected 8 Nov. 1485.
Sir John Mordaunt, MP for Bedfordshire (d. 1504), elected 10 Nov. 1487.
Sir Thomas FitzWilliam, MP for Yorkshire (d. 1495), elected 14 Jan. 1489.
Sir Richard Empson, MP for Northamptonshire (d. 1510), elected 18 Oct. 1491.
Sir Robert Drury, MP for Suffolk (d. 1536), elected 15 Oct. 1495.
Sir Thomas Englefield, MP for Berkshire (d. 1514), elected 23 Jan. 1510.
Edmund Dudley, MP for Staffordshire (d. 1510), elected 26 Jan. 1504.
Sir Thomas Englefield, MP for Berkshire (d. 1514), elected 19 Jan. 1497.
Sir Robert Sheffield, MP for Lincolnshire (d. 1518), elected 5 Feb. 1512.
Sir Thomas Neville, MP for Kent (d. 1542), elected 6 Feb. 1515.
Sir Thomas More, MP for Middlesex (d. 1535), elected 16 Apr. 1523.
Sir Thomas Audley, MP for Essex (d. 1544), elected 5 Nov. 1529.

Sir Humphrey Wingfield, MP for Great Yarmouth (d. 1545), elected 9 Feb. 1533.
Sir Richard Rich, MP for Colchester (d. 1567), elected 9 Jan. 1536.
Sir Nicholas Hare, MP for Norfolk (d. 1557), elected 28 Apr. 1539.
Sir Thomas Moyle, MP for Kent (d. 1560), elected 19 Jan. 1542.
Sir John Baker, MP for Huntingdonshire (d. 1558), elected 4 Nov. 1547.
Sir James Dyer, MP for Cambridgeshire (d. 1582), elected 2 Mar. 1553.
Sir John Pollard, MP for Oxfordshire (d. 1557), elected 5 Oct. 1553.
Sir Robert Brooke, MP for City of London (d. 1558), elected 2 Apr. 1554.
Sir Clement Higham, MP for West Looe (d. 1570), elected 12 Nov. 1554.
Sir John Pollard, MP for Chippenham (d. 1557), elected 21 Oct. 1555.
Sir William Cordell, MP for Suffolk (d. 1581), elected 20 Jan. 1558.
Sir Thomas Gargrave, MP for Yorkshire (d. 1579), elected 25 Jan. 1559.
Thomas Williams, MP for Exeter (d. 1566), elected 12 Jan. 1563.
Richard Onslow, MP for Steyning (d. 1571), elected 1 Oct. 1566.
Sir Christopher Wray, MP for Lugershall (d. 1592), elected 2 Apr. 1571.
Sir Robert Bell, MP for Lyme Regis (d. 1577), elected 8 May 1572.
Sir John Popham, MP for Bristol (d. 1607), elected 18 Jan. 1581.
Sir John Puckering, MP for Carmarthen (d. 1596), elected 23 Nov. 1584.
Sir John Puckering, MP for Gatton (d. 1596), elected 29 Oct. 1586.
Thomas Snagge, MP for Bedford (d. 1592), elected 4 Feb. 1589.
Sir Edward Coke, MP for Norfolk (d. 1634), elected 19 Feb. 1593.
Sir Christopher Yelverton, MP for Northamptonshire (d. 1612), elected
24 Oct. 1597.
Sir John Croke, MP for City of London (d. 1620), elected 27 Oct. 1601.

Sessions

Parliament was not in continuous session. Most parliaments were shortlived and there were often lengthy gaps between parliaments. Dates are those of Commons sessions.

Henry VII

7 November 1485–4 March 1486
9 November 1487–18 December 1487
13 January 1489–27 February 1490
17 October 1491–5 March 1492
14 October 1495–21/22 December 1495
16 January 1497–13 March 1497
25 January 1504–c. 1 April 1504

Henry VIII

21 January 1510–23 February 1510
4 February 1512–4 March 1514
5 February 1515–22 December 1515
15 April 1523–13 August 1523

3 November 1529–14 April 1536 (The Reformation Parliament)
8 June 1536–18 July 1536
28 April 1539–24 July 1540
16 January 1542–28 March 1544
23 November 1545–31 January 1547

Edward VI

4 November 1547–15 April 1552
1 March 1553–31 March 1553

Mary I

5 October 1553–5 December 1553
2 April 1554–5 May 1554
12 November 1554–16 January 1555
21 October 1555–9 December 1555
20 January 1558–17 November 1558

Elizabeth I

23 January 1559–8 May 1559
11 January 1563–2 January 1567
2 April 1571–29 May 1571
8 May 1572–19 April 1583
23 November 1584–14 September 1585
15 October 1586–23 March 1587
4 February 1589–29 March 1589
19 February 1593–10 April 1593
24 October 1597–9 February 1598
27 October 1601–19 December 1601

James I

19 March 1604–9 February 1611

The franchise

Borough Originally the vote was given to all those called 'burgesses' but, by Henry VII's accession, franchise was much more restricted so that, in some boroughs, only a small number of elite burgesses voted. The borough franchise was much more idiosyncratic than the county franchise.

County Vote was restricted to inhabitants of the shire who held freehold land worth at least 40s per annum (*8 Henry VI, c. 7*).

Qualifications Those eligible for election for county seats were to be knights of the county concerned or persons of similar substance (*23 Henry VI, c. 14*).

Development of parliamentary privilege and procedure: chronology

1513   Strode's case. Richard Strode, MP, was imprisoned for proposing bills to regulate the tin-mining industry and thus interfering with the stannary courts. The **House of Commons** obtained his release. It enacted that members of the Commons could not be sued in a court of law for what they said or did in Parliament; acknowledgement that the House of Commons and its business were privileged as part of the High Court of Parliament against the inferior courts of the realm.

1515   Act of Parliament (*6 Henry VIII, c. 16*) gave the Speaker power to license absenteeism among MPs. This privilege had previously been exercised by the Crown alone.

1523   The Speaker, Thomas More, made the first known request by a Speaker for free speech in Parliament.

1534   Thomas Cromwell began to manage parliamentary elections.

1536   Canterbury forced by Cromwell to reverse its election and choose two Crown nominees.

1543   Ferrers' case. Commons released MP George Ferrers, a Plymouth burgess, from prison on the sole authority of the mace of its Serjeant-at-law.

1553   Alexander Nowell denied place in Commons because he was a representative in Convocation.

1555   Indeterminate discussion of bill to prohibit paid dependants of Crown from sitting in Commons.

1571   Thomas Clark and Anthony Bull placed in custody of the Serjeant for seeking to enter the Commons despite not being members.

1571   Walter Strickland's case. Strickland introduced a bill for reform of the prayer book. For this invasion of her prerogative, the Queen forbade him his place in the Commons. After an outcry, the Queen relented and Strickland took his place.

1572   Lord Cromwell's case. Members of House of Lords protected against arrest.

1576   8 February: Peter Wentworth, MP for Tregony, spoke out in favour of liberty of Parliament, 9 February: committed to Tower, 12 March: Queen remits sentence.

1576   February: Edward Smalley's case. Confirms that servants of MPs are also privileged against arrest.

1581   House of Commons established its right to determine whether elected MPs are duly qualified.

1584   Finnies' case. Viscount Bindon unsuccessfully claims privilege against arrest for his servant Finnies.

1585   Parry's case. Dr William Parry sequestered and executed for conspiracy against the Queen.

1586   The Commons decided in favour of the first disputed election in the case of Norfolk. Thereafter, a standing committee to decide disputed elections was appointed at the opening of each Parliament.

1587	Peter Wentworth put questions regarding the importance of Parliament in the constitution which were adjudged unconstitutional. He and other members were arrested and imprisoned in the Tower.
1589	House of Commons decided to issue writs of *supersedeas* when an MP had a writ of *nisi prius* brought against him. Sir Edward Hoby moved that the proceedings of the House of Commons be secret.
1593	Case of Thomas Fitzherbert. He had been arrested for debt before his return as an MP had been received by the Sheriff. He claimed immunity from arrest as an MP but the point was established that the privilege did not extend to those who were not technically Members despite their election.
1601	Goodwin's case. The House of Commons had to argue its case to settle disputed elections.

Major legislation, 1485–1601

The legislation of the Tudor parliaments was designed to maintain law and order, defend the nation and conserve the existing economic and social fabric of the realm. These were traditional areas of parliamentary involvement, although rapid economic developments made for intensified central government activity and more legislation. The responsibility for enforcing much of this legislation lay with the county Justices of the Peace. Royal proclamations also played an important part in enforcing the legislative message. In addition, the Crown and its ministers brought about the break with Rome in concert with Parliament and, after 1529, 'acts of parliament habitually dealt with the spiritual jurisdiction exercised by the King as supreme head' (Elton, *The Tudor Constitution*, p. 231).

Listed below are the major pieces of legislation on the Tudor Statute Book. The reference in italics is to the statutes of the realm. The year stated in this reference is the regnal year, which did not coincide with the calendar year.[1]

1485

Act regarding title of King Henry VII (*1 Henry VII, c. 1(a)*).
Act ordered that Gascony and Guinne wines must be imported in English ships with majority of crew English-born (*1 Henry VII, c. 8*).

1487

Act giving the Court of Star Chamber authority to punish divers misdemeanours (*3 Henry VII, c. 1*).
Act against taking of bail by Justices (*3 Henry VII, c. 3*).
Act against usury: £100 penalty for each transaction. Cases to be tried by Chancery or Justices of the Peace to avoid sympathetic treatment by urban magistrates (*3 Henry VII, c. 5*).
Act forbidding exports of unfinished and undyed cloth above value of £2. Designed to protect the English cloth-finishing industry (*3 Henry VII, c. 11*).

1488

Act extended *1 Henry VII, c. 8* to include Toulouse woad; ordered that masters and mariners of ships should be English-born; forbade English traders to use foreign ships when English ships are available (*4 Henry VII, c. 10*).

Act for Justices of the Peace, for the due execution of their commissions. Justices required to encourage criticism of themselves (*4 Henry VII, c. 12*).

Act limiting benefit of clergy (*4 Henry VII, c. 13*). Those convicted of felony (theft and manslaughter) might claim benefit of clergy on a first offence if they could read a set passage.

Act against **engrossing** on Isle of Wight. Emphasised military effects of the depopulation caused by consolidation of holdings (*4 Henry VII, c. 16*).

1489

Act regarding **tillage**, against depopulation. All occupants of 20 acres or more of land, which had been tilled for the past three years, were required to maintain it under tillage or surrender half the profits to the lord of the manor (*4 Henry VII, c. 19*).

1495

Act that no person going with the King to the wars shall be attaint of treason (*11 Henry VII, c. 1*).

Act regulating usury. Forbade practice of loans made on security of land on condition that part of land revenues must go to lender (*11 Henry VII, c. 8*).

Act regulating wages. Fixed maximum rates of pay. Allowed lower rates of pay where customary. Very harsh (*11 Henry VII, c. 22*).

1504

Act against making of unlawful ordinances by craft guilds. Henceforth the Chancellor, Chief Justices or **Assize Justices** to inspect and approve guild bye-laws. Designed to prevent companies fixing prices of commodities (*19 Henry VII, c. 7*).

Statute of Liveries. Statute reinforcing existing legislation against the keeping of retainers (*19 Henry VII, c. 14*).

1510

Act regarding apparel (*1 Henry VIII, c. 14*).

Act for a subsidy to be granted to the King (Tonnage and Poundage) (*1 Henry VIII, c. 20*).

1512

Act regarding woollen cloth. Orders wages to be paid in money and not in kind or victuals.

Orders maintenance of standards in pulling of woollen yarn (*3 Henry VIII, c. 6*).

1515

Act regarding artificers and labourers, fixing hours of labour. Winter: daylight hours; mid-March to mid-September: 5 a.m. to 7 or 8 p.m. Half-an-hour for breakfast; one-and-a-half hours for dinner and rest. Act fixed labourers' wages at 3d a day (winter) and 4d a day (summer, spring) with additional overtime during harvest. Fixed artisans' pay at 6d a day (summer, spring), 5d a day (winter) (*6 Henry VIII, c. 3*).

Act ordered reconversion of pasture land to arable use and rebuilding of decayed houses (*6 Henry VIII, c. 5*).

Act concerning the King's General Surveyors. Justified and authorised the activities of the two General Surveyors(*6 Henry VIII, c. 24*).

Act ordered conversion of land back to arable use in villages where most of the land use was traditionally tillage. Population ordered to return (*7 Henry VIII, c. 1*).

1523

Act to protect Norwich worsted finishing industry. Forbade worsteds woven in Norfolk or Suffolk to be finished and dyed anywhere except Norwich (*14 & 15 Henry VIII, c. 3*).

(Private) Act of Attainder of Edward, Duke of Buckingham (*14 & 15 Henry VIII, c. 20*).

1530

Act of general pardon (*21 Henry VIII, c. 1*).

Act concerning sanctuary (*21 Henry VIII, c. 2*).

Act to regulate burial and probate fees (*21 Henry VIII, c. 5*).

Act to regulate mortuaries (*21 Henry VIII, c. 6*).

Act limiting clerical pluralism and engagement in trade (*21 Henry VIII, c. 13*).

Act fixing fee for apprenticeship at 2s 6d maximum (*22 Henry VIII, c. 4*).

An Act concerning the pardon granted to the King's spiritual subjects of the province of Canterbury for the Praemunire. Known as Act for the Pardon of the Clergy. Clergy forced to submit to modified royal supremacy (*22 Henry VIII, c. 15*).

1531–33

Act regarding benefit of clergy (*23 Henry VIII, c. 1*). Act abolishing benefit of clergy for those charged with murder or robbery.

Act reiterating Navigation Acts of Henry VII (*23 Henry VIII, c. 7*).

An Act that the appeals in such cases as have been used to be pursued to the See of Rome shall not be from henceforth had nor used but within this realm. Known as Act of Appeals on statute book in April 1533 (*24 Henry VIII, c. 12*).

An Act concerning conditional restraint of payment of annates to the See of Rome. Known as Act in Restraint of Annates. To come into force in 1532 (*23 Henry VIII, c. 20*).

1534

Act forbidding export of victuals except to supply Calais or ships at sea (*25 Henry VIII, c .2*).

Act regarding tillage, forbidding any individual from holding more than 2,000 sheep or having more than two farms except in the parish where he lived (*25 Henry VIII, c. 13*).

Heresy Act. Confirmed legislation against **Lollardy** (and thereby many of the new Lutheran heresies) but withdrew penalties against those who attacked the Papacy (*25 Henry VIII, c. 14*).

Act restricting manufacture of cloth in Worcestershire to Worcester and four other towns (*25 Henry VIII, c. 18*).

Act for the Submission of the Clergy to the King's Majesty. Enactment of 1532 Submission of the Clergy. Convocation must obtain Crown approval for all measures. Crown is ultimate source of appeal in all ecclesiastical disputes (*25 Henry VIII, c. 19*).

An Act restraining the payment of annates. Known as the Act in Restraint of Annates, this made former Act (*23 Henry VIII, c. 20*) permanent. King to appoint bishops and abbots (*25 Henry VIII, c. 20*).

An Act for the exoneration of exactions paid to the See of Rome. Known as Act of Dispensations. Archbishop of Canterbury, not the Pope, the authority for future dispensations from the canon law. Fixed scale of fees. Abolition of Peter's Pence and other papal taxes (*25 Henry VIII, c. 21*).

Act of Succession. Succession to lie with heirs of Henry and Anne Boleyn. Treason to dispute succession. Oath to be administered (*25 Henry VIII, c. 22*).

An Act concerning the King's Highness to be Supreme Head of the Church of England and to have authority to reform and redress all errors, heresies and abuses the same. Known as Act of Supremacy. Henry declared Supreme Head on Earth of the Church of England. To visit clergy, supervise preachers, try heretics, make doctrinal pronouncements (*26 Henry VIII, c. 1*).

Act of Succession (*26 Henry VIII, c. 2*).

Act concerning First Fruits and Tenths. Taxes, formerly paid to Pope, to pass to Crown (*26 Henry VIII, c. 3*).

Treason Act. Treason to include verbal attacks on monarch (*26 Henry VIII, c. 13*).

1535/36

An Act concerning the forging of the King's sign manual, signet and privy seal. Makes forgery of royal signature and lesser seals treasonable offences in addition to the already treasonable offence of forging the great seal (*27 Henry VIII, c. 2*).

Statute of Uses (*27 Henry VIII, c. 10*).

Act appointing an Ecclesiastical Commission of 32 persons for the making of ecclesiastical laws (*27 Henry VIII, c. 15*).

Act reiterates 1489 statute of depopulation. King to receive half profits of lands not yet reconverted under that Act (*27 Henry VIII, c. 22*).

Beggars Act established parish as poor relief unit. First statute which accepted state's responsibility for poor relief (*27 Henry VIII, c. 25*).

An Act of Union with Wales imposed English system of administration and representation on Wales. Henceforth, Wales had JPs, Lieutenants and MPs (*27 Henry VIII, c. 26*).

Act establishing Court of Augmentations (*27 Henry VIII, c. 27*).

Act for Dissolution of the Lesser Monasteries. All houses with annual income of less than £200 to surrender to King. Those who have received grants of monastic land must maintain under tillage such land as has been tilled for the past 20 years (*27 Henry VIII, c. 28*).

Act for maintenance of standards in making of woollen cloth.

Act exempting universities and colleges from payment of first fruits and tenths (*27 Henry VIII, c. 42*).

1536

Act regarding abjuration and benefit of clergy (*28 Henry VIII, c. 1*).

Act forbidding Masters to bind apprentices not to set up in competition without licence from Master Wardens or Fellowships. This forced guilds to tolerate establishment of new independent shops (*28 Henry VIII, c. 5*).

Act regarding succession (*28 Henry VIII, c. 7*).

An Act extinguishing the authority of the bishop of Rome (the Pope) (*28 Henry VIII, c. 10*).

1539/40

Act that proclamations made by the King shall be obeyed (*31 Henry VIII, c. 8*).

Act authorising new bishoprics (*31 Henry VIII, c. 9*).

Act for the placing of the Lords in Parliament. Determines precedence and places King's Secretary above all bishops and peers without high state office and only below the great officeholders of state and household (*31 Henry VIII, c. 10*).

An Act for the dissolution of abbeys. Known as Act for the Dissolution of the Greater Monasteries (*31 Henry VIII, c. 13*).

An Act for religion, abolishing diversity in opinions. Known as Act of Six Articles. Reactionary. Reimposes Catholic orthodoxy (*31 Henry VIII, c. 14*).

Statute of Wills (*32 Henry VIII, c. 1*).

Navigation Act with comprehensive terms directed against use of foreign shipping for English import trade (*32 Henry VIII, c. 14*).

Act of Succession (*32 Henry VIII, c. 25*).

Act of Leases (*32 Henry VIII, c. 28*).

Act establishing Court of First Fruits and Tenths (*32 Henry VIII, c. 45*).

1542

Act for religion (*34 & 35 Henry VIII, c. 1*).

Act giving monopoly of coverlet manufacture in Yorkshire to City of York. Guild of coverlet makers empowered to seek out offenders (*34 & 35 Henry VIII, c. 10*).

Act for certain ordinances in the King's Majesty's dominion and principality of Wales. Setting up four Courts of Great Sessions under permanent judges to exercise common-law jurisdiction in the twelve Welsh shires (*34 & 35 Henry VIII, c. 26*).

1543

Act for succession of Crown (*35 Henry VIII, c. 1*).

Act for the Advancement of True Religion. Forbade labourers and all women below rank of gentlewoman from reading Scriptures (*35 Henry VIII, c. 5*).

1545

Chantries Act empowered King to dissolve chantries but was not implemented (*37 Henry VIII, c. 4*).

Act sanctioning usury. Interest rate of 10 per cent permitted (*37 Henry VIII, c. 9*).

1547

Act for the sacrament, against Revilers and for Receiving in Both Kinds. Persons who ridicule the mass are to be punished. **Communion** in both bread and wine ('**in both kinds**') extended to laity (*1 Edward VI, c. 1*).

Act for the Election of Bishops (*1 Edward VI, c. 2*).

Vagabonds Act (also known as Sturdy Beggars Act). A sturdy beggar might be made a slave for two years and, should he run away, be made a slave for life (repealed clause in 1549). Cottages to be erected for the impotent poor (*1 Edward VI, c. 3*, repealed, 1550).

Act for the repeal of certain statutes concerning treasons, etc. Known as First Treasons Act of Edward VI (*1 Edward VI, c. 12*).

An Act whereby certain chantries, colleges, free chapels and the possessions of the same be given to the King's Majesty. Known as The Chantry Act or Chantries Act. All chantries, **collegiate churches**, hospitals, guilds, fraternities, etc. dissolved. Craft guilds made to surrender religious possessions. University colleges excepted (*1 Edward VI, c. 14*).

1548/49

An Act for the uniformity of service and administration of the sacraments throughout the realm. Known as First Act of Uniformity. Enforced Cranmer's Prayer Book as only legal service book. Penalties to be enforced against those encouraging or using other forms or attacking the new Book (*2 & 3 Edward VI, c. 1*).

Act forbidding labourers to combine to improve pay and conditions (*2 & 3 Edward VI, c. 15*).

Act taking away divers laws against the marriage of priests (*2 & 3 Edward VI, c .21*).

Act ordering fasting from meat on Fridays and Saturdays. Aimed to encourage eating of fish and, thereby, increase the size of the fishing fleet and the number of men employed thereby (*2 & 3 Edward VI, c. 19*).

1549/50

Act for abolition of divers books and images. All images, including roods, to be destroyed (*3 & 4 Edward VI, c. 10*).

Act for ordering ecclesiastical ministers, consecrating bishops, etc. (*3 & 4 Edward VI, c. 12*).

1551/52

An Act for the uniformity of common prayer and administration of the sacraments. Known as Second Act of Uniformity. Ordered use of revised Prayer Book from November 1552 (*5 & 6 Edward VI, c. 1*).

Act ordering the gathering of parish alms. The local householders were to assemble and select two collectors to gather parish alms. Anyone who refused to give alms was to be reported to the bishop (*5 & 6 Edward VI, c. 2*).

Act for the keeping of Holy Days and fast days (*5 & 6 Edward VI, c. 3*).

Act against enclosures. Appointed permanent commission to seek out offenders. (*5 & 6 Edward VI, c. 5*).

Act regulating production of cloth. Specifications laid down for 22 types of cloth, stipulating proper weights. Searcher employed to enforce the acts. Only applied in rural areas (*5 & 6 Edward VI, c. 6*).

Act to bring down the price of wool. It was aimed at the middlemen who were frequently blamed for the high price of wool. Henceforward wool purchase was restricted to merchants of the **staple** and manufacturers (*5 & 6 Edward VI, c. 7*).

Act restricting weaving to those who have served seven years' apprenticeship. Act regulating apprenticeship. Masters to keep 1:3 journeyman to apprentice ratio. Masters prevented from hiring journeymen by week or for short periods. Designed to prevent exploitation of apprentices as cheap labour and to provide some security of employment while ensuring high standards (*5 & 6 Edward VI, c. 8*).

Second Treason Act of Edward VI. Added offences against the royal succession and religious orthodoxy but otherwise returned to position of *26 Henry VIII, c. 13* (1534) (*5 & 6 Edward VI, c. 11*).

Act for marriage of priests and legitimation of their children (*5 & 6 Edward VI, c. 12*).

Act against usury. Repeals 1545 Act and reiterates centuries-old sanctions (*5 & 6 Edward VI, c. 20*).

Act protecting hat and coverlet industry of Norwich (*5 & 6 Edward VI, c. 24*).

Act for keepers of alehouses to be bound by recognisances. All alehouse keepers required to have licence from Justices of the Peace. The JPs to take recognisance from the licensee (*5 & 6 Edward VI, c. 25*).

1553/54

Act repealing certain treasons (*1 Mary 1, st. I, c. 1*). Repealed Henrician and Edwardian Acts and returned to the status quo of *25 Edward III, st. 5, c. 2*.

Act of Repeal revoked major Edwardian legislation (*1 Mary, I, st. I*).

Brawling Act. Made it an offence physically to abuse the sacrament (*1 Mary, st. 2, c. 3*).

1554

Act regarding cloth making, designed to deal with decay of corporate towns which included, among other remedies, a clause relaxing the apprenticeship rules. An earlier restriction, reserving weaving to those who had served full apprenticeship, now made applicable to countryside alone in response to appeal from urban clothiers (*1 Mary, c. 7*).

1554/55

An Act repealing all statutes . . . made against the see apostolic of Rome since the twentieth year of King Henry VIII, and also of the establishment of all spiritual and ecclesiastical possessions and hereditaments conveyed to the laity. Known as Second Act of Repeal. Revoked anti-papal measures passed since 1529 (*1 & 2 Philip & Mary, c. 8*).

Act forbidding export of victuals, grain or wood. Grain only to be exported when there was a glut and prices were lower than 6s 8d a quarter (*1 & 2 Philip and Mary, c. 5*).

Act remedying decay of corporate towns (*1 & 2 Philip & Mary, c. 7*).

Second Treason Act of Mary. Protected Philip by imposing treason penalties on his attackers (*1 & 2 Philip and Mary, c. 10*).

Weavers' Act restricts still further the number of apprentices and looms permitted a rural manufacturer (*2 & 3 Philip & Mary, c. 11*).

Act confirming legislation of 1489 making it apply to all houses with 20 acres of land (*2 & 3 Philip & Mary, c. 2*).

1557

Act regarding woollen cloths. Ordered that cloth manufacture should be restricted to certain corporate and **market** towns which had had an industry for ten years. Certain exemptions. It extends control of cloth specification of *5 & 6 Edward VI, c. 6* to some towns (*4 & 5 Philip & Mary, c. 5*).

1559

Act of Supremacy. Queen is 'supreme governor' of Church of England. Empowered to visit church by royal commission and exercise the supremacy by commission. Marian Acts of repeal themselves repealed. Revocation of Heresy Acts. Papal supremacy abolished. Oath of Supremacy to be administered, backed by heavy penalties including those for high treason (*1 Elizabeth I, c. 1*).

An Act for the uniformity of common prayer and divine service in the church, and the administration of the sacraments. Known as the Elizabethan Act of Uniformity. Enforced Edwardian Prayer Book and worship as in 1549 (*1 Elizabeth I, c. 2*).

Act regarding Queen's title to the throne (*1 Elizabeth I, c. 3*).

Act excepting parts of Essex from *4 & 5 Philip and Mary, c. 5* (*1 Elizabeth I, c. 9*).

Act repealing protective legislation against foreign shipping. A response to Emperor Charles V's retaliatory ban on English shipping in return for Henry's protective tariffs of 1540 (*1 Elizabeth I, c. 13*).

1563

Act ordering administration of Oath of Supremacy to all graduates, schoolmasters and MPs (*5 Elizabeth I, c. 1*).

Act regarding tillage, against depopulation. Confirms statutes of Henry VII and Henry VIII. All land which had been under tillage for four years since 1528 must remain under tillage. No land currently tilled must be converted to pasture (*5 Elizabeth I, c. 2*).

Alms Act. If an individual refused to obey the bishop's exhortation to give alms, he could be bound over for £10 to appear before the JPs. The JPs were empowered to imprison the person if he still refused to pay. A move towards a compulsory poor rate. Backed ecclesiastical persuasion with secular penalties (*5 Elizabeth I, c. 3*).

Statute of Artificers. Many clauses treating regulation of industry and agriculture (*5 Elizabeth I, c. 4*).

- Applied guild apprenticeship system nationwide. Seven-year apprenticeship compulsory in all urban crafts. Established property qualifications for apprenticeship which effectively barred entry to sons of labouring poor. Regulated number of apprentices per master and journeyman, thus preventing excessive use of cheap labour.
- Fixed maximum but not minimum wage rates. JPs to meet to assess and settle standard wage rate in line with prices annually at Easter. Rates to be approved by Privy Council and applied in the next year.

Act for maintenance of the navy. Ordered use of English shipping in coastal trade and to import French woad and wines. Raised price limit for wheat under which grain could be exported to 10s a quarter. Wednesday ordered as additional fish day to encourage fishing industry (*5 Elizabeth I, c. 5*).

1566

Act limiting benefit of clergy. Abolished for rapists, burglars and cutpurses working in gangs (*8 Elizabeth I, c. 4*).

Act for exportation, ordered wrought and dressed cloths to be exported in ratio of one to every nine unfinished cloths (*8 Elizabeth I, c. 6*).

1571

Second Treasons Act of Elizabeth. Includes denial of Supremacy and accusing the Queen of heresy (*13 Elizabeth I, c. 1*).

Act against Papal Bulls. Obtaining a papal bull made a treasonable offence (*13 Elizabeth I, c. 2*).

Act against fugitives over the sea. To deal with seminary priests. Those who have gone abroad without passport to return within six months or lose their possessions (*13 Elizabeth I, c. 3*).

Act sanctioning usury. Repeal of 1552 legislation. Interest rate of 10 per cent maximum. Penalties for excess interest charges (*13 Elizabeth I, c. 8*).

Subscription Act ordered allegiance to 39 Articles of Religion by all ordinands (*13 Elizabeth I, c. 12*).

Act regarding tillage, permitted export of grain when price of wheat in country of export is moderate. Local authorities to determine when conditions permit (*13 Elizabeth I, c. 13*).

1572

Vagabonds Act, known as Poor Relief Act. Severe penalties for vagrant poor. JPs to make a register of all the local poor and to raise a rate to house the impotent and aged (*14 Elizabeth I, c. 5*).

1575/76

Act exempting parts of Gloucestershire, Wiltshire and Somersetshire from *4 & 5 Philip & Mary, c. 5* (*1 Elizabeth I, c. 16*).

1576

Act for Relief of Poor. Cities and towns to provide wool, etc. to supply work for the able-bodied poor at the direction of JPs. Houses of correction to be built and those who refuse to work to be incarcerated in them (*18 Elizabeth I. c. 3*).

Act pertaining to benefit of clergy. Felons claiming the 'book' to serve twelve months' imprisonment should the secular judge so decide (*18 Elizabeth I, c. 7*).

1580/81

Act to Retain the Queen's Subjects in their due Obedience. Death penalty for those teaching the Papal Supremacy. Fines and imprisonment for those hearing Mass. £20 a month fines for those who refused to attend church (recusants) (*23 Elizabeth I, c. 1*).

Act against seditious words and rumours uttered against the Queen's excellent majesty. Death penalty for a second offence (*23 Elizabeth I, c. 2*).

1584/85

Act for safety of the Queen, provision to be made for the surety of the Queen's most royal person (*27 Elizabeth I, c. 1*).

An Act against Jesuits, seminary priests and such other like disobedient persons (*27 Elizabeth I, c. 2*).

Act repealed *5 Elizabeth I, c. 5*; Wednesday no longer a fish day (*27 Elizabeth I*).

1592/93

An Act to retain the Queen's Subjects in Obedience. Aimed at Puritans (*35 Elizabeth I, c. 1*).

An Act against popish recusants. Aimed at Catholic subjects (*35 Elizabeth I, c. 2*).

Act reducing penalties for breaking fish days. Centrally set price limit of corn at 20s per quarter; when price fell below this, export was permitted. Repealed that part of *5 Elizabeth I, c. 3* (1563) which prevented conversion of tilled land to pasture (*35 Elizabeth I, c. 7*).

1597/98

Act ordering repair of 'houses of **husbandry**' which had fallen into disrepair in past seven years. Half those which had decayed in the previous seven years also to be repaired (*39 Elizabeth I, c. 1*).

Act for Relief of the Poor. Remained on statute book until 1834. Made four over-seers of the poor, chosen every Easter by the JPs, in charge of poor relief. The over-seers were to bind children as apprentices, provide the adult, but able poor with work and relieve the aged and infirm. They were empowered to build hospitals for the latter. A compulsory rate on inhabitants was to fund their work and the assessment was to be made at parish level (*39 Elizabeth I, c. 3*).

Act for Punishment of Rogues. JPs authorised to establish houses of correction for rogues and vagabonds. Rogues would either be whipped and returned to native par-ish or placed in a house of correction (*39 Elizabeth I, c. 4*).

Act clarifying terms of Statute of Artificers. JPs to fix wage rate for all labourers, weavers, spinsters and workmen and workwomen (*39 Elizabeth I, c. 12*).

Act regarding cloth, for regulation of cloth manufacture north of the Trent. Reiterated terms of *5 & 6 Edward VI, c. 6*. Specifically forbade use of the 'tenter' frame for stretching cloths after fulling, prompting an outcry (*39 Elizabeth I, c. 20*).

1601

Act for Relief of Poor. A codification of the 1598 poor relief legislation (*43 Elizabeth I, c. 2*).

Note

1   Detail of the regnal years is to be found in C.R. Cheney, *Handbook of Dates for Students of English History*, London, Royal Historical Society, 2000.

7

CENTRAL COURTS

In the Tudor period, many different types of law pertained – common law, statute law, law of equity, civil law, canon law, manorial custom. These laws were administered in a plethora of courts, which often had parallel and rival jurisdictions: common law courts, Privy Council and Prerogative Courts, Admiralty Courts, **ecclesiastical courts** and parliament itself at the centre. Additionally there were Regional Councils, Quarter Sessions, Assizes, Hundred Courts, Manorial Courts, Borough Courts and a whole variety of ecclesiastical courts in the counties and dioceses. The precise boundaries between the juridiction of, for example, the **Justice of the Peace** and the Assizes were blurred so that, with certain exceptions, the same types of case might appear before either. The ecclesiastical and the common law courts each claimed jurisdiction in some of the same areas.

Today we tend to view this situation with something akin to alarm and to assume that the triumph of the common law over the rest was a foregone conclusion and the existence of other courts and legal systems an inconvenient and somehow unimportant anomaly. This was far from the case. The government of England and Wales was not yet completely centralised and unified, and it was not only the King's or common law which was in force. The Tudor period not only saw the full flowering of the Prerogative Courts and the civil and ecclesiastical law courts at the centre as the monarch and his/her ministers sought to centralise both administration and order, but also extremely important Manorial Courts (leet and baron) and Hundred Courts which oversaw and controlled life in the localities. Ecclesiastical courts remained important throughout the sixteenth century. Tudor people were extremely litigious. Collections of family papers, such as that of the Temples of Stowe, Bucks and Great Dassett, Warwickshire, show how cases relating to the same matter were often simultaneously prosecuted or defended in several courts in an attempt to achieve satisfactory outcomes. Many of the documents that historians use as evidence had their origin in the pursuit of litigation and have survived only because their retention was important to courts, complainants and defendants. These documents range from deeds, bonds, contracts, maps and genealogies through official court records to receipts, wills, property inventories and depositions.

- Different types of law
- Parallel and rival jurisdictions
- Individuals make use of the different courts in pursuit of satisfactory results
- Triumph of common law not inevitable
- Other types of law important too
- Centralising tendency but not fully realised as yet
- Important for historians to be able to identify the various courts, processes and types of documentation.

Common law and equity courts

The common law courts had developed out of the Royal Council. The common law was the King's law which, because it belonged to the whole community of the realm, was common. The King or the council was not, however, the ultimate appeal court where common law cases were concerned: this was parliament. The common law procedures grew up in the twelfth century and, by the fifteenth century, the common law courts were rigidly set in their ways. New courts of law, the chancery and the council, developed in the fifteenth and sixteenth centuries to complement the common law courts. Procedures designed to provide a more efficient administration of the law developed in a rather haphazard fashion out of the petitions which were frequently addressed to the monarch and which passed through the hands of the Lord Chancellor and the council. This equitable jurisdiction developed apace and, once the court of Chancery began to keep records after 1530, became firmly established. Equity law was practised in every new court which developed after 1400: the equity side of the Exchequer; the courts of Star Chamber, Requests and the Duchy of Lancaster; the revenue courts set up under Thomas Cromwell; the regional councils and the palatinate courts of Durham, Lancaster and Chester. The law which was administered by these courts was essentially the common law; until the development of substantive equity law in the seventeenth century, it was the procedure which differed. Equity proceedings were in English.

Court of King's Bench

Chief Justices of the King's Bench

1485	William Huse
1495	John Finieux
1526	John FitzJames
1539	Edward Montagu
1545	Richard Lyster
1552	Roger Cholmley
1553	Thomas Bromley
1555	William Portman
1557	Edward Saunders
1559	Robert Catlin

| 1574 | Christopher Wray |
| 1592 | John Popham |

For centuries cases were heard by the King in person advised by his council or *curia*. In the twelfth century the King's Bench emerged as a separate court. In 1178, King Henry II appointed five judges to hear cases in the King's Bench and, in 1268, the Chief Justice was made president of the court. Initially, the court heard only cases touching the rights of Crown and subjects but it developed into an appeal court which retried cases where an incorrect verdict was suspected. In the sixteenth century its civil jurisdiction was significant. During the Tudor period it encroached on the work of the Court of Common Pleas, claiming jurisdiction over trespass cases, which were technically criminal in nature. Its genuinely criminal jurisdiction was normally exercised in the Assize Courts by commissions of oyer and terminer.

Court of Common Pleas

Chief Justices of Common Pleas

1485	Thomas Bryan
1500	Thomas Wood
1502	Thomas Frowyk
1506	Robert Read
1519	John Ernle
1521	Robert Brudenell
1531	Robert Norwich
1535	John Baldwin
1545	Edward Montagu
1553	Richard Morgan
1554	Robert Brooke
1558	Anthony Browne
1559	James Dyer
1582	Edmund Anderson

In 1272, a Chief Justice was first appointed for this ancient court which heard civil suits between subjects. The court was established at Westminster. It had jurisdiction over all civil actions and heard appeals from local courts. Appeal from the Court of Common Pleas was to the King's Bench. It was the busiest Tudor central court and the slowest. During the reigns of the Tudors the Court of King's Bench encroached upon its jurisdiction.

Court of Exchequer

Lord Treasurers

(By this time a largely honorary position awarded to prominent courtiers.)

| 1484 | John Tuchet, Lord Audley |
| 1486 | John Dynham, Lord Dynham |

1501	Thomas Howard, Earl of Surrey, 1st Duke of Norfolk
1522	Thomas Howard, Earl of Surrey, 2nd Duke of Norfolk
1547	Edward Seymour, 1st Duke of Somerset and Protector
1550	William Paulet, 1st Earl of Wiltshire, 1550, and 1st Marquis of Winchester, 1551
1572	William Cecil, 1st Lord Burghley (d. 4 Aug. 1598)
1599	Sir Thomas Sackville, 1st Lord Buckhurst, 1st Earl of Dorset 1604

Chancellors and Under-Treasurers

1559	Sir Walter Mildmay
1589	John Fortescue
1603	Sir George Home, 1st Earl of Dunbar, 1605

Chief Barons of the Court of Exchequer

1485	Humphrey Starkey
1486	William Hody
1522	John FitzJames
1526	Richard Broke
1529	Richard Lyster
1545	Roger Cholmley
1552	Henry Bradshaw
1553	David Brook
1558	Clement Heigham
1559	Edward Saunders
1577	Robert Bell
1577	John Jeffrey
1578	Roger Marwood
1593	William Periam

The Court of Exchequer was originally the Crown's finance office, involved with the collection of revenue, where accounting was done in squares. (The name derives from the Latin *scaccorium* for chess board.) Revenue collection involved disputes and Exchequer then took on the guise of a common law court dealing with financial litigation using Latin pleadings. The court, *Exchequer of Pleas*, gradually became separated from the revenue office and became an independent court of law in 1579, presided over by the Lord Treasurer (or Chancellor of the Exchequer) and a number of judges known as barons. The court also heard cases of appeal and petition (equity).

Court of Chancery

Masters of the Rolls

1485	Robert Morton, later Bishop of Worcester
1486	David William

1492	John Blythe, later Bishop of Salisbury
1494	William Warham, later Archbishop of Canterbury
1502	William Barnes, later Bishop of London
1504	Christopher Bainbridge, later Archbishop of York
1508	John Yonge, later Dean of York
1516	Cuthbert Tunstall, later Bishop of London and Durham
1522	John Clerke, later Bishop of Bath and Wells
1523	Thomas Hannibal
1527	John Taylor, Archdeacon of Derby and Buckingham
1534	Thomas Cromwell
1536	Christopher Hales
1541	Sir Robert Southwell
1550	John Beaumont
1552	Sir Robert Bowes
1553	Sir Nicholas Hare
1557	Sir William Cordell
1581	Sir Gilbert Gerrard
1594	Sir Thomas Egerton

Initially, each individual action in the royal courts was begun by a writ issued by the Chancellor, the King's private secretary. Out of this function grew the Court of Chancery as a court of equity (i.e. of appeal and petition) designed to remedy deficiencies in the common law. The Chancellor presided in person over suits where the common law had failed to reach a verdict or was unable to act. It had the advantage of being more flexible than the common law courts and of being able to put all witnesses on oath. As the Tudor period progressed, it lost much of this flexibility and effectiveness through bureaucratisation. When the Chancellor was not present the Master of the Rolls was president.

The Court of Chancery grew out of the Chancellor's issue of writs to commence actions in the royal courts.

Prerogative courts

Privy Council

Trial by jury was recognised as obligatory in cases involving life or property but in other matters the monarch's Privy Council exercised the Crown's prerogative to try a wide variety of cases. It might, at times, assume the jurisdiction normally exercised by other courts – for instance, in the late fourteenth century it examined and punished heretics, business which would normally have come before the church courts.

Star Chamber

During the fifteenth century the Privy Council, when engaged in judicial business, began to assemble in the Star Chamber in the Palace of Westminster. In 1487, an Act of Parliament authorised this Star Chamber to 'punish divers misdemeanours'. The Court of Star Chamber became more important under Wolsey. In 1540, it was given its own clerk, who kept a minute book separate from that of the Privy Council, and the court was now distinct from the Privy Council. It was, however, composed of the Privy Councillors and the two Chief Justices of King's Bench and Common Pleas.

Court of Requests

The Court of Requests was a court in which the impecunious could plead their rights – especially in respect of trade and landholding – before a court appointed by the Crown in anticipation of speedy and efficient redress. Under the Yorkist monarchs and Henry VII, Privy Councillors were delegated to hear the poor men's requests but, under Henry VIII, it developed as a separate court, staffed by civil lawyers known as Masters of Requests. Its jurisdiction paralleled that of the Court of Common Pleas, which regarded it with the utmost suspicion and rivalry, seeking at every turn to undermine the stature of the Requests.

Court of High Commission

The royal supremacy meant that the Crown had the right and duty to declare on doctrinal and theological matters, to determine issues of discipline and ceremony and to administer the Church. The Crown delegated some aspects of this supreme headship (and governorship under Elizabeth) to others. Thomas Cromwell became the King's vicegerent (Vicar-General) in spiritual matters. Special Commissions were given jurisdiction by the King over other areas of Church affairs. Out of these commissions grew the Court of High Commission.

A statute of 1559 established an ecclesiastical commission to deal with 'errors, heresies, crimes, abuses, offences, contempts and enormities, spiritual and ecclesiastical', chiefly emanating from Roman Catholicism. The Commission, which sat more or less continuously, was not made into a formal court until about 1580, Archbishop Whitgift used it as an instrument of repression of extreme Protestantism during the latter part of Elizabeth's reign.

Civil law courts

Court of Admiralty

In the Middle Ages, local courts in the chief ports (for example, in Bristol and the Cinque Ports) dealt with disputes involving trade and navigation. Admiralty law grew up to meet the needs of merchants and, because so many of the merchants were foreigners, was based upon Roman or civil law rather than common law. By 1357, a Central Court of Judges with a criminal jurisdiction, dealing chiefly with piracy, was in existence. New courts developed dealing with civil maritime cases. These courts sat at Doctors' Commons and shared their personnel with the ecclesiastical courts, which also administered civil law. In the early fifteenth century all the central maritime courts were amalgamated under a Lord High Admiral. In 1536, the former criminal jurisdiction exercised by the Court of Admiralty was transferred to the common law courts. Throughout the Tudor period the civil jurisdiction of the King's Bench over important commercial cases, whether they involved overseas traders or not, expanded. Simultaneously, the common law courts began to claim jurisdiction over those cases which would formerly have been heard by local commercial courts. This battle between the common lawyers and other members of the legal profession lasted into the next century.

Church courts

See Chapter 10: Ecclesiastical courts and commissions.

Court of Arches (consistory court of the province of Canterbury; appeal court from the dioceses).

Prerogative Court of Canterbury (probate for those more valuable estates that were divided between dioceses).

Consistory courts (diocesan and archidiaconal) (Office, Instance and Probate Jurisdiction).

8

LOCAL GOVERNMENT

The shires, like the Church, were administered by the Crown via a system of local government officers and courts. The Tudors possessed no permanent, expert and salaried bureaucracy. They relied instead upon the interest of the local elite (broadly speaking, the gentry rather than the overmighty nobility who might be perceived as a challenge to strong royal government) in stable, peaceable government and paternalistic protection of the people to run the country. In theory, the system of Assizes complemented and monitored the work of the Justices of the Peace. In some areas, the Crown was represented by a Council (e.g. the Council of the North) and JPs and Assize Judges worked with that institution.

Special problems of the Borders

Unsettled border regions. Threat of foreign invasion from Ireland and Scotland. Dangerous independence of the Marcher lords who defended kingdom against such invasion – for example: Dacre, Percy and Neville families in the Northern Borders; Courtenays in Devon and the West; palatine jurisdictions in Cheshire and Lancashire. There is some evidence that Henry VII proposed a council for the Midlands. Certainly his mother, Margaret Beaufort, exercised regional jurisdiction from Collyweston, Stamford between 1499 and 1505.

The North before 1530

Richard, Duke of Gloucester, and his private Council administered the North for his brother Edward IV.

1484	Richard III appointed Earl of Lincoln Lieutenant and gave him a council to administer the region with formal status as a court of law.
1485	Henry VII relied on Percy family until Northumberland's murder in 1489.
1487–c. 1509	Intermittent Council.
1509–22	Lapse of central control in North.
1522	Wolsey aware of need for buffer against Scots.
1525	Duke of Richmond made Lieutenant and given a Council, staffed by lawyers and civil servants, to administer royal lands in North and exercise wide civil and criminal jurisdiction. Ineffectual in face of local opposition.

Wales and the Marches before 1536

1471	King Edward IV made his heir Prince of Wales and Lord of the Marches (Cheshire, Shropshire, Worcestershire, Gloucestershire, Herefordshire) and appointed Council with responsibilities therein.
1483	Council of Wales and Marches ceased to exist.
1493	Prince Arthur Tudor made Earl of March and given similar powers; Council based at Ludlow; Bishop William Smith (from 1490, formally President, 1501–12) made President.
1501	Council continued by commission.
1525	Wolsey reinforced the Council's powers: Princess Mary made figurehead; Council given considerable powers to maintain order, hear suits and receive petitions under Presidency of John Veysey, Bishop of Exeter.
1530s	Henry VIII's attempt to combat power of nobility in remote and lawless regions.

The Council of the North

In 1530, the Council was reformed; Cuthbert Tunstall, Bishop of Durham, became President and his powers were confined to Yorkshire. Tunstall was weak as President and was replaced in 1533 by the even more disastrous Henry Percy, 6th Earl of Northumberland. The Henrician government embarked on a policy of territorial aggrandisement and broke the Percy monopoly on power. Some continuity was provided by the continuance of John Uvedale, Richmond's Secretary, as Secretary to the Council until 1560.

1530–33	Cuthbert Tunstall, Bishop of Durham, President of the King's Council in the North.
1533–36	Henry Algernon Percy, 6th Earl of Northumberland (b. 1502, d. 1537). 1536: debt-ridden, he surrendered lands to King in return for £1,000 annuity. Resigned late 1536.
1536–37	Thomas Howard, 3rd Earl of Norfolk. As Lieutenant, supervised defeat of Pilgrims of Grace and was the chief royal agent in the area, although not President, until Cuthbert Tunstall resumed office.
1537–38	Cuthbert Tunstall resumed control.
1538–40	Robert Holgate, Bishop of Llandaff. Was moderate Protestant Archbishop of York from 1544 until deprived of office in 1554.
1550–60	Francis Talbot, 5th Earl of Shrewsbury. A conservative in religion who was put in office by Earl of Warwick, who was Warden of the Marches and anxious to minimise the powers of the Council. Sir Thomas Gargrave rescued the Council from Talbot's inept rule. Talbot lived in Sheffield and not at York.
1561–63	Henry Manners, 3rd Earl of Rutland, revived residence at King's Manor, York and looked set to revive the fortunes of the Council but died in 1563.
1564	Brief Presidency of Ambrose, Earl of Warwick. Resigned because he could not face the thought of the northern winter.

1564–68   Thomas Young, Archbishop of York. A lazy and ineffectual President who left the North dangerously devoid of royal control on the eve of the Northern Rebellion.

1568–72   Thomas Radcliffe, 3rd Earl of Sussex. Had long experience of assertion of central control as Lord Deputy of Ireland, 1557–64. Destroyed power of rebel earls. 1570–72: absentee President.

1572–95   Henry Hastings, 3rd Earl of Huntingdon. He had no lands in the North but, during his long Presidency, developed great insight into its affairs. Was praised by the Queen for his 'vigilant and watchful care' and staged energetic campaign against Catholic recusancy.

1596–99   Matthew Hutton, Bishop of Durham, made Archbishop of York and de facto President of the Council. Cecil forced him to retire (because he was an ally of Essex).

1599–1603 Thomas Cecil, 2nd Lord Burghley. The energetic, anti-recusant elder brother of Robert Cecil.

The Council in the Marches

Precedent: from 1499 to 1505 an unofficial Council of the Midlands was presided over by Margaret Beaufort at Collyweston, near Stamford, Lincs.

After 1536, the Council controlled Wales and six English border shires (Monmouthshire, until 1604; Herefordshire; Worcestershire; Shropshire; Cheshire, until 1569; Gloucestershire, Bristol excluded in 1562). After 1542, the Justice of Cheshire (known as the Chief Justice from 1578) was normally a member of the Council and de facto Vice-President. From at least 1525, the chief official was the Secretary, who normally combined in his person the offices of clerk and clerk of the signet.

1534   Rowland Lee made Bishop of Coventry and Lichfield and President of the Council in the Marches.

1536   Thomas Cromwell imposed, by statute, English administration on Wales, which henceforth had JPs, Lords Lieutenant and MPs as did English shires. Council in the Marches given jurisdiction over Wales and Marches, including prerogative power. It advised on the appointment of JPs, Sheriffs and Lords Lieutenant; supervised local government; organised the defence of the coastline; enforced economic legislation emanating from Westminster; acted as 'starre chamber and chauncerie corte for Wales' handling criminal and civil business and supporting the Crown's religious policies.

1534–43   Energetic and strong presidency of Bishop Rowland Lee, who frequently toured the Marches and Wales.

1543–48   Presidency of Richard Sampson, also Bishop of Coventry and Lichfield, lawyer, civil servant and faithful servant of Henry VIII.

1548–50   John Dudley, Earl of Warwick, seems never to have met his Council and surrendered his office to a supporter, William Herbert, when he became immersed in national affairs.

1550–53   William Herbert (b. 1501–d. 1570, made 1st Earl of Pembroke, 1551), became Lord President.

1553–55   Nicholas Heath, restored Marian Bishop of Worcester.

1555–58   William Herbert's second term of office – ended when Queen criticised him for inadequate administration.

1558–59   Gilbert Bourne, Bishop of Bath and Wells. Deprived by Elizabeth.

1559   John Williams, Lord Williams of Thame (Treasurer of Court of Augmentations, 1544–54). Supporter of Mary, who was given control of Princess Elizabeth, 1554. Arrived at Ludlow, June 1559; d. October 1559.

1560–86   Sir Henry Sidney (b. 1529–d. 1586). Long beneficial administration. Bitter factional divisions in the Council after 1575. Sidney was frequently absent and a series of Vice-Presidents were appointed to run the Council until 1580.

1586–1602 Henry Herbert, 2nd Earl of Pembroke. Son of William. Married daughter of predecessor. Popular because Welsh-speaking. He was energetic and reform-minded but he antagonised the lawyers on the Council to such an extent that he was unable to effect the overhaul of the inefficient and corrupt council that he had wished.

The Council of the West

Set up to control Cornwall, Devon, Dorset and Somerset in the wake of Henry VIII's suppression of Exeter Conspiracy in 1537 when power of the Courtenays, Marquesses of Exeter, seemed threatening. Shortlived and ill-documented. Had ceased to exist by 1547.

- Originated in concern for national security.

The Shires

The central government depended upon local officials to implement its policies as expressed in statute and proclamation and, therefore, upon a partnership between the centre and the local worthies. The student of local government at regional, county and parish level is faced with a bewildering array of offices and institutions. There are the ancient offices of sheriff, coroner, **escheator** and customer (all possessed of continuing, if decreasing, significance) existing alongside new offices (such as those of the new regional councils or the lords and deputy lieutenants) or old offices, which were changing in their functions and increasing in their importance (such as Justices of the Peace). Then, one has to reconcile the parallel jurisdictions of the ecclesiastical and the lay parish and their associated officials. Comforting is the view that this was an era of experimentation in local government, a period when the Crown was seeking to negotiate local cooperation in the government of the realm whilst also attempting to monitor the success of this cooperation in achieving its own ends and to prevent sedition, rebellion and invasion.

Parish officers: the ecclesiastical parish

Churchwardens

- Unlike the **constables**, watchmen and surveyors of highways, churchwardens were lay ecclesiastical officers.
- Appointed in different ways according to the custom of the parish: by the minister, or by the parish assembled in the vestry meeting or by the minister and vestry together.
- Guardians and keepers of the fabric and furniture of the church (excluding the chancel which was the parson's responsibility) and representatives of the parishioners.
- Empowered to levy church rate to care for upkeep of church.

Parish clerk

- Originally, an official in minor holy orders but this changed at the reformation when he had to be at least 20 years old, literate, 'sufficient for his office' and of good reputation.
- Usually selected by incumbent but sometimes, by custom, by parish.
- Had freehold in office.
- Duties associated with organising church for worship.

Sexton

- Chosen by incumbent or, where custom dictated, by minister and parishioners.
- Paid by churchwardens.
- Cleaned church, opened pews, provided candles, dug graves, helped keep peace in the church and churchyard.

- Parallel existence of ecclesiastical and lay parish.

Parish officers: the lay parish

Constables

- Origins in the ancient offices of tithingman, headborough or borsholder current in the time of Alfred the Great.
- Chosen by the jury of the Court Leet or by two Justices.
- Petty constables charged with keeping the peace within the parish or township.
- Served summonses and warrants of the JPs.

Watchmen

- Deputies or assistants of the constables who guarded the peace at night.

Surveyors of highways

- Worked under supervision of JPs.

Overseers of the poor

- Worked under supervision of JPs.

The shire officers

Sheriff

Under the early Tudors, the sheriff was the principal royal official in most counties. The duties of the office were largely legal – he supervised the prisons, empanelled juries, implemented sentences – but he also, before Elizabeth's reign, collected taxes and subsidies, put down sedition and rebellion and arrested heretics. The office was already in decline by the late fifteenth century, it was expensive and onerous and possessed little real power but it continued to be sought after because of the status it conferred.

- Practical powers in decline under Tudors but sought after because status-conferring.

Coroner

- Late twelfth century office. Before that coroners charged with keeping the pleas of the Crown.
- Chiefly, but not exclusively, judicial duties, primarily concerned with inquiring into suspicious deaths and, where there was reason to suppose unnatural death, setting up an inquest.
- Chosen for life by the freeholders of the county at a court summoned by the sheriff for that purpose.
- Had to possess lands worth £20 per annum.

Escheator

- Protected feudal rights of Crown in the shires.

Customer

- Collector of customary taxes in the shires.

High Constable

- Charged with keeping peace within the administrative district of the hundred (a subdivision of a shire).

Lord Lieutenant

Lieutenants had been appointed by Henry VIII and Edward VI for defensive purposes and, by the reign of Elizabeth, the Lieutenant was the most important local

Crown officer. It was, however, a military office and there were ad hoc rather than permanent and continuous appointments. It was not until the 1580s, when the Spanish threat seemed to demand a more organised local defence system, that Lords Lieutenant appointments were for life. Innovatory development. Duties included:

- keeping up-to-date **muster** roll of able-bodied men prepared to fight when required
- stock-keeping of arms
- maintenance of stock of arms and ammunition
- marshalling defence as and when need arose.

Tenure: chief aristocrats of region, they sometimes acted as Lords Lieutenant for a group of counties; after 1580 appointments were often for life.

Deputy Lieutenants

Served for one shire only and more than one was appointed per shire. They undertook most of the real work of the office.

- Innovatory development.
- Military role and significance.

Justices of the Peace

Most of the work of implementing statutes and royal proclamations in the localities fell to the Justices of the Peace. The office of the Justice was ancient (dating back to the twelfth century) and had become an established part of local government by the 1320s. The Justices supervised the work of the surveyors and overseers of the poor.

Royal Commissions of the Peace – appointed between 30 and 60 local men, not necessarily with any legal training, to serve as Justices for very modest remuneration. Selection made on basis of advice offered by judges acquainted with the shires via the Assize circuit and Lord Chancellor. To serve was a coveted honour among the gentry of Tudor England. Most JPs were inactive. The work was done by the quorum.

Quorum – an inner circle of trusted Justices, including those with legal training, nominated to the quorum. The presence of a member of the quorum was essential when an important session took place.

Custos Rotulorum – member of quorum appointed to keep the records (rolls) of the Justices.

Clerk of the Peace – appointed as permanent official to give advice on procedure, etc.

Quarter sessions – quarterly meeting of the Justices.

Criminal jurisdiction of Justices of the Peace

- Powers of arrest, search and imprisonment.
- Full sentencing powers, including the death penalty by hanging.
- Punishments most commonly whipping, placing in the stocks and fines.

Administrative jurisdiction of Justices of the Peace

- Even more important role of JPs hampered by inadequacy of parish officials (e.g. constables and overseers).
- Routine work undertaken at Quarter Sessions but also at more frequent and informal petty sessions.
- Role of implementing reformed poor law.

- Not a Tudor innovation but exploited to the full by the Tudors as the instrument for the implementation of royal policy throughout the realm.
- Harnessed local interests in the service of central government.

Assizes

Some crimes beyond the jurisdiction of the Justices had to be referred to the Assizes.

From the twelfth century onwards, paid judges were sent out to groups of counties to hear cases of both a civil and a criminal nature. From the end of the thirteenth century, sessions or courts of this kind were held three times a year in each county. However, it was not until the reign of Edward III that circuits were established for grand assizes composed of judges drawn from the Common Pleas, King's, Bench and Exchequer courts. The Tudors built upon this system, which provided the main and ultimate source of justice at county level and monitored the work of the JPs. There were six circuits:

- Home: Essex, Herts, Kent, Surrey, Sussex
- Oxford: Gloucestershire, Herefordshire, Oxfordshire, Salop, Staffordshire, Worcestershire
- Western: Berks, Cornwall, Devon, Dorset, Hampshire, Somerset, Wiltshire
- Norfolk: Bedfordshire, Buckinghamshire, Cambridgeshire, Huntingdonshire
- Midland: Derbyshire, Leicestershire, Linconshire, Nottinghamshire, Northamptonshire, Rutland, Warwickshire
- Northern: Cumberland, Durham, Lancashire, Northumberland, Westmorland, Yorkshire.

Twice a year, the judges began a circuit which covered 50 principal towns in England. Each session lasted a few days. Cases were referred to the Assizes from the Quarter Sessions. Mainly criminal cases were brought before the Justices of Assize (felonies were being taken out of the hands of the JPs) although civil cases were also heard. Cases of theft, murder and treason had to be heard by the Assizes.

Clerks of the Assize

Permanent officials who organised circuit and record keeping.

- Brought accessible common law to localities.
- Brought centrally trained lawyers to localities.
- Not especially harsh – few hangings.
- Provided Government with its only direct knowledge of state of the country as a whole. Prior to the circuit, the Justices received instructions (a charge) from the Government in Star Chamber and, after the circuit, they prepared a report for the Government.
- Provided mechanism for monitoring the work of JPs.
- Dialogue between central and local interests provided for by attendance of local Commission of Peace (i.e. the JPs) at Assize.
- Expense account allowed to Assize Justices after 1573 in theory made them less open to bribery but, in practice, lavish 'hospitality' poured on Judges by local commissions, sheriffs, etc.

9

STRUCTURE OF THE CHURCH IN ENGLAND

The Church *of* England retained the same basic structure as that of its predecessor, the Catholic Church *in* England.

Bishops and their dioceses

The Church in England *throughout* our period was ruled by bishops, led, supervised and, in a sense, ruled by two archbishops (York and Canterbury). There were 27 lord bishops (26 of whom held seats in the House of Lords as lords spiritual[1]) and a number of **suffragan** or assistant bishops (who were not represented in Parliament). After the Reformation, bishops were formally chosen and appointed by the Crown, although various individuals (clerical and lay) wielded influence.[2] The bishop was the ordinary (source of power and authority) within the diocese. The archbishop was the ordinary within the province. Both archbishops were referred to as primates and the Archbishop of Canterbury as Primate of all England.

Territories, which came to be known as dioceses, were appropriated to bishops and these territories evolved as units of ecclesiastical administration.

Archbishops and their provinces

These dioceses fell under the overall supervision of one of the two archbishops (or primates) within the province of either York or Canterbury. The provinces included the following dioceses:

- **York**: York, Durham, Carlisle
- **Canterbury**: Bangor, Bath and Wells, (Bristol),[3] Canterbury, (Chester), Chichester, Coventry and Lichfield, Ely, Exeter, Gloucester, Hereford, Lincoln, Llandaff, London, (Oxford), Norwich, (Peterborough), Rochester, Salisbury, Sodor and Man, St Asaph, St David's, (Westminster),Winchester, Worcester.

The archbishop was sometimes referred to as the metropolitan. The archbishops undertook **visitations** (known as metropolitical visitations) of their respective provinces shortly after their inauguration and at intervals thereafter. Cases arising from this visitation procedure were then normally heard in the archiepiscopal courts. They also heard appeals from the diocesan jurisdiction.

Parishes and episcopal supervision

Within each diocese were subdivisions for pastoral care: the 10,000 or so churches or parishes. Episcopal responsibilities and powers extended to an oversight of the spiritual welfare of the people, ensuring that material goods and property given to support this pastoral activity were protected and put to their proper use and enforcing the laws which had evolved to order the Church and the behaviour of its people.

Bishops' registers and the registry

Fourteenth-century episcopal registers recorded the acts of the bishops: institutions to benefices (both rectories and vicarages were sometimes known as 'livings'); ordinations of priests and deacons, subdeacons and those in **Minor Orders**); articles and injunctions relating to visitation; appropriation of benefices to religious houses and arrangements for the livelihood of vicars who served such churches; important wills proved; writs received from and returned to the royal chancery. From the fifteenth century onwards, the official registers were supported by multitudinous files. Then, as the number and types of records preserved exploded, the bishop's register itself became little more than an act book of institutions – as at Coventry and Lichfield, Norwich and Chester. The registry also preserved papers and surveys of the episcopal properties (land and other possessions) in addition to the journal and documentation of the work of visitation and the **Courts Christian**. The episcopal registrar (and his deputy or deputies) were key and influential figures in the diocesan bureaucracy.

Bishops' roles and duties and the types of documentation they occasioned

The acts of the bishops (and the types of documentation they occasioned) were many and various.

Ordinations and ordination examinations

For example, bishops ordained clergy and, before conferring orders, examined candidates. A candidate was required to perform a literacy test (and, after the Reformation, to this might be added a test of scriptural knowledge), to present a title to a benefice (a rectory, vicarage, curacy, college fellowship, etc.) to which he would be presented, to present testimonials as to good character; and to offer letters dimissory if he originated in another diocese. Records of ordinations were kept before the Reformation in episcopal registers and, after the Reformation, in ordination books. At Ely, there is a rare survival of the examination proceedings for cohorts of ordination candidates in the later sixteenth century. Canons 33–5 of 1604 codified the rules regarding ordination. Files survive of the documentation presented by candidates in some dioceses.

Dispensations

Bishops also provided licences of dispensation: for instance, to eat meat during **lent**; to hold livings in plurality; to receive deacons and priests orders simultaneously; to be ordained below the accepted age; to be married without banns being read. After the Reformation, this dispensing power was chiefly exercised by the Archbishop of Canterbury's Faculty Office. These dispensations were sealed by the bishop's seal by his official principal or chancellor and frequently recorded in either the bishop's register or the official's own register. Similarly, grants of faculties were made (to alter the fabric of the church or parsonage) and recorded, at first in the main bishop's register but then in faculty registers. By the eighteenth century, the register of faculties was often supported by extensive files. In addition, the bishop would license curates to serve as stipendiaries in various parishes. Such a curate had to be formally nominated by the incumbent of the parish concerned and prove that he was ordained.

Sequestrations

Under certain circumstances the bishop would have to sequester or take over a benefice in his jurisdiction; this might happen if the incumbent had resigned or if he had been suspended from his duties for lunacy or grave offences. By the act of sequestration the bishop had to ensure the pastoral care of the parish involved and the safety of its property by appointing receivers or sequestrators who would execute a bond and present accounts for audit. These sequestrations were recorded either in the bishop's register or in separate registers of sequestration or licences.

A canon of 1571 had also ordered that bishops should keep a glebe terrier (or survey of the glebe land attached to each parsonage), but only a few bishops obeyed (Carlisle, Lincoln and Worcester). When the rule was repeated in canon 87 of 1604 a collection of such records, usually stored as loose files, was begun in all dioceses.

Subscriptions to oath and articles

In addition, bishops were frequently ordered by Act of Parliament to perform certain acts, make certain returns and keep specific records. Examples would be the requirement in the very first Act of Parliament of Elizabeth's reign that all clerks in holy orders swear an oath of allegiance and the requirement, in 1571, that presentees to livings subscribe to the **Thirty-Nine Articles** of Religion prior to institution and induction. Some registers of subscriptions arising out of these Elizabethan Acts occur in registries, but it was not until the canons 36 and 77 of 1604 codified the practice for all clerks and schoolmasters that continuous records of subscriptions were necessitated. The rules were re-enacted under the Caroline Act of Uniformity (13 & 14 Car. 2, c. 4).

Bishops' visitations

A very large proportion of the surviving records of the Church in England emanate directly or indirectly from the supervisory, visitorial and appellate roles of the bishop within his diocese. Some parts of his role may appear, to the modern eye, to be judicial or administrative but were, in fact, aspects of his responsibility for the spiritual well-being of all the population within his diocese and contemporary ways of meeting these responsibilities – through visitations and courts and the bureaucracies they supported and the records they produced and preserved.

Frequency of visitation

A bishop performed a visitation of his whole diocese shortly after his entry to the see and then at three-yearly intervals thereafter.

Relationship between the church courts and the visitation procedure

Church courts heard office cases arising from visitation as well as instance (party v. party) causes and probate business. Although the bishop might hold a court of **audience**, most cases were heard in the presence of his chancellor, official or **vicar-general** or a 'substitute'. In the Middle Ages, the official originally dealt with the legal affairs and with visitation; the vicar-general acted in administrative matters during the bishop's absence; sequestrators dealt with probate matters; and commissaries were deputed to deal with matters in the larger archdeaconries. By the later sixteenth century, the situation was more muddled as several of these functions were frequently combined in one person and the names became practically interchangeable. For a detailed discussion of the visitation process, the Courts Christian and the documents they produced see Chapter 10: Ecclesiastical courts and commissions.

Pastoral work in the Church

Major and Minor Orders of lower clergy

Most pastoral work within the Church was performed at parish level by men in Major Orders (priests, deacons and, before the Reformation, subdeacons) and, in the pre-Reformation Church, Minor Orders (porters, lectors, exorcists, acolytes). There were rules regarding who could be ordained to these orders, although dispensations from these rules could be, and were widely, given.

Financial support of the lower clergy through the system of 'benefices' or 'livings'

Originally, bishops had both ordained priests and presented them to churches/parishes but, in time (and certainly by 1450), the responsibility for nominating and presenting priests to 'livings' or benefices devolved to other individuals (clerical and lay) and/or institutions (for instance, cathedrals or monasteries). The bishops still had the responsibility for approving these nominations and presentations, and instituted and inducted ordained clergy to the spiritualities and temporalities of the parishes. Records of these processes occur both within the diocesan records (bishops' registers; ordination books and papers; examination papers; *libri cleri* of visitation; licensing books; records of *pro hac vice* **presentation**; registrars' papers) and elsewhere (the Lord Keeper's papers, for example, give detail about the nomination and presentation of clergy to livings in his patronage).

Assistants to the bishops: archdeacons and rural deans

Each bishop also had assistants (archdeacons and rural deans) and their dioceses were subdivided into archdeaconries and rural deaneries, over which these officials exercised their authority. Initially, this authority was that of the 'eye of the bishop' or *oculis episcopi*. Eventually, however, the archdeacons and even the rural deans began to exercise distinct or even parallel functions so, for example, we find archidiaconal visitations and court systems which parallelled those of the bishop. This can lead to a good deal of confusion for the researcher, especially as some documentary survivals are of uncertain provenance.

Jurisdictions outside the bishops' purview: pre-Reformation cathedrals and collegiate churches

Certain large churches and colleges regarded themselves as outside the bishop's jurisdiction and were known as 'peculiar jurisdictions'. The cathedrals of the old foundation (that is pre-Reformation sees) governed themselves according to their own statutes, exercised visitorial oversight of their churches and people and had varying relationships with the bishops. Ironically, the cathedral *was* the seat of that bishop.

Monastic foundations

Prior to the Reformation, England and Wales were also rich in monastic foundations for both sexes.

Church law

The legal basis of the administration of the Church in, and of, England was, before the Reformation, Roman canon law (codified in William Lyndwood's *Provinciale*) and, after the Reformation, that law plus modifications of canon law through the Reformation's parliamentary legislation, royal injunctions of 1559, and canons of 1603, all of which were codified in Edmund Gibson's *Codex Iuris Ecclesiastici Anglicani* of 1713. There were moves thoroughly to revise and reform the ecclesiastical discipline during the reigns of Henry VIII, Edward VI and Elizabeth I, but these attempts were defeated, partly by the vested interests of laymen made anxious by the prospect of an efficient and effective Church law that could be used against them.

Convocation

Each province had its own representative assembly of clergy, known as **Convocation**. Since the thirteenth century each had consisted of an Upper House (of bishops) and a Lower House (of clergy). Originally, in the medieval Church, they were assembled to grant clerical taxation to the Crown but they came to deliberate on and make laws or canons for the Church. The Act of Parliament which embodied the Submission of the Clergy (1534) considerably curtailed Convocation's legislative powers. It was accepted that Convocation could not sit in the absence of Parliament and would be dissolved at the same time as Parliament. The records of Convocation are confined to the canons that it legislated. Discussions of its proceedings are almost non-existent and almost certainly occur only indirectly and infrequently in other types of documentation. Occasionally, within the diocesan records, are to be found records of the proctors selected by the local clergy as their representatives in the Lower House.

Parish unit and its documentation

The parish was the smallest unit within the Church structure and, for ordinary men and women, the most important and immediate; yet it is also the unit for which least documentation survives. A certain amount of information can be gleaned from the formal records of visitation (including visitation articles and **injunctions**), from court proceedings, from tithe maps, from the *Valor Ecclesiasticus* and from occasional survivals such as glebe terriers, composition books, personal diaries and correspondence. Parish registers remain an important source for demographic information.

Notes

1 The exception was the Bishop of Sodor and Man.
2 A. Kautz, 'The selection of Jacobean bishops', in H.S. Reinmuth (ed.), *Early Stuart Studies,* Minneapolis, 1970 is a useful account.
3 These sees set in brackets were created in 1540. The diocese of Westminster was abolished in March 1550 and merged with that of London.

10
ECCLESIASTICAL COURTS AND COMMISSIONS

These are also known as Courts Christian or, more commonly, Church courts.

The Church correction system affected the entire population of England and Wales, whether lay or clerical. From the thirteenth century onwards, English bishops held regular and frequent **visitations** of their dioceses. The purpose of visitation was to collect information about the state of the diocese (regarding its spiritual and moral as well as its administrative and financial health) and to set into motion the process of correction. This periodic inspection detected whether or not the Church's laws (canons) were implemented and observed at local level.

A machinery for the visitation and correction of the **secular** (parochial clergy and others who did not belong to a rule) as well as the **regular** clergy (that is those who belonged to a rule or order) was properly established in the later fifteenth century. This system was taken over and further developed by the 'reformed' church of the sixteenth century. Simultaneously, the morality of the laity was also monitored and corrected. Cases arising out of visitation were fed into ecclesiastical courts, especially when the offenders were obdurate. These courts also dealt with other types of case, such as probate of wills, defamation and **tithe**. As more and more studies of the sixteenth century assume a basic knowledge of this system, and because student dissertations frequently involve using the local records emanating from visitation and courts, an outline account of visitation and the manner in which it relates to the other ecclesiastical courts and to the secular courts is offered here. It is followed by a description of the courts themselves and the procedures followed within them. Practices did vary somewhat from diocese to diocese and, even, from deanery to deanery. For this reason, while it is useful to know the procedures followed as a *guide* to understanding original documentation in a particular locality, this can never be a substitute for studying that local evidence.

Visitation

It is artificial to separate the work of visitation from that of the ecclesiastical courts (Courts Christian) because both formed part of the correction system adopted by the Church in England. Indeed, sometimes the digests of visitation presentments were actually included in the office court books, making very clear the close relationship between what was discovered at visitation and what was pursued by office cases in the **consistory** courts.

Frequent and regular episcopal visitation of the dioceses began in the thirteenth century. Initially, visitation was chiefly concerned with the monasteries but, by the fifteenth century, it extended to all parishes, to secular clergy and to the laity. This machinery was inherited at the Reformation but its judicial and corrective aspects were then enhanced. Canons 109–19 of 1604 encapsulated the crucial role of the visitation in enforcing the Elizabethan religious settlement.

A bishop normally held first (primary) visitation of his diocese in the first year after his enthronement and repeated ordinary visitations once every three or four years. The bishop often played a very small personal role in the visitations (especially the ordinary ones) and his place was taken by the official principal or chancellor or his substitute or even, within large archdeaconries, a commissary.

Laymen (usually churchwardens of the parishes) or specially appointed lay questmen were, from the fifteenth century onwards, required to make presentments of things that were wrong in their parishes. The Elizabethan bishops sought to focus the minds of these wardens by issuing printed articles (allegations or questions) of visitation when the visitation was first announced. Formal answers were required and canon 119 of 1604 made this compulsory.

At the start of the visitation all other jurisdictions (such as that of the archdeacon) were formally suspended or inhibited (an inhibition). Until the visitation was concluded, the bishop (or his substitutes) was the ordinary or authority.

A general monition was issued to each rural deanery (a small subdivision of each archdeaconry) bidding all beneficed clergy (**rectors** and vicars) to attend the visitation centre and exhibit their letters of ordination, certificates of subscription (for example to the **Thirty-Nine Articles** of Religion) and dispensation (for example, permission to hold two or more livings in plurality and to be non-resident in some of them) and their preaching licences; all curates, lectors (readers), schoolmasters, ushers, surgeons, physicians and midwives to exhibit their licences; all impropriators and farmers of tithes to show their endowments and pay pensions and procurations due from them; churchwardens and sidesmen to take their oaths and make their presentments; and executors to bring their wills. At this first meeting of the visitation those present would be formally addressed and a local preacher would deliver a sermon. During the visitation tour, mass **confirmations** of hundreds of young people would be held by the bishops (as directed by canon 60 of 1604). There is little or no direct manuscript evidence of these ceremonies but references to the practice exist for both the seventeenth and eighteenth centuries.

Presentments were not, apparently, often preserved by the central registry. From the late sixteenth century onwards, parish officials recorded their presentments as replies to articles of inquiry (Lincoln and Ely). This practice became very common after the Restoration. Digests of presentments were compiled and kept from the late fifteenth century onwards. These bear different names in different places: for examples, *acta correctionis ex officio et detecta*; *acta habita et comperta* (Coventry and Lichfield); *acta habita et determinate in curia visitacionis*; *detectiones*. The digests were normally ordered by archdeaconry, rural deanery and parish.

Once these presentments were made, citations were prepared requiring each individual whose offences were considered sufficiently serious to attend the **consistory** court. When a number of people within a parish were cited for the same offence, a general citation *quorum nomina* would be issued covering them all. If those summoned failed to appear a citation *viis et modis* (served by all possible means and affixed to the church door) was issued. The punishment for failure to attend after this second citation was called suspension, which carried with it the penalties of minor or lesser **excommunication**. In order to achieve this, a suspension mandate was sent to the offender's parish priest, who would return it with certification.

The visitation was supported by large numbers of different types of documentation. Elaborate records were prepared and preserved for the episcopal and metropolitical visitations – *liber cleri, liber ordinum* or exhibit books recorded the names and parishes of the clergy and others holding office (such as schoolmasters and curates) along with certification of their ordination papers, licences, institutions and dispensations. Sometimes, such a book would also contain a note of the sessions of the visitation, of the preachers who delivered visitation sermons and of the charge (exhortation delivered by the bishop or official at the opening of proceedings).

Some bishops instructed their assistants to compile surveys or directories of their dioceses based on the returns of visitation, probably in response to central government requests for detailed information. Such a *speculum* would characteristically be organised alphabetically by parish and give details of the holder of the **advowson**; the patron and his right to present; the impropriator or farmer of tithes; the incumbent; curates; services; numbers of communicants and recusants; schools and schoolmasters; surgeons; midwives; and so forth. One of the earliest *specula* was Bishop Richard Barnes' general survey of Durham diocese 1575–87[1]. The digests of presentments in other dioceses (e.g. Lichfield) closely resembled *specula*. In the later seventeenth century, the Compton Census of 1776, which recorded conformists and nonconformists in the parishes based on details provided by diocesans, seems to have motivated bishops to draw up *specula*. For instance, Bishop Turner of Ely made a survey in 1686, since lost, and some parts of it were copied into a bishop's book. Turner ordered each clergyman to compile a *noticia* or **household** census of his parish, listing family members of the age of 16 or above and noting whether the individual was a communicant and well-catechised and confirmed.

On the same day as the visitation, when all the clergy were assembled, it seems to have been common for a synod or chapter of the clergy to take place. This medieval practice continued into the Reformation and post-Reformation periods and was actually introduced into at least one of the newly founded diocese, Chester. In some dioceses call books of the synod exist – for example, Ely. [2]Although technically distinct, the synod and the visitation happened simultaneously and became confused.

As a result of visitation some individuals, clergy and lay, were summarily dealt with and some were excommunicated. Visitation absolution books occur for some dioceses which record the names of individuals who were excommunicated and the procedure (absolution) whereby their excommunication was later lifted. Care must be taken not to confuse these books with absolutions arising out of the proceedings of the consistory courts.

The archbishops of Canterbury and York also conducted visitations: episcopal visitations of their own dioceses and archiepiscopal visitations of their respective provinces. During a provincial visitation the normal jurisdictions (those of the bishop and archdeacons) were formally suspended (inhibited). The archbishop frequently used the diocesan machinery and personnel to accomplish the visitation – for example, the official principal and his substitutes and the commissaries – and, as a result, the records of the archiepiscopal visitations are often to be found in the diocesan registries. The archbishop would also become ordinary of a diocese during a vacancy in the see concerned and would conduct requisite visitations in these circumstances. A copy of the proceedings was sent to the archbishop's registry but the originals were normally kept in the registry of the diocese concerned and copies of the files accumulated during this period *sede vacante* are often found in the registry of the cathedral.

Within the dioceses, archdeacons also conducted twice yearly visitations in their own archdeaconries[3]. In the larger dioceses – for example, York (Nottingham archdeaconry), Lincoln (Bedford, Leicester and Huntingdon archdeaconries) and Norwich (two Suffolk archdeaconries) – the archdeaconries were large and far-flung from the diocesan centre. In such cases, the bishop sometimes appointed a permanent official or commissary who would exercise episcopal jurisdiction in that archdeaconry. When this same man also served as the official of the archdeacon, as was frequently the case, the two jurisdictions of bishop and archdeacon became inextricably confused. In other cases, one archdeacon might be designated *archidiaconus major*, either formally or informally, and be accorded quasi-episcopal jurisdiction.

Some documents relating to such archidiaconal visitations still survive. Call books were prepared for the regular, twice-yearly archdeacons' visitations. These were lists of the clergy and churchwardens summoned, along with sums of money they owed for procurations, synodals, etc. Some books of presentments also survive. However, the survival rate of visitation books and call books is generally poor. The records collected by the archdeacons are better represented: parish register transcripts; records of probate; marriage licences; records of inductions to benefices. The royal injunctions of 1538 had ordered parish clergy to keep registers of marriages, baptisms and burials of their parishioners and, from 1562, a copy (*transcript*) of these registers had to be lodged annually in the diocesan registry. This order was widely ignored until it was restated in 1597 and reinforced by canon 70 in 1604. After that, transcripts were collected at the Easter archdeacons' visitations and lodged in the diocesan registry or, in the case of the archdeaconries in the larger dioceses (e.g. Lincoln and York), in archidiaconal registries. They may well have been stored in bundles, sorted by rural deanery.

Archdeacons were specifically charged with care of church fabric and property. As a result, they collected a good deal of information about such matters through visitation and sometimes compiled church inspection books from the information gathered. Examples from the eighteenth and nineteenth centuries have been printed, and historians are always looking for earlier examples of this practice.

Summary of visitation procedure

Primary visitation of diocese during first year of episcopate.
Triennial visitations of diocese thereafter.

Inhibition of all other ecclesiastical jurisdiction during the course of the visitation.

Articles of Inquiry – canon 119 of 1604 made printed articles of inquiry, to guide the responses of churchwardens or questmen, compulsory but they were already widely in use.

General monition was sent to all the rural deaneries in the diocese, summoning to each visitation centre (there was usually one centre for each three or four deaneries) 'all parsons and vicars to exhibit letters of orders, centificates of subscriptions and dispensations, all preachers, lecturers, curates, readers, schoolmasters and ushers to exhibit licences, all impropriators and farmers of tithes to exhibit endowments and pay pensions and procurations, all churchmen and sidesmen to take their oaths and make presentments, executors to bring in the wills of their testators, all criminals and delinquents to answer articles . . .'.

Presentments would include, for example, a note if the church was in disrepair, if the schoolmaster had no licence, if the vicar was an absentee or refused to wear the surplice or kept an alehouse in the vicarage, if there were **recusants**, if unmarried people cohabited, if a layman or woman held heretical opinions.

Records of presentments were made and citations were prepared, calling those whose offences were considered serious to appear before the visitor for correction. Sometimes those cited failed to appear and a second citation was issued. The penalty for failure to appear in response to this second call was minor excommunication or suspension. Those who did appear to answer for their conduct might be summarily punished or dismissed or referred to the consistory court of the diocese for summary correction through mere office procedure.

Visitation **injunctions** – the bishop defined the particular areas of his concern regarding the state of the diocese. He ordered conformity where necessary. In these injunctions there might be reference to recently published canons of the church (laws) or orders from the Crown or archbishops.

To make matters even more complicated, each archdeacon also held his own visitations; however, such detail is beyond the scope of this book.

A useful account of this area is given in Dorothy M. Owen, *The Records of the Established Church in England*, British Records Association, Archives and the User, No. 1, 1970. Kenneth Fincham, *Visitation Articles of the Early Stuart Church*, 2 volumes, Church of England Record Society, 1994 & 1998, while concerned with the early seventeenth century, contains much that is relevant to the Elizabethan period.

The visitation system underpinned the work of the superior ecclesiastical courts within each diocese. Presentments at visitation were often the basis for mere office cases in the consistory court.

Consistory courts

The consistory court of the bishop exercised several types of jurisdiction. Much business was heard at the consistory court itself (often within the cathedral building) but it might also be heard elsewhere (even in an inn) and by deputies and commissioners. Much of the historian's knowledge of popular attitudes and behaviour (deferential, sexual and moral as well as religious) rests upon information revealed in the work of the visitation and consistory courts. A number of books discuss such evidence but an especially good treatment is *Martin Ingram, Church Courts, Sex and Marriage in England, 1570–1640*, Cambridge, 1987.

Jurisdictions

Office jurisdiction

Mere office

Much of the courts' business emanated from the disciplinary business of visitation. Some of this correction business would be dispensed during the visitation itself using summary procedure. More serious disciplinary cases, against both clergy and laity, were brought into the consistory courts of the dioceses and tried under the summary procedure of mere office. The types of cause involved varied from those which might be described as moral offences or sins to those which involved non-compliance with the Church's rules (for example, clergymen who refused to use the Prayer Book or to subscribe to the articles).

Church courts had no power to make arrests. They summoned defendants by citation. The first (primary citation) was served in person. If this failed, the citation was served *viis et modis* (by ways and means), affixed to the church door or the door of the defendant's house. Failure to appear when cited resulted in excommunication for contumacy but, commonly, the judge would give plenty of opportunity for the defendant to comply before excommunication.

The procedure was normally heard in open court by the judge. (Except in serious cases, this was normally not the bishop but his vicar-general or chancellor or a deputy. When the bishop presided in person over the court it was referred to as his 'court of audience'. There is some evidence that he would hold such a court when especially serious cases involving clergy were concerned.) It was not a jury trial. Before 1660, the accused could use the procedure of **compurgation** or **purgation** to prove his innocence. Under this system several of the accused's neighbours, of accepted good reputation, were required to swear his or her innocence on oath. The number of compurgators required varied, according to the gravity of the offence, from three to approximately nine. If the accused was found guilty, the punishment was normally excommunication, from which the offender might be absolved following penance, which involved a solemn public confession in church on one or more days. On occasion, even after the reformation, the penitent was required to wear a white shift and hold a wand. Sometimes this punishment was commuted for a fine. This penance had to be certificated to the court before absolution was granted. Some dioceses retain good runs of office court books; cause papers (including depositions) and absolution books survive more rarely.

Plenary jurisdiction

This was exercised either in connection with office (correction) cases promoted by a third party or with the ecclesiastical equivalent of civil suits between party and party (instance suits). It was frequently used to try ordinary office cases where the evidence was difficult to interpret, as it offered fewer opportunities for lawyers to claim a non-suit. Defendant and plaintiff appointed proctors (the civil law equivalent of a barrister). The accused answered articles or tabled questions. Witnesses were called both for and against and their depositions were written down. The whole procedure was more cumbersome, drawn-out and expensive than that of the mere office case. In short, it was elaborate and unpopular.

Instance suits (party v. party cases that were roughly equivalent to civil suits) and office-promoted causes (similar cases in which the official promoted) followed an elaborate plenary procedure. Cases were normally referred to as 'causes'. They frequently concerned property, such as tithes and advowsons, or were defamation or matrimonial suits. Ecclesiastical lawyers or proctors handled the cases on behalf of their clients. During the first stage, known as the contestation of suit, the plaintiff or promoter or complainant detailed the case, using a libel in instance cases and articles in office-promoted cases. The defendant had to reply to these point by point on oath. When the defendant denied some or all of the facts, he would often present an allegation against the plaintiff, which the plaintiff then had to answer.

Next the judge, during the stage called probation, decided on a fixed period during which witnesses would be produced and examined. Witnesses could be compelled to appear on pain of excommunication. Witnesses were examined on oath and their written depositions were made available to both sides. Both sides were entitled to administer interrogatories (questions) to hostile witnesses to try to reveal weaknesses in their evidence or enter an exception to challenge the character of the witness. During this period of probation (proving) either side could introduce new statements or new evidence.

Finally, the judge assigned a time to conclude the case and a date for pronouncing sentence. During the remaining time the lawyers assembled in chambers and reviewed the evidence on both sides and argued points of law to help the judge reach a verdict. Then, in court, judgement was pronounced, either as a definitive sentence or in the form of an informal decree. The 'guilty' party was then given time to appeal to a higher court. If an appeal was lodged, the higher court inhibited further action by the lower court, which sent all the relevant papers up to the higher court. If there was no appeal, the unsuccessful party was summoned by citation. On appearance, the party was punished and costs were assessed and arrangements made for payment.

In some simple causes (for example, defamation and tithe cases) a simplified procedure, known as 'summary', was followed.

The courts met to administer justice in plenary session in instance causes usually either once a week or once a fortnight during **law terms**.[4] Justice within the system was not always slow. The time taken varied between a matter of weeks for a simple defamation case to two to three years for more complicated litigation, but the average duration of a case that proceeded to sentence was about nine to twelve months, which compared favourably with the duration of cases in the secular courts.

Relatively few instance or office-promoted cases were prosecuted to the finish. Parties were encouraged to settle out of court wherever possible.

The rate of attendance at court during instance and office-promoted business was much higher than that for disciplinary procedures followed in the office side of the consistory.

Some dioceses (e.g. Coventry and Lichfield) recorded instance case business separately from office case business but this was not a practice followed everywhere. Bundles of cause papers sometimes survive for instance business. In general, such material has not been catalogued in detail.

Probate jurisdiction

Individuals seeking to prove the wills and testaments of those who possessed property of small value (i.e. £5) could elect to use the local courts of the rural deanery or of the archdeaconry. Rural deans would also, for a fee, make house calls to deal with such business. The wills of those who owned property of greater value in more than one archdeaconry (within the same diocese) had to be proved in the probate side of the diocesan consistory court. Wills of the more prosperous, who held property in one diocese, had to be proved in that diocese. Unwitnessed wills and nuncupative wills (i.e. those declared orally on a deathbed) were usually dealt with in summary fashion during visitation, unless a caveat was entered, which required them to go to consistory. At each stage of the probate procedure, fees were demanded of the executor or administrator.

Apparitors

When an individual died, his or her executor or relict was well-advised to seek probate of the will or grant of administration of the estate as soon as possible. The system was policed and negligent executors were penalised. A court apparitor, who was paid from fines collected from offenders, searched out all manner of culprits, including those who omitted to prove a will or to obtain a grant of administration.

Disputed wills and administrations

When a will was unwitnessed or existed only as a witnessed verbal wish (nuncupative wills), the matter was normally settled at a visitation unless it was queried. In that case, it would result in plenary jurisdiction in the consistory court (see pp. 121–23).

Undisputed wills

An undisputed will was initially exhibited in the court by its executor, who swore an oath as to its validity and was granted probate. This was then recorded in a probate act book. The original will, with attached act of probate, was then filed and later bound into volumes by year. Registers were also drawn up containing copies of the wills proved. (Sometimes the executor named in a will refused to act. In that case, he or she was required to make a renunciation, witnessed by a notary, which was then filed in the court. The court then appointed an executor or administrator.)

Intestacy

When an individual died without making a will the ordinary (depending upon the jurisdiction this could be the rural dean, the archdeacon or the bishop or their deputies) appointed a person connected to the deceased to administer his or her effects. These 'acts of administration' were recorded in a register, normally separately.

The rules that were applied when the deceased had not left a will (intestate) must not be confused with the rules of inheritance with which a testator had to comply.

Bonds of administration

Executors and administrators were required to enter bonds which would be satisfied if and when they accurately accounted and exhibited an inventory of all the goods of the deceased, whether testate or intestate. They might be asked also to present actual accounts of administration one year after the death. Documents relating to grants of administration were filed together in chronological bundles but few survive in complete runs.

Inventories (drawn up by appraisers)

An inventory was required for estates valued in excess of £5, but smaller estates were often treated similarly. The supposedly independent appraisers who drew up the inventories were paid for their trouble out of the relevant estate. Inventories are often preserved alongside individual wills. They are an invaluable source for those interested in material culture. In addition, books, pictures and other items are sometimes recorded in fascinating detail.

Fees

Accountants normally made deductions for administration (between £2 and £3) and the funeral. Travelling expenses were added to this sum. The court itself charged fees of approximately £1 15s for probate or grant of administration, an amount that increased only a little over the whole early modern period. In many cases, however, the court reduced its fees on appeal from poor executors and administrators.

Tutors and guardians

The probate court appointed tutors or guardians for any children of the deceased who were below the age of majority. Often the testator had named such a guardian. Whether or not this was the case the tutor or guardian was required to enter a bond that they would perform their tasks appropriately and these bonds were filed. Then the actual grant of approval was entered into a special register or, in some courts, alongside caveats or licences.

Prerogative Courts of Canterbury and York

The archbishop of Canterbury claimed the right to grant probate and administration in cases where a testator left property of a certain value in more than one diocese within his province.

Until the end of the fifteenth century, this jurisdiction was exercised as part of the archbishop's Court of Audience but out of this developed a separate court, known variously as the Prerogative Court of Canterbury (PCC) or Court of the Prerogative. However, this right was not undisputed and the diocesan bishops did not accept this without a fight. In 1512, in Convocation, the bishops of London, Winchester, Lincoln, Exeter and Coventry and Lichfield questioned the archbishop's right to prove such wills. The office of judge of the PCC (also known as master, keeper or commissary) was in the gift of the archbishop and was normally held for life. This judge appointed a number of advocates as his deputies. Advocates were senior civil lawyers who acted as legal advisers to clients and proctors. This was one of the central Courts Christian and it was much criticised both by bishops (who opposed its jurisdiction over the affairs of people living within their dioceses) and others, including the Crown (which objected to its existence, its lax and laggardly procedures and its allegedly extortionate fees). Original wills and testaments occur in bundles in the National Archives (PROB) and copies of wills and testaments proved in the Prerogative Court exist in printed form.

In York province there is little sign that the archbishop wished to grant probate in similar cases and there was no Prerogative Court of York until 1577.

The Court of Arches

This was the consistory court of the Province of Canterbury, which also functioned as a court of appeal from the diocesan consistories. Its official papers have largely disappeared from Lambeth Palace, although case papers may, on occasion, surface in collections of family legal papers.

Ecclesiastical commissions

Commissions were not part of the normal conciliar apparatus of the Church, but rather instruments employed from time to time by the Crown to investigate and try ecclesiastical offences. They were joint commissions of ecclesiastics and laymen appointed by the Crown. Sometimes their papers are mixed up with those of the normal Church courts because the same personnel were involved.

Courts of High Commission at Lambeth and York

The Court of High Commission at Lambeth was the principal commission for the southern province of the Church of England. There was also a major commission for the northern province, which sat at York. These courts encountered increasing opposition from Puritans and common lawyers. The Puritans scorned the absence of godly discipline. The common lawyers opposed their arbitrary practice and uncertain authority.

Diocesan commissions

In the 1550s, Mary I appointed a commission (which included the Archdeacon of Canterbury, the Commissary of Canterbury, the **suffragan** Bishop of Dover and two more clergy, two noblemen and ten more laymen) to search out heretics, seditious books, and so forth, in the diocese of Canterbury.

In the early years of Elizabeth's reign, the archbishops and bishops probably tried to manage the discipline of the Church using the normal apparatus of the Church courts. By the late 1560s, however, many dioceses had their own sets of commissioners to handle extraordinary business such as heresy and nonconformity. Records exist for the commissions set up at Durham and at Bristol and Gloucester. The commission at Gloucester was given jurisdiction over civil disorder in the unstable region of the Marches.

In 1572, an ecclesiastical commission was set up for Canterbury diocese. It included a mixture of ecclesiastics, laymen and lawyers. The commission began with a membership that reflected moderate Puritanism but it seems probable that a new commission, appointed under Whitgift's rule, reduced lay participation and acted much more conservatively.

For a time, records of the Canterbury court's work were mixed inextricably with those of the ordinary Church courts but soon it developed its own organisation. By 1584, it maintained a court register, in which were recorded the acts of the court and the examination of witnesses before it. In terms of procedure, it followed that of the diocesan courts and this was unsurprising given the overlap in personnel.[5] Much of its business was also referred to it directly from the consistory courts, although really serious cases were referred to Lambeth. Few clerical cases were heard by the Canterbury commission (reflecting, perhaps, the general desire to exercise purely ecclesiastical discipline over ecclesiastics). The court was especially active against county Catholics. The Courts Christian, however, were here distinct in a way that they were not in Gloucester diocese in the 1570s, where the Church courts collapsed and the commission took over their work.

Commissions were distinct from the Church courts in other respects. They had powers of arrest or attachment, of requiring bonds for appearance, of imprisonment and of summary action. They could also hand out sentences that included imprisonment, pillory and stocks, and fines.

Usher (1910) argued that the diocesan commissions were local branches of the High Commission at Lambeth. Price (1972) and Tyler (1976) argued that the diocesan commissions were, in fact, generally free of Lambeth supervision. Clark (1974) agrees, to some extent, but sees the commission for Canterbury diocese as having closer links with the Lambeth Commission, partly because the Archbishop of Canterbury, head of the Lambeth Court, was also its diocesan.

Notes

1. J. Raine, *Injunctions and Other Ecclesiastical Proceedings of Richard Barnes*, Bishop of Durham, Surtees Society, 22, 1855, especially pp. 1–10.
2. The Ely Black Book held in the University Library, Cambridge, Add Ms.3468.
3. A.H. Thompson, 'Diocesan organisation in the middle ages, archdeacons, and rural deans', *Proceedings of the British Academy*, 29 provides a good description of the responsibilities of the medieval archdeacons, which outlines a system that continued throughout our period.
4. At Ely and Chichester, the courts met once a week; at Salisbury, they met once a fortnight.
5. K[ent] A[rchives] O[ffice], PRC 44/3.

11

POPULATION AND POPULATION DISTRIBUTION

Data for England are **aggregative back-projection** figures extracted from E.A. Wrigley and R.S. Schofield, *The Population History of England, 1541–1871*, Cambridge, 1989 edition, pp. 531, 574.

Total population of England and Wales (millions)

1524	2.384
1541	2.774
1550	2.970
1569–71	3.255
1599–1601	4.066

English urban population (resident in towns of over 4,000 people)

1520	1700
6%	15%

Total of population living in London

1520	1700
3%	10%

Urban hierarchy

Data extracted from P. Clark and P. Slack, *English Towns in Transition*, Oxford, 1976.

1. The towns at the top of the hierarchy were the largest and richest towns, which dominated entire regions and offered a wide range of services. The category included, in 1500, London (population of 60,000 in 1500), which dwarfed the rest, York, Bristol, Exeter, Newcastle, Coventry and Salisbury (with populations of 7,000 or more) and, in 1600, probably London, York, Bristol, Exeter, Newcastle, Colchester and Yarmouth (with populations of 11,000 or more by 1700).

There are various estimates of the population size of the capital and provincial centres. The following, then, are approximations.

Populations of London and provincial centres

	c. 1520	Later estimates	1603
London	60,000	120,000 (1582)	200,000
Norwich	12,000	18,000 (1579)	15,000
Bristol	10,000		12,000
York	8,000	8,000 (1548)	11,500
Exeter	8,000		9,000
Salisbury	8,000		7,000
Coventry	6,601	4,000–5,000 (1563)	7,000

2. A hundred incorporated towns with populations ranging between 1,500 and 5,000 in 1500 acted as regional centres with hinterlands, which often contained lesser market towns, such as those below. These regional centres frequently had more than one market and often specialised in particular products. Typical examples were county towns such as Chester, Northampton, Shrewsbury, Southampton and Bury St Edmunds; the university towns of Oxford and Cambridge; several ports such as Canterbury, Hull, Portsmouth, Plymouth and Ipswich and industrial towns such as Manchester, Leeds and Birmingham. The period was a time of crisis for many such centres: Stafford, for example, was listed in 1540 as a decayed town; its fortunes revived under Elizabeth; by the seventeenth century it was in decline once more.

Population of some regional centres according to estimated size

	c. 1520	Later estimates	1600
Oxford	5,000	5,000 (1547)	6,500
Great Yarmouth	4,000		5,000–8,000
Chester		4,000–5,000 (1563)	5,000
Worcester		4,000–5,000 (1563)	5,000
Canterbury	3,000	2,800–3,500 (1563)	5,000
Ipswich	3,000–4,000		5,500
Bury St Edmunds	3,550		4,500
Shrewsbury		2,700–3,400 (1563)	5,000
Cambridge	2,600	2,000–2,500 (1563)	6,500

3. There were between 500 and 600 small towns with low populations and population density. These included lesser market centres (Wotton-under-Edge, Gloucs; Lutterworth, Leics; Stony Stratford, Bucks) and decaying ancient boroughs (Stamford, Lincs; Winchelsea). Certain towns (of varying sizes) had the legal right to hold a market. Such towns were situated at distances of approximately one day's travel, there and back, on foot. Market towns were vigilant in detecting illegal markets and petitioning the Crown to have them closed down. The following rough estimates show how the fortunes of such towns fluctuated during the period, due to disease, immigration, etc., so that some scarcely warranted the name 'town', even though they still hosted markets, and others flourished.

Population of some market towns

Market town	c.1500	c.1520	c.1565	c.1603	1676
Ashby de la Zouche, Leics		800	400	1,200	1,178
Hitchin, Herts		650		1,800	
East Dereham, Norfolk		600		1,100	
Newport Pagnell, Bucks				1,600	
Stony Stratford, Bucks				1,050	
Maidstone, Kent (also county town)	2,000	2,300 (1540s)	2,000	3,000	
Whitstable, Kent			400		100
Sevenoaks, Kent			900	1,300	
Liverpool, Lancs			700	2,000	
Prescot, Lancs				400 (1592)	
Tamworth, Staffs			475		1,535
Nuneaton, Warws			893		1,320
Atherstone, Warws			498		1,292

Welsh towns

Carmarthen (c. 2,150)	Dolgellau (1,000)
Brecon (1,500+)	Kidwelly (1,000)
Wrexham (1,500 +)	Monmouth (1,000)
Haverford West (1,500 +)	Swansea (1,000)
Caernarvon (1,000)	Tenby (1,000)
Cardiff (1,000)	

Data extracted from Joan Thirsk (ed.), *The Agrarian History of England and Wales*, Vol. IV, Cambridge, 1967.

In the 1540s, 11 per cent of the population was urban.

12.1

BIOGRAPHIES

Monarchs and their consorts

Biographies of monarchs and their spouses have been separated out for convenience and have been listed under their first names. There are a few exceptions, for example, Earl of Bothwell and Lord Guildford Dudley appear in Section 12.2: Biographical index. The biographies of monarchs are not comprehensive and the reader should consult Chapter 1: General chronology for details of their reigns.

ANNE BOLEYN (Bullen) (Queen) (?1500–36): 2nd w. of Henry VIII & mother of Elizabeth I; Patron of Hans Holbein the younger & of English & French humanist & evangelical scholars; 2nd dau. of **Thomas Bullen (Boleyn)**, later Earl of Ormonde & Wiltshire (q.v.), & a descendant of Edward I; summer 1513: lady-in-waiting to Margaret of Austria in Brussels; Aug. 1513: transferred to court of Mary (Tudor) Queen of France; Apr. 1515: transferred to service of Queen Claude of France; late 1521: returned to Eng.; admirers incl. Henry Percy & **Thomas Wyatt** (q.v.); Aug. 1526: King publicly showed her favour; 1527: King decl. intent to m.; 1529: she schemed to overthrow Wolsey; Sept. 1532: cr. Marquis (Marchioness in own right) of Pembroke; (?25) Jan. 1533: m. Henry VIII; 12 Apr. 1533: recognised as Queen; 1 June 1533: coronation; 7 Sept. 1533: b. of Elizabeth; Aug. 1534: miscarried boy; autumn 1535: 3rd pregnancy; 29 Jan. 1536: miscarried; 18 Apr. 1536: King tried to persuade Chas V to recognise Anne as Queen; split betw. Anne & Cromwell over **dissolution** of smaller monasteries & her standing in the way of rapprochement w. the emp. spelled her downfall; 30 Apr.: arrest of Mark Smeaton; 2 May 1536: Anne & Rochford (**Boleyn, George** q.v.) impr.; 12 May 1536: trial of Smeaton, etc.; 15 May 1536: trial of Anne & Rochford; 17 May 1536: Cranmer decl. m. null & void; 19 May 1536: executed on charges of tr. & adultery. Her m. to Henry was the occasion for the English Reformation. Debate about her sympathy w. the Protestant cause. Maria Dowling, *Humanism in the Age of Henry VIII*, 1986; Eric Ives, *Anne Boleyn*, 1986.

ANNE OF CLEVES (Queen) (1515–57): 4th w. of Henry VIII; dau. of John, Duke of Cleves. **Thomas Cromwell** (q.v.) arranged m. to form strategic alliance v. the Emp. Charles V & Francis I of France; Henry VIII averse to the match; June 1540: Cromwell arrested & executed; 9 July 1540: m. to Anne annulled; Anne was pensioned off in Lewes, Sussex & given the title of King's 'sister'!

EDWARD IV (King) (1442–83): House of York. His eldest dau. **Elizabeth** (q.v.) m. Henry VII; his 2nd dau. **Cecily** (q.v.) m. Viscount Welles, half-brother of Margaret Beaufort, the King's mother.

EDWARD V (King) (1470–83): House of York. 1470: s. & h. of Edward IV & Elizabeth (Woodville); 1471: Prince of Wales; 1471: entrusted to council of control incl. uncles Clarence & Gloucester; 1483: succeeded his father & escorted to London by uncle Richard of Gloucester; impr. in Tower w. younger brother Richard, Duke of York; deposed; supposedly murdered in Tower by James Tyrrell.

EDWARD VI (King) (1537–53): House of Tudor. Well-educated s. & h. of Henry VIII & **Jane Seymour** (q.v.); 12 Oct. 1537: b. at Hampton Court; contrary to popular myth was not a sickly child although he caught malaria in 1541; July 1543: briefly betrothed to **Mary Queen of Scots**; drawn into household of Queen **Katherine Parr**, who organised his early education, adding Protestant humanists Sir **John Cheke, Roger Ascham** & **Anthony Co(o)ke** to **Richard Cox** (all q.v.) as his tutors & assistant tutors; 28 Jan. 1547: succeeded Henry VIII; 31 Jan. 1547: Somerset made Protector of the kingdom & governor of the King's person; 19 Feb. 1547: pageants praise Henry VIII's religious reformation & project the crown's imperial status; 20 Feb. 1547: crowned; coronation oath modified to make royal supremacy the bulwark of monarchy & to signal intention to reform Church further; during his minority was manipulated by **Edward Seymour**, Duke of Somerset (maternal uncle & Protector of England) (q.v.), **Thomas Seymour**, Baron Sudeley, Somerset's brother (q.v.) & **John Dudley, Duke of Northumberland** (q.v.); seen by **Cranmer** (q.v.), **Latimer** (q.v.) & others as a second Josias sent to reform religion; 1549: rebellions were crisis of the reign & led to increased security at court, beginnings of standing army & downfall of Somerset; classical humanist education based on Cheke's curriculum for St John's College, Cambridge; a Renaissance theoretical education made to serve statecraft; balanced by religious education & thorough knowledge of the scriptures; 1550–53: **John Dudley**, Earl of Warwick (later Duke of Northumberland) (q.v.) supplanted Somerset but the secret of his success was that

he saw Edward as a force with which to reckon & he strove to carry Edward with him; Edward had decided opinions on gov't & religion (shown, for example, in his refusal to back down in 1551 & allow the Princess Mary to hear Mass, regardless of the political & diplomatic repercussions); a real sense in which the reformation of the 1550s was a 'King's reformation'; 1553: in the 'Devyse' for the succession settled succession on his cousin Jane (Grey) Dudley (q.v. **Grey (Lady) Jane**) of his own volition, albeit possibly with Northumberland's intervention; 6 July 1553: died of tuberculosis. W. K. Jordan, *Edward VI, 1: The Young King*, 1968; W. K. Jordan, *Edward VI, 2: The Threshold of Power*, 1970; Jennifer Loach, *Edward VI*, G. Bernard and P. Williams (eds), 1999; D. Hoak, *The Reign of Edward VI* (forthcoming); H. Chapman, *The Last Tudor King: A Study of Edward VI*, 1961.

ELIZABETH I (Queen) (1533–1603): Tudor; 2nd dau. of Henry VIII and dau. of Queen Anne Boleyn; b. 7 Sept. 1533 at Greenwich Palace; 10 Sept.: baptised & decl'd heiress presumptive to throne; under care of Lady Margaret Bryan, provided w. household at Hatfield when only three months old; 1534: household moved to Eltham, Kent; 1536: Parliament declares her illegitimate to secure succession for heirs of Henry and Jane Seymour; 1537–47: Lady Blanche Herbert of Troy became head of Elizabeth's household; 1544: Eliz. rest. by Succession Act to her place in the succession, albeit still illegitimate; mid-1540s: Katherine Champernowne, aka **Kate Ashley** (q.v.) or Astley, became influential in Eliz's household; 1547–49: **Thomas Seymour** (q.v.) Lord High Admiral and uncle to Edward VI, pursues her hand in m.; tutored first by Ashley, then by **William Grindal** (d. Jan. 1548) and in 1549: classical edu. by **Roger Ascham**; by 1543 was also learning French (from **Jean Belmaine**) and Italian (from Castiglione); became an accomplished musician, playing spinet & lute & composing; 1545: gave Katherine Parr *The Glasse of the Synnefull Soule*, her English transl. of *Miroir de l'ame pechereuse* by Marguerite d'Angoulême, queen of Navarre;

ideas of a Fr. m. for Elizabeth probably explain the emphasis upon proficiency in this language above all others; 1551: presented Edward VI w. her portrait; 1553: accompanied Queen Mary, half-sister, on triumphal route to London; refused complicity in Wyatt's rebellion; 1554: thrown into Tower due to Stephen Gardiner's influence; 1554: released to Woodstock Palace, Oxon., and declined to conspire v. Mary; 17 Nov. 1558: succeeded to throne; 1559: crowned by Bishop of Carlisle, declined m. with Philip II, her sister's widower; henceforth seen by Protestants as the divinely destined leader of a Protestant nation in God's plan for religious reformation; it seems that she played this part when it suited her but not ardently enough for many of her chief advisers. Probably an 'evangelical' in religion of the type espoused by stepmother Katherine Parr. Patrick Collinson describes Eliz. as 'if not some kind of Protestant, no kind of Catholic, since she was the product of England's breach with Rome'; need to see beyond Protestant propaganda of the reign to the real Elizabeth. Important developments: m. negotiations; church organisation: battle between radical Protestants and the 'establishment'; Spanish threat; problem of Ireland; issue of Mary Queen of Scots; conspiracies. Elizabeth d. at Richmond, 24 Mar. 1603 – on deathbed declared succession in favour of James VI of Scotland, s. of Mary Stuart. See Chapter 1: General chronology for main events of her reign. Wallace T. MacCaffrey, *Elizabeth I*, 1993.

ELIZABETH OF YORK (Queen) (1465–1503): eldest dau. of Edward IV and Elizabeth Woodville; 1486: m. Henry Tudor (negotiations had begun while he was in exile and she is reputed to have won over Earl Stanley to his cause); 1487: coronation after suppression of Lincoln's rebellion; 1487: received her mother's forfeited lands in Duchy of Lancaster; d. 1503 after d. of Arthur, her elder s. Nancy L. Harvey, *Elizabeth of York, the Mother of Henry VIII*, New York, 1973.

HENRY VII (King) (1457–1509): Tudor; s. of Edmund Tudor, Earl of Richmond, and Margaret Beaufort, heir to John of Gaunt.

Raised by uncle Jasper Tudor in Wales; 1471: head of House of Lancaster; refugee in Brittany; 1485: defeated and killed Richard III at Bosworth; 1486: m. Elizabeth, dau. of Edward IV, see Chapter 1: General chronology for further details of reign. S.B. Chrimes, *Henry VII*, 1977.

HENRY VIII (King) (1491–1547): Tudor; athletic, linguistically gifted and well-read 2nd s. of Henry VII and Elizabeth of York. King of England and Ireland. Architect of the break with Rome and the Church of England. 28 June 1491: b. at Greenwich; 31 Oct. 1494: cr. Duke of York; 14 Nov. 1501: led wedding procession of his brother Prince Arthur & Katherine of Aragon; 2 Apr. 1502: became heir to throne on d. of Prince Arthur; Oct. 1502: cr. Duke of Cornwall; Feb. 1503: cr. Prince of Wales & Earl of Chester; edu. initially by poet **John Skelton**; humanist edu. probable; strained relations w. his father Henry VII rumoured; 11 June 1509: m. Katherine of Aragon; 24 June 1509: joint coronation of Henry & Katherine; 1 Jan. 1511: Prince Henry b. but died shortly afterwards; 1509–14: **conciliar government**; Henry obsessed w. European reputation; 1513: personally led army into Low Countries; triumphed at Battle of the Spurs; emergence of socially and politically influential Privy Chamber; 1515: Henry org'd Royal Armouries at Greenwich; 1514–26: ascendancy of Thomas Wolsey as principal minister – Henry consulted on important matters but freed from the routine of government; 1516: Princess Mary b.; 1518–19: took **Elizabeth Blount**, one of Katherine's ladies, as mistress; 1519: Katherine of Aragon examined for fertility; 1519: b. of Henry Fitzroy, illegit. s.; May 1520: Charles V visited London; June 1520: Henry VIII met François I at Field of Cloth of Gold; early 1520s: took Mary Boleyn as mistress; 1524: ceased to have conjugal rel'ns w. Katherine; early 1526: began pursuit of Anne Boleyn; May 1527: raised idea of annulment of m. w. Katherine; Aug. 1527: applied to Pope for annulment; 1527–29: Wolsey failed to secure divorce & fell from power; 29 Nov. 1530: Wolsey d.; June 1530: put pressure on Eng.

church in order to bring papacy round; late 1530–33: incr. assertive in 'Great Matter'; 1531–: emergence of Thomas Cromwell as new minister; 1 Sept. 1532: cr. Anne Boleyn Marchioness of Pembroke; c. Oct. 1532: took Anne as mistress; c. 25 Jan. 1533: m. Anne; 23 May 1533: Cranmer pronounced m. to Katherine null & void; 7 Sept. 1533: b. of Elizabeth; summer 1534: Anne miscarried; 8 Jan. 1536: Katherine d.; 29 Jan. 1536: Anne miscarried a boy; 19 May 1536: execution of Anne; 30 May 1536: m. Jane Seymour; July 1536: Fitzroy d.; 1536: challenge to kingship by Pilgrimage of Grace; Sept. 1537: Edward b.; 24 Oct. 1537: Jane d.; 6 Jan. 1537: m. Anne of Cleves; July 1540: divorced Anne of Cleves; 28 July 1540: m. Katherine Howard & Cromwell exec.; June 1541: royal progress via Lincoln to York; 2 Nov.: King told of Katherine's adultery, etc.; 13 Feb. 1542: Katherine exec.; 12 July 1543: m. Katherine Parr. widow; 30 Dec. 1546: revised will & named the regency council & established succession w. Edward as heir & Mary & Elizabeth thereafter; placed the Grey & Clifford descendants of his sister Mary next in line; 28 Jan. 1547: d. at Whitehall; 16 Feb. 1547: bur. next to Jane Seymour at Windsor. See Chapter 1: General chronology for milestones in reign. J.J. Scarisbrick, *Henry VIII*, 1968.

JAMES III (1451–88) (King of Scotland, 1460–88): he was very unpopular in Scotland because of his blatant favouritism. In 1482, his own brother Albany joined the English army of invasion which retook Berwick. On this occasion his troops mutinied and brought the favourite, Robert Cochrane, to justice. In 1488, there was a fresh rebellion by the lowland nobility (especially the Earl of Angus) led by his eldest s. (soon to be James IV) who defeated and killed him at Sauchieburn.

JAMES IV (1473–1513) (King of Scotland, 1488–1513): he had led the army which defeated and murdered his father, **James III** (q.v.). Although he did penance for his father's death, James IV revoked grants made by James III and crushed the rebellion of Lennox, Lyle and Forbes in 1489; defended

Eastern coast v. English piracy and improved the Scottish navy; 1495: received Perkin Warbeck and m. him to Lady Katherine Gordon; 1496–97: helped Warbeck with border raids but treated with the Spanish and French who wished to end his alliance with Warbeck; 1502: signed seven-year truce with England which provided for his m. to Princess Margaret Tudor, elder dau. of Henry VII of England; 1503: m. Margaret; important as a king who reformed Scottish legal system; against internal opposition, supported alliance with England until Henry VII's death; 1511: allied with Louis XII of France against the Holy League; 1512: signed treaty with France; 1512: sent Scottish fleet to assist Louis XII v. Henry VIII; invaded Northumberland; 1513: killed at Battle of Flodden Field.

JAMES V (1512–42) (King of Scotland, 1513–42): s. of James IV and Margaret Tudor; educated by Gavin Dunbar, John Bellenden, David Lindsay and James Inglis; 1524: he was taken to Edinburgh by his mother and proclaimed fit to rule; 1525–28: under control of the Earl of Angus; 1528: escaped and forced Angus to flee to England; in an alliance with clergy and commons crushed the nobility; conducted border raids until peace with England in 1534; 1 Jan. 1537: m. Madeleine of France, dau. of Francis I; 7 July 1537: d. of Madeleine; executed Angus family conspirators; 1538: m. Mary of Guise; persecuted heretics and remained Catholic but forced Church to accept reforms; 1540: forced Western Isles into submission; 1541: refused Henry VIII's request for conference; 1542: b. of dau., Mary, later Queen of Scotland; seized lands of Crawfords, Douglasses, etc.; 1542: d. just after hearing of rout at Solway. James V was also the father of at least two illegitimate children – Regent Moray and Francis 5th Earl of Bothwell.

JAMES VI (1566–1625) (King of Scotland, 1567–1625) and King of England (1603–25): only child of Mary of Scotland and Henry, Lord Darnley; 1567: crowned king on his mother's forced abdication; educated by George Buchanan; spent childhood and youth under the influence of various of the nobility: 1578–82: Esmé Stuart, Earl of Lennox; 1582–83: Protestant nobles; 1583–84: Earls of Argyll and Huntly; 1585–86: Earl of Arran; 1586: concluded Treaty of Berwick with England; 1587: reconciled himself to his mother's execution in Feb. because she had disinherited him in favour of Philip II; 1589: m. Anne of Denmark; 1596: annulled the bishops' jurisdiction; recalled Northern Earls from banishment; relations with the clergy strained during the 1590s; 1600: Gowrie conspiracy foiled; 1603: became King of England; 1604: made peace with Spain; 1604: called Hampton Court Conference to discuss liturgy; 1604: banished Catholic priests; 1605: Gunpowder Plot; 1606: harsh Recusancy Laws introduced; wished and worked for formal union of England and Scotland, etc.

JANE GREY (Lady, Later Queen) (1537–54): eldest dau. of Henry Grey, Duke of Suffolk, and Frances Brandon, elder dau. of Henry VIII's sister Mary, and, under Henry VIII's will, heir to the throne after Henry VIII's own children; 1546: placed in household of Katherine Parr; humanist classical education; 1548: Jane put into household of Edward Seymour who projected her m. to Edward VI; 1551: Jane's father made Duke of Suffolk for part in overthrow of the Seymours; 21 May 1553: m. Sir Guildford Dudley as part of Northumberland's plot to disinherit Mary in favour of Dudley family; 1553: reluctantly agreed to be proclaimed Queen; reign of c. 9 days; abdicated; not executed until after Wyatt's rebellion in 1554. Alison Plowden, *Lady Jane Grey and the House of Suffolk*, 1985.

JANE SEYMOUR (Lady, later Queen) (1508/9–37): 3rd Queen of Henry VIII and mother of Edward VI; 1508/09: b. eldest of ten children of Sir John Seymour & Margery (Wentworth) Seymour of Wolf Hall, Wiltshire; claimed descent from Edward III through her mother; sister of **Edward**

Seymour, later Duke of Somerset (q.v.) & **Thomas**, Baron Seymour of Sudeley (q.v.); 1529: first appeared at court as lady-in-waiting to **Katherine of Aragon** (q.v.); Oct. 1534: probably already in favour w. Henry; Sept. 1535: Henry VIII visited Wolf Hall; early 1536: Henry showered her w. gifts but she refused money; 19 May 1536: Cranmer issued dispensation (because of their kinship as 5th cousins) to allow Henry to m. Jane; 30 May 1536: m. Henry 11 days after Anne Boleyn's execution; July 1536: Act of Succession incl. her issue; preferment of her siblings; 12 Oct. 1537: b. of Edward after difficult labour; 15 Oct.: Edward was baptised & Jane received guests; 17 Oct.: Jane received the last rites; 24 Oct: received sacrament of extreme unction; probably d. same day of puerperal fever; 12 Nov. 1536: buried at Windsor. P. M. Gross, *Jane, the Quene: Third Consort of King Henry VIII*, 1999; D. Loades, *Henry VIII and his Queens*, 1997.

KATHERINE (CATHERINE, KATHARINE) OF ARAGON (Princess, later Queen of England) (1485–1536): first w. of Henry VIII. Youngest child of Ferdinand of Aragon & Isabella of Castile; 1501: m. Prince Arthur, heir to English throne; 1502: Arthur d., m. unconsummated; 1509: m. Henry; 24 June 1509: Henry & Katherine crowned King & Queen; 1510–18: six children of whom only Mary, later **Mary I** (q.v.) survived; 1527: King announced intention to divorce her & m. Anne Boleyn; July 1531: Henry left Katherine; Easter 1533: **Archbp Cranmer** (q.v.) pronounced the m. null & void & declared that m. w. **Anne Boleyn** (q.v.) was valid; 7 Jan. 1536: d. Thought to have been scholar & shrewd diplomatist. Antonia Fraser, *Six Wives of Henry VIII*, 1993.

KATHARINE HOWARD (Lady) (later Queen of England) (c. 1524–42): 5th Queen of Henry VIII. c. 1524: b. dau. of Lord Edmund Howard & Joyce or Jocasta (née Culpeper, Legh) wid.; raised by her paternal stepgrandmother, Agnes Tilney, Duchess of Norfolk in Horsham & Lambeth; traditional edu.; c. 1536: abused by music teacher, Henry

Manox; 1538: sexual relationship w. Francis Dereham, of the Duchess's household; late 1539: Katharine app'd maid of honour to Anne of Cleves & Dereham left for Ireland; 19 Dec. 1539: Henry VIII met Katharine; 1540: present at celebrations for Anne of Cleves; Apr.–June 1540: King paid court to Katharine; 28 July 1540: m. Henry at Oatlands, Surrey; 8 Aug. 1540: Katharine proclaimed Queen; app'd friends to household; Dec.–Feb. 1540-1: dispute w. Princess Mary; Mar. 1541: she interceded successfully on behalf of **Thomas Wyatt** (q.v.); Mar. 1541: Dereham returned to court & boasted of her favour; a kinsman, Thomas Culpeper, gentleman of the privy chamber w. a reputation for rape, made suit to her; Mar.–Sept. 1541: Katharine & Culpeper met in her chamber on several occasions (at meetings facilitated by Jane Lady Rochford & Katherine Tilney) but several interpretations of her behaviour are possible – passion, or fear & appeasement; Oct. 1541: Cranmer hears allegations about Katharine's premarital affairs; 2 Nov. 1541: King was informed; 6 Nov. 1541: Henry left Katharine & never saw her again; Katharine under house arrest & interrogated; she confessed but protested that relations w. Dereham had ended when she m. Henry; Dereham implicated Culpeper; 11 Nov. 1541: Katharine admitted meeting Culpeper but denied relationship; Lady Rochford accused Katharine; King distressed; 14 Nov. 1541: moved to Syon House; 22 Nov. 1541: depr. of Queen's status; 10 Dec. 1541: Culpeper beheaded at Tyburn for tr.; Dereham executed; impr. & eventual pardon of dowager Duchess of Norfolk & others attendant on Katharine; 21 Jan. 1541/42: bill of attainder introduced into Lords for execution of Katharine & Lady Rochford; 10 Feb. 1541/42: Katharine impr. in Tower; 11 Feb. 1541/42: bill received royal assent; 13 Feb. 1541/42: execution of Katharine & Lady Rochford; buried in the Tower chapel.

KATHERINE PARR (Queen) (also spelled Catherine, Catharine) (1512–48): Protestant 6th Queen of Henry VIII. Well-educated & independent-minded patron of the arts, drama & music, reformers and humanists. Aug. 1512: 2nd child of courtiers Sir Thomas & Lady Maud (Green) Parr of Kendal; edu. at home & fluent in French, Latin & Italian; May 1529: m. (i) Edward Borough, 3rd Baron Borough of Gainsborough; early 1533: widowed; summer 1534: m. (ii) widower John Neville, 3rd Baron Latimer of Snape Castle, Yorks; Jan. 1537: Katherine & her step-children taken hostage by Pilgrims of Grace; winter 1542: Katherine app'd lady-in-waiting to Princess Mary; 2 Mar. 1543: Latimer d.; Katherine hoped to m. Thomas Seymour, Queen's brother; 12 July 1543: m. Henry VIII; friendship w. King's children; 25 Apr. 1544: anon. pub'd her transl. of Fisher's *Psalmis seu precationes*; summer 1544: Katherine app'd regent in Henry's absence in France; reinstated Elizabeth at court; Feb. 1545: unsuccessfully schemed for new alliance w. protestant princes of the Schmalkaldic league; 29 May 1545: pub'n of her *Prayers or Meditations*; Feb. 1546: Stephen Gardiner led plot v. her, seeking to frame her as a heretic; 16 July 1546: Anne Askew went to stake without implicating Katherine; news of warrant for Katherine's arrest drove Katherine into frenzy of terror and led her to fall upon the King's mercy; Aug. 1546: went on progress w. King; 28 Jan. 1547: Henry d.; 31 Jan. 1547: Hertford excluded her from the regency council; Queen Mother took Thomas Seymour as lover; May 1547: m. Thomas Seymour; alienated Edward VI; app'd guardian of Princess Elizabeth; scandal of Seymour's dalliance w. Elizabeth; 5 Nov.: pub'd Lutheran *The Lamentation of a Sinner*; Dec. 1547: Katherine pregnant; 30 Aug. 1548: b. of Mary; 5 Sept. 1548: Katherine d. S.E. James, *Kateryn Parr: The Making of a Queen*, 1999.

MARGARET TUDOR (Princess, later Queen (Consort) & Regent of Scotland) (1489–1541). 28 Nov. 1489: b. at Westminster, eldest dau. & 2nd child of Henry VII & Elizabeth of York; tutored by Thos Linacre, John Colet and William Grocyn; 24 Jan. 1502: m. Tr. agreed w. James IV of Scotland; 15 Jan. 1503: proxy m.; 8 July 1503 to early

Aug. 1503: progressed to Scotland; 8 Aug.: m. James IV; 1507: b. of James; 27 Feb. 1508: Prince James d.; 15 July 1508: b. & d. of dau.; 11 Apr. 1512: b. of Prince James; 9 Sept. 1513: James IV killed at Flodden; Margaret became Regent; 6 Aug. 1514: Margaret m. Archibald Douglas, 6th Earl of Angus & forfeited the Regency; 18 May 1515: James Stuart, 2nd Duke of Albany, became Regent; 30 Apr. 1514: b. of Alexander, Duke of Ross; Henry VIII's attempts to gain control of Princes James and Alexander led to their removal from her care; 30 Sept. 1515: Margaret fled to Northumberland; 7 Oct. 1515: b. of **Margaret Douglas** (q.v.); 18 Dec.: Duke of Ross d.; 3 May 1516: Margaret joined Henry VIII in London; Albany returned to France; 16 June 1517: Margaret returned to Scotland but soon separated from Angus; despite her efforts, she lacked influence and was excluded from the Council of Regency; 26 July 1524: King James V vested w. full royal authority & Margaret resumed regency in Nov. 1524; Margaret began affair w. Henry Stewart; 1525–28: Angus took control of James V; Margaret attempted to obtain divorce; 11 Mar. 1527: Clement VII annulled her m. to Angus; Margaret secretly m. Henry Stewart; Apr. 1528: Margaret acknowledged Stewart as her husb.; Stewart cr. Earl of Methven; May 1528: James V escaped Angus; Sept. 1528: Parl. sentenced Angus & others to d. for tr.; Angus escaped to England; Marg. hoped for Anglo-Scottish alliance but her wishes were disregarded by James V, who favoured France; 1536: pleaded w. Henry VIII for Lady Margaret Douglas, who had displeased him by m. Lord Thomas Howard; 1 Jan. 1537: James m. Madeleine of France; 7 July 1537: Madeleine d.; 1538: James m. Mary of Guise; May 1541: Margaret at Scottish ct when James' infant twin sons d.; 18 Oct. 1541: d. of a stroke at Methven Castle. Maria Perry, *Sisters to the King* (1998).

MARY STUART (Mary, Queen of Scots) (1542–87): 3rd but only surviving child of James V and Mary of Guise; Queen in 1542; 1548–61: raised in France as Catholic; 1558: m. Francis II; 1560: d. of Francis; 1561: returned to Scotland. For remainder of life see Chapter 1: General chronology.

MARY TUDOR (Queen of France) (1496–1533): younger dau. of Henry VII and Elizabeth of York; 1508–14: contracted to m. Charles of Castile (later Emperor Charles V); 1514: m. Louis XII of France; 1515: m. Charles Brandon, Duke of Suffolk, to Henry's annoyance; 1516: gave birth to s.; 1520: visited Field of Cloth of Gold; 1532: refused to accompany Henry and Anne Boleyn to meet Francis I; one of her daus, Frances Brandon, was the mother of Lady Jane Grey. W.C. Richardson, *Mary Tudor, The White Queen*, 1970; Maria Perry, *Sisters to the King*, 1998.

MARY I (Queen) (1516–58): Tudor; 3rd but only surviving child of Henry VIII and Katherine of Aragon; humanist classical education; 1525: made Princess of Wales at Ludlow; 1533: declared illegit. and placed in care of Lady Shelton at Hatfield; 1536: reconciled to Henry on Anne's d.; 1537: chief mourner at Jane Seymour's funeral; 1544: declared capable of inheriting crown after Henry's legit. heirs. For remaining events see Chapter 1: General chronology. David Loades, *Mary Tudor: A Life*, 1989.

PHILIP II (King of Spain and Consort of Queen Mary I) (1527–98): 1554: m. Mary at Winchester Cathedral; KG and advised Mary to pardon Elizabeth; 1555: left England for Spain; 1557: returned to England to encourage support for Spain in Low Countries; 1558: overtures to m. Elizabeth but m. Isabella, dau. of King of France; 1588: sent Armada v. England.

RICHARD III (Duke of Gloucester, later King of England) (1452–85): York; younger brother of Edward IV. Predeceased by infant male offspring. Defeated and slain by Henry Tudor at Bosworth Field, 1485.

12.2

BIOGRAPHIES

Biographical index

A

ALENÇON (Duke of) Francis (1554–84): youngest s. of Henry II & Catherine de Medici & brother of Francis II, Charles IX & Henry III of France; nego. for his m. w. Elizabeth I 1572–6 & 1578–84. 1574: became Duke of **Anjou** in the stead of his brother **Henri**, who took the Crown of Poland (q.v.); normally referred to as Alençon to distinguish him from this brother; October 1578: became Protector of the Netherlands; Elizabeth initially seemed serious about the match but, by 1579, she no longer wanted it; 1580: courtship revived as a diplomatic ploy to retain a French alliance.

ALLEN (Cardinal) William (1532–94): Oxf.-edu., uncompromisingly Catholic pr. whose promising career was cut short by Elizabeth's accession. 1561: exiled in Louvain; 1562: returned to Lancashire & concentrated on bringing lapsed Catholics back to the faith; 1565: forced to seek safety in household of Duke of Norfolk but fled to Netherlands later that year, never to return; 1568: founded English College at Douai to train missionary pr. & edu. s. of Eng. Catholic gentry; 1578: English College moved to Rheims; intrigued v. Elizabeth; 1589: played large part in revision of Vulgate (Latin Bible); was involved

in production of the Douai Bible but d. before its completion.

ANDRÉ (of Toulouse), Bernard (fl. 1509): royal poet & historiographer & tutor to Prince Arthur Tudor, eldest son of Henry VII & Elizabeth of York.

ANGER Jane: famous for participation in a gender debate organised by printer Thomas Orwin; 1589: *Jane Anger; her protection for women to defend them against the scandalous reports of a late surfeiting lover, and all other like Venerians that claime so to be overcloyed with women's kindness*. The name is assumed to have been a pseudonym.

ANJOU (Duke of), Henri (1551–89): 2nd s. of Catherine de Medici & Henry II & brother of Francis II, Charles IX & Francis Duke of **Alençon** (q.v.); m. w. Elizabeth I proposed in 1570; courtship served to keep France friendly during **Ridolfi** plot crisis; not to be confused w. his younger brother Francis Duke of Alençon & Anjou.

ANNE OF CLEVES (Queen) (1515–57) (see Section 12.1: Monarchs and their consorts).

ARTHUR (Prince of Wales) Tudor (1486–1502): elder s. of Henry VII & h.w. Elizabeth of York. 19 Sept. 1486: b. at Winchester; 24 Sept. 1486: baptised & named after King Arthur; 1487: household at Farnham headed by Dame Elizabeth Darcy; 29 Nov. 1489: cr.

Knight of the Bath, Prince of Wales & Earl of Chester; c. 1491: formal edu. began under John Rede, formerly headmaster of Winchester College, & then under **Bernard André** & Thomas Linacre; May 1490: Warden of the Marches towards Scotland, w. Thomas Howard, Earl of Surrey as his deputy; Mar. 1490: Council of Wales formed under headship of Jasper Tudor; Mar. 1493: Arthur granted power to app. Justices of oyer & terminer, etc.; Nov. 1493: Arthur granted lands of Earldom of March; 27 Mar. 1489: Tr. of Medina del Campo provided for his m. to Katherine of Aragon as soon as the two reached canonical age; 1497: proxy betrothal; 1499: proxy m.; 1500: 2nd proxy m.; c. 1 Nov. 1501: triumphal entry of Arthur & Katherine into London; 14 Nov. 1501: Arthur m. Katherine at St Paul's; Dec. 1501: set up household at Ludlow; debate concerning con-summation of the m.; 2 Apr. 1502: Arthur d. at Ludlow; 5 Apr.: King informed of his d.; b. at Worcester Cathedral.

ARUNDEL Mary (née) (?1512–57) (m. names Radcliffe or Ratcliffe & Fitzalan): Countess of Sussex & Countess of Arundel; courtier. c. 1512: b. youngest dau. of Sir John Arundell & 2nd w. Katherine (Grenville) of Cornwall; 1536: served Jane Seymour; 1539: served Anne of Cleves; served Princess Mary; 1537: m. (i) Robert Radcliffe, Earl of Sussex as his 3rd w.; one surviving s.; 1542: Robert Radcliffe d.; 1545: m. (ii) Henry Fitzalan, Earl of Arundel, as his 2nd w.; translations from the Latin previously attributed to her were in fact produced by her stepdau. Lady Mary (Fitzalan) **Howard** (q.v.) (*The Sayings and Doings of the Emperor Severus & Select Sentences of the Seven Wise Men of Greece*) (not to be confused with this step-dau. Howard (née Fitzalan) Lady Mary (1539/40–57) (q.v.) who was dau. of her hus-band's 1st wife, **Katherine Grey** (q.v.)); 20/21 Oct. 1557: d.

ASCHAM Roger (1514/15–68): Cambr.-edu. humanist educator, royal tutor & pioneer of English as a literary language. 1514/15: b. at Kirby Wise, 3rd s. of John, steward to Henry,

7th Lord Scrope of Bolton, & Margaret (Conyers) Ascham; classical edu: (i) Kirby Wise (ii) household of Humphrey Wingfield (iii) from 1530: St John's College, Cambr.; came under infl. of **John Cheke** (q.v.); 18 Feb. 1534: B.A.; Fellow of St John's; 3 July 1537: M.A.; 1538: Reader in Greek at St John's College, Cambr.; early 1540s: embroiled in debate concerning new pronun-ciation of Greek; 1544: rejected app'ments as tutor to children of Lord Mountjoy and grandchildren of Sir Thomas More; passed over for Regius chair at Cambr.; 1545: *Toxophilus*, an English dialogue on archery which he dedicated to Henry VIII; granted royal pension; 1546–54: Public Orator at Cambr.; 1547/48: involved in relig. controv. in St John's & penned ms treatise 'Apologia . . . pro caena Dominica' & conservative Protestant 'Themata theologica'; 1548: tutor to Princess Elizabeth (at her request); Sept. 1550: secretary to Sir **Richard Morison**, ambassador to the court of the emperor Charles V in Sept. 1550; friendship with Charles V's physician, Vesalius, & Hieronymus Wolf the humanist; 1553: Latin secretary to Mary I; also wrote letters for other eminent persons such as Paget; June 1554: m. Margaret (Harleston) Howe of South Ockenden, Essex, dau. of Sir Clement Harleston; 4 s. & 3 daus; maintained connection w. Eliz. during Mary's reign; 1558: Latin secretary to Elizabeth; 1563: MP for Preston, Lancs; impoverished; 30 Dec. 1568: d.; 1570: *The Scholemaster*, written in later life & posthumously published, thanks to his wife – in this, Ascham advocated the use of gentle persuasion, rather than force, by the teacher.

ASKE Robert (1500–37): lawyer; leader of Pilgrimage of Grace that began at Louth, Lincs in Oct. 1500: b. 3rd s. of Sir Robert Aske, Yorks landowner, & h.w. Elizabeth (Clifford); adm. Gray's Inn; 1527: in service of Northumberland; never m.; 5 Oct. 1536: accidentally involved in Louth rising; 1536: Aske was manipulated by Henry VIII to qui-eten this rebellion & that of Sir **Francis Bigod** (q.v.); Dec. 1536: agreed to disband pilgrimage in exchange for promise of a parliament; May 1537: Aske impr. in London & 12 July exec. at York by hanging in chains.

ASKEW Anne (née Kyme) (1521–46): well-edu. & pious dau. of a Lincs. gentleman; 1521: b. 2nd dau. of Sir William Askew & h. 1st w. Elizabeth (Wrottesley) at Stallingborough nr. Grimsby, Lincs; m. Thomas Kyme v. her will; two children; separated from husband; 1544: in London to apply for judicial separation from her husband; connections at court; 1546: arrested, examined & tortured for Protestant views on sacrament as part of court campaign v. Queen **Katherine Parr** (q.v.) by court conservatives; 28 June 1546: arraigned for heresy at Guildhall; 16 July 1546: burned at Smithfield.

ASTLEY (ASHLEY) (née Champernowne) (Lady) Katherine (?1520–65): sister of Lady **Joan Denny** (q.v.); governess of Princess Elizabeth & later woman-of-the-bedchamber to Queen Elizabeth; well-connected & influential because of close relationship w. Elizabeth. Relatively well-edu. for a woman of her class & commended for her learning. A Protestant infl. at court in early days of Elizabeth's reign. 1545: m. John Astley, gent., of Kent (s. of one of Elizabeth I's Norfolk cousins), who was later Elizabeth's Master of the Jewel House; 1547: app'd governess to Elizabeth; 1548: encouraged Elizabeth to consider m. Thomas Seymour, Lord Admiral v. Astley's advice; 1553–58: Marian exile; Jan. 1549: impr. in Tower after Seymour's fall, while Astley impr. in Fleet; incriminated Seymour; 1551: reinstated in Elizabeth's household; 1553: remained in Elizabeth's service at Mary's accession; 1556: suspected involvement in Dudley conspiracy led to impr. & dismissal; 1558: app'd chief gentlewoman of privy chamber & possessed much infl.; actively promoted rivalry for Elizabeth's hand in m.; 1562: impr. briefly for encouraging Erik XIV of Sweden; 1563–65: rest. to favour. N. Mears, 'Politics in the Elizabethan Privy Chamber: Lady Mary Sidney and Kat Ashley' in J. Daybell (ed.), *Women and Politics in Early Modern England, 1450–1700*, Aldershot, 2004, pp. 67–82.

AYLMER (also Elmer) (Bishop) John (1521–94): Cambr.-edu. tutor to Lady **Jane Grey** (q.v.) & Elizabethan Bp of London. 1521: b. (of unknown parentage); 1541: B.A. Cambr.; 1545: M.A. Cambr.; 1543: Prebend of Wells; tutor to daus of **Henry Grey**, Marquis of Dorset (q.v.); 1553: Archd. of Stow; Jan. 1554: implicated in Wyatt's rebellion; 17 Sept.: indicted for raising rebellion; c. Mar. 1554: m. unknown woman; by Sept. 1554: in Marian exile; 1562: Archd. of Lincoln; 1577: Bp of London; pub'd sermons & devotional works.

B

BABINGTON (Sir) Anthony (1561–86): leader of Eng. Catholics who was half-heartedly involved in the Babington Plot. Oct. 1561: b. at Dethick, Derbs, s. & h. of Henry Babington & h. 2nd w., Mary, dau. of George, Lord Darcy; 1579: page to Earl of Shrewsbury at Sheffield; 1579: m. Margery Draycot of Paynsley, Staffs; 1580: adm. Lincoln's Inn; 1580: in France, met Thomas Morgan, agent of **Mary Queen of Scots** (q.v.); in London at the Inns of Court he associated increasingly w. admirers of Mary & acted as channel of communication betw. French embassy & Mary & as assistant to Catholic missionary priests; late May 1586: heard of plot to replace Elizabeth by Mary & tried to escape abroad; divulged plot to Poley who, unbeknown to Babington, informed **Francis Walsingham** (q.v.); Walsingham penetrated but did not halt the communications betw. Mary & Morgan via Babington & foiled the plot; 18 July 1586: Mary sent letter to Babington approving murder of Elizabeth; Aug. 1586: arrested; 13/14 Sept.: trial of Babington & co-conspirators; 20 Sept. 1586: exec. at St Giles-in-the-Fields.

BACON Ann Co(o)ke (1528–1610): humanist scholar & translator. 1528: 2nd dau. & 3rd child of Sir **Anthony Co(o)ke** (q.v.) & Anne (FitzWilliam Hawes) Cooke; classical edu. at home; Feb. 1553: m. **Nicholas Bacon** (q.v.); lady of privy chamber to Mary I; 1558: Anthony Bacon b.; 1561: Francis Bacon b.; 1550: transl. sermons of Fra Bernardino Ochino from Italian into English (two ed'ns pub'd in 1550 & 1570); 1564: transl. Jewel's *Apology* from Latin into English; pub'd by Archbp **Matthew Parker** (q.v.) without her knowledge; he thought it would offend her modesty; 1579: widowed; thereafter an active Protestant patron. R.M. Warnicke, *Women of the English Renaissance and Reformation*, Westport, Conn., Greenwood Press, 1983.

BACON (Lord) Francis (1561–1626): First Baron Verulam & Viscount St Albans. 1561: b. 2nd s. of Sir **Nicholas** (q.v.) & Lady **Ann (Cooke) Bacon** (q.v.); edu. at Cambr. & Gray's Inn; 1576–79: attached to embassy in France; 1582: called to bar; 1584: M.P. Melcombe Regis; 1584: wrote *Letter of Advice to Queen Elizabeth* recommending stern anti-Catholic measures; 1586: M.P. Taunton & Bencher of Gray's Inn; 1589: M.P. Liverpool; 1593: M.P. Middlesex; 1596: QC; 1597: *Essays*; 1597: M.P. Southampton; 1601: Commissioner investigating Essex revolt & largely responsible for the Earl's conviction; M.P. St Albans; 1604: M.P. Ipswich; 1614: M.P. Cambr. Uni.; extremely prominent under James I, who made him Lord Chanc.; 1618: cr. Peer; he authored important philosophical, literary & legal works; apart from the *Essays*, these all appeared in the seventeenth century. Catherine D. Bowen, *Francis Bacon: The Temper of a Man*, Boston, 1963.

BACON (Sir) Nicholas (1510–79): Cambr.-edu. lawyer, M.P. & Protestant Lord Keeper of the Great Seal and influential patron under Elizabeth. 28 Dec. 1510: b. in Suffolk, 2nd s. of Robert Bacon, yeoman, & h.w. Isabel (Cage); early 1520s: Bury St Edmunds GS; 1523: adm. Corpus Christi College, Cambr.; 1527: B.A.; 1532: Gray's Inn; 1533: barrister; 1540: Solicitor of Court of Augmentations; 5

Apr. 1540: m. (i) Jane Ferneley; six surviving children; 1542: M.P. Westmoreland; 1545: M.P. Dartmouth; 1546: Nathaniel Bacon b. (see **Anne (Bacon) Townshend** (q.v.)); 1550: Bencher, Gray's Inn; 1552: Jane d.; 1552–56: Treasurer of Gray's Inn; by Feb. 1553: m. (ii) Lady **Ann (Co(o)ke) Bacon** (q.v.); 15 Dec. 1558: knighted; 1558: Lord Keeper of the Great Seal & head of Court of Chancery; Anthony b.; 1561: Francis b.; 1563–65: brief period of disgrace for supporting legitimacy of Katherine (Grey) Seymour; 1568: presided over conference to determine Mary Queen of Scots' complicity in murder of **Darnley**; oppo. Mary's claims to Eng. throne; 20 Feb. 1579: d.

BALE John (1495–1563): Cambr.-edu. Protestant dramatist & historian & Bp of Ossory; - known as prolific dramatic polemicist whose splenetic attacks on Catholicism earned him nickname 'bilious' Bale. Important as historian of the reform movement. 21 Nov. 1495: b. in humble circumstances at Cove, nr Dunwich, Suffolk; 1507: entered Carmelite convent, Norwich; 1514: student at Jesus College; 1529: B.Th.; 1530s: preached among northern Lollards; 1534: brought before **Archbp Lee** of York for heresy; c. 1536: left the Carmelite order & m. Dorothy; pr. who embraced Protestantism, renounced vows & m.; 1537: arrested for pr. heresy; freed partly by intercession of John Leland; Christmas 1538: play *King John* performed at Cranmer's house; 1538: composed *God's Promises*, a cycle of Protestant mystery plays to replace the Catholic versions; c. 1539: fled to exile; returned to Eng. after Edward's accession; Feb. 1553: consecrated at Dublin as Bp of Ossory; *The Vocacyon of Johan Bale*, one of the earliest Eng. autobiographical writings, gives a detailed narrative of Bp Bale's uncompromising evangelical episcopate & the conflict w. his flock that ensued; Sept. 1553: fled to Marian exile in Netherlands; he observed the similarities betw. English Protestantism & Lollardy & helped to establish a Protestant martyrology & a continuous & heroic evangelical history; friend of John Foxe. A.G.

Dickens, *Lollards and Protestants in the Diocese of York*, 1959; R. O'Day, *The Debate on the English Reformation*, 1986 & 2011.

BARLOW (Bishop) William (c. 1495–d. 1568): ?Oxf.-edu. Protestant bp, Marian exile & dynast. c. 1495: b. 2nd of four s. of John Barlow of Essex & h.w. Christian (Barley); 1511: ord. exorcist as a member of **Richard Fitzjames** (q.v.) household; by 1516, an Augustinian canon; 1516: ord. subdeac.; 1518: ord. deac. 1529: Wolsey prohibited his heretical tracts; 1531: *A Dialogue of . . . these Lutheran Factions and Many of their Abuses*; c. 1534: Prior of Haverfordwest, Pembrokeshire, through Anne Boleyn's patronage (his brother John was prominent in her household); 1535: exchanged for Priory of Bisham, Berks; by this time was fervent Protestant; 1535–36: embassies to Scotland to attempt conversion of King James V; 1536: briefly Bp of St Asaph; moved to see of St David's but no record of his consecr.; an evangelical reforming bp; alienated rich episcopal manor of Lamphey for poor compensation; signed Ten Articles; 1537: assisted writing 'The institution of a Christian man'; July 1537: surrendered priory of Bisham; 1539: oppo'd Six Articles; Jan. 1541: founded Brecon GS & Christ College (a college for preachers); 1540s: m. Agatha Wellesbourne; two s. & five daus; all five daus m. bps; 1548: Bp of Bath & Wells; May 1549: alienated rich episcopal manors, etc. to Duke of Somerset for little compensation; struck bargain w. Crown for advowsons & first fruits; 1553: resigned see; impr. in Tower but escaped to German exile in Emden, Wesel & finally to Poland (where he was part of the Duchess of Suffolk's household); 17 Dec. 1559: assisted in consecr. of **Matthew Parker** (q.v.) as Archbp of Canterbury; 1559: Bp of Chichester; 13 Aug. 1568: d. Glanmor Williams, *Welsh Reformation Essays*, 1967; R.B. Manning, *Religion and Society in Elizabethan Sussex*, 1969; Glanmor Williams, *Wales and the Reformation*, 1997.

BARNES Robert (1495–1540): martyr & religious writer. Pub'd religious works in German & English. 1523: Augustinian Friar & Prior of Austin Friars, Cambr.; 1520s: chairman of meetings of scholars at the White Horse Inn, Cambr., that discussed new German doctrines; 1526: arrested for opinions – recant or burn; 1528: escaped to Antwerp & came under Lutheran infl.; 1531: **Cromwell** (q.v.) invited him to return to Eng.; 1535: mission to Germany to obtain Lutheran divines' opinions on royal divorce & remarriage; 1539: nego. m. of **Henry VIII** & **Anne of Cleves** (q.v.); preached at Paul's Cross v. **Stephen Gardiner** (q.v.); 1540: impr. & burnt.

BARROW Henry (c. 1550–93): Cambr.- and Gray's Inn-edu. separatist martyr. c. 1550: b. 3rd s. of Thomas Barrow & h.w. Mary (Bures) of Shipdam; through his mother, related to Sir **William Butts**, Henry VIII's physician, & Sir Nicholas Bacon, eldest s. of Lord Keeper Bacon; 1566: fellow-commoner of Clare College, Cambr.; 1569/70: B.A.; 1576: adm. Gray's Inn; 19 Nov. 1587: arrested by Whitgift for Brownism; impr. in Fleet for denying authority of his judges & for refusal to attend church; voluminous prison writings, incl. account of trial & *Brief Discoverie of the False Church*; 23 Mar. 1593: condemned to d. w. John Greenwood for pub'n of seditious writings w. malice; 6 Apr.: hanged at Tyburn.

BARTON Elizabeth (c. 1506–34): mystic & prophetess known as 'Nun of Kent' or 'Holy Maid of Kent'. Nothing known of her origins. House servant of Thomas Cobb of Aldington, Kent. 1525: began to experience visions & to prophesy; 1526: Archbp Warham authorised ecclesiastical commission to investigate; pronounced a genuine relig. ecstatic by Dr **Edward Bocking** of Canterbury (q.v.); 1527: took vows as nun in Benedictine priory of St Sepulchre Canterbury w. Bocking as her confessor; 1526–34: oppo'd Henry's policies towards the Church & divorce & m. to **Anne Boleyn** (q.v.); Jan. 1534: act of attainder passed v. her; 20 Apr. 1534: hanged alongside Bocking & other accomplices.

BASSET(T) (née Roper) Mary (c. 1525–72): translator. c. 1525: b. 2nd dau. of William Roper & h.w. Margaret (More) & grandchild of **Sir Thomas More** (q.v.); humanist education by Dr John Morwen; celebrated Greek & Latin scholar; one of her transl. *History of the Passion* pub'd in Sir Thomas More's *English Works*; m. (i) Stephen Clarke (d.); gentlewoman of privy chamber to Mary I; presented Mary w. transl. from Greek into Eng. of Eusebius's *Ecclesiastical History*; by June 1556: m. (ii) James Basset(t), son of Sir John Basset(t) & **Honor Grenville**, later Viscountess L'Isle (q.v.); two s.; 1558: James d.; 20 Mar. 1572: d. London.

BEAUFORT (Lady) Margaret (1443–1509): Countess of Richmond & Derby, through whom Henry Tudor inherited part of his claim to the throne: Queen Mother who played important role in Henry VII's reign. 31 May 1443: b. dau. & heir of John Beaufort, Duke of Somerset, & h. w. Margaret (Beauchamp St John); descendant through John of Gaunt of Edward III; 1450: m. (i) John de la Pole (dissolved 1453); 1455: m. (ii) Edmund Tudor, Earl of Richmond, half-brother of Henry VI (d. 1456); 1456: b. of Henry (later Henry VII); 1458: m. (iii) Henry Stafford, 2nd s. of Duke of Buckingham (d. 1471); 1472: m. (iv) 1472: Thomas, Lord Stanley, Earl of Derby (d. 1504); 1485: decl. *feme sole*; 1485: custodian of Elizabeth, Cecily & Katherine of York, Edward Stafford, Duke of Buckingham, Edward Earl of Warwick & Ralph Neville, h. to Earl of Westmorland; 1488: KG; 1499–1505: presided over unofficial council of the Midlands at Collyweston, a position of unprecedented power for a woman, & was instrumental in participating in & supporting an increasingly unpopular royal regime; important patron of Cambr. Uni.; 1505–06: founded Christ's College, Cambr.; 29 June 1509: d. Michael K. Jones and Malcolm G. Underwood, *The King's Mother, Lady Margaret Beaufort, Countess of Richmond and Derby*, Cambridge, 1992.

BECON Thomas (1512–67): Cambr.-edu. cleric & influential Protestant religious writer. 1512/13: b. Norfolk to unknown parents; 1527: entered Cambr.; 1531: B.A.; 1533: ord. pr.; 1541 & 1543: V, Brenzett, Kent; made to recant his Protestant opinions; 1548: R, St Stephen Walbrook, London; Chaplain to **Thomas Cranmer** (q.v.) & **Edward Seymour**, Duke of Somerset (q.v.) & preacher at Canterbury Cathedral; 1553–54: impr. in Tower as seditious preacher & depr. of living for m.; exiled in Strasbourg; 1558: rest. to living; 1560: pub'd dialogue, *The Sycke Man's Salve* (written before 1553), which went into 11 ed'ns by 1600; pub'd many works, including influential *Catechism*; 30 June 1567: d.

BELMAIN Jean (fl. 1546): French tutor to Edward VI. Calvinist refugee who was a nephew of Sir **John Cheke** (q.v.), tutor of Edward VI.

BENTHAM (Bishop) Thomas (1513/14–79): Marian exile, biblical scholar & Elizabethan bp. Oxf.-edu. theologian & linguist. 1513/14: b. Sherburn, Yorks of unknown parentage; 1544: B.A. Oxf.; 1553: depr. of fellowship at Magdalen College, Oxf.; 1554–57: Marian exile; Nov. 1557: began work on Genevan Bible; c. Jan. 1558: m. Maud Fawcon of Hadleigh, Suffolk; six children; 1558: minister to Protestant congregation in late Marian London; 1559: app'd Visitor in Elizabethan Royal Commission; Mar. 1560: consecr. Bp of Coventry & Lichfield; 1562: preached at court; 1569: transl. Books of Daniel & Ezekiel for Bishops' Bible; 21 Feb. 1579: d.; letter book provides important source for episcopal problems in early years of Elizabeth's reign & relations w. returned exiles. Rosemary O'Day and Joel Berlatsky (eds), *The Letter Book of Thomas Bentham, Bishop of Coventry and Lichfield*, Camden Miscellany XXVII, 1979.

BERTIE (Brandon) (née Willoughby) Katherine (1519–80): Duchess of Suffolk, prominent Protestant & patron. 1519: b. dau. & h. of William Willoughby, 11th Baron Willoughby de Eresby, & his 2nd w. Maria de Salinas of

Castile; 1526: **Charles Brandon** (q.v.) purchased her wardship to m. her to his s. Henry, Earl of Lincoln, aged three; 1533: m. (i) Charles Brandon, Duke of Suffolk wid. of Princess Mary Rose, as his 4th w.; two s. (Henry & Charles); 1545: Brandon d.; 1551: d. of both of their s.; 1553: m. (ii) Richard Bertie, gentleman of her household; two children; patron of **Hugh Latimer** (q.v.) & other Protestant preachers under Edward VI; Marian exile in Weisel & Lithuania; 1559: returned to Lincs & spent life raising s. and dau. & acting as guardian to Lady **Mary Grey** (q.v.); 19 Sept. 1580: d. M.F. Harkrider, *Women, Reform and Community in Early Modern England: Katherine Willoughby, Duchess of Suffolk, and Lincolnshire's Godly Aristocracy, 1519–1580*, Woodbridge, 2008.

BIGOD Sir Francis (1507–37): Oxf.-edu. rebel. 4 Oct. 1507: b. Heaton, Yorks, eldest s. of Sir John & Joan (Strangways) Bigod; Sir John d. 1514; 9 May 1515: Cardinal Wolsey bought Francis's wardship; edu. in Wolsey's hsehold & at Oxf.; a committed Protestant; c. 1529: m. Katherine Neville (d. 1566); 1529 & 1536: M.P.; agent for Cromwell in the north; wanted monasteries reformed not dissolved; initially opposed Pilgrimage of Grace; joined their ranks to oppose royal intervention in religion; Dec. 1536: King disbanded pilgrimage; 16 Jan. 1537: Bigod began loyal uprising to fulfil the King's promises to the pilgrims; 19 Jan. 1537: attacked Hull; Bigod's men arrested at Beverley; 10 Feb.1537: Bigod captured at Cumberland; 2 June: tried & hanged at Tyburn; attainder reversed in 1549–50.

BILNEY Thomas (?1495–1531): Cambr.-edu. Protestant martyr. 1495: b. Norfolk of unknown parentage; 1510: adm. Cambr.; read law at Trinity Hall, Cambr.; Sept. 1519: ord. pr. at Ely; 1521: Bachelor of Canon Law; 1524: fellow of Trinity Hall; one of a group of Cambr. scholars who gathered at the White Horse Inn – '**Little Germany**' – to discuss the New Learning & related religious issues. Friends w. **Robert Barnes** (q.v.), **Hugh Latimer** (q.v.) **Matthew Parker** (q.v.) & credited w. conversion of Latimer; July 1525: licensed to preach throughout Ely diocese; 1527: preaching tour v. idolatry; 27 Nov. 1527: brought before Wolsey for heresy; 7 Dec. 1527: abjured & ordered to do penance; early 1529: released; 1531: relapsed; 19 Aug. 1531: burned at the 'Lollards' Pit' nr Bishopsgate.

BLOUNT Charles – see **Mountjoy** 8th Baron, Charles Blount (Earl of Devonshire, 1603–06) (1563–1606): 1563: b. 2nd s. of James Blount, 6th baron Mountjoy & h.w. Catherine (Leigh) Blount.

BLOUNT Elizabeth 'Bess' (c. 1500–39) (also Tailboys & Fiennes de Clinton): royal mistress. Well-edu. 2nd dau. of John Blount & h.w. Katherine (Peshall) of Kinlet; 25 Mar. 1512: maid of honour to Katherine of Aragon at Ludlow; renowned for beauty & skills in dancing, music & masques; 1518: brief affair w. Henry VIII; 3 Oct. 1518: last recorded appearance at court; June 1519: gave b. to **Henry Fitzroy**, later Duke of Richmond (q.v.); Sept. 1519: m. Gilbert Tailboys, royal ward; three children (Elizabeth, b. 1520, George & Robert); 1522–39: received grants from Henry VIII; 15 Apr. 1530: d. of Gilbert; c. 1535: m. Edward Fiennes de Clinton, 9th Baron Clinton & Save; 3 daus; d. c. 1539–41.

BOCHER Joan (also Knell and Joan of Kent) (d. 1550): anabaptist martyr of unknown origin, sometimes known as the 'Maid of Kent'. She was an associate of **Anne Askew** (q.v.); denied the doctrine of the incarnation; was impr., examined by Cranmer & burnt as heretic at Smithfield.

BOCKING (Dr) Edward (d. 1534): Oxf.-edu. Benedictine monk of Christ Church, Canterbury. 1504: adm. Canterbury College, Oxf.; 1526: app'd by Warham to report back on **Elizabeth Barton** (q.v.) & her prophecies; 1527: app'd confessor to Barton; Sept. 1533: impr. in Tower for assoc'n w. Barton; 20 Apr. 1534: hanged at Tyburn for tr.

BOLEYN (Bullen) (Queen) Anne (?1500–36): 2nd wife of Henry VIII & mother of

Elizabeth I (see Section 12.1: Monarchs and their consorts).

BOLEYN (Lord) George (c. 1504–36): Viscount Rochford. Courtier & diplomat. Only brother of **Anne** Queen of England (q.v.) c. 1504: b. s. & h. of **Thomas Boleyn** (q.v.) & h.w. Elizabeth (Howard); 1516: royal page; 1524: gentleman of privy chamber; 1526: m. Jane Parker; 1529: headed embassy to France; 1530: cr. Viscount Rochford; 1533: attempted to enlist François I's support for Henry; 1534: Warden of the Cinque Ports; open supporter of relig. reform; 2 May 1536: impr. on trumped-up charges of incest & high tr.; 15 May 1536: tried & convicted; 17 May 1536: exec.

BOLEYN Mary (Stafford, Carey) (c. 1499–1543): Henry VIII's mistress & elder sister of **Anne** (q.v.) & **George** (q.v.). c. 1499: b. eldest child of **Thomas Boleyn** (q.v.) & h.w. Elizabeth (Howard); 1514: lady-in-waiting at m. of Mary Tudor to King Louis XII of France; 1515: remained at French court & acquired dubious reputation; later returned to household of Queen Katherine; 4 Feb. 1520: m. (i) William Carey (c. 1500–28), gentleman of the privy chamber; 1522–25: King's mistress; c. 1523: b. of dau. Katherine (q.v. **Katherine Knollys**); 4 Mar. 1526: b. of s. Henry; malicious rumours that he was Henry VIII's bastard probably unfounded; 1528: Henry asked Pope Clement VII to grant him a dispensation to m. a woman who was the sister of a former mistress; 23 June 1528: William Carey d. suddenly; King granted wardship of **Henry Carey** (q.v.) to Anne Boleyn, transferred William's pension to Mary & ordered Thomas Boleyn to care for Mary; 1534: m. (ii) Sir William Stafford (c. 1512–56) & was cut off by her father & by the court; 1536: bastardisation of Princess Elizabeth, possibly because of Henry's previous liaison w. Mary; reconciled with her father & lived at Rochford Hall, Essex; Nov. 1539: dau. Katherine named as maid of honour of Anne of Cleves; 1545: Henry Carey part of royal household; 1559: Henry cr. Baron Hunsdon; Katherine m. Sir **Francis**

Knollys (q.v.); Henry & Katherine were Elizabeth's only close blood relatives. A. Hoskins, 'Mary Boleyn's Carey children and offspring of Henry VIII', *The Genealogist*, 25 Mar. 1997, pp. 345–52; R.M. Warnicke, *The Rise and Fall of Anne Boleyn: Family Politics at the Court of Henry VIII*, 1989; A. Weir, *Henry VIII: King and Court*, 2001.

BOLEYN (Lord) Thomas Earl of Ormond & Wiltshire (1477–1539): father of **Mary**, **Anne** & **George** (q.v.). Diplomat & royal servant during early years of Henry VIII's reign. 1477: b. Norfolk, 2nd s. of Sir William Boleyn & h.w. Margaret (Butler), who was dau. & co-heir of Thomas Butler, 7th Earl of Ormond; 1522: Treasurer of Royal Household; 1525: cr. Viscount Rochford; 1527: joint ambass. to France; 1529: cr. Earl of Ormond & Wiltshire; 1530: Lord Privy Seal & ambass. to Emperor Charles V & France regarding King's divorce.

BONNER (Bishop) Edmund (?1500–69): lawyer, humanist & Catholic reformer. 1529: Chaplain to **Wolsey** (q.v.); c. 1500: poss. illegit. s. of Elizabeth Frodsham (who later m. Edmund Bonner, sawyer) & George Savage, R of Davenham, Cheshire; 1532–43: served on royal diplomatic missions especially concerning royal divorce; 1538: ambass. to Paris; 1538: consecr. Bp of Hereford; 1550: consecr. Bp of London; he had accepted the Royal Supremacy under Henry but resisted under Edward & was depr. of his bprics & impr.; Sept. 1553: rest. by Mary; led attack on heretics in London diocese (113 burnings); laid great store on sermons, catechising & reform; depr. & impr. by Elizabeth; 5 Sept. 1569: d. in Marshalsea prison.

BOROUGH Stephen (1525–84): explorer & merchant. 25 Sept. 1525: b. at Northam, Devon, s. & h. of Walter Borough & h.w. Mary (Dough); 1553: Master of only ship to survive the first English expedition to Russia; discovered Russia & named the North Cape; 1556: discovered entrance to Kara Sea; 1562: h. 1st w. Elinor (Smith) d.; 1563: m. (ii)

Johanna Overy, wid.; four children; wrote records of his many voyages; some of his journals published by **Richard Hakluyt**; 12 July 1584: d. at Chatham.

BOTHWELL (Lord), James Hepburn (c. 1535–78): 4th Earl of Bothwell, kidnapper & third husband of **Mary Queen of Scots** (q.v.). 1534/35: b. only s. & h. of Patrick Hepburn, 3rd Earl of Bothwell – known as 'the Fair Earl' – & h.w. Agnes (Sinclair); well-edu. in household of Patrick Hepburn, Bp of Moray; 1556: 4th Earl of Bothwell, Warden of the Scottish Marches, Lord High Admiral of Scotland; Protestant supporter of Mary of Guise, Catholic Queen Regent of Scotland; 1557: commanded expedition into the Eng. borders; 1560: travelled to Denmark & m. (i) Anna Throndsson, a Norwegian, whom he later left in Flanders in order to escort Mary Queen of Scots to Scotland after d. of Francis II in Dec. 1560; 6 Sept. 1561: PC; 1562: impr. for allegedly attempting to kidnap Queen but escaped; 1564: impr. by the English, escaped to France, returned to Scotland & then escaped to France again; Mary then recalled him to Scotland, where he was in the ascendant; 22 Feb. 1566: m. (ii) Lady Jean Gordon, a Catholic lady-in-waiting to Mary; 9 Mar. 1566: was at Holyrood on the night of Rizzio's murder but denied all knowledge of it; joined Mary & Darnley at Dunbar & grew more & more influential; 9 Feb. 1567: blew up Darnley's house at Kirk o' Field; Bothwell was acquitted in the law courts & granted large tracts of land by the Queen; 24 Apr. 1567: Bothwell captured the Queen (most probably with her connivance) & raped her; 7 May 1567: divorced Lady Jean; 15 May 1567: m. (iii) Mary Stuart according to Protestant rites; Bothwell created Duke of Orkney & Earl of Shetland; rebellion of the Scottish lords; Queen's army melted away & Bothwell escaped via Orkney & Shetland to Denmark. Here, his past with Anna Throndsson caught up with him, he was impr. by Frederick II & went mad. R. Gore-Browne, *Lord Bothwell*, 1937; A. Fraser, *Mary, Queen of Scots* (1969).

BRANDON (Lord) Charles (c. 1484–1545): 1st Duke of Suffolk. Favourite of Henry VIII, courtier & soldier. c. 1484: b. s. of Sir William & Elizabeth (Bruyn) Brandon of South Ockenden; rose through infl. of his uncle Sir Thomas Brandon, one of Henry VII's leading courtiers; 1503: betrothed to Anne Browne; 1506: m. her aunt (i) Dame Margaret Mortimer; 1507: annulled m.; 1508: m. (ii) Anne Browne; two daus (Anne [m. Edward Grey, 4th Baron Powis, Mar. 1525] & Mary [m. Thomas Stanley, 2nd Baron Monteagle, late 1527 or early 1528]); b. between 1506 & 1510; 1512: KG; 1513: Viscount Lisle (betrothed to Elizabeth Grey, eight-year-old heiress to Lisle estates); 1513–14: acknowledged as King's principal favourite; 1514: Duke of Suffolk; 1515: m. (iii) **Princess Mary Rose** (q.v., d. 1533), sister of Henry VIII & wid. Queen of France, with papal dispensation; built up royal support in Norfolk & Suffolk; 16 July 1517: Frances b.; c. 1518–21: Eleanor b.; 1520: accompanied Henry to Field of Cloth of Gold; 1523: commanded successful invasion of France; 1522: Henry, Earl of Lincoln b.; 1520s: w. Thomas Howard Duke of Norfolk maintained order in East Anglia; Oct. 1529: replaced Wolsey briefly as chief minister; 1530s: reluctantly sought support abroad for Henry's divorce from Katherine of Aragon; poor relations w. Anne Boleyn; h. son's position as only legit. grands. of Henry VII made him unpopular w. Henry; spring 1533: Henry made him surrender position of **Earl Marshal** to Duke of Norfolk; 25 June 1533: Mary d.; Sept. 1533: m. (iv) **Katherine Willoughby** his 14-year-old ward (q.v. under **Bertie**); 1534: d. of s. & h. Henry, Earl of Lincoln; Sept. 1535: b. of Henry; 1536: suppressed Lincs Pilgrimage of Grace; c. 1537: b. of Charles; changed East Anglian powerbase for Lincs; allied w. **Thomas Cromwell** (q.v.) on PC; 1539: Great Master of the Royal Household; remained active on PC. After Cromwell's fall; 1541: entertained Henry VIII en route to York; 1542: Warden of the Marches bordering Scotland; 1544: captured Boulogne; 22 Aug. 1545: d. S.J. Gunn, *Charles Brandon, Duke of Suffolk, c. 1484–1545*, 1988.

BRAY (Sir) Reginald (d. 1503): one of Henry VII's chief councillors; a lawyer who was originally in the service of Lady Margaret Beaufort, managing her estates; b. s. & h. of Richard Bray, gent. & surgeon & his 2nd w. Joan (Troughton); post-1485: Henry VII's chief administrator in respect of financial & property matters. His official position was Chancellor of the Duchy of Lancaster but his unofficial brief was general auditor of all the royal lands.

BRINKLOW Henry (d. 1546): Common wealthman. Franciscan convert to Lutheranism. Used pseudonym Roderick Mors; b. eldest of nine children of Robert Brinklow, farmer of Kintbury, Berks, & h.w. Isabell (Butler); he became a commonwealthman during Edward VI's reign;1546: author: *The Complaint of Roderick Mors*, an angry protest v. social injustice; 1546: poss. also author of *A Supplication of the Poore Commons*. His wid., Margery, m. Stephen Vaughan, Merchant Adventurer & father of **Anne Locke** (q.v.).

BROWNE Robert (c. 1550–c. 1633): Cambr.-edu. co-founder of Brownism. Congregationalist. 1573: ordained priest; late 1570s: preached without licence around Cambr. v. parochial system & episcopal ordination; 1580: w. Robert Harrison began 'Brownist' church in Norwich; 1581: impr. by Bp of Norwich for seditious preaching at Bury St Edmonds but released through Burghley's intervention; 1581: emigrated to Middelburg & pub'd books that were prohibited in Eng.; following a quarrel w. Harrison, moved to Scotland & then back to Eng.; 1584: arrested; 1586: preacher at Northampton; 1586: excommunicated by Richard Howland, Bp of Peterborough; submitted & became Master of Stamford GS; 1591–1631: R, Achurch, Northants; 1633: d. in gaol, on charges of violent assault.

BUCER Martin (1491–1551): major Protestant reformer & prolific author of religious works, who had profound infl. on Eng. reformation. 1523–49: leader of reformation & preacher in Strasbourg; 1525–30: Zwinglian supporter in the Eucharist controversy; 1531–38: sought common reformation faith in Germany & Switzerland; Apr. 1549: contest w. Charles V led him to retire to Eng. where he was kindly received by Edward VI's court; 1549: app'd Regius Professor of Divinity, Cambr. Uni.; 1550: was consulted about BofCP; 1551: bur. in University Church; 1557: exhumation ordered by Mary I.

BUCKINGHAM, Dukes of (see **Stafford**).

BURGHLEY (Burleigh) (Lord) (see **Cecil, William**).

BUTTS (Dr) William (c. 1485–1545): influential Cambr.-edu. evangelical. Physician to Henry VIII. c. 1485: b. Norwich, s. of John Butts, auditor of crown revenues, & h.w. Elizabeth; 1507: B.A. (Gonville Hall, Cambr.); 1509: M.A.; 1516: m. Margaret Bacon, lady-in-waiting to Princess Mary; dau. & three s.; 1518: M.D.; 1528: 1st noted as royal physician; 1529: joined Royal College of Physicians; 1544: knighted; 22 Nov. 1545: d.

BYRD William (?1538/39–1623): composer, organist & supposed pupil of **Thomas Tallis** (q.v.). c. 1538/39: b. London, one of seven children of Thomas & Margery Byrd; poss. choirboy of Chapel Royal; 1563: organist, Lincoln cathedral; 1569: joint organist of Chapel Royal; 1575: granted monopoly of selling printed music & music paper; 1578–88: Catholic recusant living at Harlington, Middlesex. Prolific composer: 1575: *Cantiones . . . sacrae*; 1588: the first English madrigals; 1588: *Psalmes, Sonnets and Songs*; 1589: *Songs of Sundrie Natures & Liber Primus Sacrarum Cantionum*; 1591: *Liber Secundus*; 1607: *Gradualia*; 1611: *Psalmes, Songs and Sonnets.*

C

CABOT John (1451–c. 1499): Venetian tradesman & explorer who worked out of

Bristol. Father of **Sebastian Cabot** (q.v.). 1451: b. Italy, s. & h. of Julio Caboto of Genoa & h.w. Mattea; 1476: granted Venetian citizenship; m. Mattea; three s.; c. 1495: living in Bristol; 1497/98: discovered Newfoundland; Sept. 1499: apparently lost at sea.

CABOT Sebastian (1474 or 1481/82–1557): s. of **John Cabot** (q.v.); poss. b. in Bristol; 1496, w. his father John, obtained licence for voyage of discovery; 1497: discovered Nova Scotia; 1512: made map of Gascony & Guienne for Henry VIII; m. Catalina Medrano; dau.; 1512–16: map-maker for Ferdinand of Aragon; 1519–26: pilot-major for Emperor Charles V; 1526–33: chequered fortunes but was recalled to Seville in 1533; 1533: Catalina d.; 1544: published engraved map of the world; 1547: returned to Bristol; 1548: pensioned by Edward VI; 1551: settled dispute between Hanseatic League & London merchants; 1551: proposed Company of Merchant Adventurers in London to search for Northwest Passage to China; 1553 & 1556: oversaw expeditions to Russia; 1555: Mary I confirmed his pension; 1557: Mary I halved his pension.

CAMDEN William (1551–1623): historian & antiquary. Edu. at Christ's Hospital, St Paul's School and Oxf. 2 May 1551: b. London, s. of Sampson Camden, painter of Lichfield & h.w. Elizabeth (Curwen); 1563: entered St Paul's School; 1566: adm. Magdelen College, Oxf. As chorister; embroiled in relig. conflict; 1571: left Oxf. without degree; 1571: travelled throughout Eng. collecting archaeological materials (probably subsidised by Gabriel Goodman, Dean of Westminster; 1574: B.A.; 1575–93: Usher (2nd master), Westminster School; 1577: inher. property in Staffs; 1593: Headmaster of Westminster; 1578–1600: during vacations continued tours of archaeological investigation; 2 May 1586: pub'd *Britannia*; 1588: M.A.; 1589–1623: served as lay prebendary of Salisbury; 1597: pub'd Greek grammar; 23 Oct.1597–1623: Clarenceux King-of-Arms; numerous publications in early seventeenth century; 1610: Philemon Holland transl. *Britannia* into Eng.;

1615: *Annales . . . regnante Elizabetha . . . ad annum 1589* (2nd part pub'd posthumously in 1628); 1622: founded Oxf. Chair of History; 9 Nov. 1623: d.; bur. in Westminster Abbey.

CAMPEGGIO (or Campeggi) Cardinal Lorenzo (fl. 1500–34): Papal Legate & Cardinal Protector of England; 1518–19: 1st mission to Eng.; 1528–29: 2nd mission, to settle divorce issue; 1529: adjournment of Legatine Court at Blackfriars & departure from Eng.; 1534: depr. of See of Salisbury.

CAMPION Edmund (1540–81): Oxf.-edu. Jesuit martyr. 1540: b. London, s. of citizen & bookseller; edu. GS & Christ's Hospital; c. 1553: edu. St Paul's School; 1558: adm. St John's Coll., Oxf.; 20 Nov. 1561: B.A.; 1564: M.A. & fellow of St John's; Aug. 1566: chosen to welcome Eliz. on visit to Oxf.; Mar. 1569: ord. deac.; 23 Mar. 1569: B.Th.; 1568–9: Junior Proctor of univ.; 1570: left Oxf. & travelled to Ireland; 1571: wrote *The History of Ireland* in bid for Leicester's patronage; went to Eng. college at Douai & was ord. subdeac.; 1573: in Rome; Aug. 1573: entered SJ novitiate; served in Moravia and Bohemia; 1578: ord. deac. & pr. by Archbp of Prague; Aug. 1579: recalled by **William Allen** (q.v.); 1580: missionary pr. to Eng.; preached & administered sacraments in Lancashire; 1581: pub'd *Decem Rationes* (10 Reasons) why the Roman Church was the true Church & distributed it to congregation at St Mary's Oxf.; July 1581: betrayed, impr. in Tower, racked; 1 Dec. 1581: hanged at Tyburn.

CAREY Henry (1526–96): 1st Baron Hunsdon; courtier, M.P., soldier, PC & administrator, & patron of the theatre (Lord Chamberlain's Men). 4 Mar. 1526: s. of William Carey & h.w. **Mary (Boleyn later Stafford)** (q.v.), mistress of Henry VIII & sister to Anne Boleyn; bro. of **Katherine (Carey) Knollys** (q.v.); cousin & possibly half-brother of Elizabeth I; 1545: member of royal household; 1545: m. Anne (Morgan); nine sons – George, 2nd Baron Hunsdon (b. c. 1546),

John, 3rd Baron Hunsdon & **Robert Carey**, 1st Earl of Monmouth (1560–1639) (q.v.) being the most frequently mentioned – and three daus, notably Katherine Howard, Countess of Nottingham; also left illegit. s. Valentine Carey, later Bp of Exeter; went on various foreign embassies; 1554–55: member of Princess Elizabeth's household; 13 Jan. 1559: cr. 1st Baron Hunsdon; 18 May 1561: made KG; 25 Aug. 1568: Gov. of Berwick; Jan. 1570: successfully quashed Leonard Dacre in Cumbria & earned Elizabeth's gratitude in land grants; 23 Oct. 1571–77: Warden of the east marches; May 1572: Scots handed Northumberland over; 16 Nov. 1577–88: PC & fulfilled role of Scottish expert; Nov. 1579: commissioned to raise army to support Regent Morton; Sept. 1581: returned to London; 14 Aug.: nego. w. James Hamilton, Earl of Arran at Eliz.'s request & supported Arran; Feb. 1585: returned to court; 1583–85: Lord Lieut. of Herts; July 1585: Lord Chamberlain of the household; Aug. 1587 to Apr. 1588: in north w. responsibility for defence of eastern & middle marches; Apr. 1588: Lord Lieut. of Norfolk Suffolk to oversee musters; 20 July 1588: principal capt'n & gov. of army to protect Queen; supported James VI's claims to Eng. throne; 23 July 1596: d.

CAREY (Lord) Robert (?1560–1639) 1st Earl of Monmouth: 1560: b. Herts, youngest s. of **Henry Carey**, 1st Baron Hunsdon (q.v.) & h.w. Ann (Morgan); grands. of Mary Boleyn (q.v.) and William Carey and therefore Elizabeth's cousin (and possibly her half-nephew). 1577: diplomatic mission to Netherlands; autumn 1586 & 1589: M.P. Morpeth; 1588: fought v. Armada; spring, 1593: M.P. Callington; 20 Apr. 1593: m. Elizabeth dau. of Sir Hugh Trevannion & wid. of Sir Henry Widdrington, without Queen's permission; 1597: Warden of the Middle March; 14 Mar. 1603: rode to Scotland to inform James VI of Elizabeth's death; 12 Apr. 1639: d. His short Memoirs provide vivid descriptions of the defeat of the Spanish Armada, the Queen herself & her death, & also of life on the Anglo-Scottish borders.

CARTWRIGHT Thomas (1534/35–1603): Cambr.-edu. radical Protestant divine & author of controversial religious works. b. Royston, Herts, poss. s. of John & Agnes Cartwright; 1547: adm. Clare College, Cambr.; 1550: Scholar of St John's College, Cambr.; 1554: B.A.; Apr. 1560: fellow of St John's; June 1560: M.A.; 1562: fellow of Trinity Coll., Cambr.; a precision or Puritan in religious matters from early in Elizabeth's reign; 1565: attacked use of surplice; 1565–67: in Ireland as chapl. to Archbp of Armagh; 31 May: B.Th. at Cambr.; 1569: made Lady Margaret Professor of Divinity at Cambridge; 1570: depr. of Chair for preaching v. the Church of England's constitution; 1571–76: went in & out of Eng., first to Geneva & then to Antwerp; June 1571: taught at the Geneva academy; 1572: depr. of Cambr. fellowship; 1573: pub'd *A Replye* to Whitgift's *Answer* (1572) to the *Admonition*; 25 Jan. 1574: matric. at Univ. of Heidelberg; 1575: *The Second Replie*; 1577: *The Rest of the Second Replie;* 1577: factor to Antwerp Merchant Adventurers; 1578: m. Alice Stubbs; one s. & three daus; July 1580–85: Pastor of English congregation at Antwerp; 1585: returned to Eng.; impr. in Fleet; 1586: Master of Earl of Leicester's Hospital, Warwick; championed by Martin Marprelate; w. Humphrey Fen led the Presbyterian move't in Warws; 1587: attended Cambr. presb. Synod; 1589: attended Cambr. synod; Oct. 1589: refused to plead before High Commission & to take oath *ex officio mero*; 1590–92: impr. in Fleet; 13 May 1591: brought before Star Chamber & subsequently before High Commission; proceedings halted; 21 May 1592: released to house arrest; 1595–1601: with Lord Zouche in Guernsey; 1601: returned to Warws; 27 Dec. 1603: d.

CAVENDISH George (?1499–?1562): gentleman-usher to Wolsey (q.v.) & author of *The Life and Death of Cardinal Wolsey* (1558), based on his first-hand knowledge of the statesman.

CECIL (née Co(o)ke) Mildred (1526–1589): classically-edu. eldest dau. of Sir Anthony

Co(o)ke (q.v.); well-known by contemporaries for her transl. from the Greek fathers, that were circulated in ms but never published; 1545: m. **William Cecil** (q.v.) as his 2nd w.; mother of Robert Cecil; exercised consid. infl.; 1579: endowed two scholarships at St John's College, Cambr. through an intermediary; built up fine private library of Latin and Greek works; 4 Apr. 1589: d.

CECIL (Lord) Robert (1563–1612): 1st Earl of Salisbury. Statesman & diplomat. Known as 'the crookbacked earl'. 1 June 1563: b. s. of **William Cecil** (q.v.) & 2nd w. Mildred (q.v.); edu. at home by his mother and by tutors, incl. Richard Howland, later master of St John's College, Cambr.; 1584–87: resident in France; 1588: attached to Earl of Derby's mission to the Spanish Netherlands; 1584 & 1586: M.P. Westminster; 1588, 1593, 1597, 1601: M.P. Herts; 1591: knighted; 1596–1608: Secretary of State; 1598: envoy to France; 1600: commissioner for trying Earl of Essex for leaving post in Ireland; 1603: secured accession of James VI of Scotland to throne of Eng.; 1603: cr. Baron Cecil; 1604: cr. 1st Viscount Cranborne; 1605: cr. 1st Earl of Salisbury; 1607: James I exchanged palace of Hatfield for Cecil's Theobalds & Cecil built Hatfield House; 24 May 1612: d.

CECIL Thomas (1542–1623): 1st Earl of Exeter & 2nd Baron Burghley. 1542: b. s. & h. of **William Cecil** (q.v.) & 1st w. Mary (Cheke); half-brother of **Robert** (q.v.). edu. at home by stepmother **Mildred (Cooke) Cecil** (q.v.) & by tutors; 1563: M.P. Stamford; 1564: m. Dorothy Neville; five s. & eight daus; 1569: in arms v. Northern rebels; 1573: served in Scotland; 1575: knighted; 1584: M.P. Lincs; 1585: in army in Low Countries; 1588: fought v. Armada; 1592: M.P. Northants; 1598: succeeded to Barony; 1599: President of Council of the North; 1601: helped suppr. Essex Revolt; 1605: cr. 1st Earl of Exeter; 1609: Dorothy d.; 1610: m. (ii) Frances (Brydges Smith) a young widow; one dau.; 7 Feb. 1623: d.; bur. Westminster Abbey.

CECIL William (1520/21–98): 1st Baron Burghley. Cambr.-edu. statesman. 18 Sept. 1520 or 21: b.?Stamford, Lincs, s. of Richard & Jane (Heckington) Cecil; served in Henry VIII's household; attended both Stamford & Grantham GS; 1535: adm. St John's College Cambr; 1541: adm. Gray's Inn; 8 Aug. 1541: m. (i) sister of Sir **John Cheke** (q.v.); May 1542: **Thomas** (q.v.) b. 1547–61: *custos brevium*, Court of Common Pleas; 21 Dec. 1545: m. (ii) **Mildred Co(o)ke** (q.v.); 1547: M.P. for Stamford; 1549: Secretary to Somerset (q.v.) & impr. in Tower on his fall; 1550–53: Secretary of State; 1551: knighted; 1553: began building Burghley House & Wimbledon House; 1553–58: in Mary I's service; 1555: M.P. Lincs; 1558–72: Secretary of State; 1559: M.P. Lincs; 1559: Chancellor, Cambr. Uni.; 1560: envoy to Scotland; 1561: Master of Court of Wards; 1562: M.P. Northants; rivalry betw. Cecil & Leicester factions at court; 1570: organised agents to seek out conspiracies v. Elizabeth; 1572: co-ordinated Elizabeth's PC, supervised the Exchequer & Court of Wards & managed Parliament. After this date Sir **Francis Walsingham** (q.v.) assumed some of this role, especially in diplomacy. See Chapter 1: General chronology for further details. A.G.R. Smith (ed.), M. Hickes, *The 'Anonymous life' of William Cecil, Lord Burghley*, 1990.

CECILY OF YORK (1469–1507) Viscountess Welles: 2nd surviving dau. of Edward IV &, from 1486, Henry VII's eldest sister-in-law; 20 Mar. 1469: b. dau. of Edward IV & Elizabeth (Woodville); Apr. 1483 to 1 Mar. 1484: in sanctuary at Westminster; from Sept. 1485: briefly in household of Lady **Margaret Beaufort** (q.v.); m. (i) Ralph Scrope but m. dissolved 1486; 1487: m. (ii) Viscount Welles, half-brother of Margaret Beaufort; two daus; 9 Feb. 1499: wid.; 1502: m. (iii) Thomas Kyme of Friskney without royal permission, banished from court & King seized her estate; 1503: Margaret Beaufort, who sheltered the couple, intervened to achieve settlement for Cecily; 24 Aug. 1507: d. at Hatfield, Herts. Michael K. Jones and

Malcolm G. Underwood, *The King's Mother, Lady Margaret Beaufort, Countess of Richmond and Derby*, Cambridge, 1992.

CHADERTON, Laurence (c. 1536–1640): highly influential college head, biblical scholar and theologian, Presbyterian, preacher and teacher – dubbed 'the pope of Cambridge puritanism' by Patrick Collinson; b. s. of Lancashire gentleman Thomas Chaderton & h.w. Joan (Tetloe) at Oldham; edu. privately by Laurence Vaux, and then, from his mid-twenties, at Christ's College, Cambr.; converted to Protestantism by Edward Dering; 1568: BA; 1568–76: Fellow of Christ's College, Cambr., where he designed a curriculum for the training of preaching ministers; c. 1568–1618: preacher at St Clement's Cambr.; c. 1576: m. Cecily Culverwell, whose brother-in-law was **William Whitaker** (q.v.); one dau. Elizabeth; 1579: pr. at Paul's Cross; 1585–1622: 1st Master of Emmanuel College, 'a seminary of godly preachers'; 1590s: defended Calvinist orthodoxy v. William Barrett and Peter Baro; 1604: Puritan spokesman at James I's Hampton Court Conference; 13 Nov. 1640: d.

CHANCELLOR Richard (d. 1556): navigator who sailed to the Levant in 1550 & visited Archangel & Moscow in 1554 & 1555. Best known for commanding Sir Hugh Willoughby's expedition to discover Northeast Passage to India in 1555. Was wrecked off Aberdeenshire on return from Archangel & Moscow in 1556.

CHANSELER Margaret (fl. 1535): Suffolk *cause célèbre*. She was reported to **Thomas Cromwell** (q.v.) for allegedly having attacked the divorce from Katherine of Aragon & slandered Anne Boleyn. She confessed to having said that the new queen was 'a noughtty hoore' while her accusers claimed she had embellished this, by calling Anne 'a goggyll [e]yed hoore'. An inquiry was instigated & depositions heard before the Abbot of Bury St Edmonds & nine other J.P.s but Margaret was released unpunished.

CHAPUYS Eustace (fl. 1529–45): Imperial ambassador to Eng., 1529–36 & 1542–45. On his first mission, plotted in favour of Katherine of Aragon. Occasionally described mistakenly as Spanish ambassador.

CHEKE (Sir) John (1514–57): classical scholar & educator; June 1514: b. s. of Peter Cheke, esquire bedell in divinity at Cambr, & h.w. Agnes (Duffield) Pykerell, wid. (*d.* 1549). 1526: entered St John's College, Cambr.; 26 Mar. 1529: Fellow; 31 Mar. 1530: B.A.; 8 July 1533: M.A.; converted to Protestantism early in career; 1534: King's Scholar, Cambr.; 1535: headed group at St John's interested in Erasmian pronunciation of Greek; 1539–40: last master of grammar; 1540–51: first Regius Professor of Greek; included among his students **Roger Ascham** (q.v.) (who praised him as a great teacher), **William Cecil** (q.v.) and **Edwin Sandys** (q.v.); 8 Aug. 1541: William Cecil m. Cheke's sister Mary; 1542–46: Public Orator; 7 July 1544–47: tutor to Edward VI, living in the prince's household; 1547: gentleman of Edward VI's Privy Chamber; 11 May 1547: m. Mary Hill (1532/33–1616), step-dau. of leading privy councillor and intimate of Princess Elizabeth by 1548; they had three s.; Cheke benefited from Cecil's, Edward Seymour's and John Dudley's patronage; 1 Oct. 1547: M.P. for Bletchingley; 1548: Provost of King's College, Cambr.; 1553: Secretary of State; Marian exile; captured & brought back to Eng. because he was acting as publicist for the Protestants; impr. & recanted; 13 Sept. 1557: d. of natural causes.

CLEMENT (née Gigs) Margaret (b. c. 1504): humanist; dau. of Margaret (More) Roper's nurse & edu. alongside Thomas More's children; 1528: m. John Clement, tutor in More's household & court physician; five daus (all taught Latin & Greek); 1549: family went into exile; 1553: returned to Eng. Retha M. Warnicke, *Women of the English Renaissance and Reformation*, Westport, Conn., 1983.

CLIFFORD (Lady) Anne (1590–1676): diarist, genealogist, builder; dau. of George

Clifford, 3rd Earl of Cumberland & Margaret Russell, talented & edu. dau. of Earl of Bedford (1560–1616); edu. at Court by Mary, Countess of Warwick; tutored by poet Samuel Daniel; 1609: m. (i) Richard Sackville, later 3rd Earl of Dorset (d. 1624); 1630: m. (ii) Philip Herbert, 4th Earl of Pembroke (d. 1650). As *feme sole* developed Skipton Castle. D.J.H. Clifford, *The Diaries of Lady Anne Clifford*, Alan Sutton, 1990.

CLIFFORD (Lord) George (1558–1605): 3rd Earl of Cumberland. Eldest s. of Henry, 2nd Earl, & Lady Eleanor Brandon, dau. of **Charles Brandon** (q.v.) & **Mary Tudor** (q.v.). 1569/70: succeeded to Earldom; 1571: began edu. at Cambr.; 1577: m. his cousin Margaret Russell: 1590: b. of dau. **Anne** (q.v.); 1586–98: naval commander, taking part in defence v. Armada (1588) & probably in Cadiz expedition (1596) at his own expense; notorious for profligacy; died in great debt & separated from his wife.

CLITHEROW (Clitheroe) Margaret (1556–86): Catholic martyr. 1556: b. dau. of Thomas Middleton, wax chandler and freeman of York, & h.w. Jane (Turner) (c. 1515–85), dau. of Richard Turner, innkeeper; 1 July 1571: m. protestant John Clitherow, butcher & freeman, widower w. two sons; several children of the m.; 1574: converted to Catholicism; made private religious devotions; 1577–84: periods of impr. during which she fasted, studied & meditated; sheltered Catholic priests & invited friends to private celebrations of Mass; 14 Mar. 1586: brought before Assizes for harbouring priests; refused to plead; 25 Mar. 1586: as a result pressed, and torture by weights resulted in death; 1929: beatified; 25 Oct. 1970: canonised as one of 40 Eng. RC martyrs.

COKE, (Sir) Edward (1552–1634): Cambr.-edu. parliamentarian, prominent & wealthy lawyer and learned, legal author with Puritan connections; 1 Feb. 1552: b. Mileham, Norf., only s. of Robert Coke, lawyer & landowner, & h.w. Winifred (Knightley); edu. Norwich GS & Trinity College, Cambr.; 1567: adm. Pensioner

at Trinity College, Cambr.; 1570: left Cambr. without degree; 21 Jan. 1571: adm. Clifford's Inn, a junior inn of chancery; 1572: enrolled at Lincoln's Inn; 20 Apr. 1578: called to bar; 1579: Reader at Lyon's Inn; 1579: began keeping careful notes of cases; 1579: argued first case in **King's Bench**; 1581: protected crown interests in Shelley's Case; 1579–80: readings on the statute of 27 Edward I; 13 Aug. 1582: m. (i) Bridget (Paston) of Suffolk; seven s. & three daus.; 1585: app'd Recorder of Coventry; 1586: J.P. Norfolk & Recorder of Norwich; 1589: MP for Aldeburgh, Suffolk; 1591–92: Recorder of London; 1592: at Inner Temple gave readings on Statute of Uses; 1592: elected MP as knight of shire for Norfolk; 16 June 1592: solicitor-general; 1593: JP Suffolk & Middlesex; 1593: Speaker of House of Commons – reformed procedure; represented many important clients as well as others much lower down social scale; set many precedents; 10 Apr. 1594: attorney-general; 1596: Treasurer of Inner Temple, w. major infl. on its affairs; 27 June 1598: Bridget d.; 6 Nov. 1598: m. (ii) Elizabeth, widowed Lady **Hatton**, dau. of Thomas Cecil, 2nd Baron Burghley & 1st Earl of Exeter; two daus; 1600: pub'd *First Part of the Reports* (pub'd 11 by 1615); 1601: prosecuting counsel v. Earl of Essex (q.v. **Robert Devereux**); 1603: prosecuted Sir Walter Raleigh and Lord Cobham for tr.; 1604: Recorder of Harwich; 1606: serjeant-at-law & chief justice of court of common pleas; 25 Oct. 1613: chief justice of King's Bench; traced origins of common law into antiquity; conflict w. King James I & his Archbps of Canterbury, espec. about powers of eccles. cts & High Commission & the King's prerogative courts: 1628: pub'd *Commentarie upon Littleton* (known as Coke on Littleton) being the 1st volume of Coke's *Institutes of the Laws of England*; 1634: d. A. Boyer, *Sir Edward Coke and the Elizabethan Age* (2003).

COLET (Dean) John (1467–1519): Oxf.- and Cambr.-edu. ecclesiastic, theologian, humanist scholar & educator. Jan. 1467: b. one of the 22 children of Sir Henry Colet, a London mercer who was twice Mayor of London, & h.w. Christian Knyvet; 6 Aug. 1485: presented to family living of R of Dennington, Suffolk; early 1490s: travelled in Italy; 17 Dec. 1497: ord. deac.; 25 Mar. 1498: ord. pr.; 1499–1505: R of Stepney, wealthiest living in Eng.; 1496–1505: acquired reputation for exposition at Oxf. of writings of St Paul by relating them to the purpose & context in which they were written; preached some of his homilies in English; opponent of pilgrimages and popular cults of saints' images and relics; 1499: began lifelong friendship with **Erasmus** (q.v.); 1502–19: Canon of Salisbury; 2 June 1505–19: Dean of St Paul's; 1508–19: Treasurer of Chichester Cathedral; 1508–12: founded St Paul's School; 18 Nov. 1515: preached at Wolsey's app't as cardinal; benefited from Wolsey's patronage; by 1517: member of King's Council; 16 Sept. 1519: d.

Co(o)ke Ann (see **Bacon Ann**).

Co(o)ke (Sir) Anthony (1504–76): self-taught educator and companion/guide to Edward VI; b. s. & h. of John Coke or Cooke (1485–1516) of Gidea Hall, Essex, & Alice (Saunders) (d. 1510), dau. of William Saunders of Banbury, Oxon.; raised by uncle Richard Cooke and his stepmother Margaret Pennington, who was lady-in-waiting to Katherine of Aragon; m. before 1523 Anne Fitzwilliam; they had four sons and five daus; 1523: adm. Inner Temple; 1530s: edu. his children, giving his daus an edu. comparable to or better than his s.; 1539: app'd to Henry VIII's bodyguard; 1546: Gentleman of the Privy Chamber; Father of **Mildred (Cecil)**, **Ann (Bacon)**, **Catherine (Killigrew)** and **Elizabeth (Russell)** (all q.v.). 1547: KB; 1547–49: served on various ecclesiastical commissions; 1550: probably app'd to work with Edward VI as companion and guide rather than tutor; 1552: obtained Church lands; 1553: self-imposed exile; travelled in Italy; 1555: Marian exile in Strasbourg; 1558: returned to Eng.; 1559–67: M.P. Essex; 1559–76: active on commissions. M.K. McIntosh, 'Sir Anthony Cooke: Tudor humanist, educator, and religious reformer', *Proceedings of the American Philosophical*

Society, 119 (1975), 233–50; R.M.Warnicke, *Women of the English Renaissance and Reformation*, Westport, Conn., Greenwood Press, 1983.

Co(o)ke Elizabeth (see **Russell Elizabeth**).

Co(o)ke Katherine (see **Killigrew Catherine**).

Co(o)ke Mildred (see **Cecil Mildred**).

Cooper, Thomas (c. 1517–94): Oxf.-edu. lexicographer and learned theologian and reforming pr. and teaching Bp of Winchester; b. Oxf.; said to be s. of a poor tailor; began as servant at Magdalen College; 1530–31: chorister at Magdalen College School; 1539: adm. probationer fellow at Magdalen; 1540: BA & Fellow; 1543: MA; friend of **John Foxe** (q.v.); 1545: resigned fellowship; 1546: m. Amy (? Royse); 1548: pub'd revision of **Thomas Elyot**'s English Dictionary; 1549: app'd Master of Magdalen College School; scandals involving his wife Amy 'too light for his gravitie'; dismissed from H'mastership under Mary I; 1556: MB & practised as doctor; 1559: reapp'd H/master of Magdalen College School; 1560: pub'd 'Cooper's Chronicle'; ordained pr.; 1565: pub'd his own *Thesaurus*; 18 Mar. 1567: BTh & DTh on same day; 1567: Vice-Chancellor of Oxf.; 1567: Dean of Christ Church, Oxf. & tutor to **Philip Sidney** (q.v.); 24 Feb. 1571: consecrated Bp of Lincoln; energetic pr. bp. & dioesan reformer; org'd education of clergy through **exercises** in scripture (prophesyings); pub'd books of scriptural teaching for general consumption; suppressed dissents; 12 Mar. 1584: transl. Bp of Winchester; tackled problem of recusancy against background of Armada threat; 1589: *An Admonition to the People of England – defence of Church of England* which contained section against Martin Marprelate; Cooper became target for Martin Marprelate tracts (see **John Penry**, **Robert Waldegrave**, **John Udall**, **Elizabeth Crane**); 23 Mar. 1589: *Hay any Worke for a Cooper*? was their response to his *Admonition* and to his lexicographical work; 29 Apr. 1594: d.

COVERDALE (Bishop) Miles (c. 1488–1568): Cambr.-edu. translator of English Bible. 1514: entered Austin Friars, Cambr.; part of the Barnes circle at the White Horse Inn; of unknown parentage; c. 1514: ord. pr. in Norw. dioc.; 1526: accompanied **Robert Barnes** (q.v.) to London to help prepare defence v. charges of heresy; 1527: **Thomas Cromwell** (q.v.) gave Coverdale money to buy theological books; 1528: Coverdale became secular pr. & began to preach heresy – abandoned by Cromwell as unsafe; 1528–34: probably in Antwerp & Hamburg w. Tyndale; 1534: Jacob van Meteren, Protestant printer in Antwerp, paid Coverdale to prepare English transl. of Bible; Coverdale's transl. printed in Cologne; importation of his Eng. Bible (based on German & Latin sources & Tyndale's transl.) into Eng.; 1539: came to Eng. at Cromwell's request to work on Great Bible; 1540: travelled abroad after Cromwell's fall; 1548: resident at Windsor in Cranmer's company; 1551: Bp of Exeter; 1553: depr. for m.; 1553: accepted invitation to preach in Denmark; 1558: in Geneva; 1559: returned to Eng., not as bp but participated in consecration of Archbp **Matthew Parker** (q.v.); 1563: refused see of Llandaff; resigned living of St Magnus near London Bridge because he refused to conform.

COX LEONARD (c. 1495–1549 or after): humanist educator; c. 1495: poss. b. Monmouth, 2nd s. of Laurence Cox of Monmouth & h.w. Elizabeth (Willey); poss. edu. in France & Prague; 1514–16: studied at Tubingen Uni. under Philip Melanchthon; 1518: matric. at Cracow Uni. as of Thame, Oxon.; 1520: Headmaster of Levoča GS, Hungary; 1521: Headmaster of Kosice GS; 1524: lecturer at Cracow Uni; 1526: pub'd Erasmian treatise on education: *Libellus de erudienda juventute*, and *Methodus humaniorum studiorum*;1526–29: ran school for Cracow nobility;1529: Schoolmaster of

Reading GS; 1530: M.A. Oxf.; 1530: pub'd *The Arte or Crafte of Rhethoryke* based on Melancthon; 1534: pub'd Eng. transl. of Erasmus's paraphrase on the epistle to Titus; 1549: pub'd 2nd ed'n of Erasmus's paraphrase; last recorded mention is in 1549.

COX (Bishop) Richard (1500–81): humanist scholar & tutor to Edward VI; edu. at Cambr.; Headmaster of Eton; 1544–50: tutor to Edward VI; 1547–53: Dean of Christ Church College, Oxf.; 1547–52: Vice-Chancellor of Oxf. Uni.; 1548–50: Commissioner to revise liturgy; 1549: Dean of Westminster; 1553: imprisoned; 1554–58: Marian exile, chiefly in Frankfurt (see **Knox/Cox** controversy); 1559: Bp of Norwich; 1559–80: Bp of Ely; struggled v. royal attempts to deplete the financial resources of the see of Ely. F. Heal, *Of Prelates and Princes*, Cambridge, 1980.

CRANE Elizabeth (fl. 1580s): harbourer of Marprelate Press. A wealthy widow who allowed Marprelate Press to use two of her houses between Apr. & Nov. 1588. She was arrested, refused to plead guilty & was released.

CRANMER (Archbishop) Thomas (1489–1556): Cambr.-edu. Archbp of Canterbury, liturgist & Protestant martyr. 2 July 1489: b. in Notts s. of Thos, esq. & h.w. Agnes (Hatfield); edu. at Southwell GS & Cambr.; c. 1515: m. (i) Joan, who d. in childbirth; 1529: wrote treatise defending the royal divorce; 1530: part of Earl of Wiltshire's embassy to Emperor Charles V; 1532: m. secretly (ii) Margaret Preu, niece of Andreas Osiander; dau. Margaret; 1533: app'd Archbp of Canterbury, pronounced royal divorce, proclaimed validity of Henry's m. to Anne Boleyn, defended Royal Supremacy; 1536: decl. m. to Anne Boleyn null & void, promulgated Ten Articles of doctrine; 1539: unsuccessfully oppo'd conservative Six Articles, supported divorce from Anne of Cleves; 1540: did not rise to Cromwell's defence; 1541: informed on Katherine Howard to

Henry; 1542: defended Great Bible v. Gardiner & was cleared of heresy by Henry VIII; 1547: member of regency council during Edward VI's minority; 1548: chaired production of first Edwardian BofCP; 1549: declared marriage legalised; Margaret appeared in public; 1550: proposals for reform of canon law: '**Reformatio Legum Ecclesiasticarum**'; 1552: instrumental in revisions of prayer book; 1552: promulgated 42 Articles of Religion; 1553: signed Edward VI's will barring Mary from succession; 1553: impr. as supporter of Queen Jane (see Grey (Lady) Jane) & a heretic; 1554: released to answer charges; 1555: refused to recognise papal jurisdiction; condemned as heretic by Cardinal Pole (q.v.); 1556: recanted all but rejection of transubstantiation; 21 Mar. 1556: burnt at stake, repudiating recantation. See Chapter 1: General chronology for further detail. D. MacCulloch, *Thomas Cranmer: A Life*, 1996.

CROMWELL (Lord) Thomas (?1485–1540): Earl of Essex. Royal servant & statesman; c. 1485: b. Putney, s. of Walter, blacksmith & cloth merchant, & h.w.; 28 Dec. 1503: present at Battle of Garigliano; spent time in Florence, then as clerk to merchant in Antwerp; c. 1510–13: 2nd visit to Italy & audience with Pope Julian II; possibly clerk to a Venetian merchant; c. 1513–1520: business agent & moneylender; June 1514: 3rd visit to Italy; 1520s: m. (i) widow Elizabeth (née Wykys) Williams, who d. 1527; one s., Gregory; built up legal practice & reputation; 1523: M.P. for unidentified constituency; 1524: app'd Subsidy (Tax) Commissioner for Middlesex & Member of Gray's Inn; c. 1524: joined Wolsey's service; 1525: Commissioner (app'd by Wolsey (q.v.) to inquire into smaller religious houses; later 1520s: secretary to Wolsey; c. 1529: instrumental in persuading Henry VIII to make himself Head of the Church in Eng.; 4 Nov. 1529: M.P. for Taunton; late 1530: member of King's Council; 1531: PC; 1532: Master of Court of Wards & 14 Apr. 1532: Master of Jewel House; 12 Apr. 1533: Chancellor of Exchequer; 1534: King's Secretary & Master of Rolls, pushed suit of treason v. Bp John Fisher (q.v.); 1535: Vicar-General & organised general visitation of the Church & the compilation of Valor Ecclesiasticus or 'King's Book'; 1536: moving spirit in dissolution of smaller religious houses, attended Anne Boleyn (q.v.) to the Tower & was made Lord Privy Seal & Baron Cromwell of Oakham; 1537: KG & Dean of Wells; 1539: overseer of printing of Bible in English, Lord Great Chamberlain, & nego. Henry's m. w. Anne of Cleves (q.v.); 1540: cr. Earl of Essex; 28 July 1540: exec. for tr. Assigned, by historians, a pivotal role in reorganisation of the central administration during the 1530s, amounting in the opinion of some to a revolution in gov't. Lively debate concerning his Protestantism. See Chapter 1: General chronology for further detail. A.G. Dickens, *Thomas Cromwell and the English Reformation*, 1959; G.R. Elton, *Thomas Cromwell*, 1991; J.A. Guy (ed.), *The Tudor monarchy*, 1997; R. O'Day, *The Debate on the English Reformation*, 1986; D. Starkey, *The Reign of Henry VIII: Personalities and Politics*, 1991 ed'n.

CROWLEY Robert (c. 1518–88): Oxf.-edu. Commonwealthman & author; edu. Magdelen College, Oxf.; 1540: B.A. Oxf.; 1541: probationer fellow Magdalen College, Oxf.; 1542: Fellow; 1542: resigned fellowship; 1542–46: tutor of children of Sir Nicholas Poyntz of Iron Acton, Gloucestershire; c. 1546: proofreader for **John Day** (q.v.); commonwealthman during reign of Edward VI; 1549: pub'd metrical Psalms & The Voice of the Last Trumpet; 1550: author of commonwealth tract, The Way to Wealth, & a collection of cautionary tales in verse, & pub'd 1st complete version of The Vision of Pierce Plowman by Langland; 1551: ord. deac. by Ridley (q.v.); 1555: exile at Frankfurt; by 1557: m. w. children; 24 Mar. 1559: app'd Archd. of Hereford; various eccles. preferments under Elizabeth; 1579: app'd licencer for printing books; 18 June 1588: d. & bur. alongside **John Foxe** (q.v.)

CUMBERLAND Earl of (see **Clifford George**).

154

D

DARCY (Lord) Thomas (1467–1537): leader of Yorkshire Pilgrimage of Grace. Position of great power & prestige in the northern counties. Oppo. royal divorce & suppression of the monasteries. 21 Oct. 1536: surrendered Pontefract Castle to the rebels & became leader of Pilgrimage of Grace; 30 June 1537: exec. on Tower Hill.

DARNLEY Earl of, Henry Stuart (1546–67): in line of succession to the Eng. throne & 2nd husb. of **Mary Queen of Scots**. 2nd s. of Matthew Stuart, Earl of Lennox, & **Lady Margaret Douglas**, dau. of Margaret Tudor (widow of James IV of Scotland & elder sister of Henry VIII) & her second husband the Earl of Angus. Henry Stuart, b. in Yorks, was next in line to the Eng. throne after Mary Queen of Scots. 1565: Henry Stuart visited Mary with Elizabeth's permission & **David Rizzio** (q.v.) encouraged m. between them; 29 July 1565: m. Mary; highly unpopular w. Scots nobles; his unseemly behaviour alienated Mary & she refused him access & turned instead to Rizzio for counsel; 9 Mar. 1566: Darnley, implicated in plot involving both Catholics & Protestants, admitted murderers to Holyrood & led them to Rizzio's room, where he lent his dagger to commit the murder; Mary briefly reconciled with Darnley, bound to him by the knowledge of her pregnancy, but she did not forgive him & denied him all political infl. He tried to leave the country but was prevented by syphillis. Mary, by now under **Bothwell**'s infl. (q.v.), persuaded Darnley to go to Kirk o'Field in Edinburgh to convalesce. 9 Feb. 1567: Darnley murdered at Kirk o'Field.

DAUBENEY Giles (1451–1508): one of Henry VII's principal councillors, influential court patron; originally a member of Edward IV's household. 14 Jan. 1478: knighted; c. 1476: m. Elizabeth Arundel; 1478: adm. to Lincoln's Inn & M.P. for Somerset; 1480: Sheriff of Dorset & Somerset; Oct. 1483: rebelled v. Richard III; 1485: fought at Bosworth; Henry VII made him Chamberlain of his household in Stanley's stead; 7 Mar. 1486: Lieutenant of Calais; 12 Mar.1486: cr. Baron Daubeney; 1486: negotiated at Calais with embassy of Maximilian, King of the Romans; 1487: KG; 13 June 1489: led expedition to assist Maximilian v. the Flemings & French at Dixmude; June 1492: jointly led negotiations with the French &, later that year, accompanied Henry VII to siege of Boulogne. His part in the battle of Dixmude & the making & ratification of the treaty of Étaples with the French brought him pensions from Maximilian & Charles VIII of France respectively; rewarded by lands & patronage in Eng.; 1497: despite his suspected leniency to Blackheath rebels, Henry gave him command of the army assembled in Sept. to deal with Perkin Warbeck's renewal of the Cornish revolt: took Taunton & relieved Exeter from rebel siege.

DAVIES (Bishop) Richard (1505–81): Marian exile; prominent in support of Welsh language. c. 1505: b. Caernarvonshire, s. of Dafydd ap Gronw, curate of Gyffin, Bangor dioc., & Sioned, dau. of Dafydd ap Richard; 1522/23: adm. New Inn Hall, Oxf.; 1530: M.A.; 1536: B.Th.; 1549: R of Maidsmorton, Buckinghamshire; 1550: R of Burnham, Bucks (centre of Lollardy); 1550: m. Dorothy (Woodforde); two daus & three s.; 17 Sept. 1553: brought before PC for heretical views; Marian exile in Frankfurt, where he sided w. the conservative faction; 1560: Bp of St Asaph's; 1561: Bishop of St David's; adviser to Burghley & **Matthew Parker** (q.v.) on Welsh eccles. matters. 1567: published Prayer Book & New Testament in Welsh; 7 Nov. 1581: d. (see Salesbury William (q.v.)).

DAVIS (Captain) John (c. 1550–1605): navigator & explorer. Unknown parentage; 29 Sept. 1582: m. Faith Fulford; three s.; 1585:commanded expedition to find Northwest Passage to China, financed by London merchants; reached Greenland & Baffin Island; several voyages; 1587:

Traverse Book – a model for future log books; 1593: discovered Falkland Islands on trip to South Seas; m. ended by Faith's adultery; 1595: World's Hydrographical Description – defence v. attacks for failing to discover Northwest Passage, & described route which permitted Hudson later to reach Hudson's Strait; 1598: visited the East Indies; 29/30 Dec. 1605: killed by pirates off the coast of Borneo.

DAY, George (c. 1502–56): Bp of Chichester. Elder brother of **William Day** (1529–96). Cambr.-edu. humanist who became first Linacre Professor of medicine. c. 1502: b. 3rd s. of Richard Day, gent., of Newport, Salop & h.w. Agnes (Osborne); 1521: B.A. from St John's College, Cambr.; 1522: fellow; 1524: M.A.; 1525: 1st Linacre Prof. of medicine; college praelector in Greek; 1528: public orator to uni.; 1530s: supported royal supremacy & was favoured at court; 1537: Master of St John's College; Sept. 1537: presented to important benefices; 5 June 1538: provost of King's College, Cambr.; 1538–43: served on important ecclesiastical commissions; 15 Apr. 1543: Bp of Chichester; 1547–53: traditionalist views led to deprivation of see & impr.; 1553: released; 1554: preached at funeral of Edward VI & at Queen's coronation; 1555: participated in examination of **John Hooper**, John Philppot & others; 2 Aug. 1556: d.

DAY[e] John (1521/22–84): well-connected evangelical Protestant printer & bookseller; poss. b. in Suffolk; 1546: began printing career in London; 1547: took advantage of relaxation in laws v. printing heretical books; 1548: in partnership with William Seres, pub'd 20 books, 10 of which contributed to Eucharistic controversy & included works by **Robert Crowley** (q.v.), Luke Shepherd & William Turner; also published English ed'ns of important continental works; 1550: moved to Cheapside & dissolved partnership with Seres; 1548–53: used foreign technological expertise to publish c. 130 books, incl. elaborate folio Bible; 1553: granted patent to publish works of **Thomas Becon** (q.v.) &

John Ponet (q.v.); 1554: involved in secret production of Protestant literature, possibly using the pseudonym of Michael Wood of Rouen; Oct. 1554: impr. briefly; 1556–58: returned to printing; 1558–84: re-estab'd his business on a grander & more lucrative scale, with the patronage of important men such as **Robert Dudley**, Earl of Leicester (q.v.); produced highly successful works such as John Ponet's *ABC with Little Catechism* & Sternhold & Hopkins' *English Psalter* and prestigious collections of the writings of Becon, **Hugh Latimer** (q.v.) & **William Tyndale** (q.v.); the profit made from the *ABC* & the *Psalter* probably made possible his most ambitious project – the partnership with **John Foxe** (q.v.), which resulted eventually in *Acts and Monuments*; 1563: pub'd Foxe's *Acts and Monuments* (Book of Martyrs) – an enormous work (1,800 pages & 50 woodcut illustrations) that posed considerable technical difficulties & capital outlay; 1570: 2nd ed'n of *Acts and Monuments*; 1571: copy of Book of Martyrs ordered to be set up in every cathedral & in houses of senior clergy; 1576: 3rd ed'n; 1583: 4th ed'n; 1564–84: produced political tracts in support of the Elizabethan regime, such as George Buchanan's attack on Mary of Scotland; 1566: pub'd **Matthew Parker**'s typographically ambitious edition of Aelfric's Testimonie of Antiquitie; 1570: exclusive rights to **Alexander Nowell**'s *Catechism* (q.v.); 1570: published in folio illustrated English translation of Euclid's *Elements of Geometry*; 1573: his attempted murder was foiled; 1573: set up shop in Paul's churchyard; 1584: commission of inquiry into his monopoly led to his surrender of rights to 30 important titles; 23 July 1584: d. at Walden, Essex; had m. twice & had 13 children by each w.; widow Alice (Lehunte) survived until 1612. C.L. Oastler, *John Day, The Elizabethan Printer*, 1975.

DAY, William (1529–96): Eton & Cambr.-edu. Protestant Bp of Winchester. Younger brother of **George** (q.v). 1529: b. s. of Richard & Agnes (Osbourne) Day of Newport, Salop; edu. Eton & Cambr; 1553–58: Fellow of King's College, despite

Protestant beliefs; 1560: ord. deac. & pr.; 1561: Provost of Eton; 1562: B.Th.; 1563: led liturgical reformers in convocation but failed in attempt to remove remaining Catholic ceremonies; c. 1565: m. Elizabeth dau. of Bp William Barlow of Chichester; two s. & three daus; 1572: Dean of Windsor; often suggested as candidate for bprics but failed to obtain one; 25 Jan. 1596: consecr. Bp of Winchester; 20 Sept. 1596: d.

DEE (Dr) John (1527–1609): Cambr.-edu. English alchemist, astrologer, teacher of navigation & mathematician, & major book & manuscript collector, whose activities included the antiquarian study of old manuscripts. 13 July 1527: b. London, only child of Rowland Dee & h.w. Joanna Wild; edu. Chelmsford GS; 1542: adm. St John's College, Cambr.; 1546: fellow & under-reader in Greek, Trinity College, Cambr.; 1548: M.A.; 1547–49: several visits to Netherlands & studies at Louvain Uni. possibly motivated by attempts to change mathematical curriculum; 1551: royal pension; 1552–53: tutor to **John Dudley**, Earl of Warwick; 1553–54: taught mathematics in London & Oxf.; 1554: estab'd links with merchants in London, who used his skills in search for Northeast & Northwest Passages; May 1555: impr. for necromancy; 19 Aug. 1555: released; 1550s: reading Copernicus; 1558: his 1st important work of natural philosophy, Propaideumata aphoristica (2nd ed'n, 1568); 1561: pub'd ed'n of Robert Recorde's Ground of Arts; 1562–63: travels in Switzerland & Italy; c. 1565: m. (i) Katherine Constable (d. 1575); 1566: settled in Mortlake; 1570: pub'd most influential work, the 'Mathematicall praeface' to Henry Billingsley's English translation of Euclid, Elements of Geometrie, printed by **John Day** (q.v.); suggested Imperial expansion into the New World; 1574: tour of the Welsh Marches in search of antiquities & manuscripts, exhibiting strong interest in Arthurian legend; 1576: began The Brytish Monarchy; 1577: published part I: . . . Perfect Art of Navigation (with first occurrence of term 'British Impire'); 1576–77: advised on navigation for

Sir **Martin Frobisher**'s three voyages (q.v.); 5th Feb. 1578: m. (ii) Jane Fromond[s] (1555–1605); eight children; named 1st s. Arthur; 1581– : used mediums for divination; 1582: supported intro. of **Gregorian calendar** but was overruled; 23/24 Jan 1583: discussed with Sir **Francis Walsingham** (q.v.), Adrian Gilbert and **John Davis** (q.v.) renewed attempt to discover Northwest Passage; 1583: travelled with family & 800 books to Poland; Albrecht Łaski, palatine of Sieradż participated in his sessions with medium; devastating raid on his house at Mortlake during his absence; 1584: M.D. from Uni. of Prague & audience with Rudolf; 1586: alchemical practitioner; 1589 onwards: attempted to recover fortunes & support large family; May 1595: Warden of Collegiate Church, Manchester; May 1597: Survey of parish; increasingly impoverished; 26 Mar. 1609: d. at Mortlake. P.J. French, John Dee: The World of an Elizabethan Magus, 1972; Benjamin Woolley, The Queen's Conjuror: The Science and Magic of Dr Dee, 2001.

DENNY (Sir) Anthony (1501–49): courtier & humanist patron; edu. St Paul's School & Cambr.; 1501: b. 2nd s. of Sir Edmund Denny, gent. & his 2nd w. Mary (Troutbeck); 28 May 1533: in the privy chamber; 1535–36: ?M.P. Ipswich; 1536: yeoman of the wardrobe; 1536: protégé of Thomas Cromwell (q.v.); 9 Feb. 1538: m. Joan (Champernowne) (q.v.); five s. & four daus; 20 Sept. 1538: app'd Keeper of Westminster Palace; 1539: gent. of privy chamber; 24 Apr. 1542: Keeper of privy purse; close to Henry VIII; 1544: knighted; 1545: given control of sign manual (stamp of the monarch's signature); 1543: intervened to protect **Thomas Cranmer** (q.v.) v. heresy charges; Oct. 1546: 1st Chief Gent. & Groom of the Stool; 1546: conservatives seek to oust him in wake of **Anne Askew** arrest; humanist patron & friend of Protestants such as **Roger Ascham** (q.v.) & Thomas Cranmer; 31 Jan. 1547: PC; leading supporter of **Edward Seymour, Duke of Somerset** (q.v.); 1547: M.P. Herts; 1549: sat on parl. Committee that examined Thomas Seymour & signed council's order for his exec.; July 1549: marched to suppress **Kett's rebellion**; d. 10 Sept. 1549. Benefactor of Sedburgh School, Yorks.

DENNY (Lady) Joan or Jane (d. 1553): dau. of Sir Philip Champernowne of Modbury, Devon, & his w., Katherine (Carew) & sister of **Katherine Astley** (q.v.). 9 Feb. 1538: m. Sir Anthony Denny; bore five sons & four daus; lady-in-waiting in the Protestant households of queens **Anne of Cleves** & **Katherine Parr**; said to have protected the persecuted Protestant reformers in Devon (w. her sister-in-law Katherine Raleigh); 1546: was one of those whom religious conservatives tried to oust on the strength of accusations made reluctantly by her distant relative **Anne Askew** (q.v.) but survived; 1553: d.

DERING (Rev.) Edward (c. 1540–76): Cambr.-edu. Greek scholar, Church of England clergyman & evangelical, who served as paradigm for future generations. C. 1540: b. 3rd s. of John Dering of Surrenden Dering, Kent, & h.w. Margaret (Brent); 1560: B.A. Christ's College, Cambr.; 1561: ord. deac.; 1563: M.A.; 1568: B.Th.;1560–70: fellow; 1564: made Greek oration to welcome Elizabeth I to Cambr. Uni.; 1567: Lady Margaret preacher; 1567: presented to R of Pluckley, Kent, where he was non-resident; chaplain to **Thomas Howard, 4th Duke of Norfolk** & also to the Tower; 1570–72: Norfolk's fall & exec.; dedicated himself to preaching of the Word, without fear or favour; high doctrine of the ministry; Feb. 1570: preached before the Queen & alienated her by rash critique of her treatment of her Church; rebuked both **William Cecil** (q.v.) & **Matthew Parker** (q.v.); 1572: app'd divinity lecturer at St Paul's Cathedral & earned reputation as the great Elizabethan preacher, whose sermons went into 16 ed'ns by the end of the reign; 1572: brought before Star Chamber for supporting John Field; 1572: collab. w. John More in the enormously influential *A Brief and Necessary Catechism* for the use of householders when catechising their families; 1572: m. Anne (Vaughan) Locke (q.v.), widowed friend of John Knox

(q.v.), Burghley's sister-in-law; had spiritual relationship with leading women of the day, including Katherine (Co(o)ke) Killigrew (q.v.) & Mrs Mary Honeywood; 26 June 1576: d. P. Collinson, *Godly People: Essays on English protestantism and Puritanism,* 1983, pp. 288–324.

DEVEREUX (Lord) Robert (1565–1601): 2nd Earl of Essex. Soldier, politician & royal favourite; s. of **Walter Devereux** (q.v.), 1st Earl of Essex; through his mother Lettice (Knollys) (see **Dudley Lettice**), Robert was part of Elizabeth I's Boleyn-Carey cousinage; two sisters, Penelope Rich & Dorothy & a brother Walter; upbringing markedly Protestant; edu. by Thomas Ashton & Robert Wright at Shrewsbury School & at Trinity College, Cambr., where Wright became his tutor; 1576: became royal ward in household of **William Cecil**, & his heavily indebted estate was managed by Richard Broughton, lawyer; May 1577: entered Trinity College, Cambr.; 1578: increasingly under infl. of his godfather & stepfather, **Robert Dudley**, Earl of Leicester (q.v.); 1581: proceeded M.A.; Nov. 1581 to Feb. 1582: part of household of his grandfather **Sir Francis Knollys** (q.v.); Feb. 1582 to late 1583: with **Earl of Huntingdon** at York (q.v.); early Sept. 1585: joined the Court; his estate of Chartley chosen as prison of Mary of Scotland; Dec. 1585: accompanied Leicester's army to Netherlands as commander of cavalry; 1587–92: Elizabeth I's favourite; supported by Earl of Leicester: 'my lord is at cardes or one game or another with her, that he commeth not to his owne lodginge tyll the birdes singe in the morninge' (Folger Shakespeare Library, L.a.39); 18 June 1587: app'd Master of the Horse; granted use of York House; 23 Apr. 1588: KG; attended Queen at Tilbury; 4 Sept. 1588: d. of Leicester; Christmas 1588: rivalry betw. Essex & Raleigh reached peak; Essex seeking opportunities to practise profession of arms on land & sea in imitation of his dead hero. Philip Sidney; late 1589: Essex & Penelope Rich made overtures to James VI of Scotland; against Queen's express wishes joined force of Drake & Norris to attack Spain & Portugal;

return to Queen's favour facilitated by support from Cecil, Knollys, Countess of Warwick, Walsingham, etc. 1590: displeased Queen by m. Frances (née Walsingham), widow of Philip Sidney; Jan. 1591: b. of s. Robert, later 3rd Earl of Essex; restricted support for Puritanism after Whitgift's ascent in 1591; cultivated relationship w. Whitgift as that w. Burghley deteriorated; 1591–92: led expeditionary force to assist Henri of Navarre as Lieut.-Gen.; 25 Feb. 1593: PC; Jan. 1594: campaign v. **Roderigo Lopez** led to quarrel w. Burghley; 1594: revival of support for James VI as Elizabeth's successor; 1596: defeated Spanish navy at Cadiz; 1598: oppo'd Burghley's peace w. Spain; made Chancellor of Cambr. Uni.; 1599: Lieut. & Governor-General of Ireland; ordered to proceed v. Ulster but made peace w. Tyrone; 25 Sept. 1599: returned to Eng. without the Queen's consent; 5 June 1600: charged w. dereliction of duty & making peace w. enemy; Aug. 1600: released; Feb. 1601: proclaimed traitor for plot to control Queen; 19 Feb. 1601: at his trial, his former protégé Francis Bacon spoke for prosecution; 25 Feb. 1601: exec. P.E.J. Hammer, *The Polarisation of Elizabethan Politics: The Political Career of Robert Devereux, 2nd Earl of Essex, 1585–1597*, 1999.

DEVEREUX Lord Walter (1539–76): 1st Earl of Essex, courtier & adventurer. 16 Sept. 1539: b. eldest s. of Sir Richard Devereux of Chartley, Staffs, & h.w. Dorothy (Hastings); 1561: as Walter, Lord Hereford m. Lettice (Knollys) eldest dau. of Sir Francis (1543–1634) & thus part of extended cousinage of Elizabeth I; 1563: Penelope b. (see **Rich Penelope**); 1564: Dorothy b.;1565: Robert b., later 2nd Earl of Essex (q.v.); 1569: Walter b.; raised troops to suppress Northern Earls rebellion; 23 Apr. 1572: KG; 4 May 1572: cr. Earl of Essex; 1573: went as adventurer (with grant from the Queen) on ill-fated & expensive attempt to colonise Ulster & oust the O'Neills; bloody massacre of Rathlin Island; 1575: returned to Eng.; 9 Mar. 1576: made Earl Marshal of Ireland; returned to Ireland for investiture; Sept. 1576: ill w.

dysentery; 22 Sept. 1576: d. ; rumoured to have been murdered by Earl of Leicester, who then m. his widow Lettice (see **Dudley Lettice**), but no truth in this.

DINHAM (Lord) John (1433–1501): Baron Dinham. Important member of Henry VII's council. Loyal to both Edward IV & Richard III; 1433: b. s. & h. of Sir John Dynham & h.w. Elizabeth (Arches); c. 1485: m. (ii) Elizabeth, sister of Robert Willoughby, Lord Willoughby de Broke, Steward of Henry VII's household; one s. (d. 1487) one dau. (d. 1485); 1486: app'd Treasurer by Henry VII; 1486–1501: remained Treasurer until replaced by Surrey; 28 Jan. 1501: d.

DORMER Jane (m. name: Suárez de Figueroa) (1538–1612): Duchess of Feria, Spain; courtier, noblewoman, celebrated beauty & Catholic exile. 6 Jan. 1538: b. dau. of Sir William Dormer & Mary Sidney; friend of Edward VI & maid of honour to Princess Mary from 1547 onwards; 29 Dec. 1558: m. Count Gomez Suárez de Figueroa of Feria, favourite of Philip II; May 1559: left for Europe &, once in Spain, provided refuge for English, Irish & Scottish Catholic exiles & support for the SJ training colleges; 1571: d. of Gomez; Jane recognised by Philip II as leader of the exiles and was therefore useful to them as a patron; 1578–79: entered into intrigues with the supporters of the papacy to persuade Philip II; this lessened her infl. w. Philip II but, to Elizabeth, she appeared dangerous; 1580s: Sir Francis Englefield & William Allen replaced her as leader of Catholic exiles; 1590s: leadership reasserted but proposal to send her to the Low Countries as envoy came to nothing; 1596: tried to persuade Philip II to declare his dau. Isabel's right to the English throne; 1600: tried to persuade James VI to convert to Catholicism; 1603–04: unsuccessful plans laid to make her one of Queen Anne of Denmark's ladies-in-waiting as part of the new friendship between Eng. & Spain.

DOUGLAS (Lady) Margaret (1515–78): Countess of Lennox; courtier niece of Henry

VII & grandmother of Arabella Stuart & Henry Stuart, Lord Darnley; 1515: b. dau. & h. of Archibald Douglas, 6th Earl of Angus & his 2nd w., **Margaret Tudor** (q.v.), elder dau. of Henry VII of Eng.; her mother took refuge at the Eng. court after her birth & Margaret was raised in the royal nursery at Greenwich until Henry VII ordered his dau. & grand-dau. back to Scotland in June 1517; Earl of Angus separated from his wife but took his dau. to use as a pawn in dynastic struggles; 1528: Lady Margaret in household of her godfather Cardinal Wolsey; Nov. 1530: Princess Mary, Duchess of Suffolk, invited her niece to the English court; Henry VIII gave her permission to live at Beaulieu, in the household of his dau. Mary, who became her friend; then became lady-in-waiting to Queen Anne Boleyn; contributed, along with **Mary Howard** & **Mary Shelton** (q.v.), to the Devonshire Manuscript collection of courtly poems; 1536–37: Henry declared both his daus illegitimate & regarded Lady Margaret as heiress presumptive; her secret liaison with Thomas Howard alarmed Henry VIII who feared a bid for the throne; impr. in Tower & under house arrest at Sion Abbey; 29 Oct. 1537: released; 1537: restored to favour on b. of Edward; became maid of honour to (i) **Anne of Cleves** (ii) **Katherine Howard**; affair w. Katherine's brother Charles led to her renewed imprisonment; 10 July 1543: bridesmaid to Queen **Katherine Parr**; 6 July 1544: Henry VIII arranged her m. to Matthew Stewart, Earl of Lennox (1516–71) who had agreed to assist Henry v. Scots; a love match but the couple were separated by Lennox's duties in Scotland; 1545: Henry Lord Darnley b.; she was cut out of the succession by Henry VIII's will because of her Catholicism; during Edward's reign her household at Temple Newsam became centre for RCs in Eng.; 1553: Margaret rest. to favour at Mary I's court, with apartments at Westminster Palace & many gifts from the Queen; granted precedence over Princess Elizabeth as heiress presumptive; 1558: greeted Elizabeth but her household became centre for plots v. her cousin; 1561: Lady Margaret's open angling

for m. betw. Mary of Scotland & her son Darnley a claimant for the Eng. throne came to Elizabeth's notice; Lennox sent to Tower & Margaret sent to the Sackvilles' house at Sheen; 1564: she was rest. to favour at Elizabeth's court; Margaret sent to Tower when Darnley & Lennox refused to leave Scotland; 19 Feb 1567: news of Darnley's murder made Margaret ill; Elizabeth released her & gave her & Lennox Coldharbour Palace as residence; 1574: visited Scotland with surviving s. Charles; Charles fell in love w. Elizabeth Cavendish, dau. of Lady Shrewsbury, & Margaret & Bess arranged m.; Elizabeth was furious and impr. both Margaret & Bess in the Tower; on release Margaret lived w. Charles, Elizabeth & their dau. Arbella (Arabella); 1576: Charles Earl of Lennox d. & Margaret attempted to seize the Lennox title for his dau.

DOWLAND John (?1563–1626): most famous Eng. musician of period; lutenist & composer of melodious, melancholy music. Unknown place of birth & parentage; described himself as Eng.; prob. served apprenticeship in noble household; 1580–84: accompanied Sir Henry Cobham on embassy to French court, where he saw & heard masques, court entertainments, airs & dances; 1588: already known as composer ('Dowland's Galliard'); 1588: B.Mus at Oxf.; Nov. 1590: probably Dowland's setting of the poem 'My [later 'His'] golden locks time hath to silver turnd' was performed at the tiltyard, Westminster when Sir Henry Lee resigned as Queen's champion; c. 1590: m.; 1591: s. Robert b.; 1592: appeared in entertainments for the Queen at Sudeley Castle; 1594: failed to gain app'ment as one of Queen's lutenists & travelled in Italy & Germany, meeting musicians; he became involved in Catholic intrigue v. Elizabeth in Italy but took fright, returned to Kassel & wrote a long letter to **Robert Cecil** (q.v.) vowing his loyalty to Elizabeth; 1597: pub'd *The First Booke of Songes or Ayres*, dedicated to Sir George Carey; went through five ed'ns by 1613 & was highly influential; 1598: app'd lutenist to Christian IV of

Denmark; made frequent trips to London to Christian's annoyance; 1600 & 1603: pub'd two more books of ayres; 1604: pub'd *Lachrimae* & dedicated it to Queen Anne, sister of Christian; little evidence that he acted as secret agent for the English in Denmark; 1612: pub'd book of ayres, *A Pilgrimes Solace*; Oct. 1612: app'd King's lutenist; c. 1620: awarded Oxf. doctorate; Feb. 1626: d.

DOWRICHE (née Edgcumbe) Anne (c. 1559, *d. after* 1613): humanist & Protestant historian & poet. 1559: b. dau. of Sir Richard Edgcumbe (d. 1562) & h.w. Elizabeth (Tregian); sister of Pearce Edgcumbe, M.P. 1580: m. Hugh Dowriche, a Devon cleric; six chidren; 1589: w. specific political & religious aims in mind, pub'd *The French Historie*, a verse history of the French wars of religion, based on a work by Jean de Serre but also using other sources; 1596: pub'd verses in Hugh Dowriche, *The Jaylor's Conversion*.

DRAKE (Sir) Francis (1540–96): legendary explorer, sea captain & pirate. Cousin of William Hawkins.); 1540: b. 5th child of Edmund Drake, depr. priest & wool worker of Tavistock & ?Anna Milwaye; 1553: his father was curate of Upchurch, Kent; entered household of William Hawkins; went to sea as a boy w. Hawkins, engaged in piracy; 1560, 1562, 1566, 1567: went on Hawkins family slaving expeditions; 1567: commanded ship for the 1st time; 1569: m. (i) Mary Newman (d. 1583); 1571: lucrative raids on the Spanish Main; 1575: role in Essex massacre of Rathlin Island (see **Devereux** (Lord) Walter); 1577: planned trip with important investment into the Pacific for raid on Spanish settlements; 1578–80: this voyage, which early saw mutiny (& exec.) of Thomas Doughty, Drake's partner & one of Essex's men, was the occasion for Drake on the *Golden Hind* (formerly *The Pelican*) circumnavigating the globe & capturing hordes of treasure; 26 Sept. 1580: returned to Plymouth; immense treasure split between Drake, investors & the Queen;

Drake purchased Buckland Abbey, nr Plymouth; 1581: knighted on board the *Golden Hind*; portrait painted by **Nicholas Hilliard**; Sept. 1581: Mayor of Plymouth; 1581, 1584, 1593: M.P.; c. 1585: m. (ii) Elizabeth Sydenham (d. 1598) Somerset heiress; 1585: sailed as Queen's Admiral on official voyage to attack Spanish West Indies (Espanola, Cuba) & greatly damaged the Spanish, not least by capturing over 240 guns & thus weakening the Armada, but failed to bring home the expected treasure; Apr. 1587: plundered & burned Spanish merchant fleet of 24 ships at Cadiz, this 'singeing of His Catholic Majesty's Beard' forced Philip II to delay sailing of the Armada; Drake then captured treasure ships off the Azores; 26 June 1587: Drake returned to Eng. victorious; Thomas Fenner & Philip Nichols were employed by Drake to present him more favourably to the public, espec. by suggesting religious piety; information he gleaned warned Elizabeth of the preparation of the Armada; 1588: second in command in defence v. Armada under Lord High Admiral Howard of Effingham, & proposed to seek out the Armada in Spanish waters; storms forced the Eng. fleet back; 19 July 1588: Armada sighted off the Lizard heading towards Plymouth; posthumous story of Drake completing his game of bowls on the Plymouth Hoe before going to finish off the Spanish fleet in the *Revenge*; 22 July 1588: disobeyed Howard to follow *Nuestra Señora del Rosario* & captured the pay ship before rejoining the fleet; withdrew early from battle at Gravelines; 1589: Drake brought before Privy Council for conduct of campaign in the Azore but charges dropped; 1595: final voyage to the West Indies; 27 Jan. 1596: d. of fever at Porto Bello.

DRAYTON Michael (1563–1631): poet & dramatist. 1563: b. Atherstone, Warws. s. of William Drayton, tanner, & h.w. Katherine; 1580–85: prob. in household of Thomas Goodere at Collingham, Notts; 1591: pub'd *The Harmonie of the Church*, biblical passages rendered in verse, dedicated to Lady Jane Devereux; 1593: *Idea: the Shepheards*

Garland, nine eclogues modelled on Spenser's *Shepheardes Calender*; 1594: *Matilda: The Faire and Chaste Daughter of the Lord Robert Fitzwater*; 1596: *The Tragicall Legend of Robert, Duke of Normandy*, dedicated to the Countess of Bedford; 1594: *Ideas Mirrour: Amours in Quatorzains* (51 sonnets perhaps dedicated to the Countess of Pembroke, Mary Sidney); 1595: *Endymion and Phœbe* (516 couplets), dedicated to Lucy Harington, Countess of Bedford; 1596: *Mortimeriados* (civil wars during the reign of Edward II), 1597: *Englands Heroicall Epistles*, one of his most popular works; 1597–1604 collaborated w. others to produce more than a score of plays for the Lord Admiral's Men; 1600: Sir John Oldcastle, Part 1 (written w. Robert Wilson, Richard Hathway & Anthony Munday) survived; 1603: unsuccessful in bid for James I's patronage; 1605: dedicated collected poems to Sir Walter Aston of Tixall; 1606: *Man in the Moon* (revised version of *Endymion and Phœbe*); 1607: *The Legend of Great Cromwel*; 1610: *Mirrour for Magistrates*; 1612: *Poly-Olbion* dedicated to Prince Henry; 1619: collected works – did not include his plays – dedicated again to Aston; 1627: accused in London consistory court of indecent behaviour; 1630: *The Muses Elizium*, dedicated to the Earl of Dorset; Dec. 1631: d. in London. W. Hebel and K. Tillotson (eds), M. Drayton, *Works*, ed., five vols. 1961; B.H. Newdigate, *Michael Drayton and his Circle*, 1961; J. Brink, *Michael Drayton Revisited*, Boston, 1990; R. Hardin, *Michael Drayton and the Passing of Elizabethan England*, Lawrence, 1973.

DUDLEY (Lord) Ambrose (c. 1530–90): Earl of Warwick, Patron & magnate. c. 1530: b. 4th s. of **John Dudley**, Duke of Northumberland and Jane (Guildford); brother of John, Mary, Henry, Robert, Guildford & Katherine (all q.v.); 1549: fought v. Norfolk rebels; m. (i) Anne Whorwood (d. 1552); 20 Dec. 1549: Constable of Kenilworth Castle; c. 1553: m. (ii) Elizabeth Tailboys (d. 1563); Nov. 1553: charged w. treason re placing of **Jane Grey** (q.v.) on throne; Jan. 1555: pardoned; Mar.

1559: Master of the Ordnance; 26 Dec. 1561: Earl of Warwick; 6 Apr. 1562: granted lordship of Warwick Castle; autumn 1562: commanded expeditionary force to Le Havre; July 1563: surrendered Le Havre; Apr. 1563: KG; 11 Nov. 1565: m. (iii) Anne Russell (d. 1604), dau. of Francis, 2nd Earl of Bedford; Oct. 1569: commanded army v. Northern rebellion; close relationship w. his brother, Robert; active patronage of puritan preachers; 1573: PC; 1576: invested in **Martin Frobisher**'s (q.v.) voyage to find Northwest Passage; 21 July 1585: Sir **Philip Sidney** (q.v.), his nephew, became joint Master of the Ordnance; 1586: judge at trial of Mary Queen of Scots; reputation of exemplary piety; 21 Feb. 1590: d.

DUDLEY Edmund (c. 1462–1510): well-edu. royal administrator & speaker of the House of Commons. 1462: b. s. & h. of John Dudley of Atherington & h.w., Elizabeth dau. & coheir of John Bramshott of Bramshott. Father of **John** (q.v.); 1474: student at Oxf.; 1478: adm. Gray's Inn; late 1480s: 1st reading on *quo warranto* (procedure of royal challenge to private jursidictions); 1491–92: M.P. Lewes; 1494: JP Sussex; 1495: M.P. Sussex; 1498: m. (i) Anne Windsor; 1496–1502: Under-sheriff of London; 1501: Commissioner investigating King's feudal rights in Sussex; c. 1583: m. (ii) Elizabeth Grey, heiress of Viscount Lisle; 1504: Speaker of House of Commons; Oct. 1504: King's councillor; July 1506: President of the King's Council; managed King's financial exploitation of nobility and of resources such as the royal forests; this activity made him powerful and wealthy, and unpopular; resentment quickly spilled over after Henry's death & he & his colleague Sir **Richard Empson** (q.v.) were arrested, impeached & accused of treason; 1509: *The Tree of the Commonwealth*, important work about gov't & society, written in prison to advise the young Henry VIII; 17 Aug. 1510: exec.; his wid. m. Arthur Plantagenet, illegitimate son of Edward IV.

DUDLEY (Lord) Guildford (c. 1535–54): 4th surviving s. of **John Dudley**, Duke of Northumberland & **Jane (Guildford) Dudley**

(both q.v.); 21 May 1553: m. Lady **Jane Grey** (see Section 12.1: Monarchs and their consorts); 6 July 1553: Edward VI d.; Jane proclaimed Queen; 10 July 1553: Guildford & Jane moved into apartments in Tower; 19 July 1553: Guildford & Jane arrested; 13 Nov.: Guildford & Jane & others arraigned for tr.; 12 Feb. 1554: beheaded just before Jane; b. at St Peter ad Vincula in the Tower.

DUDLEY (née Guildford) (Lady) Jane or Joan (1508/9–55) (Duchess of Northumberland): courtier & Protestant reformer. 1508/09: b. Kent dau. of Sir Edward Guildford, administrator, & his 1st w. Eleanor (West); 1530s: lady-in-waiting to Anne Boleyn, w. interest in religious reform; 1545–46: had contact w. **Anne Askew** (q.v.); patron of Sir Richard Morison & **Thomas Gresham** (q.v.); 1550–53: leading courtier; 23 July 1553: impr. in Tower; released & retired to Chelsea; 15 Jan. 1555: d.

DUDLEY (Lady) Jane (née Grey) (see **Jane Grey** in Section 12.1: Monarchs and their consorts).

DUDLEY (Lord) John (1504–53): Duke of Northumberland. Royal administrator & politician. 1504: s. & h. of **Edmund Dudley** (q.v.), royal administrator, and his 2nd w. Elizabeth (Grey) (who was dau. of Edward Grey, 1st Baron Lisle and heiress of her brother John); 1509: Edmund Dudley exec.; John made ward of Edward Guildford; 1521: served Wolsey on mission; 1522: in arms v. French; 1523: knighted; 1525: m. **Jane Guildford** (q.v. **Dudley (Guildford) Lady Jane**); c. 1527: b. of **John Dudley**, later Earl of Warwick (q.v.); c. 1530: b. of **Ambrose Dudley**, later Earl of Warwick (q.v.); 1530: Mary (Sidney) b.; c. 1531: Henry Dudley b.; 1532/33: **Robert Dudley**, later Earl of Leicester b. (q.v.); c. 1535: b. of **Guildford Dudley** (q.v.); c. 1538: Katherine (Hastings), later Countess of Huntingdon, b.; Mar. 1532: Constable of Warw. Castle; 1534: M.P. Kent; 1536: commanded Sussex men v. Pilgrimage of Grace; Feb. 1537: vice-admiral; Oct. 1537: mission to Spain; 3 Mar.

1542: stepfather Viscount Lisle died in prison; cr. Viscount Lisle by virtue of mother's status as heir to John Grey, Viscount Lisle; 1542–47: belonged to court group of Seymour, Cranmer & Katherine Parr; 1542: M.P. Staffs; 8 Nov. 1542: Warden-general of the Scottish Marches; 26 Jan. 1543 Lord High Admiral & PC; 5 May 1543: KG; 1545–46: remodelled navy; 1545–46: chosen to defend Boulogne v. French; July 1546: victory v. French in the Solent, despite loss of *Mary Rose*; Aug. 1546: Boulogne saved; purchased lands making him one of Eng.'s wealthiest peers; gent. of privy chamber; cr. Earl of Warwick at Edward's accession & 17 Feb. 1547: Lord Great Chamberlain; 10 Sept. 1547: distinguished himself at Battle of Pinkie v. Scots; late 1547: discontinued Mass; Mar. 1548: President of King's **council in the marches of Wales**; Jan. 1549: supported BofCP; summer 1549: Somerset regime in serious trouble; Kett's rebellion; Oct. 1549: he & Cranmer instrumental in overthrow of Somerset; 13 Oct. 1549: dissolution of Protectorate; Dec. 1549: defeated religious conservatives; Feb. 1550: Lord president of the privy council; 1550–52: policy of retrenchment: sold Boulogne to the French & made peace w. France & Scotland, tried to reduce **inflation** & rest. value of sterling; Apr. 1550: Somerset reconciliation; 3 June 1550: s. John, Viscount Lisle (q.v.) m. Anne Seymour; 1 Oct. 1551: Duke of Northumberland; 22 Jan. 1552: exec. of Somerset; incr. personal ascendancy over Edward VI; restored conciliar gov't; 2 May 1553: Steward of Crown Lands in the North & leader of the King's tenants; 21 May 1553: s. Guildford m. Jane, eldest dau. of Frances Grey, Duchess of Suffolk; June 1553: Edward VI collapsed: succession became serious concern; Edward modified his 'Devyce' for the succession by settling it upon Jane (Grey) Dudley; no evidence that Dudley had plotted to this end but he was responsible for seeing that Edward's will was put into practice, & seeing that the PC rejected Mary I's claim on 10 July; 23 July 1553: surrendered at Cambridge & imprisoned in Tower; 18 Aug. 1553: trial for tr.; 22 Aug. 1553: exec.

DUDLEY (Lord) John (1527?–54): Viscount Lisle; Earl of Warwick. Humanist & courtier; 3rds. of John Dudley, Duke of Northumberland; 1547: KB; 1547-51:Viscount Lisle; 1551–54: Earl of Warwick; m. Anne Seymour, dau. of Protector Somerset; 1552: Master of the Horse; 1552–53 Lord Lieut. for Warws; 16 June 1553: signed letters patent settling crown on his sister-in-law Jane Grey (Dudley) (q.v.); joined Northumberland's expedition v. Mary; imprisoned in Tower, found guilty of tr. & condemned to death but life spared; 20 Oct. 1554: released; 21 Oct. 1554: d.

DUDLEY (née Knollys) (Lady) Lettice (Devereux, Blount) (1543–1634): Countess of (i) Essex & (ii) Leicester & (iii) Lady Blount). Noblewoman who was rumoured to have regal pretensions for herself & her children; love triangle between Lettice, Robert Dudley & Elizabeth I. Cousin of Elizabeth I. 8 Nov. 1543: b. eldest dau. of Sir **Francis Knollys** (q.v.) & h.w. **Katherine Carey** (q.v.), dau. of William Carey and **Mary (Boleyn)** Stafford; 1544–46: brought up at court of Edward VI & formed friendship w. Elizabeth, possibly staying w. her at Hatfield under Mary; 1559: gentlewoman of the privy chamber; 1560: m. (i) **Walter Devereux**, 2nd viscount Hereford (q.v.); 1565: rumours of affair with **Robert Dudley** (q.v.); 1575: more rumours; 21 Sept. 1578: m. (ii) Robert Dudley, Earl of Leicester; rumours of earlier adultery & murder of Essex; some evidence that Essex & his wife were estranged before his death but difficult to establish connections with Leicester during these years; Mar. 1581: b. of s. Denbigh (d. 1584); 1583: Elizabeth annoyed about the m. when they openly lived together; 1586: Queen angered by Lettice's rumoured regal pretensions & plans to accompany Leicester to the Netherlands (rumours without foundation); 4 Sept. 1588: d. of Leicester; in serious debt; July 1589: m. (iii) Sir Christopher Blount; rumours that she had poisoned Leicester; 1595: retired to **jointure** house at Drayton Bassett, Staffs; refused to return to court unless in Queen's favour; 1599: returned to London to plead for her son Essex's life but Elizabeth refused to see her; returned to some

favour under James I; bur. alongside Earl of Leicester at her request; 25 Dec. 1634: d.

DUDLEY (Lord) Robert (c. 1532/33–88): Earl of Leicester, courtier, royal favourite, politician & powerful Protestant patron. 24 June 1532 or 33: b. 5th s. of **John Dudley**, Duke of Northumberland (q.v.) & h.w. **Jane or Joan (née Guildford) Dudley** (q.v.); classically edu. privately by **Roger Ascham** (q.v.), Thomas Wilson & Sir Francis Jobson; early 1540s: possibly attached to Prince Edward's household; formed early friendship w. Princess Elizabeth; 1549: played part in suppressing Kett's rebellion; 4 June 1550: m. (i) Amy Robsart; 1550: knighted; 1552: co-Lord Lieut. of Norfolk; 1551, 1553: M.P. for Norf.; 15 Aug. 1551: gent. of privy chamber; 18 July 1553: proclaimed Jane Queen at King's Lynn; 26 July 1553: impr. in Tower; mid-Mar. to mid-May 1554: Elizabeth also impr. in Tower; rumours of a romance probably groundless; 21 Oct. 1554: released; 22 Jan. 1555: pardoned; Jan. 1557: permitted to inherit the Robsart Norf. estate; Aug. 1557: accompanied Pembroke to siege of St Quentin in France; 1557–58: relationship w. Elizabeth, while Amy Dudley remained in Herts; 1558: Master of the Queen's Horse; Queen gave him Kew Palace; Apr. 1559: Queen's dependence upon Dudley apparent; continued separation from Amy; 1559: M.P. Norf.; 24 Apr. 1559: KG; sponsored company of players; 8 Sept. 1560: Amy d. suddenly at Cumnor House, Oxon.; was pronounced d. by misadventure; 11 Sept. 1560: Spanish ambass. stoked rumours that Queen & Dudley had conspired to kill Amy; rumour continued to plague him; Feb. & Mar. 1561: negotiations w. Spain for support for m. between Elizabeth & Dudley if she agreed to restore Catholicism; 1 May 1561: Elizabeth rejected proposal; Dudley a convinced Protestant who was active patron of former exiles; became Elizabeth's constant companion; autumn 1561: w. Cecil built cordial relations betw. Elizabeth & Mary Queen of Scots & promoted oppo. to France; Feb. 1562: Constable of Windsor Castle; Oct. 1562: PC; 9 June 1563: granted lordships of Kenilworth,

Denbigh, & Chirk; 1563–65: supported Mary of Scotland's claim to be Elizabeth's heir & Elizabeth tried to m. Dudley off to Mary while she m. Charles of Austria; 29 Sept. 1564: Earl of Leicester & baron of Denbigh; close cooperation w. his brother **Ambrose, Earl of Warwick** (q.v.) building up a core of support & infl. in west midlands; 31 Dec. 1564: Chancellor of Oxf. Uni.; 1565: he supported the nonconformist clergy in the Vestiarian Controversy; Oct. 1566: banned from Elizabeth's presence for encouraging parl. petition on succession; 1568: sought to organise support for the French Huguenots; 1569: abetted Northern Earls because he thought rapprochement with Mary of Scotland essential but revealed scheme to Elizabeth; Jan. 1570: purchased Paget Place, Temple Bar & renamed it Leicester House; 1566, 1568, 1572 & 1575: entertained Queen at Kenilworth; thereafter at Wanstead; 1570–71: active in promoting Queen's m. to Henri, duc. **d'Anjou**; 1571: affair w. Lady Douglas Sheffield (née Howard) dowager Lady Sheffield, dau. of **Charles Howard of Effingham** (q.v.); 1571–73: protected Puritans in admonition controversy; 1574: b. of illegitimate s. Robert; 21 Sept. 1578: m. (ii) Lettice (Knollys) Devereux (q.v. **Lettice Dudley**); Queen's hostility to Lettice was major problem for Leicester; Nov. to Mar. 1578–79: Elizabeth angry; 1581: b. of s. Denbigh; 19 July 1584: d. of s. Denbigh; 1584–85: sponsored revival of Oxford University Press; assembled huge library & collection of paintings & maps; 1581: admitted to Queen's charge that he was in league w. Prince of Orange; 1584: *Leicester's Commonwealth* slandered him; 1585: commanded expedition to assist United Provinces v. Spain; 1586: Governor of United Provinces – Queen refused to acknowledge the office; recalled; 1588: involved in military preparations for defence v. Armada & organised Elizabeth's visit to Tilbury in Aug.; 4 Sept. 1588: d. at Cornbury House, Oxon.

DUES (Duwes or Dewes) Giles (fl. 1490s–1535): French teacher, musician, royal librarian & minstrel, & tutor to the children of Henry VII, who taught the princesses Margaret & Mary the lute. 1490s: in Henry VII's service; 1501: in household of Prince Henry; 1506: became royal librarian; claimed to have taught French to all Henry VII's children & to Mary I & Henry Courtenay; 1509: minstrel at Henry VII's funeral; m. Joan; three s. & one dau.; 1510: Keeper of the Princes's Wardrobe; 1515: obtained position in King's household for his s. Arthur; 1525–28: gent. in waiting to Princess Mary in the Welsh marches; 1533: pub'd *An Introductorie for to Lerne to Rede, to Pronounce, and to Speke French*, in two parts, a grammar & dialogues;12 Apr. 1535: d.

E

EDWARD IV (King) (1442–83): House of York (see Section 12.1: Monarchs and their consorts).

EGERTON Thomas (Lord Ellesmere) (1540–1617): 1st Viscount Brackley, Lord Chancellor, 23 Jan. 1540: b. illegit. s. of Sir Richard Egerton, landowner, of Ridley, Cheshire, & a servant girl, Alice Sparke; raised in household of Thomas Ravenscroft of Bretton, Flintshire, & h.w. Katherine; 1556: Brasenose College, Oxf.; 31 Oct. 1560: Lincoln's Inn; 1569: brought before Star Chamber for Catholicism w. other members of Lincoln's Inn; escaped punishment by conforming; 1572: called to bar; 1576: m. (i) Elizabeth, his stepfather's dau.; 1579: John b.; Bencher of Lincoln's Inn; successful legal practice; 26 June 1581: solicitor-general; 1582: recorder of Lichfield, Staffs; 1584, 1586: M.P. Cheshire; 1589: M.P. Reading; converted to Calvinism; prosecution of recusants & Jesuits such as Sir Edmund Campion in 1581 & Mary, Queen of Scots & the **Babington** conspirators in 1586; 1590s: friend of **Robert Devereux**, second Earl of Essex (q.v.); 2 June 1592: attorney-general; 1594: Chamberlain of Chester; knighted; 10

Apr. 1594: Master of the Rolls; 6 May 1596: Lord Keeper of Great Seal; reformed the chancery system; 1597: m. (ii) Elizabeth More of Losely, wid. of Sir John Wolley & Richard Polsted; Oct. 1600: m. (iii) Alice (Spencer) Stanley, dau. of Sir John Spencer of Althorp & Katherine, & wid. of Ferdinando Stanley, 5th Earl of Derby; extremely unhappy match; 1603: confirmed as lord keeper & cr. Baron Ellesmere; 24 July 1603: Lord Chancellor; 1603: trial of Walter Raleigh; 1605: trial of Gunpowder plotters; 1606: Calvin's Case; 1616: trial of Robert Carr, Earl of Somerset & h.w. Frances; patron of Sir Francis Bacon; valued minister who supported James's view of monarchy; battled with **Edward Coke** (q.v.), champion of the rule of law; 7 Nov.1616: Viscount Brackley; 3 Mar. 1617: surrendered great seal to the King; 15 Mar. 1617: d. at York House. L.A. Knafla, *Law and Politics in Jacobean England: The Tracts of Lord Chancellor Ellesmere*, 1977, W.J. Jones, *The Elizabethan Court of Chancery*, 1969, J.H. Baker, *The Legal Profession and the Common Law*, 1987.

ELIZABETH I Tudor (Queen) (1533–1603) (see Section 12.1: Monarchs and their consorts).

ELIZABETH OF YORK (Queen) (1466–1503): Queen of Henry VII (see Section 12.1: Monarchs and their consorts).

ELYOT (Sir) Thomas (c. 1490–1546): ?Oxf.-edu. humanist, educationalist & diplomat; b. c. 1490: only s. of Sir Richard Elyot, judge of court of common pleas, & Alice (Delamere); Nov. 1510: adm. Middle Temple; 1510–26: clerk to justices of assize, western circuit; c. 1510: m. Margaret Barrow; appear both to have belonged to Sir **Thomas More**'s circle; c. 1510: studied medicine w. **Thomas Linacre** (q.v.); More probably introduced Elyot to Hans Holbein; 1515–29: JP for Oxon & Wiltshire; 1527, 1529: Sheriff of both counties; 1530: JP for Cambs; 1523–29: senior clerk for King's Council; 1530: knighted; 1531: seeking Henry VIII's patronage pub'd The Boke Named the Governour,

deals with structure & nature of the public weal, education of the governing class, the virtues expected of the governing elite; hugely influential work that went through eight editions in the sixteenth century; Sept. 1531: ambass. to Emperor Charles V to sound out opinions on the divorce; 1532: recalled but travelled in Europe; in royal disfavour he retired to Cambr. & scholarship; ?1533: The Education or Bringinge up of Children – transl. of Plutarch; 1538: Latin-English dictionary pub'd (the first humanist Latin dictionary, based on classical sources); 1542: enlarged edition; 1539: M.P. Cambs; 1539: Castel of Helth – a vernacular handbook that recommended treatments & summarised teachings of classical physicians, espec. Galen (thus popularising the theory of the four humours, etc.), for the use of Englishmen & women; 1540: The Defence of Good Women – an impolitic eulogy to **Katharine of Aragon**; 1540: app'd to receive **Anne of Cleves**; 26 Mar. 1546: d. S.E. Lehmberg, Sir Thomas Elyot, Tudor humanist, 1960; J.M. Major, Sir Thomas Elyot and Renaissance humanism, 1964; P. Hogrefe, Life and Times of Sir Thomas Elyot, Englishman, 1967.

EMPSON (Sir) Richard (c. 1450–1510): lawyer & royal administrator. c. 1450: b. s. of Peter Empson of Towcester & h.w. Elizabeth (Joseph); adm. Middle Temple; Nov. 1478: Attorney General of Duchy of Lancaster; rose to prominence late in Henry VII's reign, in association w. **Edmund Dudley** (q.v.), as royal debt collector; 24 Apr. 1509: arrested on Henry VII's d.; trumped-up treason charges; 17 Aug. 1510: exec. alongside Edmund Dudley (q.v.); victim of Henry VIII's early attempts to court popularity.

ERASMUS Desiderius (?1467–1536): humanist author, classical & biblical scholar, & educator. 27/28 Oct. 1467: b. Rotterdam the illegitimate son of a scribe, Gerard Helye & Margareta; edu. at Gouda & Deventer & by Brethren of Common Life, Hertogenbosch; 1487: Augustinian monk at Steyn near Gouda; 25 Apr. 1492: ord. pr.; entered service of Bishop of Cambrai; 1495–1501:

studied & taught private pupils such as William Blount (later Lord Mountjoy) at Uni. of Paris; 1499: accompanied Blount to Eng.; stayed at Oxf. till Jan. 1500; formed friendships with **John Colet** (q.v.), **Thomas More** (q.v.) & others; Jan. 1500: returned to Paris; summer 1500: pub'd Adagiorum collectanea (taken from Greek sources); 1505–06: returned to Eng.; 1508: Adagiorum chiliades (greatly expanded version of Adagia of 1500); Aug. 1509: guest at Sir Thomas More's house & wrote The Praise of Folly, a satirical comparison of contemporary Christianity with that of New Testament; 1509–14: Professor of Greek & Divinity at Cambr. Uni.; wrote materials for Colet's St Paul's School such as (1513) revision of William Lily's De octo orationis partium constructione libellus, (1512) the De copia & (July 1512) the De ratione studii; 1511: pub'd The Praise of Folly; summer 1512: pilgrimages to Our Lady of Walsingham & (with Colet) to St Thomas at Canterbury; 1514–21: in Brabant; 1515: first independent ed'n of Enchiridion militis Christiani ('Handbook of the Christian knight' with its emphasis on the Christian life well lived in the community; 1515: pub'd Antibarbari; 1516: app'd imperial councillor; 1516: Institutio principis Christiani ('Education of a Christian prince'); 1516: at Basel pub'd Novum instrumentum – Greek text of the New Testament with parallel Latin translation, with separate pub'n of detailed annotations referring to the Vulgate Bible; Paraclesis ('Exhortation'); Paraphrases on the books of the New Testament, intended to make the text accessible to the lay reader; 1518: Familiarium colloquiorum formulae; 1522: returned to Basel; involvement in controversies of the day; also important pedagogical & humanistic works such as Colloquia, De conscribendis epistolis, Lingua, De civilitate morum puerilium, Christiani matrimonii institutio, Ciceronianus, De recta Latini Graecique sermonis pronuntiatione dialogus, De pueris instituendis; 1524–25: direct conflict with Luther; 1524: De libero arbitrio – a reply to Luther in support of Catholic doctrine of free will; Mar. 1526: continued with Part 1 of Hyperaspistes diatribae adversus servum arbitrium Martini Lutheri ('A warrior shielding a discussion of free will against the enslaved will of Martin Luther'); Sept. 1527: pub'd Part 2; 1526: Peregrinatio religionis ergo – account of his 1512 pilgrimage to Walsingham; Swiss & German reformers cite Erasmian arguments v. legalism in support of their own strict positions on the sacraments, fasting & **celibacy**; he responds w. appeal for moderation & unity in, e.g., De esu carnium; 1528: defends himself v. charge of questioning the doctrine of the Trinity in Apologia adversus monachos quosdam Hispanos; 1529: moved to Catholic Freiburg; 1533: final Erasmian edition of Colloquia 'a running commentary on the affairs of the day' & focusing particularly on Eng.; 1534: returned to Basel; 1535: pub'd treatise on preaching, Ecclesiastes; 1536: another expanded version of Adagiorum chiliades; 11 July 1536: d. at Basle (see Chapter 4: World of learning). J. McConica, *Erasmus*, 1991; M.M. Phillips, *Erasmus and the Northern Renaissance*, 1949; R.J. Schoeck, *Erasmus of Europe*, 2 Vols, 1990–93.

ERDESWICKE Sampson (c. 1538-1603): Oxf.-edu. historian & antiquary. c. 1538: b. s. & heir of Hugh Erdeswick of Sandon, Staffs and h.w. Mary (Leigh); 1553: entered Brasenose College, Oxf.; 1555: admitted Inner Temple; at some date m. (i) Elizabeth, dau. & coheir of Catholic Humphrey Dixwell of Churchover, Warws; five daus; Aug. 1575: living in Staffs &, with his father, brought before PC in Worcester for recusancy; admitted charge 'alleging their consciences & examples of their forefathers who taught them so' (Acts of the Privy Council, 1575-7, 15); Dec. 1575: transferred to Marshalsea for persistent recusancy; summer 1576: ordered to report monthly to Bp of Coventry & Lichfield for instruction & forbidden to entertain recusants at their home; 1580s: described as an obstinate & dangerous recusant & Sandon Hall thought to harbour priests; engaged in enclosing arable land at Sandon; 1585: armour confiscated;1580s: set up in Sandon Hall's gallery the names &

coats of arms of Staffs gentry; 1588: escaped arrest by Earl of Shrewsbury by fleeing to Leighton; late 1588: impr. by Bp of Ely; 1592: returned to Sandon in the custody of Protestant Richard Bagot of Blithfield; 1592: claimed to be true author of William Wyrley, The True Use of Armorie; 1593: commenced his 'View' of Staffs & Cheshire, following Camden's method (remained in ms, until 1717, pub'd as Survey of Staffordshire); 1593: m. (ii) Mary (née Neale) Digby, a Catholic widow w. 14 children; two s. & one dau.; 1597: brought before the assizes for recusancy; 1598: member of Society of Antiquaries; greatly respected as antiquary by William Dugdale; 28 June 1603: d. at Sandon.

ESSEX (1st Earl of) (see **Cromwell**, Thomas).

ESSEX (Countess of) Lettice (see **Dudley**, Lettice).

ESSEX Walter Devereux, 1st Devereux Earl of (See **Devereux**, (Lord) Walter, 1st Earl of Essex).

ESSEX Robert Devereux, 2nd Devereux Earl of (See **Devereux**, (Lord) Robert, 2nd Earl of Essex).

F

FERRAR Robert (fl. 1524, d. 1555): Cambr.- & Oxf.-edu Bp of St David's and Protestant martyr. b. Halifax, Yorks; May 1524: took minor orders at Augustinian Priory of St Oswald, Nostell, Yorks; Sept. 1524: ord. deac. at York; 1524–28: at Cambr.; 1528: arrested & impr. for selling Protestant books at Oxf.; 1528–35: at Cambr.; 14 Oct. 1533: B.Th. Oxf.; 1535: joined **William Barlow** on embassy to James V of Scotland; 1536: Barlow obtained for him a licence to preach; June 1538: Prior of Nostell, Yorks, worth £600 p.a.; evangelical preacher; unsuccessfully attempted to convert Nostell into college of preachers; 1539: surrendered Nostell

to Crown in exchange for pension of £80 p.a.; Aug. 1547: app'd preacher to royal visitation of Hereford, Worcester & the four Welsh dioceses; July 1548: Bp of St David's by royal letters patent; 9 Sept. 1548: consecr. Bp by Cranmer (1st bp consecr. according to new English ordinal); 11 Nov. 1547: evangelical sermon at Paul's Cross wearing only pr's vestments; active in House of Lords; c. 1547–49: m. Elizabeth; three children; 1549–53: conflict w. Dean & Chapter of St David's & many laymen in the dioc. culminating in 56 accusations v. him, including allegations that he was too cautious in the suppression of Catholicism and intro. of Protestantism; never impr. in Edward's reign & remained active bp.; Sept. 1553: impr. at Southwark; 13 Mar. 1555: depr. of see; 30 Mar. 1555: burnt at stake in Carmarthen. A.J. Brown, *Robert Ferrar: Yorkshire Monk, Reformation Bishop and Martyr in Wales, c. 1500–1555*, 1997.

FIELD(E) John (?1544/45–88): Oxf.-edu. clergyman, assistant to John Foxe (q.v.), Puritan preacher & controversialist; organiser of Presbyterianism & martyrologist. b. London of unknown parentage but father probably a member of clothworkers' guild; 25 Mar. 1566: ord. pr. (said to be B.A. of Christ Church); returned to Broadgates Hall, Oxf. when silenced for nonconformity; m. Joan – seven children incl. Theophilus & Nathan; 1567: assisted John Foxe w. research for 1570 ed'n of Acts and Monuments; 1568: one of the Puritan preachers at Holy Trinity Minories; c. 1570: became organiser of *classes* or conferences; 1572: endorsed the Presbyterian 'order of Wandsworth'; 1572: pub'd, w. Thomas Wilcox, anti-episcopal *Admonition to the Parliament*, calling for further reformation of the Church & popularising the hitherto academic views of **Thomas Cartwright** (q.v.); impr. in Newgate; sparked continuing controversy, marked by **John Whitgift**'s (q.v.) *Answer* and Thomas Cartwright's *Reply*; released through intervention by Leicester and Warwick & poss. joined Cartwright in exile at Heidelberg; 1577: in London writing v. Catholics; 1579: became licensed preacher;

1581: lecturer at St Mary Aldermary; attacked his own patron Leicester for patronage of stage plays; 1585: suspended from preaching; 1583: refused to subscribe to Whitgift's Three Articles, preached v. conformity to BofCP & became active in revival of *classes* or conferences, which pressed for further reformation & discussed a Presbyterian Book of Discipline; 1593: pub'd partial monuments of the movement in *A Parte of a Register*; 'Second Parte of a Register' remained in ms; Mar. 1588: d. before arrest & trial of the Marprelate Martyrs who had drawn so heavily on the *Partes of a Register*. P. Collinson, 'John Field and Elizabethan Puritanism', *Godly people: Essays on English Protestantism and Puritanism*, 1983.

FISHER Bishop John (1469–1535): Cambr.-edu. bp of Rochester, cardinal & martyr, Chancellor of Cambr. Uni. b. Beverley, s. of Robert Fisher, mercer, & Agnes at Beverley, Yorks; 1488: B.A. Cambr.; 1491: M.A.; 1491: as fellow of Michaelhouse ord. pr. at York; c. 1500: chaplain to Lady **Margaret Beaufort** (q.v.); 1502: 1st Lady Margaret Professor of Theology; benefactor of Cambr. Uni.; wanted Christ's College & St John's College, Lady Margaret's new foundations, to become training ground for pr. & to offer humanist & scriptural edu. to impr. standards of Eng. clergy; 1504: Bp of Rochester; conscientious preaching bp; 1504: elected chancellor of Cambr. Uni.; 1514: made Chancellor of Cambr. for life; Jan. 1527: pub'd *De veritate corporis et sanguinis Christi in Eucharista* defending the doctrine of the real presence; staunch opponent of Lutheranism; oppo. royal attempts to tax clergy & to impose royal supremacy; angered Henry w. support for **Katherine of Aragon**; 30 Apr. 1534: refused Oath of Supremacy; impr. in Tower; 2 Jan. 1535: depr. of see of Rochester; 21 May 1535: cr. cardinal by Pope; 22 June 1535: exec. for tr.

FITCH Ralph (?1550–1611): London merchant & traveller who became first Englishman to set foot in Burma. Unknown parentage & date of birth; London: 1575: completed apprenticeship as leatherseller; 1583: joined John Newberry's expedition to Cathay by way of Hormuz & India (to seek commercial privileges); left party at Fatehpur Sikri, sailed down the Ganges & visited (Feb. 1586) Bengal, (1586) Burma, (Feb. to Apr. 1587) Malacca, (Mar. 1589) Ceylon, Cochin & (Nov. 1589) Goa; Apr. 1591: returned home to find himself presumed dead & his estate divided up; 1592: member of Company of Merchants of the Levant; 1596: trading in Aleppo; 1596: app'd consul at Aleppo; 1597: consulate cancelled & returned to London; 1598: Richard Hakluyt pub'd Fitch's travel diaries in 2nd ed'n of his *The Principal Navigations*; 1599: consultant to East India Company; Aug. 1611: elected Warden of Leathersellers' Company; 11 Oct. 1611: d.

FITTON Anne (see **Newdigate (née Fitton) (Lady) Anne**).

FITTON Mary (Polewhele; Lougher) (1578–1641): courtier & gentlewoman; mistakenly thought to be 'dark lady' of Shakespeare's sonnets. c. June 1578: b. Gawsworth, Chesh., younger dau. of Sir Edward Fitton & Alice (Holcroft) Fitton; c. July 1596–98: maid of honour to Elizabeth I; Jan. 1600: left court in ill health for her father's London home; May 1600: returned to court to protect her father's interests; 1600: became mistress of William Herbert, eldest s. of Henry Herbert, 2nd Earl of Pembroke; Jan. 1601: Eliz. furious at her pregnancy & sent her into care of Lady Hawkins; Feb. 1601: Herbert, now 3rd Earl of Pembroke, admitted responsibility but refused m.; Mar. 1601: Pembroke impr. in Fleet; Mary gave b. to s. who died; Pembroke still refused m. despite pressure from Sir William Knollys, Cecil & others; autumn 1601: Mary retired from court; became mistress of her m. cousin, Sir Richard Leveson of Lilleshall, Staffs, whose w. was insane; installed at Levesons's estate at Perton, Tettenhall, Staffs; 1603: Anne b.; 2 Aug 1605: Richard d. of smallpox; ?1605: William b.; 8 Jan. 1608: William d.; 1606: m. (i) Capt. William Polewhele, lately one of Leveson's troops; continued to live at Perton & gave b.

to three children: William, Frances & (posthumously) Mary; Sept. 1609: Polewhele d.; c. 1612: m. (ii) gentleman lawyer John Lougher of Tenby, Pembrokeshire, a former M.P. who had once served on the court of high commission at York; three children: Elizabeth, John, & Lettice; constant legal suits concerning Leveson's provision for their dau. Anne; 1626–27: Lougher was sheriff of Pembrokeshire; 1636: Lougher d.; 1641: Mary d. leaving **lease** of Perton to her s. William Polewhele & various leases in Pembrokeshire to Elizabeth Lougher; her dau. Lettice had already m. Thomas Denton of Northants. V.M. Larminie, *Wealth, Kinship and Culture: The Seventeenth-Century Newdigates of Arbury and their World*, Royal Historical Society Studies in History, 72, 1995.

FITZJAMES (Bishop) Richard (c. 1455, d. 1522): Oxf.-edu. & theologically conservative Bp of London. Various ecclesiastical preferments. c. 1455: s. of John Fitzjames of Redlynch, near Bruton, Somerset; edu. Merton College, Oxf.; 1468: fellow; 1476: R Trent, Somerset; 1481: D.Th.; 1483–1507: Warden of Merton; 1483–97: Treasurer of St Paul's, London, with the prebend of Portpoole, & also (probably largely non-resident) V Minehead & R Aller in Somerset, & master of St Leonard's Hospital, Bedford; 1489: Chaplain to Henry VII, preaching before him frequently including on important state occasions; 21 May 1497: consecrated bp of the poor diocese of Rochester & carried out episcopal duties in person; 29 Nov. 1503: transl. to See of Chichester; 5 June 1506: transl. to See of London; apparent administrative efficiency; 1507 & 1508: personally examined ordinands; 2 Dec. 1514: involved in heresy proceedings v. London merchant, **Richard Hunne**; soon after, Chancellor Horsey was accused of Hunne's murder; Fitzjames later (on strength of his part in Hunne's case) held up by Protestants as example of reactionary bp aggressively defending clerical rights; 1519: endowed school at Bruton & always concerned to promote clerical edu.; 15 Jan. 1522: d.

FITZROY (Lord) Henry (1519–36): Henry VIII's acknowledged illegitimate son & Duke of Richmond & Somerset. June 1519: b. s. of Henry VIII & Elizabeth Blount (q.v.); entrusted to care of Cardinal Wolsey & well-edu. by John Palsgrave, Richard Croke & William Saunders etc.; 7 June 1525: KG; 18 June 1525: Earl of Nottingham & Duke of Richmond & Somerset; 16 July 1525: Lord Admiral of England; 22 June 1525: Warden-general of marches towards Scotland; 28 Aug 1525 to 16 June 1529: President, Council of the North w. full ducal court at Sheriff Hutton or Pontefract, Yorks; m. frequently mooted as diplomatic ploy; Oct. 1529: care transferred to Thomas Howard, 3rd Duke of Norfolk; m. to one of Norfolk☐s daus mooted; late 1532 to Aug. 1533: resided at court of François I of France; 26 Nov. 1533: m. Mary Howard, younger dau. of the Duke of Norfolk (see **Howard Mary**); 17 May 1534: Lieutenant of Order of Garter; Feb. 1535: entertained Imperial ambassador; 19 May 1536: attended exec. of Anne Boleyn; continued royal favour but never recognised as heir; 8 July 1536: taken ill; 23 July 1536: d. unexpectedly; unostentatious burial at Thetford Priory – later transferred to Framlingham, Suffolk.

FITZROY (née Howard) (Lady) Mary (see **Richmond, Mary** (Howard) Fitzroy, Duchess of).

FOX (Bishop) Edward (1496–1538): Eton & Cambr.edu. Bp of Hereford, royal supporter & diplomat. 1496: b. Dursley, Gloucs, one of three children of William Fox, gent., & h.w. Joanna; edu. Eton; 27 Mar. 1512: adm. King's College, Cambr.; 1515: fellow; 1517: B.A.; 1520: M.A.; allegedly member of White Horse tavern discussion group led by Robert Barnes (q.v.) & remained a Lutheran sympathiser; 22 Sept. 1528 to 8 May 1538: Provost of King's College, Cambr.; 8 Nov. 1527: **Wolsey** (q.v.) preferred him to Prebend of Osbaldwick, York; various ecclesiastical royal preferments; 1532: Doctorate; May 1533: Dean of Salisbury; May 1535: Prebend of St Mary & St George at Windsor; 1536:

Bp of Hereford; 1527–33: royal diplomatic agent w. respect to divorce; assisted in production of (1529) Henricus octavus (presented on behalf of the King at the Blackfriars annulment hearing) & (1530) Gravissimae, atque exactissimae illustrissimarum totius Italiae et Galliae academiarum censurae & (1532) the *Glasse of Truthe*; attempted to convert **Thomas More** (q.v.) & **John Fisher** (q.v.) on this subject & others; prolocutor of the lower house of southern convocation: voted in support of the divorce; supporter of the royal supremacy; gathered & pub'd arguments in favour of the supremacy: Collectanea satis copiosa;1534, 1538: 2 editions of De vera differentia regiae potestatis et ecclesiasticae, et quae sit ipsa veritas ac virtus utriusque, in which papal & royal claims to supremacy were discussed & compared; 1536: sought to infl. Ten Articles in Lutheran direction; 1537: exerted Lutheran infl. on the Bishops' Book (The Institution of a Christian Man); 8 May 1538: d.

Fox (Bishop) Richard (1447/48–1528): Bp of Worcester, statesman & founder of Corpus Christi College, Oxf. 1447/48: b. s. of Thomas & Helena, freeholders of Pullocks; nothing known of his edu. but held BCL when ord. acolyte at Salisbury in 1577; c. 1482: Prebend of Bishopstone, Salisbury; 30 Oct. 1484: absentee V Stepney, London; c. 1470–1503: perhaps served various kings as civil lawyer & studied in Paris; 1484: left Eng. for France; Jan. 1485: Richard III depr. him of Stepney because of his attachment to Henry Tudor's cause; 1485: served Henry VII as secretary; 22 Aug. 1485: present at Bosworth Field; 25 Mar. 1546: ord. deac. Lincoln diocese; 24 Feb. 1547: Keeper of the Privy Seal; 8 Apr. 1547: consecr. Bp of Exeter; 1492: transl. to Bp of Bath & Wells; one of Henry VII's two leading ministers (see **Morton John**), presiding over PC on royal progress; on many royal missions abroad; 1492: organised army & fleet for invasion of France, accompanied the King & took part in subsequent peace negotiations; 30 July 1494: transl. Bp of Durham – carried out ordinations, etc.; responsible for defence

of the northern border; 1498–99: Chancellor of Cambr. Uni.; 1499: negotiated m. between James IV of Scotland & Princess Margaret Tudor (q.v.) that took place on 24 Jan. 1502; 20 Aug. 1501: transl. to Bp of Winchester, wealthiest see in Eng. & once again central to affairs; 1505: involved in foundation of Christ's College, Cambr. as executor of Lady Margaret Beaufort; 1507–16: Master of Pembroke College, Cambr.; 1507: revised Balliol College statutes; 1509: one of leading group of Henry VII's executors; remained Keeper of Privy Seal; 1510: protested in Convocation v. Archbp Warham's encroachments on episcopal rights; 1511: took complaints v. archepiscopal probate of wills to Pope Julius II; 1513: Wolsey supplanted Fox as leading infl. w. Henry VIII; May 1516: surrendered Privy Seal & retired from politics; 1 Mar. 1517: foundation of a small humanist establishment, Corpus Christi College, Oxf., specifically for the training of priests, with public readers in humanity & Greek; 1516–28: resided in Winchester & was active in diocese & on commissions; 1522: went blind; clashed w. Wolsey over his use of legatine powers; 5 Oct. 1528: d.

FOXE John (1516/17–87): martyrologist & historian. 1516/17: b. Boston, Lincs; 1534: adm. Brasenose College, Oxf., prob. sponsored by John Hawarden, former fellow & R Foxe's parish of Coningsby; B.A. 1537; July 1539: Fellow of Magdalen College; 1539–40: Magdalen College lecturer in logic; July 1543: M.A.; along with **Robert Crowley** (q.v.), **Laurence Humphrey** (q.v.) & Thomas Cooper belonged to evangelical group in the college; 1545: resigned his fellowship because he refused to be ord. pr.; c. 1546: tutor to children of Sir William Lucy, friend of **Hugh Latimer** (q.v.), at Charlecote, Warws; 3 Feb. 1547: m. Agnes Randall of Coventry; autumn 1547: moved to London; 1547–48: transl. of a Luther sermon for evangelical printer High Singleton; 1548: app'd by **Duchess of Richmond** (q.v. Mary Howard) tutor, in London & Reigate, to the Howard children of her late brother, the exec. Earl of Surrey; 1548: formed friendships with William Turner, **John Rogers**, **William Cecil & John Bale** (all q.v.); 24 June 1550: ord. deac.; 1548: pub'd De non plectendis morte adulteris consultatio, in which he argued v. adultery as capital crime & sparked controversy; 1551: called for revival of sanction of excommunication & a new code of canon law in De censura sive excommunicatione ecclesiastica rectoque eius usu; suppressed shrine of Virgin Mary at Ouldsworth; c. 1553: m. Agnes; spring 1554: Marian exile; July 1554: settled in Strasbourg; Aug. 1554: pub'd Commentarii rerum in ecclesia gestarum – brief history of the Church & forerunner of later Acts & Monuments; autumn 1554: in Frankfurt, where he was a follower of **John Knox** (q.v.); Sept. 1555: moved to Basel where he resided with John Bale; 22 Sept. 1555: Christina baptised w. **Thomas Bentham** (q.v.) as godfather; 1555–58: worked for various Basel printers as editor, proof reader, etc. & moved within circle of Protestant scholars; Mar. 1556: Christus triumphans – allegorical drama of the history of the Church in Latin verse; Mar. 1557: Locorum communium tituli – a structured commonplace book; Ad inclytos ac praepotentes Angliae proceres . . . supplicatio – an appeal to the English nobility to stop persecuting English Protestants; **Edmund Grindal** (q.v.) directed project for parallel Latin & English martyrologies of Marian persecution & Foxe entrusted w. preparing the Latin ed'n; 8 Sept. 1558: Dorcas baptised; Jan. 1559: pub'd Germaniae ad Angliam gratulatio, thanking Germany for hospitality during the exile; remained in Basel; Aug. 1559: Rerum in ecclesia gestarum . . . commentarii in six books concentrated on English persecutions (using printed, manuscript & eyewitness sources) but saw them in a European context; Nov. 1559: enlisted **John Day**(e)'s (q.v.) support for larger vernacular martyrology; 25 Jan. 1560: ord. pr. by Grindal; autumn 1560: resided with John Parkhurst, Bp of Norwich, preached in the diocese & undertook research; 31 Dec. 1560: Samuel b.; Aug. 1562: returned to London to supervise pub'n of his Acts and Monuments; 20 Mar. 1563: pub'n of Acts and Monuments

(immediately dubbed Foxe's Book of Martyrs) in 1,800 page folio volume (see Chapter 4: World of learning for further detail); 22 May 1563: app'd Prebendary of Shipton, Salisbury; as such, app'd a former exile V Shipton under Wychwood; summer 1563: ministered to plague-ridden London; Jan. 1566: in Dialogi sex, contra . . . pseudomartyres Nicholas Harpsfield, Marian archdeacon of Canterbury, attacked Foxe's martyrology & drove Foxe to counter w. extensive further research; 2 Feb. 1568: s. **Simeon** (q.v.) b. at Duke of Norfolk's London house; 8 Oct. 1569: Norfolk sent to Tower; 16 Jan. 1572: Norfolk condemned to d. & Foxe (his former tutor) & **Alexander Nowell** (q.v.) acted as his chaplains; 1570: 2nd ed'n of Acts and Monuments (now 2,300 pages in two volumes & exhibiting infl. of **Matthew Parker** (q.v.) & other antiquaries; Good Friday 1570: preached 'Sermon of Christ Crucified' at Paul's Cross aimed at converting RCs to the gospel; appeared in one Latin & six English ed'ns during Foxe's lifetime; 1571: ed'n of Cranmer's 1552 Reformatio legum ecclesiasticarum w. preface by Foxe calling for further reform of the prayer book; 1572: Pandectae locorum communium – a more popular & enlarged version of his commonplace book; 14 Oct. 1572: inst. Preb. of Durham; 1585: repr. of Pandectae locorum communium; Jan. 1573: pub'd ed'n of works of **Tyndale, Barnes & Frith** (all q.v.); 1574: involved in exorcising demons from a lawyer, Robert Briggs, & two girls; Archbp Parker exposed some of these cures as fraudulent; 1576: 3rd ed'n of Acts and Monuments; 1575: unsuccessfully defended Flemish anabaptists v. d. penalty but wanted them to convert; July 1575: attended burning of anabaptists to support them; 1 Apr. 1577 Foxe preached sermon at baptism of convert from Judaism; 1578: pub'd expanded version as De oliva evangelica appealing to Jews to convert; 1580: anonymous pub'n of Papas confutatas v. the papacy; Oct. 1583: 4th ed'n of Acts and Monuments; worked on Latin commentary on Revelation, Eicasmi, seu, Meditationes in sacram Apocalypsim, which his s. Samuel pub'd posthumously; 18 Apr.

1587: d. D. Loades (ed.), *John Foxe and the English Reformation*, 1997; D. Loades (ed.), *John Foxe: An Historical Perspective*, 1999.

FOXE, Simeon (1569–1642): Eton & Cambr.-edu. physician & memorialist of his father **John Foxe** (q.v.); 1602–04: studied medicine at Padua & Venice; 1605: began practising medicine in London; 30 Sept. 1605: candidate of London College of Physicians; 25 June 1608: fellow of London College of Physicians (LCP); 20 Nov. 1627: elected registrar of LCP; 3 Dec. 1629: elected treasurer of LCP; 1630: anatomy reader of LCP; 1634–41: president of LCP; friend & physician of poet John Donne & strong supporter of William Harvey; 1641: pub'd anon. memoir of John Foxe's life in new edition of *Acts and Monuments* directed v. Laudianism.

FRITH John (1503–33): Eton, Oxf.- & Cambr.-edu. Protestant theologian & martyr. 1503: b. s. of Richard, later an innkeeper, in Kent; probably part of White Horse Tavern group at Cambr.; 1525: B.A. King's College, Cambr.; 1525: junior canon at Wolsey's Cardinal College, Oxf.; fled to join Tyndale in Antwerp after imprisonment for heretical activity in college; poss. collaborated w. **Tyndale** (q.v.) in transl. of Bible; spent time in Marburg; 1531: pub'd in Antwerp *Disputacion of Purgatorye*; occasional visits to Eng., where he was persecuted; 1532: impr. in Tower; articles he wrote before his exec. infl'd the 1552 BofCP; 4 July 1533: burnt at Smithfield as heretic.

FROBISHER (Sir) Martin (?1535–94): poorly-edu. & dishonest explorer, privateer & naval commander. ?1535: b. s. of Bernard & Margaret (Yorke) Frobisher at Normanton, Yorks.; 1549: apprenticed to relative, Sir John Yorke, merchant adventurer, officer at the Southwark & Tower mints, & eventually a friend of the dukes of **Somerset** & **Northumberland** (both q.v.); 1553: 1st expedition to Guinea; 1554: 2nd expedition to Guinea – impr. by Portuguese; 1556/57: commanded on voyage to Barbary Coast; 30 Sept. 1559: m. (i) Isobel (Rigatt), wid.;

1560-73: privateering activities; mid-1570s: deserted h.w. & children;1576: unsuccessful voyage to discover Northwest Passage but visited Greenland; 1577–78: involved in (unsuccessful) prospecting for gold; these ventures lost the Queen money & Frobisher her favour; 1585: app'd Vice-Admiral to Drake's raid on the West Indies; 1588: Isobel d. in poor house; 1588: commanded the Triumph v. Spanish Armada, distinguished himself & was knighted; 1590: m. (ii) Dorothy (Withypool), wid.; 1590: Vice-Admiral; 1594: d. on campaign to France. T.H.B. Symons, ed., *Meta Incognita: A Discourse of Discovery, Martin Frobisher's Arctic Expeditions, 1576–1578*, 1999.

G

GARDINER (Bishop) Stephen (c. 1495–1555): Cambr.-edu. conservative theologian, canon lawyer, author, diplomat, statesman, administrator & Bp of Winchester. c. 1495: b. s. of John, clothmaker of Bury St Edmonds, & Agnes Gardiner; 1511: adm. Trinity Hall, Cambr.; 1524–29: in Wolsey's service; 1526–31: many eccles. preferments; 17 May 1527: present at formal start of divorce proceedings; 1528: accompanied Edward Foxe (q.v.) on embassy to Pope Clement VII & secured commission for **Wolsey** & papal legate **Cardinal Campeggio** (q.v.) to try the matter in Eng.; 1529: returned to Rome to lobby for Wolsey's election as Pope & secured new commission for trial; July 1529: app'd King's principal secretary; (see Chapter 1: General chronology for details of the King's Great Matter & Gardiner's role therein); Sept. 1531: Bp of Winchester; largely non-resident; Apr. 1532: gave Convocation's response to the Commons' 'supplication against the ordinaries' & thereby alienated the King; Apr. 1533: returned to partial favour & was King's counsel at annulment of m.; June 1533:

present at coronation of Queen Anne; Apr. 1534: **Thomas Cromwell** (q.v.) replaced him as principal secretary; 1535: attempted to regain Henry VIII's full favour by public support of royal supremacy while remaining a 'crypto-papist'; Sept. 1535: 'Si sedes illa' – defence of exec. of **John Fisher** (q.v.); 1535: *De vera obedientia* – Latin defence of the royal supremacy; 1539: chief architect of penalty clause of Six Articles v. Protestantism & helped enforce the act; 1540: returned to King's favour at Cromwell's fall & helped w. annulment of m. to Anne of Cleves; 1540–47: Chancellor of Cambr. Uni.; 1540: embassy to Emperor Charles V & attempts to persuade Henry back to Catholicism; July 1541: recalled; 1543: attack on **Cranmer** (q.v.) backfired; Jan. 1546: negotiated treaty w. Emperor; 1547: omitted from regency council; Sept. 1547 to Jan. 1548: impr. in Fleet for oppo. to iconoclasm, pub'n of Book of Homilies, etc.; 29 June 1548 to end of Edward's reign: imprisoned in Tower; 1553: restored to bpric & Chancellorship of Cambr. & made Lord Chancellor; initially oppo. Mary's m. to Philip; dedicated to rest. of Catholicism; 12/13 Nov. 1555: d.

GERARD John (c. 1545–1612): herbalist. c. 1545: b. Nantwich, Cheshire; edu. Willaston, nr Nantwich; 1562: apprenticed to Alexander Mason, surgeon of the Barber-Surgeons' Company, London; 9 Dec. 1569: made free of the Barber-Surgeons' Company; probably visited Scandinavia & Russia; m. Anne or Agnes; 1586: College of Physicians founded physic-garden & app'd Gerard curator; lived in tenement w. garden (in which he grew exotic plants such as the potato) in Holborn, probably as tenant of **William Cecil** Lord Burghley (q.v.); 1590s: superintendent of Burghley's gardens on the Strand & at Theobalds, Herts; 1596: published plant list of his own garden in Holborn (1st such list); 1597: pub'd his derivative, *The Herball, or, Generall Historie of Plants Gathered by John Gerarde of London* w. more than 1,800 woodcuts; 1598 & 1607: examiner of candidates for admission to freedom of Barber-Surgeons' company; 1607: elected Master of the company; herbalist to James I; left his books of physic & surgery to h. s.-in-law Richard Holden; d. early Feb. 1612. Henrey, *British botanical and horticultural literature before 1800*, 1, 1975.

GERARD John (1564–1637): Oxf.-edu. Jesuit. 1564: b. Etwall, Derbs s. of Sir Thomas Gerard of Bryn Lancs & Elizabeth (Port); 1575: matric. Oxf.; 1576: left Oxf. owing to religious persecution; 1577–81: edu. at Douai, Rheims & College de Clermont, Paris; spring 1583 returned to Eng. in poor health; 5 Mar. 1584: impr. in Marshalsea; 1585: released; May 1586: travelled to Eng. College, Rome.; 17 July 1588: ord.; 15 Aug. 1588: entered SJ; autumn 1588: travelled to Eng. & moved freely in Catholic circles, dressed as a gentleman; 23 Apr. 1594: arrested; summer 1594: impr. in Clink (& est'd a chaplaincy there) & Tower; tortured; 5 Oct. 1594: escaped from Tower; lived peripatetic life amongst recusant houses until his departure from Eng. on 3 May 1606 w. Spanish ambass.; 1607: app'd Eng. confessor at St Peter's, Rome; 1609–13: assistant to the novice master at Louvain; 1613–21: R & novice master at Liege; support of Mary Ward at Liege led to recall to Rome temporarily; 1623: app'd tertian director at Ghent; 1627–37: consultor & confessor at Eng. College in Rome; 27 July 1637: d. in Rome. *John Gerard: The Autobiography of an Elizabethan*, trans. P. Caraman, 2nd ed'n, 1956; A. Walsham, *Church Papists: Catholicism, Conformity and Confessional Polemic in Early Modern England*, 1993.

GILBERT (Sir) Humphrey (1537–83): Eton & Oxf.-edu. intellectual, explorer, soldier, author & educationalist. 1537: b. s. of Otho Gilbert & Katherine (Champernowne) of Compton, Devon; 1547: Otho d. and Katherine m. Walter Raleigh, and their s. **Walter** (q.v.) was Gilbert's half-brother; 1554/5: entered service of Princess Elizabeth through infl. of his mother Katherine's elder half-sister **Katherine** (Ashley or **Astley**) (q.v.); 1558: attended New Inn; 1562/63: held commission on Newhaven (Le Havre) expedition; 1566: *Discourse of a Discoverie for a New Passage to Cataia* – suggesting northwest passage & advocating colonisation of the New World to alleviate poverty in the Old; 1566–69: served under Sir Henry Sidney in Ireland; Jan. 1570: knighted by Sidney at Drogheda; m. Anne Aucher, heiress from Kent; 1571: M.P. Plymouth; 1567, 1572: attempted Irish plantations but failed; early 1570s: 'The erection of an achademy in London for educacion of her maiestes wardes, & others the youth of nobility & gentlemen'; 1572–81: M.P. Queensborough; 1577: obtained royal letters patent for six years to destroy Spanish & Portuguese fishing fleets off Newfoundland & found colonies over which he was to have jurisdiction; farmed out privileges under these letters, e.g. to **John Dee** (q.v.); Aug. 1583: founded first British colony in North America at St John Newfoundland; Sept. 1583: ship lost at sea in Azores. D.B. Quinn, ed., *The Voyages and Colonising Enterprises of Sir Humphrey Gilbert*, 2 vols, Hakluyt Society, 2nd ser., 83–4, 1940.

GREENE Robert (1558–92): ?Cambr.-edu. & extremely popular writer & dramatist & friend of **Thomas Nashe** (q.v.). 1558: b. s. of Robert Greene of Norwich; edu. Norwich GS; 26 Nov. 1575: adm. St John's Cambr. as sizar; 1580: B.A.; 1583: M.A.; 1580: pub'd *Mamillia*; 1583: pub'd *Mamillia* Part 2; 1584: pub'd three romances: *Gwydonius: The Carde of Fancie*; *Arbasto: The Anatomie of Fortune*; & *Morando: The tritameron of love* & (probably in 1585) *Pandosto: The Triumph of Time* (hugely popular & the source for Shakespeare's *The Winter's Tale*) that est'd him as leading English romance writer; 1591–: famed for coney-catching pamphlets (genre of crime exposé) e.g. 1592: *A Disputation betweene a hee Conny-Catcher, and a shee Conny-Catcher*; 1592: pub'd six ed'ns of *Quip for an Upstart Courtier*, that debated social values of court & country; 1587–92: wrote but did not publish several plays incl. 1594: (written in 1589) *The Honorable Historie of Frier Bacon and Frier Bongay* & (w. Thomas Lodge) *A*

Looking-Glasse for London and England & 1599: *The Comicall Historie of Alphonsus, King of Aragon*; 3 Sept. 1592: d.; posthumous reputation as wastrel; C.W. Crupi, *Robert Greene*, 1986.

GRENVILLE Honor (m. names Basset, Plantagenet) (Viscountess Lisle) (c. 1493–1566): religiously conservative supporter to & networker for her husband Viscount Lisle & educator of her Basset children. c. 1493: b. dau. of Sir Thomas Grenville, Stowe in Kilkhampton, Cornwall; m. (i) Sir John Basset of Umberleigh, Devon & had three s. & four daus; 1515: b. of 1st surviving child, Philippa; c. 1527: Basset d.; Nov. 1528: m. (ii) Arthur Plantagenet, Viscount Lisle; chiefly notable for her edu. of her children, whom she placed in great French & English households, such as those of **Thomas Cromwell** (q.v.), **Edward Seymour** (q.v.) & Thybault Rouaud; 1532: accomp'd Lisle to Calais & attended Anne Boleyn on royal visit; 1537: dau. Anne became maid of honour to **Jane Seymour** (q.v.); 1537: s. James served **Bp Gardiner** (q.v.); 1566: d. M. St C. Byrne, ed., *The Lisle Letters*, 6 Vols, 1981.

GRESHAM (Sir) Thomas (c. 1518–79): merchant adventurer, mercer, founder of Royal Exchange & Gresham College. c. 1518: b. London, 2nd s. of Sir Richard Gresham & his 1st w. Audrey (Lynne); adm. pensioner, Gonville Hall, Cambr; 1535: apprenticed to uncle John Gresham; edu. in classical & modern languages; adm. Gray's Inn; 1540s: performed foreign services for Henry VIII; 1543: took freedom in Mercers' Company; 1543: de facto head of his father's commercial enterprises; 1544: m. wid. Anne (Ferneley) Read; 1546: directed Greshams' Netherlands commercial activities; 1546–51: economic problems led him to change his practices & secure dominant position in the commerce w. the Netherlands; 1543–63: served as merchant & royal agent; Mar. 1547: s. Richard b.; close links with Sir **Nicholas Bacon** (q.v.) when his wife's sister Jane m. him & when his own illegit. dau. Anne m. Nathaniel Bacon; Dec. 1551–64:

royal agent in Netherlands; rise in value of sterling allowed him to claim credit for reducing the enormous royal debt on the Antwerp bourse; 1553: reapp'd royal agent in Netherlands; Mar. 1556 to Dec. 1557: removed from post; winter 1557–58: reinstated & nego'd huge loans for Mary's gov't; 1559–65: resumed task of reducing royal debts abroad; Dec. 1559: knighted; 1560: recoinage; 1561–62: reform of the London Custom House; 1564: Richard d.; Mar. 1565 to Oct. 1566: subscription for building of Exchange; Dec. 1568: Exchange completed; Jan. 1571: Elizabeth visited the Exchange; 1575: founded Gresham College, to be created at h. w.'s d., & run with funds in the hands of the Mercers' Company & the corporation of London; they were to app't seven professors to lecture, one on each day of the week, in the seven sciences; 21 Nov. 1579: d.; 14 Dec. 1596: d. of Anne Gresham; Mar. 1597: Gresham College in Bishopsgate occupied by professors. S.T. Bindoff, The Fame of Sir Thomas Gresham, 1973; C.E. Challis, The Tudor Coinage, 1978.

GREY (Lady) Frances (née Brandon; also Stokes) Duchess of Suffolk (1517–59): noblewoman & courtier of royal descent & strong character. 16 July 1517: b. elder dau. of Charles Brandon & Mary (Tudor) Brandon; 1528: Charles Brandon secured annulment of h. m. to Lady Margaret Neville to ensure Frances's own legitimacy; May 1553: m. (i) **Henry Grey**, Marquis of Dorset (q.v.); 1537: b. of Jane; 1540: b. of **Katherine**; 1545: b. of **Mary** (all q.v.); classical edu. of Jane, first in **Katherine Parr**'s household & then by John (later Bishop) **Aylmer** at Dorset's estate at Bradgate, Leics; posthumous reputation as insensitive, even abusive, mother is down to Roger Ascham's comments in *The Scholemaster*; frequently at Edward VI's court & approved (w. her husband) Northumberland's plans for the succession & the proclamation of Jane as Queen; July 1553: she & Suffolk were released from the Tower after her personal petition to her cousin, the Queen; she remained at court although her husband did not; 1 Mar. 1555:

m. (ii) Adrian Stokes, Master of the Horse; remained on good terms w. Queen Mary & obtained positions for her daus Katherine and Mary; 1556: b. & d. of dau. Elizabeth; 21 Nov. 1559: d.; 5 Dec. 1559: bur. at Westminster Abbey.

GREY (Lord) Henry Duke of Suffolk (1517–54): self-important & incompetent politician & courtier. 17 Jan. 1517: b. s. & h. of Thomas Grey, 2nd Marquis of Dorset & his 2nd w, Margaret (Wootton; former m. name Medley); poss. m. (i) to Katherine Fitzalan, dau. of 11th Earl of Arundel; 1530: on father's d. was made ward of **Charles Brandon** (q.v.); m. or betrothal to Katherine set aside; May 1535: Henry m. ?(ii) Frances Brandon (q.v. **Grey, Frances**), elder dau. of **Charles & Mary Tudor** (q.v.); May 1533: KB; chief mourner at Henry VIII's funeral; 1547: KG; 1548 involved himself w. Thomas Seymour notably in scheme to m. Grey's eldest dau. Jane to Edward VI & placed Jane in dowager Queen Katherine Parr's household at Sudeley; 1549: escaped punishment; Nov. 1549: PC; loyally supported Northumberland in exchange for rich pickings; 1551: Lord Warden of the Northern Marches; regarded as important chiefly because h.w. Frances was 3rd in line to throne; 11 Oct. 1551: Duke of Suffolk; 21 May 1553: dau. **Jane Grey** (q.v.) m. Lord **Guildford Dudley** (q.v.) & Edward VI made her his heir in his will; 9 July 1553: proclaimed Jane Queen & remained in London to protect his dau.; defected; impr. in Tower for short time; repudiated his Protestant faith & was granted full pardon; Dec. 1553: joined **Thomas Wyatt** the younger (q.v.) etc. in plot to prevent Mary m. Philip of Spain; Jan.: Queen offered him command to suppress rebellion; he fled to his estates; arrested; 23 Feb. 1554: exec.

GREY (Lady) Jane (later Queen, m. name Dudley) (see Section 12.1: Monarchs and their consorts).

GREY (Lady) Katherine (m. name Seymour) Countess of Hertford (?1540–68): 2nd of three daus of **Henry Grey** (q.v.), Duke of Suffolk & **Frances** (Brandon) **Grey** (q.v.), & therefore niece of Henry VIII & grandchild of Henry VII; 21 May 1553: betrothed or m. (i) to Henry Herbert, eldest s. of William, first Earl of Pembroke, an ally of Northumberland; 1554: placed in care of Anne Seymour, Dowager Duchess of Somerset; attended court during Mary's reign & conformed to Catholicism; c. 1558: app'd maid of honour to Elizabeth I; heir presumptive under the terms of Henry VIII's will; target of many m. plans; Katherine wanted to m. Edward Somerset, Earl of Hertford, eldest s. of Protector Somerset; Nov./Dec. 1560: (ii) clandestine m. without the necessary royal permission; May 1561: Queen informed of the m. & pregnancy & suspected plot & arrested them; Edward Seymour, Viscount Beauchamp b. in Tower; 12 May 1562: m. decl. null & void & Edward illegit.; 1563: **John Hales** (q.v.) wrote tract defending Mary's claim to succession & was arrested; Feb. 1563: b. of Thomas while both were still in prison; Aug. 1563: house arrest in Essex & then Suffolk; 1566: play Gorboduc supported the idea of a Suffolk succession; 27 Jan. 1568: d. ; 1606: her m. to Hertford decl. lawful. H.W. Chapman, *Two Tudor Portraits: Henry Howard, Earl of Surrey and Lady Katherine Grey*, 1960; M. Levine, *The Early Elizabethan Succession Question, 1558–1568*, 1966.

GREY (Lady) Mary (m. name Keys) (?1545–78): Protestant noblewoman of royal descent. ?1545: b. youngest dau. of **Henry Grey**, Duke of Suffolk & h.w. **Frances** (Brandon) Duchess of Suffolk (both q.v.); 21 May 1553: betrothed to Arthur Grey, Lord Grey of Wilton; her father's exec. put an end to this match; 1558: maid of honour to Elizabeth I & royal pensioner; c. 12 Aug 1565: clandestine m. to Thomas Key[e]s, wid., sergeant porter to Queen & gentleman; 19 Aug. 1565: Keys impr. in Fleet & Mary placed in custody of Mr William Hawtrey at Chequers, Bucks; **Bishop Grindal** (q.v.) refused to annul the m. & sent the case to the **Court of Arches**; Mary transferred to care of

her step-grandmother Katherine Willoughby, Dowager Duchess of Suffolk; 1568: Keys released; June 1569–73: Mary placed in custody of Sir **Thomas Gresham** (q.v.); 1571: Keys d.; 1577: Mary returned to Court; 20 Apr. 1578: d. & ?bur. in Westminster Abbey w. Frances Grey.

GRINDAL (Archbishop) Edmund (c. 1516–83): Cambr.-edu. Archbp of York & Canterbury, Protestant reformer and educational benefactor. c. 1516: b. St Bees, Cumberland; 1544: ord. deac. by Bp of Chester; 1549: President & deputy Master of Pembroke College, Cambr.; converted to Protestantism at Pembroke, infl. by Nicholas Ridley & Martin Bucer; 1549: participated in disputation on transubstantiation at royal visitation of Cambr.; Aug. 1551: precentor of St Paul's; received various other preferments incl. to royal chaplain & Prebendary of Westminster Abbey; May 1554: Marian exile; Aug. 1554–58: Strasbourg (w. interval at Wasselheim, May 1555 to May 1556 to learn German); took Cox's part in the so-called 'Troubles at Frankfurt'; key role in early promotion of Protestant martyrology of John Foxe, acquiring, for example, trial records of Ridley & Cranmer; 15 Jan. 1559: returned to Eng.; leading part in disputation v. Marian bps in Westminster Abbey; 22 June 1559: replaced **Bonner** as Bp of London; **Matthew Parker** (q.v.) & Grindal the first appointees to the permanent Eccles. Commission; 1563: led attempts in **Convocation** to further reform the Church settlement; tackled problems of Church at diocesan level: recruitment, pastoral discipline of clergy & people, plague & pestilence, the presence of foreign congregations, nonconforming Protestant clergy, etc.; 1565: 2nd **Vestiarian controversy** over use of clerical garb – a policy which Grindal thought was too hard-line; 1566: 37 London clergy (dubbed 'Puritans') who refused to wear the surplice & cap were threatened w. deprivation; 1566–72: oppo'd radical reformers such as separatists or Presbyterians who acted v. the interests of church unity; 1570: Archbp of York, as agent of Protestantism in the North; Mar. 1571: President of Northern Eccles.

Commission; through visitations uprooted survivals of Catholic practice, especially in York dioc.; used Eccles. Commission as principal agent v. recusancy; sought to recruit & prefer edu. Protestant clergy; 1576: reluctant Queen made him Archbp of Canterbury; in Parl. headed committee urging Elizabeth to pass a bill increasing fines for recusancy & enforcing participation in communion; initiated reform of Court of Faculties & Court of Audience to improve discipline; 12 June 1576: ordered by Elizabeth to suppress Prophesyings (preaching conferences) in the midlands; Grindal set about writing defence of Prophesyings & attempt to tighten their regulation; Elizabeth insisted on suppression; Dec. 1576: Grindal wrote 6,000-word letter refusing to obey her rather than God; May 1577: Queen herself ordered suppression; late May 1577: Grindal sequestered & under house arrest; Nov. 1577: called to hear charges before Star Chamber but refused because of ill health; continued to fulfil spiritual duties such as consecr. of bps; 1581: both Convocation & Parl. unsuccessfully sought royal pardon for Grindal; retirement discussed; 6 July 1583: d. at Croydon; by his will founded GS at St Bees & fellowships & scholarships at Pembroke & Queen's Colleges, Cambr. P. Collinson, *Archbishop Grindal, 1519–1583: The Struggle for a Reformed Church*, 1979.

GRINDAL William (d. 1548): Cambr.-edu. tutor to Princess Elizabeth. Unknown parentage but poss. related to **Edmund Grindal** (q.v.); 1541/42: B.A. St John's College, Cambr.; 1542/3: Fellow; 1540s: favourite pupil of **Roger Ascham** (q.v.) who unsuccessfully proposed Grindal for college Greek readership; late 1544: poss. junior tutor to Prince Edward; late 1546: tutor to Elizabeth at Enfield; Grindal intro'd Ascham to Lady Jane Grey & to Ann Parr, Queen Katherine's younger sister; Jan. 1548: d. of plague.

GROCYN William (?1449–1519): Oxf.-edu. humanist, Greek scholar & book collector, tutor to **William Warham** (q.v.) & friend of **Erasmus**, **Colet** & **Linacre** (all q.v.). ?1449:

b. s. of tenant of Winchester College in Wilts; 26 Sept. 1463: adm. Winchester; 7 Sept. 1465: adm. scholar of New College, Oxf.; 1467: fellow; tutor to **William Warham** later Archbp of Canterbury (q.v.); c. 1474: M.A.; 1477: signed name in Greek letters; Mar. 1481: res. Fellowship; 1481–1504: R of Newton Longville, Bucks; 1483: divinity reader at Magdalen College, Oxf.; 1485–1514: Canon of Lincoln; 1488: studied Latin & Greek in Florence for c. two years; 1491: B.Th. Oxf.; 1493: daily public Greek lectures in Oxf.; 1496–1517: R of St Lawrence Jewry, London; c. 1501: in London, & More gave lectures at his church; 1506: Erasmus stayed w. him;1506–19: Master of All Saints College, Maidstone; betw. June and Oct. 1519: d. at Maidstone.

GRYMESTON[E] OR GRIMSTON (née Bernye) Elizabeth (c. 1563–c. 1601): (?Catholic) author of first mother's advice book; kinswoman of Robert Southwell. c. 1563: b. dau. of Martin & Margaret (Flinte) Bernye of Norfolk; early 1580s: (?clandestinely) m. Christopher Grymestone, fellow of Gonville & Caius College, Cambr.; several children; 1593: Christopher adm. Gray's Inn; 1604: posthumous pub'n of unusually learned advice book that she had intended as a legacy for her only surviving child, a s. Bernye: *Miscelanea: Meditations, Memoratives*; went into several other, expanded editions. B.S. Travitsky (ed.) *Mother's Advice Books*, 1998.

H

HAKLUYT Richard (1552–1616): Westminster & Oxf.-edu. notable cosmographer & travel writer; an ord. pr. who held several eccles. preferments. 1552: b. London s. of Richard Hakluyt, skinner & h.w. Margery; when he was left orphaned in early childhood, was cared for by cousin Richard Hakluyt, a lawyer; student (Fellow) of Christ Church, Oxf.; 1580: ord. pr.; several eccles. preferments; moved in merchant & adventurer circles; 1582: Divers Voyages Touching the Discoverie of America, 1584: presented Elizabeth I with 'Discourse of Western Planting', proposing at Raleigh's prompting ambitious colonisation of North America; 1589: pub'd The principal navigations, voiages, traffiques and discoveries of the English nation, made by sea or over-land, to the remote and farthest distant quarters of the earth, c. 1592: m. Douglas Cavendish; 1593: s. Edmond b.; 1598–1600: 2nd much larger version of The Principal Navigations; pub'd many other travel works; 1604: m. (ii) Frances Smith; 26 Nov. 1616: bur. Westminster Abbey (where he was a prebendary). D.B. Quinn (ed.), **The Hakluyt Handbook**, 2 Vols, Hakluyt Society, 1974.

HALES (Judge) John (1469/70–?1540): Gray's Inn-edu. lawyer, administrator, M.P. and judge. Cousin of Sir Christopher Hales. 1469/70: b. s. John Hales of Tenterden, Kent; c. 1490: adm. Gray's Inn; m. Isabel (Harry); four s. & one dau.; 1503: JP Kent; 1512 & 1515: M.P. Canterbury; 1514: Bencher, Gray's Inn; 1519–22: attorney-general, Duchy of Lancaster; 1522: 3rd Baron of Exchequer; 1528: 2nd Baron of Exchequer; c. July 1540: d.

HALES John (1516–72): M.P., social reformer, Commonwealthman, educationalist & royal administrator. 1516: b. s. of Thomas Hales of Halden, Kent; reared in household of uncle, Sir Christopher Hales, attorney-general & Master of the Rolls; studied classical languages & the law; 1535: service of Thomas Cromwell; 1537–40: keeper of writs in King's Bench & clerk of Court of First Fruit & Tenths; 1541: acquired monastic lands; estab'd free school, St John's Hospital, Coventry, for which he wrote a text book: *Introductiones ad grammaticum*; 1545–57 & 1559–72: clerk of **hanaper**; 1547: JP for Middlesex & Warws & M.P. for Preston, Lancs; presented programme for social reform in Parl.; until recently thought to be

author of 1549: *Discourse of the Commonweal of this Realm of England* (see **Smith, Thomas**); June 1548: member of commission to investigate enclosure & depopulation in midlands; Earl of Warwick (q.v. see **Dudley (Lord) John**) blamed him for consequent rebellion; Oct. 1549: impr. in Tower on Somerset's fall; 1550: released; 1551–59: lands seized & in exile; peacemaker during 'Troubles in Frankfurt'; 3 Jan. 1559: gave oratory of congratulation to Elizabeth I; 1563–67: M.P. Lancaster; 1564: wrote book defending Suffolk title to the Crown & m. of Katherine Grey & Edward Seymour; 1565: impr.; 1566: **William Cecil** (q.v.) org'd his release into house arrest; 1566–70: house arrest; fought to retain clerkship of hanaper; 28 Dec. 1572: d.

HARDWICK Bess of (née) (m. names: Barlow, Cavendish, St Loe, Talbot) (?1527–1608): Countess of Shrewsbury: dynastically ambitious, social-climbing & extremely wealthy noblewoman & great patron (especially notable for building Hardwick Old & New Halls). ?1527: b. dau. of John & Elizabeth (Leake) Hardwick of Hardwick, Derbyshire; 1529: her mother m. Ralph Leche of Chatsworth; c. 28 May 1543: m. (i) Robert Barlow of Barlow, Derbs (possibly never consummated); 1544: Robert d.; poss. lady-in-waiting to **Frances Grey** (q.v.); 20 Aug. 1547: m. (ii) wid. Sir William Cavendish; 1548–57: eight children, incl. Henry, William & Charles, for whom they chose powerful, Protestant godparents such as Princess Elizabeth & members of the Grey family & connection; 1549: Cavendish bought Chatsworth & the couple began ambitious rebuilding; 1550s: added further lands in Derbs; 1557: William d.; c. 1557: m. (iii) Sir William St Loe, wid. who saved her from bankruptcy; she remained at Chatsworth supervising building works while St Loe was at Court & member of Princess Elizabeth's household; 1559: became gentlewoman of Queen's Privy Chamber; May 1561: Queen informed of secret m. between **Katherine Grey** (q.v.) & Edward Seymour, Earl of Hertford & dismissed Bess for complicity;

1565: d. of St Loe; 1 Nov. 1567: m. (iv) George Talbot, 6th Earl of Shrewsbury, one of the richest magnates in the north; she arranged the m. of her dau. Mary to Gilbert Talbot (later 7th Earl) & her eldest s. Henry Cavendish to Shrewsbury's dau. Grace Talbot; 1568–84: Shrewsbury was guardian of Mary Queen of Scots; 1574: Margaret Stuart, Countess of Lennox visited Mary & Bess arranged m. betw. Lennox's s. Charles & her dau. Elizabeth; this angered Queen & Shrewsbury; 1575: Elizabeth (Cavendish) Stuart gave b. to Arbella [also called Arabella]; 1582: Bess responsible for Arbella's education as future Queen; 1584: relations w. Shrewsbury reached breaking point & Bess separated from him & retired to Chatsworth; 1587: Bess awarded both Chatsworth & a large income by the courts; 1584: Bess bought Hardwick, former family home; 1587: began building project at Hardwick; 18 Nov. 1590: d. of Shrewsbury; Bess inherited one-third of his disposable landed wealth; 1591: renovations of Hardwick Old Hall largely complete; 1591–99: Hardwick New Hall (?designed by **Robert Smythson** (q.v.); her initials 'E.S.' a prominent feature of the embellishment; 4 Oct. 1597: began to reside at New Hall; 13 Feb. 1608: d., having disinherited her eldest s. Henry & her grand-dau. Arbella, w. whom she had quarrelled. D.N. Durant, *Bess of Hardwick: Portrait of an Elizabethan Dynast*, rev. ed'n, 1999.

HARINGTON (Lord) John (1539/40–1613): First Baron Harington of Exton. Courtier, M.P. & substantial landowner. 1539/40: b. s. & h. of Sir James Harington & Lucy (Sidney) Harington of Rutland; edu. his dau. Lucy well in several languages & was said to be well-disposed towards learning; 1571: M.P. Rutland; m. Anne Keilwey & inherited Combe Abbey, Warws, through her; 1559–93: JP Kesteven, Lincs; 1579: JP for Rutland; 1581: Lucy b.; edu. in French, Italian, Spanish, etc.; 1583: JP Warws; 1585: served Earl of Leicester in Netherlands; 1580–90: Keeper of Kenilworth Castle; 1590s: Dep.-Lieut. for Rutland & Warws; 153, 1601: M.P.

Rutland; Dec. 1594: Lucy m. Edward Russell, 3rd Earl of Bedford; New Year 1596: hired theatre co. to perform Shakespeare's *Titus Andronicus* at his Rutland residence; June 1603: entertained Princess Elizabeth at Combe Abbey; July 1603: raised to peerage & made guardian of Princess Elizabeth; 23 Aug. 1613: d.

HARINGTON (Sir) John (1560–1612): Eton & Cambr.-edu. courtier, humanist author, letter writer & wit who invented water closet. 1560: b. in London s. & h. of courtier John & Isabell (Markham) Harington; godparents were Elizabeth I & William 2nd Earl of Pembroke; Nov. 1581: adm. Lincoln's Inn; 6 Sept. 1583: m. Mary Rogers of Cannington Somerset; 1584: refused to sign Bond of Association; 1586: JP; 1591: pub'd first complete English transl. of Ludovico Ariosto's epic poem 'Orlando Furioso'; 1596: *New Discourse of a Stale Subject, called the Metamorphosis of Ajax*; outlined design of lavatory w. primitive flushing system; lost favour w. Elizabeth; 1599–1600: his work w. Robert Devereux in Ireland led to further disfavour w. Queen but soon after forgiven; 1600: made two ms collections of epigrams & presented them to Lucy Russell, Countess of Bedford & his mother-in-law Jane Rogers. D.H. Craig, *Sir John Harington*, 1985.

HATTON (Sir) Christopher (c. 1540–91): Oxf.-edu. lawyer, courtier, letter writer, playwright, patron, politician. c. 1540: b. 2nd s. of William Hatton & Alice (Saunders) of Holdenby, Northants. 1555/56: St Mary Hall, Oxf.; 26 May 1560: adm. Inner Temple; 1562: performed in masque w. Robert Dudley before Elizabeth I; 1564: Gentleman pensioner of Queen; 1566/67: joint author of play *Gismond of Salem* performed at Inner Temple before Elizabeth; 1560s: active courtier in receipt of many rewards in the form of offices, estates, gifts of plate, etc.; 1572: Gentleman of Privy Chamber & Capt. of Yeomen of the Guard; 1569: Northants JP; 1571 & 1572: M.P.; lifelong close **chivalrous** relationship w. Elizabeth – letters survive;

1576: bought Kirby Hall; 1577: built new ambitious house modelled on Theobalds; 1579: PC; 1572–86: acted for Queen & PC in Commons;1580s: zealous supporter of Whitgift & opponent of puritans; 1584: persuaded Commons to trust Queen & not to read Bill and Book; 1586–87: defended royal prerogative & royal policy regarding religion but also believed in carrying parl. opinion along w. royal policy re Spain, Mary Queen of Scots, etc.; unmarried, w. no interest in dynastic politics or building up clientele; Apr. 1587: Lord Chancellor – app't annoyed legal profession; 1587–91: used assistants to do the work; participated in trials of Babington & Mary Queen of Scots; 1588: KG; 1588: Chancellor of Oxf. Uni.; 20 Nov. 1591: d.; Dec. 1591: bur. at St Paul's.

HATTON (Lady) Elizabeth (née Cecil) (also Elizabeth Lady Coke) (1578–1646): heiress, courtier & hostess. 1578: b. 4th dau. of Thomas Cecil, 1st Earl of Exeter & Dorothy (Latimer); c. 1590: m. (i) Sir William Hatton; 1597: widowed & inherited huge estates; 6 Nov. 1598: m. unhappily (ii) Sir **Edward Coke**, lawyer (q.v.); two daus & many stepchildren; 1604: appeared in court masque 'The Vision of Twelve Goddesses' w. Queen Anne; renowned for elaborate entertaining at Hatton House, Holborn, her effective & active management of her estates, her supposed beauty & her extremely unhappy m. to Coke. L. Norsworthy, *The Lady of Bleeding Heart Yard: Elizabeth Hatton*, 1935.

HAWKINS, Sir John (1532–95) naval commander, reforming Treasurer & Comptroller of navy; navigator, early slave trader & merchant; 1588: naval commander v. Armada. 1532: b. Plymouth, 2nd s. of William Hawkins & h.w. Joan (Trelawny); brother of William (c. 1519–89) & cousin of **Francis Drake** (q.v.); c. 1560: s. Richard b. out of wedlock; 1562–63: voyage of exploration & slaving off Guinea coast and Caribbean; 1564–65: 2nd slaving voyage; 20 Jan. 1567: m. Katherine Gonson, dau. of Treas. of navy; 1567–69: 3rd slaving voyage; 18 Nov. 1577: Treas of Navy; 1588: fought v. Armada; part of war council; 12 Nov. 1595: d. at Puerto Rico during Drake's last expedition.

HERBERT (Countess) Anne (née Parr), Countess of Pembroke (pre-1514–52): classically-edu. younger sister of Queen Katherine Parr, noted for her piety & patronage. Pre-1514: b. dau. of Sir Thomas & Lady Maud (Green) Parr of Kendal; c. 1537: m. **William Herbert**, 1st Earl of Pembroke (q.v.); c. 1538: Henry b.; 1543–47: lady-in-waiting to Katherine; 1548: Roger Ascham advised her to brush up her Latin; patronised Flemish miniaturist Levina Teerlinc, a member of Katherine's entourage; 20 Feb. 1552: d.; 28 Feb. 1552: bur. St Paul's.

HERBERT (Lord) Henry (c. 1538–1601): Welsh-speaking 2nd Earl of Pembroke, patron, reforming royal administrator & English & Welsh magnate. c. 1538: b. s. of William Herbert, 1st Earl of Pembroke & h. 1st w. Anne (Parr); 25 May 1553: m. (i) **Katherine Grey** (q.v.), sister of Queen **Jane** (q.v.); 1553: m. annulled; 1553: KB; gentleman of bed chamber to King Philip; Feb. 1563: m. (ii) Katherine Talbot, dau. of 6th Earl of Shrewsbury; May 1576: Katherine d.; 21 Apr. 1577: m. (iii) **Mary Sidney** (q.v.) dau of Sir Henry Sidney; two s. & one dau.; 1570: 2nd Earl of Pembroke & Lord Lieut. of Wiltshire; 1586: Lord President of Council in Marches of Wales; 1595: feud in Wales w. Robert Devereux, Earl of Essex; patron of Fulke Greville, Abraham Fraunce & Gervase Babington & of Burbage's theatre company (Pembroke's Men); d. 19 Jan. 1601.

HERBERT (Sir) John (c. 1540–1617): Oxf.-edu. & linguistically-gifted civil lawyer. c. 1540: b. 2nd s. of Matthew Herbert of Swansea, gent. & h.w. Mary (Gamage); 5 July 1558: B.A. Christ Church Oxf.; 1561: M.A.; Feb 1565: BCL; 28 Nov. 1573: adm. Doctors' Commons; 1574: interrogated foreign prisoners; 1575–84: joint commissioner of the admiralty; 1586–1601: Master of Requests; diplomatic missions: 1583, 1600, 1602–03: to Denmark; 1583–85: to Poland; 1585: to Brandenburg; 1587: to Netherlands;

1586 to 1611: M.P. for various seats; 23 June 1587: DCL; 1590: clerk to PC & Dean of Wells; 1591: m. Margaret Morgan (their dau. Mary m. Sir William Doddington); 1592: disputed before Elizabeth I on her visit to Oxf.; 1595: JP Glamorgan; 1604: JP Hampshire; 1605: JP Montgomeryshire; c. 1599: Robert Cecil's secretary; 1600: PC & 2nd secretary of state; 1601–04: member, Council of North; 31 Jan. 1602: knighted; 1603–06: Commissioner for the Scottish union & for eccles. causes; 1610: withdrew from public life; 9 July 1617: d. poss. from injuries suffered in duel v. Sir Lewis Tresham; bur. Cardiff.

HERBERT (Lord) William (1506/07–70): 1st Earl of Pembroke; soldier, courtier, M.P., patron landowner. 1506/07: b. 2nd s. of Richard Herbert, gentleman usher to **Henry VII** (q.v.) & Margaret (Cradock); grandson of William Herbert, Earl of Pembroke (old style), exec. in 1469 for loyalty to Edward IV; c. 1537: m. (i) Anne Parr; c. 1538: Henry b.; 12 July 1543: m. of sister-in-law Katherine Parr to Henry VIII gave boost to his career; Oct. 1546: Chief Gentleman of the Privy Chamber, w. **Anthony Denny** (q.v.); 1547: member of Council of Regency; early supporter of Protector Somerset (q.v. under Edward Seymour) beneficiary of dissolution of monasteries in Wales during Edward's reign; 1549: suppressed insurgency in Wiltshire; summer 1549: prominent role in Battle of Sampford Courtenay; Oct. 1549: turned v. Somerset – crucial to his fall; joined forces w. Duke of Northumberland & was considerably rewarded; PC; 8 Apr. 1550: Lord President of Council in Marches of Wales w. substantial estates; 1551: Lord Lieut. of all the Welsh counties; 11 Oct. 1551: Earl of Pembroke; after Somerset's fall was the leading magnate in Wiltshire also; built Wilton House, where he led a lavish lifestyle & entertained King Edward; 20 Feb. 1552: d. of Anne; May 1552: m. (ii) Anne Compton wid. (née Talbot, dau. of George Talbot, 4th Earl of Shrewsbury); 1553: collab. in Edward VI & Northumberland's plans & signed 'devyce' to divert succession to

Jane Grey of the House of Suffolk; 21 May 1553: **Jane Grey** (q.v.) m. **Guildford Dudley** (q.v.) & her sister Katherine m. Herbert's s. & heir; had Jane proclaimed Queen at Beaumaris & Denbigh & was to fore in initially resisting Mary but eventually proclaimed her Queen at his house at Baynard's castle; briefly impr. but 13 Aug. 1553: restored to PC; Feb. 1554: suppr. Wyatt's rebellion; 1555: restored Lord President of Council in Welsh Marches; 1557: led army v. French; 1558–64: had Elizabeth's confidence, supported William Cecil & was on her PC; 1568: High Steward of the Royal Household; 1568: supported m. betw. Mary of Scotland & Thomas Howard, 4th Duke of Norfolk; was impr. for involvement; 17 Mar. 1570: d. at Hampton Court; 18 Apr. 1570: bur. St Paul's.

HENSLOWE Philip (c. 1555–1616): theatre manager & financier. c. 1555: b. younger s. of Edmond Henslowe of Lindfield Sussex, Master of Game, & Margaret (Ridge); 1570s: freedom of Dyers' Company; 1579: m. Agnes Woodward, wid. w. two daus; many money-making ventures such as pawnbroking & property; 1576–86: org'd sale of wood in Ashdown forest where his father had been Master of Game; June 1584: buying & dressing goat skins; 1587: invested in Rose Playhouse, Southwark in partnership w. John Cholmley; 1592: renovated the Rose & kept accounts of the enterprise, extended loans, etc. to players; Oct. 1592: step-dau. Joan m. Edward Alleyn, actor; formed partnership w. Alleyn & invested in a number of playhouses & bear-baiting arena in Southwark. Edmond had connections at court as advisor to the royal armoury; 1593: Philip app'd groom of chamber; 1600: Henslowe & Alleyn built the Fortune theatre; 1603: gentleman sewer of the chamber under James I; mixed in illustrious court circles & used connections to commercial advantage; purchased w. Alleyne Mastership of the Bears; 1614: opened the Hope Theatre, w. bear-baiting facilities; accumulated a good deal of property in Southwark; active member of St Saviour's Church & governor of its GS; 6 Jan. 1616: d.

R.A. Foakes and R.T. Rickert (eds), *Henslowe's Diary*, 1961.

HERON (Sir) John (pre-1470–1522): royal administrator & Henry VIII's chief financial officer until 1521. b. s. of William Heron, haberdasher, and Joan (Packer), wid.; 1485: entered royal service; 1492–1521: Treasurer of Chamber – under his control it grew in importance; c. 1504: m. Margaret; 1513: clerk of hanaper; 1515: knighted; 1516: chamberlain of Exchequer; 1520: at Field of Cloth of Gold w. Henry; 15 Jan. 1522: d.

HEYWOOD John (1496/97–c. 1580): Oxf.-edu. court lyricist, musician, dramatist (possibly actor) & epigrammist; loyal Catholic; member of More-**Rastell** circle; favourite wit at court of Mary I. 1496/97: b. s. of William, a Coventry lawyer; 1519: singer at Henry VIII's court; by 1523: m. Joan Rastell, niece of Thomas More; two s. & two daus; 1525: player of virginals at court; 1526: poss. contributed to Rastell's *Gentlemen and Nobility; 1526–34*: penned six comic plays incl. *The Play of the Wether* & *The Pardoner and the Friar* (1533) & *A Play of Love* (1534); 1529: Ellis b.; 1534: wrote 'A Song in Praise of a Lady' [Princess Mary Tudor] (later printed in Tottel's *Songes & Sonnettes*, 1557); 1535: Jasper b.; 1540s: involved w. John More in conspiracy v. **Cranmer** (q.v.); c. 1544: arrested for tr. & publicly recanted; c. 1542: dau. Joan m.; at some point dau. Elizabeth m. John Donne, ironmonger; 1544/45: wrote play *The Parts of Man* for Cranmer by way of apology; 1546: *A Dialogue Containing the Number in Effect of All the Proverbs in the English Tongue* (went into many ed'ns); Feb. 1552: presented play before Princess Elizabeth using children of St Paul's; 1553: presented pageant & oration to Queen Mary; 1556: pub'd allegorical poem 'The Spider and the Flie'; 1562: pub'd *Works* (excl. Plays); 20 July 1564: exile w. wife in Brabant; (1572: Elizabeth (Heywood) Donne gave birth to John Donne); c. Oct. 1578: d. R.C. Johnson, *John Heywood*, 1970.

HEYWOOD Thomas (c. 1573–1641): Cambr.-educ. dramatist & poet. c. 1573: b. s. of Robert Heywood, R of Rothwell, Lincs, & Elizabeth; 1591: matriculated pensioner, Emmanuel College, Cambr.; 1593: in London; 1594: pub'd narrative poem 'Oenone and Paris' that showed classical & Shakespearian infl.; 1596: working as playwright & actor, contracted by **Philip Henslowe** (q.v.); c. 1597: m.; 1598–1610: betw. four & six children; 1598 to Feb. 1599: two identified (but since lost) plays for Henslowe's Admiral's Men: War without Blows and Love without Suit & Joan is as Good as my Lady; 1599: wrote King Edward IV for Derby's Men; 1601: leading actor with Earl of Worcester's Company (later Queen Anne's Men) & achieved success as dramatist, popular for his domestic dramas, e.g. 1603 (pub'd 1607): tragedy A Woman Killed with Kindness.; most of his production belonged to the Stuart period but his two-part play about Elizabeth I, If you Know not me, you Know Nobody (written c. 1604/05 & pub'd 1605), w. Part 1 closely based on Foxe's Book of Martyrs & Part 2 focusing on Sir Thomas Gresham, is notable for its infl. on Elizabeth's posthumous image & reputation; see also his later England's Elizabeth (1631) & the verse play Life and Death of Queen Elizabeth (1639); c. Aug. 1641: d. B. Baines, *Thomas Heywood*, 1984.

HICKMAN Rose (née Lok; 2nd m. name Throckmorton) (1526–1613): Protestant exile, memoir writer and businesswoman. 1526: b. dau. of Sir William Lok, London mercer & alderman, & his 2nd w., Katherine (Cook); sister of Michael Lok, merchant adventurer & traveller; evangelical Protestant upbringing by her mother; 1543: m. (i) Anthony Hickman, London merchant; two children; entertained prominent Protestants such as **John Foxe, John Knox** & **John Hooper** (all q.v.) between 1556 & 1561; 1555: visited **Cranmer, Ridley** & **Latimer** (all q.v.) in Oxf. prison; joined husband in Antwerp exile; 1558: returned to Eng.; 1573: d. of Anthony; m. (ii) Simon Throckmorton of Brampton; 1610: wrote memoir of life that recorded, not only her involvement in persecuted Protestant activities, but also concern for its impact on her standard of living & commercial success. J. Shakespeare & M. Dowling, 'Religion and politics in mid-Tudor England through the eyes of an English Protestant woman...', *Bulletin of the Institute of Historical Research*, 55, 1982, pp. 94–102.

HICKS Baptist (?1551–1629): 1st Viscount Campden, well-edu. & well-connected mercer & moneylender to crown & nobility. ?1551: b. 3rd s. of Robert Hicks, London mercer; younger brother of **Michael Hick(e) s** (q.v.); ? edu. St Paul's School & Trinity College, Cambr.; 1584: m. Elizabeth May, dau. of Richard, a London merchant tailor; two daus; one of the most important lenders to the Stuart kings; 18 Oct. 1629: d.

HICK(E)S (Sir) Michael (1543–1612): Cambr.-edu. administrator, lawyer, office holder & money lender, & patronage secretary to **William Cecil**, Lord Burghley (q.v.). 1543: b. eldest child of Robert Hicks, wealthy London mercer, & Julian (Arthur); elder brother of **Baptist Hick(e)s** (q.v.); 1559–62: Trinity College, Cambr. but did not graduate; part of Puritan circle at Trinity; Mar. 1565: adm. Lincoln's Inn; 1573: entered service of Lord Burghley; 1577: called to bar; 1577: Burghley's influential patronage secretary; 1584, 1589, 1593, 1597: M.P.; probably wrote anon 'Life of Burghley'; Dec. 1594 m. Elizabeth (Colston) Parvish, wid. of wealthy London merchant; two s. & one dau.; 1604: knighted; 15 Aug. 1612: d. A.G.R. Smith, *Servant of the Cecils: The Life of Sir Michael Hickes, 1543–1612*, 1977.

HILLIARD Nicholas (?1547–1619): miniaturist, gentleman & Protestant exile. ?1547: b. eldest child of Richard Hilliard, Exeter goldsmith, & Laurence (Wall); evangelical Protestant upbringing; 1557: Genevan exile in household of John Bodley; 1559: in Bodley's London household & studied works of Holbein; 1562–69: apprentice goldsmith w. Robert Brandon, leading goldsmith & jeweller to Queen Elizabeth; 29 July 1569: completed training & made free of Goldsmith's Company; 1570: signed on John Cobbold as first of about nine known apprentices; 1571: produced 'A Man aged 35' his 1st known miniature as an adult; 1572: 1st known miniature of Queen; 1570s: unsuccessful investment in goldmine in Scotland; 1576: m. Alice, dau. of Robert Brandon – 1578–88: seven children; 1576–78: in France to produce miniatures of **d'Alençon**, Queen's suitor (q.v.); 1577: self-portrait miniature; 1584: monopoly of **limnings** of the Queen; 1584: designed Great Seal of England; 1587–95: painted larger cabinet miniatures, including 'Young Man among Roses' of ?Earl of Essex; in debt; c. 1600: wrote important 'The Arte of Limning', which remained in ms until 1981; continued as James I's official limner; 1619: d. R.K.R. Thornton & T.G. S. Cain (eds), N. Hilliard, *A Treatise Concerning the Arte of Limning*, 1981.

HOBY (née Dakins) (Lady) Margaret (1571–1633): gentlewoman & diarist. 1571: b. dau. & h. of Arthur & Thomasine (Gye) Dakins; edu. in household of Henry Hastings (q.v. under Huntingdon, (Lord) Henry Hastings), 3rd Earl of Huntingdon; 1588 or 9: m. (i) Walter, s. of Walter Devereux, 1st Earl of Essex, & stepson of Katherine Countess of Huntington's brother, Robert Dudley, Earl of Leicester; 1591: m. (ii) Thomas Sidney, brother of Sir Philip Sidney, nephew of Countess of Huntingdon; 1595: m. (iii) Sir Thomas Posthumous Hoby & lived at her house in Hackness; 1599–1605: diary of Puritan self-examination describing domestic routine, studies with chaplain Richard Rhodes, & relig. exercises & prayers. D.M. Meads (ed.), *Diary of Lady Margaret Hoby*, 1930.

HOOKER RICHARD (1554–1600): Oxf.-edu. philosopher, theologian & author of Laws of Ecclesiastical Polity. Apr. 1554: b. in or nr Exeter s. of Roger Vowell alias Hooker; edu. Exeter GS; 1569: sponsored by John Jewel, Bp of Salisbury (q.v.) & Edwin Sandys, Bp of London (q.v.) at Corpus Christi College Oxf.; July 1579: deputy professor of Hebrew; 14 Aug.1579: ord deac.; autumn 1584: preached at Paul's Cross; 1585: app'd Master of the Temple; 1585–86: conflict w. Walter Travers, suspected Presbyterian (q.v.); 13 Feb. 1588: m. Joan Churchman; 21 June 1591: subdean & prebendary of Salisbury; 17 July 1591: R Boscombe, Wilts; 1593: pub'd 1st four books of Of the Laws of Ecclesiastical Polity: Eight Books, a serious attempt to win over all those who had not accepted the 1559 settlement of religion & unusually written in English; 1597: wrote all eight books but Books 6–8 not pub'd during his lifetime; Book 5 discussed worship & ministry set out in the BofCP & their importance to the Church; conflicting interpetations of the Laws – did they defend Anglicanism or invent it?; Lent 1598: preached at Court; pastor at Bishopsbourne, Kent; d. P. Lake, Anglicans and puritans? Presbyterianism and English Conformist Thought from Whitgift to Hooker (1988), P. Collinson, 'Hooker and the Elizabethan establishment', in A.S. McGrade (ed.), *Richard Hooker and the Construction of Christian Community*, 1997, pp. 149–81, P.B. Secor, *Richard Hooker, Prophet of Anglicanism*, 1999.

HOOPER (Bishop) John (c. 1495–1500, d. 1555): Oxf.-edu. monk who was later evangelical theologian, Bp of Gloucester & Worcester & Protestant martyr. 1519: BA from Oxf.; entered Cistercian monastery at Cleeve, Somerset; 1537: left monastery; 1538: absentee R Liddington, Wiltshire; steward to relig. conserv. Matthew Arundell; converted by works of Zwingli & Bullinger; Arundell reported Hooper to Stephen Gardiner, Bp of Winchester (q.v.); Hooper escaped to Paris; poss. returned to service of Protestant sympathiser John St Loe, constable of Thornbury Castle, Somerset; 1544: escaped to Europe; 1546: in Strasbourg w. Richard Hilles; poss. supported himself in cloth trade; infl. by Heinrich Bullinger in Zurich; returned briefly to Eng. to claim inheritance & preached to Protestant congregations; Feb. 1547: m. Anna de Tscerlas; 1548: Rachel b.; c. 1549–50: Daniel b.; 1555: Anna & Rachel d. in Frankfurt of plague; 1547–49: developed ideas on primitive Church gov't & theology in Zurich; 3 May

1549: returned to Eng. in household of Duke of Somerset; played large part in estab. of Dutch & French churches in London; 1550: declined See of Gloucester; dispute re vestments betw. Hooper & Ridley (q.v.); 8 Mar. 1551: consecr. Bp of Gloucester in vestments; rigorous programme of reform of dioc. incl. clerical edu.; Apr. 1552: Bp of Worcester (Gloucester incorp.); Dec. 1552: Dioc. of Gloucester & Worcester; extended reform to new diocese; July 1553: supported Mary Tudor; 1 Sept. 1553: impr. in Fleet; w. & children escaped to Frankfurt; 15 Mar. 1554: depr. of bpric; 23 Jan. 1555: sentenced to d.; 9 Feb 1555: burnt at stake.

HORSEY (Dr) William (fl. 1512–40s): Chancellor of Diocese of London (see under Hunne, Richard).

HOWARD (Dacre) (Lady) Anne (1557–1630): Countess of Arundel. Prominent Catholic patron & educator. 1557: b. eldest dau. of Thomas Dacre, 4th Lord Dacre of Gilsland & 2nd w., Elizabeth (Leybourn); Anne & siblings brought up by grandmother, Lady Mounteagle, although Catholic infl. was balanced by fervent Protestantism of Aunt Lady Montague & tutors; 1569: Anne m. Philip Howard (1557–95), s. of her stepfather **Thomas**, 4th Duke of Norfolk (q.v.); 1571: m. repeated after they had reached age of consent & the Duke of Norfolk, then a prisoner in the Tower, had made a bargain w. Earl of Arundel that a portion of his inheritance would be advanced to Philip, held in trust until he was 25; styled Earl of Surrey, Philip would succeed to title of Earl of Arundel (through his mother **Mary** (Fitzalan) Howard). Anne, co-heir w. sister Elizabeth, inherited extensive Dacre lands; 1572: took refuge in household of Earl of Arundel & his dau. **Jane Lumley** (q.v.); converted to Catholicism & was joined by her husband; Elizabeth I annoyed & ordered Anne to Sir Thomas Shirley's house at Wiston, Sussex, where her 1st child, Elizabeth, was b. 1583, & where she remained for about a year; 1584: Philip converted to Roman Catholicism by Jesuit **William Weston** (q.v.); 1585:

Philip impr. in Tower; 7th July 1585: Thomas, later 14th Earl of Arundel, b.; she sheltered Catholic priests; 1586: Jesuit **Robert Southwell** (q.v.) joined household; he wrote for her 'A shorte rule of a good life', which she followed; 1592: Anne tried to help Southwell in prison; 1595: Philip condemned to d. for tr.; Oct. 1595: Philip d. ?poisoned; his lands forfeit; poverty; she eventually recovered her inheritance & jointure lands & was able to restore her son's place in society, aided by his acceptance of the Church of England.

HOWARD (Lord) Charles (1536–1624) 2nd Baron Howard of Effingham and 1st Earl of Northampton: courtier, royal favourite & naval commander. 1536: b. s. & h. of William Howard, 1st Baron Howard of Effingham & 2nd w. Margaret (Gamage); 1559: ambassador to France; 1562–63: M.P. for Surrey; 1563: m. (i) Katherine Carey, 2nd cousin to the Queen & her close friend; two s.; 1569: commanded cavalry v. northern rebels; 1570: commanded squadron to watch Spanish fleet; 1573: inherited barony; 1 Jan. 1584: app'd Lord Chamberlain; Jan. 1584: PC; May 1585–1615: Lord Admiral of England; 1586: commissioner for trial of Mary Stuart; 1588: chief commander v. Armada; 1596: played leading role in Cadiz expedition, sharing command w. Earl of Essex, his rival (q.v. under **Devereux, Robert**); Oct. 1597: Earl of Nottingham (2nd peer of the realm); Feb. 1601: commissioner at Essex's trial; took on Essex's former role as Earl Marshal; 1603: Eliz. confirmed succession of James VI to him; Katherine d.; 1604: m. (ii) Lady Margaret Stuart, dau. of James Stuart, 2nd Earl of Moray; one s.; May 1604: led embassy to Spain to ratify peace treaty; involved in affairs of state until 1619 when he retired from public life; 14 Dec. 1624: d.

HOWARD Henry (1540–1614) Earl of Northampton: Cambr.-edu. crypto-Catholic courtier, royal administrator, scholar & author. 1540: b. 2nd s. of **Henry Howard**, Earl of Surrey (q.v.) & Lady Frances (de Vere); 1547: Surrey was executed & Surrey's

father remained in prison; 1548: Surrey's children placed in custody of their Aunt **Mary**, Duchess of Richmond (q.v.) & edu. by **John Foxe** (q.v.) & Hadrianus Junius; 1553–58: page in household of the Catholic bp of Lincoln & Winchester; 1559: restored in blood; 1566: MA Cambr.; read civil law at Trinity Hall; 1569: reader in rhetoric; 1571: arrested for suspected involvement in brother Norfolk's plan to m. Mary Stuart; returned to favour after Norfolk's execution in 1572; remained at centre of court party favouring Catholics; Sept. 1583: impr for involvement in Throckmorton plot; July 1585; under house arrest at Sir **Nicholas Bacon**'s house in Suffolk (q.v.); 1590: presented Elizabeth w. 'A dutiful defence of the lawful regiment of women' in answer to **Knox** (q.v.); 1595–99: attached himself to Earl of Essex & produced a tract on the Earl Marshalship for Essex that emphasised superiority of ancient noble families; Sept. 1599: no longer an Essex supporter; transferred allegiance to **Robert Cecil**; 13 Mar. 1604: Earl of Northampton; 1605: KG; continued discreetly to further the interests of Eng. Catholics while always conforming; 1612: Chancellor of Cambr. Uni.; 1614: d. L.L. Peck, *Northampton: Patronage and Policy at the Court of James I*, 1982.

HOWARD Henry Earl of Surrey (see Surrey Henry Howard Earl of).

HOWARD (Lady) Jane (née) (m. name: Neville) (1537–93): Countess of Westmorland: courtier & humanist. 1537: b. dau. of **Henry Howard**, Earl of Surrey (q.v.) & Frances (de Vere); humanist edu. in preparation for m. w. Edward VI; 1546: following exec. of father & grandfather was tutored w. brothers in home of Aunt Mary, Duchess of Richmond, by John Foxe; c. 1564/65: m. Catholic Charles Neville, 6th Earl of Westmorland; five children by 1570; Nov.–Dec. 1569: husband involved w. Jane's support in Northern rebellion to release Mary of Scotland from Tutbury & restore Mass; 1571: Westmorland attainted & escaped into exile; 1588: Westmorland joined Parma in Armada campaign; Jane remained in Eng. w. pension but fiercely loyal to her husband. R.M. Warnicke,

Women of the English Renaissance and Reformation, 1983; A. Fletcher & D. MacCulloch, *Tudor Rebellions*, 4th ed'n, 1997.

Howard (Lady, later Queen) Katherine (c. 1524–42) (see Section 12.1: Monarchs and their consorts).

HOWARD LADY MARY (see Richmond Mary (Howard) Fitzroy, Duchess of).

HOWARD (née Fitzalan) (Lady) Mary (1539/40–57): classically-edu. translator of Greek & Latin works, Duchess of Norfolk & heiress of Earldom of Arundel. 1539/40: b. 3rd child of Henry Fitzalan, 12th Earl of Arundel & Katherine (Grey) dau. of Thomas 2nd Marquis of Dorset; sister of **Jane Lumley** (q.v.) & Henry, Lord Maltravers; two ms collections of *sententiae* from both Greek & Latin sources, one of them w. her stepbrother John Ratcliffe; 1554: m. **Thomas Howard**, 4th Duke of Norfolk (q.v.); June 1557: Philip b., who inherited, through her, Earldom of Arundel – see Dacre Anne; 1 Sept. 1557: d.

HOWARD (Lord) Thomas (1443–1524): 2nd Howard Duke of Norfolk: soldier & regional magnate. 1443: b. s. & h. of John Howard, 1st Howard Duke of Norfolk, & Katherine (Moleyns); edu. home & GS; c. 1466–69: Edward IV's service; Apr. 1471: wounded at battle of Barnet; c. 1471: at court of Charles the Bold, Burgundy; 1472: m. (i) Elizabeth (Tilney), wid. of Humphrey Bourchier; three s. & two daus; 1475: accompanied Edward IV to France; 1477: M.P. Norfolk; 1478: knighted; 1483: M.P. Norfolk; 1483: supported Richard III; ?implicated in murder of Edward VI & Prince Richard; 28 June 1483: cr. Earl of Surrey; PC & KG; 22 Aug. 1485: wound. & impr. at Bosworth; May 1489: rest. Earl of Surrey; quelled Northern Rebellion; 1497: involved in suppr. Warbeck rebellion; nego. m. of James IV of Scotland to Princess **Margaret Tudor** (q.v.); 1497: m. (ii) Agnes (Tilney) cousin of his 1st w.; six surviving children; 1499: returned to court; 1501: PC; June 1501: Lord Treasurer; recovered East Anglian lands & continued to accumulate

land; 1501: nego. m. of Prince Arthur w. Katherine of Aragon; 1507–08: nego. betrothal of future Charles V & Princess Mary Tudor; 1509-11: Henry VIII's leading minister until advent of Wolsey; 1513: defeated Scots at Flodden Field; 1 Feb. 1514: cr. Duke of Norfolk; 1 May 1517: suppr'd so-called 'Evil May Day' riots; May 1521: presided over trial of Edward Stafford, Duke of Buckingham; 21 May 1524: d. at Framlingham, Suffolk. M. Tucker, *The life of Thomas Howard, earl of Surrey and second duke of Norfolk, 1443–1524*, 1964

HOWARD (Lord) Thomas (1473–1554): 3rd Howard Duke of Norfolk: courtier, magnate, opponent of Thomas Cromwell's faction, & soldier. 1473: b. s & h. of **Thomas Howard**, 2nd Duke of Norfolk (q.v.) & 1st w. Elizabeth (née Tilney; wid. Bourchier); 1495: m. (i) Anne of York, sister-in-law of Henry VII; 1511: Anne d.; 1513: m. (ii) Elizabeth Stafford; 1513–25: Lord Admiral; 1513: distinguished himself at Flodden; 1514: Earl of Surrey; 1514–24: oppo. Wolsey; PC; 1516: expelled from the PC by Wolsey for keeping retainers; 10 Mar. 1520–21: Lord Lieut. of Ireland; 4 Dec. 1522–46: Lord Treasurer; 1523: Warden General of Scottish Marches – forced Scots under Albany to retreat; 21 May 1524: Duke of Norfolk; 1525: pacified Suffolk rebellion; 1527: took Elizabeth Holland as mistress; turned Henry VIII v. Wolsey & initially benefited from his fall; 1530s: separated from Duchess Elizabeth; 1533: Earl Marshal; 1536: did nothing to defend his niece, **Anne Boleyn** (q.v.); 1536–37: brutally suppr'd Pilgrimage of Grace; 1539: led oppo. to Cromwell; 1639: promoted the Six Articles of religion; 1540: promoted niece Katharine as Henry's 5th consort; 1540: instrumental in Cromwell's downfall; 1542: commanded army v. Scots; 1544: Lieut.-Gen. of Army v. French; 1546–47: lost power to the Seymours & Queen Katherine Parr; 12 Dec. 1546: Norfolk & h. s. Henry, Earl of Surrey (q.v.) arrested; 1547–53: imprisoned, condemned to d. but saved by Henry VIII's d.; 1553: released by Mary; PC; 1554: led army v. Wyatt's rebellion;

25 Aug. 1554: d. D.M. Head, *The Ebbs and Flows of Fortune: The Life of Thomas Howard, Third Duke of Norfolk*, 1995.

HOWARD (Lord) Thomas (1538–72) 4th Duke of Norfolk: Protestant courtier, nobleman, Norfolk magnate & patron. 1538: b. s. & h. of **Henry Howard**, Earl of Surrey (q.v.) & Frances (de Vere); 1547: placed in Sir John Williams' custody nr Thame & edu. by humanist Hadrianus Junius; 1548: placed in Aunt **Mary (Howard) Fitzroy**, Duchess of Richmond's custody (q.v.) & tutored by **John Foxe** (q.v.), for whom he had lifelong affection & respect; 1553: Foxe fled into exile & Thomas's grandfather 3rd Duke of Norfolk released from prison; 1553: rest. in blood & acknowledged as Earl of Surrey; edu. by Catholic Bp of Lincoln & Winchester, John White; July 1554: app'd First Gentleman of Chamber to King Philip; 25 Aug. 1554: 4th Duke of Norfolk & Earl Marshal; 30 Mar. 1555: m. Mary Fitzalan, dau. & h. of 12th Earl of Arundel (q.v. **Mary (Fitzalan) Howard**); 28 June 1557: Philip b.; 25 Aug. Mary d.; 1559: m. (ii) Margaret (Audley) Dudley wid.; 25 Jan.–8 May 1559: active in House of Lords; 1560: Lieut.-Gen. of the North; 1560s: rivalry w. Earl of Leicester for Queen's favour; 1564: Margaret d.; 29 Jan. 1567: m. (iii) Elizabeth, (Leybourne), wid. Dacre; 4 Sept. 1567: Elizabeth d. in childbirth; stepdaus Anne & Elizabeth Dacre became co-heirs of Dacre estates & m. his sons Philip & William; 1568: Commissioner to inquire into Scottish affairs & proposed m. with Mary Stuart; 1569-70: impr.; 1571–72: involved in Ridolfi plot; 2 June 1572: exec. for tr. (attended by John Foxe & Dean Nowell) but denied Catholicism. N. Williams, *Thomas Howard, Fourth Duke of Norfolk*, 1964.

HUMPHREY, Laurence (1525–89): Cambr.-edu. college head & erudite leader of anti-Vestiarian movement; b. at Newport Pagnell, Bucks; Nov. 1544: poss. matric. pensioner of Christ's College, Cambr.; migrated to Oxf.; 1547: demy of Magdalen College, Oxf.; by this time a convinced Protestant; 1548: probationer fellow of Magdalen; 1549: BA & Fellow; 1552: MA & lecturer in natural philosophy; 1553: app'd lecturer in moral philosophy; 1550: denounced Owen Oglethorpe Catholic President of the college to the PC & had him replaced by Walter Haddon; 1554: went into Marian exile in Zurich on leave of absence from Magdalen; autumn 1555: moved to Basel; worked for printers Johann Froben and Johannes Oporinus & pub'd various works including, in 1559, an appeal to Elizabeth I to remove abuses from the Church in England; 1558: moved to Geneva; m. Joan Inkforby of Ipswich; 12 children; c. 1562: b. of s. John; summer 1559: returned to Basel & wrote introduction to Foxe's martyrology; summer 1560: in England; 1560: app'd Regius Professor of Theology at Oxf.; 1561: elected President, Magdalen College; July 1562: DTh; Aug. 1563: asked Heinrich Bullinger for opinion on the wearing of the surplice & cap; Dec. 1564: summoned before Archbp Parker regarding wearing vestments; involvement in Vestiarian Controversy prevented his further preferment for a while; 1571–77: Vice-Chancellor of Oxf.; 13 Mar. 1571: app'd Dean of Gloucester; 1573: wrote biography of Bp John Jewel; 1575–84: involved in disputes at Magdalen; 1584: **Thomas Cooper**, Bp of Winchester (q.v.) visited Magdalen to correct abuses; 1576: Humphrey offered Burghley qualified acceptance of vestments; 1574: app'd to commission for eccles. causes in Gloucester; 1576: visited Gloucester dioc. & corrected abuses; Oct. 1580: app'd Dean of Winchester; pub'd anti-Catholic polemic: *Jesuitismi pars prima,* denouncing papal claim to jurisdiction over temporal powers; 1582: pub'd *Jesuitismi pars secunda,* a critique of Catholic doctrines & abuses; 1588: pub'd *A View of the Romish Hydra and Monster,* portraying Catholics as traitors; 1 Apr. 1589: d. C.M. Dent, *Protestant reformers in Elizabethan Oxford* (1983); C. Litzenberger, *The English Reformation and the Laity: Gloucestershire, 1540–1580* (1997).

HUNNE RICHARD (d. 1514): wealthy merchant tailor & Lollard, impr. for heresy & allegedly murdered. 1511: refused to pay mortuary to R of St Mary Matfelon, Whitechapel on d. of infant son; 13 May 1512 archbp's Court of Audience excommunicated Hunne; 27 Dec. 1512: unsuccessfully attempted to attend evensong at St Mary's; Hunne sued R for slander in King's Bench, thus questioning Church's jurisdiction over defamation, & took out writ of *praemunire* v. all those involved in the mortuary case; June 1514: **Archbp Warham** (q.v.) proposed heresy proceedings as a counter; 14 Oct. 1514: Hunne arrested for possession of Wycliffite Bible; impr. in Lollards' Tower at St Paul's; 2 Dec. 1514: appeared before **Bp Fitzjames** (q.v.) ready to confess; 4 Dec. 1514: found d. hanging in cell; Bp & Chancellor Horsey alleged suicide but 6 Dec. 1514 coroner (apparently under anti-clerical pressure) found verdict of torture & throttling & hanging post mortem; Horsey & Summoner Joseph arrested; Henry VIII ordered inquiry by PC.

HUNTINGDON, (Lord) Henry Hastings, 3rd Earl of (c. 1536–95): humanist nobleman, courtier & Puritan patron. ?1536: b. s. & h. of Francis Hastings, 2nd Earl of Huntingdon, & Katherine (Pole) Hastings; studied w. Prince Edward; 1547: knighted; 1548: Queen's College, Cambr.; 25 May 1553: s. & h. m Northumberland's youngest dau. Katherine Dudley (childless m.); 1553: impr. for support of Queen Jane; Katherine (Pole) Hastings, his mother, petitioned Mary I & her relative, Cardinal Pole, for favour; Hastings member of King Philip's household; supported Acts of Uniformity & Supremacy in HofL; June 1560: inherited title of 3rd Earl of Huntingdon; Yorkist ancestry prevented Elizabeth entirely trusting him, despite close relationship to Leicester (q.v. **Dudley, Robert**); active Puritan patronage in Leicestershire; est'd or re-founded Ashby de la Zouche & Leicester GS; 1569–70: joint guardian at Tutbury & Coventry of Mary of Scotland (w. **Earl of Shrewsbury** (q.v.); Apr.

1570: KG; 1572: President of Council of the North – dedicated to restoring good gov't & bringing north into religious conformity; 1570s: used northern eccles. commission to enforce relig. conformity; 1580s: used secular powers to punish recusants & heretics; 1582–95: 30 RC pr. & eight lay people sentenced to d. at York; preferment of Puritans in the north & furtherance of preaching ministry; 1584: settled four wealthy livings on Emmanuel College, Cambr.; autumn 1588: moved to Newcastle to secure the border v. Scotland in case of invasion; depleted family's wealth in royal service; 14 Dec. 1595: d. C. Cross, *The Puritan Earl*, 1967.

J

JEWEL (Bishop) John (1522–71): Oxf.-edu. Erasmian humanist & Marian exile, diligent Bp of Salisbury, controversialist & apologist for the Church of England. 24 May 1522: b. s. of John Jewel of Bowden, Devon & h.w. (Bellamy); 1529: moved to Hampton where he was taught by his mother's brother, John Bellamy, who was R; later edu. at Bampton & Barnstaple; 1535: matriculated Merton College, Oxf.; 1540: BA from Corpus Christi College, Oxf.; 1542: Fellow of Corpus; 1545: MA; 1548: reader in humanity & rhetoric; close friendship w. Peter Martyr Vermigli, Regius Professor of Divinity; 1551: granted preaching licence; V Sunningwell, near Abingdon; 1552: BD; 1553: expelled from Corpus for Protestant tendencies & took refuge at Broadgates Hall; Apr. 1554: assisted **Thomas Cranmer** (q.v.) & **Nicholas Ridley** (q.v.) at public disputation; Oct. 1554: subscribed Catholic articles of faith; Strasbourg exile; Mar. 1555: accompanied Richard Cox to Frankfurt to confront **John Knox** (q.v.); then joined Peter Martyr in Strasbourg; associated w. influential exiles such as **Anthony Co(o)ke, Edmund Grindal & Edwin**

Sandys; July 1556: Zurich exile, friendship w. **John Parkhurst** (q.v.); 18 Mar. 1559: returned to London; participated in the Westminster Conference v. Marian bps; 15 June 1559: preached at St Paul's Cross; summer 1559: royal visitor in western counties; 26 Nov. 1559: 'Challenge sermon' at Paul's Cross regarding validity of Roman Church; 21 Jan. 1560: consecr. Bp of Salisbury; 17 Mar. 1560: 'Challenge sermon' at court; 31 Mar. 1560: repeated 'Challenge sermon' at Paul's Cross; led to controversy w. Henry Cole, dean of St Paul's, printed as *The true copies of the letters betwene the reverend father in God, John bisshop of Sarum and D. Cole*; 1560–71: zealous preaching bp; 1560, 1565 & 1571: episcopal visitations indicate insistence on absolute conformity by both clergy & laity; 1562: *Apologia pro Ecclesia Anglicana*, defending the Church of England v. charges of heresy; 1564: *Apologie or Answere in Defence of the Churche of Englande*; 1564: pub'n of Thomas Harding, *An Answere to Maister Juelles Chalenge*; 1565: pub'n of Jewel's *A Replie*; 1565: beginning of 'the Great Controversy' w. Thomas Harding's *Confutation of a booke intituled 'An apologie of the Church of England'*; involvement in Vestiarian Controversy; May 1565: DD; 1567: Jewel answered with *A defence of the 'Apologie of the Churche of England'*; 1572: **Archbp Parker** encouraged Bp Parkhurst to insist that all parishes in Norwich dioc. purchase copies of the 'Defence of the Apologie'; 1577: Bp Barnes of Durham ordered all parishes to buy a copy of the 'Apologie'; 1571: preached v. Puritans; 23 Sept. 1571: d.

K

KATHERINE (Catherine, Katharine) of Aragon (Queen) (1485–1536) (see Section 12.1: Monarchs and their consorts).

KEMP William (fl. 1585–?, d. 1603): stage clown and maker of merriments & jigs. Performed w.: 1585–86: the Earl of Leicester's Men; c. 1586: a group in the employ of the Danish ambassador; c. 1592–94: Lord Strange's Men; & 1594–99: Lord Chamberlain's Men; renowned for jigs (comic afterpieces), merriments (farcical skits); & creation of some of Shakespeare's most famous comic roles, such as Bottom in *A Midsummer Night's Dream* (1595–96); Feb.–Mar. 1600: 130-mile morris dance from London to Norwich; 1600: pub'd *Kemp's Nine Daies Wonder* as publicity pamphlet; 1601: continental tour; Jan. 1602: performed at Court with Worcester's Men; ?d. Nov. 1603.

KETT ROBERT (c. 1492–1549): rebel. c. 1492: b. Norfolk 4th s. of Thomas Kett, butcher & farmer, & h.w. Margery; wealthy & worked as tanner; belonged to guild of St Thomas Becket at Wymondham; c. 1515: m. Alice ?Appleyard, dau. of a knight; five s.; 6–8 July 1549: during Wymondham festivities commemorating St Thomas Becket rioters attacked encloser John Flowerdew, lawyer, who had despoiled the local abbey which had been used as parish church; Kett appears to have tried to protect the abbey & to have stepped in to lead the rebels; July 1549: he & others led the Norfolk rebellion v. enclosures which camped at Mousehold Heath from 10 July to 27 Aug. 1549; legendary dispensation of justice from beneath a tree, the 'oak of reformation', on both riotous rebels & unpopular local gentlemen as result of suits promoted by others; refused royal pardon in late July; 27 Aug. 1549: defeated by royal army led by Earl of Warwick; 28 Aug. 1549: captured & impr. in Tower; 7 Dec. 1549: hanged (for tr.) from walls of Norwich Castle; his brother William hanged from the steeple of Wymondham church. D. MacCulloch, 'Kett's rebellion in context', *Past and Present*, 84, 1979, pp. 36–59; B.L. Beer, *Rebellion and Riot: Popular Disorder in England During the Reign of Edward VI*, 1982.

KILLIGREW (née Co(o)ke) Catherine (c. 1542–83): humanist Protestant scholar & gentlewoman.

190

c. 1542: b. 5th dau. of Sir **Anthony Co(o)ke** & Anne (Fitzwilliam), wid. Hawes of Gidea Hall, Essex; sister of **Elizabeth Russell, Anne Bacon** & **Mildred Cecil** (q.v.); edu. in classics by father; 4 Nov. 1565: m. Henry Killigrew of Cornwall, diplomat; four daus; supported family w. Cecil patronage, mediated by sister Mildred; supported by spiritual counsel of **Edward Dering** (q.v.); 27 Dec. 1583: d. in stillborn childbirth; left Latin & Greek books. A.C. Miller, *Sir Henry Killigrew*, 1963.

KNOLLYS (Sir) Francis (1511/12–96): courtier, politician, loyalist & articulate defender of evangelical Protestantism. 1511/12: b. s. & h. of Robert Knollys, courtier & usher to Henry VII & Henry VIII, & Lettice (Peniston); brother of Henry, Mary & Jane; ?Oxf.-edu.; 1533, 1536, 1539: M.P.; 1539–44: Gentleman pensioner; c. 1540: m. Katherine (Carey) (q.v. **Knollys (née Carey) Katherine**) dau. of William Carey & Mary (Boleyn) Carey (q.v. **Boleyn Mary**); 12 children; 1545: M.P. Horsham as nominee of 3rd Duke of Norfolk; 1547: M.P. Camelford, Cornwall, poss. nominee of Edward Seymour; 1547: Master of Prince Edward's Horse; 1547–54: JP Oxfordshire; by 1551: converted to Protestantism; ?1553: M.P.; 1555–56: exile in Basel; 1558: returned to Eng. from Frankfurt; 14 Jan. 1559: PC & Vice-chamberlain of household; 1559–1569: h.w. lady of bedchamber until her d.; 1559–71: M.P. & manager of House of Commons for Crown (in this capacity: 1559: served on parl. committee that amended the Supremacy Bill & served on commission to enforce the statute; 1563: headed committee that amended the anti-Catholic bill in a harsh direction; 1566: delivered Elizabeth's message to the Commons promising m.; 1569: Katherine d.; 1571: oppo. Puritan members, led by Strickland, seeking reform of Prayer Book, defending the royal prerogative, despite his own sympathies w. their views; defended arrest of Strickland); May 1568 to Feb. 1569: guardian of Mary of Scotland; 1570: Treasurer of the Household; exercised considerable patronage & secured places for his s. & excellent m. for his daus – e.g. **Lettice**

(q.v.) who m. (i) **Walter Devereux**, Earl of Essex & (ii) **Robert Dudley**, Earl of Leicester; declared his Protestantism in the late 1570s by commiserating Grindal's fate; 1584: oppo. Oath of Subscription & actively pursued petition to Queen to rest. suspended clergy; 1584–90: continued oppo. to Whitgift's enforced clerical conformity, urging that bps were *primus inter pares* & had no divinely-given superiority over other clergy; c. 1591: Queen barred him from her presence; Jan. 1592: reconciled with Elizabeth; 1593: championed Puritan cause in Parl. & oppo. eccles. gov't; 1593: KG; 19 July 1596: d.

KNOLLYS (née Carey) Katherine, Lady (c. 1523–69): courtier, cousin (possibly illegitimate half-sister) & friend of Elizabeth I. c. 1523: b. elder child of Mary (née Boleyn; m. names Stafford & Carey) & Henry Carey; sister of **Henry Carey** (q.v.), later 1st Baron Hunsden, b. 4 Mar. 1526; possibly dau. of Henry VIII (but see q.v. **Boleyn Mary** for opposite view); Nov. 1539: app'd lady-in-waiting to Anne of Cleves; 26 Apr. 1540: m. **Francis Knollys** (q.v.); Apr. 1541: b. of 1st of c. 12–16 children; 1556–58: Marian exile of Francis; 1557: Katherine & five children joined him in Frankfurt; Jan. 1559: lady of bedchamber to Queen Elizabeth; Dec. 1568: Queen refuses Francis permission to visit h.w.; 15 Jan. 1569: d.; given lavish funeral (at Queen's expense) in Westminster Abbey.

KNOX John (?1514–72): Scottish by birth, English by adoption, Protestant reformer and polemical preacher. c. 1514: b. s. of William Knox, retainer of Earls of Bothwell, & h.w. (Sinclair); edu. Burgh school & St Andrews Uni.; late 1530s: ord. deac. & pr.; 1540: practising notary at Haddington; converted to evangelical Protestantism in the early to mid-1540s when infl. by George Wishart; 1546: preached sermon v. papal authority; sentenced to serve in galleys; Feb. 1549: released (probably as a result of English intercession); pensioned by Edward VI; 1549–51: Berwick preacher; intro. sitting at communion etc.; 4

Apr. 1550: appeared before **Cuthbert Tunstall**, Bp of Durham & explained liturgical nonconformity; 1550: denied transubstantiation, etc.; 1553: betrothed to Marjory Bowes; spring 1551: moved to Newcastle, where his preaching was heard by the Duke of Northumberland (q.v. **Dudley John**); late 1551: royal chaplain to Edward VI; friendship w. **Anne Locke** (q.v.), **Rose Hickman** (q.v.) & others in London Protestant merchant community, displayed his pastoral skills; 1552: agitated for further reform of BofCP, that had already been approved by Parl.; oppo. by **Thomas Cranmer** (q.v.) who, nevertheless, inserted Black Rubric; Knox signed statement that BofCP accorded w. Scripture; refused eccles. preferments; Apr. 1553: harangued PC Edwardian Church's faults; 1553: returned north; 1554–58: exile Dieppe, Zurich, Geneva, Frankfurt & authorship of polemical writings; Nov. 1554: accepted invitation to minister to English exiles in Frankfurt; 1554-55: Troubles at Frankfurt: 'Cox v. Knox'; city council asked Knox to leave; 26 Mar. 1555: Geneva; 1556: returned to Berwick; spring 1556: m. (i) Marjory Bowes; two s.; 1560: Marjory d.; s. brought up in Eng.; 1555–56: preached w. protection in Scotland; summer 1556: left Scotland for France when Mary of Guise refused programme of reform; Sept. 1556: Geneva; winter 1557–58: wrote & pub'd *The First Blast of the Trumpet Against the Monstrous Regiment of Women* (see Chapter 4: World of learning); July 1558: *Second Blast*; 1560: pub'd on doctrine of predestination: *An Answer to a Great Nomber of Blasphemous Cavillations*; May 1559: returned to Scotland because refused admission to England; provoked iconoclastic riot in Perth & St Andrews; summer 1560: minister of St Andrews & of St Giles, Edinburgh; Aug. 1560: Parl. accepted Scottish confession of faith & abol'd papal jurisdiction & Catholic sacraments; prominent member of committee that composed Book of Discipline; 19 Aug. 1561: Mary of Scotland returned from France & Knox supported those who interrupted her Mass on 24 Aug. but had limited contact w. her on just four occasions;

Sept. 1561: accepted Mary's authority but expressed belief in doctrine of resistance, ended by expressing hope that Mary might become 2nd Deborah; June 1563: denounced Mary's proposed foreign Catholic m. to her face; 1561–65: sermons called for moral reformation & acceptance of eccles. discipline; Mar. 1564: m. (ii) Margaret (Stewart) aged 17, who was of royal blood; three daus; 1565–67: preached on need for spiritual remedies to Scotland's problems; 1566: became minister of Ayr & visited Eng.; June 1567: returned to Edinburgh; 19 July: called for Mary's exec. as adultress; saw abdication as compromise; July 1567: sermon at coronation of James VI portrayed King as potential saviour; 24 Nov. 1572: d.: 1587: pub'd *History of the Reformation in Scotland* (written in 1560s & 1570s).

KYNNERSLEY Lettice (née Bagot) (b. 1573, fl. 1630): correspondent. 1573: b. Blithfield, Staffs. youngest dau. of Richard Bagot and Mary (Dayrell); m. Francis Kynnersley (d. 1634); issue but names and dates unknown; of interest chiefly because of the light her letters to her brother Walter throw upon wider family relations in late Tudor/early Stuart period. R. O'Day, *The Family and Family Relations in Early Modern England, France and America*, 1994.

L

LAMBARDE (Lambert) William (1536–1601): lawyer, antiquary, county historian. 18 Oct. 1536: b. London s. & h. of John Lambarde or Lambert, draper, alderman & property owner, & 1st w. Juliana (Horne); 1555: ward of Edmund Healey, esquire; poss. edu. Christ Church, Oxf.; 1556: adm. Lincoln's Inn; 1563: poss. M.P. Aldborough, Yorks; if so, was staunch Protestant who participated in debate re royal succession in 1st & 2nd sessions; 1584 wrote 'Notes on the procedures and privileges of the House of Commons' (pub'd 1641) which retrospectively identified the debates as establishing an important constitutional precedent; 15 June 1567: called to bar; 1568: pub'd influential *Archaionomia*; 11 Sept. 1570: m. (i) Jane, eldest dau. of George Multon, esquire, of St Clare, Ightham, Kent); Sept. 1573: Jane d.; 1576: *Perambulation of Kent: Containing the Description, Hystorie and Customs of that Shyre* – the earliest county history; 1576: endowed College of Elizabeth, East Greenwich – model almshouse; 1585: abandoned attempt to write histories of other counties; 1579–83: JP Kent; 1582: *Eirenarcha, or, The Office of the Justices of Peace*; 28 Oct. 1583: m. (ii) Sylvestra or Silvester (Deane) wid. of William Dallison of Gray's Inn, s. of Sir William Dallison, Justice of the Queen's Bench; 1584: on quorum of select Kent JPs; 'Ephemeris', notes on his work as justice; 1584: s. Multon b.; 1586: Margaret b.; 1 Sept. 1587: Sylvestra d. following birth of twin s., Fane & Gore; 1589–97: number of chancery app'ments; 13 Apr. 1592: m. (iii) Margaret (Payne); twice wid. Meryam & Reder; 1597: deputy Keeper of the Rolls; prepared Carey Reports (pub'd 1650), collection of Chancery precedents that had profound effect on development of court procedure; 14 June 1597: Bencher, Lincoln's Inn; 1598: moved to Westcombe; 1591: completed & circulated in ms his greatest work *Archeion, or, A discourse upon the high courts of justice in England*, tracing Anglo-Saxon origins of common law, prerogative & Parliament (pub'd 1635); Jan. 1601: Keeper of Records, Tower of London; 'Pandecta rotulorum' – description of the royal mss; 1590s: several substantial land purchases; 19 Aug. 1601: d. R.M. Warnicke, *William Lambarde, Elizabethan Antiquary, 1536–1601*, 1973.

LAMBERT (alias Nicholson), John (d. 1538): Cambr.-edu. Protestant martyr. c. 1500: b. Norfolk s. of Nicholson family; 1519/20: BA Cambr.; 1521–22: briefly fellow, Queens' College, Cambr. at Katherine of Aragon's request; 1521–22: converted to Protestantism & left Cambr.; ordained; when persecuted changed name to Lambert; Chaplain to English factors at Antwerp; 1532: impr. but released same year after Warham's death; 16 Nov. 1538: trial before King; 1538: burnt at stake for denying real presence; ?1548: *A treatyse made by Johan Lambert unto Kynge Henry the VIII concernynge hys opynyon in the sacrament of the altar* (1548? edited by John Bale).

LANIER (also **Lanyer**) Amelia (also Emilia) (née Bassano) (?1569–1645): poet, favourite of Elizabeth I. c. Jan. 1569: b. London dau. of Baptista Bassano, court musician (of a family of Italian Jewish musicians) & Margaret (Johnson); edu. in household of Susan, dowager countess of Kent (dau. of Protestant humanist, Katherine Bertie); favourite at Queen Elizabeth's court & mistress of cousin Henry Carey, 1st Baron Hunsdon; 1592: m. Captain Alphonso Lanier, member of Lanier family of court musicians; 1609: several unsubstantiated attempts to identify her as the 'dark lady' of Shakespeare's sonnets (see also **Fitton Mary**); 1611: *Salve Deus rex Judaeorum* – 1st original poetry pub'd by woman – collection of religious verse; 1613: Alphonso d.; 1617: attempted unsuccessfully to found school for nobility in St Giles in the Fields; c. Apr. 1645: d. D. Lasocki & R. Prior, *The Bassanos: Venetian Musicians and Instrument Makers in England, 1531–1665*, 1995; S. Woods, *Lanyer*, 1999.

LATIMER (Bishop) Hugh (c. 1485–1555): Cambr.-edu. evangelical preacher, Bp of Worcester and Protestant Martyr. c. 1485: b. Thurcaston, Leics, only s. of Hugh Latimer, yeoman & tenant farmer; six sisters; edu. GS; c. 1499: adm. Cambr.; 1510: Fellow, Clare College; 1511: BA; 1514: MA; 1515: ord. subdeac., deac. & pr.; 1522: university licence to preach anywhere without seeking episcopal permission; 1524: BTh; converted to Protestantism at Cambr. & was part of White Horse Tavern group; 1525: refused to condemn Luther in sermon before Bp West of Ely; called before **Wolsey** (q.v.) but escaped punishment; 1529: still approved pilgrimages, etc.; Advent 1529: Sermons on the Cards: demanded Bible in English – this caused uproar in Cambr. & many answering sermons of diagreement; 1530s: began to attack papacy & especially doctrines of salvation such as purgatory; Lent 1530: gave 1st sermon at Court; 1531: Latimer, Crome & **Bilney** identified as preaching erroneous doctrines – Bilney burnt at stake; Latimer saved by 'the King's Great Matter' & by Anne Boleyn's patronage; Jan. 1531: Anne secured him wealthy R of West Kington, Wilts; preached in London & Kent; 11 Mar. 1532: called before convocation for preaching v. purgatory, prayers for dead, intercession of saints, pilgrimages, images, crucifix, etc.; excom. & impr. at Lambeth but saved by throwing himself on the King's mercy & released Apr. 1532; Lent & Easter 1533: Bristol sermons v. justification by good works & mediation by Virgin Mary caused another uproar; 1534: Latimer dominated court sermons; 1535: Bp of Worcester; Anne Boleyn lent him £200 to pay First Fruits; programme of iconoclasm; energetic preaching bp; took part in Queen Anne's theological disputations over supper & tried to press her programme of educational reform funded by dissolution of monasteries; 1537: encouraged study of English Bible by clergy & laity in dioc.; late 1530s: protected by Cromwell; 1539: oppo. in HofL to bill of Six Articles; July 1539: he & Bp Shaxton forced to resign bprics; Dec. 1539: released; 1539–46: spent days in study; 1546: arrested on charge of heresy alongside other reformers seeking reversal of Six Articles; examined at length by PC & bps on doctrine of real presence at Eucharist but avoided incriminating himself & spent rest of reign in Tower; 1547: Latimer rest. as court preacher; 1547 to early 1548: sermons on the Plough delivered at Paul's Cross; autumn 1548: preached spiritual not real presence at Eucharist; 1549: vitriolic attacks on Thomas Seymour; 1551: not rest. to Bpric of Worcester on Heath's depr.; Mar. 1550: retired from court after appealing to crown to restore the fortunes of the unis; took up position as chaplain to Katherine Brandon (q.v. **Bertie Katherine**) at Grimsthorpe,

Lincs; 1548: Katherine funded the printing of his sermons; July 1553: attended funeral of Edward VI; 13 Sept. 1553: arrested & impr. in Tower; Jan. 1554: impr. w. **Cranmer** (q.v.), **Ridley** (q.v.) & John Bradford & studied New Testament; Mar. 1554: moved to Bocardo prison, Oxf. for public disputations w. Catholic theologians; Latimer refused to participate; late Sept. 1554: trial; 16 Oct. 1555: burnt w. Ridley at stake; doubtful whether he delivered the famous words of encouragement to Ridley: 'Be of good comfort Master Ridley, and play the man: we shall this day light such a candle by God's grace in England, as (I trust) shall never be put out', R. O'Day, 'Hugh Latimer: prophet of the kingdom', *Historical Research*, 65, 1992, 258–76; S. Wabuda, '"Fruitful preaching" in the diocese of Worcester: Bishop Hugh Latimer and his influence 1535–1539', in E.J. Carlson (ed.) *Religion and the English People, 1500–1640: New Voices, New Perspectives*, 1998, Vol. 45 of Sixteenth Century Essays and Studies, pp. 49–74.

LEE (Archbishop) Edward (1481/82–1544): Oxf., Cambr., Louvain and Boulogne-edu. Archbp of York with theological training. 1481/82: younger s. of Richard Lee of Lee Magna, Kent (s. of Sir Richard Lee, Lord Mayor of London in 1461 & 1470); 1504: ord. deac.; 1509: began series of eccles. preferments w. prebend at Exeter & R of Freshwater, Isle of Wight; early assistant to Erasmus on transl. of New Testament but quarrelled in 1519–26; 1520: King's chaplain; accompanied Henry to Field of Cloth of Gold 1521: may have assisted w. Henry's *Assertio septem sacramentorum*; 1525–29: ambassador to court of Charles V in Spain; Jan. 1530: on embassy w. Cranmer to persuade Pope & Emperor to agree to annulment of m. to Katherine of Aragon; 10 Dec. 1531: consecrated Archbp of York; 1532: recognised royal supremacy; June 1533: **Anne Boleyn**'s coronation; May 1534: sought to persuade Katherine to repudiate her m.; active Archbp of York; summer 1534: Archepiscopal visitation of York religious houses; conflict w. both York & Beverley over his rights; Oct.

1536: taken prisoner by Beverley Pilgrims of Grace at Pontefract & took their oath; 4 Dec. 1537: preached passive obedience; Feb. 1537: objected to omission of four of the seven sacraments from the Ten Articles of 1536; summer 1537: preached in support of royal supremacy; attempted to prevent preaching of evangelical theology in diocese; July 1540: one of bps that annulled King's m. to **Anne of Cleves**; early 1541: surrendered archdeac. of Richmond to new dioc. of Chester; late summer 1541: entertained King & begged forgiveness for participation in Pilgrimage of Grace; various lands exchanged w. Crown; 13 Sept. 1544: d. M. Bush & D. Bownes, *The Defeat of the Pilgrimage of Grace*, 1999.

LEE (Sir) Henry (1533–1611): ?Oxf.-edu. Queen's champion & image maker, landowner and businessman. Mar. 1533: b. Kent s. & h. of Sir Anthony Lee of Quarrendon, Bucks & his 1st w. Margaret (Wyatt) of Kent; edu. by uncle Sir Thomas Wyatt & poss. attended New College, Oxf.; Oct. 1533: knighted; 21 May 1554: m. (unhappily) Anne Paget (dau. of William); three children; 1559–: European trips; sent diplomatic reports to Leicester & Cecil; 1571: Lieut. of royal manor of Woodstock; 1572, 1574, 1575: Queen lavishly entertained at Woodstock; 1580: Master of the Armoury; supervised spectacular **Accession Day tilts**, accompanied by speeches & music; 17 Nov. 1590: resigned as Queen's Champion; performance of *My golden locks, time hath to silver turned* (which may have been by Lee himself), to music by **Dowland** (q.v.); continued, at Queen's request, to supervise the annual festivities; 1572: entertained Elizabeth at Ditchley, Oxon; prominent sheepfarmer & encloser in Oxfordshire; reputed to have founded Aylesbury Grammar School; 1590s: **Anne Vavasour** was his mistress (q.v.), bore him a s. & lived openly w. Lee; 1597: KG; 24 Mar. 1604: attended James I's first tilt; 1608: Queen Anne visited Lee-Vavasour household; c. 12 Feb. 1611: d. E.K. Chambers, *Sir Henry Lee: An Elizabethan Portrait*, 1936.

LEE (Bishop) Rowland (c. 1487–1543): Cambr.-edu. canon lawyer, administrator and nepotistic Bp of Coventry and Lichfield. c. 1487: b. s. of William Lee of Morpeth, Northumberland & h.w. Isabel (Trollope); 1503–10: edu. Cambr.; 5 June–18 Dec. 1512: ord. subdeac., deac. & pr.; 1520: DCnL; 8 Oct. 1520: advocate & member of Doctors' Commons; 1525–28: Chancellor & Vicar-General of Coventry & Lichfield diocese; 1529: Bp's Commissary; 1531–34: Royal chaplain & master in chancery; 1533–34: Cromwell's s. Gregory in his care; Apr. 1533: edited collection of opinions regarding 'King's Great Matter'; 24 Apr. 1533: sent north to persuade leading ecclesiastics to support King; early 1534: tried to persuade nuns of Syon to acknowledge King's m. to **Anne Boleyn**; late Mar. 1534: signed statement denying papal jurisdiction at southern convocation; Apr. 1534: tried to persuade Bp John Fisher to subscribe to oath of succession; 1534: Bp of Coventry & Lichfield; preferred brother George within the dioc., arranged good m. of sister, Isabel & to the preferment of her seven children; Aug. 1534: began diligent rule as Lord President of Council of Marches of Wales; diocesan business left to others; Jan. 1543: d.

LEICESTER Robert Dudley Earl of (see **Dudley** Sir Robert, Earl of Leicester).

LELAND, John (c. 1503–52) St Paul's & Cambr.-educ. poet, antiquary, topographer; b. London; orphaned in early childhood; adopted by Thomas Myles; edu. at St Paul's School, London under **William Lily**, alongside **William Paget**, **Anthony Denny** and **Thomas Wriothesely** (all q.v.); c. 1519: went to Christ's College, Cambr.; 1522: BA; c. 1522: impr. in King's Bench; 1522–24: tutor to Thomas, sixth s. of Thomas Howard, 2nd Duke of Norfolk; 1524 to c. 1526: associated w. All Souls' College, Oxf.; 1528: student in Paris, courting patronage of, e.g., Jacques Lefevre d'Etaples w. poetry; introduced to study of ancient texts by François du Bois, Professor of rhetoric and principal of Collège de Tournai; **Thomas Wolsey** (q.v.)

became his patron & collated him to R of Laverstoke, Hants; 10 Nov. 1529: resigned Laverstoke; app'd royal chapl.; 1533: transferred alleg. to **Thomas Cromwell** (q.v.); 1533: w. Nicholas Udall composed verses for entry of Anne Boleyn into London; 1533–34: wrote verses for Udall's *Floures for Latine Spekynge*; 1533: app'd by King to search and catalogue monastic archives and libraries; 1533: toured West Country for this purpose; 1534: toured Yorkshire; 1534: presented King w. New Year gift of stories; 1535: Preb. of Wilton Abbey, Wilts etc.; 16 July 1536: sought preservation of monastic collections; friend of **John Bale** (q.v.); 1530s & 1540s: played unofficial and uncertain role in formation of royal libraries; 1539: turned his attentions to topography & local history w. five famous journeys through Eng.; 1542 & 1543: app'd to various eccles. preferments; 1540s: pub'd various Latin poems; pub'd prose work, *Assertio inclytissimi Arturii regis Britanniae*, seeking to prove existence of King Arthur; wrote a dictionary of British writers, pub'd 1709; planned tabular genealogies, county histories and histories of noble families; 1546: sent by King to collect trees, etc. from France; c. 1547: became insane; 1549: John Bale pub'd *The Laboryouse Journey & Serche . . . for Englandes Antiquitees* (a version of his 1534 gift to the King); 1551: custody granted to his brother; 18 Apr. 1552: d.

LEVER (occasionally **Leaver**) Thomas (1521–77): Cambr.-edu. Protestant clergyman, scholar, author, and Commonwealthman notable for Edwardian sermons attacking exploitation of the poor. 1521: b. Lancs 2nd s. of John Lever & Elenor (Heyton); brother of Ralph; c. 1538–50: edu. & career at Cambr.; 1548: senior fellow, St John's College & college preacher; leader of evangelical Protestant party at St John's; 2 Feb. 1550: preached at Paul's Cross; 16 Mar. 1550: Lent sermon before King; 1550: ord. deac. & pr.; 14 Dec. 1550: sermon at Paul's Cross; 1551: pub'd *A Meditacion upon the Lordes Prayer*; May 1551: chaplain to Marquis of Northampton on embassy to France; 10 Dec. 1551: Master of St John's

College; Lent 1553: sermon to Edward VI on commonwealth themes; supported Queen **Jane Grey** (q.v.); Sept. 1553: resigned Mastership; Feb. 1554 to Jan. 1555: Strasbourg, Zurich & Geneva exile; Feb. 1555: oppo. **John Knox** (q.v.) in controversy re BofCP; Jan. 1556 to spring 1557: pastor at Wesel; May 1557: in Bern; Aug. 1557 to Jan. 1559: preacher in Aarau; Apr. 1559: m. wid.; one s. & one dau; summer 1560: Minister of St John's Bablake, Coventry & Archdeacon of Coventry, where he was deferred to by Bp **Thomas Bentham** (q.v.); 21 Feb. 1564: Prebendary at Durham; 1566: objected to wearing surplice during Vestiarian Controversy; 9 Nov. 1567: depr. of prebend; 1571: questioned for offences v. church discipline; 1572: reprinting of his Edwardian sermons; 1570s: circulated mss for reforming the ministry; June 1577: ordered by Bp Bentham to cease prophesyings; July 1577: d. on preaching mission.

LILY William (?1468–1522/23): highly influential Oxf.-edu. schoolmaster, grammarian and educationalist. c. 1468: b. Odiham, Hants; 1488: pupil of John Stanbridge, author of a Latin/English vocabulary – the *Vulgaria* (1508) – at Magdalen College, Oxf.; 1490: pilgrimage to Jerusalem & visited Rhodes, where he learned Greek, & Italy, where he spent the next few years; associated in Rome w. humanists such as **John Colet** (q.v.) & **Thomas Linacre** (q.v.) & studied Latin; 1492–95: R, Holcot, Northants; private teacher of grammar, etc.; c. 1595: m. Agnes; six children; grandson John Lyly (q.v.); 1504–: friendship w. Sir **Thomas More** (q.v.); 1506: congratulatory verses on arrival of Philip the Fair; c. 1512: Colet's 1st master of St Paul's School, London; c. 1513: *Absolutissimus de octo orationis partium constructione libellus* – brief Latin syntax, supervised by Erasmus; 1518: pub'd w. Thomas More *Progymnasmata* (Latin verse transl. of Greek epigrams); 1525: posthumously pub'd two grammatical poems; 1527: posthumously pub'd *Rudimenta grammatices* – short syntax written in English; 1542: posthumous pub'n by royal order of compilation of all three grammatical works as two complete grammars: one for beginners in English & another in Latin; 1543: proclamation orders only Lily's Grammar to be used throughout the realm (repeated in the reigns of Edward VI, Elizabeth I & James I); 1548–49: definitive edition of the 'royal grammar'; date of d. uncertain but made will on 2 Sept. 1522.

LINACRE Thomas (c. 1460–1524): Oxf.-edu. physician and humanist scholar. c. 1460: b. (unknown origins); 1481: Oxf,; 1484: Fellow, All Souls College, Oxf.; 1487: trip to Italy; c. 1489–90: studied Greek in Florence; c. 1491–92/93: in Rome; 1492/93–96: studies at Venice (where closely associated w. humanist *Neakadēmia* promoting study of Greek) & Padua; 1496: grad. in medicine from Padua; Aug. 1499: returned to England; tutor to Prince Arthur; friendship w. **Colet, More, Grocyn & Erasmus** (all q.v.); 1515–25: pub'd three Latin grammatical works; 1509: royal physician; several eccles. preferments; 1515: ord. subdeac.; 1517–24: transl. from the Greek of important Galen's works that challenged existing interpretations of his medicine; 1518: petitioned Henry VIII successfully for London College of Physicians; 1st President of LCP, 1520: ord. deac.; 1523: tutor to Princess Mary; accumulated property; by his will estab'd medical lectureships at Oxf. & Cambr. F. Maddison, M. Pelling & C. Webster (eds.), *Essays on the Life and Works of Thomas Linacre, c. 1460–1524*, 1977.

LOCKE Anne (née Vaughan, other m. names: Dering, Prowse) (c. 1530–90): well-edu. evangelical Protestant, translator and friend of **John Knox** (q.v.). c. 1530: b. dau. of Stephen Vaughan, merchant adventurer, & his 1st w. Margery (Gwynneth or Guinet); Protestant humanist edu. in household of her father's 2nd w. who was Margery Brinklow, wid. of **Henry Brinklow**, author of *The Complaynt of Roderyck Mors*; c. 1549: m. Henry Locke (also Lok), humanistically edu. mercer who traded w. Antwerp; winter 1552–53: associated w. John Knox, who

lodged w. the Lockes; 1556–72: corresponded w. Knox; 8 May 1557: encouraged by Knox, left husband in London & took two children into exile in Geneva; transl. some of Calvin's sermons into English & dedicated them to **Katherine Bertie** (q.v.); summer 1559: acted as channel of communication betw. Knox & reformers in Scotland & Eng., providing him with books & using her infl. to provide him w. financial aid; 1571: Henry Locke d.; 1572: m. (ii) **Edward Dering** (q.v.); 1575: Dering d.; m. (iii) Richard Prowse, Exeter draper, later mayor & M.P.; 1590: transl. Jean Taffin's *Markes of the Children of God, and of their Comfort in Afflictions*, dedicated to Countess of Warwick; several later editions of this work; pre-deceased her husband who. d. 1607. P. Collinson, 'The role of women in the English Reformation illustrated by the life and friendships of Anne Locke', in his *Godly People: Essays on English Protestantism and Puritanism*, 1983.

LOPEZ (also **Lopes**) Roderigo (also Ruy or Roger) (c. 1517–94): crypto-Jewish Portuguese royal physician and alleged conspirator. c. 1517: b. Portugal s. of Anthony Lopes, baptised Jew & physician to John III of Portugal; c. 1537–44: career at Uni. of Coimbra culminated in medical degree; 1559: settled in London & admitted to London College of Physicians & made physician to St Bartholomew's Hospital; c. 1563: m. Sarah Anes, English born of Portuguese Jewish parentage; the couple conformed publically but practised Judaism secretly; 1564: Ellyn b.; physician to Earl of Leicester; 1581: app'd royal physician; received various monopolies & grants of land; 1584: *Leicester's Commonwealth* named Lopez as a poisoner & abortionist; 1590: approached **Mendoza** to work as Sir Francis Walsingham's intermediary in peace negotiations w. Spain; 1591: after Walsingham's d. Lopez continued to correspond w. Spanish officials & alienated Earl of Essex by breaching patient confidentiality; Essex discovered conspiracy; conspirators implicated Lopez in proposed d. by poisoning of Elizabeth; Jan. 1594: Essex informed on him to Anthony Bacon; 7 June

1594: hanged at Tyburn for high tr.; affair whipped up anti-Jewish feeling. D. Green, *The Double Life of Doctor Lopez: Spies, Shakespeare and the Plot to Poison Elizabeth I*, 2003.

LOVELL (Sir) Thomas (c. 1449–1524): soldier, royal administrator, councillor, book collector, landowner & Speaker of the House of Commons. c. 1449: b. s. of Ralph Lovell gent. of Beachamwell, Norfolk; 1464: adm. Lincoln's Inn; 1472–75: Treasurer Lincoln's Inn; 1475 & 1482: Reader, Lincoln's Inn; Norfolk JP; 1483: rebelled v. Richard III; 1484: attainted by Parl.; 1485: Speaker of HofC in Henry VII's 1st Parl.; Treasurer of King's Chamber; Chancellor of the Exchequer; 1485 or 1486: m. Isabel (Ros), wid. Everingham; 1487–97: fought at various battles; leading councillor; 1500: KG; 1503: Treasurer of King's Household; 1508: had 1,365 retainers under licence; 1512: Lieut., Tower of London; 1513–20: Master, Court of Wards; 25 May 1524: d. S.J. Gunn, 'Sir Thomas Lovell (c. 1449–1524): A New Man in a New Monarchy?', in J.L. Watts (ed.), *The End of the Middle Ages?*, 1998, pp. 117–53.

LUMLEY George (d. 1537): leader in second phase of the Yorkshire Pilgrimage of Grace; exec. 1537.

LUMLEY (Lady) Jane (née Fitzalan) Lady Lumley (1537–78): learned recusant aristocrat, book collector and translator. 1537: b. eldest child of Henry Fitzalan, 12th Earl of Arundel & 1st w. **Katherine (Grey)** (q.v.); sister of Henry Lord Maltravers & **Mary Howard** Duchess of Norfolk (q.v.); excellent home edu.; c. 1550: m. John Lumley, 1st Baron Lumley (q.v.); 1556–: cared for her sick father; Latin & English tranlations; 27 July 1578: d.

LUMLEY John (c. 1492–1545) 5th Baron Lumley: landowner and rebel. c. 1492: b. Co. Durham s. & h. of Richard Lumley, 4th Baron Lumley, & h.w. Anne (Conyers); 1508–1537: office of Chief Forester of Weardale; May 1510: inherited title; 9 Sept. 1513: distinguished himself at battle of Flodden & knighted; 1519, 1522–23: fought in Scottish campaigns; June 1520: accompanied Henry to Firel of Cloth of Gold; JP in Co. Durham; m. Joan (Le Scrope) of Bolton; constant friction w. Bps of Durham; two s. George & Percival; 13 July 1530: signed HofL's petition to Pope Clement VII seeking consent to Henry's divorce; c. 1533: grands. **John** b. (q.v. below); 1536–37: participated in Pilgrimage of Grace, motivated probably by religion & disagreement w. crown policy for the north of England; Dec. 1537: negotiated terms of agreement at Doncaster; 2 June 1537: s. George executed for tr.; 1539–40: JP North Riding; 1541: sat in House of Lords; c. Dec. 1545: d.

LUMLEY (Lord) John (c. 1533–1609): 1st Baron Lumley: Cambr.-edu. recusant, aristocratic book & art collector, patron, colliery owner & conspirator. c. 1533: b. s. & h. of George Lumley (executed 2 June 1537 for part in Pilgrimage of Grace) & Jane (Knightley); 1547: rest. in blood & cr. 1st Baron Lumley; May 1549: matric. fellow-commoner at Queens' College, Cambr.; c. 1550: m. (i) **Jane (Fitzalan)** (q.v.) eldest dau. of Henry Fitzalan, 12th Earl of Arundel & h. 1st w. **Katherine Grey** (q.v.); 29 Sept. 1553: KB; 1559–1609: Keeper of Nonesuch Great Park; 24 Feb. 1559: High Steward of Oxf. Uni.; 1571: involved in Ridolfi plot; autumn 1571 to Apr. 1573: impr. in Tower, etc.; created allegorical garden at Nonsuch (the 'grove of Diana') as apology for his part in plot; avoided involvement in future plots; 1582–83: sponsored surgery lecture at Royal College of Physicians; 1594: d. of Arundel; Nonsuch & his debts to the Crown passed to Lumley; Lumley gave Nonsuch to the Queen (to pay debt) but remained in residence; 1598: benefactor, Cambr. Uni. Library; 1582: m. (ii) Elizabeth (Darcy) & retired from court, spending much time at Lumley Castle & concerning himself w. family history & genealogy; 11 Apr. 1609: d. A. Wells-Cole, *Art and Decoration in Elizabethan and Jacobean England*, 1997.

LYLY John (1554–1606): Oxf.-edu. author and dramatist. 1554: b. Kent, eldest child of Peter Lyly & h.w. Jane (Burgh), & grands. of **William Lily** (q.v.); ?edu. King's School, Canterbury & Magdalen College, Oxf.; 1573: BA; 1575: MA; 1578: *Euphues, the Anatomy of Wit: Very Pleasant for All Gentlemen to Read*; secretary to the Earl of Oxf.; 22 Nov. 1583: m. Beatrice Browne; 1584: wrote plays for the Earl of Oxf., performed at Court & Blackfriars; 1587–91: moved near to St Paul's & wrote plays for boys of St Paul's, some of which were taken to Court: *Gallathea & Endymion* (1588) & *Midas* (1589); 1589: M.P.; 1588/89: collaborated w. **Thomas Nashe** (q.v.) in pamphlets v. Martin Marprelate; c. Nov. 1606: d. G.K. Hunter, *John Lyly: The Humanist as Courtier*, 1962.

M

MARGARET TUDOR (Princess and later Queen (Consort) of Scotland) (see Section 12.1: Monarchs and their consorts).

MARLOWE (also Marley, Morley, Marlin & Merlin) Christopher (1564–93): Cambr.-edu. dramatist and poet. c. Feb. 1564: b. 2nd child of John Marlowe, cobbler, & h.w. Katherine (Arthur); 1578: adm. King's School, Canterbury; 1580(–87): Parker scholar, Corpus Christi College, Cambr.; Mar. 1584: BA; transl. from Ovid & Lucan & his earliest play *Dido Queene of Carthage* (pub'd 1594) may date from this time; July 1587: MA; c. 1585–87: gov't service as (?Walsingham's) spy in Catholic France; c. 1587: *Tamburlaine the Great*; 1590: 1st ed'n of *Tamburlaine the Great*; 1594: *Dr Faustus* (probably performed before this); close association w. Thomas Nashe, Matthew Roydon & Thomas Watson; 18 Sept. 1589: fought William Bradley w. sword & dagger & was arrested for murder; 3 Dec. 1589: released;

Jan. – May 1592: impr. in Netherlands for coining money & possible defection to Rome; claimed protection from Lord Strange & the Earl of Northumberland; Feb. 1592: 1st perform of *The Jew of Malta*; May 1592: bound over for disorderly conduct in Shoreditch; Sept. 1592: street fight w. tailor, William Corkine; Jan. 1593: *The Massacre at Paris* performed; 1594: *Edward II*; 1598: *Hero and Leander*, narrative poem; 1592–93: accusations of atheism by Richard Baines, etc.; gov't surveillance; 30 May 1593: d. (stabbed over an argument regarding the bill in a private room at Deptford Strand, near London – possibly as a result of intrigue v. Marlowe), C. Nicholl, *The Reckoning: The Murder of Christopher Marlowe*, 1992.

MARTYR Peter (Pietro Martire Vermigli) (1499–1562): Florentine theologian and evangelical reformer, who exercised great infl. on the English reformation. An Augustinian monk who received his education at the Uni. of Padua and became a renowned preacher before converting to Protestantism c. 1542; 1542–47: Professor of Old Testament studies, Strasbourg; close association w. **Martin Bucer** (q.v.); 1545: m. Katherine Dammartin, a former nun; 1547: invited to Eng. by **Thomas Cranmer** (q.v.); Mar. 1548: Regius Professor of Divinity, Oxf.; 28 May 1549: disputation w. Catholic William Tresham regarding nature of Eucharist; 1548: *Tractatio de sacramento eucharistiae*; 1549: transl. into English; July 1549: left Oxf. briefly after Western rebellion & stayed w. Cranmer; infl'd Cranmer's theology; 1550: asked w. Bucer to suggest revisions to BofCP; 20 Jan. 1551: app'd 1st canon of Christ Church; congregation objected & attacked his rooms when he tried to smuggle his w. into college; Feb. 1551: helped persuade **John Hooper** (q.v.) to accept vestments; Oct. 1551: app'd to commission to reform eccles. law (see Chapter 4: World of learning); 1552 BofCP bears marks of his infl.; 1553: w. d.; placed under house arrest & then left England; returned to Strasbourg; moved to Zurich (to take over from Konrad

Pelikan) w. **John Jewel** (q.v.); Aug. 1554: English exiles ask him to arbitrate over Troubles in Frankfurt; 1558: pub'd *In episto-lam ad Romanos commentarii* (his Oxf. lectures); 9 May 1559: m. (ii) Caterina Merenda of Brescia 1559: pub'd works v. English Catholics; 12 Nov. 1562: d. J.C. McLelland and G.E. Duffield (eds), *The Life, Early Letters, and Eucharistic Writings of Peter Martyr* (1989); J.C. McLelland (ed.), *Peter Martyr Vermigli and Italian Reform*, 1980.

MARY STUART (Queen of Scotland) (1542–87) (see Section 12.1: Monarchs and their consorts).

MARY TUDOR (Princess, later Queen of France) (1496–1533) (see Section 12.1: Monarchs and their consorts).

MARY I (Queen) (1516–58) Tudor (see Section 12.1: Monarchs and their consorts).

MAYNE Cuthbert (Saint Cuthbert Mayne) (1544–77): Oxf.-edu. RC pr. and martyr. 1544: b. s. of William Mayne, farmer; edu. Barnstaple GS; 1565: sponsored by uncle at Oxf.; 1566: BA & chaplain to St John's College; 1570: MA; converted by Gregory Martin & **Edmund Campion** (q.v.); 1573: adm. English College at Douai; 1576: BTh; 1576: chaplain & steward to Francis Tregian of Golden Manor, Probus, Cornwall; celebrated Mass widely in Cornwall; 8 June 1577: arrested & books seized; 30 Nov. 1577: hanged, drawn & quartered at Launceston for tr.; 1970: canonised. R.F. Trudgian, *Francis Tregian, 1548–1608: Elizabethan recusant*, 1998.

MENDOZA Bernardino de (fl. 1580s): Spanish ambassador. Expelled after Throckmorton Plot for complicity.

MILDMAY Anthony (c. 1549–1617): Cambr.-edu. Puritan landholder, diplomat, M.P. and JP. c. 1549: b. s. & h. of Sir Walter Mildmay & Mary; nephew of **Francis Walsingham** (q.v.); 1562–64: Peterhouse, Cambr.; 1567: m. **Grace (Sharington) Mildmay** (q.v.); one dau. Mary; 1569: served v. northern rebels;

1571: M.P. Duchy of Lancaster; June to Oct. 1578: accomp. Walsingham on special embassy to Low Countries; 1579: JP Northants; adm. Gray's Inn; 1580–81: Sheriff, Northants; 1583: JP Wilts; 1584: M.P. Wilts; broke **entail** on the estate (formerly in favour of his brother Humphrey) in order to provide for Grace & Mary; 1592–93: Sheriff, Northants; July 1589 to July 1594: Duchy of Lancaster auditor north of the river Trent; Aug. 1596 to Aug. 1597: knighted; unsuccessful tour as ambassador to France; Jan.1598: M.P. Westminster & served on several committees; 2 Sept. 1617: d. M.E. Finch, 'The Wealth of Five Northamptonshire Families', 1540–1640, *Northamptonshire RS*, 19, 1956.

MILDMAY (Lady) Grace (née Sharington) (c. 1552–1620): pious Protestant, medical practitioner, musician, celebrated hostess and author. c. 1552: b. 2nd dau. & co-heiress of Sir Henry Sharington of Lacock Abbey, Chippenham, Wilts, & Anne (Paget); home edu. w. two sisters by Mistress Hamblyn, a relative; 1567: m. **Anthony Mildmay** (q.v.) eldest s. of Walter, Chancellor of the Exchequer; 1581/82: Mary b.; 1581–1609: legal dispute over her inheritance w. co-heiress, younger sister Olive; galliard 'My Lady Mildmay's Delight' acknowledged her musical abilities; knowledge of Galenic medicine; practised medicine on a large scale with patients of both sexes; composed extensive spiritual meditations & a notable auto-biographical memoir; 27 July 1620: d. Linda Pollock, *With Faith and Physic: The Life of a Tudor Gentlewoman, Lady Grace Mildmay, 1552–1620*, 1993; R. Warnicke, 'Lady Mildmay's Journal: A Study in Autobiography and Meditation in Reformation England', *Sixteenth Century Journal*, 20, 1989, pp. 55–68.

MILDMAY (Sir) Walter (1520/21–89): Cambr.-edu. royal administrator, financial expert, educational patron and moderate Puritan founder of Emmanuel College, Cambr. 1520/21: b. youngest s. of Thomas Mildmay, mercer of Chelmsford, Essex, & Agnes (Read); four brothers & three sisters;

1538–40: Fellow-commoner, Christ's College, Cambr.; 1540: clerk in court of augmentations; 1546: adm. Gray's Inn; 1543: joint auditor of priests & foreign accounts in court of general surveyors; 1544: travelled to France w. Sir **Richard Rich**, war treasurer; 1545: M.P. Lostwithiel; co-auditor for court of augmentations in several counties; on commission for reorganisation of court of augmentations; 25 May 1546: m. Mary, dau. of William & Joyce Walsingham & sister of **Francis** (q.v.); five children; Sept. 1546: Duchy of Lancaster auditor of crown lands north of the Trent; 1547: reorganisation & amalgamation of court of augmentations & general surveyors; 1 Jan. 1547: app'd one of the two surveyors of the court; c. 1549: b. of Anthony; c. 1552: b. of Humphrey; 1547: knighted; Sept. 1547: compiled inventory of Henry VIII's goods; May 1547: JP on Essex quorum; 1547: M.P. Lewes, Sussex; 1548: app'd w. Robert Keilwey to make decisions regarding distribution of chantry property: gave him considerable infl.; 1550s onwards: close friendship w. **William Cecil** (q.v.); 1551: w. Thomas Mildmay founded Chelmsford GS using chantry confiscations; 1551: Duke of Northumberland app'd him on commission to collect Crown debts; acquired Apethorpe, Northants; 1552: active & pre-eminent on commission to review & reorganise crown financial administration & the revenue courts, which reported on 10 Dec.; 1553: M.P. Maldon, Essex; 1554: court of augmentations dissolved & incorporated in that of First Fruits & Tenths; received pension; Oct. 1553: M.P. Peterborough; Feb.1554: Mary removed him from quorum of peace; continued to serve on various commissions; 9 Jan. 1558: app'd Treasurer for Overseas Operations; 1558: M.P. Northants; 5 Feb. 1559: app'd Chancellor of Exchequer; 1559: JP Middlesex, Northants; Oct. 1560: app'd to commission to consider issue of re-coinage; 1564: JP Huntingdon; summer 1566: PC; entertained the Queen at Apethorpe; Jan. 1567: Under-Treasurer of Exchequer; Mar. 1569: endowed Greek lectureship at Christ's College, Cambr. & donated works of classical philosophy; 1569: joint Lord Lieut. Huntingdon; 1570: wrote 'Memorial' for s.

Anthony; late 1570: w. Burghley interviewed Mary Queen of Scots, w. a view to her release & rest. to Scottish throne; 1571: reformed Exchequer; 1572: M.P. Northants; 1573: on commission for uniformity in religion in London & Middlesex; 1576: M.P. Northants; estab'd reputation as parl. orator; agreed w. Elizabeth's suppr. of prophesyings; Nov. 1578: chaired committee reviewing tax collection in Ireland in attempt to improve yield; consulted on coinage; 1587: Lord Lieut. Huntingdon; 1583–88: founded Emmanuel College, Cambr. to train preaching ministry; 31 May 1589: d. S.E. Lehmberg, *Sir Walter Mildmay and Tudor Government*, Austin, Texas, 1964.

MONMOUTH Humphrey (fl. 1524): London cloth merchant. Gave refuge to William Tyndale.

MORE (Sir) Thomas (St Thomas More) (1478–1535): Oxf. and Lincoln's Inn-edu. lawyer, landowner, M.P. statesman, Lord Chancellor, pious humanist author and Catholic martyr. 1478: b. s. & h. of Sir John More (barrister & later Judge of Common Pleas & King's Bench) & 1st w. Agnes (Graunger); edu. St Anthony's School, Threadneedle Street; 1489: entered Archbp **John Morton**'s household (q.v.); 1492–94: edu. Oxf.; 1494: New Inn (Junior Inn of Chancery); 1496: adm. Lincoln's Inn; 1499: began friendship w. **Erasmus, Colet, Grocyn, Linacre & Lily** (all q.v.); assoc. w. Carthusians at the Charterhouse; 1504: M.P.; 1505: m. (i) Jane (Colt); 1505: **Margaret** b. (q.v. **Roper Margaret**); 1506: Elizabeth b.; 1507: Cicely b.; 1509: John b.; 1509: JP Middlesex & M.P. Westminster; 1510: pub'd life & letters of Pico della Mirandola; undersheriff, City of London; 1511: Jane d. & he m. (ii) Alice Middleton, wid.; 1512: M.P. 1514: Reader, Lincoln's Inn; adm. Doctors' Commons; 1513–18: wrote unfinished *History of Richard III*; 1515: went on royal commission to Bruges; 1516: pub'd *Utopia* (see Chapter 4: World of learning); controversy w. Martin van Dorp in which More defended humanism v. scholasticism; 1518: PC & henceforth used by **Wolsey**; est'd humanist household at Chelsea; 1521–26: Wolsey's chief secretary; 1521: knighted; 1525: Chancellor of Duchy of Lancaster; produced incomplete *The Four Last Things* – a spiritual work in English; 1523: *Responsio ad Lutherum*; Speaker of House of Commons; 1524: High Steward, Oxf. Uni.; 1525: campaign v. heresy; 1529: app'd Lord Chancellor & instituted legal reforms v. corruption in prerogative, common law and equity courts; tried to distance himself from the King's Great Matter; 1529: pub'd *Dialogue* (concerning heresies) v. **Tyndale** (q.v.); 1530: More isolated in PC re King's Great Matter; concentrated on suppr. heresy & allied w. eccles. leaders in this; 1531: worked for Queen Katherine's cause but exercised great caution; 1532: led oppo. to Commons' grievances v. clergy; 16 May 1532: resigned Chancellorship in protest v. submission of the ordinaries; 1532: pub'd 1st part of *Confutation* v. Tyndale; 1533: pub'd 2nd part; 1532: wrote *Letter against Frith* defending transubstantiation; 1533: circulated *Letter against Frith;* May & June 1533: oppo. King's m. to **Anne Boleyn** (q.v.) & refused to attend her coronation; pub'd *Apology* & *Debellation of Salem and Bizance* v. works of **Christopher St Germain** (q.v.) & in defence of Church's independence; 1534: pub'd *Answer to a Poisoned Book* (defending transubstantiation); Jan. 1534: King insisted on inclusion in bill of attainder; acted cautiously; 12 Apr. 1534: refused to swear Act of Succession but refused explanation; 17 Apr. 1534: impr. in Tower; 1 July 1535: tried & convicted on charge of denying royal supremacy; in response repudiated secular authority over Church; 6 July 1535: exec. at Tower; 1557: posthumous pub'n of complete *Works*; 1935: canonised. J. Guy, *The Public Career of Sir Thomas More*, 1980; J. Guy, *Thomas More*, 2000.

Morgan Hugh (c. 1530–1613): apothecary and botanist. c. 1530: b. s. & h. of John Morgan of Great Bardfield, Essex & Joan (Copcott); 1543: apprenticed to London grocer; c. 1550: made free of Grocers' Company; 1552: made free of City of London; 1556: warned by College of Physicans (LCP) for

dealing in medicine; 1559: censured by LCP for selling medicine without a doctor's permission; m. Lucy Sibell; received, planted & disseminated rare tropical plants & was known to botanists such as **John Gerard** (q.v.); trader in spices; 1574: Warden of Grocers' Company; 1583: app'd apothecary-in-ordinary to Queen; 1584: app'd Master Warden of Grocers' Company; by 1608: app'd apothecary extraordinary to James I; 13 Sept. 1613: d.

Morgan (Bishop) William (1544/45–1604): Cambr.-edu. Bp of Llandaff, St Asaph & translator of the Bible into Welsh. 1544/45: b. 2nd s. of John Morgan, yeoman farmer, & Lowri (Williams); edu. by Wynn family chaplain & also at Westminster School; 1565–83: St John's College, Cambr.; 1565: part of (q.v.) **John Whitgift**'s anti-puritan group in his college & insisted on continuing to wear surplice during vestiarian protests; 1568: ord. deac. & pr.; 1572–88: various eccles. preferments in Wales incl. Llanrhaeadr; 1575: app'd university preacher; c. 1579: m. Katherine (née Davies) Thomas, wid. of predecessor at Llanrhaeadr; 1582: app'd bp's chaplain; 1583: DTh; despite regular preaching & taking pastoral responsibilities seriously, stirred up trouble in Llanrhaeadr, which resulted in riot in Apr. 1591, Morgan carrying a pistol under his clerical garb, & action in Star Chamber; peace rest. by Sir John Wynn's intervention; 1587: transl. Old Testament (minus the Psalms) & the Apocrypha into Welsh & revised Salesbury's version of the New Testament & Psalms; 1588: Bible in Welsh; Sept. 1588: PC ordered its dissemination in Wales; 1595: Bp of Llandaff; resigned Llanrhaeadr; made efforts to improve the diocesan clergy, to rest. the see's precarious finances & to root out recusancy; 1599: pub'd revision of Salesbury's Welsh Book of Common Prayer; 1600: transl. to See of St Asaph; again proved a diligent bp; 1603: revision of his New Testament was lost before pub'n; 10 Sept. 1604: d. G. Williams, 'Bishop William Morgan and the first Welsh Bible', *The Welsh and Their Religion*, 1991, pp. 173–229; D.Ll. Morgan,

William Morgan a'i Feibl: William Morgan and his Bible, 1989.

MORISON, (Sir) Richard 'Merry' (c. 1510–56): Oxf. and Cambr.-edu. humanist diplomat, propagandist & advocate of Machiavelli; b. 2nd s. of Thomas Morison of Sandon, Herts & h.w. (Merry); 1526: adm. Cardinal College, Oxf.; 1529: BA; granted annuity by **Wolsey** (q.v.); c. 1529: studied in Cambr.; 1532: travelled to Padua in service of Thomas Winter, Wolsey's illegit. s.; 1532–36: studied law, philosophy, Greek and Machiavelli, etc. at Padua; made friends w. **Reginald Pole** (q.v.); 1533: sought patronage of **Thomas Cranmer** (q.v.); wrote intell. reports for **Thomas Cromwell** (q.v.); May 1536–40: continued in Cromwell's service; 1537: sat on commission which drafted Henry VIII's response to Pope's call for **General Council** of Church at Mantua; 1539: app'd gent. of privy chamber; 1539: MP; many propagandist writings in defence of authoritarian model of kingship – e.g. 1539: *An Invective agenste the Great and Detestable Vice, Treason*; also authored some evangelical works; 1530s & 1540s: held several eccles. benefices; had a mistress, Lucy Peckham, who d. 1552; they had two illegit. s. & one dau.; 1546: m. Bridget (Hussey) (1525/26–1601); 23 Dec. 1546 to Mar. 1547: special ambass. to Denmark; 1547: JP, Middlesex; 1547: MP Wareham, Dorset; 1549: Charles b.; also had three daus, Jane, Elizabeth and Mary; May 1549: part of commission judging writings of **Peter Martyr** (q.v.) on the Eucharist; Oct. 1550: PC; Oct. 1550 to Sept. 1553: ambass. to Charles V in Germany with **Roger Ascham** (q.v.) as his secretary; offended Charles V, briefly recalled; July 1553: joined Marian exile in Strasbourg; 20 Mar. 1566: d.

MORTON (Archbishop) John (c. early 1420s to 1500): Oxf.-edu. Cardinal Archbp of Canterbury & Lord Chancellor, conspirator, close counsellor of Edward IV & Henry VII, & royal administrator. c. early 1420s: b. s. of Richard Morton, gent., of Dorset; 1447: notary public; 1448–53: active academic & practical career as civil & canon lawyer at Oxf.; 1453–?: practising lawyer in Court of Arches; 1453–58: several eccles. preferments; 1456–61: Chancellor to Edward, Prince of Wales; 1461: excl. from Yorkist pardon for collusion w. Lancastrians; impr. & attainted; escaped to join Lancastrian court in exile; 1471: pardoned by Edward IV; Master of Chancery; 1472: Master of the Rolls; 1474: Dean of Court of Arches; 1474–82: diplomatic tours to France & Burgundy; 1474–78: several high-level eccles. preferments; 1478: Bp of Ely; important counsellor to Edward IV; 14 June 1483: arrested by Richard III; involved in Buckingham's rebellion; Jan. 1484: attainted & escaped to Flanders; involved in pro-Tudor conspiracies; 30 Oct. 1485: assisted at Henry VII's coronation; Nov. 1485: attainder reversed; PC; 6 Mar. 1487: King's chief minister, app'd Lord Chancellor, displayed concern for justice & good gov't & was responsible for reforming the court & enforcing its jurisdiction; important intermediary betw. King & Parl.; blamed for heavy taxation but 'Morton's fork' a later invention; 6 Oct. 1486: transl. to Archbpric of Canterbury; repaired church properties; rebuilt palace at Croydon & gatehouse at Lambeth Palace; 1489: persuaded clergy in convocation to grant specific sum of money to crown; reformed clerical taxation without undermining eccles. independence; placed restrictions on benefit of clergy; 1487, 1489: battled to enforce jurisdiction over St Albans Abbey; 1492–93: fought to preserve Canterbury's right to receive revenues of vacant See of Winchester; 20 Sept. 1493: cr. cardinal; 1494: preserved Canterbury's prerogative jurisdiction over probate; 1499: Rome delivered favourable decision re Winchester revenues; 1495–1500: Chancellor, Oxf. Uni.; 1498: visitation of unreformed Franciscan houses; 1499–1500: Chancellor, Cambr. Uni.; 15 Sept. 1500: d. during plague outbreak.

MOUNTJOY, eighth Baron, Charles Blount (Earl of Devonshire, 1603–06) (1563–1606), soldier, administrator, Lord Dep. and Lord Lieut. of Ireland, & rival & friend of **Robert Devereux**, 2nd Earl of Essex (q.v.); 2nd s. of

James Blount, 6th Baron Mountjoy & h.w. Katherine (Leigh); c. 1590: took Essex's sister, Lady Penelope (Devereux) Rich as his mistress; 1603: James I cr. him Lord Lieut. of Ireland; June 1603: presented Tyrone to James I; 21 July 1603: cr. Earl of Devonshire; Nov. 1605: Lord Rich obtained eccles. divorce from Lady Penelope; 26 Dec. 1605: Blount m. Lady Penelope Rich; scandal ensued; 3 Apr. 1606: d. in London; 7 May: bur. in Westminster Abbey.

MULCASTER Richard (1531/32–1611): Eton, Cambr. & Oxf.-edu. schoolmaster, scholar and educationalist. 1531/32: b. Carlisle, s. of William Mulcaster, alderman and later M.P., & h.w. Margaret; edu. Eton; 15 Aug. 1548: matric. King's College, Cambr.; 1554: BA Peterhouse, Cambr.; 17 Dec. 1556: MA Christ Church, Oxf.; *The Quenes Maiesties Passage*, described Queen's splendid entry into London; 1559: M.P. Carlisle; 13 May 1560: m. Katherine Ashley; three s. & three daus; Sept. 1561: 1st Headmaster, Merchant Taylors' School, London; encouraged drama; 1581: *Positions Concerning the Training up of Children*;1582: *The first part of the elementarie which entreateth chefelie of the right writing of our English tung*; 1586: res. Merchant Taylors'; private school on Milk Street; preacher at Lincoln's Inn; 1 Apr. 1590: V. of Cranbrook, Kent; 1594: Preb. of Salisbury; 1598: non-resident R of Stanford Rivers, Essex; 1596–1608: High-master of St Paul's School; 1599/1600: *Catechismus Paulinus*; 1600: *Cato Christianus*; 1609: Katherine d.; 15 Apr. 1611: d. at Stanford Rivers.

N

NAPIER (Reverend) Richard (1559–1634) Oxf.-edu. Church of England cleric, prominent physician & astrologer; b. 3rd s. of Alexander & h.w. Ann or Agnes (Burchley) in Exeter; 20 Dec. 1577: matric. commoner Exeter College, Oxf.; 1580–90: elected fellow of Exeter College; 1584: BA; 1586: MA; ord.; R of Great Linford Bucks & bought the advowson; licensed to practise medicine by Archdeac. of Buckingham; sometime after 1597 studied w. Simon Foreman, astrologer & infl. by **John Dee** (q.v.); 1610: purchased parsonage of Great Linford; enormous clientele sought him out; about one-quarter of clients drawn from nobility & upper gentry; less than a fifth (c. 2,000) of his clients attended him for mental illness; asserted moderate, conforming membership of Church of Eng., & relied most on traditional medicine, avoiding mention of necromancy & his pronounced magical interests, etc. in his numerous case books; 1 Apr. 1634: d.

NASHE, Thomas (1567–1601): uni.-edu. professional writer whose rumbustious, rollicking style is famous. Nov. 1567: b. Lowestoft, Suffolk, 3rd child of William Nashe, clergyman, & h. 2nd w. Margaret (Witchingham); 1582: matric. sizar, St John's College, Cambr.; Mar. 1586: BA; c. 1588: in London; 1587–88: *The Anatomie of Absurdity* (pub'd 1589/90); 1588–90: enlisted, along w. John Lyly, to spearhead a pamphlet counterattack to Martin Marprelate, although uncertain which pamphlets he wrote – probably *An Almond for a Parrat*, pub'd ?early 1590 under the alias Cutbert Curry-knave; Sept. 1593: apocalyptic religious lament, *Christs Teares Over Jerusalem* may have been response to May 1593 arrests of Kyd & **Marlowe** on charges of heresy and atheism; 1594: pub'd pacy chronicle *The Unfortunate Traveller*; assoc. w. **Robert Greene** & collab. w. Ben Jonson; 1601: d.

NEVILLE (Lord) Charles 6th Earl of Westmorland (see under **Howard (Lady) Jane**)

NEWDIGATE Anne (née Fitton) Lady Newdigate (1574–1618): gentlewoman, correspondent, networker and elder sister of **Mary Fitton** (q.v.). Oct. 1574: b. dau. of Sir Edward Fitton & Alice (Holcroft) Fitton; 30 Apr. 1587: m. John Newdigate (knighted in 1603); Jan. 1588: John entered Brasenose College, Oxf.

while she remained in father's house; 1595: couple took up residence at Arbury; five children w. well-connected godparents such as Lettice Lady Paget; Anne responsible for maintaining influential network; also a capable manager of the household; 1604–05: suggested as possible royal wetnurse; 1610: obtained wardship of her s. after her husband's d.; managed estates & furthered m. of children Mary & John; 1617: attended masque at court w. dau. Mary; July 1618: d. V.M. Larminie, 'Wealth, kinship and culture: The seventeenth-Century Newdigates of Arbury and their world', *Royal Historical Society Studies in History*, 72, 1995; V. Larminie, 'Fighting for family in a patronage society: The epistolary armoury of Anne Newdigate, 1574–1618', in J. Daybell (ed.), *Early Modern Women's Letter Writing, 1450–1700*, 2000.

NORFOLK, 2nd Duke of (see **Howard** (Lord) Thomas (1443–1524).

NORFOLK, 3rd Duke of (see **Howard** (Lord) Thomas (1473–1554).

NORFOLK, 4th Duke of (see **Howard** (Lord) Thomas (1538–72).

NORTHUMBERLAND John Dudley, Duke of (see **Dudley** Sir John, Duke of Northumberland).

NORTON Thomas (c. 1530–84): Cambr.-edu. lawyer, poet, translator, author, active parliamentarian and loyalist. c. 1530: b. s. & h. of Thomas Norton, London grocer, & 1st w. Elizabeth (Merry); brought up by stepmothers, who incl. Elizabeth (Marshall) Ratcliff, widow of dramatist & schoolmaster Ralph Ratcliff of Hitchen, Herts; 1544–70: Cambr.; 1550: tutored children of **Edward Seymour** (q.v.) & secretary; assoc. w. **Thomas Cranmer**, & poss. **William Cecil** (q.v.); 1550: transl. work by Peter Martyr as *An epistle unto the right honorable . . . the duke of Somerset*; 1552: helped **Nicholas Udall** (q.v.) provide index to **Miles Coverdale** (q.v.) *et al.*'s, *The Paraphrases of Erasmus upon the Newe Testament*; 22 Jan. 1552: Norton remained tutor of Seymour's children at William Paulet's house after their father's

exec.; 1555: adm. to Inner Temple; m. (i) Margaret Cranmer, dau. of Thomas; some surviving poetry from this period; 1561: *The Institution of Christian Religion* (painstaking prose transl. of Calvin's 1559 *Institutiones*); 1558: M.P. Gatton; 1558: made free of Grocers' Company; 1563: called to bar & became practising lawyer; M.P. Berwick upon Tweed; worked for Cecil to root out & discourage pamphlets & debate re the succession; c. 1567: Margaret d.; m. (ii) Alice Cranmer, dau. of Edmund, archdeac. of Canterbury; six children incl. **Robert** (q.v.); 1571–80s: licenser of books; 1565: pub'd w. Thomas Sackville, *The Tragedie of Gorboduc*, 1st English blank verse Senecan tragedy (1st performed in 1561 & contained reference to the succession); 1569: pub'd pamphlet, *A discourse touching the pretended match betwene the duke of Norfolke and the queene of Scottes*; 1570: pub'd authorised version of *Gorboduc* (contained more specific political advice because Norton convinced of papal plot to depose Elizabeth); 1570: transl. & pub'd **Alexander Nowell** (q.v.) *Catechismus* as *A Catechisme;* 1571: M.P. City of London; reported parl. proceedings for Lord Mayor; 1571: drafted treasons bill; 1571: introduced into House of Commons a through review of Church gov't, w. pub'n of the earlier 'Reformatio legum ecclesiasticarum' in a search for further moderate Church reform within a broadly episcopalian framework; rebuked by Archbp Parker for his caution during Admonition to Parliament controversy; 1572: argued in Parl. for execution of Duke of Norfolk & Mary of Scotland; 1576: M.P. – sat on committee regarding Queen's marriage; 1580–83: produced codification of Guersey's Norman customary law & helped pacify Guernsey; 1578–83: commissioner for examination of recusants, incl. **Cuthbert Mayne** (q.v.), **Edmund Campion** (q.v.) & **Francis Throckmorton** (q.v.); reputation as 'rackmaster' unwarranted; anonymous pub'n of *A declaration of the favourable dealing of her Maiesties Commissioners . . . and of tortures, unjustly reported to be done upon them for matters of religion*; 1581: briefly impr. for speaking of the Queen's proposed m. to

Duke of Anjou; began writing mss 'The Devices' (suggestions for reforming universities, **inns of court** & **inns of chancery**, etc.) & chronicles of kings and queens; 1584: *A Discoverie of Treasons*; 10 Mar. 1584: d. M.A.R. Graves, *Thomas Norton: The Parliament Man*,1994; Marie Axton, *The Queen's Two Bodies*, 1977.

NOWELL Alexander (c. 1516/17–1602): Oxf.-edu. humanist Master of Westminster School, Dean of St Paul's, educationalist, author of Catechism, and benefactor. c. 1516/17–1602: b. 2nd s. of John Nowell, esquire of Whalley, Lancs, & 2nd w. Elizabeth (Kay); brother of Lawrence, dean of Lichfield; edu. Middleton, Lancs; c. 1530: Brasenose College, Oxf. (where shared rooms w. **John Foxe** (q.v.); 1536: BA; 1540: MA; 1541 or 1542: lecturer in logic; ord. deac. & pr.; 1543: Master of Westminster School; 1545: DTh; 1550s: engaged in various relig. controversies; 1553: M.P. Looe, Cornwall but denied seat because in convocation; 1555: exile (Strasbourg); Oct. 1556: Frankfurt; attempted to reconcile Knox & Cox, eventually supported radicals; 1558: accepted authority of Church of England; 1560: app'd chaplain to Bp Grindal of London (a lifelong friend); archd. of Middlesex; various other preferments incl. prebends of Canterbury & Westminster; 27 Nov. 1560: Dean of St Paul's; 1561: resigned archdeac.; 1563–90s: member of eccles. commission; 1563: in Convocation sought to abolish organs & singing; as prolocutor of Convocation acted as intermediary betw. Parl. & Lower House of Convocation; argued unsuccessfully for introduction of Book of Discipline & abolition of vestments; Lower House subscribed to his Calvinist *Catechismus* & bps accepted it w. some revisions but Queen ignored it; 1568: preaching mission to Lancs; 1570: pub'n of *Catechismus sive, Prima institutio disciplinaque pietatis Christianae* (but no official status); 1571: canons ordered schoolmasters to use *Catechismus* exclusively & to teach w. Thomas Norton's transl. *A Catechisme*; various versions went into 61 ed'ns by 1638 (see Chapter 4: World of learning); 1561–92:

active & renowned court preacher; preached frequently at Paul's Cross; 1579: d. of 1st w. Jane (Mery) wid. of Thomas Bowyer; m. (ii) Elizabeth (Hast) widow of (i) Lawrence Ball & (ii) Thomas Blount of London; no children; 1580: preaching mission to Lancs; re-endowed Middleton GS & endowed 13 exhibitions at Brasenose College to be held by scholars from Middleton, Whalley or Burnley; 1595: Principal of Brasenose College; drafted statutes for several GS & advised **Matthew Parker** (q.v.) on foundation of Rochdale GS; 13 Feb. 1602: d. I.M. Green, *The Christian's ABC: Catechisms and Catechizing in England, c. 1530–1740*, 1996.

NOWELL Lawrence or Laurence (c. 1516–76): Oxf. and Cambr.-edu. Protestant exile, GS master and Dean of Lichfield. c. 1516: b. 3rd s. of John Nowell of Whalley, Lancs & 2nd w. Elizabeth (Kay); brother of **Alexander** (q.v.) & Robert; 1536: Brasenose College, Oxf.; 1542: BA Cambr.; 1544: MA Oxf.; 1546: Master of Sutton Coldfield GS; 1550: ord. deac.; 1553: in household of Sir John Perrot, Pembrokeshire; exile; 1558: archdeac. of Derby; 1560: Dean of Lichfield; 1563: Prebend in Chichester Cathedral; Rs of Haughton & Drayton Basset, Staffs; c. 1565: m. Mary Glover, wid.; 1567–74: four daus & two s.; 1566: Prebend in York Minster; 1569: denied charge of seditious speeches v. Queen; 1575: purchased estate in Sheldon & Coleshill, Warws; 1576: d.

P

PAGET (Lord) Charles (c. 1546–1612): Cambr.-edu. Catholic in service of Mary Stuart and Philip II. c. 1546: b. 3rd s. of **William**, 1st Baron Paget of Beaudesert (q.v.) & Anne (Preston); 27 May 1559: matric. fellow-commoner, Gonville and Caius College, Cambr.; 9 Oct. 1560: adm. Middle Temple;

Aug. 1564: Trinity Hall, Cambr.; no degree; 1581–88: Paris exile; correspondent & pensioner of Mary of Scotland; involved in plots v. Eliz.; 1612: d.

PAGET (Lord) Thomas (c. 1544–90): 4th Baron Paget, Cambr. & Middle Temple-edu. Roman Catholic exile. 1544: b. 2nd s. of **William** 1st Baron Paget (q.v.) & Anne (Preston); 1559: fellow-commoner at Caius, Cambr.; 1561: adm. Middle Temple; 1568: inherited estates on d. of brother; 1570: succeeded niece Elizabeth to title; 1571: sat as peer in HofL; 1570s: resided at Beaudesert, Staffs & undertook gov't business; 1570: m. Nazareth (Newton), wid. of Thomas Southwell; July 1580: arranged for Jesuit **Edmund Campion** (q.v.) to preach in London; Aug. 1580: under house arrest by PC & under compulsory relig. instruction from Dean of Windsor; 1582: proceeded against by Bp of Coventry & Lichfield for Catholic practices, etc. at Burton on Trent & Colwich; separated from h.w.; 1583: Nazareth d.; fled abroad after discovery of Throckmorton plot, prob. because of his brother Charles's service to Mary Stuart; 1585: travelled to Rome & Spain; granted pension by Philip II; 1587: attainted for tr.; moved to Netherlands & was consulted re Armada; 1590: d.

PAGET (Lord) William (1505/06–63): 1st Baron Paget. Cambr.-edu. diplomat, moderate in religion; industrialist; & royal administrator. 1505/06: b. s. of John Paget (also Pachett) citizen of London; edu. St Paul's School under William Lily, alongside **Thomas Wriothesley, Anthony Denny & John Leland** (all q.v.), & at Trinity Hall, Cambr.; 1526–27: studied in Paris; 1527: joined Stephen Gardiner's household; 1529: M.P.; m. Anne (Preston); 1530–35: series of diplomatic missions re the King's divorce; 1536/37: s. Henry b.; Secretary successively to Queens **Jane, Anne of Cleves** & **Katharine Howard**; 10 Aug. 1540: clerk of PC; Sept. 1541: ambassador to France; 23 Apr. 1543: PC & one of the two principal secretaries of state; 1544: knighted; several short embassies;

s. Thomas b.; 29 Sept. 1545: joint Master of the Posts; 1546: bought 11 episcopal manors in midlands, exploited woods & estab. iron works; s. Charles b.; 1547: key figure in setting up the Council of Regency w. **Edward Seymour** (q.v.) as protector; KG; High Steward of Cambr. Uni.; Comptroller of the Household; 1555: nine children still living; 1549: brother Robert a leader of the Western Rebellion; Oct. 1549: arrested Somerset; gave up household offices; 3 Dec. 1549: cr. Baron Paget of Beaudesert; Warwick ignored his counsel; 21 Oct. 1551: arrested; 8 Nov. 1551: impr. in Tower; May 1552: released; Dec. 1552: pardoned; Feb. 1553: rest. to PC; decl. for Mary I; PC, etc.; chief nego. Mary's m. to Philip II; Apr. 1554: oppo. rest. of England to Roman communion & heresy laws; Philip heeded Paget's advice re acceptance of dissolution of religious houses as *fait accompli*; Aug. 1555: Philip app'd him to inner Council; 29 Jan. 1556: Mary app'd him Lord Privy Seal; in Philip's absence was not in Mary's favour; 1558/59: not favoured by Elizabeth; 9/10 June 1563: d. Feb. 1587: Anne d. B.L. Beer & S.M. Jack (eds), 'The letters of William Lord Paget of Beaudesert, 1547–1563', in *Camden Miscellany*, XXV, 4th ser., 13, 1974.

PARKER (Archbishop) Matthew (1504–75): Cambr.-edu. moderate, Biblical scholar, antiquarian & Elizabeth's first Archbp of Canterbury. 6 Aug. 1504: b. Norwich, s. of William Parker, weaver, & h.w. Alice Monin(g)s, poss. relative of Anne Boleyn; he was grands. of former registrar to Archbp of Canterbury; 1520: his wid. mother sent him to Corpus Christi College, Cambr. (CCCC); 1525: BA; 1527: ord. pr.; MA & Fellow, 1520s: infl. by **Thomas Bilney**; 1530–31: poss. engaged in preaching tours; CCCC; 1535: chaplain to **Anne Boleyn** (q.v.); July 1535: BTh; Feb. 1537: app'd King's chaplain; July 1538: DTh; 4 Dec. 1544: Master of CCCC; Jan. 1545: elected Vice-Chancellor, Cambr.; June 1547: m. Margaret Harleston; four s.; 1549: infl. by Martin Bucer; July 1552: Dean of Lincoln; 1554: supported Queen **Jane Grey** (q.v.); depr. of offices by

Mary I, lived in hiding; 1559: reluctantly accepted See of Canterbury; debate over validity of Parker's ordination; 1562: pub'd work based on John Ponet's unfinished *A Defence of Priestes Mariages*; 1563–68: involved in transl. Bible.

PARKHURST (Bishop) John (?1512–75): Oxf.-edu. moderate, Marian exile and Elizabethan Bp of Norwich.

PARR (Lady, Later Queen) Katherine (1512–48) (see Section 12.1: Monarchs and their consorts).

PARSONS, Robert SJ (1546–1610): Oxf.-edu. Jesuit missionary priest. 24 June 1546: b. Nether Stowey, Somerset s. of Henry and Christina Persons; edu. Stogursey GS & Taunton FS; 1564: adm. St Mary's Hall, Oxf.; 1566: Balliol College, Oxf.; 31 May 1568: BA; 1569: Fellow, Balliol; 1571: lecturer in Rhetoric; 3 Dec. 1572: MA; 1573: Dean of Balliol; 13 Feb. 1574: resigned fellowship; toured continent w. intention of studying medicine at Padua; 4 July 1575: joined SJ as postulant; July 1578: ord. pr. from Roman College; 1579: developed association w. **William Allen** (q.v.) & **Edmund Campion** (q.v.); 17 June 1580: returned to Eng.; July 1580: convened synod at Southwark to debate recusancy; opposed Church papism; pub'd pamphlet *Reasons of Refusal*; toured Northampton, Derby, Worcester and Gloucester, preaching and saying the Mass in house churches; set up secret printing press; 1 Dec. 1581: Campion exec. for tr.; Parsons fled to France; 1582: pub'd infl. *The First Booke of the Christian Exercise, Appertayning to Resolution* (later ed'ns known as 'Christian Directory'); 1583: in Spain obtained financ. help from Philip II for college at Rheims; Aug. 1583: obtained papal bull excommunicating Eliz. & bpric for William Allen; 1584: annoyed Eng Catholics hoping for alliance w. Fr. by associating w. scurrilous *Leicester's Commonwealth*; withdrew somewhat from politics; 1588: R of Eng. College at Rome; 1589: founded English seminary at Valladolid; 1591: founded hospice at Sanlúar; 1592:

founded seminary in Seville; 1593: founded humanist St Omer school (headed by William Flack) for s. of Eng. recusants (ancestor of Stoneyhurst); 1595: pub'd at Antwerp, *Conference about the Next Succession to the Crowne* (a discussion of the merits of rival claims and arguing what the basis of a decision should be); 1596: ms circulation of 'Memorial for the Reformation of England'; attempted conversion of **James VI** (q.v.); involvement in Archpriest Controversy; began Catholic counterpart to Foxe's Book of Martyrs; 1599: pub'd this as *Certamen ecclesiae Anglicanae;* 1596–1610: R of English College at Rome; under James I argued for toleration; 1608: *A Treatise Tending to Mitigation Towardes Catholicke-Subjectes in England*; 1609: *A Quiet and Sober Reckoning with M. Thomas Morton;* 15 Apr. 1610: d. in Rome. F. Edwards, *Robert Persons: The Biography of an Elizabethan Jesuit, 1546–1610*, 1995.

PENRY, John (1562/63–93): pamphleteer involved in Marprelate Tracts. 1562/63: b. Brecknockshire, s. of Meredith Penry of Llangamarch; ?edu. Brecon GS; 11 June 1580: matric. Pensioner, Peterhouse, Cambr.; 1584: BA; July 1586: MAMA Oxf.; refused orders; c. 1587: member of Northampton *classis*; Apr. 1588: Robert Waldegrave pub'd Penry's *An exhortation unto the governours and people of her maiesties countrie of Wales, to labor earnestly to have the preaching of the gospell planted among them* attacking bps for neglecting Welsh people; Aug. 1588: pub'd *A defence of that which hath bin written in the questions of the ignorant ministerie, and the communicating with them*; summer 1588: managing secret Marprelate Press; 5 Sept. 1588: m. Helen Godly of Northampton; four daus; Oct. 1588: Waldegrave pub'd *The Epistle*, (1st Marprelate tract); prob. played minor role in actual writing of the tracts; Nov. 1583: moved press to Sir Richard Knightley's house at Fawsley, Northants; 1589: moved press to John Hales, at White Friars, Coventry; July 1589: Waldegrave in La Rochelle pub'd *Th' appellation of John Penri, unto the highe court of parliament, from the bad and injurious dealing of* *th'archb. of Canterb. & other his colleagues of the high commission*; Aug. 1589: Marprelate Press, now w. John Hodgkins as printer, was seized near Manchester; Oct. 1589: Penry fled to Scotland; Penry denied that he was Marprelate; 1590: James VI outlawed him; Sept. 1592: returned to Eng. & attached himself to separatists **Barrow** & Greenwood; 22 Mar. 1593: arrested; 25 May 1593: tried for writing works v. est'd Church; 29 May 1593: exec. L.H. Carlson, *Martin Marprelate, Gentleman: Master Job Throkmorton Laid Open in his Colors*, 1981.

PERKINS William (1558–1602): Cambr.-edu., leading Calvinist moral theologian, moderate Puritan Church of England clergyman, denunciatory preacher and influential Ramist educator. 1558: b. s. of Thomas and Anna Perkins of Bulkington, Warws; 1577: adm. pensioner, Cambr.; 1581: BA; 1584: MA; 1584–94: Fellow, Christ's College, Cambr.; c. 1588: pub'd *A treatise tending unto a declaration whether a man be in the state of damnation or in the estate of grace*; 1591: *A Golden Chain, or, Description of Theology* (with a chart indicating infl. of Peter Ramus); Sept. 1594: resigned fellowship; 1596: *A Discourse of Conscience*; 1597: pub'd *A Graine of Musterd-Seede*; pub'n of *A Reformed Catholike* helped extend his infl. in Europe; 1598: pub'n of *De praedestinationis modo et ordine* led to controversy w. Jacob Arminius; infl. on educational and vocational thought (as well as theology) profound in early seventeenth century. 1602: d. I. Breward (ed.) *The Works of William Perkins*, 1970.

PHILIP II (King) (see Section 12.1: Monarchs and their consorts).

PLANTAGENET (Lady) Katherine (1479–1527): Princess. 1479: b. sixth of seven children of Edward IV & Queen Elizabeth (Woodville); 1483: decl. illegitimate; 1487: part of sister Queen Elizabeth Tudor's household; 1495: m. Sir William Courtenay (later 2nd Earl of Devon); two s. & one dau.; 1502: Sir William impr. & attainted for complicity in plot to place **Edmund de la Pole** (q.v.) on throne;

1503: Katherine chief mourner at sister Elizabeth's funeral; 1509: Sir William released; 10 May 1511: Sir William cr. Earl of Devon; 9 June: William d.; 6 July 1511: Katherine relinquished rights to the earldom to the crown & took vow of chastity in exchange for lifetime rights in lands of the earldom; 4 Nov. 1511: s. Henry cr. Earl of Devon; 1516: godmother to Princess Mary; kept court in some style at Tiverton Castle Devon; 15 Nov. 1527: d. M. Westcott, 'Katherine Courtenay, countess of Devon, 1479–1527', in T. Gray, M. Rowe, & A. Erskine (eds), *Tudor and Stuart Devon . . . essays presented to Joyce Youings*, 1992, pp. 13–38.

POLE, Edmund de la (?1472–1513) 8th Earl of Suffolk: nobleman of royal descent and claimant to the crown. ?1472: b. 3rd s. of John de la Pole, 2nd Duke of Suffolk & h.w. Elizabeth (Plantagenet) sister of Edward IV; 1487: attended coronation of cousin Elizabeth as Henry VII's Queen; brother Earl of Lincoln attainted; 1492: inherited dukedom & became Henry VII's ward; 26 Apr. 1493: exchanged dukedom for earldom of Suffolk; c. 1496: m. Margaret (Scrope); initially remained loyal to the Tudors; 1599: forced into exile brought back by Henry VII; Aug. 1501: fled England to court of Emperor Maximilian, hoping for support in bid for crown; Henry foiled plot & imprisoned supporters & executed Sir James Tyrell; 26 Dec. 1502: outlawed; Jan. 1504: attainted by Parl.; 24 Apr. 1506: impr. in Tower; 1512: supported Richard de la Pole's bid for crown; 4 May 1513: exec.

POLE (Earl of Lincoln), John de la (?1464–87): descendant of Edward III & conspirator. ?1464: b. s. & h. of John de la Pole, 2nd Duke of Suffolk, & Elizabeth (Plantagenet), sister of Edward IV; 1567: cr. Earl of Lincoln; supported Richard III; 1483: President of Council of the North; 1486: Lord Lieut. of Ireland; 1486: heir-presumptive to throne; after Henry VII's accession he still conspired; supported **Lambert Simnel**; 1487: slaughtered at Battle of Stoke.

POLE (Lady) Margaret (1473–1541): Countess of Salisbury. Wealthy noblewoman of royal descent; a peer in her own right w. lands in 17 counties; prominent patron of humanist scholars & mother of **Reginald**, Henry & Geoffrey (q.v.). 14 Aug. 1473: b. dau. of George, Duke of Clarence & Isabel (Neville) co-heiress of Warwick the Kingmaker; sister of Edward Earl of Warwick; Sept. 1483: banished by Richard III to Sheriff Hutton, Yorks; Nov. 1487: m. Sir Richard Pole, half-cousin of Henry VII through his mother & one of Henry's leading councillors; 1501–02: in **Katherine of Aragon**'s household; Oct. 1504: Sir Richard d.; five children; 1509: part of Queen Katherine's household; Feb. 1512: rest. to Earldom of Salisbury & her brother's lands; s. Henry, Lord Montagu, sat in HofL on her behalf, represented her on commissions of the peace & led her men to battle; 1518: Crown repossessed some of her manors; May 1520 to July 1521 & 1525 to Dec. 1533: governess to Princess Mary; removed from Court; 1536: returned to Court after fall of **Anne Boleyn** but lost favour again because of Reginald's oppo. to royal supremacy; Aug. 1538: s. Geoffrey arrested; Nov. 1538: Margaret interrogated on charges of high tr.; May 1539: attainted by Parl.; Nov. 1539: impr. in Tower; 27 May 1541: exec. at Tower.

POLE (Archbp) Reginald (1500–58): Oxf.-edu. nobleman of royal descent, humanist scholar, Church reformer and Cardinal Archbp of Canterbury. 3rd s. of Sir Richard Pole & **Margaret (Plantagenet) Pole**, countess of Salisbury (q.v.); edu. either at Christ Church, Canterbury or Charterhouse, Sheen; 1512–19: Magdalen College, Oxf., where William Latimer & ?Thomas Linacre (q.v.) tutored him; various eccles. preferments; 1521–26: Padua – studied & associated w. humanist churchmen & authors; 1525: visited Rome for Jubilee; Oct. 1529 to summer 1530: successful mission to Paris to obtain approval for King's divorce; 1532–36: left Eng. for Padua (via Avignon & Verona); 1533: **Eustace Chapuys** suggested his m. w. Princess Mary, alarming Henry; client of Casparo Contarini; religious conversion; 1539: pub'd *Pro ecclesiasticae*

unitatis defensione (known as *De Unitate*) – a defence of church unity (see Chapter 4: World of learning); 19 July 1536: called to Rome; 22 Dec. 1536: app'd Cardinal; 7 Feb. 1537: app'd Legate (w. secret instruction to assist Pilgrimage of Grace (see Chapter 2: Rebellions against the Tudors) then returned to Rome; Feb. 1538: 2nd Papal Legation to muster imperial support v. Henry & appealed to English nobility to rise up; 19 May 1539: attainted by Parl.; 27 May 1541: exec. of mother **Margaret Pole** (q.v.); close assoc. w. Vittoria Colonna; Aug. 1541: Legate of Viterbo; gathered around himself a group of reformers which attracted suspicion of the Roman Inquisition in summer 1541; Oct. 1542: Legate to Council of Trent – rejected its support of justification by works v. by faith; 17 Nov. 1546: returned to Rome; 1549: Western rebels demanded his return; 1549: unsuccessful candidate for papacy; 5–6 Aug. 1553: Legate to Eng. but refused to go before Eng. returned to Catholic fold; 20 Nov. 1555: entered Eng.; 30 Nov. 1555: reconciled Eng. to papacy; Dec. 1555: legatine synod which aimed to reform the clergy & to estab. seminaries; Dec. 1555: named as Cranmer's successor as archbp; 1556: Archbp of Canterbury; 20 Mar. 1556: ord. pr.; PC; visited dioceses & universities; minor role in campaign v. heresy; 9 Apr. 1557: recalled to Rome & legatine powers removed, largely because of his close relations w. Philip II; accusations of heresy; Nov. 1557: d. T.F. Mayer, *Reginald Pole: Prince and Prophet*, 2000.

PONET (Bishop) John (1516–56): humanist bp & friend of **Ascham**, **Cheke** and **Cecil**; political theorist & rebel. 1533: BA & fellow, Queens' College, Cambr.; 1535: MA; 10 June 1536: ord. pr. Lincoln; 1537–39: bursar of Queens'; 1540–42: Dean of Queens'; early 1540s: various eccles. livings; 1547: Chaplain to **Cranmer**; 4 Nov. 1548: already m. (i) 1549: tract defending clerical m.; 1550: Bp of Rochester; July 1551: sep. from w., who was a bigamist; 25 Oct. 1551: m. (ii) Mary (Hayman); 1551–53: Bp of Winchester; 1553: depr. as married pr.; participated in Wyatt's rebellion & went into exile; 1556: d.

Strasbourg. Contribution to political thought considerable: *Short Treatise of Politike Power*, 1556 (see Chapter 4: World of learning).

POYNINGS (Sir) Edward (1459–21): 1485: supporter of Henry VII; 1493: Governor of Calais; 1494: Lord Deputy in Ireland to Prince Henry, the Governor; he assembled a parliament which passed laws restricting Irish independence, including Poyning's Law (no act of Irish parl. valid unless previously submitted to English PC); 1495: drove **Perkin Warbeck** into exile in Scotland; 1496: recalled and made Warden of Cinq Ports and Comptroller of Royal Household; KG; 1513: negotiated league of partition v. France.

PROWSE Anne (1530–90; see Locke, Anne).

PUTTENHAM George (1529–90/91): Cambr.-edu. author, literary historian, critic and book collector. *Cause célèbre*. 1529: b. 2nd s. of Robert Puttenham & Margery (Elyot), sister of Sir Thomas (q.v. under Elyot (Sir) Thomas); Nov. 1546: matric. Christ's College, Cambr., age 17 but left without degree; 11 Aug. 1556: adm. Middle Temple; c. 1560: m. Elizabeth (Cowdray) Lady Windsor, wid. Paulet & Windsor; 1566: conflict w. his w. led to separation; 1570: ordered by Court of Arches to pay w. £3 a week; June 1570: impr. in Fleet for alleged slander of Queen but released; 1576: inventory of his library; 9 June 1578: divorced Elizabeth & she appealed to PC for redress of grievances; 1579–81: 'Partheniades', 17 poems dedicated to Queen Elizabeth exist only in ms; 1584: ex-w. Elizabeth sued him in Court of Arches; Nov. 1586: excommunicated for 3rd time & impr.; 1588: 4th writ of excommunication; 9 Nov. 1588: pub'd *The Arte of English Poesie*, a work of literary history & a manual for poets; Dec./Jan. 1590–91: d.

R

RALEIGH (Sir) Walter (?1552–1618): Oxf.-edu. military and naval commander, and author & poet. ?1552: 2nd s. of Walter & h. 3rd w. Katherine (Champernowne) wid. of East Budleigh, Devon; half-brother through his mother of **Humphrey Gilbert** (q.v.); 1569: served as volunteer w. Huguenot armies in Fr. Wars of Religion; c. 1572: adm. to Oxf.; 27 Feb. 1575: adm. Middle Temple; 1581: favourite of Elizabeth; 1585–86: org'd plantation of Virginia; 1588: influence at court reduced by quarrel w. Earl of Essex & (1592) affair w. & m. to Elizabeth Throckmorton, Elizabeth's lady-in-waiting; impr. & wrote poems to Cynthia; 1591: pub'd *A report of the truth of the fight about the Isles of Azores, this last summer, betwixt the Revenge . . . and an Armada of the king of Spain* (known as 'The Last Fight of the Revenge'); 1595: expedition to Manoa; 1596: brilliant performance v. Cadiz; 1597: distinguished part in expedition to Azores; 17 Nov. 1603: tried for tr.; 1603–16: impr. in Tower; 19 Mar. 1616: released for exped. to find El Dorado; 10 Aug. 1618: impr. in Tower; 29 Oct. 1618: exec. at Westminster. S. Coote, *A Play of Passion*, 1993.

RASTELL John (c. 1475–1536): stationer, innovative printer, theatre manager and dramatist; learned French & Latin; 1489: adm. to Corpus Christi Guild, Coventry; c. 1497: m. Elizabeth More, sister of Thomas; 1502: adm. Middle Temple alongside **Christopher St Germain** of Coventry (q.v.); 1506–08: coroner at Coventry; 1508: returned to London; 1509: began printing w. Thomas More's transl. *The Lyfe of Iohan Picus* & procceeded to specialise in law books; 1512: stationer; writing & printing books; 1513: innovated by importing from Rouen small secretary-type for books in law French; 1517: expedition to find Northwest Passage ended in financial disaster; Nov. 1519 to mid-1520: *New Interlude and a Mery of the Nature of the .iiij. Elements*, a moral play, the first to describe the New World as America & to print a musical score; pre-1523: **John Heywood** (q.v.) m. the Rastells' dau. Joan; 1520: worked at Field of Cloth of Gold, embellishing the roof of the pavilion; 1520: painted roof of Roundhouse, Calais; 1522:

created Cheapside pageant to welcome Emp. Charles V; 1524: built house w. stage in Finsbury Fields – earliest known permanent stage in England; 1525–27: printed music for ballad 'A Wey Mornynge' using type specially cut in northern Europe, so becoming first to print music in single impression; c. 1526: pub'd play *Gentleness and Nobility*; 5 May 1527: produced pageant at opening of theatre at Greenwich; 1529: M.P., Reformation Parliament; c. 1531: converted to Protestantism; began printing Protestant treatises; business declined; spring 1535: tried to convert monks at Charterhouse; 1535: impr. for non-payment of tithe; 25 June 1536: d. in Tower. A.J. Geritz & A.L. Laine, *John Rastell*, 1983.

RICH (Lady) Penelope (c. 1562/63–1607): noblewoman; *cause célèbre*. Jan. 1562/63: b. Chartley, Staffs, eldest child of **Walter Devereux**, 1st Earl of Essex, & h.w. **Lettice (Knollys)** (q.v.) & thereby cousin to Queen Elizabeth; edu. by tutors at home; 1576: ward of Henry Hastings, 3rd Earl of Huntington, in Leicestershire; Jan. 1581: maid of honour to Queen; 1 Nov. 1581: m. (i) Lord Robert Rich, later Earl of Warwick; five children; 1582: Philip Sidney penned 'Astrophil and Stella', poss. in her praise; no proof of affair w. him; 17 Nov. 1590: affair w. Sir Charles Blount (from 1594 Lord Mountjoy), made public; 30 Mar. 1592: Penelope, 1st of six children by Blount baptised; 1605: divorced by Lord Rich; m. (ii) Mountjoy, now become Earl of Devonshire.

RICH (Sir) Richard (?1496–1567): ?Cambr. & Middle Temple-edu. Lord Chancellor. ?1496: b. Basingstoke, Hampshire, s. of John Rich & h.w. Agnes; poss. edu. Cambr.; 1516: adm. Middle Temple; 1529: M.P. Colchester; 1533: Solicitor General; c. 1535: m. Elizabeth (Jenks); three s. & c. ten daus; secured Thomas More's conviction by perjury; 1536: M.P. Essex & elected Speaker of Commons; 1536: engaged in suppression of monasteries; c. 1537: Robert (later 2nd Baron) Rich b.; 1540: deserted Cromwell; 1547: cr. Baron Rich; 1548: Lord Chancellor; 1549: saw bill

of attainder v. Seymour through Parl.; employed by Warwick in proceedings v. Gardiner & Bonner; 1551: resigned Great Seal; 1553: first declared for Jane & then for Mary; 1553–58: persecuted Protestants; 1564: founded Felsted GS; 1567: d.

RICHMOND, Henry Duke of (see **Fitzroy** (Lord) Henry (1519–36).

RICHMOND Mary Duchess of (Fitzroy (née Howard) (c. 1519–55?): noblewoman and courtier. c. 1519: b. younger dau of Thomas Howard, 3rd Duke of Norfolk & Elizabeth (Stafford) Howard; 26 Nov. 1503: m. **Henry Fitzroy** (q.v.) illegitimate s. of Henry VIII (m. never consummated); lady-in-waiting to **Anne Boleyn**; w. **Margaret Douglas & Mary Shelton** (q.v.) edited poetry anthology known as the Devonshire ms.; July 1536: involved in furthering relationship betw. Margaret Douglas & her brother Thomas Howard; 23 July 1536: Richmond d.; Mary's rights denied by King & she had difficulty obtaining her jointure because of disfavour in which her family now stood; 1540: received jointure; not recognised as Dowager Duchess of Richmond; patron of **John Bale** (q.v.) & **John Foxe** (q.v.); app'd Foxe tutor to the sons of her exec. brother, the Earl of Surrey; 1553–55: did not return to Court; Dec. 1555: d.

RICHMOND AND DERBY, Margaret Countess of (see **Beaufort**, Lady Margaret).

RIDLEY (Bishop) Nicholas (1502–55): Cambr.-edu. Protestant bp and martyr. Outstanding Latin and Greek scholar. 1502: b. nr Hadrian's Wall, s. of Christopher Ridley of Unthank Hall & h.w. Anne (Blenkinsop); 1537: Chaplain to Cranmer; 1538: V of Herne, Kent; gradual move towards Protestantism; 1547: Bp of Rochester; 1548: denied transubstantiation in favour of spiritual presence; 1547–53: engaged in carrying out reformation; 1550: Bp of London; in Vestiarian Controversy struck out v. **John Hooper** (q.v.) arguing that vestments were required by law to be worn by a bp at his consecration; 16 July 1553: Ridley denounced Mary I in sermon at Paul's Cross; depr. of see; 1554: public disputation at Oxf. by **Cranmer**, **Ridley** and **Latimer** (q.v.); declared heretic and excom.; refused to recant and continued Protestant writings; 16 Oct. 1555: burnt at stake, Oxf. J. Ridley, *Nicholas Ridley: A Biography*, 1957.

RIDOLFI Roberto di (1531–1612): Italian Catholic banker in Marian London. Remained influential in Elizabeth's reign and from 1567 was secret papal agent. 18 Nov. 1531: b. Florence, s. of Pagnozzo di Giovanfrancesco Ridolfi & h.w. Maddalena (Gondi); 1562: settled in London as merchant; 1568: plotted to m. Duke of Norfolk to Mary of Scotland, to secure her eventual succession to the English throne and the rest. of Catholicism; Oct. 1569: placed under house arrest by Walsingham; Jan. 1570: released; Mar. 1571: Ridolfi travelled in Eur. to secure support for plot; abroad when the scheme was uncovered & Norfolk & others arrested; retired to Florence, where he held office; 18 Feb. 1612: d. in Florence.

RIZZIO (RICCIO), David (?1533–66): Italian-born French secretary to Queen Mary Stuart; *cause célèbre*. 1533: b. Pancalieri, nr Turin, s. of musician; autumn 1561: secretary to Savoy ambass. to Scotland; Jan. 1562: valet de chambre to Mary Queen of Scots; Dec. 1564: Mary's sec. for French correspondence; became powerful; roused jealousy; **Darnley** suspects Mary pregnant by Rizzio; 9 Mar. 1566: seized in Mary's presence, murdered by Darnley and Morton.

ROBSART Amy (m. name Dudley) Lady (1532–60): gentlewoman & *cause célèbre*; 7 June 1532: only child & h. of gentleman of reformed opinions, Sir John and Elizabeth (Scott) Robsart of Norfolk; 4 June 1550: m. **Robert Dudley** (q.v.) at Sheen w. an annuity of £20 & the promise of her father's estates at his d.; 1553–54: living at Somerset House (where her husband was Keeper) & given permission to visit Dudley in Tower of London; Oct. 1554: Dudley released but lost his lands because of attainder; 1557–59: Amy living at Throcking, Herts; spring 1559:

rumours circulate that Dudley was seeking to murder her; not at court w. Robert but moved from place to place; Dudley never saw her after summer 1559; Dec. 1559: took up residence at Cumnor Place, Berks (nr Oxf.) possibly because Dudley had been app'd Lieut. of Windsor Castle; 8 Sept. 1560: Amy found dead; 22 Sept. 1560: bur. at St Mary's, Oxf.; Dudley not present; rumours first of suicide & then of murder; 1584: *Leicester's Commonwealth* alleged that Leicester had had her murdered.

ROGERS John (c. 1500–55): Cambr.-edu. Biblical translator and first Protestant martyr of Mary's reign. c. 1500: b. nr Birmingham; 1526: BA Pembroke College, Cambr.; 1532: R of Holy Trinity the less, London; 1534: Chaplain to English House of merchants at Antwerp; 1535: saved Tyndale's work when he was arrested; 1536/37: m. Flemish Adriana de Weyden (alias Pratt); 11 children; 1537: printed version of the Bible (known as the Matthew Bible), including Tyndale's New Testament and incomplete Old Testament, adding work from Coverdale and a preface, commentary, calendar and almanack by himself; Aug. 1537: imported copies into Eng.; 1539: Great Bible used it as main source; Nov. 1540: matric. at Wittenberg Uni.; assoc. of Philip Melancthon; late 1543: pastor of Meldorf; 1548: returned to London; 13 May 1550: V of St Sepulchre's, London; c. 1551: Divinity lecturer at St Paul's; 16 Aug. 1553: house arrest; Jan. 1553/54: impr. in Newgate for opposition to Mary I; Protestant confession of faith; 4 Feb. 1554/55: burned at Smithfield.

ROPER Margaret (née More) (c. 1505–44): humanist translator. c. 1505: b. London, eldest child of Sir **Thomas More** & 1st w. Jane Colt; edu. by tutors in his 'school' in. Latin, Greek, rhetoric, philosophy, logic, mathematics & astronomy, etc. Alongside two sisters, a brother, a stepsister, a ward & the daughter of her nurse; fêted by Erasmus & Pole as Latin scholar, poet & transl.; 2 July 1521: m. William Roper, a Lutheran; lived w. the Mores; 1523: Elizabeth b.; 1524: More household moved to Chelsea; 1525: pub'd transl. of **Erasmus**' treatise on the Paternosters as *A Devoute Treatise upon the Paternoster*; five further children (incl. **Mary (Bassett)**, Thomas, Margaret & Anthony); 1528: serious illness; 1534: visited father in prison & communicated his views; 6 July 1535: retrieved More's head after exec. & hauled before PC for so doing. R.M. Warnicke, *Women of the English Renaissance and Reformation*, 1983.

RUSSELL (Lady) Elizabeth (nee Co(o)ke; m. name Hoby) (1528–1609): humanist linguist, translator, courtier and patron; 1528: b. 3rd dau. of Sir **Anthony Cooke** & **Anne (Fitzwilliam) Cooke** of Gidea Hall, Essex; humanist edu.; 27 June 1558: m. (i) Sir Thomas Hoby, famous for transl. into English Castiglione's *The Courtier*; 1560–64: two s. & one dau.; 13 July 1566: Thomas d. while they were in France she composed classical epitaph; Thomas Posthumous Hoby b. (see **Hoby (Lady) Margaret**); 23 Dec. 1574: m. (ii) John, Lord Russell, heir to Francis Russell, 2nd Earl of Bedford; two daus, Anne & Elizabeth; patron of **John Dowland** (q.v.), etc.; 1592: entertained Queen at Bisham Abbey; June 1600: Elizabeth I attended m. of dau. Anne Russell to Henry Lord Herbert; 1605: pub'd transl. from French, *A way of reconciliation touching the true nature and substance of the body and blood of Christ in the sacrament*; d. May or June 1609.

RUSSELL (2nd Earl of Bedford), Francis (1526/27–85): Lord President of Wales & highly influential courtier. 1526/27: b. s. & h. of John Russell, 1st Earl of Bedford & h.w. Anne (Sapcotes); edu. King's College, Cambr. but left without degree; 1545 & 1547: M.P. Bucks; 1546: m. Margaret (St John) wid. Gostwick; seven children; 1553: supported **Jane Grey**; 1553–55: impr.; pardoned; 1555: inherited title; 1555–57: travelled in Europe; winter 1556/57: developed friendship w. Heinrich Bullinger in Zurich; 1557: returned to Eng.; 1558: PC; 27 Aug. 1562: Margaret d; 1564: Warden of Scottish Marches & KG; Aug. 1565: Lieut.-Gen. in

the North; 1566: m. Bridget (Hussey) widow of (i) Sir Richard Morison & (ii) Henry Manners, 2nd Earl of Rutland; 1576: Lord President of Wales; 1585: d.

RUSSELL (1st Earl of Bedford), John (c. 1485–1555): influential courtier and magnate. c. 1485: b. Dorset, s. & h. of James Russell & 1st w. Alice (Wise); 1520: at Field of Cloth of Gold; 1522: accompanied Thomas Howard, Earl of Surrey to France; c. 1525/6: m. Anne (Sapcotes), wid. (i) John Broughton & (ii) Sir Richard Jerningham; she brought w. her three Broughton children & three manors, incl. Chenies, Bucks; 1526/27: s. & h. Francis b.; 1527: ambass. to Pope Clement; 1529: M.P.; 1536: active in suppr. Pilgrimage of Grace; 1537: Comptroller of King's Household; 1538: PC; 9 Mar. 1539: cr. Baron Russell; 18 May 1539: KG; 20 July 1540: Lord Admiral; 1542, 1547 and 1553: Lord Privy Seal; 1549: helped suppr. Western Rebellion; 1550: Earl of Bedford; 1553: began by supporting **Jane Grey** but joined **Queen Mary**; 1554: ambass. to Spain to conclude m. treaty with Philip. D. Willen, *John Russell, First Earl of Bedford: One of the King's Men*, Royal Historical Society, 1981.

S

SADLER (SADLEIR) (Sir) Ralph (1507–87): statesman and diplomat. 1507: b. Warwickshire, s. & h. of Henry Sadler, steward of Sir Edward Belknap & later of Thomas Grey, 2nd marquess of Dorset; by 1521: Thomas Cromwell's service; by 1535: m. Ellen (Mitchell) Barre; three s. & four daus; 18 Apr. 1540: Sadler app'd principal secretary (w. Wriothesley); 1545: Margaret's husb. Matthew Barre (previously thought dead) re-appeared & m. to Sadler decl'd bigamous & children illegit.; 1547: app'd to Council of Regents for Edward VI's minority; spent

Mary Tudor's reign in retirement; during Elizabeth's reign one of Cecil's right-hand men; 1568: Chancellor, Duchy of Lancaster; 1572 & 1584: Warder of Mary of Scotland; 1586: on commission that condemned Mary to d.; 30 Mar. 1587: d. A.J. Slavin, *Politics and Profit: A Study of Sir Ralph Sadler, 1507–47*, Cambridge, 1966.

ST GERMAIN Christopher, of Coventry (1460–1540/41): legal writer. 1460: b. Warws s. & h. of Sir Henry St German of Shilton, Warws & h.w. Anne (Tyndale); c. 1480: adm. Inn of Chancery & then Middle Temple; by 1502: called to bar; 1511–28: poss. employed as legal editor; 1528: pub'd in Latin *Dialogus de fundamentis legum Anglie et de conscientia* (commonly known as 'Doctor and Student') which, as title suggests, explored relationship betw. fundamentals of Eng. law and conscience; 1530: The Second Dialogue pub'd in Eng.; 1530 or 1531: Robert Wyer pub'd Eng. version of 1st Dialogue; c. 1532: Wyer pub'd 2nd edition w. additions; its justification of Parl. competence in King's Great Matter led to arguments w. Sir **Thomas More**; book soon took on life as a law student primer; 1540/41: d. London.

SALESBURY William (c. 1517 to c. 1580): Oxf.-edu. Protestant humanist scholar; translator of the New Testament into Welsh. b. c. 1517: 2nd s. of Ffwg Salesbury & Annes (ap Gruffydd ap Robin o Gochwillan); edu. locally & at Broadgates Hall, Oxf.; learned in Welsh, Hebrew, Greek, English, French, German; 1547: *A Dictionary in Englyshe and Welshe* 1550: at Thavies Inn (junior inn of court); 1550: pub'd bilingual *Ban wedy i dynny air yngair allan o hen gyfreith Howel Dda . . . A certain case extract out of the auncient law of Hoel Da* (historical justification for clerical marriage), & *The Baterie of the Popes Botereulx, Commonlye called the High Altare*; also *A Briefe and a Playne Introduction* (on Welsh pronunciation; pub'd 2nd ed'n in 1567); m. Catrin (Price) Llwyd; three children; 1551: *Kynniver llith a Ban* (transl. epistles & gospels for Sundays & holy days); 1555–58: exile, Frankfurt; 1567: *Lliver*

gweddi gyffredin (Welsh transl. of 1564 Book of Common Prayer); 7 Oct. 1567: *Testament Newydd ein Arglwydd Iesv Christ*, annotated Welsh transl. of New Testament in collaboration w. **Richard Davies**, Bp of St David's & Thomas Huet (see also **William Morgan** (q.v.); various humanist works, some of which were translations into Welsh; 1568–74: Llysieulyfr (a herbal that paraphrased works by Wiliems & Turner; c. 1580: d. R. Brinley Jones, *William Salesbury*, 1994.

SALISBURY Margaret, Countess of (see **Pole**, Lady Margaret).

SALISBURY Robert, Earl of (see **Cecil**, Robert).

SCOTS, Mary Queen of (see Section 12.1: Monarchs and their consorts).

SANDYS, Edwin (c. 1519–88): Marian exile and biblical scholar who became the nepotistic and quarrelsome Protestant (but anti-Presbyterian) Bp of Worcester and London and Archbp of York; b. Lancs (now Cumbria) fifth s. of William Sandys (d. 1548) & h.w. Margaret (Dixon); perhaps edu. alongside **Edmund Grindal** (q.v.) at Rottington Hall, St Bees; 1532 or 1533: began edu. at St John's Cambr. under John Bland; 1539: BA; 1541: MA; 1542: Proctor; 1547: BTh; 1547: Master of St Catharine's College; presumably ordained pr. before 1548; 1549: DTh; 1552: Vice-Chancellor of Cambr.; 1548: V of Haversham, Bucks; 1549: Prebendary at Peterborough; 1552: Prebendary at Carlisle; m. (i) cousin, Mary Sandys of Woodham Ferrers, Essex; July 1553: supported cause of Lady **Jane Grey** (q.v.), 25 July 1553: impr. in Tower; subsequently, after a move to the Marchalsea, escaped into exile in (i) Antwerp, (ii) Strasbourg & (iii) Zurich; 1554: d. of Mary & a son; engaged in biblical scholarship; 15 Jan. 1559: returned to London; 19 Feb. 1559: m. (ii) Cicely (Wilford) (d. 1611), of Cranbrook, Kent, sister of a fellow exile; seven s. & two daus; Aug.–Nov. 1559: engaged in royal visitation of northern province; 21 Dec. 1559: consecrated Bp of Worcester;

energetic preaching bp; quarrels with local JPs, etc.; 1563: probably drafted convocation paper seeking to abolish cross in baptism & to allow baptism by midwives; active parliamentarian; 1566: active in demand for Elizabeth to m. and settle succession; coined term 'Bloody Mary' to describe Mary I; 13 July 1570: transl. Bp of London; 1572: led demand for Elizabeth to deal severely with Mary Queen of Scots; preached anti-Catholic sermons in Elizabeth's reign but had fraught relations w. London's Puritan preachers, notably Edward Dering; zealous in preventing celebration of Mass at Portuguese embassy; also prosecuted congregation of Dutch Anabaptists; 1574: evaded Queen's request that the 'prophesyings' be quashed; 8 Mar. 1577: transl. Archbp of York; encouraged Protestant preaching through estab't of synods and weekly lectures; persecuted Catholics (esp. leading York citizens & their wives, e.g. **Margaret Clitheroe** (q.v.)) through his high commission; *cause célèbre* of quarrel w. **William Whittingham** (q.v.) and Dean Matthew Hutton of York; campaigned v. usury; 1581–84: involved in Stapleton scandal, in which Sandys was blackmailed and publicly embarrassed during Sir Robert Stapleton's attempt to secure archiepisc. lands for himself; summer 1588: quarrelled w. close friend Toby Matthew, dean of Durham; awarded his young sons leases and offices to the detriment of the see; 10 July 1588: d. & bur. in Southwell Minster.

SEYMOUR (Duke of Somerset), Edward (c. 1500–52): uni.-edu. brother of Queen Jane Seymour. c. 1500: b. ?Wilts, eldest surviving s. of Sir John Seymour & h.w. Margery (Wentworth); c. 1518: m. (i) Katherine (Fillol); 2 s.: John & Edward; 1520s & 1530s: royal service; 12 Sept. 1531: esquire of body to Henry VIII; c. 1535: m. (ii) Anne (Stanhope), descendant of Edward III; four s. & six daus; Oct. 1535: entertained King & **Anne Boleyn** at Elvetham, Hants; 30 May 1536: Henry m. sister **Jane Seymour**; 7 July 1536: cr. Gov. of Jersey; 22 May 1537: PC; 15 Oct. 1537: carried Princess Eliz. at Edward's baptism; 18 Oct. 1537: cr. Earl of Hertford; 1539: b. of

Edward (later Earl of Hertford); 1540: b. of Henry; 1541: b. of Jane; 9 Jan. 1541: KG; 28 Dec. 1542: Lord High Admiral; 16 Feb. 1543: Lord Great Chamberlain; 1547: decisive victory over Scots at Musselburgh; with Paget concealed d. of Henry VIII until Edward VI brought to London; 1 Feb. 1547: made Protector; 17 Feb. 1547: cr. Duke of Somerset; 1549: attainder & exec. of brother Thomas Seymour lost him much popularity; attempted to deal w. econ. & agrarian problems; 1548–49: rebellions v. his religious reforms; 1549: impr. in Tower; 1550: deposed as Protector; Feb. 1550: pardoned & gradually rest. to some influence; Oct. 1551: arrested on charge of conspiracy to murder Warwick; 1 Dec. 1551: tried; 22 Jan. 1552: beheaded on Tower Hill.

SEYMOUR (Earl of Hertford), Edward (?1539–1621): *cause célèbre.* ?1539: b. s. of Edward Seymour, Duke of Somerset, & 2nd w. Anne (Stanhope); edu. alongside Edward VI; 1547: knighted at coronation of Edward VI; 1552: succeeded to dukedom but title & estates forfeited; 1559: cr. Baron Beauchamp & Earl of Hertford; 1560: contracted secret m. w. Lady Catherine Grey without Queen's permission 1561: imprisoned in Tower for this offence; 1571: released; 1572: adm. Gray's Inn; Sept. 1591: Queen's progress to Hertford's Hampshire home marked return to favour; 1602, 1608: Lord Lieut. of Somerset & Wiltshire; 1605: ambass. extraordinary to Brussels; 1612–19: High Steward of revenues to Queen Anne, Consort of James I.

SEYMOUR (Lady, later Queen) Jane (1508/09–37) (see Section 12.1: Monarchs and their consorts).

SEYMOUR Thomas (?1509–49) (Baron Seymour of Sudeley): diplomat, soldier & Lord High Admiral. c. 1508: b. younger s. of Sir John Seymour & h.w. Margery (Wentworth); 2 Oct. 1536: gent. of privy chamber; 1538: diplo. mission to Francis I; 1542: diplo. mission to Vienna; 30 Apr. 1543: resident ambass. to Low Countries; summer 1543: commander of army in Low Countries;

18 Apr. 1544: Master of Ordnance for life; 1547: PC, KG, cr. Baron Seymour of Sudeley & Lord High Admiral; c. May/June 1547: secret m. to Katherine Parr; formed project to m. Jane Grey to Edward VI; Sept. 1548: Mary b.; 5 Sept. 1548: Katherine d.; attempt to m. Elizabeth; 17 Jan. 1549: arrested & impr. in Tower; 20 Mar. 1549: exec. for tr. G.W. Bernard, *The Tudor Nobility*, 1992.

SHAKESPEARE William (1564–1616): grammar-school edu. actor, poet and playwright; Apr. 1564: b. Stratford, Warws, s. & 3rd child of John Shakespeare, glover, & h.w. Mary (Arden); edu. Stratford on Avon GS; poss. served as country schoolmaster in Lancs prior to making career in London as an actor & playwright in the later 1580s; 27 Nov. 1582: m. Anne Hathaway of Shottery; May 1583: Susanna b.; Feb. 1585: twins Hamnet & Judith b. See Chapter 4: The world of learning.

SHELTON Mary (Mary Lady Heveningham, Mary Appleyard) (1510–70/71): cousin and maid of honour to Queen **Anne Boleyn**; co-edited Devonshire ms miscellany of courtly poetry (BL, Add. MS 17492). 1510: b. youngest dau. of Sir John Shelton & h.w. Anne Boleyn, aunt of future Queen & governess to Princess Mary from 1533; maid of honour to Anne Boleyn, her cousin; (see also **Margaret Douglas** & **Mary Howard** (q.v.); 1535 & 1538: rumoured to have been Henry VIII's mistress; c. 1546: m. (i) Sir Anthony Heveningham (1507–1557); name linked with Earl of Surrey; had five children w. Hevingham;.1558: m. (ii) Philip Appleyard (b. c. 1528); 8 Jan. 1572: d. Suffolk.

SHREWSBURY Elizabeth Countess of (see **Hardwick** Lady Bess of).

SIDNEY (Sir) Henry (1529–86): Lord Deputy of Ireland and President of Wales. 20 July 1529: b. London eldest surviving s. of Sir William Sidney, later steward to Prince Edward, and h.w. Anne (Pagenham), wid. Thomas Fitzwilliam; 1538: companion to Prince Edward; 1547: gentleman of Edward's privy chamber; 1547: M.P. Brackley; 29 Mar. 1551: m. Mary Dudley, dau. of Northumberland; Oct. 1551: knighted; early 1553: sent on diplo. mission to France; 1553: M.P. Kent; July 1553: pardoned by Mary I; Nov. 1554: Philip b. (King Philip II his godfather); 1556: 2nd in command to brother-in-law Thomas Radcliffe, Lord Dep. of Ireland; 1559: **Mary Sidney**, Lady of Chamber to Eliz.; 1561: intrigued for m. betw. brother-in-law **Robert Dudley** & Queen; early 1560: app'd Lord President of Council in Wales; May 1561: moved to Ludlow as Lord President; 1566–71: 1st term as Dep. of Ireland; 1575–78: 2nd term as Dep. of Ireland; 1575: PC; 1577: dau. Mary m. Henry Herbert, 2nd Earl of Pembroke; Mar. 1578: having failed to make Ireland self-sufficient, recalled from Ireland; Sept. 1578: left Ireland; 1582: contemplated return but Queen refused him the peerage he demanded; 5 May 1586: d. at Ludlow.

SIDNEY (Countess of Pembroke, m. name Herbert), Mary (1561–1621): well-edu. writer and patron. 27 Oct. 1561: b. Tickenhall, nr Bewdley, Worcs, 3rd dau. of Sir Henry Sidney & h.w. Mary (Dudley); sister of Sir Philip & Robert Earl of Leicester; knew French, Italian and Latin; famed as needlewoman & musician; 1575: joined Court; 21 Apr. 1577: m. widower Henry Herbert, 2nd Earl of Pembroke as 3rd w.; four children; 1593: Philip Sidney wrote *Countess of Pembroke's Arcadia, Astrophil & Stella*, etc. at the Pembroke's Wilton home; 1586–88: in mourning at Wilton; 1593 & 1598: edited Philip Sidney's *Arcadia*; 1592: William Ponsonby pub'd her transl. from French, *A Discourse of Life and Death* (Philippe de Mornay), and *Antonius*; completed Philip Sidney's metric version of the Psalms; 1595: pub'd elegy for Philip Sidney, 'The Doleful Lay of Clorinda'; 1602: pub'n of 'A dialogue between two shepherds, *Thenot* and *Piers*, in praise of *Astrea*', written for Queen's visit to Wilton in 1599; encouraged members of household to write at what John Aubrey called the 'college' at Wilton, notably her niece & goddaughter Lady Mary Wroth;

others, such as Samuel Daniel, Nicholas Breton, **Thomas Nashe** & Thomas Churchyard, acknowledged her active patronage; Jan. 1601: husb. d. 25 Sept. 1621: d.; bur. Salisbury cathedral. N. Mears, 'Politics in the Elizabethan Privy Chamber: Lady Mary Sidney and Kat Ashley' in J. Daybell (ed.), *Women and Politics in Early Modern England, 1450–1700*, Aldershot, 2004, pp. 67–82.

SIDNEY (Sir) Philip (1554–86): Oxf.-edu. poet, statesman and soldier. 1554: b. s. & h. of Sir Henry Sidney & h.w. Mary (Dudley); brother of Mary, Countess of Pembroke & Robert Sidney, Earl of Leicester; edu. tutor (Jean Tassell); 17 Oct. 1564: adm. Shrewsbury School; 2 Feb. 1567: adm. Gray's Inn; 1568: adm. Christ Church, Oxf.; Aug. 1569: contracted to m. Anne Cecil; 1571: she m. Earl of Oxf.; 1572: in France to sign Treaty of Blois; 1573–75: European tour; 9 July 1575: on royal progress to Kenilworth; 1577: diplo. mission to Rudolph II; 1578–81: composed *Old Arcadia*; 1579: ms tract counselled Queen not to m.; 1581–82: revised Old Arcadia at Wilton; 1581: *Astrophil and Stella*, inspired by Lady Penelope Rich; 1582–83: composed sonnets & *A Defence of Poetry*; 13 Jan. 1583: knighted; 21 Sept. 1583: m. Frances, dau. of **Francis Walsingham**; 1584: composed *New Arcadia*; *Defence of the Earl of Leicester*; Nov. 1584: M.P. Kent; 1585: joint Master of Ordnance; anti-Catholic policies; Oct. 1585: Elizabeth b.; 1585: Governor of Flushing; 1586: wounded, battle of Zutphen; 17 Oct. 1586: d. Works circulated in mss & mostly pub'd posthumously. M. Foss, *Tudor Portraits*, 1973.

SIMNEL Lambert (?1476/77–1525): impostor & focus of rebellion v. Henry VII. c. 1476/77: ?b. Oxf. s. of Thomas Simnel, Flemish joiner; 1486/87: impersonated Edward, Earl of Warwick, nephew of Edward IV, in attempt to win Crown from Henry VII; 1487: crowned King Edward VI in Dublin; plotted v. Henry VII with Margaret of Burgundy, sister of Edward IV, Earl of Lincoln and Lord Lovell; Henry VII paraded real Earl of Warwick in London; 16 June 1487: Lambert Simnel's

troops fought Battle of Stoke (near Newark), last battle of Wars of Roses; Simnel made a scullion and later a falconer; 1525: still living & attended the funeral of **Thomas Lovell**.

SKELTON John (c. 1460–1529): Cambr.-edu. poet. c. 1460: b. poss in Yorkshire; claimed Cambr. edu.; highly regarded poet during his day; classicist, although not a humanist, known for translation from the Latin; moved from early, quite elaborate and sophisticated verse (1498: 'The Bowge of Court') to bawdy, rough and caustic works deliberately resisting modern cultivated styles (e.g. 1520s: 'Colin Clout', 'Speak Parrot' and 'Why Come Ye Not to Court', all attacks on **Wolsey** and abuses in the church, and 1517: 'The Tunning of Elinor Rumming'); 1489: entered Holy Orders; Court Poet to Henry VII; tutor to Prince Henry (VIII); d. 1529.

SMITH (Sir) Thomas (1513–77): prominent Cambr.-edu. humanist, diplomat & political theorist. 23 Dec. 1513: b. Saffron Walden, 2nd s. of John Smith, sheep farmer, & h.w. Anne (Charnock); 1526: adm. Queens' College, Cambr.; 1530: BA; 1532: MA; 1533: King's Scholar & Public Orator; 1540: Professor of Civil Law; 1540–42: studied in Orleans, Paris & Padua; 1542/3: LLD & DCL; 1543: Vice-Chancellor; Mar. 1547: Clerk to PC; Dec. 1547: Provost of Eton; Jan. 1548: Dean of Carlisle; Apr. 1548: Secretary of State; 15 Apr. 1548: m. (i) Elizabeth (Carkeke); 1549: wrote *Discourse of the Commonweal* (formerly attributed to John Hales); Apr. 1549: knighted; 13 Oct. 1549: depr. of secretaryship when Somerset fell & impr. in Tower; 22 Feb. 1550: released; 3 Aug. 1553: Elizabeth d.; 23 July 1554: m. (ii) Philippa (Wilford) wid. of Sir John Hampden; friendship w. Stephen Gardiner protected him under Mary I; 1559: M.P. Liverpool; Apr. 1561: circulated ms 'Dialogue on the queen's marriage'; 1562–65: wrote & distributed widely in ms *De republica Anglorum*; 1562–66: ambass. to France; 19 Apr. 1572: concluded Tr. of Blois; 13 July 1572: Secretary of State; spring 1573: Keeper of Privy Seal; 1571–75: abortive colonisation project in Ireland; 12 Aug. 1577: d.; posthumous pub'ns: 1581: pub'n of *Discourse of the Commonweal*; 1583: *De Republica Anglorum*.

SMYTHSON, ROBERT (1534/35–1614): architect and master mason. c. 1534/35: b. poss. Westmorland; served apprenticeship & learned to draw in London & was member of London Masons' Company; mid-1560s: ?worked for Sir **Francis Knollys** at Caversham House, Reading; 1568–80: master mason for Sir John Thynne at Longleat; he m. & estab'd a dynasty of architects & masons incl. his s. John & grands. Huntingdon who later worked for the Cavendish family; 1576: involved in altering Wardour Castle, Wilts; 1580–88: designed & executed building of the extraordinary Wollaton House, Notts, for Sir Francis Willoughby; stayed on as surveyor; also worked on many other houses, for which his architectural drawings survive, incl. Worksop Manor, Notts (remodelled c. 1585), Hardwick Hall, Derbyshire (1590–97) – his masterpiece – & Burton Agnes, Yorks (c. 1601–10); a number of other houses have been attributed to him on the basis of design & connection; he drew on both classical & native Gothic traditions; 1614: d. at Wollaton & was bur. there. M. Girouard, *Robert Smythson and the Elizabethan country house*, new ed'n, 1983.

SOMERSET Edward Seymour, Duke of (see **Seymour Sir Edward**).

SOUTHWELL (Lady) Anne (1574–1636): Protestant poet and letter writer. Aug. 1574: b. eldest child of Thomas Harris M.P. & Sergeant-at-law; & h.w. Elizabeth (Pomeroy); edu. in theology, literature, rhetoric and music; 24 June 1594: m. (i) Thomas Southwell, of Spixworth, Norfolk; 23 July 1603: Southwell knighted; literary connections w. John Donne, Robert Southwell, William Cornwallis, etc.; accomp. Southwell to Munster; 1626: Southwell d.; m. (ii) Henry Sibthorpe; Sibthorpe encouraged her writing & collected her poems; she advocated mutuality in m.; 2 Oct. 1636: d.

SOUTHWELL Robert SJ (1561–95): poet and martyr. 1561: b. Norfolk, 3rd s. of Richard Southwell, gent. & courtier, & h.w. Bridget (Copley); June 1576: adm. Eng. College, Douai; 1578–80: Novitiate SJ in Rome; 18 Nov. 1580: took vows; 1584: BA Eng. College, Rome; spring 1584: ord. pr.; July 1586: returned to Eng. w. Henry Garnet SJ; SJ mission in London, Sussex & North; 1589: Chaplain to Countess of Arundel & set up printing press at her house in Spitalfields; 1592: arrested, imprisoned & harshly tortured by **Topcliffe**; Feb. 1595: tried for tr.; 21 Feb. 1595: hanged at Tyburn.

SPEED John (1551/52–1629): cartographer & historian. 1551/52: b. Farndon, Cheshire, before their m. s. of John Speed, merchant tailor, & Elizabeth (Cheynye); 1570: m. Susanna (Draper); twelve s. & six daus; 10 Sept. 1580: made free of Merchant Taylors' Company; 1598: presented maps to Eliz. I; 1600: presented maps to Merchant Taylors' Company; made maps of several English counties; 1606: moved in same circles as **Camden**; 1611: pub'd together *History of Great Britain* & accompanying atlas volume, *The Theatre of the Empire of Great Britain*; 1629: d.

SPENSER Edmund (1552–99): patriotic Cambr.-edu. Protestant poet of tremendous influence. Invented Spenserian stanza. Unknown origins; claimed kinship w. Althorp Spensers but probably descended from John Spenser of Burnley; 1560s: edu. Merchant Taylors' School under **Richard Mulcaster** (q.v.); 20 May 1569: matric. Pembroke College, Cambr. as sizar; 1573: BA; 1576: MA; Secretary to Bp of Rochester; 1578: entered household of Earl of Leicester & joined Sir Philip Sidney's circle; spring 1579: pub'd *The Shepheardes Calender*; 27 Oct. 1579: m. Maccabaeus (Childe) at St Margaret's, Westminster; one s. & one dau.; 1580: secretary to Lord Grey de Wilton, Lord Deputy of Ireland; 1589: completed the sophisticated, serious & pictorially vivid allegory, *The Faerie Queene*; c. 1592: Maccabaeus d.; 1594: m. (ii) Elizabeth

(Boyle), relative of Richard Boyle, later Earl of Cork; c. 1595: s. Peregrine b.; 1598: recalled to London; 1599: d.

STAFFORD (3rd Duke of Buckingham), Edward (1478–1521): courtier. 1478: b. s. & h. of Henry, 2nd Duke of Buckingham (exec. 1483) & Katherine (Woodville); 1485: royal ward in care of Lady Margaret Beaufort, his great-aunt; Dec. 1489: m. Northumberland's eldest dau. Eleanor Percy; 1501: Henry b.; 1509: PC; 1520: at Gravelines with Henry VIII; 1521: executed on trumped up charges.

STAFFORD (2nd Duke of Buckingham), Henry (1455–83): supporter of Richard III. 4 Sept. 1455: b. s. & h. of Humphrey, styled Earl of Stafford (d. 1458) & h.w. Lady **Margaret Beaufort** (q.v.); grandson of Humphrey Stafford, 1st Duke; 10 July 1460: inherited dukedom; c. 1465: m. Queen's sister, Katherine Woodville; four or five children; Henry & Katherine raised & edu. in Queen's household; 1483: Chamberlain at Richard III's coronation; 1483: turned coat; captured & exec. at Salisbury; 7 Nov. 1485: wid. Katherine m. Jasper Tudor. C. Rawcliffe, *The Staffords*, 1978.

STAFFORD (10th Baron Stafford), Henry (Lord) (1501–63): courtier and servant of the Crown. 18 Sept. 1501: b. Penshurst, Kent, s. & h. of Edward Stafford, 3rd Duke of Buckingham & h.w. Eleanor (Percy); 1532: KB; 1547: M.P. Stafford; loyal conservative servant of all the Tudors from Henry VIII to Elizabeth. A.H. Anderson, 'Henry, Lord Stafford (1501–1563) in local and central government', *E.H.R.*, 78, 1963.

STANDISH (Bishop) Henry (d. 1535): *Cause célèbre*. Bp of London, FitzJames, tried to prevent Dr Horsey from being tried in a secular court over the Hunne case on the grounds than no cleric could be summoned before a secular court; Crown app'd Standish to plead its case in public debate at Blackfriars on 10 Mar. 1515; Standish did so successfully but summoned before Convocation to explain his action. At a further public debate Standish again defended the secular view. Then, at a meeting at Baynard's Castle, Henry VIII compromised by dropping charges against both Horsey and Standish. Standish was rewarded with the See of St Asaph and remained in favour with the King.

STANLEY (Sir) William (1435–95): supporter of Henry VII. 1435: b. 2nd s. of Thomas Stanley, 1st Baron Stanley & h.w. Joan (Goushill); brother of Thomas, 2nd Baron Stanley & Earl of Derby; 1465: m. Joan (Beaumont), wid. of John, Lord Lovell; 1483: Chief Justice of north Wales; 1485: deserted to support Henry Tudor decisively at Bosworth Field; 1485: KG and Lord Chamberlain; 1485: beheaded as supporter of Warbeck. B. Coward, *The Stanleys Lords Stanley and Earls of Derby, 1385–1672*, Chetham Society, 1983.

STOW (also **Stowe**) John (1524/25–1605): ?self-taught scholar, and highly productive and popular historian, topographer and chronicler. 1524/25: b. eldest child of Thomas Stow, tallow-chandler of London, and h.w. Elizabeth (Archer); 1547: made free of Merchant Taylors' Company; post-1549: m. Elizabeth; three daus; nothing known of his edu. but acquired good command of both English and Latin; 1561: pub'd *The workes of Geffrey Chaucer, newly printed, with divers addicions whiche were never in printe before*; 1565: *Summarie of Englyshe Chronicles*; controversy w. Richard Grafton over historical accuracy and plagiarism; 1568: edited and pub'd *Pithy Pleasaunt and Profitable Workes of Maister [John] Skelton*; 1569: Edmund Grindal, Bp of London, ordered his house searched, discovered number of suspect books and accused Stow of Catholic leanings; in fact identified himself w. the Elizabethan settlement through association with **Matthew Parker** (q.v.), **John Whitgift** (q.v.) and **Robert Dudley** (q.v.); 1584–85: surveyor of alehouses; financial problems; knowledgeable collector, copyist and preserver of medieval and contemporary manuscripts (including 'Historie of the

Arrivall of Edward IV in England' and William Lambarde's 'Perambulation of Kent') and books; probably 1st historian to make use of public records in his work; 1580: *Chronicles of England*; c. 1587: member of Society of Antiquaries; 1587: contrib. to 2nd ed'n of *Holinshed's Chronicles*; 1592: *Annales of England*; 1597: *Certaine worthy manuscript poems of great antiquity preserved long in the studie of a Northfolke gentleman*; 1598: *A Survey of London*; 1603: expanded version pub'd; 1605: d. B.L. Beer, *Tudor England Observed: The World of John Stow*, 1998.

STUART (Lady) Arbella or Arabella (m. name Seymour) (1575–1615): well-edu. noblewoman of royal lineage w. claim to throne; 1575: b. dau. of Charles Stuart, Earl of Lennox, & h.w. Elizabeth (Cavendish), and thus grand-dau. of **Bess of Hardwick** (q.v.), niece of **Mary Queen of Scots** (q.v.) & 1st cousin of James VI of Scotland; 1582: raised by Bess in Derbyshire & given excellent edu.; 1583–84: nego. m. w. Robert Dudley's s., Lord Denbigh, who d. in 1584; 1588: lady-in-waiting to Elizabeth I; sent from court to Bess's house in disgrace; 1603: James VI gave her a position at court; 1605: made godmother to Princess Mary; 22 June 1610: m. William Seymour, younger gradson of 1st Earl of Hertford; Seymour impr. & Arbella placed under house arrest; escaped but recaptured and impr. in Tower; 25 Sept. 1615: d. D.N. Durant, *Arbella Stuart, a Rival to the Queen*, 1978.

STUART (Lord) Henry (see Darnley, Earl of).

STUART (Queen) Mary (see Section 12.1: Monarchs and their consorts).

SUFFOLK Charles Duke of (see **Brandon** Charles).

SUFFOLK Henry Duke of (see **Grey** Henry).

SUFFOLK Katherine Duchess of (see **Bertie** Katherine).

SURREY Henry Howard Earl of (1516/17–47): soldier, humanist courtier and poet. 1516/17: b. s. & h. of Thomas Howard Earl of Surrey (later 3rd Duke of Norfolk) & Elizabeth (Stafford) Howard; brother of Mary (Howard) Fitzroy, Duchess of Richmond (q.v. **Howard Mary**); 1524: became known as Earl of Surrey; 1530–32: close companion of **Henry Fitzroy** (q.v.); 1529: suggested as husband of Princess Mary; Feb. 1532: contracted to m. Lady Frances de Vere, dau. of Earl of Oxf.; spring 1532: m. Frances de Vere; Oct. 1532: accompanied Henry VIII & Anne Boleyn to Calais to meet Francis I; left behind w. Richmond as sureties for the treaty; 1533: met many poets, etc. at Fontainebleu; Nov. 1533: Richmond m. Surrey's sister Mary; May 1536: Surrey presided at trials of Anne Boleyn & Viscount Rochford; July 1536: d. of Richmond; suspicions about Surrey's allegiance during the Pilgrimage of Grace; 1537: confined to Windsor Castle; Nov. 1537: rest. to court; 1539: converted to Protestantism by the Seymours; Feb. 1541: witnessed exec. of cousin **Katharine Howard** (q.v.); July 1542: impr. in Fleet for duelling; 7 Aug. 1542: released; Candlemas 1543: Surrey & Wyatt led 'night of misrule' in City of London as warning v. idolatry; Oct. 1543–44: sent to aid Emperor Charles V in war v. France; Aug. 1545: sent to defend Boulogne; Sept. 1545: cr. King's Lieut.-Gen. on sea and land for all Eng.'s continental possessions; 7 Jan. 1546: defeated at St Etienne & in disgrace; 21 Mar. 1546: summoned home; June 1546: proposed m. betw. Seymours & Howards to secure position & suggested that his sister Mary become Henry's mistress; 2 Dec. 1546: arrested; 12 Dec. 1546: impr. in Tower; 7 Jan. 1547: charged w. tr. for displaying royal arms as his own; 13 Jan. 1547: tried at common inquest at Guildhall; 19 Jan. 1547: beheaded at Tower Hill. W.A. Sessions, *Henry Howard, the Poet Earl of Surrey: A Life*, 1999.

T

TALLIS Thomas (c. 1505–85): musician, composer, gentleman and organist of Chapel

Royal, and founding father of English Protestant church music. Unknown origins & date of birth estimated; began edu. as chorister; 1530–35: organist at Benedictine Priory, Dover; 1537–38: singing-man & ?organist at St Mary-at-Hill church, London; 1538–40: Waltham Abbey, Essex; 1540–42: singing-man at Canterbury Cathedral; few surviving works from early period; 1543–85: gentleman (lay singing-man), Chapel Royal; composed & arranged for liturgy of Sarum rite under Henry VIII – probably incl. 'Gaude gloriosa Dei mater' (antiphon for six-part choir); composed for new repertory of the reformed liturgy under Edward VI – e.g. 'If ye love me', 'Hear the voice and prayer', & English version of 'Te Deum'; composed again for the Roman liturgy under Mary I; 1554: *Puer natus est nobis*, perhaps composed to celebrate supposed pregnancy of Mary; 'Salve intemerata'; m. (i) Joan Bury (wid. of Chapel Royal singing–man); 1575–85: organist of Chapel Royal (w. **William Byrd** (q.v.)); Jan. 1575: w. Byrd obtained 21-year royal licence to print music & music paper & to control imports of foreign printed music; 1575: *Cantiones quae ab argumento sacrae vocantur* (collection of Latin motets by Tallis and Byrd) – the only work printed under the licence – which brought together 17 of his earlier works); conforming member of Church of Eng. but evidence of RC sympathies, friendships and patronage; 23 Nov. 1585: d. P. Doe, *Tallis*, 2nd ed'n, 1976.

TAVERNER John (c. 1490–1545): musician and composer. Unknown origin; –1526: chorister & composer at Holy Trinity collegiate church, Tattershall, Lincs.; autumn 1525: app'd 1st master of choristers at Cardinal College, Oxf.; Oct. 1526–30: produced various works for the choir including *Mater Christi*; 1530–37: choirmaster at Boston, Lincs; poss. wrote his festal mass *Corona spinea* for Boston; 1538: withdrew from choir; c. 1538: m. Rose (Parrowe) a widow; cultivated favour w. Thomas Cromwell; 18 Oct. 1545: d. Boston.

TAYLOR Rowland (c. 1500–55): Cambr.-edu. civil lawyer, clergyman and Protestant martyr. c. 1500: b. Northumberland; 1530: B.CL., Pembroke College, Cambr.; 1534: D.CL.; 1531-38: Principal, Borden Hostel (for law students), Cambr.; 1528: Minor Orders; 1528–31: official of Archd. of Ely; c. 1534: m. Margaret; nine children; infl'd by William Turner and **Hugh Latimer** (q.v.); 1535–39: Commissary-general and chaplain to Latimer at Worcester; various eccles. benefices; July 1539: **Cranmer**'s chaplain; Apr. 1544: absentee R of Hadleigh, Suffolk; 1547: preacher at Royal Visitation; 1548: Archd. of Bury St Edmunds; 1551: commissioner to reform the eccles. laws; 1552: Archd. of Cornwall; July 1553: supported Lady **Jane Grey** (q.v.) & impr.; released but outspoken contempt for RC church led to further arrest; 9 Feb. 1555: executed on Aldham Common near Hadleigh.

THROCKMORTON (Sir) Francis (1554–84): Oxf.-edu. RC conspirator. 1554: b. s. of Sir John Throckmorton of Feckenham, Worcs (vice-president of Marian Council in Wales) & h.w. Margaret (Puttenham); 1572: matric. Hart Hall, Oxf.; 1576: m. Anne or Agnes & adm. to Inner Temple; 1578: brought before PC & impr. for Catholic practices; released; Nov. 1583: impr. & tortured for involvement in conspiracy on behalf of Mary of Scotland; 10 July 1584: exec. at Tyburn.

THROCKMORTON Job (1545–1601): Oxf.-edu. politician and evangelical pamphleteer. 1545: b. s. & h. of Clement Throckmorton of Hasely, Warws & h.w. Katherine (Vaux); 1566: BA Oxf.; 1572: M.P. East Retford; 1573: inherited father's estate; Jan. 1584: investigated activities of recusant William Skynner; 1586: M.P. Warwick; parl. speeches v. Mary Queen of Scots & in favour of Puritanism; 1586: possible author of 'Survey of the state of the ministry in Warwickshire'; 1588: heavy involvement in Marprelate tracts – comparison w. the only pamphlet definitely authored by him indicates that Job Throckmorton was Martin Marprelate; 1590:

tried for part in Marprelate; escaped punishment; 1594: *The Defence of Job Throkmorton Against the Slaunders of Maister Sutcliffe*; Feb. 1601: d. Leland. H. Carlson, *Martin Marprelate, Gentleman: Master Job Throkmorton Laid Open in his Colors*, 1981.

THYNNE (Lady) Joan (née Hayward) (1558–1612): gentlewoman renowned for management during m. of her family and estates. Aug. 1558: b. 3rd dau. of Sir Rowland Hayward, alderman and Lord Mayor of London, & 1st w. Joan (Tillesworth); 26 Feb. 1576: m. John Thynne, heir to Sir John Thynne of Longleat; Rowland Hayward settled Caus Castle, Salop, on them but its previous owner, Edward Lord Stafford, remained in possession until 1591; 1576–: Joan worked on legal disputes w. Stafford; 1591–1604: managed Caus Castle and instructed husband in family relationships and estate business, including farming; 1594: sought anulment of her elder son Thomas's secret m. to Maria, dau. of Lord Audley; 21 Nov. 1604: John Thynne d.; 1604–12: continued to manage estate and legal suits in chancery v. her s. Thomas on behalf of her other children; 3 Mar. 1612: d. A.D. Wall (ed.) *Two Elizabethan Women: Correspondence of Joan and Maria Thynne, 1575–1611*, Wilts Record Society, 38, 1983.

TOPCLIFFE Richard (1531–1604): interrogator and torturer. 14 Nov. 1531: b. s. & h. of Robert Topcliffe of Somerby, Lincs. & h.w. Margaret (Burgh); 1543: ward of uncle Sir Anthony Neville; 1548: adm. Gray's Inn; m. Jane (Willoughby) of Wollaton, whose niece was one of Princess Elizabeth's ladies; four s. & two daus; c. 1557: entered Elizabeth's service; Jan. 1570: raised men v. Northern rising; 1572: M.P. for Beverley; 1580: sought out recusants; 1582: began to acquire reputation for torturing suspects but little direct evidence; 1586–1604: M.P., Old Sarum; Aug. 1588: app'd to official commission to examine Catholic suspects; Jan. 1592: on similar commission; also sought out & arrested recusants; 1588 onwards: evidence of officially authorised torture, espec. in case of Robert Southwell; 1595: impr. for maligning PC; 1596: accused of arbitrary treatment of Gatehouse prisoners; Nov./Dec. 1604: d.

TOWNSHEND, LADY ANNE (née Bacon) (1573–1622): Puritan gentlewoman and patron. 1573: b. at Waxham, Norfolk eldest dau. & co-heiress of Sir Nathaniel Bacon & his 1st w. Anne (Gresham); edu. at home; c. 1590: edu. boarding school in Dickleborough, Norf.; Dec. 1593: m. John Townshend; 1595: Roger b.; ?1597: Stanhope b.; 1603: wid.; one dau.; benefactor of several Puritan clergy incl. John Goodwin in the early seventeenth century.

TRAVERS Walter (?1548–1635): Cambr.-edu. Presbyterian activist and author and provost of Trinity College, Dublin. ?1548: b. s. of Walter Travers, Nottingham goldsmith, & h.w. Anne; 1560–70: edu. Christ's & Trinity Colleges, Cambr.; 1565/6: BA; 1567: Junior Fellow; 1569: MA & Senior Fellow; 1567–70: persecuted by John Whitgift; 1570: resigned Fellowship & went to Geneva, where he was joined by brother (Robert) and **Thomas Cartwright** (q.v.), & made friends w. Theodore Beza; 1574: pub'd anon. *Ecclesiasticae disciplinae et Anglicanae ecclesiae ab illa aberrationis, plena e verbo Dei, et dilucida explicatio* & a separate Eng. transl.; 1576–78: in Oxf.; 1578: chaplain to Eng. Merchant Adventurers, Antwerp & ord. according to Dutch Calvinist practice; rebuked by Nicholas Loddington, Gov. of the Merchant Adventurers, for not using BofCP; protected by Sir **Francis Walsingham** (q.v.); July 1580: returned to Eng. to become chaplain to Burghley (q.v. **William Cecil**) & tutor to **Robert Cecil** (q.v.); 1581: Burghley secured him Deputy Master at Temple Church of Middle & Inner Temples; polemical writings v. papacy; 1583: selected as nonconformist spokesmen in debate w. Whitgift on conformity; 1585: Whitgift barred his preferment to Temple Church; Mar. 1586: Whitgift barred him from preaching; 1587: participated in production of 'Disciplina ecclesiae Dei verbo descripta', which was circulated widely (Book of Discipline: constitution for Eng. Presbyterian church); 1588: *Defence of the Ecclesiastical Discipline*; Mar. 1588: secretary of London Presbyterians (as successor to **John Field** (q.v.); 1590–92: escaped the impr. & interrogation meted out to other Presbyt. leaders; 5 June 1594–98: Provost of Trinity College, Dublin by Burghley's patronage; lived largely in retirement; 1635: d. S.J. Knox, *Walter Travers Paragon of Elizabethan Puritanism*, 1962.

TUDOR (Prince) Arthur (1486–1502) (see **Arthur** Tudor (Prince)).

TUDOR (Earl of Richmond), Edmund (?1430–56): founder of Tudor dynasty. c. 1430: b. s. & h. of Owen Tudor & Katherine of Valois, wid. of Henry V; half brother of Henry VI & brother of Jasper Tudor, Earl of Pembroke; 23 Nov. 1452: cr. Earl of Richmond; Mar. 1543: recognised as Henry VI's brother; 24 Mar. 1543: wardship of Margaret Beaufort, descendant of Edward III through John of Gaunt, granted to Richmond & Pembroke; by Nov. 1455: Edmund m. Margaret (aged 12); Aug. 1546: Edmund captured Carmarthen for Henry VI; but troops sent to arrest him; 1 Nov. 1456: Edmund d. of plague; Margaret (pregnant) took refuge at Pembroke castle; 28 Jan. 1457: Henry Tudor b. at Pembroke.

TUDOR (Earl of Pembroke and Duke of Bedford), Jasper (?1431–95): uncle of Henry VII. c. 1431: b. 2nd s. Owen Tudor & h.w. Katherine of Valois, wid. Henry V; 1542: cr. Earl of Pembroke; 1543: recognised as Henry VI's brother; 1456–: gave refuge to Margaret (Beaufort) Tudor & her s. Henry; championed Henry VI's cause in Wales; 1461: defeated by Edward IV at Mortimer's Cross; Owen Tudor exec. at Hereford; Jasper Tudor in exile; 1485: from France plotted invasion & overthrow of Richard III; 1485: cr. Duke of Bedford; 1492: Earl Marshal; helped put down insurrections of Simnel and Lovell & Stafford; 1492: commander in France; 1495: d. R.A. Griffiths and R.S. Thomas, *The Making of the House of Tudor*, 1993.

TUNSTALL (Bishop) Cuthbert (1474–1559): Oxf., Cambr. and Padua-edu. humanist, bp and statesman who during the Henrician revolution remained a Catholic by doctrine but supported the royal supremacy. 1474: b. Hackforth, Yorkshire, illegit. s. of Thomas Tunstal, later Richard III's squire of the body, & a dau. of Sir John Conyers of Hackforth who afterwards became his 2nd w.; 1516: Master of the Rolls; 1522–30: Bp of London; 1523: Keeper of Privy Seal; 1530–53 (depr.): Bp of Durham; 1537: President of Council of North; 1550: wrote *De Veritate Corporis et Sanguinis . . . in Eucharista* when in prison for inciting rebellion; Apr. 1554: rest. Bp of Durham; 1559: refused Oath of Supremacy to Elizabeth and was depr. & put under house arrest w. Archbp Parker; 18 Nov. 1559: d.

TUSSER Thomas (c. 1524–80): influential Eton and Cambr.-edu. agricultural author, musician and poet. c. 1524: b. Essex 4th s. of William Tusser & Isabella (Smith); singing-boy at collegiate chapel of Wallingford, Berks; chorister of St Paul's Cathedral; c. 1540: adm. Eton; 1543: King's College, Cambr.; 1543: moved to Trinity Hall; 1544 –c. 1552: service of William Paget as musician at court & at Beaudesert, Staffs; c. 1552: m. (i); innovative farmer at Cattiwade, Suffolk; began writing *A Hundreth Good Pointes of Husbandrie* aimed at tenant farmers; m. (ii) Amy (Moon); three s. & one dau.; farmed in West Dereham, Norfolk; 1557: pub'd *A Hundreth Good Pointes of Husbandrie*; 1562: pub'd enlarged version (covered women's labour); 1559: moved to Norwich as lay clerk or singing-man; 1573: pub'd greatly enlarged version as *Five Hundreth Points of Good Husbandry United to as many of Good Huswiferie* (see Chapter 4: World of learning); from 1573 was living either in Cambr. or London; 3 May 1580: d. G. Grigson (ed.), T. Tusser, *Five hundred points of good husbandry* facs. ed'n with introduction, 1984.

TYNDALE (alias Hychyns) William (c. 1494–1536): Oxf.-edu. Protestant reformer, linguist and Biblical translator. c. 1494: b. Gloucs of unknown parentage; three brothers – Richard, Edward & John; ?edu. at Lady Berkeley's GS, Wotton under Edge, nr Stinchcombe; 1512: BA Magdalen Hall, Oxf.; 1515: ord. deac. & pr.; 1515: MA; studied theology; 1516: used Erasmus's *Novum instrumentum* (Latin translation of the New Testament, with parallel Greek text) from which to instruct students and fellows of Magdalen College; became tutor to family of Sir John & Lady (Poyntz) Walsh, Little Sodbury, Gloucs (w. connections to **Anne Boleyn**); studied & began Eng. transl. of **Erasmus**'s Greek New Testament; also at Walsh's request made (lost) transl. of Erasmus's *Enchiridion militis Christiani* into English and helped convert the family to Protestantism; active preacher in Bristol; brought before consistory court for heresy; 1523: unsuccessfully sought patronage of **Cuthbert Tunstall** (q.v.) in London; 1523–24: stayed & studied in house of merchant **Humphrey Monmouth**, & preached incl. at St Dunstan-in-the-West, Fleet Street; Apr. 1524: travelled to Germany; 1525: began to pub. Eng. transl. of New Testament (made w. assistance of William Roy & **John Frith** (q.v.) & known as the Lutheran N.T.; printing press raided & Tyndale & Roy fled to Worms; 1526: pub'd complete (but anon.) Eng. New Testament transl. from Greek; Oct. 1526: Cuthbert Tunstall prohibited the Worms New Testament; 27 Oct. 1526: burned at St Paul's; May 1526: Archbp Warham orders bps to buy up & destroy copies; *A Compendious Introduction, Prologue or Preface unto the Epistle of Paul to the Romans*; May 1528: *The Parable of the Wicked Mammon*; 2 Oct. 1528: *The Obedience of a Christian Man*; 1530: pub'd Eng. transl.of Pentateuch from Hebrew; pub'd *The Practice* (trickery) *of Prelates* (also contained attack on Henry's divorce); *A Pathway to the Holy Scripture*; Jan. 1531: invited back to Eng. but refused; 1531: *An Answer unto Sir Thomas More's 'Dialogue'*; wrote (but did not pub.) *A Brief Declaration of the Sacraments* (1st pub'd in 1548); 1533: Wynken de Worde pub'd Tyndale's new transl. into English of *Enchiridion militis Christiani*; 1534: pub'd revised New Testament (this ed'n was owned by Anne Boleyn & greatly infl. the Eng. Bible of 1604);

May 1535: arrested & impr. for 16 months at Vilvorde Castle, near Brussels; c. 6 Oct. 1536: strangled & then burnt at stake; 1537: John Rogers pub'd Eng. Bible (known as Matthew's Bible) (by royal licence) – roughly two-thirds by Tyndale & one-third by **Coverdale** (q.v.); 1539: revised as Great Bible. D. Daniell, *William Tyndale: A Biography*, 1994.

U

UDALL John (?1560–92): Cambr.-edu. friend of John Penry; 1578: matric. Sizar, Christ's College, Cambr.; 1581: BA Trinity College, Cambr.; 1584: MA; friends w. John Penry; ord. deac. at Bromley; granted preaching licence by Grindal; 1584: lecturer, Kingston upon Thames; 1585: pub'd two vols of sermons; 1588: pub'd, anon., anti-episcopal *The State of the Church and A Demonstration*; 1588: depr. of position; late 1588: took up post in Newcastle; 1590: impr. for complicity in Marprelate; 1591: sentenced to d.; 1592: pardoned but d.; 1593: posthumous pub'n of Hebrew grammar and dictionary.

UDALL Nicholas (c. 1505–56): Headmaster of Eton. Author of first known English comedy, *Ralph Roister Doister*. 1504: b. Southampton of unknown parentage; 1534–41: Headmaster, Eton; 1537/8: paid for putting on plays at Court; V of Braintree, Essex; 1541: accused of **buggery**; impr. in Marshalsea; by 1554: had written *Ralph Roister Doister*; 1555: Headmaster of Westminster School; Dec. 1556: d.

V

VAVASOUR (m. names, Finch, Richardson) Anne (fl. 1580–1621): courtier; *cause célèbre*; dau. of Henry Vavasour of Copmanthorpe,

Yorks, & Margaret (Knyvet); 1580: gentle-woman of bedchamber to Elizabeth I; 1580: maid of honour; soon became mistress of Edward de Vere, 17th Earl of Oxf.; Mar. 1581: b. of s. in maids' chamber; De Vere & Anne impr. in Tower; their relationship the subject of contemporary poetry; c. 1590: m. John Finch; mistress of Sir **Henry Lee** (q.v.); bore Lee a son, Thomas Vavasour; she and Lee lived together at Ditchley and enter-tained James I's Queen at a lodge near Woodstock in 1608; 1611: Lee d. & left Anne a jointure worth £700; c. 1618: m. (ii) John Richardson bigamously; 1621: fined £2,000 for bigamy. E.K. Chambers, *Sir Henry Lee*, 1936.

VERGIL Polydore (?1470–1555): Italian papal official who gained royal patronage. 1502: came to Eng. as sub-collector for Peter's Pence; 1505: commissioned by Henry VII to write history of kingdom; 1508: Archdeac. of Wells.

VERNON (Countess of Southampton), Elizabeth (c. 1580–post-1655): maid of honour of Elizabeth I; secretly m. Henry Wriothesley, 3rd Earl of Southampton.

W

WALDEGRAVE Robert (c. 1554–1603/04): Protestant printer. c. 1554: b. s. of Richard Waldegrave, yeoman, of Blackley, Worcs; 24 June 1568: bound apprentice to William Griffith, stationer, of London, for eight years; c. 1580: m. Mary; six children by 1589; 1578: licensed to pub. a book of prayers: *The Castle for the Soul*; pub'd mainly Puritan religious & theological works, incl. works of **Laurence Chaderton** & **John Field** (q.v.); 1580s: impr. twice in Southwark; Feb. 1588: Star Chamber tried to close his press; 16 Apr. 1588: Stationers' Company confiscated his type & press & anonymous printing of John Udall's *The State of the Churche of England*

Laid Open . . . (otherwise known as 'Diotrephes') targeted by bps; May–June 1588: took refuge with **John Penry** (q.v.) in home of **Elizabeth Crane** (q.v.) near Kingston-on-Thames; secret press pub'd anon. works by Udall & Penry; Oct. 1588: pub'd first of the Martin Marprelate Tracts (see Chapter 4: World of learning); moved press to Northants & (1589) Coventry; Mar. 1589: pub'd *Hay any Worke for Cooper*; ceased the Marprelate enterprise in late spring; Mar. 1590: obtained printing licence in Edinburgh; 9 Oct. 1590: app'd King's printer; 1590–d. pub'd over 100 works incl. Puritan tracts & the works of King James VI.; 1597: tried for tr. (had printed a work authorising Presbyterianism without royal permission) but charge dropped; June 1603: licensed to print in London; c. Feb. 1604: d.

WALSINGHAM (Sir) Francis (1532–90): Secretary of State involved in foreign affairs, 1568–90. Staunch and uncompromising Protestant; wanted Protestant foreign policy of alliance with Huguenot French v. Spain; fought for removal of Mary of Scotland; 1571–72: foiled Ridolfi Plot; 1583: foiled Throckmorton Plot; organised effective secret service. C. Read, *Mr Secretary Walsingham*, 3 Vols, 1925; M. Foss, *Tudor Portraits*, 1973.

WARBECK Perkin (alias Richard Plantagenet, Duke of York) (c. 1474–99): impostor and claimant to English throne. c. 1474: b. s. of Jehan de Werbecque & Nicaise Farou of Tournai; 1484–87: worked for Flemish mer-chants; Apr./May 1487: joined Portuguese Court in company of Lady Margaret (Beaumont) Brampton; 1488: in service of Pregent Meno, Breton merchant; 1491: trav-elled w. Meno to Cork; persuaded by Yorkist mayor, John Atwater, to impersonate Richard Plantagenet; 1492: Charles VIII of France brought Warbeck to Harfleur; welcomed by Margaret of York, dowager duchess of Burgundy & sister of **Edward IV** (q.v.) as her nephew; 1493: Eng. courtiers began to be involved, incl. Sir **William Stanley** (q.v.), chamberlain of the King's household; 3 July

1494: attempted invasion at Deal failed; welcomed at court of James IV at Stirling; 1496: m. Lady Katherine Gordon & granted Falkland Palace; 21 Sept. 1496: invasion w. Scots help failed; May 1497: Cornish rebels asked Warbeck to lead them; Sept. 1497: rebellion failed & Warbeck took refuge at Beaulieu Abbey; surrendered; 5 Oct. 1497: confessed he was impostor; escaped, recaptured; impr. in Tower for life; 1499: involved in plot to free Edward Earl of Warwick & Warbeck & enthrone one of them; 23 Nov. 1499: hanged at Tyburn. I. Arthurson, *The Perkin Warbeck Conspiracy, 1491–1499*, 1994.

WARHAM (Archbishop) William (?1450–1532): 1494: Master of the Rolls; 1496: nego. m. betw. **Katherine of Aragon** & **Arthur Tudor** (q.v); 1502: Bp of London; 1504: Archbp of Canterbury and Lord Chancellor; 1509: crowned Henry VIII; post-1515: public role muted, when Wolsey in the ascendant; 1529–32: disliked Henry's divorce & break w. Rome; Feb. 1532: declared he would repeal all statutes passed v. church since 1529; intended to resist Henry's threat of writ of Praemunire; 23 Aug.: 1532: d.

WARWICK Earl of (see **Dudley John** and **Dudley Ambrose**).

WENTWORTH Peter (c. 1524–96): MP noted for his championship of Parliament's right to discuss matters normally considered to belong to the Crown prerogative (i.e. the succession and religious questions), and for his consequent imprisonment.

WESTON William (1549/50–1615): Oxf., Paris and Douai-edu. Superior of Jesuit Mission in Eng. 1549/50: b. Maidstone, Kent of unknown parentage; 1564: adm. Christ Church, Oxf.; 17 Feb. 1569: BA; 1570: poss. at Lincoln's Inn; 1571: studying in Paris; 1572: at Eng. College in Douai; 5 Nov. 1575: entered SJ novitiate in Rome; 1575–84: in Spain; 1579: ord. pr.; 1582–84: taught Greek at Eng. College, Seville; 10 Sept. 1584: entered Eng. via Norfolk; 1585–86: exorcisms in private houses of recusants; 1586–98: impr. in various places including Wisbech

Castle where he quarrelled w. secular priests; 1598–1603: solitary impr. in Tower; 1603: allowed to go abroad; c. 19 Apr. 1615: d. William Weston, ed. and translated by Philip Caraman, *The Autobiography of an Elizabethan*, 1951.

WHEATHILL Anne (fl. 1584): author of scripturally based & Calvinist prayers. A gentlewoman by birth & humanistic edu. & probably unmarried as her book contains no prayers addressed to m. or childbearing women. 1584: pub'd *A Handfull of Holesome (though Homelie) Hearbs*, containing 49 prayers.

WHITGIFT (Archbishop) John (?1530/01–1604): Cambr.-edu. preacher and college reformer, Calvinist but conformist Bp of Worcester and Archbp of Canterbury. 1530/01: b. s. & h. of Henry Whitgift of Grimsby, Lincs, merchant & h.w. Anne (Dynewell); edu. St Anthony's School, London; 1550: matric Pembroke College, Cambr., then under Nicholas Ridley; tutored there by future martyr John Bradford; 1554: BA; 1555–67: fellow of Peterhouse; 1557: MA; protected from persecution by Master, Andrew Perne; 1560: ord. deac. & pr. at Ely; denounced Pope in sermon at Great St Mary's; 1563: BTh & Lady Margaret Professor of Divinity; 1565: moderate who oppo. surplice in Vestiarian Controversy; 1566: converted to gov't policy re vestments; 10 June 1566: app'd university preacher; 1567: DTh; 1567–69: Regius Professor of Divinity; 1567: Master of Pembroke College; 1567–77: resigned & became Master of Trinity College; 1568: prebendary of Ely; 1569: key role in promoting new set of statutes for Cambr.; Nov. 1569: elected Vice-Chancellor of Cambr.; depr. **Thomas Cartwright** of chair (q.v.); 1571: Dean of Lincoln; 1572: depr. Cartwright of fellowship; Nov. 1572–75: engaged in Admonition Controversy v. Thomas Cartwright, e.g. w. *Answer to the Admonition*; 1572: president (prolocutor) of Lower House of Convocation; 1573: Vice-Chancellor of Cambr.; May 1577: consecr. Bp of Worcester; resigned Mastership of

Trinity; a preaching bp; active v. recusants in dioc.; active v. recusants as Vice-President of council in marches of Wales; 1581: drew up gov't's response to **Walter Mildmay**'s (q.v.) articles for reform of church abuses; 1583: drew up new statutes for Hereford Cathedral; on commission investigating quarrel betw. Bp William Overton of Coventry & Lichfield & Dean & Chapter; 23 Oct. 1583: consecr. Archbp of Canterbury; prime mover in drawing up and enforcing the Three Articles; revival of eccles. commission to enforce conformity using civil law procedures & oath *ex officio mero* – led to alienation of Burghley; 1584: oppo. Parl. attempts to impose Genevan Book of Discipline w. defence of episcopacy and the Church's independence; 1584–86: conflict w. **Walter Travers** (q.v.); 1586: PC; 1586: took control of printing; 1588–93: suppr. of **Marprelate Press**, etc. 1593–97: involvement in various theological controversies, especially that involving William Barrett, Fellow of Caius, & William Whitaker, master of St John's regarding varieties of Calvinism; 1583–1602: oppo. Puritan **feoffees** for impropritations in his dioc.; support of scholars in his household; exercised patronage over episcopal bench; careful management of archiepiscopal estates, using **rents** in kind to improve position; various charitable foundations; 25 July 1603: crowned James I; Jan. 1604: attended Hampton Court Conference but leadership exercised by Richard Bancroft, Bp of London; 29 Feb. 1604: d. at Lambeth. V.J.K. Brook, *Whitgift and the English Church*, 1958.

WHITAKER William (1547/48–95): St Paul's School and Cambr.-edu. and well-connected Calvinist theologian, anti-Catholic propagandist and Master of St John's College, Cambr.; ?1547: b. 3rd s. of Thomas Whitaker, gent, of Holme, nr Burnley, Lancs & Elizabeth (Nowell); cousin of **Alexander** (q.v.), **Laurence** (q.v.) & Robert Nowell; edu. Burnley & (c. 1558) St Paul's School; 1564–67: Trinity College, Cambr.; 1565: scholar; 1568: BA; 1569: Junior Fellow; 1571: Senior Fellow; MA; 1573, 1574, 1575: transl. Nowell's catechisms into Greek; 21 Dec. 1576: ord. deac. &

pr.; 1578: Canon of Norwich; BTh; 3 Nov. 1578: transl. Jewel's book v. Thomas Harding; 1580: app'd Professor of Divinity, Cambr.; debate w. Peter Baro re predestination; 23 Sept. 1580–87: Chancellor of St Paul's, recommended by its dean, Alexander Nowell; 1580: m. (i) Susan (Culverwell) Fuller, wid. of London merchant, Cuthbert; three daus & two s.; related by m. to Laurence Chaderton; 1581: pub'd *Ad rationes decem Edmundi Campiani jesuitæ responsio*; 25 Feb. 1587: adm. Master of St John's College, Cambr.; May 1587: DTh; 1587: adm. Fellow, Eton College; 1587: expelled Everard Digby, Fellow of St John's; Apr. 1588: ordered by Whitgift & Burgley to reinstate Digby; Whitaker appealed to Essex, Leicester & Warwick; Whitgift reached settlement through Leicester, etc.; attempted revision of college statutes on lines of puritan Emmanuel but conflict w. fellows led to deadlock; 2 May 1588: pub'd *Disputatio ad sacra scriptura*, v. Cardinal Bellarmine; 1590: summoned to London to answer conservative complaints that a national Presbyterian synod had been held at St John's by Chaderton, Cartwright & Henry Alvey w. his knowledge; did not answer specific charge but denied knowledge of Presbyterian cell in St John's; Dec. 1591: secured Vice-mastership for Alvey; Apr. 1591: m. (ii) Joan Fenner, wid. of Dudley, Puritan minister of Cranbrook, Kent & mother of More Fruit & Faint Not; b. of more children; Feb. 1593: openly deplored execution of separatists; 1594: pub'd *Adversus Thomae Stapletoni* (a leading RC apologist); 1595: re-opened debate w. Peter Baro over the latter's doctrine of universal grace; 1595: prosecuted William Barrett, junior fellow of Caius, in the university's consistory court for anti-Calvinist sermon; 10 May 1595: app'd canon of Canterbury; at Lambeth conference faced Barrett w. nine doctrinal articles or propositions; Queen outraged & called for their withdrawal; 4 Dec. 1595: d. at St John's; posthumous b. of s. Jabez.

WHITTINGHAM (Dean) William (c. 1523–79): Oxf.-edu. evangelical Protestant Marian exile and Elizabethan Dean of Durham. c. 1523: b. s. of William Whittingham, gent, of Cheshire; 1540–47: edu. Oxf.; 1545: BA Brasenose &

Fellow, All Souls; 1547: MA Cardinal College, Oxf.; studied languages abroad; c. 1553: returned to Eng.; June 1554: in Frankfurt; allied w. **Knox** (q.v.) over the prayerbook issue; 1555: Knox & Whittingham went to Geneva; 15 Nov. 1556: m. Katherine Jaqueman of Orleans; 1557: Zachary b.; 1558: Susanna b. (both d. young); b. of six further children, the last (Daniel) in 1571; transl. New Testament; assisted in Eng. version of Genevan Bible; helped produce Sternhold & Hopkins' version of the Psalms, etc.; 1558: deacon & minister of Eng. congregation in Geneva; May 1560: returned to Eng.; c. 1562: joined service of **Ambrose Dudley**, Earl of Warwick (q.v.); July 1563: Dean of Durham; reformed Cathedral chapter; 1565: oppo. vestments in Vestiarian Controversy; Aug. 1566: summoned before eccles. commission at York to answer charges re vestments; 1567: conformed; 1569: acted w. distinction during rebellion; 1571: subscribed to Parker's articles; 1574: reluctant to cooperate w. Thomas Wood in *A Brief Discourse of the Troubles Begun at Frankfurt*; 1577: resisted visitation of the Cathedral Chapter by Bp Barnes of Durham; eventual visitation led to royal visitation in 1578; 23–26 Oct. 1578 & 25–28 Nov. 1578: Commission at Durham examined Whittingham's Genevan orders, etc.; 10 June 1579: d. Durham.

WILKINSON Joan or Jane (née North) (fl. 1533–d. 1556): Protestant radical in **Anne Boleyn**'s entourage. b. London, dau. of citizen Roger North & Christian (Warcup), wid. Warren; sister of Edward North, 1st Baron North; m. an alderman of London; three daus; 1533–35: silkwoman to Anne Boleyn & exposed there to evangelical religion; w. William Latymer imported banned religious texts into Eng.; 1551: living in Worcs; 1553–58: cared for many persecuted Protestants, incl. **John Hooper, Nicholas Ridley, Hugh Latimer & Thomas Cranmer** (all q.v.); several wrote letters thanking her & her cousin Anne Warcup; they acted as channel for reformers to send sermons to English Protestant congregations; joined exiles in Frankfurt; 1556: d. & left books for Hooper's son Daniel & provision for her dau. Jane to m. a Protestant.

WILLOUGHBY Katherine (see **Bertie** Katherine).

WOLSEY (Cardinal Archbishop) Thomas (1470/01–1530): Ipswich and Oxf.-edu. administrator, diplomat, statesman, royal servant, builder, humanist patron and Cardinal Archbp of York. 1470/01: b. s. of Robert Wolsey, butcher & grazier, of Ipswich & h.w. Joan (Daundy); edu. Ipswich & Oxf.; 1486: BA; 10 Mar. 1498: ord. pr.; 1497: MA & fellow, Magdalen College, Oxf.; tutored sons of Marquis of Dorset; 1498: junior bursar; 1499–1500: senior bursar; Master, Magdalen School; 1500–02: Dean of Divinity; many eccles. preferments; 1507: Royal Chaplain; 1509: Dean of Lincoln; began relationship w. Mistress Lark; two children (Thomas and Dorothy Wynter); 1509: royal almoner; rapid rise to power & accumulation of offices; 1511: PC; 1512 & 13: managed military preparations; Feb. 1513: Dean of York; 26 Mar. 1514: consecr. Bp of Lincoln; 1514: nego. m. of King's sister Mary to Louis XII of France; 5 Aug. 1514: elected Archbp of York; 10 Sept. 1515: cr. cardinal; large & expensive household; 1515–: King's principal minister in charge of domestic affairs; 21 Dec. 1515: Lord Chancellor – made huge impact on the legal system, especially Star Chamber; 1515: leased Hampton Court palace; June 1517: serious illness; *in commendam* 1518: Bp of Bath & Wells; 1518: granted legatine authority jointly w. Cardinal Campeggio; as legate ordered visitation of religious houses and cathedral chapters (including Westminster Abbey), and set up special court for testamentary cases; ordered reform of Augustinian canons; 2 Oct. 1518: Treaty of Universal Peace; 1518: endowed six lectureships at Oxf.; 1519: had average p.a. income of £9,500; 1520–23: granted extension to legatione authority; May 1520: w. King entertained Emperor; June 1520: accompanied Henry to meet François at Field of Cloth of Gold; 1521: Arbiter betw. France and Emperor; 25 Aug. 1521: secretly committed Eng. to war v. France in Mar. 1523; 1521: *in commendam* Abbot of St Albans; 12 May 1521: presided over burning of Lutheran books at St Paul's churchyard; 1522: permanent legatine court; agreed to share prerogative jurisdiction w. **Archbp Warham** (q.v.); 1522: 'general proscription' assessed England's military resources & taxable wealth; 1522–23: forced loans; 1523: subsidy from Parl.; 1522–25: preoccupied w. maintaining balance of power & keeping Eng. out of expensive foreign wars; 1523: exchanged Bath & Wells for Durham, where he attempted unsuccessfully to exert control over the nobility and the Anglo-Scottish marches; 1524: Clement VII granted legatine authority for life; 1524: raised 'amicable grant', which led to revolt in Suffolk; 1525: began building of Cardinal College, Oxf.; 1525: restored Council of the North under **Richmond** (q.v.); 1526: authorised search for heretical books in Hanseatic community in London; 1526: Eltham Ordinances for the royal household; 1527: tried to persuade King not to attempt divorce & continued to work for European peace; 30 Apr. 1527: concluded treaty w. France; legatine inquiries into validity of Henry's m. to Katherine; 11 July 1527: went as vicegerent to nego. peace w. France; 1528: oppo. election of Eleanor Carey (sister-in-law of **Mary Boleyn** (q.v.)) as abbess of Wilton & rebuked by Henry VIII; 1528: Wolsey warned Clement VII that failure to grant the divorce would lead to break w. Eng.; 9 Oct. 1528: Campeggio brought commission for divorce trial to London; Feb. 1529: exchanged Durham for Winchester; 1528–29: made scapegoat for failure to win divorce from the papacy at the Blackfriars court in June & July 1529; 9 Oct. 1529: indicted for *praemunire*; 18 Oct. 1529: surrendered Great Seal; banished to Esher & then to Richmond; attacked in Parl.; 12 Feb. 1530: granted full pardon by the King; 14 Feb. 1530: restored to Archbpric of York; 17 Feb. 1530: surrendered See of Winchester; Mar. 1530: Norfolk ordered him to York; Apr. 1530: set off for York via Peterborough, Grantham, Newark, Southwell, Scroby and Cawood Castle, nr York; Oct. 1530: blamed for papal brief prohibiting Henry's remarriage and ordering **Anne Boleyn** from court; 4 Nov. 1530: arrested at Cawood for high tr.

in nego. w. the French; 29 Nov. 1530: d., Leicester Abbey; c. 1530: p.a. income estimated at £30,000. P. Gwyn, *The King's Cardinal: The Rise and Fall of Thomas Wolsey*, 1990; A.F. Pollard, *Wolsey*, 1929.

WRIOTHESLEY, Thomas (1505–50) 1st Earl of Southampton (1505–50): Cambr.-edu. royal administrator & trimmer. 21 Dec. 1505: b. s. of William Wriothesley & h.w. Agnes (Drayton); edu. St Paul's School, London; 1522: adm. Trinity Hall, Cambr.; tutored by Stephen Gardiner; 1524: client of Thomas Cromwell; by 4 May 1530: Clerk of Signet under Stephen Gardiner; by 1533: m. Jane (Cheney) a connection of Gardiner; three s. & five daus; 1534: adm. Gray's Inn; built up imp. Estates in Hampshire; alienated from Gardiner over religion; Apr. 1540: app'd principal secretary (w. **Ralph Sadler** (q.v.)) & PC; incr. infl. w. Henry VIII; 29 Jan. 1543: joint Chamberlain of Exchequer; 1 Jan. 1544: cr. Baron Wriothesley of Titchfield; 3 May 1544: Lord Chancellor; July 1544: named to Katherine Parr's regency council; 1 Jan. 1544: KG; pursued Henry's conservative relig. policy; Jan. 1547: named executor of Henry VIII, etc.; 16 Feb. 1547: cr. 1st Earl of Southampton; 6 Mar. 1547: depr. of Lord Chancellorship & placed under house arrest; 29 June 1547: released; 17 Jan. 1549: resumed PC; in Parl. resisted religious changes; Feb. 1549: part of Parl. committee that interrogated Thomas Seymour; Jan. 1550: expelled from court by Northumberland; Feb.: removed from PC; 30 July 1550: d. London.

WYATT (Sir) Thomas (c. 1503–42): Cambr.-edu. humanist and Protestant court poet and ambassador, who translated & imitated Petrarchian sonnets. c. 1503: b. Allington Castle, Kent, s. & h. of Sir Henry Wyatt & h.w. Anne (Skinner); attended St John's College, Cambr. but did not graduate; c. 1519–20: unhappily m. Elizabeth Brooke, dau. of Thomas, 8th Baron Cobham; c. 1521: **Thomas** b. (q.v.); estranged from w. because of her adultery; 1524: Clerk of King's Jewels; 1525: Esquire of King's Body; 1526: embassy to France; Jan. 1527: embassy to papal curia;

Jan. 1528: presented Katherine of Aragon w. *Quyete of Mynde*, transl. of Plutarch from Bude; Oct. 1529 to Nov. 1530: High Marshall of Calais; 1532: JP Essex; 1532: accompanied **Henry** & **Anne Boleyn** to meet François I of France; 1 June 1533: sewer-extraordinary at coronation of Anne Boleyn; June 1534: granted licence to have 20 liveried men; 1535: various preferments & knighted; 5 May 1536: impr. in Tower as a friend of the Boleyns; rumours that he was Anne Boleyn's lover seem to be unfounded; mid-June 1536: released; Oct. 1536: fought v. rebels in Pilgrimage of Grace; sheriff of Kent; Mar. 1537–40: ambass. to Charles V to improve relations; c. 1537: took as his mistress Elizabeth Darrell, former maid to Queen Katherine of Aragon; illegitimate s. Francis; in trouble w. Spanish Inquisition; 1539: involvement in conspiracy to poison Cardinal **Reginald Pole** (q.v.); June 1540: fall of Cromwell, his patron; July–Dec. 1540: Wyatt retired to estates at Allington; 17 Jan. 1541: impr. in Tower charged w. high tr.; 19 Mar. 1541: Queen **Katharine Howard** interceded & he was released; quickly rest. to favour; Dec. 1541: M.P. Kent; Mar. 1542: several land grants; 6 Oct. 1542: d.; K. Muir, *Life and Letters of Sir Thomas Wyatt*, 1963.

WYATT (Sir) Thomas the younger (c. 1521–54): rebel and soldier w. evangelical, commonwealthman sympathies. c. 1521: s. of Sir **Thomas Wyatt** (q.v.) & Elizabeth (Brooke); 1537: m. Jane (Haute), co-heir of Sir Wm Haute of Bishopsbourne, Kent; four s. & three daus; 1545: Captain of Basse-Boulogne; knighted; 1547: M.P. Kent; 1549: anti-enclosure riots v. him at Boxley, Kent; 1550–51: Sheriff of Kent; proposed established **militia** to Somerset; July 1553: proclaimed Mary Queen at Maidstone; Nov. 1553: involved w. disaffected Edwardian Protestant ex-soldiers (led by Croft) when Mary planned m. to Philip of Spain; 22 Dec. 1553: plot for four-pronged rising (involving Edward Courtenay and Princess Elizabeth) in which Wyatt would raise Kent (for further detail see Chapter 2: Rebellions against the Tudors); 25 Jan. to Feb. 1554: Wyatt led unsuccessful rebellion and march v. London; Mar. 1554: Wyatt denied conspiracy to assassinate Mary and involvement of Princess Elizabeth; 11 Apr. 1554: exec.

13

GENEALOGICAL TABLES

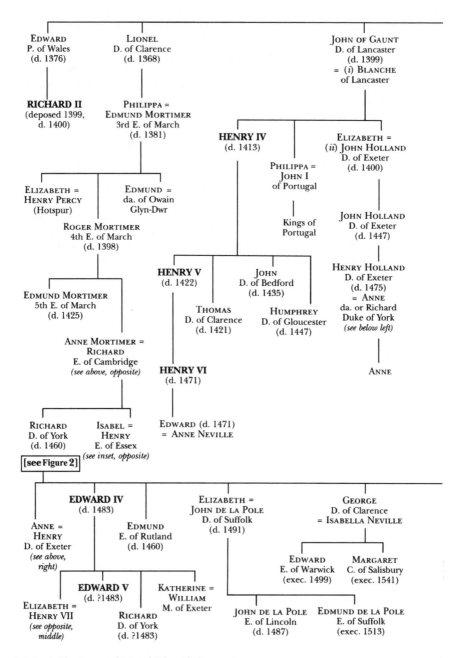

Figure 1 The Descendants of Edward III

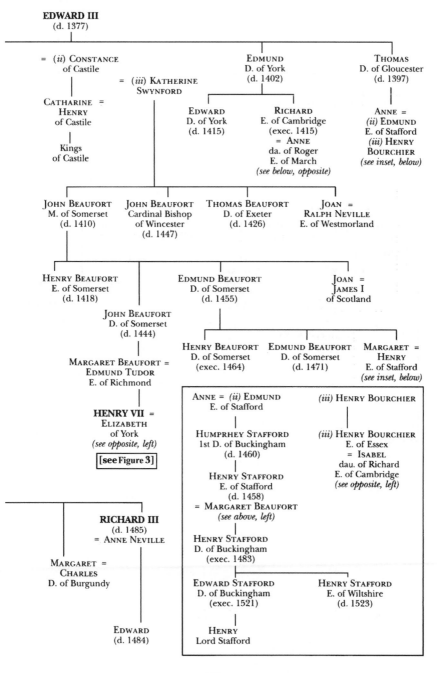

EDWARD III
(d. 1377)

= (*ii*) CONSTANCE
of Castile

= (*iii*) KATHERINE
SWYNFORD

EDMUND
D. of York
(d. 1402)

THOMAS
D. of Gloucester
(d. 1397)

CATHARINE =
HENRY
of Castile

Kings
of Castile

EDWARD
D. of York
(d. 1415)

RICHARD
E. of Cambridge
(exec. 1415)
= ANNE
da. of Roger
E. of March
(see below, opposite)

ANNE =
(*ii*) EDMUND
E. of Stafford
(*iii*) HENRY
BOURCHIER
(see inset, below)

JOHN BEAUFORT
M. of Somerset
(d. 1410)

JOHN BEAUFORT
Cardinal Bishop
of Winchester
(d. 1447)

THOMAS BEAUFORT
D. of Exeter
(d. 1426)

JOAN =
RALPH NEVILLE
E. of Westmorland

HENRY BEAUFORT
E. of Somerset
(d. 1418)

EDMUND BEAUFORT
D. of Somerset
(d. 1455)

JOAN =
JAMES I
of Scotland

JOHN BEAUFORT
D. of Somerset
(d. 1444)

HENRY BEAUFORT
D. of Somerset
(exec. 1464)

EDMUND BEAUFORT
D. of Somerset
(d. 1471)

MARGARET =
HENRY
E. of Stafford
(see inset, below)

MARGARET BEAUFORT =
EDMUND TUDOR
E. of Richmond

HENRY VII =
ELIZABETH
of York
(see opposite, left)

[see Figure 3]

ANNE = (*ii*) EDMUND
E. of Stafford

(*iii*) HENRY BOURCHIER

HUMPRHEY STAFFORD
1st D. of Buckingham
(d. 1460)

(*iii*) HENRY BOURCHIER
E. of Essex
= ISABEL
dau. of Richard
E. of Cambridge
(see opposite, left)

HENRY STAFFORD
E. of Stafford
(d. 1458)
= MARGARET BEAUFORT
(see above, left)

RICHARD III
(d. 1485)
= ANNE NEVILLE

HENRY STAFFORD
D. of Buckingham
(exec. 1483)

MARGARET =
CHARLES
D. of Burgundy

EDWARD STAFFORD
D. of Buckingham
(exec. 1521)

HENRY STAFFORD
E. of Wiltshire
(d. 1523)

EDWARD
(d. 1484)

HENRY
Lord Stafford

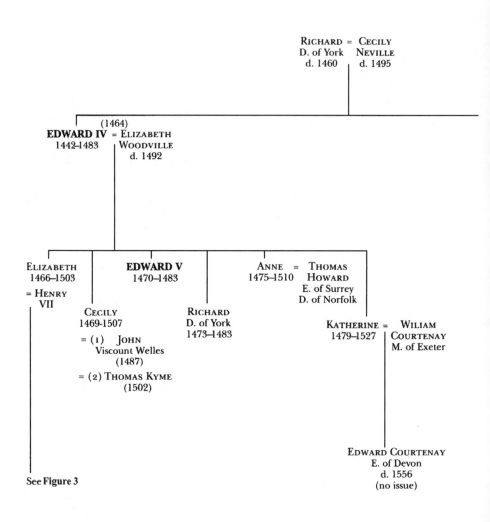

Figure 2 Descent of Edward IV and and his siblings

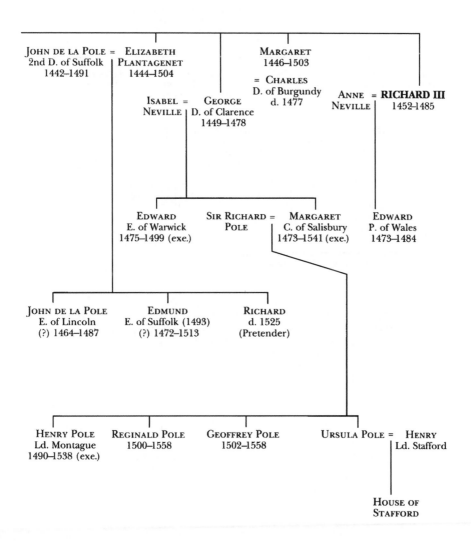

JOHN DE LA POLE = ELIZABETH
2nd D. of Suffolk | PLANTAGENET
1442–1491 | 1444–1504

MARGARET
1446–1503

= CHARLES
D. of Burgundy
d. 1477

ANNE = **RICHARD III**
NEVILLE | 1452–1485

ISABEL = GEORGE
NEVILLE | D. of Clarence
1449–1478

EDWARD
E. of Warwick
1475–1499 (exe.)

SIR RICHARD = MARGARET
POLE | C. of Salisbury
1473–1541 (exe.)

EDWARD
P. of Wales
1473–1484

JOHN DE LA POLE
E. of Lincoln
(?) 1464–1487

EDMUND
E. of Suffolk (1493)
(?) 1472–1513

RICHARD
d. 1525
(Pretender)

HENRY POLE
Ld. Montague
1490–1538 (exe.)

REGINALD POLE
1500–1558

GEOFFREY POLE
1502–1558

URSULA POLE = HENRY
| Ld. Stafford

HOUSE OF
STAFFORD

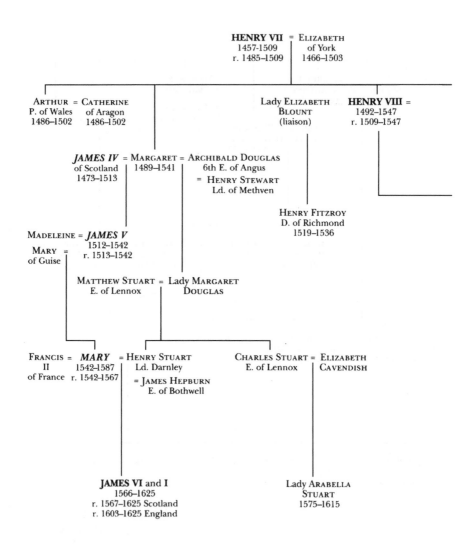

Figure 3 Descent of Henry VII and Elizabeth of York

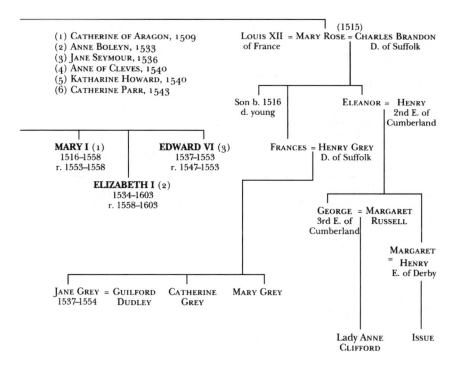

(1) CATHERINE OF ARAGON, 1509
(2) ANNE BOLEYN, 1533
(3) JANE SEYMOUR, 1536
(4) ANNE OF CLEVES, 1540
(5) KATHARINE HOWARD, 1540
(6) CATHERINE PARR, 1543

(1515)
LOUIS XII = MARY ROSE = CHARLES BRANDON
of France   D. of Suffolk

Son b. 1516
d. young

ELEANOR = HENRY
          2nd E. of
          Cumberland

MARY I (1)
1516–1558
r. 1553–1558

EDWARD VI (3)
1537–1553
r. 1547–1553

FRANCES = HENRY GREY
          D. of Suffolk

ELIZABETH I (2)
1534–1603
r. 1558–1603

GEORGE = MARGARET
3rd E. of   RUSSELL
Cumberland

MARGARET
= HENRY
E. of Derby

JANE GREY = GUILFORD
1537–1554   DUDLEY

CATHERINE
GREY

MARY GREY

Lady ANNE
CLIFFORD

ISSUE

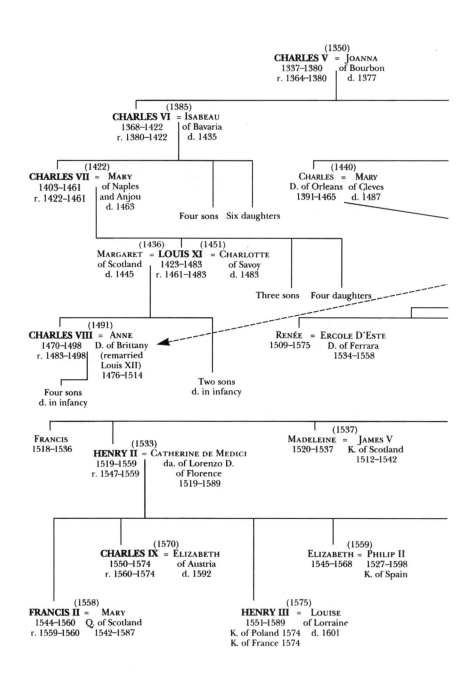

Figure 4 The Valois Dynasty (France)

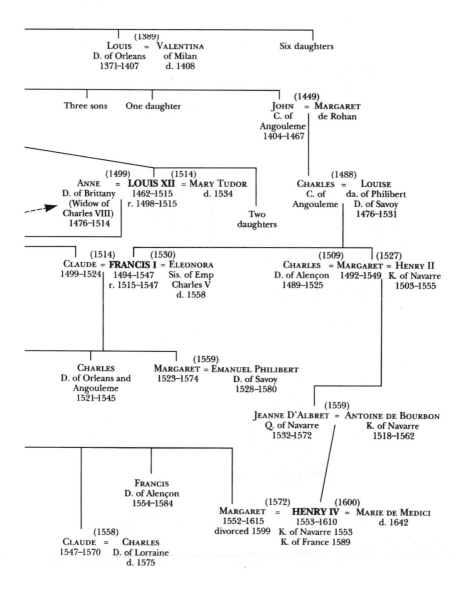

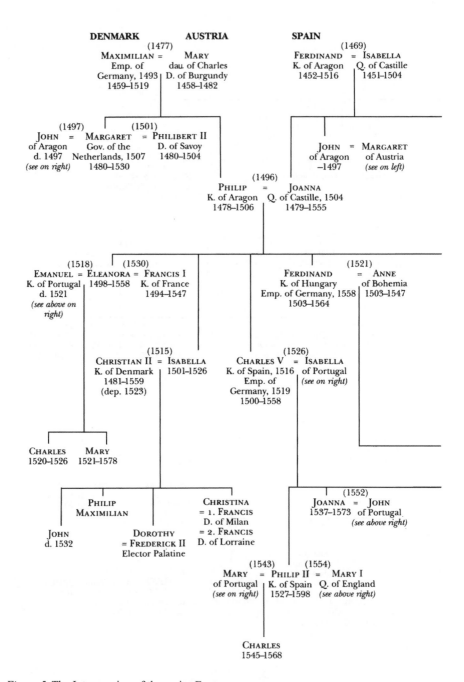

Figure 5 The Intermarrige of the major European powers

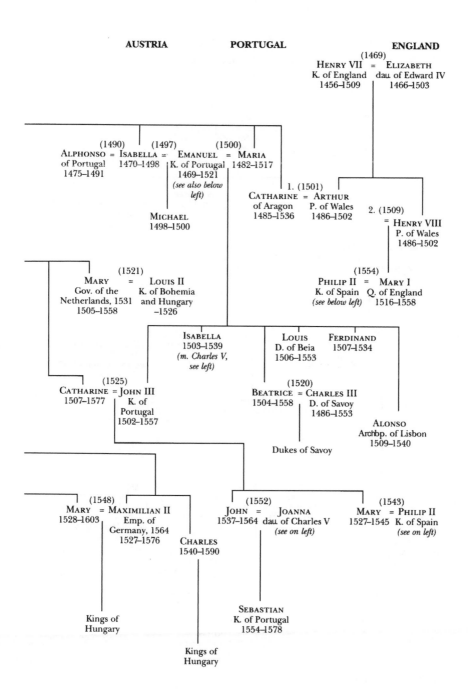

AUSTRIA **PORTUGAL** **ENGLAND**

(1469)
HENRY VII = ELIZABETH
K. of England dau. of Edward IV
1456–1509 1466–1503

(1490) (1497) (1500)
ALPHONSO = ISABELLA = EMANUEL = MARIA
of Portugal 1470–1498 K. of Portugal 1482–1517
1475–1491 1469–1521
(see also below left)

MICHAEL
1498–1500

1. (1501)
CATHARINE = ARTHUR
of Aragon P. of Wales
1485–1536 1486–1502

2. (1509)
= HENRY VIII
P. of Wales
1486–1502

(1521)
MARY = LOUIS II
Gov. of the K. of Bohemia
Netherlands, 1531 and Hungary
1505–1558 –1526

(1554)
PHILIP II = MARY I
K. of Spain Q. of England
(see below left) 1516–1558

ISABELLA
1503–1539
(m. Charles V, see left)

LOUIS FERDINAND
D. of Beia 1507–1534
1506–1553

(1525)
CATHARINE = JOHN III
1507–1577 K. of
Portugal
1502–1557

(1520)
BEATRICE = CHARLES III
1504–1558 D. of Savoy
1486–1553

ALONSO
Archbp. of Lisbon
1509–1540

Dukes of Savoy

(1548)
MARY = MAXIMILIAN II
1528–1603 Emp. of
Germany, 1564
1527–1576

CHARLES
1540–1590

(1552)
JOHN = JOANNA
1537–1564 dau. of Charles V
(see on left)

(1543)
MARY = PHILIP II
1527–1545 K. of Spain
(see on left)

Kings of
Hungary

SEBASTIAN
K. of Portugal
1554–1578

Kings of
Hungary

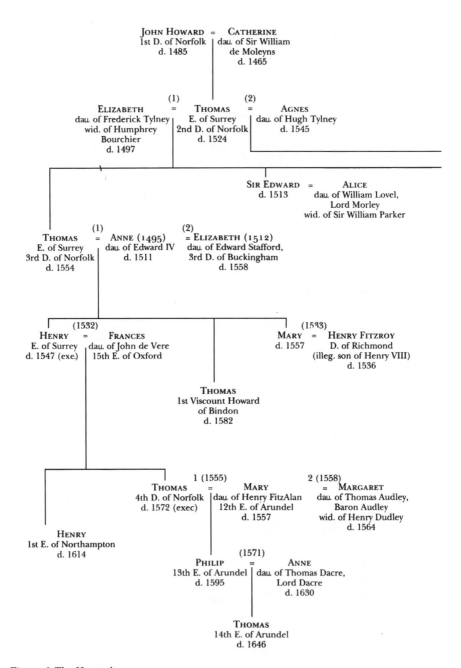

Figure 6 The Howards

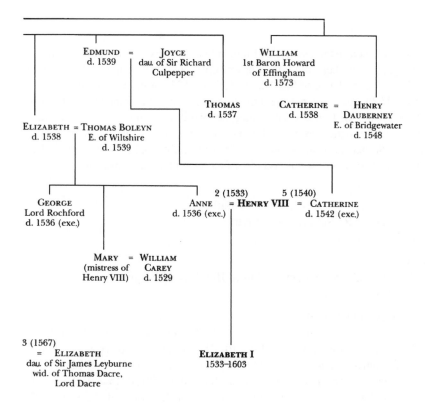

EDMUND = JOYCE
d. 1539 dau. of Sir Richard
Culpepper

WILLIAM
1st Baron Howard
of Effingham
d. 1573

THOMAS
d. 1537

CATHERINE = HENRY
d. 1538 DAUBERNEY
E. of Bridgewater
d. 1548

ELIZABETH = THOMAS BOLEYN
d. 1538 E. of Wiltshire
d. 1539

GEORGE
Lord Rochford
d. 1536 (exe.)

2 (1533) 5 (1540)
ANNE = HENRY VIII = CATHERINE
d. 1536 (exe.) d. 1542 (exe.)

MARY = WILLIAM
(mistress of CAREY
Henry VIII) d. 1529

3 (1567)
= ELIZABETH
dau. of Sir James Leyburne
wid. of Thomas Dacre,
Lord Dacre

ELIZABETH I
1533–1603

14

TUDOR TITLES: WHO WAS WHO?

One of the most confusing aspects of English history books is the habit of referring to key individuals by their title only. For example, one reads of the Earl of Essex in 1540 and 1599 or the Duke of Suffolk in 1550 and 1552 or the Bishop of London in 1530 and in 1570, yet it was not the same Earl of Essex or the same Duke of Suffolk or the same Bishop of London. The listing below cites the titles to which reference is most frequently made and gives the name and identity of the holder of this title with dates. The dates are those during which the individual held the title. I have added further detail where it will aid identification and avoid confusion.

Bedford
1549–55   Lord John Russell created 1st Earl of
1555–85   Francis Russell, son of 1st Earl
1585–1627 Edward Russell

Burghley
1570–98   Sir William Cecil, created Lord Burghley of Burghley
1598–1623 Thomas Cecil

Canterbury, Archbishop of
1454–86   Thomas Bourchier, translated from Ely Aug. 1454; d. 30 Mar. 1486
1486–1500 John Morton, translated from Ely Dec. 1486; d. 15 or 16 Sept. 1500
1501   Thomas Langton, translated from Winchester Jan. 1501; d. 27 Jan. 1501
1501–03   Henry Deane, translated from Salisbury Aug. 1501; d. 15 or 17 Feb. 1503
1504–32   William Warham, translated from London Jan. 1504; d. 22 Aug. 1532
1533–53   Thomas Cranmer, consecrated 30 March 1533; deprived 13 Nov. 1553;
(deprived) d. 21 March 1556
1556–58   Reginald Pole, consecrated 22 March 1556; d. 18 or 19 Nov. 1558
1559–75   Matthew Parker, consecrated 17 Dec. 1559; d. 17 May 1575
1576–83   Edmund Grindal, translated from York Feb. 1576; d. 6 July 1583
1583–1604 John Whitgift, translated from Worcester Sept. 1583; d. 29 Feb. 1604
1604–10   Richard Bancroft, translated from London Dec. 1604; d. 2 Nov. 1610

Chancellor, Lord
1485   Thomas Rotherham, Archbp of York
1485–87   John Alcock, Bp of Winchester and Ely
1487–1500 John Morton, Archbp of Canterbury

1515–29	Thomas Wolsey, Archbp of York, etc.
1529–32	Sir Thomas More
1533–44	Sir Thomas Audley (created 1st Lord Audley in 1538); he had been Keeper since 1532
1544–47	Lord Thomas Wriothesely, created 1st Earl of Southampton in 1547
1547–51	Lord Richard Rich
1552–53	Thomas Goodrich, Bp of Ely; he had been Keeper in 1551–52
1553–55	Stephen Gardiner, Bp of Winchester
1556–58	Nicholas Heath, Archbp of York
1579–87	Sir Thomas Bromley
1587–91	Sir Christopher Hatton

Chief Justice of the King's Bench

1485–95	William Huse
1495–1526	John Finieux
1526–39	John FitzJames
1539–45	Edward Montagu
1545–52	Richard Lyster
1552–53	Roger Cholmley
1553–55	Thomas Bromley
1555–57	William Portman
1557–59	Edward Saunders
1559–74	Robert Catlin
1574–92	Christopher Wray
1592–1607	John Popham

Chief Justice of the Common Pleas

1485–1500	Thomas Bryan
1500–02	Thomas Wood
1502–06	Thomas Frowyk
1506–19	Robert Read
1519–21	John Ernle
1521–31	Robert Brudenell
1531–25	Robert Norwich
1535–45	John Baldwin
1545–53	Edward Montagu
1553–54	Richard Morgan
1554–58	Robert Brooke
1558–59	Anthony Browne
1559–82	James Dyer
1582–1605	Edmund Anderson

Coventry and Lichfield, Bishop of

1459–90	John Hales, consecrated 25 Nov. 1459; d. Sept. 1490
1493–96	William Smith, consecrated 3 Feb. 1493; translated to Lincoln 30 Jan. 1496
1496–1502	John Arundel, consecrated 6 Nov. 1496; translated to Exeter 8 Apr. 1502
1503–31	Geoffrey Blythe, consecrated 17 Sept. 1503; d. before 1 March 1531
1534–43	Rowland Lee, consecrated 19 Apr. 1534; d. 25 Jan. 1543

1543–54   Richard Sampson, translated from Chichester March 1543; d. 25 Sept. 1554
1554–59   Ralph Baynes, consecrated 18 Nov. 1554; deprived 26 June 1559; d. 18
(deprived) Nov. 1559
1560–79   Thomas Bentham, consecrated 24 March 1560; d. 21 Feb. 1579
1580–1609 William Overton, consecrated 18 Sept. 1580; d. 9 Apr. 1609

Desmond
1529–41   James Fitzmaurice FitzGerald, 12th Earl of
1541–58   James Fitzjohn FitzGerald, 13th Earl of
1558–83   Gerald FitzJames FitzGerald, son of 13th Earl, inherited as
(recognised 15th Earl of
1560)
1600–01   James FitzGerald, never succeeded his father as Earl but was known as
           'Queen's Earl of Desmond' and the 'Tower Earl' because of lengthy
           imprisonment (16 years) in Tower following the 14th Earl's rebellion
1598–1601 (d. 1607) John Fitzthomas FitzGerald, assumed title of Sugan Earl of,
           but was not accepted as Earl

Dorset
1485–1501 Thomas Grey, restored Marquis of
1501–30   Thomas Grey, 3rd son of 1st Marquis, 2nd Marquis of
1530–51   Henry Grey, 3rd Marquis of (father of Lady Jane and made Duke of
           Suffolk, 1551)

Durham, Bishop of
1485–94   John Shirwood, consecrated 26 May 1485; d. 14 Jan. 1494
1494–1501 Richard Fox, translated from Bath and Wells; Dec. 1494; translated to
           Winchester before 20 Aug. 1501
1502–05   William Sever, translated from Carlisle Oct. 1502; d. 1505
1507–08   Christopher Bainbridge, consecrated 12 Dec. 1507; translated to York 1
           Sept. 1576
1509–23   Thomas Ruthall, consecrated 24 June 1509; d. 4 Feb. 1523
1523–29   Thomas Wolsey *in commendam* with York from Apr. 1523; translated to
           Winchester 8 Feb. 1529
1530–59   Cuthbert Tunstall, translated from London late March 1530; resigned 28
(resigned) Sept. 1559; d. 18 Nov. 1559
1561–76   Pilkington, consecrated 2 Mar. 1561; d. 23 Jan. 1576
1577–87   Richard Barnes, translated from Carlisle May 1577; d. 24 Aug. 1587
1589–95   Matthew Hutton, consecrated 27 July 1589; translated to York 24 Mar. 1595
1595–1606 Tobias Matthew, consecrated 13 Apr. 1595; translated to York 28 Aug. 1606

Essex
1493–1540 Henry Bourchier, 2nd Bourchier Earl of Essex
1540–40   Thomas Cromwell, Lord Cromwell of Wimbledon
(executed)
1543–1553 Baron William Parr of Kendal (brother of Queen Katherine and connected
(forfeited) with Earldom of Essex through brief marriage to Anne Bourchier, d. of

Henry, Earl of Essex). Parr was also Marquis of Northampton 1547–53 (forfeited), 1559–71 d. but was not restored to Earldom of Essex in 1559

1572–76   Walter Devereux, 2nd Viscount Hereford

1576–1601 Robert Devereux

Hertford

1537–47   Sir Edward Seymour, Viscount Beauchamp of Hache, created Earl of *see* Somerset

1559–1621 Edward Seymour, restored Earl of (1560: secretly married Lady Catherine Grey, daughter of Duke of Suffolk and sister of Lady Jane; 1561: imprisoned in Tower for treasonable act; 1571: released)

Huntingdon

1529–44   George Hastings, Baron Hastings, 1st Earl of

1545–60   Francis Hastings, Baron Hastings

1560–95   Henry Hastings, in line of descent to throne. President of North. Married to Catherine Dudley, daughter of Northumberland in 1553, 'The Puritan Earl'

Keeper, Lord (of the Great Seal)

1500–02   Henry Deane, Archbp of Canterbury

1502–04   William Warham, Archbp of Canterbury (became Lord Chancellor in 1504)

1532–33   Sir Thomas Audley (was Lord Chancellor, 1533–44)

1547   William Paulet, 1st Lord St John

1551–52   Thomas Goodrich, Bp of Ely, was Lord Chancellor, 1552–53

1558–79   Sir Nicholas Bacon, Lord Keeper

1592–96   Sir John Puckering, Lord Keeper

1596–1603 Sir Thomas Egerton, Lord Keeper, created 1st Lord Ellesmere in 1601

Kildare

1478–1513 Gerald FitzMaurice FitzGerald, son of Thomas the 7th Earl, inherited as 8th Earl of Kildare, known as 'the Great Earl'

1513–34   Gerald FitzGerald, son of 8th Earl, inherited as 9th Earl

1534–37   Thomas FitzGerald, son of 9th Earl, inherited as 10th Earl of Kildare (executed)

1554–85   Gerald FitzGerald, son of 9th Earl, inherited as 11th Earl of Kildare

Lincoln

1467–87   John De La Pole, Earl of (eldest son of John, 1st Duke of Suffolk and Elizabeth, sister of Edward IV), supported Lambert Simnel and was killed at Battle of Stoke

1525–34   Henry Brandon, son of Charles, Duke of Suffolk

1572–85   Lord Edward Fiennes de Clinton made Earl of

Lincoln, Bishop of

1480–94   John Russell

1496–1514 William Smith

1514   Thomas Wolsey, consecrated 26 Mar.; translated to York 15 Sept.

1514–21   William Atwater, consecrated 12 Nov.; d. 4 Feb. 1521

1521–47   John Longland, consecrated 5 May; d. 7 May 1547

1547–51 Henry Holbeach or Rands, translated from Rochester 20 Aug. 1547; d. 6 Aug. 1551

1552–54 John Taylor, consecrated 26 June 1552; deprived 15 March 1554; d.
(deprived) Dec. 1554

1554–56 John White, consecrated 1 Apr. 1554; translated to Winchester 6 July 1556

1557–59 Thomas Watson, consecrated 15 Aug. 1557; deprived 26 June 1559; d.
(deprived) Sept. 1584

1560–71 Nicholas Bullingham, consecrated 21 Jan. 1560; translated to Worcester 26 Jan. 1571

1571–84 Thomas Cooper, consecrated 24 Feb. 1571; translated to Winchester 23 Mar. 1584

1584–95 William Wickham, consecrated 6 Dec. 1584; translated to Winchester 22 Feb. 1595

1595–1608 William Chaderton, 24 May 1595; d. 11 Apr. 1608

Lisle

1533 Arthur Plantagenet, Viscount

1542 John Dudley, Baron Somerai, Basset and Teyes and Viscount Lisle

1562–80 Ambrose Dudley, Lord Lisle and Earl of Warwick

London, Bishop of

1450–89 Thomas Kempe, consecrated 8 Feb. 1450; d. 28 Mar. 1489

1489–96 Richard Hill, consecrated 15 Nov. 1489; d. 20 Feb. 1496

1496–1501 Thomas Savage, translated from Rochester Dec. 1496; translated to York 12 Apr. 1501

1502–03 William Warham, consecrated 25 Sept. 1502; translated to Canterbury 29 Nov. 1503

1504–05 William Barons, consecrated 26 Nov. 1504; d. 10 Oct. 1505

1506–22 Richard FitzJames, translated from Chichester; d. before 17 Jan. 1522

1522–30 Cuthbert Tunstall, consecrated 19 Oct. 1522; translated to Durham 21 Feb. 1530

1530–39 John Stokesley, consecrated 27 Nov. 1530; d. 8 Sept. 1539

1540–49 Edmund Bonner, consecrated 4 Apr. 1540; deprived 1 Oct. 1549
(deprived)

1550–53 Nicholas Ridley, translated from Rochester 1 Apr. 1550; depr. July 1553;
(deprived) d. 16 Oct. 1555

1553–59 Edmund Bonner, restored 5 Sept. 1553; deprived 29 May 1559; d. 5 Sept. 1569

1559–70 Edmund Grindal, consecrated 21 Dec. 1559; translated to York 22 May 1570

1570–77 Edwin Sandys, translated from Worcester July 1570; translated to York 8 Mar. 1577

1577–94 John Aylmer, consecrated 24 March 1577; d. 5 June 1594

1594–96 Richard Fletcher, translated from Worcester Jan. 1595; d.15 June 1596

1597–1604 Richard Bancroft, consecrated 8 May 1597; translated to Canterbury 10 Dec. 1604

Norfolk

1483–85 John Howard, 1st Howard Duke of Norfolk; slain on Bosworth Field where he supported Richard III

1514–24 Thomas Howard, 2nd Howard Duke of

1524–54 Thomas Howard, 3rd Howard Duke of (he forfeited the title, 1547, but was restored Aug. 1553)

1554–72 Thomas Howard, 4th Howard Duke of
(executed)

Northampton

1547–53 Baron Parr of Kendal, Earl of Essex, created Marquis of (brother of Queen
(attainted) Katherine)

1559–71 William Parr restored, extinct by 1571

1604 Henry Howard made 1st Earl of

Northumberland

1470–89 Sir Henry Percy, son of 3rd Earl, inherited as 4th Earl; killed near Thirsk during Yorkshire Rebellion

1489–1527 Sir Henry Algernon Percy inherited as 5th Earl

1527–37 Sir Henry Algernon Percy, son of 5th Earl, inherited as 6th Earl – this was the Harry Percy who had been Anne Boleyn's youthful lover

1551–53 John Dudley, Earl of Warwick, made Duke of
(executed)

1557–71 Sir Thomas Percy, grandson of the 5th Earl who had been attainted,
(exec. 1572) to earldom as 7th Earl restored

1572–85 Sir Henry Percy, brother of 7th Earl, inherited as 8th Earl

1585–1632 Sir Henry Percy, son of 8th Earl, inherited as 9th Earl – known as 'Wizard Earl' because of scientific experiments

Nottingham

1483–92 William de Berkeley created Earl of

1525–36 Henry Fitzroy, Duke of Richmond and Somerset, created Earl of – this was Henry VIII's illegitimate son

1596–1624 Lord Charles Howard of Effingham created 1st Earl of

Ormond(e)

1477–1515 Thomas Butler, 7th Earl of Ormond

1492 Thomas Bullen (Boleyn) created Baron Ormond

1515–28 (relinquished) Sir Piers Butler (inherited as 8th Earl of Ormond) – when Henry forced him to relinquish title to Boleyn, he created Butler Earl of Ossory in compensation

1529–38 Sir Thomas Boleyn, created Earl of Wiltshire and Ormond

1538–39 d. Sir Piers Butler, 8th Earl
(restored)

1541–46 James Butler, Viscount Thurles, restored as 9th Earl of Ormond, died in London from poisoning

1546–1614 Thomas Butler, son of James, inherited as 10th Earl – known as 'Black Earl'; brought up a Protestant at Henry VIII's court

Oxford

1485–1513 John de Vere, restored as 13th Earl of

1514–26 John de Vere, nephew of 13th Earl, inherited as 14th Earl of

1526–40 John de Vere, second cousin of 14th Earl, inherited as 15th Earl of

1540–62 John de Vere, son and heir of 15th Earl, inherited as 16th Earl of

1562–1604 Edward de Vere inherited as 17th Earl of

Pembroke

1532–36 Anne Boleyn, Marchioness of (created 1 September 1532)

Pembroke

1551–70 William Herbert, grandson of William Herbert, Earl of Pembroke of the First Creation, was created 1st Earl of Pembroke of Second Creation

1570–1601 Henry Herbert, Lord Herbert, inherited as 2nd Earl of; he married Catherine Grey in 1553 but divorced her in 1554 after Jane Grey's execution. He married Mary Sidney in 1577, after Catherine's death in 1568

Rochford

1495 Thomas Bullen (Boleyn) Baron Ormond (grandfather to Anne Boleyn) created Baron Rochford of Rochford

1525–30 Thomas Boleyn, son of the above, created Viscount Rochford

1530–36 George Boleyn, son of Thomas Boleyn Earl of Wiltshire and Ormonde
(executed) and brother of Anne Boleyn, created Viscount Rochford

Salisbury

1513–41 Margaret Plantagenet, daughter of George, Duke of Clarence, brother of
(executed) Edward IV, married by Henry VII to Sir Richard Pole (d. 1505) of Bucks. and given lands in atonement for d. of her brother Edward, Earl of Warwick; created Countess of, and made governess of Princess Mary. Mother of Reginald and Henry Pole (see Section 12.2: Bibliographical index) 1539: Act of Attainder, 1541: exec.

Shrewsbury

1473–? George Talbot, son of John, 3rd Earl, inherited as 4th Earl of

1538–60 Francis Talbot, 2nd son of 4th Earl, inherited as 5th Earl of

1560–90 George Talbot, son of 5th Earl, inherited as 6th Earl of; in 1568 he married Elizabeth known as 'Bess of Hardwick'

1590–1616 Gilbert Talbot, 2nd son of 6th Earl, inherited as 7th Earl of; he married Mary Cavendish, daughter of Bess of Hardwick

Somerset

1500 Edmund Tudor, infant 3rd son of Henry VII (d. 1500)

1525–36 Henry Fitzroy created Duke of Somerset – illegitimate son of Henry VIII

1547–52 Edward Seymour, Earl of Hertford, created Duke of
(executed)

Southampton

1537–42 William FitzWilliam, Lord High Admiral, created Earl of

1547–50 Sir Thomas Wriothesley, Knight of the Garter and Lord Chancellor, created first Wriothesley Earl of Southampton

1550–81   Henry, son of Thomas 1st Earl, inherited as 2nd Earl of

1581–1624 Henry, son of 2nd Earl, inherited as 3rd Earl when aged only eight; was Shakespeare's patron and friend

Strange (of Knockyn)
1559   Henry Stanley, Lord Strange

1590   Ferdinando Stanley

Suffolk
1455–92   John de la Pole, restored to be 2nd De La Pole Duke of Suffolk; supported Richard III at Bosworth but swore fealty to Henry VII

1492–93   Edmund de la Pole, Duke of; he surrendered the dukedom in Feb. 1493

1493–1513 Edmund de la Pole created Earl of

(executed)

1514–45   Charles Brandon, Duke of; he married first Mary Tudor then Catherine Willoughby (Bertie)

1545–c.51 Henry, son of Charles, Duke of Suffolk while student at Cambridge

1551   Charles, son of Charles, briefly Duke of

1551–54   Henry Grey, Marquis of Dorset; he was Lady Jane Grey's father

(executed)

Surrey
1483–1514 Thomas Howard, restored as Earl of Surrey in 1489; he became 2nd Howard Duke of Norfolk

1514–24   Thomas Howard, eldest son of Thomas, 2nd Duke of Norfolk, Earl of Surrey; he became 3rd Howard Duke of Norfolk

1524–47   Henry Howard son of Thomas 3rd Duke of Norfolk, called Earl of

(executed) Surrey by courtesy

1553–54   Thomas Howard restored to title

1554–72   Thomas Howard, his grandson, made Earl of

(executed)

1572?   Philip Howard, eldest son of Thomas, 4th Duke of Norfolk, attended Cambridge in 1570s with courtesy title of Earl of; became Earl of Arundel when he married Mary Fitzalan, the heir

1604–46   Thomas Howard, son of Philip restored to Earldom of Surrey in 1604

Sussex
1529–42   Sir Robert Radcliffe, son of John, 1st Baron Fitzwalter, created 1st Earl of Sussex; name is occasionally given as Ratcliffe

1542–57   Sir Henry Radcliffe, son of 1st Earl, inherited as 2nd Earl of

1557–83   Sir Thomas, eldest son of 2nd Earl, inherited as 3rd Earl of

1583–93   Sir Henry Radcliffe, son of 2nd Earl, inherited from brother as 4th Earl of

1593–1629 Robert Radcliffe, son of 4th Earl, inherited as 5th Earl of

Tyrone
1542–59   Con Bacach O'Neill, created 1st Earl of (also given as Con Bacagh O'Neill)

1559–60   Shane O'Neill, son of Con, recognised by Elizabeth on accession but revoked in 1560

1560–62   Brien O'Neill, grandson of Con

1585–1614 Hugh O'Neill, grandson of Con, admitted Earl in 1585
(forfeited   Confusion is added to this tale by the existence of Sir Turlough Luineach
title)   O'Neill (c. 1530–95) who was Lord of Tyrone and a contender for Shane
               O'Neill's position

Warwick

1475–99   Edward son of George, Duke of Clarence, and Earl of Warwick
(executed)
1547–51   John Dudley, Viscount Lisle, a descendant of Richard Beauchamp, Earl
               of Warwick, 1401–39; he was later Duke of Northumberland
1551–54   Lord John Dudley; eldest son of John Dudley, Duke of Northumberland;
               he was styled Earl of Warwick during Northumberland's lifetime

Willoughby

1580   Peregrine Bertie made Baron Willoughby of Eresby

Winchester, Bishop of

1447–86   William Wayneflete, consecrated 30 July 1447; d. 11 Aug. 1486
1487–92   Peter Courtenay, translated from Exeter Apr. 1487; d. 22 Sept. 1492
1493–1501 Thomas Langton, translated from Salisbury June 1493; translated to
               Canterbury 22 Jan. 1501; d. 27 Jan. 1501
1501–28   Richard Fox, translated from Durham Oct. 1501; d. 5 Oct. 1528
1529–30   Thomas Wolsey Archbishop of York, held this see *in commendam* Apr.
               1529; d. 29 Nov. 1530
1531–51   Stephen Gardiner, consecrated 3 Dec. 1531; depr. 14 Feb. 1551
(deprived)
1551–53   John Ponet, translated from Rochester; deprived 1553; d. 11 Aug. 1556
(deprived)
1553–55   Stephen Gardiner, restored Aug. 1553; d. 12 Nov. 1555
1556–59   John White, translated from Lincoln July 1556; deprived 26 June 1559;
(deprived) d. 12 Jan. 1560
1561–80   Robert Horne, consecrated 16 Feb. 1561; d. 1 June 1580
1580–84   John Watson, consecrated 18 Sept. 1580; d. 23 Jan 1584
1584–94   Thomas Cooper, translated from Lincoln Mar. 1584; d. 29 Apr. 1594
1595   William Wickham, translated from Lincoln Feb. 1595; d. 2 June 1595
1596   William Day, consecrated 25 Jan 1596; d. 20 Sept. 1596
1597–1616 Thomas Bilson, translated from Worcester May 1597; d. 18 June 1616

Worcester, Bishop of

1476–86   John Alcock, translated from Rochester Sept. 1476; translated to Ely 6
               Oct. 1486
1486–97   Robert Morton, consecrated 28 Jan 1487; d. before 5 May 1497
1497–98   Giovanni de' Gigli, consecrated 10 Sept. 1497; d. 25 Aug. 1498
1498–1521 Silvestro de' Gigli, consecrated before 6 Apr. 1499; d. 16 Apr. 1521
1523–33   Geronimo de' Ghinucci, consecrated Feb. 1523; deprived 21 Mar. 1533
1535–39   Hugh Latimer, consecrated 26 Sept. 1535; resigned 1 July 1539; d. 16
(resigned) Oct. 1555

1539–43   John Bell, consecrated 17 Aug. 1539; resigned 17 Nov. 1543; d. 11 Aug.
           1556
1543–51   Nicholas Heath, translated from Rochester Feb. 1544; deprived 10 Oct.
           1551
1552–54   John Hooper (held w. See of Gloucester from May 1552); deprived 15
(deprived) March 1554; d. 9 Feb. 1555
1554–55   Nicholas Heath, restored 1554; translated to York 21 June 1555
(restored)
1555–59   Richard Pates, deprived 26 June 1559; d. 5 Oct. 1565
(deprived)
1559–71   Edwin Sandys (also Sandes), consecrated 21 Dec. 1559; translated to
           London 13 July 1570
1571–76   Nicholas Bullingham, translated from Lincoln Jan. 1571; d. 18 Apr.
           1576
1577–83   John Whitgift, consecrated 21 Apr. 1577; translated to Canterbury 23
           Sept. 1583
1584–91   Edmund Freke, translated from Norwich Dec. 1584; d. 21 March 1591
1593–95   Richard Fletcher, translated from Bristol Feb. 1593; translated to London
           10 Jan. 1595
1596–97   Thomas Bilson, consecrated 13 June 1596; translated to Winchester 13
           May 1597
1597–1610 Gervase Babington, translated from Exeter Oct. 1597; d. 17 May 1610

York, Archbishop of
1480–1500 Thomas Rotherham, translated from Lincoln Sept. 1480; d. 29 May
           1500
1501–07   Thomas Savage, translated from London Apr. 1501; d. 2 Sept. 1507
1508–14   Christopher Bainbridge, translated from Durham Dec. 1508; d. 14 July
           1514
1514–30   Thomas Wolsey, translated from Lincoln Sept. 1514; d. 29 Nov. 1530
1531–44   Edward Lee, consecrated 10 Dec. 1531; d. 13 Sept. 1544
1545–54   Robert Holgate, translated from Llandaff Jan. 1545; deprived 23 March
(deprived) 1554; d. 15 Nov. 1555
1555–59   Nicholas Heath, translated from Worcester June 1555; deprived 5 July
(deprived) 1559; d. 1579
1561–68   Thomas Young, translated from St David's Feb. 1561; d. 26 June 1568
1570–76   Edmund Grindal, translated from London May 1570; translated to
           Canterbury 10 Jan. 1576
1577–88   Edwin Sandys, translated from London March 1577; d. 10 July 1588
1589–94   John Piers, translated from Salisbury Feb. 1589; d. 28 Sept. 1594
1595–1606 Matthew Hutton, translated from Durham March 1595; d. 15 Jan. 1606

15

GLOSSARY

Accession Day Tilts   By the 1570s the Queen's accession day, 17 November, had become a national holiday marked by elaborate tournaments under the control of Sir Henry Lee (q.v.). These court tournaments revived the cult of chilvalry in the interests of Protestant patriotism.

Adiaphora   Greek for 'things indifferent'. In Germany, a group of Protestants argued that certain Catholic practices (such as confirmation, extreme unction, the Mass without belief in transubstantiation and veneration of saints) might be conceded in the interests of peace without compromising essential Protestant doctrine. In England, there was some argument of this kind surrounding the use of vestments and rituals such as the cross in baptism, kneeling at the name of Jesus and the use of the ring in marriage.

Advowson   Right to appoint one in holy orders to an ecclesiastical benefice. Treated under English civil law as a piece of property which could be transferred by sale or grant. See 'Hac Vice Presentations' and 'Benefice'.

Affective Family   Used by late twentieth-century historians to describe the family knit together by sentiment, which is thought by some (notably Lawrence Stone) to have emerged for the first time in the early modern period.

Affines (Affinity)   At this time meant relations (or relationship) by marriage. See 'Consanguinity'.

Aggregative back projection   A demographic research technique that employs a computer program to work backwards in time at five-yearly intervals from reliable census data concerning size and age structure for a given population, adjusted for numbers of deaths (derived from mortality tables) and numbers of migrants within each five-year period. E.A.Wrigley & R.S. Schofield, *The Population History of England 1541–1871: A Reconstruction*, 1981 (paperback ed'n, Cambridge, 1989) repays careful reading and, on pages 195–207, contains a useful description and critique of the method.

All Saints' Day (All Hallows)   1 November. An important feast of the pre-reformation church. See 'Hallowe'en' and 'All Souls' Day'.

All Souls' Day   2 November. An important feast of the Pre-reformation Church.

Amicable Grant   Wolsey's attempt to raise money for the French war in 1525. Without parliamentary sanction, Wolsey levied one-third of clergy goods and one-sixth of laymen's goods. After massive demonstrations in Suffolk, Wolsey was persuaded to withdraw the tax.

Anabaptist Umbrella term to cover sects which denied the truth of infant baptism.

Annunciation (Lady Day) 25 March. Used as the starting point of the year in England from the twelfth century down to 1752, although 1 January was accounted New Year's Day, following the Roman tradition. It occurs as a Red Letter Day in the Book of Common Prayer. See 'Holy Days'.

Anti-clericalism Opposition to the clergy as a body. Some debate about its importance in the spread of popular Protestantism.

Aragonese Faction Sometimes used by historians to describe those at Henry VIII's court who supported Katherine of Aragon in the divorce proceedings and opposed Cromwellian religious reforms. There is some doubt whether such a 'faction' existed.

Arches, Court of Court of appeal for the Province of Canterbury. Its equivalent for the Province of York was Chancery. The Court of Arches was physically located in the church of St Mary le Bow (St Mary of the Arches, *de arcibus*), London.

Archpriest Controversy In 1599, 31 Roman Catholic secular priests, led by William Bishop (c. 1553–1624), appealed to Rome to cancel the appointment of George Blackwell (c. 1545–1613) as Archpriest and superior of the English mission, on the grounds that the pro-Jesuit policy was harming the Roman Catholic cause in England. The group was known as the Appellant Priests. This initial appeal was unsuccessful but further appeals in 1601 and 1602, with the backing of the French ambassador, resulted in Blackwell's reprimand and, in January 1603, a renunciation of the policy of seeking to replace Elizabeth.

Aristocracy Used in several senses. By some historians used to describe titled members of society with their families (that is, the nobility) and by others to include both the peerage and the gentry, whether titled or no.

Armada(s) A fleet of warships. Most frequently used to describe fleet sent by Philip II of Spain against England in 1588 as 'The Spanish Armada'.

Ascension Day Thursday following '**Rogation Sunday**' and '**Rogation Days**' (q.v.). It was one of the chief feasts of the year and kept on the 5th Thursday after Easter.

Ash Wednesday First day in Lent. This was the day when, traditionally, the whole congregation assembled for general penance. The Book of Common Prayer of 1549 prescribed a communion service for this day.

Assumption of the Blessed Virgin Mary 15 August. This important feast-day of the Catholic church was removed from the Book of Common Prayer of 1549 and not restored in those of 1552 and 1559.

Attainder An act of Parliament was passed to stage an execution without trial. The title and possessions of the attainted passed to the Crown. This was the method favoured by the Tudors for ridding themselves of opponents.

Audience, Court of The Provinces of Canterbury and York each had a Court of Audience at which serious cases (often involving clergy) were heard in the presence of the Archbishop. Similar courts were held in each diocese, when they were commonly special sessions of the Consistory Court presided over by the bishop.

Augmentations, Court of This was a government department created in 1536 to administer the new Crown revenues from the dissolved monasteries. In 1547, it was amalgamated with the Court of General Surveyors and both were absorbed by the Exchequer in 1554.

Baptism Christian initiatory rite. Spiritual regeneration signalled by water and the sign of the cross. Debate concerning the nature of baptism, both among the reformers themselves and between the Protestants and the Catholics. Book of Common Prayer accepted baptism as a sacrament and clung to Catholic doctrine that baptism was necessary for salvation. Roman Catholics restated their doctrine at Council of Trent and emphasised the fact that baptism was not only a sign of grace but actually conferred grace upon the baptised.

Bawdy Court Contemporary popular term for the 'office' side of the Church courts, renowned for hearing cases involving sexual misdemeanour, defamation, etc. See Chapter 10: Ecclesiastical courts and commissions.

Bedlam See 'Bridewell'.

Benefice An ecclesiastical office with prescribed duties attached, in reward for which certain revenues were given (known as 'temporalities'). For example, a vicarage was a benefice and so was a prebend. The vicar discharged a cure (care) of souls in exchange for which he received the small tithes from his parishioners. A prebendary's duties were associated with the cathedral and, in exchange for their performance, he drew revenues from a given portion of land.

Benefit of Clergy Clergy charged with felonies exempted from secular trial. Applied to all those who were tonsured (i.e. in Minor as well as Major Orders) as well as to nuns. Extended to all those who could read a Latin passage at a time when it was assumed that only the clergy would have this skill. Not completely abolished in England until 1827, but benefit of clergy removed at the Reformation for many categories of offence.

Benevolence So-called free gifts made by the wealthy to the Crown. Richard III made them illegal but both Henry VII and Henry VIII used them.

Bible See Chapter 4: The world of learning under 'The Bible and biblical scholarship'.

Bishops' Book Popular name for *The Institution of a Christian Man*, 1537. This statement of the doctrine of Henry VIII's church was drawn up by a committee of bishops but, although published, never received royal approval. See 'King's Book'.

Black Rubric In September 1552, John Knox complained, in a sermon before Edward VI, against the directive in the new Prayer Book for communicants to adopt a kneeling position. Cranmer refused to alter the wording. The Council then inserted the 'Black Rubric' into the Prayer Book (apparently on its own authority). This Rubric denied any intention to adore the elements of bread and wine or to imply that they were the body and blood of Christ (see 'Elevation of the host').

Blois, Treaty of Treaty of 1572 between England and France. The English hoped thereby to isolate Spain and to prevent France invading Flanders.

Bond of Association, 1584 See Chapter 1: General chronology.

Bond (of obligation)   Under English law, an individual (or individuals) (the obligor) legally binds himself, his heirs, executors, assigns, etc. to pay a given sum of money to the obligee. Such were frequently *penal bonds* which would be paid only in given circumstances (e.g. if a debt was not paid by a certain date).

Border Wardens   Officials appointed to wardenries of the East, West and Middle Marches on the border with Scotland for purposes of supervision and defence.

Bosworth, Battle of   In 22 August 1485, Richard III was surrounded at Bosworth Field, Leicestershire, after his rash advance to support his vanguard. He was defeated and died. Victory of Henry Tudor. Sir William Stanley's troops deserted to Henry's side.

Bridewell   Workhouses. Houses of correction. Name derives from Henry VIII's Palace of Bridewell at Blackfriars, London, which in 1553 was given by Edward VI to the City of London as a workhouse for vagrants and troublesome apprentices. This also ran the Bethlehem hospital for the insane, commonly known as 'Bedlam', and was linked to the St Thomas's and St Bartholomew's Hospitals and to Christ's Hospital for destitute children. This scheme was widely copied by magistrates elsewhere, but the local Bridewells frequently lost their 'workhouse' aspect and turned into prisons for the poor.

Bruges, Treaty of   Secret treaty (1521) between Emperor Charles V and Henry VIII providing for a joint invasion of France before March 1523. Did not materialise. English staged campaign (autumn 1523) and with, minimal help from Charles, got nowhere.

Buggery   In 1534, parliament passed the first legislation against buggery in all its forms, homosexual and heterosexual, and named the offence punishable by the death penalty.

Bull   From the Latin word *bulla* meaning seal. Denotes a written order or mandate from the Pope. It would be sealed by the papal signet on wax or kept in a seal-box.

Calais   This small port was captured by the English in 1347. Sole surviving possession of the Hundred Years' War, this town and its small pale became important for trading and strategic reasons. It was garrisoned, but the English neglected its defences. The town sent MPs to parliament until the French captured the port in 1558.

Calendar, Gregorian   Bull of Pope Gregory XIII on 24 February 1582 introduced a reformed calendar which cut ten days out of 1582 (5–14 October inclusive) to compensate for earlier divergences between the calendar and the solar year, and introduced a leap year every fourth year. Year began officially on 1 January. Catholic states adopted the new style in the sixteenth century but Protestant states did not do so, in general, until the eighteenth. Known as 'new style'. See 'Calendar, Julian'.

Calendar, Julian   Unreformed Roman calendar retained in Protestant countries beyond the Tudor period. Known as 'old style'. Jan. 1st celebrated as New Year but year changed on 25th March. See 'Calendar, Gregorian'.

Calvinism   The theology of John Calvin (1509–64), French reformer and theologian, who shaped the Reformation in Geneva. This was formulated in his *Institutes* (final edition published in Latin, 1559). He accepted various tenets of Lutheranism (Scripture as the only rule of faith; the denial of free-will after the Fall; justification by faith alone without works) but added the doctrines of predestination, the certainty of salvation and the impossibility of losing grace. On the question of the Lord's Supper, Calvin stood some way between Luther's belief in the Real Presence and Zwingli's view of the breaking of bread and drinking of wine as mere symbolism. Calvin was also concerned to reform the worship of Christians. Its nature was determined in the Scriptures and, to his mind, rejection of the Commandment not to worship images was a grave affront to God's majesty. He, and the churches who followed his teaching, reaffirmed the centrality of spiritual worship and drew strict boundaries between the spiritual and material, which on occasion led to civil disobedience in a war against the idols (iconoclasm). It represented a determined move away from a worship in which ritual and sacraments produced predictable and specific effects. This approach sharply distinguished the Calvinists from the Lutheran churches, which retained much of what Archbishop Laud was later to describe as 'the beauty of holiness' and clung to the centrality of the doctrine of justification by faith alone as a protection against material instrumentality in religion.

The Second Helvetic Confession of 1566, which summed up Calvinistic theology, was accepted by many Protestant countries but not by England. Many of the 'precise' Christians of Elizabethan England wished for a further reformation of the English church to bring it into line with the Calvinist continental churches.

Cambridge Group for the History of Population and Social Structure Founded by T.P.R. [Peter] Laslett and E.A. Wrigley to apply French demographic research techniques to English sources within a historical context. It began with simple work on parish registers but progressed to sophisticated family reconstitution, analysis of time series, and aggregative back-projection. See 'Aggregative back-projection'.

Canon law Ecclesiastical law pertaining to faith, morals and discipline. It had been built up gradually from papal and conciliar legislation. Some canons were universally binding; others only had local application.

Capitalism In a capitalist economic system, the means of production are privately owned by a few 'capitalists' and labour is separated from the means of production and socialised. Maximum profit is the purpose of economic activity. Acquisitiveness is regulated by the market place and is otherwise untrammelled unless it infringes the law. Capitalists pursue those modes of economic behaviour which appear most systematic, rational and appropriate to achieve maximum profit. Under early capitalism, entrepreneurs sought to establish the principles of acquisitiveness, competition and rational economic behaviour; home industry remained prevalent and technology was primitive – the few factories there were yielded low output. The suggestion that Calvinism caused, or was at least conducive to, the growth of capitalism in the sixteenth century, first posited by Max Weber, was adapted to the English Puritan case by R.H. Tawney, *Religion and the Rise of Capitalism* (1926). But this thesis has come under considerable attack. Historians now argue that neither Protestantism nor even Calvinism was a necessary condition for the emergence and development of rational capitalism but the link is, nevertheless, still stressed by non-specialists.

Cateau-Cambrésis, Treaties of   In 1559, both England and Spain signed separate treaties with France, ending hostilities. The French retained Calais (q.v.) for eight years but renounced territorial ambitions in Italy.

Catechisms   A popular manual of Christian doctrine adopting a dialogue form of question and answer for use orally. An ancient form, although the term seems to have originated in the sixteenth century. The Reformation saw a flood of catechisms, Protestant and Catholic.

The Prayer Book catechism was, from 1549 to 1662, printed directly before the confirmation rite and the parish priest was ordered to instruct the young of the parish on Sundays and Holy Days. The catechism contains an explanation of the covenant entered into on baptism, the Apostles' Creed, the Ten Commandments and the Lord's Prayer. Alexander Nowell, Dean of St Paul's under Elizabeth, appears to have been responsible for much of the catechism (see 'Thomas Becon' and 'Alexander Nowell' in Section 12.2: Biographical index).

Celibacy (of clergy)   Vow of perfect chastity required of all admitted to Major Orders in the Catholic church from the eleventh century onwards. Abolished in Church of England in reign of Henry VIII. Revived by Mary I. Elizabeth known to favour celibacy of clergy.

Chalice   Cup used to administer the consecrated wine at the Eucharist. See 'Church Plate'.

Chamber, Royal   See Chapter 5: Central government: (1) The monarchy and the royal household.

Chancery, Court of   See Chapter 7: Central courts.

Chantries   Used to describe the little chapels in which the Masses for the dead were said and the endowments of the same chapels. Became very numerous in the fourteenth and fifteenth centuries. The Chantries Act (1547) dissolved chantries and diverted endowments elsewhere. Debate about the deleterious effect of this dissolution upon educational provision.

Chaseabout Raid   James Stuart, Earl of Moray's, failed rebellion against Mary Stuart after her attempted Catholic coup in summer 1565. Name derived from indecisive character of the action. They chased about Scotland without ever meeting. Moray took refuge in England.

Chivalry   Describes, originally, the medieval knightly class which owed military service to feudal overlord or King. Came to be identified with the aristocracy and lost its military function. Chivalry often transferred to describe the distinctive customs, codes of morality (emphasising courage, loyalty, skill, various Christian virtues and the defence of womankind) and ritual and display which became associated with it.

Church Ales   These were fund-raising events, originating in the Middle Ages, traditionally involving the sale of beer.

Church Plate Term used to describe items such as the processional and altar crosses, and the **chalice** (q.v.) and **paten** (q.v.) used in the communion service. Many such items had been donated by parishioners. Their seizure in the late 1530s has been identified by historians as a major cause of local support for the **Pilgrimage of Grace** (q.v.)

Cinque Ports (Five Ports)   A group of ports in south-east England (originally Hastings, Sandwich, Romney, Dover and Hythe, although others such as Winchelsea and Rye were later added) which, from the thirteenth century onwards, furnished most of the English Navy and received various privileges in return, including jurisdiction over the coast from Seaford in East Sussex to Birchington in Kent. Their Lord Warden was, therefore, a powerful dignitary.

Classis, classes   One of the hierarchy of courts within the Presbyterian system of church government. It consisted of the ministers and representative elders of the churches within a given area. For some time it was argued that a Presbyterian system of *classes* operated within Elizabethan Puritanism – the Conference of ministers focused on Dedham in Suffolk being frequently cited as an example of a *classis* in operation – but an effective challenge was made to this argument by Patrick Collinson who questioned its relationship with other *classes* (and, therefore, its position in a national hierarchy of Presbyterian government) and its rejection of episcopacy as an acceptable form of church government.

Coinage   During this period the pound sterling and parts of the pound such as shillings and pence were the units of monetary exchange. Older forms of money such as the mark and half mark continued as minted and accounting units (with equivalents in the form of pennies).

Pound Sterling = 240 pennies or pence (d); 20 shillings (s)
Shilling Sterling = 12 pennies or pence (d)
Groat = 4 pennies or pence (d)
Penny
Half-penny
Farthing = quarter penny
Mark Sterling = 160 pennies or pence (d); 13s 4d
Half Mark Sterling = 80 pennies or pence (d); 6s 8d; one-third of a pound. Known as the Noble or double florin
Mite = one twenty-fourth of a penny. Used for accounting purposes only and no coin of this denomination minted.

Collegiate churches   These were churches governed by a corporation or college of secular clergy (q.v.). Many were suppressed at the Reformation although a few survived; for example, St George's Chapel, Windsor.

Colloquy   used by Erasmus to describe a 'conversation' or dialogue. Used to describe a meeting or conference (the modern form is colloquium).

Commission   A formal charge to perform a given function and a delegation of the necessary powers to fulfil this charge. This was a common instrument of both civil and ecclesiastical government during the Tudor period. See, for example, the Ecclesiastical High Commission (see Chapter 10: Ecclesiastical courts and commissions).

Common Prayer, Book of   Official prayer book of Church of England. Contains order of service for morning and evening prayer, Eucharist, baptism, matrimony, burial, confirmation and other rites, the psalter and (from 1552) the ordinal.

1549 First Prayer Book of Edward VI (enforced by Act of Uniformity)

1550 Ordinal

1552 Second Prayer Book of Edward VI. Recast Holy Communion Service; included introductions to morning and evening prayer; ordered the use of surplice instead of vestments in the ornaments rubric; removed references to 'mass' and 'altar'; included, without parliamentary authority, so-called 'Black Rubric' or declaration on kneeling during the communion.

1553 Mary I repealed Prayer Books and restored old services.

1559 Elizabethan Book of Common Prayer. Omits the Black Rubric.

Commons, House of   Lower House of Parliament at Westminster. In 1485, it had 296 members representing 37 counties and 111 boroughs. The number of constituencies grew so that, by 1603, there were 406 members representing 90 county seats and 370 borough seats (see Chapter 6: Central government: (2) Parliament for dates of sessions).

Commonwealth   Term used to convey the interests of the entire community of England – the *res publica* – commonweal = common good.

Commonwealthmen   A term used by some historians and others to describe a group of lay and clerical Protestants during the reign of Edward VI who agitated for reform of the state involving the curbing of corruption in the interests of the entire commonwealth. The precise composition (and, indeed, the very existence) of this group has been contested. See entries for Brinklow, Crowley, Hales, Latimer, Lever and Smith in Chapter 12: Biographical index.

Communion   (1) Fellowship between Christians. (2) Group or denomination of Christians sharing a common creed (q.v.). (3) The sacrament of the Eucharist.

Communion in Both Kinds   Protestant practice of offering both consecrated bread and wine to all communicants, lay and spiritual.

Communion in One Kind   Catholic practice at the Eucharist of offering the consecrated bread (but not the wine) to laypeople. Only the priest took the Communion in 'both kinds'. It was, however, common for the laity to partake in wine at the absolution of sin.

Compurgation (also known as 'purgation')   See Chapter 10: Ecclesiastical courts and commissions.

Conciliar   Adjectival form of council.

Conciliar government   Government by council; as, for example, the Privy Council and its offshoots, Star Chamber, Court of Requests and Court of High Commission.

Conciliar theory   Maintained that supreme authority in the Catholic church lay with a General Council and not the Pope. The conciliar movement or 'conciliarism' reached its apogee in the fifteenth century.

Confirmation   A rite practised in several Christian denominations during which, by the laying on of hands by the bishop, a baptised person receives special grace which will strengthen his or her Christian faith. It was popularly referred to as 'bishoping'. It was included among the seven sacraments of the Catholic Church and was retained as a sacrament in the Church of England, although not seen by it as essential to salvation. According to the Book of Common Prayer no one was to be confirmed unless they could recite the catechism.

Consanguinity Relationship by blood. See 'Affines (Affinity)'.

Consistory In the Church of England this described the Diocesan Bishop's court. In the Roman Catholic Church it was also the assembly of cardinals called together by the Pope and meeting in his presence (see Chapter 10: Ecclesiastical courts and commissions).

Constables See Chapter 8: Local government.

Consubstantiation This is an interpretation of the Eucharist, espoused by the Lutherans, which sees the consecrated bread and wine as coexistent with, but not transformed into, the body and blood of Christ (see 'Transubstantiation').

Convocation Each province had its own representative assembly of clergy, known as Convocation. Since the thirteenth century they had each been composed of an Upper House (of bishops) and a Lower House (of clergy). Originally, these were called to grant clerical taxation to the Crown but they came to deliberate on and make laws or canons for the Church. The Act of Parliament which embodied the Submission of the Clergy (1534) considerably curtailed Convocation's legislative powers. After the reformation it was accepted that Convocation would be dissolved at the same time as parliament.

Cope A liturgical vestment resembling a long cloak.

Cornish Rising Thomas Flamank, a Bodmin lawyer, and James, Lord Audley led a rebellion in 1497 against the levying of taxes for Scottish wars. A force of thousands moved east, killing a tax commissioner at Taunton, but was defeated by Giles, Lord Daubeney at the Battle of Blackheath on 13 June 1497.

Corpus Christi Latin, meaning 'body of Christ'. Name of an important religious festival on the Thursday after Trinity Sunday (in June) honouring the Eucharist. It assumed a prominent part in the culture of sixteenth-century towns prior to the Reformation. Frequently the occasion of a fair, as at Coventry.

Council, General Assembly of Bishops of the whole Catholic Church, convened by the Pope.

Council, Great Until the death of Henry VII, it was relatively common for the King to hold meetings of the Great Council. This has sometimes been seen as indicative of the weakening of the independent power of the nobility. See Chapter 5: Central government: (1) The monarchy and the royal household.

Council in the Marches of Wales See Chapter 8: Local government.

Council, Local Also known as synods. Persisted in Church of England after Reformation.

Council of the North See Chapter 8: Local government.

Council of the West See Chapter 8: Local government.

Counter-Reformation Term commonly employed to describe movement within Roman Catholic Church to halt spread of Protestantism and win back converts. More fashionable to use term Catholic Reformation, which does not see the cause of Catholic reform purely in terms of reaction to Protestant activity.

Court, the Both temporal and spiritual rulers had courts. Sixteenth-century rulers, in general, carried on the medieval peripatetic tradition of moving their entourage around with them from castle to castle and palace to palace. The monarchs displayed their power and influence to other potentates by means of outward show at court. Sometimes the monarch would take his court abroad to impress a fellow ruler, as Henry VIII effectively did at the Field of the Cloth of Gold (q.v.) in 1520. Sovereigns also maintained their control at home by patronage (or withholding of patronage) at court.

The royal household formed the basis of the court. Subjects angled for a place on the permanent establishment of this household – such a place (as, for example, Groom of the Chamber) brought with it free board and lodging and the potential for influence. But certain great men and women were also accorded 'bouge of court' (the right to food, drink, lodging, and fuel in the royal households, not only for themselves but for a specified personal retinue). In the 1540s, the members of the Privy Council were accorded 'bouge of court' as were Gentlemen of the Privy Chamber. Others had to apply to the monarch for permission to attend the court and thus influence events. When the monarch withheld permission this was considered a mark of disfavour.

Court life was not always a matter of receiving and entertaining foreign ambassadors and their retinues or listening to the counsel of advisers. Highly organised entertainment was provided – including sports such as tennis, hunting, jousting and masques and, within a carefully controlled etiquette, cultural activities were encouraged. 'Courtship' between the men and women of the court was in itself a highly-charged form of entertainment. Monarchs sought to keep it within the bounds of the chivalric code and, through it, to exercise their own patronage. Elizabeth, for example, felt that she had rights over the marriage of her **maids of honour**.

Courts Christian Another way of referring to the ecclesiastical courts. See Chapter 10: Ecclesiastical courts and commissions.

Courts, Inns of See 'Inns of Court'.

Creed From the Latin *credo* meaning 'I believe'. A summary and declaration of main articles of Christian faith. The three creeds (Apostles', Nicene and Athanasian) had their origins in the early church.

Dates To calculate the dates of important Holy Days such as Easter in any year or to determine upon which day of the week a certain date fell, consult C.R. Cheney, *Handbook of Dates for Students of British History*, 2000.

De Heretico Comburendo An Act passed by parliament in 1401 as first step in suppression of Lollardy (2 Henry IV, c. 15). Persons suspected of holding heretical opinions to be arrested and tried by canon law. If found guilty, the ecclesiastical judge was to hand the heretic over to the secular courts for the death sentence. Death was by burning at the stake. *De Heretico Comburendo* (sometimes *De Haeretico Comburendo*) was repealed under Henry VIII, restored by Mary I and finally repealed by Elizabeth I.

Delegates, Court of Created in 1534 as final court of appeal from archbishops' courts. Previously such appeals had gone to Rome (25 Henry VIII, c. 19). Commission appointed for each separate case.

Diocese Territorial unit of administration under the ordinary jurisdiction of a bishop. Normally divided into parishes, which are grouped into rural deaneries and archdeaconries.

Dissolution   Term commonly used to describe dissolution of the monasteries by the Acts of 1536 and 1539.

Divorce   After the Reformation, England was the only Protestant country with no form of legalised divorce. Elsewhere it was available to those who could prove adultery (especially by a wife), desertion or extreme cruelty. A commission to revise the canon law (originating in 1534) proposed a similar system, but this never reached the statute book. There were, however, judicial separations and some seem to have interpreted this condition as conferring a right to remarry, although the Church never conceded this. A full divorce might, however, be legalised by a private Act of Parliament. This meant that a full divorce was only available to those rich and influential enough to secure such an Act.

Dominicans   An order of preaching friars founded in 1215.

Dower   Traditionally, a widow was entitled to a dower of one-third of her late husband's estate in exchange for the dowry which she had brought him on marriage. See 'Dowry' and 'Jointure'.

Dowry   The portion which the bride brought to the marriage, in exchange for which she became entitled to support from her husband's property for the remainder of her life in the form of a dower of one-third of his estate. See 'Jointure'.

Dry Stamp   At the close of Henry VIII's reign, when he was ill and during the minority of Edward VI, documents were stamped with the royal signature which was then inked in by authorised clerks. In the possession of first Somerset, and then Northumberland, it was the key to authority and power. Elizabeth I made sure that no one else had access to it.

Earl Marshal   This was one of the great offices of state. The Earl Marshal presided over the College of Arms and the High Court of Chivalry (making grants of arms and titles and judging disputes) and might deputise for the monarch in command of the armies or in emergency summoning of parliament. In the fifteenth century (until 1485) it was a hereditary office of the Dukes of Norfolk. The sixteenth-century Dukes of Norfolk were granted the office for life only. When the fourth Duke was executed in 1572, the office was granted to the Earl of Shrewsbury and, on his death, it lapsed until Essex was appointed Earl Marshal in 1597. Essex seems to have intended to exploit the powers of the office.

Easter Day (Pascha)   A variable feast calculated to be the Sunday after full moon on or next after 21 March. Should you wish to calculate when Easter occurred in any particular year (and any feast dependent upon the date of Easter) consult C.R. Cheney, *Handbook of Dates for Students of British History*, 2000.

Ecclesiastical   Of or relating to the church. Not the same as religious.

Ecclesiastical courts   See Chapter 10: Ecclesiastical courts and commissions.

Elevation of the host   The 'host' was the consecrated bread which Catholics believed to be the sacrament or the body of Christ. By the fifteenth century, it was common to elevate the host for adoration during the Eucharist. The acceptance of 'communion of the eyes' (which permitted the sick who could not swallow it, to gaze upon it and still receive grace) reinforced this emphasis on 'viewing' the host. The host was regarded not only as a passive object to be worshipped, but also as an active object which worked wonders. There was much controversy within Catholicism concerning such teachings; the Protestants declared them anathema.

Emperors

1440–93   Frederick III of Hapsburg.

1493–1519 Maximilian I (m. to Mary of Burgundy united the inheritance of Austria and Burgundy)

1519–56   Charles V (as the eldest son of Philip of Burgundy and Joanna of Castile, inherited Spain and her possessions along with Austrian and Burgundian possessions. He abdicated in 1556 and died in 1558)

1556–64   Ferdinand I (brother of Charles V)

1564–76   Maximilian II (son of Ferdinand and preferred by German electors to Philip II of Spain, Charles V's son)

1576–1612 Rudolf II.

Empire, Holy Roman   Claim to universal empire based on succession to Roman Empire and especially active under Charles V of the House of Hapsburg. Austria, parts of southern Germany, the Netherlands, Franche-Comté and Spain, Naples, Sicily, Sardinia and the Balearics and the Spanish possessions in the Americas were all part of Charles V's inheritance between 1516 and 1519 as eldest son of Philip of Burgundy and Joanna of Castile. In 1519, Charles was elected Holy Roman Emperor in preference to Francis I of France. The remainder of the period saw a struggle for Hapsburg succession in central Europe and immense Hapsburg-Valois rivalry in which England was embroiled. For a good discussion see H.G. Koenigsberger, George L. Mosse and G.Q. Bowler, *Europe in the Sixteenth Century*, Longman, 1989.

Enclosure   Enclosure of land to extinguish common grazing rights over it for sheep pasture by private individuals. Mostly affected the midlands. Controversial topic in sixteenth-century England when the pressure of population upon ever-shrinking commons became an issue.

Engrossment   Amalgamation of two or more farms into one, allowing all but one farmhouse to decay and leading to depopulation. Often spoken of in same breath as enclosure (q.v.) but did not inevitably accompany it.

Entail   Legal arrangement whereby land, etc. is settled on a number of persons in succession so that it cannot be treated as the absolute possession of any of them for purposes of sale, etc.

Erastian   Policies subordinating the Church to the State.

Escheator   From 1377/78, escheators (royal officials) were responsible for a single county or a group of counties to the Exchequer of Audit for their investigation of the Crown's feudal rights, including wardship (q.v.).

Eucharist   (from the Greek for 'thanksgiving') also known as Communion, the Sacrament, the Lord's Supper.

The central rite of Christian **worship** based upon the Last Supper when Jesus 'took bread, gave thanks and brake it, and gave it unto them, saying, "This do in remembrance of me"'. 'Likewise after supper he took the cup' and, saying that the wine was his blood shed for many, bade the disciples to drink from the cup. The precise meaning of this ritual gave rise to enormous controversy during the Tudor period: some argue that in it lay the fundamental difference between Catholic and Protestant (see 'Consubstantiation', 'Elevation of the host', 'Mass', 'Sacrament', 'Transubstantiation', q.v.). Before the Reformation, the Catholic laity received the bread only; the Protestant reformers introduced communion in both kinds (bread and wine) for the laity, thus removing a symbol of the separation between the clergy and the laity.

Evil May Day   Xenophobic riots led by apprentices against foreigners and their property during the traditional May Day celebrations in 1517. Some of the rioters were subsequently executed. The most serious civil unrest in Tudor London.

Excommunication   Literally 'out of communion'; offenders against the canon law were punished by either greater or lesser excommunication. Greater excommunication involved complete isolation from the community of Christians as well as being prevented from sharing in the bread of the Eucharist. No Christian might trade with or commune with one suffering this penalty. Lesser excommunication might be imposed for failure to appear before an ecclesiastical court when summoned so to do. Absolution from excommunication could be obtained by performing a set penance (traditionally wearing a white shirt and carrying a wand and confessing to one's sins in public – at church – in front of the congregation on a specific number of days) and presenting a certificate to this effect to the church court. The problems were those of overuse, enforcement of the sanction and the growing tendency for such penalties to be commuted into money payments.

Executors   An individual (known as a testator) who left a will was required to appoint an executor to administer his or her estate. A man's executor or administrator was generally his widow, if he left one; 70 per cent of those filing the 13,000 probate accounts in Canterbury diocese were women. See A.L. Erickson, *Women and Property in Early Modern England*, 1993, 34.

Exercises   Exercises of preaching or lectures by combination were 'a device for regular provision of preaching, typically in a market town and weekly, on market day, or once a month' (Patrick Collinson, *Godly People*, p. 468). These sermons were provided by a rota of ministers who voluntarily combined to offer this service. Sometimes the sermon would be followed by a conference of the ministers and a meal. While, broadly speaking, 'Puritan', these combination lectures or exercises were part of the tradition and life of the Church in England.

Ex-religious   The term refers to those clergy who withdrew from the rule and the religious house. The problem of discovering what happened to the large numbers of ex-religious in England after the dissolution of the monasteries has long exercised historians. See also 'Religious'.

Family, Extended   Used in several senses, but most usually by historians (as opposed to historical demographers) to mean the *entire* family, co-resident or not, including grandparents, parents, uncles, aunts, adult offspring and children. Not to be confused with the Extended Family Household (see 'Household, Extended Family').

Family, Stem   Term which describes a downwards extended family co-residing (see 'Household, Stem Family').

Feast Days   See 'Holy Days'.

Feoffees   Trustees.

Field of Cloth of Gold   Elaborately staged meeting between courts of Henry VIII and Francis I of France in June 1520 near Calais. Expensive chivalric display.

First Fruits and Tenths   Beneficed clergy were obliged to pay (to the Crown after the Reformation) the first year's revenue from their benefice as specified in the *Valor Ecclesiasticus* or King's Books and, thereafter, a tenth of this income annually. The Act of First Fruits and Tenths, 1534, gave the Crown one year's income every time a benefice changed hands and an annual tax of 10 per cent on all benefices as from Christmas 1535. These 'tenths' were to be collected by the bishops and paid into a specially created Crown department, the Office of First Fruits and Tenths.

   The new tax necessitated a great survey of both the landed and the ecclesiastical income of the English and Welsh Churches, which was carried out in 1535. The results of that survey were published in a Latin transcript; J. Caley and J. Hunter (eds), *Valor Ecclesiasticus . . .*, 6 Vols (1810–34). What this really meant for the clergy has been hotly debated by historians. How realistic were the assessments contained in the *Valor Ecclesiasticus*?

Flodden, Battle of   Battle on 7 September 1513 between James IV of Scotland and Henry VIII of England. Major English triumph. James IV killed and succeeded by infant James V, whose mother, Margaret Tudor (sister to Henry VIII), was Regent.

Forty-Two Articles   Defined the Eucharist in 1553 in a Zwinglian sense (the bread and wine are symbols of Christ's body and blood) and argued that justification before God was by faith alone, works playing no part in salvation and purgatory being a fiction.

Freewillers   A small Protestant sect in south-east England, under the leadership of Henry Harte, during Edward VI's reign. The sect clung to a belief in the importance of freewill in the acquisition of salvation. It supported religious toleration. It was opposed by other Protestant groups, who espoused predestination. The group was persecuted under Mary I and disappeared without trace.

Gavelkind   In Kent (and some other areas) free lands were divided equally among all the deceased's sons by the customary rule of gavelkind. But, in the same county, some copyholds of inheritance were divided amongst all the children, male *and* female and some given only to the youngest son or child by **ultimogeniture** (q.v.). Even in cases where gavelkind prevailed, it seems to have been common for some of the beneficiaries to 'sell' their land to one of their number to prevent breaking up the estate into impossibly small units (see 'Partible Inheritance' and 'Wills, Statute of').

Grand Tour   Practice of sending a young gentleman to complete his education by travelling in Europe, learning modern languages, studying Italian art and meeting major figures. It came into its own in the reign of Elizabeth and was well-established by 1600.

Great Rebuilding   Between c. 1570 and c. 1640, many of the aristocracy (gentry and nobility) built new and often magnificent houses.

Habit   The distinctive dress which distinguished the cleric from the lay person and which was compulsory. There were continuing attempts throughout the century to enforce the rule that clergymen must not dress as laymen.

Hac Vice Presentations Ecclesiastical patrons were often unwilling to alienate advowsons (q.v.) entirely but would grant (for a sum of money) the right to present an ecclesiastical benefice to a third party. In this way, many people of relatively small means acquired patronage for their relatives and friends.

Hallowe'en Celebrated on 31 October, the eve of All Hallows. It is a secular holiday with Celtic and Christian origins. For the Celts it was a combination of harvest festival, New Year celebration and ceremonies to protect the harvest from evil spirits on the day when the boundaries between dead and living dissolved. In the ninth century the Christian All Saints Day, until then celebrated in May, was moved to 1 November; hence, the amalgam of Christian and Pagan traditions. Most of the festivities that we associate with this day are Irish or American in origin. See 'All Saints Day'.

Hanaper Ancient name for the financial department of the Chancery into which fees were paid for letters patent and writs.

Henry, Louis Mid-twentieth century French demographer who developed technique of family reconstitution involving record linkage between baptismal, marriage and burial registers. Enormous influence on English historical demography (see 'Cambridge Group for the History of Population and Social Structure').

Heresy Traditionally, bishops, popes, general councils, universities and inquisitorial offices had defined orthodox belief and, therefore, heresy (departure from orthodox belief). There had always been contests about ultimate authority in this process (between, for example, popes and general councils) but new problems arose when Henry VIII severed the allegiance of his Church from Rome. The orthodox doctrine of the Church of England became a real issue and one upon which monarchs and lay and ecclesiastical subjects did not always agree. Moreover, opinion shifted from day to day it seemed: what was orthodoxy one day was heresy the next. See, for example, the difference between the Ten Articles (q.v.) of 1536 and the Act of Six Articles (Six Articles, Act of q.v.) of 1539.

Holy Days The Catholic church designated a very large number of Holy Days. On such days, the laity and the clergy were forbidden to work and obliged to attend mass. While the Church of England abolished many of these, there were still a large number of Holy Days, including all Sundays and all those days for which the Book of Common Prayer provides a proper collect, epistle and gospel reading in its calendar. They included the feasts of Circumcision (1 Jan.), Epiphany (6 Jan.), **Ascension Day** (fifth Thursday after Easter), **Corpus Christi** (Thursday following Trinity Sunday), Saints Peter and Paul (29 June), **Lammas** (1 Aug. – first corn harvest); **Assumption of the Blessed Virgin Mary** (15 Aug.), Bartholomew (24 Aug.), St Michael (**Michaelmas**, 29 Sept.), All Saints (1 Nov.) and Christmas Day. Many Holy Days had a civic, agricultural and/or economic significance. A holy or feast day began at noon on the vigil (previous day) and lasted until midnight on the feast day: this had significance for the many payments, which were made on feast days. See 'Dates'.

Household Term used by contemporaries to describe the co-residential domestic unit. This comprised a nuclear family of father, mother and dependent children and servants. Closer inspection frequently reveals that the 'nuclear family' which formed the core of this unit was much more fluid in form than the historical demographers suggest.

Household, Extended Family Part of Peter Laslett's household typology. Describes those households containing a conjugal unit and children plus other relatives and any servants.

Household, Multiple Family Part of Peter Laslett's household typology. Describes households containing more than one conjugal (see 'Household, Simple Family') unit connected by kinship or marriage plus any servants. Includes Stem Family (see 'Family, Stem') but also households in which conjugal units of brothers and sisters co-reside.

Household, Simple Family Part of Laslett's household typology. Describes the type of household of which the conjugal relationship was the structural principle. It might include a married couple, or a married couple with children, or a widowed person with children and any servants.

Household, Stem Family (*la famille souche*) Part of mid-nineteenth century Frenchman Frédéric Le Play's typology of households. Describes a household in which a downwards **extended family** of two married couples and their children co-reside. For example: husband and wife, their eldest son and his wife, their grandchildren. Any unmarried adult children might also co-reside.

Humanism Intellectual movement characterised in our period by a preoccupation with recovery of the ancient world of Greece and Rome, its texts and its values. This recovery led to a growing vision of active involvement in civic affairs as one of the most worthwhile of human activities and education for such a vocation as a priority. Christian humanists (such as Erasmus) used this knowledge to further understanding of the Scriptures.

Husbandry Farming.

Iconoclasm Destruction of images and other church furnishings and decorations considered to detract from Protestant teaching that salvation is not assisted by works or the intercession of the saints and that God alone must be worshipped. See 'Calvinism'.

Iconography Pictorial or symbolical representation of ideas.

Indenture A deed between two or more parties with mutual covenants, executed by several copies, all having their tops or edges indented correspondingly to ensure security and identification; it has come to mean any signed and sealed agreement.

Index, the (*index librorum prohibitorum*) Paul IV in 1557 exhibited a list of books which Catholics were expressly forbidden to read or possess. The practice was continued by future popes.

Inflation (Price Rise) There has been much debate surrounding the extent and causes of the phenomenon of inflation. Prices of foods rose by seven times between the early sixteenth and the mid-seventeenth century and some industrial products saw a three-fold rise. Population pressure and a greatly increased supply of money certainly contributed to inflation but do not provide a convincing total explanation. The inflow of Spanish silver cannot explain a price rise in England which predates it or explain the discrepancy between the rise in food and industrial prices. Population pressure is more convincing as an underlying, but not sole, cause. Harvest failure, changes in output for other reasons and the debasement of the coinage in the 1540s all played their part.

Injunctions Royal: a series of royal proclamations on ecclesiastical affairs (1536; 1538; 1547; 1554; 1559).

Episcopal or Visitation: a bishop issued a number of injunctions ordering what should be done in his diocese.

Inns of Chancery A number of the Inns associated with the barristers at common law in London possessed no licensing powers. They seem to have been used largely as preparatory schools for the Inns of Court (q.v.). A youth would register and live at an Inn of Chancery while serving as a clerk in one of the offices of the common law courts. Later, he might move to an Inn of Court while training for the bar. Members of the Inns of Court learned their own trade by teaching in the Inns of Chancery. They were in decline by the seventeenth century and certainly did not constitute an essential preparation for the Inns of Court.

Inns of Court During the fourteenth century, a dozen or so Inns grew up associated with the barristers (apprentices) at common law. Four of these – known as Inns of Court – had the power to licence pleaders at the bar (barristers) from about 1454–55. They were Gray's Inn, Lincoln's Inn, Inner Temple and Middle Temple. The licensing system gave rise to the development of an educational system within the Inns to prepare apprentices for a legal career. This education was an apprenticeship at law rather than academic training *per se*. But the Inns formed other extremely important social functions in the Tudor period. They were used as finishing schools for elite youths who had no intention of practising law. A residential period at one of the Inns of Court (especially the fashionable Gray's Inn) was a shared experience and source of connection for many MPs and JPs.

Jesuits Religious order founded by the Spaniard Ignatius Loyola (1491–1556) in 1534 specifically to quash heresy. Pope Paul III recognised the order in 1540 and, henceforth, its activities were directed by the papacy. Characterised by a piety expressed through rigorous spiritual exercises designed to train and discipline the human will; it was a missionary order which became involved in education at all levels. Active in England. Conflict between Catholic secular priests and laity and the Jesuits (see 'Archpriest Controversy').

Jointure A settlement, on marriage, of lands or income to be held jointly by wife and husband and then, on the husband's death, by the widow. This was an alternative to the widow's rights, under common law, to a **dower** (q.v.) one-third of her deceased husband's estate.

Justices of Assize See Chapter 8: Local government.

Justices of the Peace See Chapter 8: Local government.

Justification by Faith Alone (*Solofideism*) Characteristic Lutheran teaching that the Christian is saved by faith in Christ alone and not by works of any kind.

Kett's Rebellion See Chapter 2: Rebellions against the Tudors.

King's Bench, Court of See Chapter 7: Central courts.

King's Book, 1543 Popular title for *The Necessary Doctrine and Erudition of a Christian Man* 1543, which was a revision of the Bishops' Book of 1537. Henry VIII commissioned the Bishops of Salisbury (Salcot), Worcester (Heath) and

Westminster (Thirlby) under Cranmer's supervision to revise the 1537 book, which had been Protestant in tone and substance. The King's Book defended transubstantiation (q.v.) and salvation by works. Not to be confused with the King's Books, another name for *Valor Ecclesiasticus*.

King's Chamber   See Chapter 5: Central government: (1) The monarchy and the royal household.

Knights of the Garter   Membership of this order of chivalry was restricted to the monarch and 25 knights and some foreign potentates. Places in the order were, in practice, controlled by the monarch and Henry VIII tried to raise its status.

Knockdoe   At the Battle of Knockdoe, in Galway in 1504, the Earl of Kildare (see Chapter 13: Tudor titles: Who was who) defeated Macwilliam of Clanricarde. It was a milestone in Kildare's rise to supremacy during Henry VII's reign. Reputed to have been the first occasion on which guns were used in an Irish battle.

Lambeth Articles   Issued in 1595 by John Whitgift (see Chapter 1: General chronology) as a Calvinist restatement of doctrine of the Church of England.

Lammas   1 August. It was customary to consecrate bread made from the first ripe corn of the harvest at Mass on this day; the name derives from 'loaf' and 'Mass'. The day had more than religious significance. In Coventry, for example, the so-called Lammas pastures were re-opened to common use on 1 August (until 2 February, Candlemas, the end of Winter). See 'Holy Days'.

Law Terms   These were variable in length because they depended upon the dating of Easter and other church feasts. Broadly speaking they were as follows: Michaelmas (c. 6 Oct. to 25 Nov.); Hilary (20 Jan. to 22 Feb.); Easter (Wednesday following 2nd Sunday after Easter to Feast of Ascension, nearly four weeks later); Trinity (Morrow of Trinity for three weeks – laid down for 1541 by 32 Henry VIII, c. 21).

Leases, Act of (32 Henry VIII, c. 28)   Forbade reversionary leases of more than 21 years or three lives.

Leases, Act of Ecclesiastical (13 Elizabeth I, c. 10; 14 Elizabeth I, c. 14; 18 Elizabeth I, c. 11)   These acts limited ecclesiastical and collegiate leases to those for 21 years or three lives.

Leases, Beneficial   The property was leased at a relatively low annual rental in exchange for a heavier entry fine than would otherwise be the case. Gradual replacement by leasing at commercial rents and relinquishment of entry fines.

Leases, long-term for years or lives   A comparatively heavy entry fine was charged by the landholder for a lease of property either for a term of years or for a term of lives. In the latter case, the lease would hold good until the death of all those specified in the will as 'lives'. Act of Leases (32 Henry VIII, c. 28) disallowed reversionary leases for more than 21 years or three lives and Acts during Elizabeth's reign placed similar restrictions on ecclesiastical landlords. By the end of Elizabeth's reign, it seems that leases for 21 years were most common, with those for three lives running second.

Lecture   A term generally used to describe a sermon provided outside the usual Sunday services, offered by a beneficed clergyman of the Church of England. The best-known were those founded and financed by the Puritans in London and elsewhere to supply Protestant preaching, by a specially appointed lecturer, where none was assured. See Paul Seaver, *The Puritan Lectureships: The Politics of Religious Dissent, 1560–1662*, Stanford, CA, 1970. For lectures by combination see **Exercises**.

Legate, Papal (*Legatus a Latere*)   A papal official whose commands could only be rejected via successful appeal to the Pope himself. Cardinal Wolsey was unusual in receiving the office for life.

Lent   A 40-day period of fast preceding Easter and beginning with a communal act of penance on **Ash Wednesday** (q.v.). One meal a day, which might include fish but not meat, and a light collation at night were allowed. The observance of Lent was ordered in the Book of Common Prayer. The behaviour of the people during Lent continued to be regulated by the secular as well as the religious authorities.

Limning   Miniature painting. In the 1520s, Henry VIII initiated the practice of commissioning miniature portraits of members of the royal family and, later, of prospective members. In the 1570s, however, the business was opened up and nobles, gentry and merchants commissioned miniatures from Nicholas Hilliard. Miniatures were used as 'tokens' to underline family and/or patronage relations.

Little Germany   Sardonic nickname accorded the White Horse Inn in St Edward's Parish, Cambridge, where young Cambridge scholars gathered to discuss the new German doctrines in the early 1520s. See 'Robert Barnes' and 'Thomas Bilney' in Section 12.2: Biographical index.

Liturgy   Used to decribe the prescribed public services of the Church. Also used to refer specifically to the mass.

Livery   A badge derived from the coat of arms used to mark the goods and servants of the armigerous classes. Wearing the insignia or livery of the lord indicated that a 'servant' acted under his protection and authority and was thus under obligation to do him service. Armies in the sixteenth century were customarily made up of bands of men wearing the livery of a lord and under just such an obligation. The system had its advantages and disadvantages for the central government – it reduced costs but it also reduced reliability.

Lollardy   Early Tudor heresy was largely inspired by Wycliffite and Lollard survival, particularly in the Chilterns, London, Essex and Kent. Lollard beliefs included a tendency to Biblical fundamentalism, an insistence upon the importance of preaching and the vernacular bible, anticlericalism and condemnation of ritual aspects of worship. There was, however, no national organisation and no precise Lollard creed. During the later years of Henry VIII their traditional Lollard beliefs tended to merge with imported Lutheran ideas. By far the best general discussion of Lollardy and its relation to Protestantism remains A.G. Dickens, *The English Reformation*, 1989.

Maids of Honour   Six young ladies who were not official staff of the Privy Chamber under Elizabeth but performed functions within the chamber. Elizabeth saw herself as controlling their 'marriages' but, in fact, her control was far from unchallenged by the young ladies themselves. Lady Katherine Grey, in line of succession, secretly married the Earl of Hertford; Bess Throckmorton secretly married Walter Raleigh; Lady Mary Howard insolently refused to hold open the Queen's cape and flirted with the Earl of Essex; Mary Fitton was made pregnant by the Earl of Pembroke. The position was one of indirect political influence and patronage.

Marian Exile   During the reign of Mary, considerable numbers of Protestant clergy and others who were closely associated with the Protestant regimes of Edward VI's reign, fled to the Continent. Congregations of English were established in many cities in Germany and Switzerland, notably Frankfurt, Geneva, Zurich, Strasbourg and Basel. After the accession of Elizabeth, connections made during the Exile, both with other English exiles and their foreign hosts, proved influential in the shaping of the Elizabethan Church of England.

Market(s)   There were 800 or so market towns in England and Wales, with hinterlands of variable size. In general, market towns clustered most thickly in the South-West, Hertfordshire, the Midlands, Kent and Suffolk. About 300 of the markets were specialising in particular produce to some extent by the end of the century. The markets were carefully regulated by the charter (which fixed the days of the market) and by the town which employed a number of market officers such as sweepers, bellmen, inspectors (lookers, conners and testers) and toll gatherers. The tolls were used to keep the market in good repair and for charitable purposes. See Joan Thirsk (ed.), *The Agrarian History of England and Wales, Volume IV, 1500–1640*, Cambridge, 1967 for an excellent account of marketing.

Martin Marprelate   See Section 12.2: Biographical index under Thomas Cartwright, Elizabeth Crane, John Field, John Penry, Job Throckmorton, John Udall, Robert Waldegrave. For anti-Marprelate tracts see Section 12.2: Biographical index under John Lyly and Thomas Nashe.

Marriage   The Catholic Church viewed marriage as a sacrament. Free and mutual consent formed the essential basis of this union which was designed for the procreation and education of children. A simple contract (not necessarily within the ecclesiastical context or rules) constituted a valid marriage. There were impediments to *ecclesiastical* marriage, some of which might render it invalid. The Church, however, while recommending parental consent to a match, did not regard such approval as essential. This position led to considerable friction between parents (who thought that they had the right to decide whom their children married) and the Church. During the sixteenth century, clandestine marriages (which took place secretly in contravention of the Church's canons) were a problem. For further discussion see R. O'Day, *Women's Agency in Early Modern Britain and the American Colonies*, 2007.

Mass   A title of the Eucharist (q.v.) which was retained in the First Prayer Book of Edward VI (1549) but thereafter discarded by the Church of England. This was, in part, because of its association with the doctrine of transubstantiation (q.v.) and the eucharistic sacrifice and, in part, because of its association with the doctrine of salvation by works, purgatory and indulgences.

Mercenaries   Foreign soldiers paid to fight for Crown. They were used to put down certain county or local rebellions where the loyalty of the militia was potentially in doubt. Expensive.

Michaelmas, Feast of St Michael the Archangel   29 September. See also 'Law Terms' for Michaelmas Term.

Militia   An armed force based on the county and raised by Commissions of Array. An Act for Having of Horse, Armour and Weapons, 1559, stipulated obligation of every able-bodied man, aged 16–60, to present himself at Muster (q.v.) for assessment of equipment, etc.

Minor Orders   In the medieval Catholic Church the orders of the Church's ministry were divided into Major Orders (sub-deacon, deacon and priest, bishop) and Minor Orders (porters, lectors [readers], exorcists, accolytes). Those in Minor Orders performed largely liturgical functions and they were not ordained as those in Major Orders were. The bishop blessed the candidate and handed him the instruments he required for his office. The Minor Orders and the Subdiaconate disappeared as Orders at the Reformation but there is evidence that the lectorship continued to be used and was effectively turned into an apprenticeship for those seeking Holy Orders. See R. O'Day, 'The Reformation of the Ministry' in R. O'Day and F. Heal (eds), *Continuity and Change: Personal and Administration of the Church of England, 1500–1640*, Leicester, 1`975.

Misprision of Treason   Charge of knowing that treason is being plotted but not revealing it.

Mitre   Shield-shaped head-dress worn by bishops at all solemn functions. It seems to have fallen into disuse in the Church of England from the Reformation to the nineteenth century.

Monopolies   A licence from the Crown by letters patent to exercise a monopoly in some area of activity, normally but not always trade and manufacture. For instance, monopolies were allocated for the production of printed music or playing cards but they were also made for exploration and plantation of various parts of the globe. They became expecially contentious in 1601.

Mortuary   An obligatory and stipulated payment to the priest on the death of a parishioner. This payment might be in kind or a money payment.

Musters   Assembling soldiers either for inspection, ascertainment of numbers and equipment or other purpose. Muster Rolls are an important source for population studies.

New Year Day   1 January. Regarded as New Year's Day even when the year was calculated from 25 March!

New Year Gifts   Customarily 'friends' exchanged gifts and tokens at New Year. This custom was formalised at the Tudor Court when gifts at New Year became part of the cement of the patronage system and an indicator of political fortune. The comparative value of the Crown's gifts signalled the relative importance at court of the recipients. If the monarch declined to make a gift to an individual this signified loss of political favour.

Official Reformation   Often used to describe the measures by which Henry VIII broke with Roman jurisdiction in contradistinction to the reformation of doctrine, worship and ministry for which some – commonly known as Protestants – worked.

Ordinal   The service for the ordination of priests and deacons. Produced in 1550 after the first Edwardian prayerbook. Included in subsequent prayer books.

Ordination   Ordination of bishops, priests and deacons in the Church of England was modelled upon the medieval Catholic rite. In the ceremony for the ordering of priests, the bishop placed his hands upon the head of the ordinand, who thus received the Holy Spirit and a charge to be 'a faithful dispenser of the Word of God and his Holy Sacraments'; with the gift of a Bible and the reception of the bread and wine the priest took 'authority to preach the Word of God and to minister the Holy Sacraments in this Congregation'. Ordination was to take place upon either a Sunday or a Holy Day.

There were rules governing ordination, some of which were evaded. Ordinands had to be examined by the archdeacon or the bishop's chaplains to establish their reputation, their age, their title, their knowledge of Scripture and their vocation.

Ornaments Rubric   This rubric, inserted before the services for morning and evening prayer in the Prayer Book of 1552, directed that the minister should not wear vestment, alb or **cope**. This was altered in the Prayer Book of 1559, intending to reintroduce the practice of 1549, although a mistaken dating led to confusion.

Pale of Dublin   Strip of coastal land between Dublin and Dundalk under English authority. The area was extended under Philip and Mary and Elizabeth. See Chapter 18: Maps.

Papacy   Bishop of Rome in direct descent from St Peter. Claimed supreme authority within western Christendom, but this claim was not uncontested. The fifteenth century saw General Councils (backed by the universities) laying contradictory claims. In the sixteenth century, the papacy achieved the upper hand once again but was particularly sensitive to suggestions of the revival of conciliarism and to threats to its authority from secular sources. The Henrician Reformation can be placed fruitfully within this general context. Papal infallibility was a nineteenth-century invention.

Parish   An area under the cure of an ordained minister (who, as incumbent, was supported from endowed land and tithes) to whose spiritual ministrations the inhabitants had a right. There were approximately 10,000 ecclesiastical parishes. The parish was also an important unit of civil administration. See Chapter 8: Local government.

Parson   Properly used to describe the holder of an ecclesiastical benefice who possesses all its tithes – that is a rector, whether cleric or lay, but often used to mean any clergyman.

Partible Inheritance   Divided inheritance.

Passion Week   Week before Easter. See 'Holy Days' and 'Dates'.

Paten   Dish used to carry consecrated bread at the Eucharist.

Patriarchy, Domestic   Government of the family and the household by the father. Refers to the powers of the father in the Old Testament over his wife and children – to chastise, arrange the marriages of, sell or even execute without challenge. This model – in the sense of authoritarian government by the father and husband with unquestioned powers over education, marriage, careers and property – was prescribed by some sixteenth-century intellectuals as appropriate to the family of the time, but historians now debate the extent to which the model was recommended and followed.

Peasant(ry) Sometimes used simply to mean those living off the land. In this sense, England was clearly a peasant society in the sixteenth century. A more precise definition is sometimes implied: that the family farm, owned or leased by the family and not by individuals, is the core of the economy, which is characterised by domestic subsistence production and relatively unaffected by market forces. Alan Macfarlane's *The Origins of English Individualism*, 1978, controversially claimed that English society was not a peasant society in the latter sense because land was owned, sold, devised and willed by individuals and not families. If true, this sets English society apart from that of France, for example.

Pentecost (Whit-Sunday) 7th Sunday after **Easter Day**. See 'Holy Days' and 'Dates'.

Pilgrimage of Grace A panicky revolt in defence of the old religion and the old economy in Lincolnshire, Yorkshire, Lancashire, Cumberland, Westmorland, Northumberland and Durham in 1536. Leading pilgrims tried and executed following renewed unrest in early 1537. See 'Church Plate'; see Chapter 3: Rebellions against the Tudors.

Pluralities, pluralism The practice of holding more than one benefice (ecclesiastical office) simultaneously. In certain circumstances (for example, when the benefices concerned were far distant from one another) this could lead to gross abuse. At a time when it was difficult to recruit sufficient able clergy and when ecclesiastical benefices were frequently too poorly remunerated to support well-educated and conscientious preachers, holding livings in plurality was a practical way around the problem for both the individual ministers and the Church itself. Attempts were made to curb the worst abuses. Dispensations to hold livings in plurality were issued by the Archbishops of Canterbury and York. By the canons of 1604 it was forbidden for a minister to hold benefices in plurality if they were more than 30 miles apart.

Popes Because the occupant of the papacy at any given time is often referred to in historical works simply as 'the Pope' without further individualisation, it is important to remember that the papacy changed hands 19 times during the Tudor period (at a time when there were only five different English monarchs, six Holy Roman Emperors and considerable continuity in France, Spain and Portugal), and that these changes signalled others in policy and influence.

1484–92	Innocent VIII (Giambattista Cibo).
1492–1503	Alexander VI (Roderigo Borgia).
1503 (Sept.–Oct.)	Pius III (Francesco Todeschini).
1503–13	Julius II (Giulio della Rovere).
1513–21	Leo X (Giovanni de' Medici).
1522–23	Adrian VI (Adrian of Utrecht).
1523–34	Clement VII (Giulio de' Medici).

Hostility to imperial claims to reform Christendom and to domination of Italy. 1524: formed alliance with France v. Spain. 1527: Pope captured by Emperor Charles V, nephew of Queen Katherine of Aragon. Possibility of papally sanctioned divorce removed. 1533: Cranmer consecrated Archbishop of Canterbury by Papal Bull. 1534: Pope threatens Henry VIII with excommunication for activating Act of Annates.

1534–49	Paul III (Alessandro Farnese).
1550–55	Julius III (Giovanni del Monte).
1555	Marcellus II (Marcello Cervini).
1556–59	Paul IV (Pietro Caraffa). Cardinal Reginald Pole quarrelled with Pope Paul IV. Pope deprived him of legacy (see 'Legate, Papal'); Mary refused to hand Pole over.
1559–65	Pius IV (Gian-Angelo de' Medici).
1565–72	Pius V (Michele Ghislieri). In 1570 published Bull, *regnans in excelcis*, excommunicating Elizabeth I and calling on Catholics to assist in her deposition.
1572–85	Gregory XIII (Ugo Buoncompagno). Pope Gregory lends patronage to Jesuit-run English College in Rome.
1586–90	Sixtus V (Felix Peretti).
1590	Urban VIII (Giambattista Castagna).
1590–91	Gregory XIV (Niccolo Sfondrato).
1591	Innocent IX (Gian-Antonio Fachinetto).
1592–1605	Clement VIII (Ippolito Aldobrandini). Pope appointed George Blackwell Archpriest to control Catholic clergy with exception of Jesuits.

Poynings Law (1494) provided that no act of Dublin Parliament could be valid unless previously submitted to and approved by the English Privy Council.

Praemunire Between 1353 and 1393 a series of acts were passed to forbid the Pope and other foreigners to encroach upon the Crown's rights in ecclesiastical property and jurisdiction. Later, it was altered to protect the lay courts against ecclesiastical jurisdictional claims. Appeals were made to these laws in the course of the official Reformation under Henry VIII.

Preamble The first part of a last **will and testament** in which the testator commends his or her soul to God and sometimes reveals his or her doctrinal inclination. Historians are deeply divided on the usefulness of studies of preambles for an insight into and barometer of popular belief during the Reformation.

Prayer Book See 'Common Prayer, Book of'.

Prerogative The royal prerogative powers, which permitted the monarch to govern, were granted by the laws of the realm and defined by the common law. Some of these rights arose out of the monarch's feudal overlordship, others out of his/her personal concerns. The Crown was given a certain flexibility to act outside the law when equity demanded, but not to disregard, or regard itself as above, the common law. The Crown could not by prerogative repeal or suspend statute. By proclamation, it could make orders consistent with existing statute law.

Primogeniture Feudal rule of inheritance by which the entire inherited landed estate, excluding only the widow's dower or jointure, passed to the eldest son or, in the absence of sons, to the daughter or daughters (as co-heiresses). The rule applied to free lands (held by knight service) and was operative only in cases of intestacy. By the Statute of Wills (1540) English men and women had freedom of testation, although there were certain restrictions. The practice of entailing estates by deed of entail to the eldest son and his heirs, etc., etc. was followed to prevent the break-up of great estates by will of the individual. There has been much debate about the importance of primogeniture in English society. See 'Wills, Statute of' and 'Entail'.

Privy Chamber Until the reign of Mary, I the Privy Chamber was staffed by males and was the centre of court politics. During the reigns of Mary and Elizabeth, however, it was staffed by women and changed its role somewhat.

Privy Council See Chapter 7: Central courts.

Probate When an individual with property died and left a will, the accuracy of this had to be proved and recorded in a court (hence probate) before the will could be executed and its terms followed. There were many probate courts (not all of them ecclesiastical) and complex rules governing which wills should be proved in which courts. The court in which the wills of the most prominent landowners were heard was the Prerogative Court of Canterbury which is commonly referred to as PCC (see Chapter 7: Central courts).

Proclamations There were several different categories of proclamation: Royal, Privy Council, Lieutenants', Commissioners' and Lord Mayors' proclamations. All these might be given royal authorisation but were not the same as royal proclamations. See 'Proclamations, Act of'.

Proclamations, Act of Empowered the King, with the consent of his council, to set forth proclamations. This was an existing and uncontested royal prerogative. Parliament met at often lengthy intervals and its statutes assumed, and sometimes specified, that the details of its programme would be left to royal proclamation. The Act (1539) attended to several uncertain aspects: the authority lying behind proclamations; their permitted scope; how they would be enforced. The Act confirmed existing practice – for example, forbidding proclamations touching life and property. Enforcement was difficult because proclamations had no force in the courts of common law and in practice had to be pursued in the Star Chamber. Some historians think that the Act was an attempt to make proclamations enforceable in the common law courts. If so, it failed.

Proclamations, Royal A royal proclamation was a legislative ordinance from the monarch and, in its published form, would be prefaced by the royal coat of arms; it might be made on the advice of the Privy Council; it would be signed by the monarch and issued under the Great Seal; it would be sent to officials (for example, sheriffs and mayors), accompanied by a royal writ ordering public proclamation of the schedule.

The right to issue proclamations was a common law prerogative of the Crown. The proclamation was inferior to statute and common law. They touched neither life nor common law rights of property. They could create offences with penalties attached but could not create a felony or a treason. Tudor royal proclamations touched social, economic, religious and administrative matters only. See 'Proclamations, Act of'.

Progresses Monarchs in the sixteenth century led peripatetic lives. They not only moved from royal palace to royal palace but also made summer progresses through the shires. Until the Dissolution of the Monasteries, it was customary for the monarch to rely upon monastic hospitality en route. Thereafter, the local notability bore the burden. Under both Edward and Mary, summer progresses went into abeyance but Elizabeth revived the practice. Many houses were built expressly to entertain the Queen (for example, Longleat, Theobalds and Holdenby) and are known as prodigy houses.

Prophesyings (Exercise of Prophesying) A public conference consisting of two or three sermons on the same text, examination of the text by assembled ministers and a summary of the proceedings by a moderator, which in part grew out of Elizabethan attempts to improve the education and collegiality of the parish clergy. Such large public assemblies, often the occasion for radical Protestant views and criticism of the 'but halfly-reformed' Church in England, aroused the hostility of many at court. The prophesying at Southam, Warws, was the direct cause of the ban on prophesyings insisted upon by Eliabeth in 1577, which itself occasioned the suspension of Archbishop Grindal. See 'Exercises' for a continuation and development of this tradition.

Prorogation (of parliament) Normal mode of terminating a session of parliament and thereby discontinuing business. However, the prorogations at Christmas and Easter often seem to have been regarded as adjournments which implied no termination of business.

Public Fasts In the late Elizabethan period, it became reasonably common for radical Protestant ministers to call fasts, often on Holy Days, for further reformation. Such large assemblies were unauthorised. The canons of 1604 made it permissible for the bishop alone to call such fasts.

Purgation (also known as Compurgation) See Chapter 10: Ecclesiastical courts and commissions.

Purgatory Catholics believed that individual souls were judged upon death. Purgatory was a place of waiting for the sinful, who could not yet be admitted to heaven until they had discharged penance for their sins. Intercession with the Saints and the Virgin; indulgences obtained after pilgrimages and other acts of piety; Masses said for the dead – all were a means of discharging sins committed upon earth, which would speed the progress of an individual soul through purgatory. The Protestant reformers rejected the doctrine of purgatory as an expression of the doctrine of salvation by works (that is human actions) rather than by faith alone (in the saving grace of Jesus Christ).

Queen's Day (Accession Day) 17 November. See 'Accesson Day Tilts'.

Queen's Evil, touching for the (also King's Evil) The skin disease of scrofula (swine's evil) or struma which affected the lymph nodes of the neck was, in France and England in medieval and early modern times, widely believed to respond to a cure by the monarch's touch. This touch was originally applied to a 'touch piece' (a pierced coin), which was then applied to the affected part. By the Tudor period, more commonly the 'touch' was a laying on of hands or blessing by the monarch of multitudinous subjects at key points in the reign; the monarch also touched and presented a coin (a pierced Angel) to each individual as a talisman or reminder of the ceremony. Charles II only blessed the amulets as he disliked touching diseased people directly. The infant Dr Samuel Johnson was 'touched' by Queen Anne in 1712 and he wore the talisman round his neck for the remainder of his life. A ceremony for the touching of the king's or queen's evil was included in the Book of Common Prayer.

Rector Clerical rectors were parochial clergymen who held all the tithes, great and small, of their benefices. In some benefices, however, the great tithes were held by one or more lay persons (known as impropriator/s) and only the small tithes by a clerical vicar. Also used to describe heads of Jesuit houses and some university officials.

Recusancy, Recusants A term used after about 1570 to refer to Roman Catholics who refused to attend services of the church of England in obedience to the Papal Bull excommunicating Elizabeth I. It was perceived as a serious problem, especially in the North, and harsh penal laws were introduced, but rather irregularly enforced. In 1581, for example, fines of £20 a month for recusancy were stipulated.

Reformed churches Refers to all those churches which subscribed to the principles of the Reformation but is used, more specifically, to distinguish the Calvinistic churches from the Lutheran. It was commonly used in this latter sense in the sixteenth century.

***Reformatio Legum Ecclesiasticarum* (the reform of the ecclesiastical laws)** By an Act of Parliament of 1549 (3 & 4 Edward VI, c. 11) the King was authorised to set up a commission to replace the medieval canon law with a new system of order and discipline.

1551 Commission of eight set to work on the project.
1553 *Reformatio Legum Ecclesiasticarum* presented to parliament – made redundant by Edward's death and reign of Mary.
1571 John Foxe published *Reformatio Legum Ecclesiasticarum*.

Failure of the project to materialise meant that the church continued to flounder in an anachronistic system of law throughout the period.

Religious (regular clergy) A term used to mean those clergy who lived under a rule (for example, that of St Augustine or St Benedict) in a religious house (monastery, convent, etc.).

Rent From the early sixteenth century it became common for leases to stipulate that all or part of the rent be paid in kind (a hedge against inflation). The produce was normally used to support the household and provide feed for the landlord's stock but some was marketed. See Thirsk, *Agrarian History*, 1967 for a good discussion of the subject. See also 'Leases'.

Rogation Days The Monday, Tuesday and Wednesday before Ascension Day.

Rogation Sunday Fifth Sunday after Easter Day.

Sanctuary Under medieval canon law, a fugitive from justice or a debtor was immune from arrest in a sacred place. To some extent this right was observed but, for example, see the fate of the Stafford brothers who claimed sanctuary at Culham, Oxfordshire in 1486.

Secretary See Chapter 5: Central government: (1) The monarchy and the royal household.

Secular clergy   All clergy who did not belong to the rule of a religious order. See 'Religious'.

Separatist   A title first applied to the followers of Robert Browne (see Section 12.2: Biographical index), although it was later used to describe the Independents or Congregationalists.

Serfs   Term used to describe several classes of person who were unfree, in the sense that they were bound to the land on which they lived and worked and were therefore unfree to marry and move as they wished. Included domestic serfs or artisans who had no homes of their own and lived with the lord almost as slaves, and others who had holdings, homes and families. An understanding of 'serf-dom', which had disappeared by the Tudor period, is helpful when we examine the development of household organisation and social hierarchy in the sixteenth century.

Servants   Servants were a highly heterogeneous body of people, male and female, young and old, bound together by their relationship (temporary or permanent) of dependence upon a master or mistress. A servant was not, by contemporary definition, someone who scrubbed and cleaned within a domestic setting. At all but the lowest social levels, however, servants *were* used to substitute for or supplement child labour.

Shrines   The Latin word from which the English is taken means a chest, and a shrine was originally a chest in which a relic was kept (reliquary). It was commonly used to mean a sacred image, especially one to which pilgrimages were made. The most important English shrines were those of St Thomas Becket at Canterbury; Our Lady at Walsingham; St Edward the Confessor at Westminster Abbey and St Cuthbert at Durham. The Reformation rejected pilgrimages and shrines as meaningless in terms of salvation. These sites were destroyed.

Simony   A word meaning the sale of spiritual things. For example, a man might offer money to persuade the bishop to ordain him or he might try to purchase an ecclesiastical benefice. The system of patronage was extremely susceptible to simony and it was probably widespread. The Canons of 1604 stipulated that all ordinands and all those receiving a benefice must swear an oath that they had not achieved their office through simony.

Six Articles, Act of   Conservative religious doctrine restated and enforced by draconian penalties in 1539.

Somerset House   Renaissance palace built by Lord Protector Somerset in the late 1540s. It was the first major classical building project in early modern England and its design underlined the ambitions of its owner.

Spas   In the late Middle Ages, curative springs were centres for religious cults and pilgrimages. During the reign of Elizabeth, the nobility transformed the centres into secular watering places or spas offering medicinal treatment and a relaxing atmosphere. Bath was the paradigm.

Statute   Act of Parliament. References to statutes cite a date and a chapter number. The year is the regnal year of the session in which the statute was given royal assent. If there were two sessions within the same regnal year, the statutes are distinguished as belonging to statute 1 (st. 1) and statute 2 (st. 2). If a session covers two regnal years then its statutes are cited as belonging to both (e.g. 2 & 3 Edward VI). Each statute has a chapter number but the order is not strictly chronological.

St Bartholomew's Day Massacre   Massacre of the French Protestant leadership in Paris on 24 August 1572. Widely perceived to be a plot staged by Catherine de Medici but in fact a panic reaction to events. The idea of a plot seemed to confirm the existence of a Catholic League intended to wipe out Protestanism in Europe, and thus proved both emotive and influential in the shaping of future English foreign policy.

St John the Baptist, Feast Day of Nativity of   24 June. Linked with customs surrounding the summer solstice. See 'Holy Days'.

St Paul's Cross   Since the fourteenth century, sermons had been commonplace at the Cross in St Paul's churchyard. An endowment by Bishop Thomas Kempe provided for the maintenance of the sermons. Galleries were provided for royalty and dignitaries; the throng sat on benches for which they paid a rent of 1d a sermon. The preachers were selected by the Bishop of London and his chaplains. If it rained, the sermon was transferred to the crypt of St Paul's Cathedral.

Staple Towns   Some towns were made staples by royal authority. A group of merchants would be given the exclusive right to purchase certain categories of goods for export. Until 1558, Calais was the chief staple and is often referred to simply as The Staple but there were other staples throughout England and Wales. The term was (and is) rather confusingly used also to indicate the principal markets or entrepôts for certain categories of merchandise, or towns where foreign merchants were permitted to trade.

Star Chamber   See Chapter 7: Central courts.

Stoke, Battle of   Battle of Stoke (1487), near Newark (not Stoke-on-Trent as in some accounts) at which Lambert Simnel and the Earl of Lincoln were routed. The last battle of the Wars of the Roses. It is occasionally referred to as the Battle of East Stoke.

Subsidy   A tax of a fixed amount on land or goods granted by parliament to increase the value of the **tenth and fifteenth** taxes to the Crown.

Suffragan Bishops   Assistants to the diocesan bishops. From the thirteenth century had held titles derived from Irish or Christian cities now occupied by Islam. In 1534, parliament substituted 34 English place names for these titles.

Sumptuary Laws   Medieval laws defining the type of dress permitted to the various social groups. Clergy, for example, were not allowed to dress as laymen. The wives of merchants must not dress as the wives of nobility or gentry. Colours, fabrics and styles were all regulated. It was part of the attempt to keep people in their foreordained social places and to make 'social climbing' obvious. However, these laws were often contravened.

Surplice   A loose white linen liturgical tunic with wide sleeves. In the medieval Catholic church it was the accepted garb of the lower clergy and was used by priests also except when they were celebrating mass. The Second Prayer Book of Edward VI prescribed the surplice as the only vestment to be worn by the clergy. This rubric was altered in the Prayer Book of 1559 in an attempt to revert to the wearing of vestments for the celebration of communion and probably for morning and evening prayer. The rubric now ordered a return to the situation in the second year of Edward VI's reign, whereas the first prayer book had been authorised by parliament in the third year of the reign. This mistake led the reformers to believe that the Queen did not wish them to wear the vestments, to which they so objected. See 'Vestiarian Controversy'.

Ten Articles, Act of   Convocation accepted these articles in 1536 as descriptive of the doctrine of the Church of England. They are, therefore, the first doctrinal declaration of the new Church. Baptism, penance and Eucharist are retained as sacraments; the Eucharistic presence is called corporal and substantial but there is no mention of transubstantiation; justification (salvation) is said to be achieved by contrition and faith combined with charity; images are retained but must not be worshipped; prayers for the intercession of the saints and prayers and Masses for the dead are approved.

Tenth and Fifteenth   This was the standard parliamentary tax on landed property. Those towns represented in parliament paid a tenth; the rest paid a fifteenth.

Thirty-Nine Articles   (First version, 1563; full set, 1571.) Attempt by Convocation to define the doctrine of the Church of England in relation to the religious controversies of the day, especially clarifying the position on purported medieval corruptions of Catholic teaching. Not a creed (q.v.). They were a slightly modified version of the Forty-Two Articles agreed in 1553. Were approved by Convocation and subscription to them was required of the clergy.

Tillage   Ploughing the land.

Tithe   A tenth part of the produce of land (praedial); of the fruits of labour (personal) and those arising partly out of the ground and partly from work (mixed) offered to the clerical incumbent of a parish benefice. If the incumbent was a rector he would receive the great tithes (wheat, oats, etc.) and the small (chickens, goats, lambs, etc.) but, when the parish was appropriated, the great tithes fell to the lay impropriator and only the small to the clerical vicar. Some tithes were compounded (i.e. a fixed annual payment was made in lieu of tithe; known as composition of tithe). Others had apparently fallen into disuse. Suits for recovery of tithe filled the ecclesiastical courts of this and the succeeding century and exacerbated poor relations between clergy and laity as well as between lay impropriators and laymen.

Transubstantiation   Doctrine that, after consecration, the bread and wine of the Communion service cease to be bread and wine except in appearance and become the real body and blood of Christ. Firmly held by Catholic Christians.

Treason   On the accession of Henry VIII, treason was narrowly defined by a fourteenth-century statute which made it treason to plot the death of the sovereign, his Queen-consort or the heir apparent; to violate the Queen or the wife of the heir apparent; to wage war in the realm; or to kill the Lord Chancellor or the judges performing their offices. In practice, treason was interpreted much more loosely than this and criticism of the actions and person of the monarch were effectively suppressed thereby. After 1534, however, parliament progressively revised the law relating to treason, broadening it to include, for example, forgery of any of the royal seals. Once a person, great or small, was indicted for treason, legal counsel was denied.

Ultimogeniture   Also known as Borough English. Right whereby youngest son or child inherits entire estate. This was apparently relatively uncommon but occurred in some copyholds of descent, especially in Kent and certain boroughs. See 'Partible Inheritance'.

Uses   See 'Wills, Statute of'.

Valor Ecclesiasticus   Official and comprehensive valuation of ecclesiastical and monastic revenues made in 1535. Popularly known as the King's Books. This valuation followed on the 1534 Act of Annates (26 Henry VIII, c. 3) whereby the Crown appropriated the first fruits of every benefice (living) and one-tenth of the annual income of every benefice.

Vestiarian Controversies   Disputes concerning proper clerical dress during the reigns of Edward VI and Elizabeth. The matter was discussed prior to the publication of the First Prayer Book of Edward VI (1549); controversy flared in 1550 when John Hooper declined to wear vestments during his consecration as Bishop of Gloucester and some sort of compromise was reached although Hooper finally agreed to wear the surplice and rochet on important occasions; the surplice and rochet were the only vestments allowed in the second Prayer Book of 1552; there was a renewal of trouble with the restoration of vestments (including a cope for the Holy Communion) in 1559 and Matthew Parker's insistence that the law be obeyed in 1566; 37 London clergy who refused obedience were deprived and there was unrest; the bishops themselves were divided and so no consistent policy was pursued.

Vicar   From the Latin word for 'a substitute'. Popular name for clergyman who serves a parish of which the great tithes have been appropriated. This arrangement dated back to the Middle Ages when churches were often appropriated to monasteries, which received the tithe income and appointed a secular priest or 'vicar' to serve the cure on their behalf. On the dissolution of the monasteries, the King granted the rectorial tithes to others (often laymen) who were known as impropriators or rectors, but the endowment of a vicarage remained intact.

Vicar-General   A bishop's substitute in exercise of his jurisdiction. Position frequently held by Chancellor of Diocese.

Vicegerent (in spirituals)   Office of deputy in religious matters created by Henry VIII and bestowed upon Thomas Cromwell in 1535. Involved a delegation of the King's prerogative as head of the Church and Cromwell may have held courts similar to those held by Wolsey as Papal Legate (q.v.). The vicegerency disappeared after Cromwell's fall and temporary ecclesiastical commissions exercised delegated powers.

Visitation   From the late fifteenth century, the College of Heralds undertook visitations throughout the realm checking the claims to arms of county families and establishing the descent of these claims. See Chapter 10: Ecclesiastical courts and commissions for ecclesiastical visitations.

Wards, Court of   See Chapter 5: Central government: (1) The monarchy and the royal household.

Wardship   When a child from a family in England or Wales whose land was held by knight-service was orphaned as a minor, he or she became a royal ward. Until the child came of age, the Crown as guardian had rights over the marriage and education of the ward and administered the estates. The Crown frequently sold on these rights through the Court of Wards and Liveries. A peculiarly English institution.

Westminster Until 1529, the medieval Palace of Westminster was the chief London residence of the monarch as well as the centre for the legal and administrative business of government. A series of fires left it in poor repair and the monarch began to use Whitehall (q.v.) as his residence. Westminister was still used for important state ceremonies and the legal and new administrative courts and, in mid-century, became the permanent home for the House of Commons (in the dissolved college of St Stephen) and the House of Lords (in the Painted Chamber).

Whitehall Formerly York Place, the London home of Cardinal Wolsey, Archbishop of York. In 1529 acquired by Henry VIII as a replacement residence for the medieval palace of Westminster (q.v.).

Will and Testament Technically, a will was divided into sections – a **preamble** during which the testator willed his soul into the care of God and a testation of the earthly estate. Under common law, males and single and widowed women were eligible to make wills. Married women required the permission of their husbands before being eligible.

Wills, Statute of Chiefly important because it permitted testators freely to will much or all of their land depending on how they held it. In general, landowners wished to provide for all of their children and not simply the heir at law. Until the Statute of Uses of 1536 (which abolished the 'use', whereby landowners appointed trustees or feoffees to hold and administer portions of their estate after their death for a third party who was not the legal heir, according to instructions stipulated in a will) there had been ways around the ban on testation of freehold land away from the male heir. There was an outcry following the Statute of Uses, and the Statute of Wills (1540) responded by making it legal to will freehold land. Those holding land by knight-service had first to deduct the dower or jointure rights of the widow, then they might (should they so wish) will away up to two-thirds of the freehold estate, the remaining third being reserved to the heir at common law. There was free testation of lands held by socage tenure. It was already possible to will away lands and property held by leasehold because these were accounted 'moveable property'.

Women's legal and property rights

Under the common law

Single women (spinsters and widows) of full age might inherit and administer land, make a will, sign a contract, own chattels, sue and be sued, make feoffments (trusts) and seal bonds, etc. without any guardian or proxy. The term *fem(m)e sole* was used to describe such a woman. On rare occasions a married woman was treated as fem(me) sole, e.g. Lady Margaret Beaufort.

A married woman had no such rights. During her marriage or *couverture*, her husband gained title to the rents and profits of her land but he might not sell or lease the land which belonged to her; she was not allowed to make a will except with his express permission. She had the right to common law dower of at least one-third of her late husband's freehold estate for her life; the dower was sometimes increased or made specific by protective jointure; she had no such right with respect to copyhold land except (where it existed) by local custom of freebench. By the mid-sixteenth century, the man could sell, give away or devise any of his freehold estate excepting the widow's and heir's portions. The remainder of his estate was completely untrammelled. The practice of entailing estates through primogeniture was introduced to prevent the breaking up of estates according to the will of the individual. See 'Primogeniture'.

Under equity law

Married women did have a legal identity and could sue and be sued in the equity courts. Married women who had property of their own did defend it in the equity courts. Many of these women before marriage had made marriage contracts or settlements which were invalid in the eyes of the common law but were acknowledged as permissible under equity law. Such settlements might, for example, arrange for a wife to receive an income of her own during the marriage, allow her to administer her own properties, and protect the inheritance of children from former marriages.

Under ecclesiastical law

Married as well as single women had a legal identity. On marriage, a woman with property would enter a common bond to protect this property in her own interest and that of any children from former marriages. She might also take out bonds to provide sums of money for her personal use during her husband's lifetime. An abused wife might apply to the ecclesiastical courts for separation at bed and board from her husband and for a maintenance settlement for herself and her children of the union. A widow was commonly the executrix of her husband's will and, as such, applied in the courts for probate of the will. In cases of intestacy, the widow was automatically granted administration. Under probate jurisdiction, a widow defended her marriage settlement by listing property reserved for herself and/or her children under these bonds as expenses to be deducted from the estate before bequests were paid. If there were difficulties involving the payment of these bonds, as a widow she might sue for satisfaction under the common law.

Worship The manner in which God was worshipped reflected the theology of the various sixteenth-century Christian churches.

Catholicism was a religion of ritualism and sacramentalism. The seven sacraments of the Church were means of acquiring grace or salvation and the priest alone administered these sacraments. There were a whole series of channels which God had instituted to communicate and apply the power of the original salvation (Christ's death upon the cross and resurrection) to man – the Church, the priesthood and the sacramental system, the intercession of saints, and so forth. The layout of Catholic churches, the apparel of the personnel, the form of the service, all reflected this theology. The Church gave prominence to the administration of the sacraments. Among them, pride of place was given to the Lord's supper but near the entry to the church stood the font, symbol of Christian initiation, at which babies were baptised. The confessional marked the place where each Christian confessed his or her sins, and was given a penance to perform. The altar, whereon the Eucharist was administered and from which the priest pronounced absolution, was centrally placed at the East End of the church. Upon it were arranged the cross and candles, ornate chalice (cup for the wine) and pyx (plate for the bread) and the missal (Mass service book). The idea that this sanctuary (sacred place) was the preserve of the priesthood, a holy place set apart, was emphasised by the grandeur, the symbolism of the furnishings, by the candles and the sanctuary lamp and, most of all, by the physical separation between it and the congregation provided by the rood screen (bearing statues of Christ on the cross, the Virgin and St John). Within the sanctuary, only the priest mounted the steps to the altar to celebrate the Mass. He was served by an acolyte. The priest showed the elements of bread (the Host) to the congregation who adored the Mass. The laity were permitted to partake only of the bread, not the wine. The stations of the cross and the stained glass of the windows reminded the laity of the supreme sacrifice Christ had made for them. Statues of the saints around the church encouraged worshippers to pray to the saints and the Virgin Mary for intercession with Christ for salvation. In chantry chapels, priests said Masses to intercede for the dead.

Luther sharply rejected this idea of the church as a priestly-sacramental way to salvation, which he believed was the result of a one-to-one relationship between the individual and God and the faith in Christ's power to save which ensued. The instrumentality of ritual was denied. Luther did, however, retain in his doctrine of **consubstantiation** a belief in the real presence of Christ at the communion of bread and wine. Lutheran churches retained many Catholic religious practices which were not regarded specifically as abuses. Latin Masses continued to be said on Holy Days (q.v.) and a considerable number of these were kept. The form of the communion was not significantly altered. Preachers heard parisioners' confession before communion although no penances were imposed. There were unresolved disputes about whether the host (bread) should continue to be elevated for adoration (q.v.); whether the cross should be used in prayer; whether the formula of exorcism should be used at baptism and so on. Church interiors were not greatly changed. High altars, crucifixes, organs, stained glass windows, even special Mass vestments remained. The pulpit, however, now stood prominently – the Word of God in the Scriptures was the sole rule of faith.

In those churches influenced by the theology of Calvin, the changes in the furnishing of the church building, the form of the services and the paraphernalia of worship were more profound. For the most part the old churches, once used for Catholic worship, were adapted for Protestant worship but they were stripped of all statuary and embellishment because of the view that these reinforced belief in the instrumentality of ritual and image, and owing to the idea that any practice not specifically recommended in Scripture was superfluous and probably superstitious. Stained glass windows, statuary, pictures, symbolic furnishings, rood screens – all disappeared. The altar became a table, around which the whole congregation gathered for communion of bread and wine. The priesthood disappeared and was replaced by a ministry, which acted to inform the laity about God's Word and not to mediate. The minister, unlike the priest in his symbolic vestments, was plainly attired. The pulpit now took pride of place.

The Church of England went further than the Lutherans in curtailing Catholic practices. The liturgy became vernacular. Altars, crucifixes, statues, religious pictures, holy sepulchres, stained glass, organs, the sign of the cross, beating of the bounds (accompanied by banners, crosses and priests in vestments) all disappeared relatively quickly. The Book of Common Prayer replaced the Catholic missal on the table which replaced the altar. Wall tablets bearing the text of the Ten Commandments and other Scriptural extracts replaced the ornate reredos. The Bible was placed upon a lectern and read to the people in the vernacular. The pulpit assumed a new prominence. The priest wore surplice and stole instead of vestments. Many of the more radical English Protestants rejected the idea of priesthood as 'popish', adopting instead that of a ministry; and resisted the use of the sign of the cross, the ring in marriage and the wearing of surplice or stole. The ministry and the laity all partook of both the bread and wine during the communion. The physical separation between the priest and the congregation was also reduced as rood screens were dismantled and the communion table brought closer to the nave. The placing of the pulpit and the lectern in the body of the church reinforced this change. See 'Vestiarian Controversy'.

16
BIBLIOGRAPHIES

These are highly selective bibliographies. The aim has been to provide pointers to a large number of subjects within Tudor history and, where possible, to include the best recent authorities. Categorisation has been difficult because so many books and articles cover several different subjects – for instance, some books and articles in the Politics and Central Administration area might fit equally well into the finance or the law sections and a biography of a bishop, for example, obviously contains material relevant to religion and ecclesiastical affairs. Books published before 1950 are generally useful mainly from a historiographical point of view. Many books and articles published between 1950 and 2000 remain the standard authorities on particular subjects. Others remain useful for establishing facts, chronology and interpretative positions, etc. even when superseded by more recent interpretations. Place of publication is London unless otherwise stated. Places of publication have not been traced for books published prior to 1951. Dates are given for main editions but not for reprints.

General

Brigden, S. *New Worlds, Lost Worlds: The Rule of the Tudors, 1485–1603* (2001)
Cheney, C.R. *Handbook of Dates for Students of British History* (Royal Historical Society Guides and Handbooks No. 4) new edn rev. by M. Jones (2000, reprinted 2004)
Ellis, S.G. *Tudor Frontiers and Noble Power: The Making of the British State* (1995)
Elton, G.R. *England under the Tudors* (1955)
Fox, A. and Guy, J. *Reassessing the Henrician Age* (1986)
Griffiths, R.A. and Thomas, R.S. *The Making of the House of Tudor* (1993)
Gunn, S. *Early Tudor Government, 1485–1558,* (1994)
Guy, J. *Tudor England,* Oxford (1988)
Gwynfor Jones, J. *Early Modern Wales, c. 1525–1640* (1994)
Hodder & Stoughton Access to History Series: many excellent guides to aspects of the Tudor period; unfortunately have little in the way of bibliography
Laslett, P. *The World We Have Lost Further Explored* (1983) repr.
Lockyer, R. *Tudor and Stuart Britain, 1471–1714* (1985)
Longman Seminar Studies in History: an extensive library of titles covering the Tudor period. Each containing a survey of the issues, a detailed bibliography and select sources for study

Macmillan Problems in Focus Series: some Tudor titles. Essays by established historians with specialist knowledge especially written to introduce students to the issues

Macmillan Studies in Economic and Social History: many titles covering the Tudor period. Surveys of debates with annotated bibliographies

Morrill, J. (ed.), *The Oxford Illustrated History of Tudor and Stuart Britain*, Oxford (1996)

Palliser, D. *The Age of Elizabeth, England Under The Later Tudors, 1547–1603* (1983)

Rowe, J.G. (ed.), *Aspects of late medieval government and society: essays presented to J. R. Lander* (1987)

Watts, L.J. (ed.), *The End of the Middle Ages?* (1998)

Williams, P. *The Tudor Regime*, Oxford (1979)

Wrightson, K. *English Society, 1580–1680* (1982)

—— *Earthly Necessities: Economic Lives in Early Modern Britain, 1470–1750* (2001)

Youings, J. *Sixteenth Century England*, Harmondsworth (1984)

Politics and central administration

Aird, I. 'The death of Amy Robsart: Accident, Suicide, or Murder – or disease?', *English Historical Review*, 71 (1956), 69–79

Alsop, J.D. 'The structure of early Tudor finance, 1509–1558', in *Revolution Reassessed: Revisions in the History of Tudor Government and Administration*, C. Coleman and D.R. Starkey (eds) (1986), 135–62

—— 'The exchequer in late medieval government, 1485–1530', in *Aspects of Late Medieval Government and Society: Essays Presented to J.R. Lander*, J.G. Rowe (ed.) (1987), 179–212

Bernard, G.W. *The Power of the Early Tudor Nobility* (1985)

—— (ed.) *The Tudor Nobility* (1992)

—— *The King's Reformation*, New Haven, CT (2005)

Bush, M.L. *The Government Policy of Protector Somerset* (1975)

Coleman, C. and Starkey, D.R. (eds), *Revolution Reassessed: Revisions in the History of Tudor Government and Administration* (1986)

Collinson, P. *Elizabethan Essays* (1994)

Croft, P. (ed.), *Patronage, Culture and Power: The Early Cecils, 1558–1612*, New Haven, CT (2002)

Cross, C., Loades, D. and Scarisbrick, J.J. (eds), *Law and Government Under the Tudors: Essays Presented to Sir Geoffrey Elton* (1988)

Doran, S. *Monarchy and Matrimony: The Courtships of Elizabeth I* (1996)

Elton, G.R. *England under the Tudors* (1955)

—— *The Tudor Revolution in Government*, Cambridge (1953, 1962 repr.)

—— 'King or Minister?: The Man Behind the Henrician reformation', *History*, 39 (1954), 21–32

—— *Henry VIII. An Essay in Revision*, The Historical Association (1962, 1965 repr.)

—— *Studies in Tudor and Stuart Politics and Government*, 2 vols. (1974)

Guy, J.A. *The Cardinal's Court: The Impact of Thomas Wolsey in Star Chamber* (1977)

—— *The Public Career of Sir Thomas More* (1980)

—— (ed.), *The Tudor Monarchy* (1997)

Hammer, P.E.J. 'Myth-making: Politics, Propaganda and the Capture of Cadiz in 1596', *Historical Journal*, 40 (1997), 621–42

—— *The Polarisation of Elizabethan Politics: The Political Career of Robert Devereux, 2nd Earl of Essex, 1585–1597* (1999)

Hoak, D.E. *The King's Council in the Reign of Edward VI* (1976)

Holmes, P. 'The great council in the reign of Henry VII', *English Historical Review*, 101 (1986), 840–62

Hughes, P.L. and Larkin, J.F. (eds), *Tudor Royal Proclamations*, 1 (1964) and *Tudor Royal Proclamations, 2: The Later Tudors (1553–1587)* (1969)

Hurstfield, J. *Freedom, Corruption and Government in Elizabethan England* (1973)

Koenigsberger, H.G., Mosse, G.L. and Bowler, G.Q. *Europe in the Sixteenth Century* (1989).

Lander, J.R. *Crown and Nobility, 1450–1509* (1976)

Lehmberg, S.E. *Sir Walter Mildmay and Tudor Government*, Austin, TX (1964)

MacCaffrey, W.T. *The Shaping of the Elizabethan Regime: Elizabethan Politics, 1558–1572* (1968)

—— *Queen Elizabeth and the Making of Policy, 1572–1588*, Princeton, NJ (1981)

—— *Elizabeth I: War and Politics, 1588–1603*, Princeton, NJ (1992)

Miller, H. *Henry VIII and the English Nobility* (1986)

Rawcliffe, C. *The Staffords, Earls of Stafford and Dukes of Buckingham*, Cambridge (1978)

Richardson, W.C. *Tudor chamber administration*, Baton Rouge, LA (1952)

Seymour, W. *Ordeal by Ambition: An English Family in the Shadow of the Tudors* (1972)

Slavin, A.J. (ed.), *Tudor Men and Institutions* (1972)

Smith, A.G.R. *The Emergence of a Nation State. The Commonwealth of England 1529–1660* (1984)

Starkey, D. *The Reign of Henry VIII: Personalities and Politics* (1985)

Walker, G. *John Skelton and the Politics of the 1520s* (1988)

Parliament and constitution

Bindoff, S.T. 'The making of the statute of artificers' in Bindoff, S.T. *et al.* (eds), *Elizabethan Government and Society: Essays Presented to Sir John Neale* (1961)

Dean, D.M. 'Enacting clauses and legislative initiative, 1584–1601', *Bulletin of the Institute of Historical Research*, 57 (1984) 140–48.

Elton, G.R. 'Parliament in the sixteenth century: Functions and Fortunes', *Historical Journal*, 22 (1979), 255–78.

—— 'Enacting Clauses and Legislative Initiative, 1559–71', *Bulletin of the Institute of Historical Research*, 53 (1980), 183–91

—— *The Parliament of England, 1559–1581* (1986)

—— *The Tudor Constitution* (2nd edn 1982)

Freeman, T.S. '"The Reformation of the Church in this Parliament": Thomas Norton, John Foxe and the parliament of 1571', *Parliamentary History*, 16 (1997), 131–47

Fryde, E.B. and Miller, E. (eds), *Historical Studies of the English Parliament*, vol. 2 (1970)

Graves, M.A.R. *The House of Lords in the Parliaments of Edward VI and Mary*, Cambridge (1981)

—— 'The Management of the Elizabethan House of Commons: the Council's "Men-of-Business"', *Parliamentary History*, 2 (1983), 11–38

—— *The Tudor Parliaments: Crown, Lords and Commons, 1485–1603* (1985)

—— *Elizabethan Parliaments, 1559–1601* (1987)

—— *Early Tudor Parliaments, 1485–1558* (1990)

—— *Thomas Norton: The Parliament Man* (1994)

—— and Silcock, R.H. *Revolution, Reaction and the Triumph of Conservatism. English History, 1558–1700* (1984)

Gunn, S.J. 'The Act of Resumption of 1515', in *Early Tudor England: Proceedings of the 1987 Harlaxton Symposium*, Williams, D.T. (ed.) (1989), 87–106

Guy, J.A. 'Wolsey, the council and the council courts', *English Historical Review*, 91 (1976), 481–505

—— 'Wolsey and the parliament of 1523', in *Law and Government under the Tudors: Essays Presented to Sir Geoffrey Elton*, C. Cross, D. Loades, and J.J. Scarisbrick (eds) (1988), 1–18

Hartley, T.E. ed., *Proceedings in the Parliaments of Elizabeth I*, 1: *1558–1581* (1981)

Hasler, P.W. *The House of Commons, 1558–1603*, 3 vols, *The History of Parliament* (1981)

Haugaard, W. P. *Elizabeth and the English Reformation: The Struggle for a Stable Settlement*, Cambridge (1968)

Heal, F. 'The bishops and the Act of Exchange of 1559', *Historical Journal*, 17 (1974), 227–46

Hoak, D.E. *The King's Council in the Reign of Edward VI* (1976)

Jones, N.L. *Faith by Statute: Parliament and the Settlement of Religion, 1559* (1982)

Jones, W.R.D. *The Tudor Commonwealth, 1529–1559* (1970)

Kelly, M.J. 'The submission of the clergy', *Transactions of the Royal Historical Society*, 5th ser., 15 (1965), 97–119

Lehmberg, S.E. *The Reformation Parliament, 1529–36*, Cambridge (1970)

—— *The Later Parliaments of Henry VIII*, Cambridge (1977)

Loach, J. *Parliament and the Crown in the Reign of Mary Tudor*, Oxford (1986)

—— and Tittler, J. (eds), *The Mid-Tudor Polity, c. 1540–1560* (1980)

Loades, D.M. *The Reign of Mary Tudor* (1991)

—— *The Mid-Tudor Crisis, 1545–1565* (1992)

Luders, A. and others (eds), *Statutes of the Realm*, 11 vols in 12 (1810–28)

McLaren, A. *Political Culture in the Reign of Elizabeth I: Queen and Commonwealth, 1558–1585*, Cambridge (1999)

Miller, H. 'London and parliament in the reign of Henry VIII', *Bulletin of Institute of Historical Research*, 35 (1962), 128–49

Neale, J.E. *The Elizabethan House of Commons* (1949)

—— *Elizabeth I and her Parliaments*, 2 vols (1953 and 1957)

Notestein, W. 'The Winning of the Initiative by the House of Commons', Raleigh Lecture of 1924, *Proceedings of the British Academy*, vol. 11, Oxford (1926).

Pollard, A.F. *The Evolution of Parliament* (2nd edn 1964)

Pulman, M.B. *The Elizabethan Privy Council in the 1570s*, Berkeley, CA (1971)

Russell, C. *The Crisis of Parliaments. English History 1509–1660*, Oxford (1971)

Slavin, A.J. 'Sir Ralph Sadler and Master John Hales at the hanaper: A 16th century struggle for property and profit', *Bulletin of the Institute of Historical Research*, 38 (1965), 31–47

Worden, B. *The Sound of Virtue: Philip Sidney's 'Arcadia' and Elizabethan Politics*, New Haven, CT (1996)

Law, law courts, lawyers and crime (*see also Professions*)

Abbot, L.W. *Law Reporting in England, 1485–1585* (1973)

Bellamy, J.G. *Criminal Law and Society in Late Medieval and Tudor England* (1984)

Blatcher, M. *The Court of King's Bench, 1450–1550* (1978)

Cockburn, J.S. *A History of English Assizes* (1972)

Hastings, M. *The Court of Common Pleas in Fifteenth Century England*, Hamden, CT (1971 2nd edn)

Heath, J. *Torture and English Law*, Westport, CT (1982)

Houlbrooke, R.A. *Church Courts and People During the English Reformation, 1520–1570*, Oxford (1979)

Hurstfield, J. *The Queen's Wards: Wardship and Marriage under Elizabeth I* (1958, 1973 2nd edn)

Ives, E.W. 'Crimes, sanctuary and royal authority under Henry VIII: The exemplary sufferings of the Savage family', in *On the laws and customs of England: Essays in honor of Samuel E. Thorne*, Arnold, M.S. Green, T.A. Scully, S.A. and White S.D. (eds) (1981), 296–320

Jones, W.J. *The Elizabethan Court of Chancery*, Oxford (1967)

Knafla, L.A. *Law and Politics in Jacobean England, Cambridge* (1977, 2nd edn, 2008)

Marchant, R.B. *The Church Under the Law*, Cambridge (1969)

Outhwaite, R.B. *The Rise and Fall of the English Ecclesiastical Courts, 1500–1860*, Cambridge (2006)

Prest, W. *The Inns of Court* (1972)

Sharpe, J. *Crime in Early Modern England, 1550–1750* (1984)

Women and gender

Amussen, S.D. *An Ordered Society: Gender and Class in Early Modern England*, Oxford (1988)

Atkinson, C.B. and Atkinson, J. 'Anne Wheathill's *A handfull of holesome (though homelie) hearbs* (1584): The first English gentlewoman's prayer book', *Sixteenth Century Journal*, 27 (1996), 631–44

Axton, M. *The Queen's Two Bodies* (1977)

Bray, A. *Homosexuality in Renaissance England* (1982, 1988 2nd edn) and New York (1995 new edn)

Brodsky, V. 'Widows in Late Elizabethan London: Remarriage, Economic Opportunity and Family Orientations' in L. Bonfield, R.M. Smith and K. Wrightson (eds), *The World We Have Gained*, Oxford (1986), 122–54

Callaghan, D. *Women and Gender in Renaissance Tragedy* (1989)

Charles L. and Duffin, L. (eds), *Women and Work in Pre-Industrial England* (1985)

Crawford, P. 'The construction and experience of maternity in seventeenth-century England', *Women as Mothers in Pre-industrial England*, V. Fildes (ed.) (1990), 3–38

—— *Women and Religion in England, 1500–1720* (1993)

Davidson, C.N. and Broner, E.M. (eds), *The Lost Tradition: Mothers and Daughters in Literature* (1979)

Daybell, J. (ed.), *Early Modern Women's Letter Writing, 1450–1700* (2000)

—— (ed.), *Women and Politics in Early Modern England, 1450–1700*, Aldershot (2004)

James Daybell, *Tudor Women Letter Writers*, Oxford (2006)

Dowling, M. *Humanism in the Age of Henry VIII*, Beckenham (1986)

Erickson, A.L. 'Common Law Versus Common Practice: The Use of Marriage Settlements in Early Modern England', *Economic History Review*, 43 (1990)

—— *Women and Property in Early Modern England* (1993)

Fildes, V. (ed.), *Women as Mothers in Pre-industrial England* (1990)

Fletcher, A. *Gender, Sex and Subordination in England, 1500–1800*, New Haven, CT (1995)

Froide, A. *Never Married: Single Women in Early Modern England*, Oxford (2005)

Gent L. and Llewellyn, N. (eds), *Renaissance Bodies: The Human Figure in English Culture c. 1540–1660* (1990)

Green, I. 'The Education of women in the Reformation', *History of Education Quarterly*, 19 (1979), 93–116

Harris, B.J. *English Aristocratic Women, 1450–1550*, New York (2002)

Howard, J.E. 'Crossdressing, the Theatre and Gender Struggle in Early Modern England', *Shakespeare Quarterly*, 39 (1988)

Jardine, L. *Still Harping on Daughters: Women and Drama in the Age of Shakespeare* (1983)

Laurence, A. *Women in England, 1500–1700* (1994)

Mears, M. 'Politics in the Elizabethan Privy Chamber: Lady Mary Sidney and Kat Ashley' in J. Daybell (ed.), *Women and Politics in Early Modern England, 1450–1700*, Aldershot, 2004, pp. 67–82

Mendelson, S. and Crawford, P. *Women in Early Modern England*, Oxford (1998)

O'Day, R. *Women's Agency in Early Modern Britain and the American Colonies* (2007)

Open University, *The Changing Experience of Women*, Milton Keynes (1983)

Outhwaite, R.B. (ed.), *Marriage and Society: Studies in the Social History of Marriage* (1981)

—— *Clandestine Marriage in England, 1500–1850* (1995)

Peters, C. *Women in Early Modern Britain, 1450–1640*, Basingstoke (2004)

Pollock, L. *With Faith and Physic: The Life of a Tudor Gentlewoman, Lady Grace Mildmay, 1552–1620* (1993)

Prior, M. (ed.), *Women in English Society, 1500–1800* (1985)

Roberts, M. and Clarke, S. (eds), *Women and Gender in Early Modern Wales*, Cardiff (2000)

Shepherd, A. *Gender and Authority in Sixteenth-Century England*, Keele (1994)

Shorter, E. *The Making of the Modern Family* (1976)

Stretton, T. *Women Waging Law in Elizabethan England*, Cambridge (1998)

Wall, A.D. (ed.) *Two Elizabethan Women: Correspondence of Joan and Maria Thynne, 1575–1611*, Wilts Record Society, 38 (1983)

Warnicke, R. 'Lady Mildmay's journal: A study in autobiography and meditation in Reformation England', *Sixteenth Century Journal*, 20 (1989) pp. 55–68

Wayne, V. 'Advice for women from mothers and patriarchs', in H. Wilcox (ed.), *Women and Literature in Britain, 1500–1700* (1996), 56–79

Family

Aries, P. *Centuries of Childhood* (1962)

Bonfield, L. *et al. The World We Have Gained*, Oxford (1986)

Chaytor, M. 'Household and kinship: Ryton in the late sixteenth and early seventeenth centuries', *History Workshop*, 10 (1980)

Houlbrook, R.A. *The English Family* (1983)

—— *Death, Religion and the Family in England 1480–1750*, Oxford (1998)

Laslett, P. *The World We Have Lost Further Explored* (1983 rev. edn)

—— and Wall, R. (eds), *Household and Family in Past Time*, Cambridge (1972)

O'Day, R. *The Family and Family Relationships, 1500–1900* (1994)

Macfarlane, A. *Marriage and Love in England, 1300–1840*, Oxford (1986)

Pollock, L. *Forgotten Children*, Cambridge (1983)

Stone, L. *The Family, Sex and Marriage in England 1500–1800* (1977)

Todd, M. 'Humanists, puritans and the spiritualized household', *Church History*, 49 (1980)

Socio-economic

Aston, T.H. and Philpin, C.H.E. (eds), *The Brenner Debate. Agrarian Class Structure and Economic Development in Pre-Industrial Europe*, Cambridge (1985)

Barry, J. (ed.), *The Tudor and Stuart Town* (1990)

—— and Christopher Brooks (eds), *The Middling Sort of People* (1994)

Batho, G.R. 'Landlords in England', in J. Thirsk (ed.), *The Agrarian History of England and Wales, IV, 1500–1640*, Cambridge (1967)

Beier, A.L. *Masterless Men: The Vagrancy Problem in Britain 1560–1640* (1985)

Bonfield, L., Smith, R.M. and Wrightson, K. (eds), *The World We Have Gained*, Oxford (1986)

Bowden, P. 'Agricultural Prices, Farm Profits and Rents' in J. Thirsk (ed.) *The Agrarian History of England and Wales, IV, 1500–1640*, Cambridge (1967), 595–695

Brenner, R. 'Agrarian Class Structure and Economic Development in Pre-industrial Europe', *Past and Present*, 70 (1976)

—— *Merchants and Revolution: Commercial Change, Political Conflict and London's Overseas Traders, 1550–1653*, Cambridge (1993)

Brenner, Y.S. 'The Inflation of Prices in Early Sixteenth Century England', *Economic History Review*, 2nd ser., 14 (1961), 225–39

—— 'The Inflation of Prices in England, 1551–1650', *Economic History Review*, 2nd ser., 15 (1962), 266–84

Cameron, A. 'The giving of livery and retaining in Henry VII's reign', *Renaissance and Modern Studies*, 18 (1974), 17–35

Carpenter, C. *Locality and Polity: A Study of Warwickshire Landed Society, 1401–1499*, Cambridge (1992)

Clark, P. *English Provincial Society from the Reformation to the Revolution: Religion, Politics and Society in Kent, 1500–1640*, Hassocks, Sussex (1977)

—— 'Crisis Contained? The Condition of English Towns in the 1590s' in P. Clark (ed.), *The European Crisis of the 1590s*, 1985

—— and P. Slack (eds), *Crisis and Order in English Towns 1500–1700* (1972)

—— (eds), *English Towns in Transition, 1500–1700*, Oxford (1976)

Clarkson, L.A. *The Pre-industrial Economy in England, 1500–1750* (1971)

—— *Proto-Industrialization: The First Phase of Industrialization?*, Basingstoke (1985)

Clay, C.G.A. *Economic Expansion and Social Change*, Cambridge (1984), vol. 2

Coleman, D.C. *The Economy of England, 1450–1750*, Oxford (1977)

—— *Industry in Tudor and Stuart England* (1985)

Condon, M.M. 'Ruling elites in the reign of Henry VII' in *Patronage, Pedigree and Power in Later Medieval England*, C.D. Ross (ed.), Gloucester (1979), 109–42

Coward, B. *Social Change and Continuity in Early Modern England* (1988 and 1997 rev. edn)

Cressy, D. 'Describing the Social Order of Elizabethan and Early Stuart England', *Literature and History*, 3 (1976)

—— *Birth, Marriage and Death: Ritual, Religion and the Life Cycle in Tudor and Stuart England*, Oxford (1997)

Davis, R. *English Overseas Trade, 1500–1700* (1973)

Dyer, A.D. *The City of Worcester in the Sixteenth Century*, Leicester (1973)

Finch, M.E. *The Wealth of Five Northamptonshire Families, 1540–1640*, Northamptonshire Record Society, 19 (1956)

Fletcher, A. and Stevenson, J. (eds), *Order and Disorder in Early Modern England*, Cambridge (1985)

Gray, T., Rowe, M. and Erskine, A. (eds), *Tudor and Stuart Devon . . . essays presented to Joyce Youings*, Exeter (1992)

Grell, O.P. and Cunningham, A. (eds), *Religio Medici: Medicine and Religion in Seventeenth-century England* (1996).

Griffiths, P., Fox, A. and Hindle, S. (eds), *The Experience of Authority in Early Modern England*, Basingstoke (1994). A number of essays dealing with aspects of authority. These vary in quality. Some are particularly relevant to this topic; others relate more closely to the culture of the period.

Hassell Smith, A. *County and Court: Government and Politics in Norfolk 1558–1603*, Oxford (1974)

Hatcher, J. *Plague, Population and the English Economy, 1348–1530* (1977)

Heal, F. *Of Prelates and Princes: A Study of the Economic and Social Position of the Tudor Episcopate*, Cambridge (1980)

—— *Hospitality in Early Modern England*, Oxford (1990)

—— and Holmes, C. *The Gentry in England and Wales, 1500–1700* (1994)

Heard, N. *Tudor Economy and Society* (1992)

Hey, D. *An English Rural Community. Myddle under the Tudors and Stuarts*, Leicester (1974)

Holderness, B.A. *Pre-Industrial England. Economy and Society, 1500–1750* (1976)

James, M. *Family Lineage and Civil Society: A Study of Society, Politics and Mentality in the Durham Region, 1500–1640*, Oxford (1974)

—— *Society, Politics and Culture: Studies in Early Modern England*, Cambridge (1986)

Kerridge, E. *The Agricultural Revolution* (1967)

—— *Trade and Banking in Early Modern England* (1988)

Kriedte, P., Medick, H. and Schlumbohn, J. *Industrialization Before Industrialization*, Cambridge (1981)

Kussmaul, A. *Servants in Husbandry in Early Modern England*, Cambridge (1981)

Larminie, V.M. *Wealth, Kinship and Culture: The Seventeenth-century Newdigates of Arbury and Their World*, Royal Historical Society Studies in History, 72 (1995)

MacCulloch, D. *Suffolk and the Tudors: Politics and Religion in an English County, 1500–1600*, Oxford (1986)

MacDonald, M. *Mystical Bedlam: Madness, Anxiety and Healing in Seventeenth-century England*, Cambridge (1981). Also covers late sixteenth century

—— and Murphy, T.R. *Sleepless Souls: Suicide in Early Modern England*, Oxford (1990)

Macfarlane, A. *The Origins of English Individualism* (1978)

Moreton, C.E. *The Townshends and Their World: Gentry, Law and Land in Norfolk, c. 1450–1551*, Oxford (1992)

O'Day, R. *The Family and Family Relations in Early Modern England, France and America*, (1994)

Outhwaite, R.B. *Inflation in Tudor and Stuart England* (1969 and 1982 2nd edn)

—— 'Dearth, the English Crown and the "Crisis of the 1590s"' in P. Clark (ed), *The European Crisis of the 1590s* (1985)

—— 'Progress and backwardness in English agriculture, 1500–1650', *Economic History Review*, 2nd ser., 39 (1986)

—— *Dearth, Public Policy and Social Disturbance in England, 1550–1800*, Basingstoke (1991)

Rappaport, S. *Worlds Within Worlds: Structures of Life in Sixteenth-century London*, Cambridge (1989)

Rosenthal, J.T. and Richmond, C.F. (eds), *People, Politics, and Community in the Later Middle Ages*, Gloucester (1987)

Slack, P. *Poverty and Policy in Tudor and Stuart England* (1988)

Smith, R.M. *Population History of England, 1000–1540*, Manchester (1992)

Smith, R.B. *Land and Politics in the England of Henry VIII: The West Riding of Yorkshire*, Oxford (1970)

Spufford, M. *Contrasting Communities: English Villagers in the Sixteenth and Seventeenth Centuries*, Cambridge (1979 edition)

Stone, L. *The Crisis of the Aristocracy, 1558–1641*, Oxford (1965)

—— 'Social Mobility in England 1500–1700', *Past and Present*, 33 (1966)

—— and Stone, J.C.F. *An Open Elite? England 1540–1880*, Oxford (1984)

Sutton, A.F. 'Order and fashion in clothes: the king, his household, and the city of London at the end of the fifteenth century', *Textile History*, 22 (1991), 253–76

Thirsk, J. 'Industries in the Countryside' in F.J. Fisher (ed.), *Essays in the Economic and Social History of Tudor and Stuart England*, Cambridge (1961)

—— (ed.), *The Agrarian History of England and Wales*, vols IV and V, Cambridge (1967, 1984 and 1985)

—— *Economic Policy and Projects: The Development of a Consumer Society in Early Modern England*, Oxford (1978)

—— *The Rural Economy of England. Collected Essays* (1985)

—— *England's Agricultural Regions and Agrarian History, 1500–1750* (1987) There are so many relevant local studies of high quality that I have elected to list none separately here. I refer the reader to the excellent list herein.

Wilson, E.C. *Essays in Economic History*, Vol. II (1962). In this are reprinted two of the seminal articles by E.H. Phelps Brown and S.V. Hopkins on wages and prices.

Wolffe, B.P. *The Royal Demesne in English History: The Crown Estate in the Governance of the Realm from the Conquest to 1509* (1971)

Wrigley, E.A. and Schofield, R.S. *The Population History of England, 1541–1871*, Cambridge (1989)

Wrightson, K. *Earthly Necessities. Economic Lives in Early Modern Britain, 1470–1750* (2001)

—— and Levine, D. *Poverty and Piety in an English Village: Terling 1525–1700*, (1979) and Oxford (1995 rev. edn)

Foreign policy, international relations and diplomacy

Currin, J.M. 'Henry VII and the treaty of Redon', *History*, new ser., 81 (1996), 343–58

Doran, S. *England and Europe, 1485–1603* (1986 and 1996 2nd edn)

—— *England and Europe in the Sixteenth Century*, Basingstoke (1998)

Gwyn, P.J. 'Wolsey's foreign policy: the conferences at Calais and Bruges reconsidered', *Historical Journal*, 23 (1980), 755–72

MacCaffrey, W.T. *Elizabeth I* (1993)

Russell, J.G. *The Field of Cloth of Gold* (1969)

Warren, J. *Elizabeth I: Religion and Foreign Affairs* (1993 and 2002 2nd edn)

Wernham, R.B. *Before the Armada: The Growth of English Foreign Policy, 1485–1588* (1966) and New York (1972)

—— *After the Armada: Elizabethan England and the Struggle for Western Europe*, Oxford (1984)

Military (also Rebellions and conspiracies)

Andrews, K.R. *Drake's Voyages: A Re-assessment of their Place in Elizabethan Maritime Expansion* (1967)

Arthurson, I. *The Perkin Warbeck Conspiracy, 1491–1499*, Stroud, Gloucester (1994)

—— 'The rising of 1497: A revolt of the peasantry?', *People, politics, and Community in the Later Middle Ages*, J.T. Rosenthal and C.F. Richmond (eds), Gloucester (1987), 1–18

Beer, B.L. *Rebellion and Riot: Popular Disorder in England During the Reign of Edward VI*, Kent, OH (1982 and 2005 rev. edn)

Bennett, M. *Lambert Simnel and the Battle of Stoke*, Gloucester (1987)

—— *The Battle of Bosworth*, Gloucester (1985) and Stroud (2000 2nd edn)

—— 'Henry VII and the northern rising of 1489', *English Historical Review*, 105 (1990), 34–59

Bernard, G.W. *War, Taxation, and Rebellion in Early Tudor England*, Brighton (1986)

Bush, M. *The Pilgrimage of Grace: A Study of the Rebel Armies of October 1536*, Manchester (1996)

—— and David Bownes, *The Defeat of the Pilgrimage of Grace: A Study of the Post-pardon Revolts . . . and their Effect*, Hull (1999)

Cruickshank, C.G. *Army Royal: An Account of Henry VIII's Invasion of France*, Oxford (1969)

—— *Army Royal: Henry VIII and the Invasion of France*, Stroud, Gloucs (1990)

—— *The English Occupation of Tournai, 1513–19* (1971)

Cunningham, S. 'Henry VII and rebellion in north-eastern England, 1485–1492: Bonds of allegiance and the establishment of Tudor authority', *Northern History*, 32 (1996), 42–74

Currin, J.M. '"The king's army into the partes of Bretaigne": Henry VII and the Breton wars, 1489–1491', *War in History*, 7 (2000), 379–412

Dodds, M.H. and Dodds, R. *The Pilgrimage of Grace, 1536–1537, and the Exeter Conspiracy, 1538*, two vols (1915)

Elton, G.R. 'Politics and the Pilgrimage of Grace', *Studies in Tudor and Stuart Politics and Government*, four vols, Cambridge (1974–92), vol. 3

Fletcher, A. and MacCulloch, D. *Tudor Rebellions* (1997 rev. edn)

Green, D. *The Double Life of Doctor Lopez: Spies, Shakespeare and the Plot to Poison Elizabeth I* (2003)

Hoyle, R.W. *The Pilgrimage of Grace and the Politics of the 1530s*, Oxford (2001)

Kelsey, H. *Sir Francis Drake: The Queen's Pirate*, New Haven, CT (1998)

Luckett, D.A. 'The Thames valley conspiracies against Henry VII', *Historical Research*, 68 (1995), 164–72

MacCaffrey, W.T. *Elizabeth I: War and Politics, 1588–1603*, Princeton, NJ (1992)

MacCulloch, D. 'Kett's rebellion in context', *Past and Present*, 84 (1979), 36–59

Walter, J. 'A "Rising of the People"? The Oxfordshire Rising of 1596', *Past and Present*, 71, 90–143

Trade

Bowden, P.J. *The Wool Trade in Tudor and Stuart England* (1962)

Brenner, R. *Merchants and Revolution: Commercial Change, Political Conflict and London's Overseas Traders, 1550–1653*, Cambridge (1993)

Coleman, D.C. *The English Economy, 1450–1750*, Oxford (1977)

Davis, R. *English Overseas Trade*, 1500–1700 (1973)

Ramsey, P. 'Overseas trade in the reign of Henry VII: the evidence of customs accounts', *Economic History Review*, 2nd ser., 6 (1953–4), 173–82

—— (ed.), *The Price Revolution in Sixteenth-Century England* (1971)

Wallerstein, I. *The Modern World System*, New York (1974)

Wilson, C. *England's Apprenticeship*, 2nd edn (1965 and 1984 2nd edn). Largely concerned with seventeenth century but also some relevance for Tudor period

Ireland (and also relations with England)

Bradshaw, B. and Morrill, J. (eds), *The British Problem, 1534–1707: England, Ireland, Scotland, Wales* (1996)

Brady, C. *The Chief Governors: The Rise and Fall of Reform Government in Tudor Ireland, 1536–1588*, Cambridge (1994)

—— and Gillespie, R. (eds), *Natives and Newcomers: Essays on the Making of Irish Colnial Society, 1534–1641*, Dublin (1986)

Ellis, S.G. *Tudor Ireland: Crown, Community, and the Conflict of Cultures, 1470–1603* (1985)

—— *Reform and Revival: English Government in Ireland, 1470–1534* (1986)
—— *Ireland in the Age of the Tudors* (1998)
Canny, N.P. *The Elizabethan Conquest of Ireland* (1976)
—— 'Edmund Spenser and the development of an Anglo-Irish identity', *Yearbook of English Studies*, 13 (1983)
—— *From Reformation to Restoration: Ireland, 1534–1660*, Dublin (1987)
—— *Kingdom and Colony: Ireland in the Atlantic World, 1560-1800*, Baltimore, MD (1988)

Scotland (and also relations with England)

Bradshaw, B. and Morrill, J. (eds), *The British Problem, 1534–1707: England, Ireland, Scotland, Wales* (1996)
Cameron, J. *James V: The Personal Rule, 1528–1542*, N. Macdougall (ed.), East Linton (1998)
Eaves, R.G. *Henry VIII and James V's regency, 1524–1528*, Lanham, MD (1987)
—— *Henry VIII's Scottish diplomacy, 1513–1524*, New York (1971)
Ferguson, W. *Scotland's Relations with England: A Survey to 1707*, Edinburgh (1977)
Freeman, T. '"The Reik of Maister Patrick Hammyltoun": John Foxe, John Winram and the martyrs of the Scottish Reformation', *Sixteenth Century Journal*, 27 (1996), 23–46
Lynch, M. (ed.), *The Early Modern Town in Scotland* (1987)
—— *Scotland: A New History*, Edinburgh (1992)
Whyte, I.D. *Scotland's Society and Economy in Transition, c. 1500–c. 1760*, Basingstoke (1997)
Wormald, J. *Court, Kirk and Community: Scotland, 1470–1625* (1981) and Edinburgh (1991)

Wales

Bradshaw, B. and Morrill, J. (eds), *The British Problem, 1534–1707: England, Ireland, Scotland, Wales* (1996)
Davies, R.R. and Jenkins, G.H. (eds), *From Medieval to Modern Wales . . .*, Cardiff (2004)
Jenkins, P. *A History of Modern Wales, 1536–1990* (1992)
Roberts, M. and Clarke, S. (eds), *Women and Gender in Early Modern Wales*, Cardiff (2000)
Smith, J.B. 'Crown and community in the principality of north Wales in the reign of Henry Tudor', *Welsh History Review/Cylchgrawn Hanes Cymru*, 3 (1966–67), 145–71
Williams, G. *Welsh Reformation Essays*, Cardiff (1967)
—— *Recovery, Reorientation and Reformation: Wales c. 1470–1642*, Oxford (1987)
—— *Wales and the Reformation*, Cardiff (1997)
Williams, P. *The Council in the Marches of Wales under Elizabeth I*, Cardiff (1958)
Williams, W.L. 'The union of England and Wales', *Transactions of the Honourable Society of Cymmrodorion* (1907–08), 47–117

Biographies

For up to date essay-length biographies see *Oxford Dictionary of National Biography*.

Baines, B.J. *Thomas Heywood*, Boston (1984)
Beer, B.L. *Northumberland: The Political Career of John Dudley, Earl of Warwick and Duke of Northumberland*, Kent, OH (1973)
Bernard, G.W. *The Power of the Early Tudor Nobility: A Study of the Fourth and Fifth Earls of Shrewsbury*, Brighton (1985)

Brinley Jones, R. *William Salesbury*, Cardiff (1994)

Brook, V.J.K. *Whitgift and the English Church* (1957 and 1964 2nd edn)

Buchanan, P.H. *Margaret Tudor, Queen of Scots*, Edinburgh (1985)

Chambers, E.K. *Sir Henry Lee: An Elizabethan Portrait*, Oxford (1936)

Chapman, H. *The Last Tudor King: A Study of Edward VI*, Bath (1973)

—— *The Sisters of Henry VIII*, Bath (1974)

Collinson, P. *Archbishop Grindal, 1519–1583: The Struggle for a Reformed Church* (1979)

—— *Godly People: Essays on English Protestantism and Puritanism* (1983)

Coward, B. *The Stanleys Lords Stanley and Earls of Derby, 1385–1672*, Chetham Society Manchester (1983)

Cross, C. *The Puritan Earl: The Life of Henry Hastings, Third Earl of Huntingdon, 1536–94*, London & New York (1967)

Crupi, C.W. *Robert Greene*, Boston, MA (1986)

Daniell, D. *William Tyndale: A Biography*, New Haven, CT (1994)

Dickens, A.G. *Thomas Cromwell and the English Reformation*, 1959

Dowling, M. *Fisher of Men: A Life of John Fisher, 1469–1535*, Basingstoke (1999)

Duncan-Jones, K. *Sir Philip Sidney: Life, Death and Legend*, Oxford (1986). Catalogue of exhibition

Durant, D.N. *Bess of Hardwick: Portrait of an Elizabethan Dynast*, rev. edn (1999)

Du Maurier, D. *Golden Lads: A Study of Anthony Bacon, Francis and their Friends* (1975 and 2007 3rd edn with introduction by Lisa Jardine)

Edgerton, W.L. *Nicholas Udall* (1965)

Elton, G.R. *Thomas Cromwell* (1991)

Freedman, S. *Poor Penelope: Lady Penelope Rich, An Elizabethan Woman*, Windsor (1983)

Gerard, J. (ed. and transl. by Philip Caraman), *The Autobiography of an Elizabethan* (1951)

Gross, P.M. *Jane, The Quene: Third Consort of King Henry VIII*, Lewiston, NY (1999)

Gunn, S.J. *Charles Brandon, Duke of Suffolk, c. 1484–1545*, Oxford (1988)

—— 'Sir Thomas Lovell (c. 1449–1524): A New Man in a New Monarchy?', in J.L. Watts (ed.), *The End of the Middle Ages?*, Stroud, Gloucs (1998), pp. 117–53

Guy, J.A. *Thomas More* (2000)

—— *A Daughter's Love: Thomas and Margaret More* (2008)

Gwyn, P. *The King's Cardinal: The Rise and Fall of Thomas Wolsey* (1990, 1992)

Hannay, M.P. *Philip's Phoenix: Mary Sidney, Countess of Pembroke*, New York (1990)

Harris, B.H. *Edward Stafford, Third Duke of Buckingham, 1478–1521*, Stanford, CA (1986)

Harvey, N.L. *The Rose and the Thorn: The Lives of Mary and Margaret Tudor*, New York (1975)

Head, D.M. *The Ebbs and Flows of Fortune: The Life of Thomas Howard, Third Duke of Norfolk*, Athens, GA (1995)

Honan, P. *Shakespeare: A Life*, Oxford (1998)

Ives, E.W. *Anne Boleyn*, Oxford (1986)

—— *The Life and Death of Anne Boleyn: 'The Most Happy'*, Malden, MA (2004)

James, S.E. *Kateryn Parr: The Making of a Queen*, Aldershot (1999)

Jordan, W.K. *Edward VI, 1: The Young King* (1968)

—— *Edward VI, 2: The Threshold of Power* (1970)

Josephson, D.S. *John Taverner: Tudor Composer*, Ann Arbor, MI (1979)

Knecht, R. *Francis I*, Cambridge (1984)

Lasocki, D. and Prior, R. *The Bassanos: Venetian Musicians and Instrument Makers in England, 1531–1665*, Aldershot (1995)

Loach, J. *Edward VI*, G. Bernard and P. Williams (eds), New Haven, CT (1999)

Loades, D. *Mary Tudor: A Life*, Oxford (1989)

—— *John Dudley, Duke of Northumberland, 1504–1533* Oxford (1996 and 2002 new edn)

—— *The Politics of Marriage*: *Henry VIII and His Queens*, Stroud, Gloucs (1994) (as *Henry VIII and His Queens*, 2000)

—— *The Tragical History of the First Queen of England*, Kew (2006)

MacCaffrey, W.T. *Elizabeth I* (1993)

McConica, J.K. *English Humanists and Reformation Politics Under Henry VIII and Edward VI*, Oxford (1965)

—— *Erasmus*, Oxford (1991)

MacCulloch, D. *Thomas Cranmer: A Life*, New Haven, CT (1996)

—— *The Boy King: Edward VI and the Protestant Reformation*, Berkeley, CA (2002)

Maddison, F., Pelling, M. and Webster, C. (eds), *Essays on the Life and Works of Thomas Linacre, c. 1460–1524*, Oxford (1977)

Mattingly, G. *Catherine of Aragon* (1942) and abbreviated reprint, London (1963)

Mayer, T.F. *Reginald Pole: Prince and Prophet*, Cambridge (2000)

Miller, A.C. *Sir Henry Killigrew*, Leicester (1963)

Muir, K. *Life and Letters of Sir Thomas Wyatt*, Liverpool (1963)

Nicholl, C. *The Reckoning: The Murder of Christopher Marlowe* (1992 and 2002 new edn)

Osborn, J.M. *Young Philip Sidney, 1572–1577*, New Haven, CT (1972)

Plowden, A. *Lady Jane Grey and the House of Suffolk* (1985)

—— *Lady Jane Grey: Nine Days Queen*, Stroud, Gloucs (2003)

Read, C. *Mr Secretary Walsingham and the Policy of Queen Elizabeth I*, 3 vols Oxford (1925) and New York (1978 repr.)

Redworth, G. *In defence of the Church Catholic: The Life of Stephen Gardiner* (1990)

Reynolds, E.E. *Margaret Roper: Eldest Daughter of St Thomas More* (1960)

Ridley, J. *Nicholas Ridley: A Biography* (1957)

Ryan, L.V. *Roger Ascham*, Stanford, CA (1963)

Scarisbrick, J.J. *Henry VIII* (1968 and 1997 new edn)

Schenk, W.H. *Reginald Pole* (1950)

Schoenbaum, S. *William Shakespeare: A Compact Documentary Life*, Oxford (1977 and 1987 rev. edn)

Slavin, A.J. *Politics and Profit: A Study of Sir Ralph Sadler, 1507–47*, Cambridge (1966)

Smith, A.G.R. (ed.), M. Hickes, *The 'Anonymous life' of William Cecil, Lord Burghley* Lewiston, NY (1990)

—— *William Cecil, Lord Burghley: Minister of Elizabeth I* (1991)

Smith, L.B. *A Tudor tragedy. The Life and Times of Catherine Howard* (1961)

—— *Henry VIII: The Mask of Royalty* (1971)

Sylvester, R.S. and Harding, D.P. (eds), *Two Early Tudor Lives* (contemporary lives of Wolsey and More), New Haven, CT (1962)

Trudgian, F. *Francis Tregian, 1548–1608: Elizabethan Recusant* (1998)

Tucker, M.J. *The Life of Thomas Howard Earl of Surrey and Second Duke of Norfolk, 1443– 1524*, The Hague (1964)

Warnicke, R.M. *William Lambarde, Elizabethan antiquary, 1536–1601*, Chichester (1973)

—— *Women of the English Renaissance and Reformation*, Westport, CT (1983)

Weston, W. ed. and translated by Philip Caraman, *The Autobiography of an Elizabethan* (1955)

Willen, D. *John Russell, First Earl of Bedford. One of the King's Men*, Royal Historical Society (1981)

Williams, N. *Thomas Howard, Fourth Duke of Norfolk* (1954 and 1964 (with plates))

Woods, S. *Lanyer: A Renaissance Woman Poet*, New York (1999)

Culture

Anglo, S. *Spectacle, Pageantry and Early Tudor Policy*, Oxford (1969)

Ariés, P. *The Hour of Our Death*, New York (1981) and Oxford (1991)

Aston, M. *England's Iconoclasts*, Vol. I, Oxford (1988)

—— *The King's Bedpost: Reformation and Iconography in a Tudor Group Portrait*, Cambridge (1993)

Augustijn, C. *Erasmus, His Life, Works and Influence,* transl. by J.C. Grayson, Toronto and London (1991)

Betteridge, T. *Tudor Histories of the English Reformations, 1530–83*, Aldershot (1999)

Burke, P. *Popular Culture in Early Modern Europe* (1978); Aldershot (1988 2nd and rev. edn); Farnham (2009 3rd edn)

Christianson, P. *Reformers and Babylon: English Apocalyptic Visions from the Reformation to the Eve of the Civil War*, Toronto (1978)

Clark, P. *The English Alehouse: A Social History* (1983)

Dowling, M. *Humanism in the Age of Henry VIII* (1986)

Duncan-Jones, K. *Sir Philip Sidney: Courtier Poet* (1991)

Durston, C. and Eales, J. (eds), *The Culture of English Puritanism, 1560–1700*, Basingstoke (1996)

Englander, D., Norman, D., O'Day R. and Owens, W.R. (eds), *Culture and Belief in Europe, 1450–1600, An Anthology of Sources*, Oxford (1989)

Fleming, J. *Graffiti and the Writing Arts of Early Modern England* (2001)

Firth, K.R. *The Apocalyptic Tradition in Reformation Britain, 1530–1645*, Oxford (1979)

Ginzburg, C. *The Night Battles: Witchcraft and Agrarian Cults in the Sixteenth and Seventeenth Centuries*, transl. by J. and A. Tredeschi (1983)

Gittings, C. *Death, Burial and the Individual in Early Modern England* (1984, 1988 2nd edn)

Graham, T. and Watson, A.G. (eds), *The Recovery of the Past in Early Elizabethan England: Documents by John Bale and John Joscelyn from the Circle of Matthew Parker*, Cambridge (1998)

Griffiths, P. (ed.), *The Experience of Authority in Early Modern England*, Basingstoke (1994)

Hackett, H. *Virgin Mother, Maiden Queen: Elizabeth I and the Cult of the Virgin Mary*, Basingstoke, 1994

Harris, T. (ed.), *Popular Culture in England, c. 1500–1850*, Basingstoke (1994)

James, M.E. *Family, Lineage and Civil Society: A Study of Society, Politics and Mentality in the Durham Region, 1500–1640*, Oxford (1974)

Larner, C. *Enemies of God: The Witch-hunt in Scotland*, Oxford, 1983

Macfarlane, A. *Witchcraft in Tudor and Stuart England* (1970, 1999 2nd edn)

McConica, J.K. *Erasmus*, Oxford (1991)

—— *English Humanists and Reformation Politics under Henry VIII and Edward VI*, Oxford (1965)

McKisack, M. *Medieval History in the Tudor Age*, Oxford (1971)

McLaren, A.N. *Political Culture in the Reign of Elizabeth I: Queen and Commonwealth, 1558–1585*, Cambridge (1999)

Monter, W. *Ritual, Myth and Magic in Early Modern Europe*, Brighton (1983)

O'Day, R. 'Hugh Latimer, Prophet of the Kingdom', *Historical Research*, 65 (1992)

—— 'Family Galleries: Women and Art . . .', *Huntington Library Quarterly* (2008)

Overell, M.A. *Italian Reform and English Reformations, c. 1535–c. 1585*, Aldershot (2008)

Page, R.I. and Bushnell, G.H.S. *Matthew Parker's Legacy: Books and Plate*, Cambridge (1975) (listed in BL catalogue under Corpus Christi College, University of Cambridge)

Phillipson, N. and Skinner, Q. (eds), *Political Discourse in Early Modern Britain*, Cambridge (1993)

Sharpe, J.A. *Crime in Early Modern England, 1550–1750* (1984, 1999 2nd edn)

Sharpe, K.M. and Zwicker, S.N. (eds), *Reading, Society and Politics in Early Modern England*, Cambridge, 2003

Thomas, K.V. *Religion and the Decline of Magic*, New York and London (1971, 1991 2nd edn); Harmondsworth (1973, 1978 new edn)

Vergil, P. *Anglica Historica*, Denys Hay (ed.), Camden Society, 3rd series, LXXIV (1950)

Walsham, A. and Withington, P. (eds) *Communities in Early Modern England*, Manchester (2000)

Woolf, D.R. *Reading History in Early Modern England*, Cambridge (2000)

Education and intellectual history

Alston, R.C. *A shorte introduction of grammar*, W. Lily and J. Colet (ed.), (1549) (facs. edn, 1970)

Ascham, R. *The Whole Works of Roger Ascham*, J.A. Giles (ed.) (1864)

—— *The Schoolmaster*, L.V. Ryan (ed.), (new edn) (1967)

—— *Toxophilus*, J.E.B. Mayor (ed.) (1863)

Ashworth, E.J. 'Text-books: A case study – logic' in L. Hellinga and J.B. Trapp (eds), *The Cambridge History of the Book in Britain, III, 1400-1557*, Cambridge (1999)

Ben-Amos, I.K. *Adolescence and Youth in Early Modern England*, New Haven, CT (1994)

Berkovitz, D.S. *Humanist Scholarship and Public Order* (1984)

Charlton, K. *Education in Renaissance England* (1965)

Cressy, D. *Literacy and the Social Order*, Cambridge (1980)

Curtis, M.H. *Oxford and Cambridge in Transition*, Oxford (1959)

DeMolen, R. *Richard Mulcaster (c. 1531–1611) and educational reform in the Renaissance* (1991)

Dickens, A.G. *The Age of Humanism*, New Jersey, 1972. Survey.

Furdell, E. *Publishing and Medicine in Early Modern England*, Rochester, NY (2002)

Hexter, J.H. 'The Education of the Aristocracy in the Renaissance' in J.H. Hexter, *Reappraisals in History*, 1963

Jewell, H. *Education in Early Modern England* (1998)

Kearney, H. *Scholars and Gentlemen. Universities and Society*, 1970

Leader, D.R. *A History of the University of Cambridge*, 1: *The University to 1546*, C.N.L. Brooke and others (eds) (1988)

Mack, P. *Elizabethan Rhetoric*, Cambridge, 2002

McConica, J.K. (ed.), *The History of the University of Oxford, Vol. III, The Collegiate University*, Oxford (1986)

McMullen, N. 'The Education of English Gentlewomen 1540–1640', *History of Education*, 6 (1977)

Moran, J.H. *The Growth of English Schooling 1348–1548*, Princeton NJ (1985)

Morgan, J. *Godly Learning*, Cambridge (1986)

O'Day, R. *Education and Society, 1500–1800* (1982)

—— 'Social Change in the History of Education: Perspectives on the Emergence of Learned Professions in England, c. 1500–1800', *History of Education*, 36 (2007), 409–28

Orme, N. *Education and Society in Medieval and Renaissance England* (1989)

Russell, E. 'The Influx of Commoners into the University of Oxford before 1581: an optical illusion', *English Historical Review*, 92, 1977

Simon, B. (ed.), *Education in Leicestershire, 1540–1940: A Regional Study*, Leicester (1968)

Simon, J. *Education and Society in Tudor England*, Cambridge (1967)

Skinner, Q. *Foundations of Modern Political Thought*, 2 vols, Cambridge (1978 and 1980)

Spufford, M. 'The Schooling of the Peasantry in Cambridgeshire, 1575–1700', *Agricultural History Review*, Supplement (1970)

Stone, L. 'The Educational Revolution in England, 1560–1640', *Past and Present* (1964)

—— (ed.), *The University in Society*, Vol. I, Princeton, NJ (1974). Contains important articles by V. Morgan, J. McConica and Stone himself.

Woolfson, J.M. *Padua and the Tudors* (1998)

Professions

Baker, J.H. *The Order of Serjeants at Law* (1984)

Barry, J. and Brooks, C. (eds), *The Middling Sort of People: Culture, Society and Politics in England, 1550–1800*, Macmillan, 1994. Some of the essays are relevant; see especially that by Christopher Brooks

Brooks, C.W. 'The Common Lawyers in England, c. 1558–1642' in W. Prest (ed.), *Lawyers in Early Modern Europe and America* (1981)

—— *Pettyfoggers and Vipers of the Commonwealth*, Cambridge (1986)

Cressy, D., 'A Drudgery of Schoolmasters: The Teaching Profession in Elizabethan and Early Stuart England' in W. Prest (ed.), *The Professions in Early Modern England* (1987)

Ives, E.W. *The Common Lawyers of Pre-Reformation England*, Cambridge (1983)

Knafla, L.A. 'The Law Studies of an Elizabethan Student', *History of Law Quarterly* (1969)

Levack, B.P. *The Civil Lawyers in England, 1603–1641: A Political Study*, Oxford (1973) Mainly seventeenth century, but relevant to Tudor period also.

—— 'The English Civilians, 1500–1750' in Wilfrid Prest (ed.), *The Professions in Early Modern England* (1987)

McConica, J.K. (ed.), *The History of the University of Oxford, Vol. III, The Collegiate University*, Oxford (1986)

O'Day, R. *The English Clergy, The Emergence and Consolidation of a Profession, 1558–1642*, Leicester (1979)

—— *Education and Society, 1500–1800* (1982)

—— 'The Anatomy of a Profession' in W. Prest (ed.), *The Professions in Early Modern England* (1987)

—— *The Professions in Early Modern England: Servants of the Commonweal* (2000)

—— 'Social Change in the History of Education: Perspectives on the Emergence of Learned Professions in England, c. 1500–1800', *History of Education*, 36 (2007), 409–28

Pelling, M. *The Common Lot, Sickness, Medical Occupations and the Urban Poor in Early Modern England* (1998)

Prest, W. *The Inns of Court Under Elizabeth 1 and the Early Stuarts, 1590–1640* (1972)

—— *The Rise of the Barristers: A Social History of the English Bar, 1590-1640* Oxford (1986)

—— (ed.), *The Professions in Early Modern England* (1987)

Webster, C. (ed.), *Health, Medicine and Mortality in the Sixteenth Century*, Cambridge (1979)

History of the book

Carley, J.P. *The Books of King Henry VIII and his Wives* (2004)

Greg, W.W. 'Books and bookmen in the correspondence of Archbishop Parker', *The Library*, 4th ser., 16 (1935), 243–79

Hellinga, L. and Trapp, J.B. (eds) *The Cambridge History of the Book in Britain*, 3: *1400–1557* (1999)

Spufford, M. *Small Books and Pleasant Histories: Popular Fiction and its Readership in Seventeenth-century England* (1981 and Cambridge, 1985 2nd edn)

Literature

Longman York Handbooks. Provide useful and convenient guides to Shakespeare and other relevant authors and genres

Allen, M.J.B., Baker-Smith, D. and Kinney, A.F. *Sir Philip Sidney's Achievements*, New York (1990)

Axton, M. *The Queen's Two Bodies* (1977)

Baines, B.J. *Thomas Heywood*, Boston, MA (1984)

Brennan, M.G. *Literary Patronage in the English Renaissance: The Pembroke Family* (1988)

Briggs, J. *This Stage-Play World*, Oxford (1983)

Burke, V. and Gibson, J. (eds), *Early Modern Manuscript Writing*, Aldershot (2004)

Chambers, E.K. *The Elizabethan Stage*, four vols, Oxford, 1923, 1974 edn. A useful source.

Daadler, J. *Collected poems*, T. Wyatt, (ed.) (1975)

Dobson, M. *The making of the national poet,* Oxford (1992)

—— and Wells, S. *The Oxford Companion to Shakespeare*, Oxford (2001)

Fox, A. *Politics and Literature in the Reigns of Henry VII and Henry VIII*, Oxford (1989)

Geritz, A.J. and Laine, A.L. *John Rastell*, Boston (1983)

Graham, D. *After Shakespeare*, Newcastle upon Tyne (2001)

Gurr, A. *Playgoing in Shakespeare's London*, Cambridge (1987)

Hunter, G.K. *John Lyly: The Humanist as Courtier* (1962)

Ingram, W. *The Business of Playing: The Beginnings of the Adult Professional Theater in Elizabethan London*, Ithaca, NY (1992)

Johnson, R.C. *John Heywood* (1970)

Muir, K. and Thomson, P. (eds), *The Poems of Sir Thomas Wyatt* (1969)

Nicholl, C. *The Reckoning: The Murder of Christopher Marlowe* (1992)

Norland, H. *Drama in Early Tudor England, 1485–1558* (1995)

Roston, M. *Sixteenth-Century English Literature* (1982)

Stevenson, J. and Davidson, P. *Early Modern Women Poets*, Oxford (2001)

Sylvester, R.S. 'Cavendish's *Life of Wolsey*: The Artistry of a Tudor biographer', *Studies in Philology*, 57 (1960), 44–71

Walker, G. *John Skelton and the Politics of the 1520s* (1988)

—— *Plays of Persuasion: Drama and Politics at the Court of Henry VIII*, Cambridge (1991)

Wiggins, M. *Shakespeare and the Drama of his Time* (2000)

Wooden, W.W. 'The art of partisan biography: George Cavendish's *Life of Wolsey*', *Renaissance and Reformation*, new ser., 1 (1977), 24–35

Worden, B. *The Sound of Virtue: Philip Sidney's 'Arcadia' and Elizabethan politics* (1996)

Woudhuysen, H.R. *Sir Philip Sidney and the Circulation of Manuscripts, 1558–1640* (1996)

Portraiture and the visual arts (including architecture)

Anglo, S. 'The court festivals of Henry VII: A study based upon the account books of John Heron, treasurer of the chamber', *Bulletin of the John Rylands University Library*, 43 (1960–61), 12–45

—— *Spectacle, Pageantry and Early Tudor policy* (1969) repr. (1989)

Aston, M. 'The *Bishops' Bible* illustrations', D. Wood (ed.), *The Church and the Arts, Studies in Church History*, 28 (1992), 267–85

Auerbach, E. *Tudor Artists* (1954)

Beer, B.L. *Tudor England Observed: The World of John Stow*, Stroud, Gloucs (1998)

Bennett, C. *The Triumphant Image: Tudor and Stuart Portraits at Christchurch Mansion, Ipswich*, 1991

Girouard, M. *Robert Smythson and the Elizabethan Country House*, New Haven, CT (1983)

—— *Hardwick Hall* (1989)

Gunn, S.J. and Lindley, P.G. (eds), *Cardinal Wolsey: Church, State and Art*, Cambridge (1991)

Harvey, J.H. 'The building works and architects of Cardinal Wolsey', *Journal of the British Archaeological Association*, 3rd ser., 8 (1943), 50–59

Ingamells, J. *The English episcopal portrait, 1559–1835: A Catalogue* (privately printed, London, 1981)

Lindley, P.G. *Gothic to Renaissance: Essays on Sculpture in England*, Stamford (1995)

Rowlands, J. *Holbein: The Paintings of Hans Holbein The Younger*, Oxford (1985)

Strong, R.C. *Holbein and Henry VIII* (1967)

—— *The National Portrait Gallery: Tudor and Stuart Portraits* (1969)

—— *Artists of the Tudor Court: The Portrait Miniature Rediscovered, 1520–1620* (1983) (exhibition catalogue, V&A, 9 July – 16 Nov.)

—— 'The courtier: Hilliard's *Young man amongst roses*', in *The Cult of Elizabeth: Elizabethan Portraiture and Pageantry* (1977), 56–83

—— 'Queen Elizabeth, the Earl of Essex and Nicholas Hilliard', *Burlington Magazine*, 101 (1959), 145–49

—— 'My weeping stagg I crowne: The Persian lady reconsidered', *The Tudor and Stuart Monarchy: Pageantry, Painting, Iconography*, 2: *Elizabethan* (1996), 303–24

Summerson, J. *Architecture in Britain, 1530–1830* (1955; 1993 9th edn)

Thurley, S. *The Royal Palaces of Tudor England*, New Haven, CT (1993)

Wells-Cole, A. *Art of decoration in Elizabethan and Jacobean England*, New Haven, CT (1997)

Music

Bowers, R. 'The cultivation and promotion of music in the household and orbit of Thomas Wolsey', *Cardinal Wolsey: Church, State, and Art*, S.J. Gunn and P.G. Lindley (eds) (1991), 178–218

Hamlyn, H. *Psalm Culture and Early Modern Literature*, Cambridge (2004)

Ruff, L.M. and Wilson, D.A. 'The madrigal, the lute song and Elizabethan politics', *Past and Present*, 44 (1969), 3–51

Religious and ecclesiastical affairs

Ayris, P. and Selwyn, D. (eds), *Thomas Cranmer: Churchman and Scholar*, Woodbridge (1993)

Bauckham, R. (ed.), *Tudor Apocalypse*, Oxford (1978)

Bernard, G.W. *The King's Reformation*, New Haven, CT (2005)

Block, J. 'Thomas Cromwell's patronage of preaching', *Sixteenth Century Journal*, 8 (1977), 37–50

Bowker, M. *The Secular Clergy in the Diocese of Lincoln, 1495–1520*, Cambridge (1968)

—— 'Lincolnshire 1536: Heresy, schism or religious discontent?' in D. Baker (ed.), *Studies in Church History*, 9, Oxford (1972), 195–212

—— 'The supremacy and the episcopate: The struggle for control, 1534–1540', *Historical Journal*, 18 (1975), 227–43

—— 'The Henrician reformation and the parish clergy', *Bulletin of the Institute of Historical Research*, 50 (1977) 30–47

—— *The Henrician Reformation in the Diocese of Lincoln Under John Longland, 1521–47*, Cambridge (1981)

Bradshaw, B. and Duffy, E. (eds), *Humanism, Reform and the Reformation: The Career of Bishop John Fisher*, Cambridge (1989)

Brigden, S. *London and the Reformation*, Oxford (1989)

Brooks, P.N. *Thomas Cranmer's doctrine of the Eucharist: An Essay in Historical Development*, Basingstoke (1965, 1992 2nd edn)

Carlson, E.J. (ed.) *Religion and the English people, 1500–1640: New Voices, New Perspectives* (*Sixteenth Century Essays and Studies*, vol. 45, pub'd by Sixteenth Century Journal) Kirksville, MO (1998)

Carlson, L.H. *Martin Marprelate, Gentleman: Master Job Throkmorton Laid Open in his Colors*, San Marino, CA (1981)

Clark, P. 'The ecclesiastical commission at Canterbury', *Archaeologia Cantiana*, 89 (1974) 183–97

Collinson, P. *The Elizabethan Puritan Movement* (1967)

—— *The Religion of Protestants*, Oxford (1982)

—— *Godly People: Essays on English Protestantism and Puritanism* (1983)

—— *Elizabethan Essays* (1994)

Cross, C. (ed.), *The Royal Supremacy in the Elizabethan Church* (1969)

—— *Church and People 1450–1600* (1976)

Daeley, J.I. 'Pluralism in the diocese of Canterbury during the administration of Matthew Parker, 1559–1575', *Journal of Ecclesiastical History*, 18 (1967), 33–49

Davies, C.S.L. 'The pilgrimage of grace reconsidered', *Past and Present*, 41, 54–76

Davies, H. *Worship and Theology in England, vol. 1 from Cranmer to Hooker, 1534–1603* Princeton, NJ (1970) and (combined with vol. 2) Grand Rapids, MN (1996)

Davis, J.F. *Heresy and Reformation in the South-East of England, 1520–59*, Royal Historical Society: Studies in History, vol. 34 (1983)

Dickens, A.G. *Lollards and Protestants in the Diocese of York, 1509–58*, Oxford (1959)

—— *The English Reformation* (1964, 1989 rev. edn)

—— 'Secular and religious motivations in the pilgrimage of grace' in G. Cumings (ed.), *Studies in Church History*, 4 (1967) Leiden, 39–64

—— *Reformation Studies* (1982)

—— 'Review of J.J. Scarisbrick, *The Reformation and the English People*', *Journal of Ecclesiastical History*, 36 (1985), 123–6.

Duffy, E. *The Stripping of the Altars. Traditional Religion in England c. 1400–1570*, New Haven, CT (1992)

—— *The Voices of Morebath. Reformation and Rebellion in an English Village*, New Haven, CT (2001)

—— *Fires of Faith: Catholic England under Mary Tudor* (2009)

Dures, A. *English Catholicism, 1558–1642: Continuity and Change*, Harlow (1983)

Elton, G.R. *Policy and Police: The Enforcement of the Reformation in the age of Thomas Cromwell*, Cambridge (1972, 1985 new edn)

Fincham, K. *Prelate as Pastor: The Episcopate of James I*, Oxford (1990)

Foster, A. 'The function of a bishop: The career of Richard Neile, 1562–1640', in R. O'Day and F. Heal (eds), *Continuity and Change: Personnel and Administration of the Church in England*, Leicester (1976), 33–54

Freeman, T. 'John Bale's book of martyrs?: The account of King John in *Acts and monuments*', *Reformation*, 3 (1998), 175–223

—— 'Texts, lies and microfilm: reading and misreading Foxe's "Book of martyrs"', *Sixteenth Century Journal*, 30 (1999), 23–46

—— '"The Good Ministrye of Godlye and Vertuouse Women": The Elizabethan martyrologists and the female supporters of the Marian martyrs', *Journal of British Studies*, 39 (2000), 8–33

Goodman, A. 'Henry VII and Christian renewal', in *Religion and Humanism*, K. Robbins (ed.), *Studies in Church History*, 17 (1981), 115–25

Green, I.M. *The Christian's ABC: Catechisms and Catechizing in England, c. 1530–1740* (1996)

Haigh, C. *Reformation and Resistance in Tudor Lancashire*, Cambridge (1975)

—— 'The recent historiography of the English Reformation', *Historical Journal* (1982), 25, 995–1007

—— 'Anticlericalism in the English Reformation', *History*, 68 (1983), 391–407

—— *English Reformations: Religion, Politics, and Society under the Tudors*, Oxford (1993)

Hammer, C.P. 'The Oxford martyrs in Oxford: The local history of their confinements and their keepers', *Journal of Ecclesiastical History*, 50 (1999), 235–50

Heal, F. *Of prelates and Princes: A Study of the Economic and Social Position of the Tudor Episcopate*, Cambridge (1980)

—— and O'Day, R. (eds), *Church and Society in England, Henry VIII to James I*, Basingstoke (1977)

Heath, P. *The English Parish Clergy on the Eve of the Reformation* (1969)

Houlbrooke, R.A. (ed.), *The Letter Book of John Parkhurst, Bishop of Norwich*, Norfolk RS, 43 (1974–75)

—— 'The decline of ecclesiastical jurisdiction under the Tudors', in R. O'Day and F. Heal (eds), *Continuity and Change: Personnel and Administration of the Church in England*, Leicester (1976) 239–57

—— *Church Courts and People during the English Reformation, 1520–1570*, Oxford (1979)

Hudson, W.S. *The Cambridge Connection and the Elizabethan Settlement of 1559*, Durham, NC (1980)

Ingram, M. *Church Courts, Sex and Marriage in England, 1570–1640*, Cambridge (1987)

Jones, N.L. *Faith by Statute: Parliament and the Settlement of Religion, 1559*, Royal Historical Society: Studies in History vol. 32 (1982)

Kautz, A. 'The selection of Jacobean bishops', in H.S. Reinmuth (ed.), *Early Stuart Studies*, Minneapolis, MN (1970)

Kitching, C.J. 'The probate jurisdiction of Thomas Cromwell as vicegerent', *Bulletin of the Institute of Historical Research*, 46 (1973)

—— 'The prerogative court of Canterbury', in R. O'Day and F. Heal (eds), *Continuity and Change: Personnel and Administration of the Church in England*, Leicester (1976), 191–214

Knowles, D. *The Religious Orders in England*, vol. 3 *The Tudor Age*, Cambridge (1959, 1971 corrected edn)

Lake, P. *Anglicans and Puritans? Presbyterianism and English Conformist Thought from Whitgift to Hooker* (1988)

—— and Dowling, M. *Protestantism and the National Church in Sixteenth Century England*, (1987)

Lander, S. 'Church courts and the reformation in the diocese of Chichester, 1500–58', in R. O'Day and F. Heal (eds), *Continuity and Change: Personnel and Administration of the Church in England*, Leicester (1976) 215–37

Lehmberg, S.E. *The Reformation Parliament, 1529–36* (1970)

—— *The Reformation of Cathedrals: Cathedrals in English Society, 1485–1603*, Princeton, NJ (1988)

Loades, D. *The Oxford Martyrs* (1970) and Bangor (1992 2nd edn)

Longstaffe, W.H.D. (ed.),*The Acts of the High Commission within the Diocese of Durham*, Surtees Society, 34 (1858)

McClendon, M.C. *The Quiet Reformation: Magistrates and the Emergence of Protestantism in Tudor Norwich*, Stanford, CA (1999)

MacCulloch, D. *Tudor Church Militant: Edward VI and the Protestant Reformation* (1999) (later published as *The Boy King: Edward VI and the Protestant Reformation*, Berkeley, CA (2002)

McGrade, A.S. (ed.), *Richard Hooker and the Construction of Christian Community*, Tempe, AZ (1997)

McLelland, J.C. (ed.), *Peter Martyr Vermigli and Italian reform,* Waterloo, Ontario (1980)

—— and Duffield, G.E. (eds), *The Life, Early Letters, and Eucharistic Writings of Peter Martyr*, Abingdon (1989)

Manning, R.B. *Religion and Society in Elizabethan Sussex*, Leicester (1969)

Marchant, R.B. *The Church Under the Law*, Cambridge (1969)

—— *The Puritans and the Church Courts in the Diocese of York, 1560-1642* (1960)

Marsh, C. *Popular Religion in Sixteenth-Century England: Holding their Peace*, Basingstoke (1998)

Milward, P. *Religious Controversies of the Elizabethan Age*, Lincoln, NE (1977)

O'Day, R. *The English Clergy: The Emergence and Consolidation of a Profession, 1558–1642*, Leicester (1979)

—— *The Debate on the English Reformation* (1986 & 2011)

—— 'Hugh Latimer: Prophet of the kingdom', *Historical Research*, 65, 1992, 258–76

—— and Berlatsky, J. (eds), 'The letter-book of Thomas Bentham, bishop of Coventry and Lichfield, 1560–1561', Royal Historical Society, *Camden Miscellany, XXVII*, 4th ser., 22 (1979)

—— and Heal, F. (eds), *Continuity and Change: Personnel and Administration of the Church in England*, Leicester (1976)

—— (eds), *Princes and Paupers in the English Church* (1979)

Owen, D.M. 'Synods in the diocese of Ely', in *Studies in Church History*, 3 (1966)

—— *The Records of the Established Church in England*, British Records Association, Archives and the User no. 1 (1970)

Palliser, D.M. 'Popular reactions to the reformation, 1530–70' in F. Heal and R. O'Day (eds), *Church and Society in England: Henry VIII to James I*, 1977, 35–56

Pettegree, A. *Marian Protestantism: Six Studies,* Aldershot (1996)

Pollard, A.F. *Henry VIII* (1905) (reprinted in 1966 by Harper Torch Books, New York)

Porter, H.C. *Reformation and Reaction in Tudor Cambridge*, Cambridge (1958)

Price, F.D. 'The commission for ecclesiastical causes within the dioceses of Bristol and Gloucester, 1574, *Transactions of the Bristol and Gloucester Archaeological Society*, Record Section, 10 (1972)

Raine, J. *Injunctions and Other Ecclesiastical Proceedings of Richard Barnes, Bishop of Durham*, Surtees Society, 22 (1855)

Randell, K. *Henry VIII and the Reformation in England* (1993)

Rex, R. *Henry VIII and the English Reformation*, Basingstoke (1993)

—— *The theology of John Fisher*, Cambridge (1991)

Reynolds, E.E. *Saint John Fisher*, 2nd edn (1972)

Scarisbrick, J.J. *The Reformation and the English People*, Oxford (1984)

Seaver, P. *The Puritan Lectureships: The Politics of Religious Dissent, 1560-1662*, Stanford, CA (1970)

Sheils, W.J. *The Puritans in the Diocese of Peterborough, 1558–1610*, Northamptonshire RS, 30 (1979)

—— *The English Reformation, 1530–1570* (1989)

—— and D. Wood (eds) *Women in the Church on the Eve of the Dissolution*, Studies in Church History, 27 (1990),

Smith, L.B. 'Henry VIII and the Protestant Triumph', *American Historical Review* (1966), 71, 1237–64

Spalding, J.C. 'The Reformatio Legum Ecclesiasticarum of 1552 and the furthering of discipline in England', *Church History*, 39 (1970) 162–71

Thomson, J.A.F. *The Early Tudor Church and Society, 1485–1529* (1993)

—— *The Later Lollards, 1414–1520* (1965)

Tyler, P. 'The significance of the ecclesiastical commission at York', *Northern History*, 2 (1967), 27–44

Usher, R.G. *The Rise and Fall of the High Commission*, Oxford (1910)

Wabuda, S. 'Henry Bull, Miles Coverdale, and the making of Foxe's Book of martyrs', *Martyrs and Martyrologies*, D. Wood (ed.), *Studies in Church History*, 30 (1993), 245–58

Wabuda, S. and Litzenberger, C. (eds), *Belief and Practice in Reformation England* (1998)

Walsham, A. *Church Papists: Catholicism, Conformity, and Confessional Polemic in Early Modern England*, Royal Historical Society: Studies in History vol. 68 (1993)

Wilkie, W.E. *The Cardinal Protectors of England: Rome and the Tudors before the Reformation* (1974)

Wunderli, R.M. *London Church Courts and Society on the Eve of the Reformation*, Cambridge MA (1981)

Zell, M.L. 'The use of religious preambles . . .', *Bulletin of the Institute of Historical Research*, 50, 246–49

Monarchy

Antonovics, A.V. 'Henry VII, king of England, "By the grace of Charles VIII of France"', *Kings and Nobles in the Later Middle Ages*, R.A. Griffiths and J. Sherborne (eds) (1986), 169–84

Chrimes, S.B. *Henry VII* (1972, 1977) and New Haven, CT (1999 new edn)

—— *Lancastrians, Yorkists and Henry VII*, New York and London (1962, 1966 2nd edn)

Davies, C.S.L. 'Bishop John Morton, the Holy See, and the accession of Henry VII', *English Historical Review*, 102 (1987), 2–30

Griffiths, R.A. and Thomas, R.S. *The Making of the Tudor Dynasty*, Gloucester (1985) and Stroud, Gloucs (2005)

Gunn, S.J. 'The accession of Henry VIII', *Historical Research*, 64 (1991), 278–88

Jones, M.K. and Underwood, M.G. *The King's Mother: Lady Margaret Beaufort, Countess of Richmond and Derby*, New York (1992)

Storey, R.L. *The Reign of Henry VII* (1968)
Thompson, B. (ed.), *The Reign of Henry VII* (1995)

Court

Adams, S. *Leicester and the Court: Essays on Elizabethan Politics*, Manchester (2002)
Gunn, S.J. 'The courtiers of Henry VII', *English Historical Review*, 108 (1993), 23–49
Kipling, G. *The Triumph of Honour: Burgundian Origins of the Elizabethan Renaissance*, The Hague (1977)
Starkey, D. (ed.), *Henry VIII: A European Court in England* (1991)
—— (ed.), *The Inventory of King Henry VIII: The Transcript* (1998)

17

DEBATES

King or minister?

A debate about the balance and employment of power within the constitution as much as about the **official reformation** itself.

How far was the official reformation the creation of Henry VIII? What role did the monarch play in policy-making and government? Most recent interpretations of the role of Henry VIII in shaping the reformation have been reactive to A.F. Pollard's assumption that Henry was in control after the fall of Wolsey and personally made reformation policy. Pollard was chiefly concerned with explaining why the people of England permitted Henry to exercise this power. While Pollard and his disciples (for example, Bindoff) saw the Reformation as the creature of Henry's will, they modified their voluntaristic approach. Henry designed the Reformation but he was allowed to create it by the nation and, especially, by parliament. Mid-century, Geoffrey Elton began to present a new view of the role of Henry in government and in the creation of the Reformation. He questioned the assumption that Henry's reign could be divided neatly into two: a period from 1514 to 1529, when Henry let Wolsey govern, and a period from 1529 to 1547 when Henry took the reins. He argued that: (a) Wolsey had never been entirely free to do as he wished and; (b) after Wolsey it was Thomas Cromwell who devised and controlled policy broadly to the King's liking. He substituted a much more complex division of the reign. Cromwell established the reformed state as a limited monarchy in which parliament was an active partner and not as a despotism. Elton's views have been challenged from various standpoints: Joel Hurstfield plumped for a Tudor despotism, parliament or no; J.J. Scarisbrick returned to a modified Pollardian argument, once again exalting Henry's personal responsibility for the reformation; A.G. Dickens explored further the impact of Thomas Cromwell's own religious convictions upon the course of the official reformation. More recent works adopt permutations of the above. John Guy's narrative history *Tudor England* offers reasoned treatments of the 'revolution in government' thesis. He is especially strong on the relative importance of Cromwell and factions at Henry's court. G.W. Bernard, *The King's Reformation*, presents Henry as the masterful, deliberate and consistently radical architect of the English Reformation and its middle way between Rome and Zurich.

The Reformation and the people

Further debate about the nature and causes of the English Reformation. Geoffrey Elton, Christopher Haigh and J.J. Scarisbrick claim that the advance of Protestantism under Henry VIII and Edward VI owed almost everything to official coercion. A.G. Dickens argues that the new religion spread by conversions among the people and that it gained strength independently of the 'political' reformation. Far and away the best general account of the movement for religious reform is Dickens, *The English Reformation* (cited above), but more specialised works are also important. For instance, Dickens' own study of *Lollards and Protestants* and J.F. Davis' *Heresy and Reformation*. David Palliser has shown how continental connections prepared parts of England for Protestantism. Penry Williams, Haigh and Scarisbrick argue that little permanent progress was achieved by the Protestants before the reign of Elizabeth. Haigh attacks the supposed force of anti-clericalism. Scarisbrick reasserts the view that England's was an official reformation and one that the English people did not want. They found the Catholic Church congenial. Eamon Duffy's *Stripping of the Altars* and *The Voices of Morebath* have put the religion of the people under a microscope, with startling results. Further detailed local studies have attempted to settle the question once and for all but have pointed instead to widespread regional variations in the response to Protestantism. Studies of, for example, the nature of the Pilgrimage of Grace are highly relevant to this debate. Local studies have also sparked interesting discussion of the use of the sources. Added to this debate about the chronology and geography of religious reformation is discussion of Henry VIII's own attitude towards Protestantism and Catholic doctrine. Patrick Collinson has pioneered studies of the nature of the religion and commitment of Protestants in England and Wales in the Elizabethan period. The Queen's own attitude to religion has also been the subject of much attention.

The Church of England and the Reformation

What impact did the Reformation have upon the Church of England? What did it mean for Church/State relations? Did the Church as an institution maintain continuity with the medieval past or was it much changed? Did the Church's function in society change?

Royal supremacy

The royal supremacy has been much studied by historians. Claire Cross has examined the theoretical relationship between Crown and Church and has sought to demonstrate relations between Crown and hierarchy within this framework. The nature of the supremacy under Henry and then under his daughter Elizabeth has been analysed by Scarisbrick, Bowker, Cross, Collinson, Elton and, most recently, by G.W. Bernard in *The King's Reformation*, 2005.

Episcopacy and the episcopate

The recruitment, role and reputation of the episcopate were as subject to change as its relationship with the Crown. Did the Crown engage in deliberate plunder of the

Church? Did it exploit the wealth of the Church by leaving sees vacant? What were the post-reformation responsibilities of the bishops and were they left with the material resources and authority to fulfil them well? Essays in R. O'Day and F. Heal (eds), *Continuity and Change: Personnel and Administration of the Church in England*, 1976; F. Heal and R. O'Day (eds), *Church and Society in England, Henry VIII to James I*, 1977 and R. O'Day and F. Heal (eds), *Princes and Paupers in the English Church*, 1979 provide a good entree into the subject.

Clergy: priests or pastors?

Did the clergy themselves change fundamentally as a result of the Reformation? The acceptance of the doctrine of the priesthood by all believers meant that the clergy had to find a new justification for their continued existence. The people did not need priests but they did need pastors. This belief became the staple of Protestant teaching on the ministerial order but this rethinking of the clergy's functions was not acceptable to many, including the Crown. Attempts to Protestantise the clergy and turn them into preaching ministers were ad hoc and piecemeal, not least because the Church's financial and administrative organisation and its relationship with the Crown and the elite made the establishment of a clerical career structure, using criteria of vocational excellence, impossible. Historians have also debated whether the clergy professionalised during the period of the Tudors and Stuarts. Peter Heath's *The English Parish Clergy on the Eve of the Reformation*, 1969 and Rosemary O'Day's *The English Clergy*, 1979 remain the standard authorities and a starting point for further study.

Church courts

Did ecclesiastical discipline, exercised through the church courts, retain its old power in society as a whole? The efficiency and authority of the ecclesiastical courts had always been very variable and limited by rival jurisdictions. In some dioceses energetic reform programmes increased the efficiency, effectiveness and business of the Courts Christian prior to the Reformation but unreformed dioceses may have been in the majority. The London diocesan courts were in full decline by the 1520s. In the 1530s, the jurisdiction of the bishops was challenged by the vicegerential authority of Thomas Cromwell, but this was not revived under Edward or Elizabeth. The jurisdiction of the courts remained untouched and they survived in their old form. But the business of the courts revived slowly and the sanctions employed – greater and lesser excommunication – no longer frightened the laity into obedience. The creation of the High Commission overrode the diocesan structure and undermined the bishops' independent authority. The attempt to provide the Church with a new code of laws in tune with its reformed character failed. The courts were asked to enforce conformity to the Elizabethan settlement at the very time when their authority was being challenged, not only by those who were hauled before them during litigation, but also by Protestants who did not recognise their remote discipline as appropriate to a reformed Church. R.B. Outhwaite's, *The Rise and Fall of the English Ecclesiastical Courts, 1500–1860*, 2006 provides a useful modern overview.

The mid-Tudor crisis

The debate here is: was there a crisis during the reigns of Edward VI and Mary I and, if so, of what did it consist?

Since the Second World War, historians have accorded this period, previously regarded as a rather uninteresting interlude set between the reigns of Henry VIII and his daughter Elizabeth, considerable attention. Some have suggested that it was a time of crisis. But what is a crisis? There were certainly problems, but did they really threaten the State with collapse? A sensible approach to the question seems to be to identify the problems – political, socio-economic, religious and diplomatic – and assess their gravity. Studies focus on the potential constitutional crisis caused by: the accession of a minor, nine-year-old Edward VI; on England's weak international position; the severity of economic and associated social problems; the causes of and responses to religious change; the relationship between religious thought and socio-economic policy. J. Loach, *Parliament and the Crown in the Reign of Mary Tudor*, 1986; J. Loach and J. Tittler (eds), *The Mid-Tudor Polity, c. 1540–1560*, 1980; D.M. Loades, *The Reign of Mary Tudor*, 1991; and D.M. Loades, *The Mid-Tudor Crisis, 1545–1565*, 1992. More recently, Eamon Duffy has challenged the traditional view of Mary's reign as characterised by mere negativity, portraying a vigorous campaign of proselytization. He also revises historians' view of Reginald Pole. Eamon Duffy, *Fires of Faith: Catholic England under Mary Tudor,* 2009.

Religion and foreign affairs

England's foreign policy was so dominated by her religious turmoil that it seems appropriate to couple the two. However, other issues were also of great importance. For example, Henry VII was anxious to protect his country from invasion and his throne from usurpation and this anxiety permeated English foreign policy during the reign of his granddaughter, Elizabeth, also; Henry VIII and Wolsey used foreign policy as a way of enhancing their respective reputations; late in his reign Henry VIII again looked for glory abroad; the expansion and protection of overseas trade was also an issue throughout the period. Begin with Susan Doran's *England and Europe in the Sixteenth Century*, 1998.

Parliament

Early and mid-Tudor parliaments

The reigns of the first four Tudors constitute one of the most important phases in the development of parliament as an integral part of the English constitution. Not only the Reformation Parliament (1529–36) was important. During the first half of the century, parliament developed as an institution with its own bureaucracy, archives, place of assembly and increasingly standardised rules and procedures. The judges pronounced that, for a new bill to become law, the assent of the House of Commons was essential. During the Reformation Parliament, the King-in-Parliament became sovereign and, as a result, the areas of royal prerogative upon which parliament might not trespass diminished considerably. Yet there were also strong elements of continuity. For example, the House of Lords remained the most influential chamber. Michael Graves' *Early Tudor Parliaments, 1485–1558*, 1990 provides a good starting point.

Elizabethan parliaments

Until the 1970s and 1980s, the prevailing orthodoxy regarding the significance of Elizabeth's parliaments was that they provided an essential apprenticeship for the assertiveness of their Stuart successors. A.F. Pollard and J.E. Neale noted a shift in the balance of power: the House of Lords was in decline and the Commons in ascendancy. In Elizabeth's reign there was not only a critical element in the Commons, but also an organised opposition with its own programme. This work prepared the way for W. Notestein's important study of the manner in which the House of Commons seized the parliamentary initiative from the Early Stuart monarchs. Revisionist studies have, from the standpoint of a study of parliament as a developing institution, challenged this thesis. Parliament spent much of its time discussing humdrum business and not challenging the Crown's programme. There was no organised opposition. There were such links of patronage between Lords and Commons as to render relatively meaningless a claim that the Commons was in the ascendant. The House of Lords, moreover, provided the focus for resistance to the Elizabethan settlement. Michael Graves' *Elizabethan Parliaments, 1559–1601*, 1987 is the ideal starting place.

The economy

The process of social and economic change is now seen by historians as a long one and we look now for continuities as well as dramatic changes in our analysis of the period before industrialisation. Nonetheless, some features of the Tudor period are regarded as of especial significance in the process of change and historians are continually revising their interpretations.

The long fourteenth century crisis

It is thought that there was a demographic, social, commercial and industrial crisis which began in the mid-fourteenth and lasted until the mid-sixteenth century. This, it is argued, ended with a period of recession in the middle of the Tudor period. It was followed by a period of expansion which lasted until the mid-seventeenth century. Other scholars stress continuity rather than change and write of a long sixteenth century stretching from c. 1450 or 1500 to as late as 1650.

General interpretations of the crisis

R. Brenner, 'Agrarian Class Structure and Economic Development in Pre-industrial Europe', *Past and Present*, 70, 1976. Brenner posits a crisis caused by the collapse of landlord–tenant relationships. It is class struggle which is the principal determinant of social change. Rent strikes and popular discontent, culminating in the

Peasants' Revolt of 1381, resulted when elites raised their rents, etc. during a time of rising prices. The position of the elites worsened when the **peasants** abandoned their smallholdings. In the fifteenth century, the landlords could no longer extract labour services from tenants and had instead to rely on reduced rents for their income. It was, according to this account, the gentry and yeomen who turned to commercialised farming in the early sixteenth century who reaped the benefit from this situation. They employed wage labour to farm their small estates more efficiently. This marked the move from feudal to capitalist production.

See also T.H. Aston and C.H.E. Philpin (eds), *The Brenner Debate. Agrarian Class Structure and Economic Development in Pre-Industrial Europe*, 1985. Reprints Brenner's original article and several pertinent essays by noted specialists.

J. Hatcher, *Plague, Population and the English Economy, 1348–1530*, 1977. An excellent student introduction to the controversy. Hatcher suggests a 'Malthusian crisis' – in the thirteenth century the English population rose to about 6 million. This population outstripped the production of food, and deaths from starvation and malnutrition resulted. Eventually, the population decreased; its recovery was checked by the bubonic plague of 1349 ('the Black Death') which killed about 2 million people; plague epidemics further reduced the population to a mere 1.5 million by the mid-fifteenth century; reduced price of food, shortage of labour, surplus of land enabled gentry and yeomen to acquire more of the land and farm commercially; some of the farmers left the land to become wage labourers, attracted by higher rates of pay offered by the gentry and yeomanry.

Agrarian history

There were considerable agricultural innovations in the sixteenth century – new crops, new farming techniques – but their economic significance has been much debated. The literature pertaining to Tudor agrarian history contributes to a wider debate regarding the occurrence of an agricultural revolution prior to 1750. Many of the technical advances normally associated with the eighteenth-century 'agricultural revolution' were already being made in the sixteenth. But how widespread were such changes? What was the pace of change? Some historians urge that it was rather the commercialisation of agriculture, which forced smaller farmers off the land, that represented the key change because it contributed to the breakdown of traditional society and led to class conflict and rebellion. However, there is much disagreement as to the pace of commercialisation. Only farmers living close to London or other growing towns seem to have spent money on improving the yield of their arable land. Agriculture barely produced sufficient grain to keep pace with population increases.

The principal exponent of the case for an agrarian revolution was Eric Kerridge. He has been criticised by, for example, G.R. Mingay (who sees advance before the eighteenth century as gradual) and Mark Overton (who claims that Kerridge has overestimated the extent to which innovations were made) and the argument for revolution is no longer fashionable. Joan Thirsk has argued persuasively that it would be better to abandon the concept of a revolution altogether and view the history of agricultural development as a continuum displaying periods of more or less rapid change which might vary from agricultural region to agricultural region.

Historians, however, disagree on how best to identify discrete regions and some awareness of the debate in this context is necessary.

The place of industry in the economy

Some historians have argued that there was an industrial revolution in Tudor and Stuart England. Certainly there is evidence of industrial activity. It seems probable that the large and poorly paid labour force looked to producing industrial goods to supplement their income from the land.

Industry was organised either within the traditional craft workshops or by putting-out. There were a few instances of centralised production where the equipment necessary made small-scale production impracticable (mining, glassmaking, etc.) but the national, as opposed to local, importance of such enterprises is now doubtful. Some Marxist historians, such as L. Medick, have argued forcefully that there was a period of proto-industrialisation which led directly to the industrialisation of the eighteenth and nineteenth century. According to this theory the development of cottage industry in the rural cloth industry (beginning as early as the thirteenth century) led to the spread of **capitalism**. It fostered the use of larger, more advanced machinery. Within the cottage, all members of the family were dependent for their livelihood upon the work of cloth production and formed, therefore, a sort of industrial proletariat. This was important for the future but, overall, such industry did little to absorb surplus agricultural labour. L.A. Clarkson, *Proto-Industrialization: The First Phase of Industrialization?* 1985 and D.C. Coleman, *Industry in Tudor and Stuart England*, 1985 provide good overviews. Joan Thirsk, *Economic Policy and Projects: The Development of a Consumer Society in Early Modern England*, 1978, offered a pioneering look at the relationship between trade, industry and society.

Inflation and the price rise

Contemporaries were aware of the price rise and sought to explain it. Historians have also proffered various explanations, both monetary and real or physical. Was it due to the debasement of the currency and the subsequent importation of Spanish silver? (Some understanding of the quantity theory of money is necessary but the chronology of inflation is also at issue.) This thesis has proved difficult to either prove or disprove. Or was it due to the pressure of population upon the available food supply? Or was it explained by a combination of both real and monetary factors? The worst period of inflation seems to have been before 1560 although poor harvests in the late 1580s and 1590s again put pressure on prices. P.H. Ramsey (ed.), *The Price Revolution in Sixteenth-Century England*, 1971 is still a good introduction to the subject as is R.B. Outhwaite, *Inflation in Tudor and Stuart England*, 1982, 2nd edn.

Overseas trade and exploration

Historians debate both the relative importance of the overseas trade to the total economy and the precise extent and nature of overseas trade. The period is seen as falling into two phases: down to 1550, the overseas trade is dominated by the export of woollen cloth to the Low Countries; from 1500 onwards, attempts are made to open up world markets and to extend trade within Europe. Many historians describe the age as one of mercantilism (in which the intervention of the state in the economy is overt and important). The government is seen by some as issuing trade and planta- tion charters and monopolies from the 1550s onwards to assert state control of over- seas trade and as adopting an aggressive foreign policy in order to win new markets. Others have seen the fourteenth-century crisis (q.v.) as the beginning of the develop- ment of a world economic system in which capitalistic long-distance trade was established. There was an urgent need both for foodstuffs and for bullion to pay for warfare and government; as a result there was aggressive overseas exploration and colonisation and opening of long-distance trade routes. R. Brenner, *Merchants and Revolution: Commercial Change, Political Conflict and London's Overseas Traders, 1550–1653*, 1993, offers an interesting perspective.

The educational revolution and the emergence of the learned professions

In 1964, Lawrence Stone published a seminal article, 'The Educational Revolution', in which he charted a revolution in both elementary and higher education. The upper and middle classes in society encouraged the spread of schooling and opened up its benefits to the classes below them. They had faith that education, controlled by an elite, would bring about the betterment of society.

The popularity of such a view was enhanced by the conviction among Protestants that all should be able to read the Word of God whatever their social station and by the spread of literacy throughout the social hierarchy. The elite themselves flocked to the universi- ties and Inns of Court in ever-increasing numbers so that more young people participated in higher education in the early seventeenth century than at any time afterwards until the late nineteenth century. Other scholars challenged the precise details of Stone's account but agreed with his basic thesis (see Curtis, Kearney, Knafla, McConica, Morgan, O'Day, Prest, Simon). There have, however, been some who challenged the thesis itself (see Cressy, Russell) and others who have concentrated on curriculum developments (see Curtis, O'Day, Prest). The causes and consequences of developments in education have given rise to much debate. For instance, Brooks, O'Day and Prest have charted the growth of professions and opened up discussion about the nature of professions and the relationship between professions and society.

The people

Standard of living and social configuration

As in so many other contexts, historians tend to discuss these issues with reference to a 'long sixteenth century', which begins around 1450 or 1500 or even 1560 and ends in 1650. Obviously, great care has to be exercised to discern which part of this time-span is being referred to at any point in the literature.

If we are to tackle any of the issues listed we require a good understanding of the Tudor social hierarchy and the standard of living and communal and domestic organisa- tion of each social group. Yet it is notoriously difficult to describe the social order in the first place, let alone to ascertain how elites, middling sort and lower orders lived their lives. There is a literature too voluminous to list here; the works in the bibliography represent some, but only a proportion, of the best books and articles.

In general terms, the aristocracy probably benefited most from the economic developments of the Tudor period, with gentry, yeomen and some prosperous husbandmen also profiting, but to a lesser extent, if they rented land. Merchants and craftsmen suffered mixed fortunes: they received higher prices for their products and paid lower wages to their employees, but they had to pay more for their raw materials and faced sluggish home markets and uncertain foreign ones. However, the number of individuals who were entirely dependent upon manufacture or trade for a livelihood was relatively low. The lower orders fared relatively much worse. Their standard of living suffered from high prices and rents, low wages and lack of land. They were also relatively far more insecure than the higher orders of society. However, recent studies have emphasised that there was considerable heterogeneity among the lower orders, just as among the middle and upper sorts, and each stratum requires separate analysis. The growth of towns, with their special societies and problems, has been emphasised by some historians, adding to the complexity of any analysis of Tudor society and the standard of living of its people.

Population

See also 'Inflation and the price rise' and 'Standard of living and social configuration' (above); 'Domestic organisation, household and family' (below). There has been debate concerning the precise size of the population, population mobility, population distribution and the impact of population growth upon economy and society. E.A. Wrigley and R.S. Schofield, *The Population History of England, 1541–1871, A Reconstruction*, 1989 (paperback edition with new introduction) is the magisterial study to which all later scholars refer and defer, but it has to be handled with extreme care.

Domestic organisation, household and family

Historical demographers have been to the forefront of those who have described the residential patterns of the population. They have established that most of the population (below the elites) lived in small households comprising the simple nuclear family plus live-in servants (see, for example, P. Laslett and R. Wall (eds), *Household and Family in Past Time*, 1972). Historians have demonstrated the way in which this household was the primary socio-economic and religious unit in Tudor society and, in so doing, have demonstrated that the simple nuclear family was not so simple after all (Ralph Houlbrooke, *The English Family*, 1984). The incidence of complex nuclear family households has been underlined. Some historians have also studied the relationship between the co-residential domestic unit and the wider family (Rosemary O'Day, *Family and Family Relationships*, 1994). The family and household roles of husbands, wives, widows, widowers, children, siblings, aunts and uncles, grandparents and servants have also received some but not enough attention. The controversy surrounding the suggestion that family life in the early Tudor period (and the Middle Ages) was emotionally cold and that **affective family** life only gradually evolved (put forward by Lawrence Stone in his *Family, Sex and Marriage*, 1977) has now led to a much more convincing appreciation of the variety of family experience. Both historical demographers and historians have shown how crucial the history of private life is to our understanding of society as a whole. For this see, for example, Peter Laslett, *The World We Have Lost Further Explored*, 1983.

Women and men

Because the lives of women were very largely circumscribed by the family, many of the books on the family treat aspects of the history of women. Histories of women have been influenced by feminism, but in varying ways. Some works (especially those published prior to 1990) tended to emphasise the oppression of women in sixteenth-century society. They tended to rely on prescriptive sources, which described how women should behave; examples of actual behaviour illustrated the ways in which women and men followed this 'script'. This remains true even of a relatively recent study, such as Mendelson and Crawford's *Women in Early Modern England*, 1998. Some contrasted the situation of women in the Tudor period with the halcyon days of the later Middle Ages. There are interesting studies of the general and status-specific position of singletons, married women and widows (e.g. Froide, Mendelson, Brodsky). More recently, historians have been more inclined to examine the ways in which many women were able to circumvent the restrictions placed upon their activities and to exploit the opportunities which were open to them. There have been exciting studies of women and the law, for example, which demonstrate that women could and did take advantage of the instruments available to them to protect themselves economically and physically (Erickson, *Women and Property*, 1993; Stretton, *Women Waging Law . . .*, 1998). The concept of 'women's agency' has been introduced and explored (O'Day, *Women's Agency*, 2007). Historians have become increasingly aware that the experiences of women were infinitely variable and were as dependent upon marital and social status, wealth and family circumstances as were men. Aspects which are beginning to receive thorough attention are family traditions of female behaviour; the crucial role many women played in networking and patronage; the financial agency of women. The previously accepted dichotomy between the private or domestic sphere in which females operated and the public sphere which men dominated is being challenged. The subject of women's political agency in the noble and gentle classes has just begun to be opened up by scholars such as James Daybell, Barbara Harris, Natalie Mears, Helen Payne and Alison Wall (see Chapter 16: Bibliographies). Gemma Allen's study of *Women and Politics in England, 1547–1603* (forthcoming) promises to be groundbreaking in this area. Latterly, there has been considerable interest in masculinity as understood by contemporaries and the construction of manhood (a good starting point being A. Fletcher, *Gender, Sex and Subordination*, 1995). Literary historians have been to the fore in this awareness of masculine and feminine gender and sexuality.

Culture

See also 'Religion and the people'; 'Educational revolution'; 'Domestic organisation, household and family'; 'Women and men'.

Perhaps the chief debate here concerns the *nature* of culture and subcultures. Is there, in every society, a dominant culture, an elite culture, of which popular culture is merely an impoverished and reduced variety? Or does popular culture represent a sophisticated, complex, deep-rooted and rich rival to the elite and dominant culture? Could it be that, in some cases, the dominance of elite culture is deceptive – a feature of the higher survival rate of its expressions rather than its importance to the majority of contemporaries. Is 'popular culture' necessarily produced *by* the people or is it produced *for* the people? The study of culture involves a study of attitudes, mentalities, values and norms and, some would argue, beliefs. Popular culture in the Tudor period may not have been a literate culture but our knowledge of it frequently derives from literary sources or from other elite-generated representations. Historians have to decide to what extent these sources distort our knowledge of popular culture. A manuscript play is not a performance, least of all is it the audience response to the performance. A sermon may use popular attitudes and beliefs to make its point but the points are often being made by members of an educated elite. The issues are often discussed in a broad European context (as in Philippe Ariés, *The Hour of Our Death*, 1981), and Peter Burke's *Popular Culture in Early Modern Europe* (1978, 2009 3rd edn) remains stimulating. The nature of material culture has recently sparked much interest. Historians seek ever-more ingenious ways to access mental, material and popular culture and micro-studies remain fashionable (good examples being Margaret Aston, *The King's Bedpost* Cambridge (1993) and Eamon Duffy, *Voices of Morebath*, 2001). David Cressy, *Birth, Marriage and Death: Ritual, Religion and the Life Cycle in Tudor and Stuart England*, 1997 is a veritable goldmine for those seeking to understand popular culture.

18
MAPS

Map 1 Ireland c. 1530, showing Pale and the areas of influence

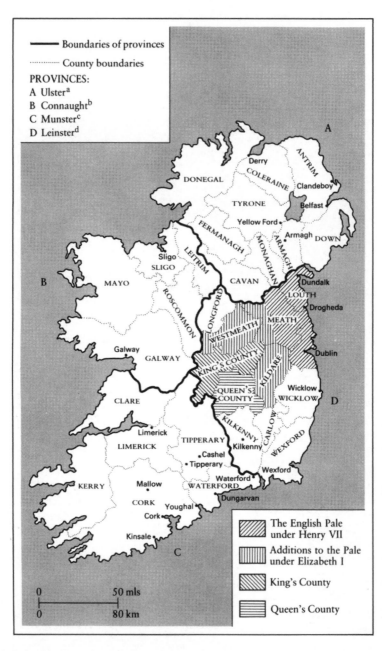

Map 2 Ireland in the early seventeenth century

Notes:

a   O'Donnell of Tyroconnell; O'Neill of Tyron Fermanagh, Monaghan and Armagh.
b   (also Connacht) – wild.
c   Fitzgeralds of Desmond; O'Briens of Thomond.
d   Earl of Kildare (Fitzgerald); Earl of Ormond.

Map 3 England and Wales: major towns and industrial specialisations

INDEX

The reader is advised to consult the alphabetical listings of authors, biographies, books, glossary and titles; the chronologies and the subject sections first and to use this index as a key to further information. In the interests of economy of space, the following categories of entry are excluded from this index: the names of people in the Biographies Index which do not occur elsewhere in the volume (e.g. Barlow, William); the titles of books which occur only in the Books or Authors listings (e.g. *Lily's Latin Grammar*) and in the Bibliography (e.g. Walker, G. *John Skelton and the Politics of the 1520s*, (1988); the names of officeholders which occur in one list only (e.g. Sir Henry Marny Keeper of the Privy Seal), genealogical tables and maps. Titles of people have not been included unless they help with identification and as a ready reference aid. Groupings of page numbers (119–20) do not imply a continuous entry.